ROADS TO DOMINION

CRITICAL PERSPECTIVES

A GUILFORD SERIES

Edited by Douglas Kellner
University of Texas, Austin

PSYCHOANALYTIC POLITICS, SECOND EDITION:
JACQUES LACAN AND FREUD'S FRENCH REVOLUTION
Sherry Turkle

POSTNATIONAL IDENTITY: CRITICAL THEORY AND
EXISTENTIAL PHILOSOPHY IN HABERMAS,
KIERKEGAARD, AND HAVEL
Martin J. Matustik

THEORY AS RESISTANCE: POLITICS AND CULTURE
AFTER (POST)STRUCTURALISM
Mas'ud Zavarzadeh and Donald Morton

MARXISM IN THE POSTMODERN AGE: CONFRONTING
THE NEW WORLD ORDER
*Antonio Callari, Stephen Cullenberg,
and Carole Biewener, Editors*

AFTER MARXISM
Ronald Aronson

THE POLITICS OF HISTORICAL VISION:
MARX, FOUCAULT, HABERMAS
Steven Best

LEWIS MUMFORD AND THE ECOLOGICAL REGION:
THE POLITICS OF PLANNING
Mark Luccarelli

ROADS TO DOMINION: RIGHT-WING MOVEMENTS AND
POLITICAL POWER IN THE UNITED STATES
Sara Diamond

ROADS TO DOMINION

Right-Wing Movements and Political Power in the United States

◆ ◆ ◆

SARA DIAMOND

THE GUILFORD PRESS
New York   London

Published by The Guilford Press
A Division of Guilford Publications, Inc.
72 Spring Street, New York, NY 10012

Printed in the United States of America

This book is printed on acid-free paper.

Last digit is print number: 9   8   7   6   5   4   3   2   1

Library of Congress Cataloging-in-Publication Data

Diamond, Sara.
    Roads to dominion: right-wing movements and political power in
the United States / Sara Diamond
        p.   cm. — (Critical perspectives)
    Includes bibliographical references and index.
    ISBN 0-89862-862-8 (hard) — ISBN 0-89862-864-4 (pbk.)
    1. Conservatism—United States.   2. United States—Politics and
government—1945–1989.   3. United States—Politics and
government—1989–   I. Title.   II. Series: Critical perspectives
(New York, N.Y.)
JC573.2.U6D53   1995
320.5'2'0973—dc20   95-12887
                                                          CIP

For the ones who inspire me

Acknowledgments

Many thanks to those who helped bring this book into being. This work had its first incarnation as my doctoral thesis in sociology at the University of California at Berkeley. On that project, Franz Schurmann and Michael Rogin were exceptionally helpful.

While I wrote the thesis I was happy to be invited to add to Douglas Kellner's Critical Perspectives series. Colleagues Gerry O'Sullivan and Val Burris read the first draft and wrote many pages of valuable suggestions for revision. Another friend and colleague, Chip Berlet, also read the first draft, and we had many thought-provoking phone conversations about it. Guilford Press editor Peter Wissoker was a pleasure to work with.

Finally, thanks go to my life-long companion, Richard Hatch, without whom this book and countless other things truly would not have been possible.

Contents

PART III
THE REAGAN ERA AND BEYOND, 1980–1995

. . .

Introduction

For millions of Americans, the 1992 Republican National Convention in Houston, Texas was a shocker. Before a nationwide prime-time television audience, syndicated pundit and 1992 Republican primary challenger Patrick Buchanan, television preacher Pat Robertson, and Vice-President Dan Quayle rallied thousands of flag-waving delegates behind thunderous battle cries for a "cultural war" for "family values." Outside the Houston Astrodome, young zealots handed out leaflets denouncing "queers" and "feminazis." Inside, some of the party's long-time business leaders and elected officials found themselves overwhelmed by the religious fervor of a new crop of party loyalists.

Patrick Buchanan drew the battle lines in his opening night convention speech in Houston. He warned of a coming "religious war" that would plague the United States from within. "It is a cultural war, as critical to the kind of nation we shall be as the Cold War itself, for this war is for the soul of America," he roared. Two nights later, Pat Robertson echoed Buchanan's call to war when he accused Democratic candidate Bill Clinton of pushing "a radical plan to destroy the traditional family."

From all points of the political spectrum, Americans sat up and took notice as the Republicans endorsed a platform marked by the priorities of the GOP's Christian right wing. For the first time, in 1992, the platform included a plank that unequivocally opposed abortion under all circumstances, and another that denounced the Democrats' support for gay rights legislation. Allies of Patrick Buchanan, who had garnered a quarter to a third of Republican votes in the 1992 state primaries, secured a plank favoring tougher law enforcement against undocumented immigrants from Mexico.

Buchanan, Pat Robertson, and, along with them, the party's Old Guard, lost one battle in the cultural war in 1992. They lost, for a season, their claim on the White House. But two years later the Right was back

1

in the saddle after the 1994 elections delivered both houses of Congress to the Republicans for the first time in forty years. Among those who joined the new Republican Congressional majority were several dozen veteran Christian Right activists, including seven "pro-life" women. Among 600 state and local races monitored by a liberal lobbying group, the Christian Right won victories for 60 percent of the candidates the movement backed. In Oregon and Idaho, anti-homosexual activists lost state ballot measures that would have preemptively banned gay civil rights laws. But in California voters approved, by an overwhelming majority, a ballot measure to deny social services to "illegal" immigrants. Nationwide exit polls indicated that evangelical Christians comprised about 30 percent of those who voted in 1994.

Gone were the days when born-again Christians shunned worldly affairs. Gone, too, were the days when Christian Right activists stood outside the halls of power, petitioning to get in. Now, at long last, they took their seats inside the Republicans' proverbial big tent. And they were there to stay.

Gone also were the days when the specter of communism, and one's willingness to fight it, was the benchmark separating patriots from infidels. The 1990s saw the disappearance of state socialism as a sustainable alternative within a tightening global capitalist economy. The end of a cycle of progressive revolutions brought no end to armed conflict around the world. But the end of the Cold War did spell an end to the U.S. Right's half-century obsession with its own role as international policeman. The end of Soviet-style Communism coincided with the Right's renewed focus on traditional moral order and ethnic–cultural homogeneity inside the borders of the United States.

By the end of the twentieth century, the press reported routinely on the influence of right-wing movements. We read about fatal shootings of abortion doctors and bombings of synagogues by racist skinheads. We also read about hundreds of ordinary churchgoers who ran for elected office for the first time in their lives, who took charge of local school boards and sponsored anti-gay rights ballot initiatives. We read about campaigns to remove books from libraries, to ban public funding of sexually explicit art, to prevent passage of an historic national health care reform bill. Each of these news events was part of a much bigger story. Each was a landmark along the road to political power.

This book is about how right-wing movements in the United States, from the 1940s to the present, moved from the sidelines of U.S. politics to center stage. How did the American right wing transform itself from a small clique of post-World War II conservative intellectuals into well-heeled, grassroots movements representing millions of ordinary citizens? Along the way, what shifts and compromises have movement strategists made? How have heated questions about racism, foreign military adventures and nuclear weapons, income taxes, gender roles—even the content of grade-school textbooks—all figured into the unfolding drama in the history of right-wing movements over the past fifty years? How and why have movement activists developed mutually beneficial ties with political elites even while working to replace them?

Although this is a book about the development of right-wing movements over time, my goal is not to recall each and every episode in that history. Nor is it my intention to answer the complicated question of why certain types of people join certain types of movements. I assume people join movements they see as representing both their interests—economic and otherwise—and their ideological preferences for how the world ought to be. Setting aside questions of motives and sincerity, this narrative will reveal how and why outsiders like Pat Robertson became players within institutions like the Republican Party. But in this book I propose to do more than tell the rich history of the U.S. Right.

During many years of research, I have discovered some recurring patterns that help explain how the movements under scrutiny have, variably, grown and declined. These patterns shed light on how social change happens; specifically, how social movements accrue and deploy power within formally democratic political systems. Through the documentary record movements have left behind, we can see their close interactions with policymaking elites—sometimes as enemies, other times as allies.

The nature of these interactions is crucial to our ability to understand and even predict the influence of social movements on the day-to-day policies we all must live with. Whether we have access to health care and quality public education, whether we can live in racial harmony, whether we can feel proud about our country's behavior in the international arena—all of these are questions determined in no small part by the strength and influence of social movements.

In this book, I explain the U.S. Right's development not just through a narrative of its history but also by analyzing how its movements have interacted with government agencies over time. I call my perspective a *state interaction* approach because I see political movements as central, not marginal, to routine political decision making. In order to make this book accessible to many kinds of readers, I have refrained from the sort of jargon and abstract generalizations that make much academic writing unreadable. Having said this, though, I am indebted to the work of social movements theorists over the past two decades. My approach was influenced by sociology's *political process model*, which attributes the success of social movements to three sets of factors: advantageous shifts in the political–economic context, the mobilization of tangible and intangible resources, and the awakening of a collective sense of efficacy and belief in the possibility of change.[1]

My approach to right-wing movements is consistent with the political process model because I emphasize context, including party politics and the role of countermovement forces; resources, internal and external to a movement; and the motivating force of belief systems or ideology. Beyond this, there are some other essential elements of my presentation of right-wing movement history that I need to advise readers about from the start. Some of these elements are definitional and others are conceptual.

The first question is about how I view social movements in relation to the rest of political society. Although some of the characters in this book have espoused unwholesome ideas and have employed some eccentric means to achieve their ends, nevertheless I see their activism as part and parcel of how routine politics takes place. Though personally I am not sympathetic to the subjects of this study, neither is my purpose here to condemn nor endorse one movement over another, one strategy or set of tactics over another. My purpose is to explain how and why diverse right-wing movements have traveled their respective paths toward political power.

As with any social movement, some of the leaders of the U.S. Right have distinguished themselves through their influential writings, through attracting large followings, through developing particularly astute plans of action at key points in time. At intervals, I highlight the contributions of some of the Right's most important historical figures. Mostly, though, what drives movements is the sum total of countless small actions by thousands of unsung activists. In this history of the Right, therefore, I refer more often to organizations than to individual leaders, for a couple of reasons. Beyond the importance of extraordinary leaders, it is through organizations that large numbers of unnamed movement activists wage their campaigns and projects.

Organizations are agents of social change and they are also among the most crucial resources movements have. As we will see in the case of the U.S. Right, a political movement is successful to the extent that it can accommodate many different types of organizations, so that activists of different dispositions can find useful outlets for their talents. Over time, a social movement's set of organizations will naturally change, as that movement develops different pieces of its agenda and faces new opportunities and obstacles in its path.

My approach to explaining the growth of right-wing movements is historical and comparative. This point is an obvious one but worth mentioning as most scholarship about the Right has been ahistorical and noncomparative. Only by understanding where movement activists have come from can we see where they are headed. And only by understanding how activists have developed their world views and plans of action, variably, in conflict and collaboration with other social forces, can we fully appreciate why movements make the strategic choices they do. I have written this history of the U.S. Right with a triple focus on its movements' *ideologies* (or politically salient belief systems), *actions* (intended and realized), and broader *significance* for the rest of society.

Along these three dimensions, I have found that the political thinking, actions, and importance of movements revolve largely around questions of state power and public policymaking. But before elaborating on what I mean to explain in this history of right-wing movements' relationships with government agencies and political elites, I first must define the terms I use throughout this book.

DEFINING RIGHT-WING MOVEMENTS AND STATE POWER

Readers may justifiably wonder what I mean by "right-wing movements" and how I propose to treat a range of political actors, from neo-Nazis to neoconservatives, in a single study. Other scholars have resolved problems of defining right-wing movements more expeditiously than I can. Some have focused narrowly on a single social movement during a single time period. Others have adopted, wholesale, the vague label many on the Right apply to themselves, "conservative."[2]

Beginning in the 1950s, some of the most influential social scientists established an enduring set of analytical blinders with their rhetorical descriptions of "extremists" and the "radical right."[3] Under this paradigm, grassroots right-wing activists have been portrayed as operating outside the democratic system, despite their use of mostly legitimate pressure tactics like voting, lobbying, and persuading supporters through media campaigns, and despite their mutually beneficial ties with established political elites. "Radical" and "extremist" are pejorative terms. They reveal their originators' sympathy for the political status quo but elucidate little else. The "radical–extremist" frame limits an honest study of movements to those few who fit the description. It implies that movements so designated operate outside normal political processes and ought not to be taken seriously, which is generally not the case. As we will see in this book, relatively few on the Right have relied on extremist tactics or promoted ideas that thoroughly challenge those of mainstream society.

Unfortunately though, during the 1990s a number of liberal and centrist interest groups resurrected the radical–extremist Right paradigm for their media campaigns against politically active evangelical

Christians. The result was a disservice to the general public. The distortions inherent in the radical–extremist labeling effort blunted public awareness of how and why the Christian Right's millions of constituents became indispensable to the Republican Party. Instead, some critics of the Christian Right promoted a view of conspiracies by small right-wing cliques to stage manage what was truly a mass movement. Such faulty analysis of their political opponents is a liability for countermovement activists.

Apart from the pitfalls of mislabeling, even the best scholarly research has tended to focus disproportionately on social movements opposed to the status quo. My view of right-wing movements departs from this perspective. As we will see in this book, right-wing movements hold mixed stances toward prevailing power structures. They are partially *oppositional* and partially what I call *system-supportive*. As we will see below, such mixed stances are, nevertheless, consistent. Depending on the policy issue, movements hold predictable positions on what they believe government agencies and elected officials ought to accomplish.

This variability complicates definition. At one level, the frequently used "conservative" label applies to a range of anticommunist and, later, New Right actors who referred to themselves as "the conservative movement" and who argued about who really belonged in their camp. But "conservatism" implies reticence toward change, and that sentiment does not capture what many self-described "conservatives" are all about. Participants in the Christian Right, for instance, sought change, not the status quo; they wanted to alter legislation to reflect their religious values throughout society. Yet they were not truly "radical" either. Like their secular New Right counterparts, they collaborated with the architects of U.S. Cold War foreign policy. They persistently endorsed capitalism and the inherent inequality of its opportunities and results.

For lack of more accurate and encompassing terms, then, I use "right wing," "rightists," and "right-wing movements" to include a range of political activists who, nevertheless, bear a coherent set of policy preferences. Naturally, movements involving scores of organizations, thousands of committed activists, and many more supporters are not monolithic. What has unified the Right is a consistent set of principles in three realms of social endeavor: the economy, the nation-state in global context (military and diplomatic), and the moral order of behavioral norms and hierarchies on the bases of race and gender.

We will see throughout this book that these three realms correspond to the preoccupations of right-wing movements with protecting "free market" or "libertarian" capitalism; promoting anticommunism and, generally, U.S. military hegemony over much of the rest of the world; preserving traditional morality and supreme status for native-born white male Americans and for the nuclear family. Libertarianism, anticommunist militarism, and traditionalism have been the three pillars of the U.S. Right. But these are tendencies, not absolutes. Each of the right-wing movements analyzed in this book ranks the priority of these three areas of commitment, and the specific policy issues implied by them, in distinct ways. What cuts across the diversity of right-wing movements are some consistent notions about the proper role of the *state* in society.

Here I must digress a bit and say what I mean by the *state* and *state power*. These are academic concepts, but they are also essential tools for defining right-wing movements and explaining the broad significance of their beliefs and actions.

In common parlance, we think of the government as that set of agencies and office holders—some elected, others appointed—who make and carry out decisions that profoundly effect our daily lives. For sociologists, though, the *state* is a concept with greater explanatory utility than the *government*. Historically, states developed for several purposes: to manage production and trade within and across geographic boundaries, to enforce order between disparate cultural groupings and nations, to distribute political rights and material benefits to citizens. The *state* includes rotating office holders and more permanent bureaucratic agencies, plus political parties and all the other extra-governmental players who help determine the distribution of power within a society.

Power is the ability to affect the actions or ideas of others, through various combinations of coercion and persuasion. Who holds power and how they deploy it are among the most crucial features of any given society. Some analysts view state power as indistinguishable from a society's wealthiest class. The renowned Italian Marxist Antonio Gramsci defined the state as the entire range of activities and institutions by which a "ruling class" both coerces and wins the consent of the governed. This view of the state implies a consent-winning role for powerful educational and cultural institutions, such as churches, schools and the mass media. These institutions are strongly influenced by society's dominant economic elites. But they also partially reflect and serve the interests of other classes. Along with political parties and elections, legislatures and judiciaries, these consent-winning institutions are among the most important sites where class conflict is contained, if not resolved.

In this book I use the term *government* when I refer to specific administrations. I use the terms *state*, *state actors*, and *state institutions* more inclusively in reference to a more enduring strata of political elites and the myriad agencies through which they wield and preserve their power. An echelon of *para-statal* agencies (from the Greek root "para" meaning "alongside") often act as quasi-independent extensions of the state. Theoretically, these can include system-supportive churches, media outlets and social movement organizations.

State power is the capacity to shape and implement public policy and, by definition, political movements are those seeking state power. This might imply that political movements are oppositional toward existing regimes or toward the state generally. But historically, the activism of right-wing movements has been both oppositional and system-supportive, often in combination. This is why I define right-wing movements not by their relationship to the state but rather by their views of what functions the state should and should not perform. As mentioned above, right-wing movements have granted priority to the principles of economic libertarianism, military strength and traditional moral order. Each of these principles implies a corresponding role for the state.

In the economic sphere, libertarianism calls for limited state intervention. Individuals should conduct economic transactions unregulated, as they please. The state should not intervene to *distribute* wealth among social classes but, rather, should allow whatever distribution pattern that emerges through natural market forces. Yet this libertarian ideal of nonintervention belies a different reality: most rightists have supported de facto state intervention to the advantage of the upper classes. A small number of purist libertarians have opposed protectionist trade policies and massive tax-supported Pentagon spending. Most of the Right has supported what Noam Chomsky called the "Pentagon system." Through regressive and high tax rates, the middle and lower classes have paid for state funding of capitalists' research and development in profitable high-technology industries.[4] State subsidies not withstanding, the Right's "free market" tenet has been politically useful. The Reagan–Bush administration came to power on a popular program that included "supply-side" tax cuts for the rich.

Supply-side economics faltered in part because of an irresolvable contradiction between the drive to cut popular government entitlements, like Social Security, and the drive for massive military spending to defeat communism. Questions about what communism was, in real life and in the minds of its adherents, are beyond the scope of this book. Here I adopt the distinction Joel Kovel made in his insightful book *Red Hunting in the Promised Land* between Communism and communism. Following Kovel, I use uppercase "C" *Communism* to refer to actually existing governments and movements and lowercase "c" *communism* to refer to the varied movements and political currents organized around the ideal of a classless society. Anti-Communism was opposition to Communist bloc states and real live Communists. Anticommunism was, and remains, what Kovel calls the "reigning ideology of the West." Anticommunism was, and is, a package of beliefs about the moral superiority of the United

States, about the importance of protecting American lives above all others, and about the necessity of ensuring international order through military force. Beyond application to particular crises, anticommunism has been a dichotomous and reactive way of seeing the world: good guys verus bad guys; bright, true Americans versus dark, suspicious aliens and criminal elements.[5]

Anticommunism became the American Right's dominant motif not just because it justified the enforcement of U.S. dominion internationally but also because it wove together disparate threads of right-wing ideology. At an elite level, anticommunism was about preserving economic inequality, the libertarian strain in right-wing thinking. At a more mass level, anticommunism was about obedience to authority and repression of domestic political dissent and deviant tendencies in the broader culture.

In the realms of culture and morality, *traditionalists* back the state as enforcer of a religious moral order, through laws regulating sexual practices, reproduction, childhood education, and mass media content. At the same time, traditionalists, wary of social change and supportive of class, race, and gender hierarchies, have tended to oppose state initiatives to *distribute* civil rights and liberties among traditionally subordinate groups. Historically, traditionalists opposed racial integration. They opposed the legislation of equal rights for women, let alone access to safe and legal abortion. They longed for the "good old days," when the schools taught the virtues of Western civilization, when the government, ostensibly, kept its nose out of family affairs.

A pattern is evident. To be right-wing means to support the state in its capacity as *enforcer* of order and to oppose the state as *distributor* of wealth and power downward and more equitably in society. Throughout the history of U.S. right-wing movements, we will see this recurring pattern as one organization after another worked to bolster capitalism, militarism, and moral traditionalism.

It would make sense to organize an historical study of the Right around these three sets of policy priorities. But the actual right-wing movements in contemporary U.S. history do not fit neatly into these three categories. Nor is it an easy task to classify movements spanning decades, representing hundreds of organizations and thousands, if not millions, of supporters. For the sake of accuracy and in order to narrate the Right's history in a comparative sense, in this book I use a typology of four broad but distinct movements:

1. The conservative movement, also referred to as the anticommunist movement. By the 1970s, the conservative New Right added to its anticommunist focus a heavy emphasis on issues of moral traditionalism,

in concert with the emerging Christian Right. The conservative movement was also home to a minority contingent of libertarian intellectuals.

2. The racist Right, including classic Ku Klux Klan-type groups, the broader-based segregationist movement, the Americanists of the 1970s and, later, the paramilitary white supremacist movement.

3. The Christian Right, with its roots in an evangelical subculture and, later, its ties to the nominally secular New Right.

4. The neoconservative "movement," with roots in Cold War liberalism and the Democratic Party. By the 1980s, neoconservatives made common cause with the New Right. (I use quotations in the case of the neoconservative "movement" because it was a small, loosely connected but influential group of intellectuals who held provisional status on the Right.)

Within each of these four broad movements, smaller sub-movements and specific organizations have grown and declined over time. For the racist Right, for example, the segregationist Citizens' Councils were the dominant sub-movement during the 1950s and 1960s; later, during the 1980s, the Aryan Nations assumed prominence. As a subset of the larger Christian Right, the anti-abortion movement rose in the 1970s and persisted into the 1990s. The conservative movement evolved from its early emphasis on anticommunism to its New Right phase when issues of traditional morality became important. The neoconservatives forged links with the New Right to achieve foreign policy objectives during the 1980s, but that alliance began to break apart after the Cold War.

For each of these four major movements, we will see how changing political openings and obstacles determined their successes and failures over time. Throughout this book, I use the concepts of *political context* or *political opportunities* to mean several sets of circumstances. These include large-scale trends such as shifts in the economy, major policy doctrines, electoral realignments, and changing culture norms; government actions such as wars, landmark court cases, and legislative reforms; plus efforts by political elites to directly *facilitate* or *repress* social movements. Facilitation and repression can take strong or subtle forms.

The pattern I have observed is that movements tend to mobilize most strongly in response to changes initiated or at least formalized by state policymakers. We will see, for example, that the Christian Right, though opposed to homosexuality from the start, mobilized furiously against gay rights after local jurisdictions enacted anti-discrimination measures to protect the civil rights of homosexuals. Similarly, the segregationist Citizens' Councils formed and grew in direct response to federal government mandates for public school integration.

These were cases in which the Right mobilized in opposition to government policy changes. At other times, right-wing movements have operated as reliable allies of the state, particularly in the realm of foreign and military policy. In numerous cases, right-wing movements have influenced state policymaking along both ideological and partisan lines. Right-wing movements have devoted major resources toward media and educational campaigns, and as they have gained strength, they have challenged established elites through elections.

In turn, factions of the political establishment have found it expedient to facilitate the growth of system-supportive movement organizations. By facilitation I refer not only to the Right's indispensable corporate benefactors. I refer also to the numerous ways in which policymakers grant legitimacy to their loyal constituents: by including them in government operations, by endorsing their efforts, and by indicting their opponents.

THE CHAPTERS AHEAD

There was more than a touch of historical symbolism in the choice of Patrick Buchanan as opening keynote speaker at the Republicans' 1992 convention. Here was a man who represented three generations of activism on the Right. By virtue of his post-Cold War advocacy of a non-interventionist U.S. foreign policy, Buchanan's ideas made him a throwback to the America First movement of the 1940s. But like many of his political generation, Buchanan had cut his activist teeth in the movement of young anticommunist stalwarts who backed Barry Goldwater for president in 1964. Following Goldwater's landslide defeat, his young conservative admirers went about their business quietly laying the organizational groundwork for the rise of the New Right in the 1970s. Buchanan himself was hired by would-be president Richard Nixon as a speech writer and liaison to the activist Right. Later Buchanan would serve as President Reagan's Director of Communications. From the 1960s through the 1980s, Buchanan was a persistent advocate for anticommunist militarism, unrestrained capitalism, and Christian moralism.

In 1992 Buchanan took the political pundits by surprise when he challenged incumbent President George Bush and won a quarter to a third of Republican votes in the state primaries he entered. Buchanan arrived at the Houston convention as a leading spokesman for the "family values" program. His opening night speech signalled the Christian Right's success in moving the party further to the right.

At the risk of over-dramatizing the role of one person, Buchanan's Old Right philosophy, his activist career and service to the Republicans, and his advocacy for the Christian Right epitomize much of the Right's trajectory over the past half century. To recount and explain this history, I have divided this book into three parts, corresponding to three sweeps of time: the Cold War and civil rights era from 1945 to 1964; the period when the New Right rose to power, 1965 to 1979; and the Reagan era and its aftermath, 1980 to the present.

The context for the chapters in Part I is the immediate aftermath of World War II and the onset of the Cold War in the late 1940s and early 1950s. Chapter 1 traces the Right's transformation from pre-war isolationism to post-war support for militarist anticommunism. Along the way, the early conservative movement soft-pedaled its tradition of blatant nativism, anti-Semitism, and racism. Instead, the movement's intellectual leaders forged what they called a "fusionist" coalition between the libertarians, traditionalists, and anticommunists among them. William F. Buckley's founding of *National Review* magazine in 1955 was an event that signified the willingness of conservatives to work together despite ideological differences.

By then both the Truman and Eisenhower administrations had led the United States into a massive superpower conflict, under the auspices of which the United States waged the Korean war and set the stage for further military intervention in Asia. The 1949 Chinese Revolution convinced right-wing policymakers of the threat posed by Communist movements around the world. At home Senator Joseph McCarthy and other powerful politicians launched a wave of repression against real Communists and countless more left-of-center U.S. citizens from every walk of life.

It was after politicians established the anticommunist agenda as the nation's top foreign and domestic preoccupation that the anticommunist movement mobilized intensely to press the cause further. Chapter 2 chronicles both the elite-oriented and mass-based wings of the anticommunist movement. At the elite level, a network of pro-Taiwan "China Lobby" groups worked to prevent international diplomatic recognition for Communist China. The American Security Council, formed in 1955, had two early missions: private intelligence gathering against labor unions and dissidents, and, in collaboration with government agencies, the dissemination of anticommunist propaganda in military schools and for the general public.

The exposure of military leaders' use of John Birch Society literature in anticommunist training sessions caused a scandal resulting in the ouster of the popular General Edwin A. Walker. The mass-based John Birch Society, born in 1958, was scorned by most political elites. They were repelled by the Society's frequent accusations that respectable figures from President Dwight Eisenhower to Supreme Court Justice Earl Warren were secret agents of a "communist conspiracy." The Birch Society represents a classic case of a movement organization that was tactically oppositional to, but nevertheless system-supportive of the overall parameters of U.S. anticommunist policy.

The Society's heyday coincided with one of the largest reactive citizen mobilizations in recent U.S. history. The 1954 Supreme Court decision mandating an end to segregated public schools came at a time when the black-led civil rights movement was on the march. Chapter 3 reviews the profound changes in southern and national politics on questions of legal racial equality. Before World War II southern political elites were solidly Democratic and segregationist. After the war, the migration of large numbers of African Americans into northern cities gave liberal Democrats new incentives to recruit black voters by backing modest civil rights goals. Southern members of Congress, state governors, mayors, and prominent businessmen fought back. Throughout the South, they facilitated the mobilization of Citizens' Councils involving hundreds of thousands of mostly middle-class white activists. These Citizens' Councils slowed, but ultimately could not prevent, the integration of schools and other public facilities.

Yet they kept organized racism alive and well. After the federal government's passage of the landmark 1964 Civil Rights Act and the 1965 Voting Rights Act, Citizens' Councils and John Birch Society leaders formed the nucleus for Alabama Governor George Wallace's 1968 presidential campaign. Wallace's successful appeal to nearly ten million voters that year convinced Republicans to pursue a "southern strategy," making themes of racial antagonism a cornerstone of its drive to dominate the South for the next two decades.

Chapter 4 traces the roots of the early Christian Right to the evangelical movement of the Cold War era. The movement was then pre-political in that it was not yet linked to state policymaking processes as were the other right-wing movements of the period. Instead evangelicals focused on consolidating missionary and broadcast resources in competition with the mainline denominational churches, which the evangelicals criticized as soft on communism. It was the strong organizational apparatus the evangelicals were then building that would eventually make them useful allies of New Right conservatives beginning in the 1970s.

In the second period of this history, from the mid-1960s through the 1970s, the most important features of the political context were the U.S. war in Southeast Asia, the ascension of the Republican Party's most conservative faction, the rise of the 1960s counterculture and protest movements, and the inflationary economy of the 1970s. Part II of this book begins by tracing the conservative movement's recuperation following presidential candidate Barry Goldwater's 1964 defeat.

Central to the movement's endurance was its persistent anticommunism. The so-called New Right of the 1970s represented a reassertion of the old "fusionist" era's blend of anticommunism, traditionalism, and libertarianism, though the first two concerns took precedence over the third. (A contingent of libertarians with the Young Americans for Freedom broke ranks with the Right over the Vietnam war and the draft and formed a small Libertarian Party.) I explain the mobilization of the New Right as the combined result of increased corporate funding of conservative think tanks, lobbies, and political action committees; movement leaders' development of new, effective, and multiple-type organizations; and tailor-made issues in the realms of both foreign affairs and domestic morality.

The New Right's successful overtures to an increasingly politicized evangelical constituency—which is the subject of Chapter 7—were accompanied by the declining influence of the organized racist Right. Chapter 6 treats the 1968 George Wallace presidential campaign and distinguishes between the millions of people who voted for him and the small number of campaign activists who proceeded to form ineffective splinter parties in the 1970s. Under the banner of "Americanism," Wallace stalwarts combined a nationalistic brand of anticommunism, with racism, anti-Semitism, and anti-elitist conspiracy theories. Neither of the Americanists' two dominant organizations, the Liberty Lobby and the John Birch Society, were able to broaden their base beyond a few hundred thousand supporters. With declining influence, the movement's hard core moved toward survivalism and arcane teachings on white racial superiority. A new sub-movement of Identity Christian and Posse Comitatus tax protesters paved the way for the racist Right's violent resurgence in the early 1980s.

In the 1970s, at the furthest end of the right-wing spectrum from the Americanists, neoconservatism emerged as an influential tendency among prominent, disillusioned and formerly liberal intellectuals. Chapter 8 reviews the neoconservatives' roots in the liberal anticommunist activism of the 1950s and 1960s. Several crucial developments moved the neoconservatives rightward. These included a shift among some civil rights activists from integrationism to demands for equality of results, as well as the New Left's rising influence within—and also against—the Democratic Party, symbolized by the "days of rage" outside the 1968 party convention in Chicago. Leading noeconservatives broke with the party's liberal wing once George McGovern was nominated in 1972. From there, hawkish neoconservatives joined a coalition of New Right groups to defeat the Strategic Arms Limitation Treaty, and to forge a "shadow cabinet" of policy advisers for Ronald Reagan's 1980 presidential campaign.

In Part III of the book, we see Reagan's election as a dream fulfilled for the conservatives, the Christian Right and neoconservative defectors to the Republican Party. Libertarian activists opposed the new administration's intense militarism and camaraderie with the Moral Majority. But the libertarian perspective was reflected in the top priority the Reagan cabinet gave to a "supply-side" economic plan to cut taxes and spending. Chapter 9 describes the outrage of conservatives over the administration's failure to drastically expand Pentagon spending, cut taxes and balance the budget all at the same time. Throughout the 1980s, the movement consistently opposed Reagan's handling of economic policy but supported and collaborated in the administration's "low intensity" guerrilla wars, especially in Central America.

Similarly, the Christian Right had its hopes crushed when the Reagan administration failed to make good on campaign promises to outlaw abortion and reinstate school prayer. Chapter 10 documents the Christian Right's collaboration, with the New Right, on behalf of right-wing paramilitary forces from Central America to southern Africa to the Philippines. Limited success at the national level on social policy issues, combined with the need for greater intra-movement accountability following the embarrassing TV preacher scandals of the late 1980s, contributed to the Christian Right's strategic shift toward decentralized local activism. Pat Robertson's 1988 presidential bid expanded the Christian Right's grassroots organizational structure and tactical repertoire and deepened the movement's influence within the Republican Party.

Meanwhile, as we will see in Chapter 11, the organized racist Right continued to fracture, in two directions. The economic crisis in the U.S. Farm Belt enhanced the recruitment opportunities for Posse Comitatus tax protesters and for a violent echelon of Klansmen and Identity preachers united as the Aryan Nations. This wing of the white supremacist movement faced stiff government repression following a crime spree by its terrorist underground, the Order. At the same time, the Liberty Lobby's Populist Party boosted the electoral career of "former" Ku Klux Klan leader David Duke, who was elected to the Louisiana state legislature in 1989. Two years later, Duke won a majority of the white vote when he was, nevertheless, defeated in his race for the governor's seat. Apart from the foibles of the organized racist Right movement, the Duke phenomenon demonstrated the persistent salience of racism in electoral politics.

Softer versions of racism made their way into right-wing movements' post-Reagan-era faction fights, as detailed in Chapter 12. The withering of communism as a unifying enemy for the Right heightened inherent philosophical differences between the influential neoconservatives and a group of self-described "paleoconservatives." New Right activists with sympathies in both camps took the feud seriously, particularly as it was exacerbated by the Bush administration's 1991 Persian Gulf war, the first major U.S. foreign policy crisis after Communism's demise.

While conservatives bickered among themselves, evangelical Christians continued to build the strongest grassroots movement on the political scene. The Christian Right flexed its political muscles at the 1992 GOP convention and again in November through victories in scores of state and local races nationwide. Upon George Bush's departure from the White House, Republicans faced a quandary: how to maintain the activist resources and commitment offered by politically active evangelicals without further alienating those voters who were disturbed by the Christian Right's "family values" agenda. By the mid-1990s it was clear that the Republican Party would not abandon its reliable evangelical echelon.

In the Epilogue, I offer some final thoughts on the legacy of the Right's fifty-year quest for power. A postscript lets readers know how I collected data for this book. My intent is to encourage the study of social movements—in this case, those of the Right—as integral to the workings of our political system.

As this book was going to press public awareness of right-wing movements rose to an all-time high following the April 19, 1995, bombing of the federal building in Oklahoma City. Scores of people were killed in the blast. The first suspect arrested was a young man named Timothy McVeigh who was believed to be connected to a network of violent militia groups. Time would tell the full extent of McVeigh's connections and motivations.

But in the wake of the bombing, pundits, politicians, and groups with varying agendas tried to link the incident to all sorts of things: to the popularity of right-wing talk radio, to anti-abortion violence, to the growing clout of the Christian Right, even to the Republican-controlled Congress with its drumbeat of anti-government rhetoric. Speculation ran rampant, and hard data about the militia movement was in short supply.

What we did know was chilling. In the two years following the government's deadly raid on the Branch Davidian compound in Waco, Texas, thousands of people were arming themselves for more confrontations with federal agents. Credible estimates place the numbers of militia members in the tens of thousands, with probably many more thousands of armchair supporters tuned into the movement's radio broadcasts and computer forums.

Here was a movement that had quickly mobilized a motley crew of gun enthusiasts, tax protestors, veterans of the John Birch Society and white supremacist groups, plus newcomers with no previous experience in right-wing movements. Here was a movement representing some of the most alienated and disenfranchised members of society. Unlike some of the right-wing groups treated in this book, the militias feared and rejected ties with political elites and, instead, sought to reclaim some sense of power over and against a government they saw as tyrannical.

The rapid rise of the militias was made possible by the long march of their predecessors on the Right. This book sets the stage for our understanding of some of the tragic and perplexing events we now witness.

PART I

THE COLD WAR
AND CIVIL RIGHTS ERA,
1945–1964

CHAPTER 1

Delayed Reaction

THE RIGHT AFTER WORLD WAR II

World War II reconfigured the global political economy and set the stage for some major shifts in U.S. politics at home and abroad. After dropping the world's first atomic bombs on Japan, the United States emerged from the war as leader of the Free World: prosperous and unified, ready to do battle with the great "Communist threat" to the east. Despite its heavy losses in the war against fascism, the Soviet Union also emerged victorious. For better or worse, Soviet state socialism and the incipient revolution in China presented models for the anti-colonial national liberation movements of the next three decades. None of the political forces active before World War II could remain the same.

Right-wing movements in the United States were no exception. In the aftermath of World War II, self-described conservative activists faced three challenges. First, on the international scene, anticommunists both in and out of government questioned the Truman administration's resolve to defeat purported Soviet expansionism. Second, the activists were concerned by the domestic economy and the issue of whether New Deal policies represented a threat to liberty on a par with communism. Third was the possibility that an expanding interventionist and welfare state would necessarily challenge the provincial hegemony of southern Democrats and the system of racial segregation they had maintained since Reconstruction.

Among its many effects, World War II had relegated these crucial questions to a subordinate place on the national agenda. Many right-wing activists had opposed the United States' entry into World War II as vociferously as they had opposed the New Deal economic policies of the 1930s and 1940s.[1] Our historical analysis of the contemporary Right begins after 1945, with a resurgent oppositional activism that was, essentially, a delayed reaction to the rise of the welfare state of the 1930s. It was after 1945 that anticommunism became the driving ideological force and policy determinant among both political elites and social movement actors. The Cold War consensus on the need to defeat communism set the parameters within which the Right debated the relative merits of containment versus rollback doctrine. Within that same context, many traditional right-wing isolationists came to see foreign and military interventionism as imperative.[2]

At the same time, the Cold War set an agenda for domestic politics. While both Republicans and Democrats vied for the chance to direct U.S. foreign policy, leaders within each party had to decide how best to mobilize the electorate. Cast as a moral struggle between two competing sets of worldviews, the Cold War itself highlighted the discrepancy between U.S. democratic ideals and the reality of disenfranchisement for racial minority groups. The Democratic Party became a generally favorable vehicle for the emerging civil rights movement; the party sought to solidify support among actual and potential African American voters, many of whom migrated north after the war.[3] Many Republicans opposed federally mandated remedies for racial inequality and sought new party members among disaffected southern Democrats for whom civil rights initiatives were as threatening as the "communist menace."[4]

Apart from the beginning salience of the civil rights issue, the hallmark of the Right's post-war transformation was its shift from a traditionally non-interventionist foreign affairs stance to varying degrees of support for U.S. interventionism abroad. Certainly, conservatives' anticommunist impulses pre-dated the onset of the Cold War. But the conclusion of World War II left the political fate of much of the world uncertain. With the defeat of expansionist fascism, communism remained a real alternative for much of the world's population, and the United States determined to stop it. As conservative movement intellectuals engaged themselves in the post-war debates on how best to defeat communism, their anticommunist priority came to be fused with their pre-war pillars of moral traditionalism and anti-New Deal libertarian economics. This chapter, covering the late 1940s and early 1950s, traces the ideological and organizational development of what conservatives themselves termed a "fusionism" between disputing libertarians and traditionalists. Anticommunism became the unifying principle for the conservative intellectuals who, by the 1950s and 1960s, would become opinion leaders and significant Republican partisans.

THE RIGHT BEFORE AND AFTER WORLD WAR II

The construction of the post-war American Right was largely the work of conservative intellectuals, as opposed to a more grassroots-based echelon of activists who would become influential in the 1950s and beyond. Intitially, it was a group of conservative intellectuals who viewed with trepidation the expansion of the welfare state and some seemingly related trends: racial minorities' nascent demands for civil rights, the spread of secularism, and the growth of mass, popular culture.

These concerns were less prominent on the Right during the first part of the twentieth century. The early decades were marked by cycles of nativist activism waged against newly arrived immigrants from Europe and Asia. It was during the 1920s that the Ku Klux Klan, then largely an expression of nativist bigotry, reached its heyday of membership and influence.[5] Then in the 1930s the Depression spread economic hardship across ethnic, religious, regional, and even class lines, swelling the ranks of the Left and the trade union movement.

This is not to minimize the prominence of a proto-fascist movement active inside the United States during the 1930s and 1940s. More than one hundred American fascist organizations were active during the Depression era.[6] The pro-Hitler German American Bund circulated German Nazi literature inside the United States.[7] Bundists and some Ku Klux Klansmen attempted to forge associations,[8] even as Klan membership dropped drastically after the 1920s.[9] While Klan groups continued to meet informally throughout the 1940s, in 1944 the Knights of the Ku Klux Klan formally disbanded rather than pay a large bill assessed of them by the Internal Revenue Service.[10] (After the war, the Klan found itself in competition with the more respectable and mass-based Citizens' Councils of the 1950s. The Klan would play a violent role in the effort to thwart the civil rights movement.)[11]

During the Depression era, and predating the rise of popular televangelists by several decades, radio priest Father Charles E. Coughlin built a loyal following of millions of listeners. Coughlin's weekly on-air sermons interwove indictments of Wall Street bankers with dire warnings of creeping communist conspiracies. In the early years of Coughlin's popularity, he fancied himself a veritable confidant to President Franklin D. Roosevelt. But over time, Coughlin became one of the New Deal's most vitriolic critics. On the eve of the United States' entrance into World War II, Coughlin published anti-Jewish tracts and endorsed fascism as a viable alternative to Communism. Throughout his years on the air, Coughlin's claim to fame was his appeal to precisely those working-class ethnic immigrant groups who had been the targets of nativist prejudice.

Now they, too, could ally themselves in a putative struggle to preserve American sovereignty.[12]

Coughlin's anti-elitist diatribes were echoed by other well-known demagogues of the 1930s. William Dudley Pelley built the avowedly fascist American Silver Shirts into a paramilitary organization with 15,000 members modeled after Nazi Germany's SS batallions. In his public messages, Pelley mixed wild tales about aliens from outer space with standard racist and anti-Jewish appeals. Gerald Winrod, a fundamentalist minister from Kansas, preached against Jews, Catholics, and communists. The circulation of his *Defender* magazine grew from 40,000 in 1934 to 100,000 in 1936.[13] The Reverend Gerald L. K. Smith was a far-right preacher who began his career with the Silver Shirts before becoming a protégé to Huey Long, the demagogic Louisiana governor and, later, U.S. Senator who rallied millions behind a Share-Our-Wealth scheme to simply tally the national net worth and divide it evenly to the citizenry. Until his assassination in 1935, Long was a thorn in the side of the Roosevelt administration. But he did not pander to nativism and racial bigotry, as Smith did when he tried unsuccessfully to assume Long's mantle.[14] Added to the followings of right-wing preachers, support for what one scholar called "native American fascism" came from many, but certainly not all, German American and Italian American groups.[15]

Amid the flurry of right-wing activity, President Roosevelt's package of New Deal reforms—intended to alleviate the hardships of the Depression—fueled American fascists' claims that the country was headed toward state socialism. This fear drove a number of prominent businessmen to back fascist activities, including a plan to draft U.S. Marine Major General (Ret.) Smedley Butler to lead a military coup d'etat against Roosevelt. Butler rejected the businessmen's financial offer and reported the plot to members of Congress.[16]

The Justice Department, in 1942–1944, also prosecuted several prominent American fascists on sedition charges. Most notorious was Lawrence Dennis, a former State Department official who had become a prolific publisher of pro-fascist books and magazine articles.[17]

As in Europe, nationalistic concern about economic solvency and racial purity was the bedrock of domestic American fascism. On both sides of the Atlantic, fascism appealed to both mass and elite contingents. In the United States, pro-Nazi groups and the Ku Klux Klan opposed government policies that would protect the civil rights of ethnic minorities or entangle the United States in wars that, rightists argued, would benefit only the mythical "rich Jews."

The elite contingent of the Depression-era Right focused on New Deal economics and debates about the overall direction of U.S. foreign policy. In 1934 a coalition of conservative Democrats, Republicans, and business leaders formed the American Liberty League to rally opposition to President Roosevelt's New Deal reforms, especially pro-labor legislation.[18] One League spokesperson described the Great Depression as a "health tonic" that would rid the economic system of harmful poisons.[19] With financial backing from the Du Pont family, General Motors, Sun Oil, and other corporations, the League tried unsuccessfully to undermine Roosevelt's 1936 reelection campaign. But Roosevelt's campaign team successfully used the League's known corporate sponsorship for negative publicity against presidential challenger Alf Landon and other League-affiliated Republicans.[20]

Campaigns by the American Liberty League were followed by those of another corporate-sponsored anti-New Deal group. The Committee for Constitutional Government, formed in 1937 to oppose Roosevelt's Supreme Court appointments,[21] outlasted the Roosevelt administration as a leading post-war business lobby against New Deal labor and tax policies.[22] Later, during the 1950s, the Committee was among a number of groups that lobbied for a constitutional amendment to limit the power of Congress to impose taxes, especially on income, inheritance, and gifts.[23] During the Eisenhower administration, the Committee joined numerous right-wing groups who backed Senator John Bricker's (R-OH) proposed amendment to limit the presidential power to make treaties, while increasing the input of Congress in foreign affairs.[24] Both efforts, one to weaken the redistributive power of Congress to tax, the other to weaken presidential power to enforce international relations, enjoyed substantial support but ultimately failed.

Isolationist Roots

The American Right of the Depression era was characterized by (1) the strident racism and anti-Semitism of its large, mass-based organizations and (2) the anti-New Deal economic agenda of its corporate lobbies. Both camps were strongly nationalistic, and both shared an aversion to U.S. government intervention abroad. Much later, in the 1990s, when Patrick Buchanan rallied supporters of his 1992 Republican primary race behind the slogan "America First," he raised both the specter of the Right's return to its isolationist roots and some of the general public's recollections of what the old America First Committee was all about.

Founded by a small group of businessmen and law students in 1940,[25] the America First Committee was largely a publicity organization dedicated to keeping the United States out of World War II. During its brief existence, the Committee produced a flood of literature, gathered hundreds of thousands of signatures on anti-war petitions, and sent anti-interventionist speakers to hundreds of community meetings around the country. By the time it formally disbanded—following the Japanese bombing of Pearl Harbor in December 1941—the Committee boasted some 450 chapters and at least a quarter of a million members.[26] Many among them, including AFC leader and Chairman of the Board of Sears Roebuck, General Robert E. Wood, resented being labeled "isolationist."[27] At best, the label implied naiveté. At worst, isolationism implied an unwillingness, on the part of its advocates, to right international wrongs or to take patriotic pride in the United States' projection of military strength. As World War II intensified, isolationism became discredited, even among those right-wing activists who still opposed U.S. participation in the war. General Robert E. Wood, who later was a founder of the anticommunist American Security Council in the 1950s, claimed not to be an "isolationist."[28] Charles A. Lindbergh defended the America First Committee position as "a policy not of isolation, but of independence; not of defeat, but of courage."[29]

In the heat of national debate prior to the United States' entrance into World War II, America Firsters found themselves labeled disloyal, or naive, or even outright admirers of Adolf Hitler.[30] The charge against America First as anti-Semitic was made plausible by Lindberg's widely publicized 1941 speech in which he identified Jews, along with the Roosevelt administration and the British, as advocates of U.S. intervention.

> Instead of agitating for war, the Jewish groups in this country should be opposing it in every possible way, for they will be the first to feel its consequences. Tolerance is a virtue that depends upon peace and strength. History shows that it cannot survive war and devastation. A few far-sighted Jewish people realize this, and stand opposed to intervention. But the majority still do not. Their greatest danger to this country lies in their large ownership and influence in our motion pictures, our press, our radio, and our Government.[31]

While the America First Committee refused to reprimand Lindbergh, many individual America Firsters disapproved of the use of anti-Jewish rhetoric.[32]

After the America First Committee disbanded following Japan's bombing of Pearl Harbor, isolationist sentiment on the Right became less vocal but persisted. One important venue for isolationist writers was the *Human Events* newsletter, founded in 1944 by anti-interventionist journalists Felix Morley and Frank Hanighen, with William Henry Chamberlin on board as contributing editor. With an initial donation of $3,000 from Sun Oil Company Vice-President Joseph N. Pew, *Human Events* took its name from the opening line of the Declaration of

Independence and began with 117 subscribers.[33] In its early years, one occasional contributor among the otherwise conservative lineup was Socialist Party presidential candidate and anti-interventionist Norman Thomas.[34] By the 1960s, *Human Events* would grow to become a major right-wing newspaper, a supporter of Cold War foreign policy, and a leading backer of Barry Goldwater's presidential candidacy. But during World War II and its aftermath, *Human Events* served as a forum in which right-wing critics of foreign policy expressed their major concerns.

In their initial statement of policy, dated March 1, 1944, Morley, Hanighen, and Chamberlin spelled out their opposition to an enlarging state apparatus and U.S. interventionism abroad:

> True Liberalism will survive neither subordination to a despotic bureaucracy at home, nor entanglement in any Balance of Power system directed from abroad by those over whom American public opinion has no control.
>
> The present political, social, and economic strains will not be resolved—they will on the contrary be intensified—if the unconditional surrender of our present enemies finds the United States implicated in unauthorized, unpredictable, and unlimited military commitments in every quarter of the globe.[35]

With a pessimist's tone, Morley predicted that post-war policy would be "strongly imperialistic" and that, for starters, the United States would seek to dominate oil resources in the Persian Gulf.[36] *Human Events* opposed, early on, U.S. participation in a proposed United Nations on the grounds that George Washington had warned against such "entangling alliances."[37] At the same time, even before World War II had ended, *Human Events* editor William Henry Chamberlin warned readers that "Among all the belligerent powers the Soviet Union seems to stand the best prospect of realizing its war aims. Soviet objectives in Europe can be summed up in boundary changes and the establishment of a sphere of influence which the Red Army is already in a position to underwrite."[38] After the war Chamberlin devoted numerous *Human Events* essays to the problem of unchecked "Soviet expansionism" and pointed to the difficulties traditional isolationists would face in confronting the post-war enemy.[39]

THE BEGINNINGS OF THE CONSERVATIVE TRANSFORMATION

The difficulty Chamberlin identified derived from potential contradictions in the stance of conservatives toward the state. They were unequivocally opposed to redistributive New Deal economics, but the Cold War would require a strong state to influence foreign affairs. Following President Roosevelt's death, *Human Events* concerned itself with the general direction of state intervention in domestic affairs. In early 1947 *Human Events* published Edna Lonigan's daunting summation of the challenges conservatives faced:

> The New Deal is dead but the evil that it did lives on. Because it is now without a leader, a party, or even a symbol, we tend to forget how deep were the changes it made, and how much effort will be needed to repair the damage wrought.
> State Socialism, however begun, soon shifts to an oligarchy in which a small elite assumes control of the productive life of the nation.
> The New Deal democracy was not a representative party, based on free individual choices, but a pyramid of blocs—farmers, labor, Jews, Negroes, Southern Democrats, little businessmen, etc.; there was the right bait for all of them.[40]

Human Events editor Frank Hanighen was more succinct, describing the "paramount issue" of the day as "man versus the state."[41]

This theme resonated with the content of a landmark book by Austrian economic theorist Friedrich A. Hayek, *The Road to Serfdom*, published in 1944. Hayek expounded the essential tenets of a philosophy that would guide libertarian economic thinking for decades. Hayek took aim at "collectivism" and any sort of economic planning that would usurp "competition." He warned that "the road" to German National Socialism had been paved by the kind of welfare state policies gaining ground in Britain and the United States in the 1940s.

> The common features of all collectivist systems may be described, in a phrase ever dear to socialists of all schools, as the deliberate organization of the labors of society for a definite social goal.
> The various kinds of collectivism, communism, fascism, etc., differ among themselves in the nature of the goal toward which they want to direct the efforts of society. But they all differ from liberalism and individualism in wanting to organize the whole of society and all its resources for this unitary end and in refusing to recognize autonomous spheres in which the ends of the individuals are supreme. In short, they are totalitarian in the true sense of this new word.[42]

Hayek's book was widely reviewed and published in excerpt form by *Reader's Digest*.[43] Echoing Hayek's warning that "classical liberal" economics was the surest safeguard against both German-style fascism and

Soviet-style Communism, another Austrian economist, Ludwig von Mises, produced a series of economic treatises.

Libertarian Underpinnings

Mises' writings did not enjoy the same kind of mass popularity as Hayek's *The Road to Serfdom*, but both theorists provided a framework for the delayed reaction of libertarian intellectuals in the late 1940s and early 1950s. At this point, conservatism did not constitute a veritable social movement. Corporate-backed intellectuals established organizations through which they were able to consolidate thinking along conservatism's libertarian dimension. But only after philosophical libertarianism was complemented by traditionalism and anticommunism would conservatives become capable of attracting a broader base.

Hayek and Mises were both early associates of the Foundation for Economic Education (FEE), founded in 1946 by Leonard Read, a former manager of the Los Angeles Chamber of Commerce. From FEE headquarters in Irvington-on-Hudson, New York, Read assembled a group of corporate sponsors and academic economists and began diligently publishing books and tracts on libertarian philosophy and economics.[44] Read had been influenced by Albert Jay Nock, the early twentieth-century libertarian, anti-statist publisher of *The Freeman*, which Read brought under the publishing auspices of FEE during the 1950s.[45] FEE's approach was not to expend resources on particular pieces of state interventionist economic policy, but rather to educate and build a consensus among opinion leaders about the moral and practical superiority of unrestrained capitalism.

> The victory against socialism will finally come about not by beating down this moral, political, economic, and social error but, instead, by upholding its opposite. There is no limit to the forms error can take. Fighting error alone is an endless, futile undertaking. Knock down one error and new errors are always on hand to take its place. . . . Mere error-fighting by itself, without a positive approach, leaves this problem: Even after convincing a person of his mistake, you have given him no place to turn except to some other error among countless errors. The technique for libertarians is to uphold the free market, voluntary society, private property, limited government concept. Uphold it expertly, proudly, attractively, persuasively![46]

Rather than developing an individual subscriber base, FEE used a policy of controlled circulation. A business executive could make a large donation to FEE and request to have *The Freeman* sent to hundreds of employees.[47] By 1952, FEE was sending *The Freeman* and other publications to a mailing list of 28,712.[48] By the 1950s, FEE had established a large budget, reporting revenues of $287,000 in 1954, $433,000 in 1955, and $601,000 in 1956.[49] FEE reported the bulk of its donations as coming from the states of California, Illinois, Michigan, Texas, and Ohio.[50] Though FEE did not publicize dollar amounts from individual or corporate donors, during the 1950s its trustee list included numerous economics professors, university deans and presidents, oil and utility company executives (most prominently, J. Howard Pew of Sun Oil), the Chairman of the Board of United Fruit Company, and an Executive Vice-President of the Chase Manhattan Bank.[51] FEE's affluence and longevity represented significant corporate-based approval for Read's view that government should play as limited a societal role as possible.

> I would have government defend the life and property of all citizens equally; protect all willing exchange and restrain all unwilling exchange; suppress and penalize all fraud, all misrepresentation, all violence, all predatory practices; invoke a common justice under law; and keep the records incidental to these functions. Even this is a bigger assignment than governments, generally, have proven capable of. Let governments do these things and do them well. Leave all else to men in free and creative effort.[52]

Around the time of FEE's inception, a group of European and American classical liberal intellectuals, some of whom had met before the war, held a conference in Mont Pelerin, Switzerland. The ten-day conference in April 1947 was followed by another in 1949 and, thereafter, by yearly conferences held in cities on both sides of the Atlantic. Frederich Hayek was the founder and, for many years, the chairperson of this international strategy group of libertarian economists, activists, and business leaders, who dubbed themselves the Mont Pelerin Society.[53] Years after its founding, libertarian economist Milton Friedman credited the Society with serving as a "rallying point" for classical liberals.[54] Historian George Nash cites the influence of European thinkers in the Mont Pelerin Society as a factor that prevented many U.S. conservative intellectuals of the 1950s and 1960s from drifting toward the kind of xenophobia that attracted some grassroots activists.[55] Renowned conservative philosopher Russell Kirk argued that the Society's friendliness toward "conservative, traditional and religious opinions and institutions" as well as its "detestation of the total state," made it an asset in the "merging of the best elements in the old conservatism and the old liberalism."[56]

FUSIONISM

It is unlikely that libertarianism alone could have sustained the post-war Right. Rather, both participants and observers of the conservative movement credit the unifying current known as "fusionism" for the contemporary Right's successful growth and endurance. Fusionism represented the kind of breakthrough ideological transformation that can either help catalyze a new movement or lead an already existing one through a period of impasse. Fusionism, simply put, was the historical juncture at which right-wing activists and intellectuals focused, diversely, on the libertarian, moral–traditionalist, and emerging anticommunist strains of conservative ideology, recognized their common causes and philosophies, and began to fuse their practical agendas.[57]

Fusionism was not a process that occurred independently of human agency. Perhaps because conservatives in the late 1940s were few in number and politically weakened by the mass popularity of World War II interventionism and New Deal domestic policy, the influence of a few key individuals and publications was strong. Among those most prominent in the fusionist era dialogues were the "traditionalist" Russell Kirk, and Frank Meyer, an ex-Communist who became a leading advocate of anti-statist individualism and libertarianism in the 1950s. Kirk's book *The Conservative Mind*, released in 1953 by Henry Regnery's publishing house, became a classic on a par with Hayek's *The Road to Serfdom*. Kirk directed the attention of conservative readers to the threat posed by all things "socialist" from the French Revolution forward. His definition of "conservatism" revolved around preservation of an established moral order and hierarchies of inequality. Kirk's formulation posed an apparent contradiction to the libertarians' concern with individualism and the notion of "man versus the state." But Kirk also stressed private property rights as the essence of human freedom.[58]

Over several decades, Kirk's *The Conservative Mind* would popularize, for countless right-wing activists, some of the same commitment to notions of traditional moral standards and timeless truths found in the work of Leo Strauss. An obscure political philosopher who taught for many years at the University of Chicago, Strauss was mentor to a generation of intellectuals, including prominent neoconservatives of the 1980s and 1990s like William Bennett, Allan Bloom, and Irving Kristol. In his teaching and in his writings—his best known-book was *Natural Right and History*—Strauss stressed reliance on the belief, propounded by the ancient philosophers, in a natural social order, something distinguishable from the kind of relativistic, even hedonistic, moral codes that shifted with the changing of the political guard. Strauss' thinking was complex. A small number of conservative thinkers studied Strauss' work in depth and drew from it politically relevant convictions: that freedom is not purely an end in itself but a means to securing a virtuous society, that the passage of historical time may coincide little with the achievement of social progress. Where classic Marxism held that history moves societies inexorably in a progressive direction, Straussians suspected the opposite was true: that modernity brought with it the threat that utopians would rationalize even their most egregious policies on a thesis of ends justifying means.[59]

Reverence for the past and an enduring social order balanced the fusionists' adjoining commitment to individualism, especially in the marketplace. These themes came together in the 1950s as conservatives applied them to their critique of establishment institutions. In 1951, a young William F. Buckley, Jr. published his first book *God and Man at Yale*, a scathing critique of left-liberalism and secularism within the academy. At the same time, Buckley lamented academia's supposed abandonment of the free enterprise–private property credo.[60] *God and Man at Yale* raised a storm of controversy,[61] and Buckley became the first president of the Intercollegiate Society of Individualists, founded in 1953 by Frank Chodorov, a libertarian editor of both *Human Events* and *The Freeman*. The Society, which later changed its name to the Intercollegiate Studies Institute (ISI), built chapters on college campuses across the country and became the major vehicle for the recruitment and training of students into the conservative movement, until Buckley started Young Americans for Freedom in 1960. In founding ISI, Chodorov's operative theory was his belief that "opposition breeds conviction" and that New Deal "socialists" had, "with admirable astuteness," gone "to work particularly on the fertile mind of youth."

> Long before the New Deal came upon us, thousands of these college-bred Socialists had taken their training into fields where it could be put to use: as labor leaders, ministers, teachers, lawyers, writers. They were opinion-makers. They worked themselves into positions of importance in these fields, and further entrenched themselves by hiring more recent graduates of the Socialist clubs.[62]

The secret to gaining political power would be to combat liberals within the labor, professional, and intellectual institutions, starting with the academy. ISI focused on distributing literature by, and arranging college speaking engagements for, the leading conservative intellectuals of the time: Richard Weaver, Russell Kirk, Frank Meyer, Leonard Read, and others.[63] Many student editors of ISI publications later became influential political leaders in their own right.[64]

While Buckley, as founder of the *National Review* magazine, would become the best-known unifier of traditionalists and libertarians on the

Right, the leading intellectual proponent of fusionism was Frank Meyer, an ex-communist turned anti-statist libertarian. In a 1955 article in *The Freeman*, Meyer critiqued Kirk's *Conservative Mind* for its subordination of individual freedom to the goal of conserving community values.[65] Buckley's brother-in-law, L. Brent Bozell, a Catholic traditionalist, contended that the libertarians and fusionists put too much emphasis on individual liberty and not enough on virtue, either voluntary or coerced. The rhetorical debates inspired by the conflict between traditionalism and libertarianism raged for decades in *National Review*, *Modern Age*, and other conservative journals of opinion.

From both a practical and philosophical standpoint, Frank Meyer proposed what he called a "dialectical" synthesis of traditionalism and libertarianism. Meyer argued that advocates of "both implicitly accept, to a large degree, the ends of the other."[66] His logic ran like this: without a basis in moral values, personal freedom is meaningless; and without freedom of choice, society's pursuit of virtue and order would lead to "totalitarian authority."[67]

Anticommunism was the major factor in what fusionist and *National Review* publisher William Rusher called the "strategic integration" of conservative thought.[68] Communism and, by extension, the liberalism of the New Deal Democrats provided the threat of an external enemy. Anticommunism provided a perspective from which both libertarians and traditionalists could see each other's points of view. Economic libertarians could see that the threat of socialism required a response more profound than mere fiscal policy or theory. Traditionalists could see that cherished institutions and moral persuasion alone could not stem the tide toward socialism.

Pragmatic empathy alone, however, does not explain how libertarians and traditionalists overcame their differences and melded their tendencies. Fusionism represented the maturity of intellectuals who were willing to hold in mind two seemingly contradictory ideas, libertarianism and traditionalism. They were willing to see their nascent movement as broad enough to contain diversity and willing to acknowledge that no single person or small group had "the answer."

If libertarianism on the economic front represented an anti-statist position, that tendency was counterbalanced by traditionalism. With its emphasis on the preservation of moral order or community standards, traditionalism implicitly called for some sort of state role to enforce prevailing values through law. Anticommunism may have had as an objective the limitation of statist intervention in the "free market," but anticommunism also made imperative a role for the state in enforcing existing class and power relations, both within U.S. society and in the realm of international affairs.

The Birth of *National Review*

If there was a single pivotal event in the cementing of the fusionist ties between Cold War-era conservative intellectuals, it was the 1955 founding of the *National Review* magazine by publisher William F. Buckley, Jr.[69] Prior to that event, conservative intellectuals had no central outlet for rigorous debate among themselves, let alone a means of communication to preach to the unconverted. From its inception, *National Review* projected itself as an iconoclastic publication, one determined not to remain marginal but to pull mainstream thinking in its own direction. In his opening "Publisher's Statement," Buckley made his often-quoted announcement that *National Review* "stands athwart history, yelling Stop at a time when no one is inclined to do so."

> There are, thank Heaven, the exceptions. There are those of generous impulse and a sincere desire to encourage a responsible dissent from the Liberal orthodoxy. And there are those who recognize that when all is said and done, the market place depends for a license to operate freely on the men who issue licenses—on the politicians. They recognize, therefore, that efficient getting and spending is itself impossible except in an atmosphere that encourages efficient getting and spending. And back of all political institutions there are moral and philosophical concepts, implicit or defined. Our political economy and our high-energy industry run on large, general principles, on ideas—not by day-to-day guess work, expedients and improvisations. Ideas have to go into exchange to become or remain operative; and the medium of such exchange is the printed word.[70]

Buckley was explicit about the need for conservatives to think strategically; they should not react haphazardly to events as they occurred but, rather, should systematically propagate antiliberal ideology and policy views. Among the magazine's six stated priorities, *National Review* set out to critique and combat (1) "the growth of government"; (2) communism, described as "the century's most blatant force of satanic utopianism"; (3) the "cultural menace" of "conformity of the intellectual cliques" in education and the arts; (4) the "identifiable team of Fabian operators. . .bent on controlling both our major parties"; (5) "politically oriented unionism"; and (6) "the fashionable concept of world government, the United Nations [and] internationalism."[71]

Reflecting fusionism's diversity of conservative opinion, *National Review* offered regular contributions by traditionalists (including Russell Kirk on educational trends and Buckley's brother-in-law L. Brent Bozell on affairs in Washington, D.C.); libertarian-oriented analysts John Chamberlain, Karl Hess and Frank Meyer; and, on foreign affairs, James

Burnham, an ex-leftist who promoted a rigid "rollback" doctrine for U.S. victory in the Cold War.[72] Issue after issue, *National Review* focused on several problems crucial to the emerging conservative movement. On foreign policy, Burnham and others tracked developments among the decolonializing Third World nations and spurred debates on how best the United States could prevail in the superpower arms race. Bozell, Meyer, and others analyzed the conservative movement's rocky relationship with the Republican Party of the 1950s and 1960s, and they offered a fairly consistent viewpoint in support of southern states' resistance to the civil rights movement and federal initiatives to effect desegregation.

On Cold War foreign policy, *National Review* contributors divided into several camps, but debate between them was amicable. Maintaining the Right's disposition toward isolationism, William Henry Chamberlin called veteran America First organizers Charles Lindbergh and General Robert E. Wood "principled and patriotic" opponents of the United States' entry into World War II. Chamberlin claimed long-term U.S. interests would have been better served if the Roosevelt administration had opted to let "two dictators," Stalin and Hitler, battle each other. Likewise, Chamberlin wrote, the United States should have allowed the Japanese and Chinese nationalists to fight it out with the Chinese Communists and the Soviet Union.

> Neither isolationism or interventionism is a rational goal in itself. Under changing circumstances, each may be desireable as the more serviceable to the interests of the United States. Certainly isolationism, with its flat rejection of foreign alliances and overseas commitments, is not a safe or even a practicable policy for the United States now, when the Communist empire has weighed down the scales of world power so heavily that only United States power can maintain a precarious balance. To advocate isolationism today is, therefore, to aid, albeit unconciously, the Communist grand design of world domination.[73]

This was the logic through which the crucial shift from isolationism to interventionism was made: abstention from international conflict could no longer be defended in a context in which the United States was the only power strong enough to counterbalance the Soviet Union. In its Cold War context, interventionism maintained the isolationists' preference for unilateralism, decisive action, and preoccupation with the errors of liberal Democrats.

The remaining question was how best to defeat communism, the form and extent of intervention necessary. In "Liberation: What Next?", an article that provoked a series of published rebuttals and counter-arguments, James Burnham advocated that the policies of "containment" and "coexistence" with the Soviet Union be replaced with an all-out strategy he called "liberation." The goal would be to force the Soviet Union's military withdrawal from Eastern Europe, return the USSR to its pre-1939 borders, reunify the two Germanys and forge friendly relations with Germany and the rest of Eastern Europe.[74] *National Review* contributors Frank Meyer and William S. Schlamm expressed strong disapproval of the idea that the United States ought to withdraw its occupation forces from Europe. They argued that the end result of Burnham's plan would be to make atomic warfare the only credible deterrent to Soviet military moves in the region of Eastern Europe.[75] Schlamm disputed Burnham's claim that Eastern Europe was the most critical axis of the superpower struggle, and argued instead that the United States needed to be preoccupied with three regional trouble spots: Europe, Asia, and Latin America.[76] By the 1960s, Burnham's "rollback" line would dominate the thinking of anticommunist movement activists. Anticommunism itself smoothed the apparent contradiction between fighting a superpower arms race with the Soviet Union and "liberating" Third World nations from communist guerrilla insurgencies.

National Review contributors also initiated a debate on the relative merits of supporting the Republicans' Eisenhower–Nixon ticket of 1956. William S. Schlamm argued against, claiming that Eisenhower was just another liberal with Republican trappings. James Burnham argued for, because the two-party system requires that coalitions be built long before elections are held. Therefore, Burnham concluded that conservatives' abstention from the election or the formation of a third party would only isolate the Right and give the upper hand to its opponents in both parties.[77]

On southern politics and the question of federal intervention to achieve integration, *National Review* opinion makers were less divided. Though the magazine was founded after the landmark 1954 Supreme Court decision mandating the desegregation of public schools, throughout the late 1950s and 1960s, *National Review* editorialized in favor of states' rights in the handling of "the Negro problem." On this matter, it seemed, the "traditionalism" of the southern "way of life" outranked the libertarian notion of "individual freedom," at least for African Americans. In a characteristic editorial, "Why the South Must Prevail," Buckley was explicit on the threat civil rights initiatives posed to the tradition of white supremacy:

> The central question that emerges—and it is not a parliamentary question or a question that is answered by merely consulting a catalogue of the rights of American citizens, born Equal—is whether the White

community in the South is entitled to take such measures as are necessary to prevail, politically and culturally, in areas in which it does not predominate numerically. The sobering answer is *Yes*—the White community is so entitled because, for the time being, it is the advanced race. The question, as far as the White community is concerned, is whether the claims of civilization supersede those of universal suffrage.

National Review believes that the South's premises are correct. If the majority wills what is socially atavistic, then to thwart the majority may be, though undemocratic, enlightened. It is more important for any community, anywhere in the world, to affirm and live by civilized standards, than to bow to the demands of the numerical majority.[78]

The Legacy of Fusionism

During the immediate post-war period, the Right was more of an intellectual ideological current than a proper social movement. At this stage, conservatives knew which state policies and political forces they opposed, but they had only begun to articulate alternatives. From the 1930s through the end of the 1940s, opponents of New Deal statism maintained a bloc within Congress,[79] but relations between characteristically right-wing state actors and outsider movement activists were tenuous. Right-wing movement interaction with the state was limited to the ideological terrain and had yet to effect a strong impact in the realms of political parties and executive-level policymaking. It was not until the Cold War period of the 1950s that state actors began incorporating para-statal institutions, including social movement organizations, in efforts to combat communism. The groundwork laid by fusionist intellectuals, who opposed state intervention in the economy but supported state action to repress communism, facilitated the eventual mobilization of system-supportive outsiders within policymaking processes.

From 1945 through the 1950s, libertarians and traditionalists put aside some of the inherent philosophical differences that divided them and began to make common cause against welfare statism at home and communism as represented by the Soviet Union and, later, China. Ultimately, the end result of the fusionist compromise, and of all the practical debates that enlivened the pages of *National Review*, was the development of a sophisticated and flexible movement, one that could accommodate some degree of diversity and internal contradiction without splitting apart at the seams.

In the coalition that came together, the role of anticommunist ideology and objectives was probably decisive. Simultaneous with the rise of an explicitly anticommunist movement (Chapter 2), that constituency within the Democratic Party known as "Cold War liberals" espoused a mixed agenda: militarism and other forms of strong state interventionism abroad to thwart communism, but also strong state initiatives at home to secure domestic economic welfare, civil rights for African Americans and organizing rights for anticommunist trade unions (Chapter 8). While some defectors from the 1930s Communist movement found their ideological home with the Cold War liberals and, later, among the neoconservatives of the 1970s and 1980s, a small but significant number joined forces with the fusionists early on. These included the prominent ex-leftists who became *National Review* contributors: Max Eastman, John Dos Passos, Will Herberg, and James Burnham.[80] Their collaboration in the fusionist coalition lent credibility to the urgency of the anticommunist cause and helped smooth the Right's transition from isolationism to interventionism.

If New Deal welfare statism constituted the core of political hegemony following World War II, its most vulnerable periphery was the socialist Left. By the time *National Review* was started in 1955, the Cold War was in full swing. State institutions and politicians themselves had already marshalled a variety of tactics against "subversive" U.S. citizens, against the Soviet Union, and against its real and perceived allies around the world. Professional Cold Warriors would eventually enjoy the collaboration of a multifaceted anticommunist movement, one that would galvanize substantial popular support and pave the way for the Right's ascent within the Republican Party.

CHAPTER 2

From McCarthy to Goldwater

THE ANTICOMMUNIST MOVEMENT OF THE 1950s AND 1960s

Not until the Cold War was in full force would the early conservative movement's fusionist thinkers find a context within which to express themselves, first on the pages of *National Review* and *Human Events*, later at meetings of the Republican Party faction that drafted Barry Goldwater as its 1964 presidential candidate. It was during the 1950s and 1960s that conservatives moved from near obscurity on the political landscape to prominence as a vocal minority.

By the early 1950s, anticommunism had become the raison d'être of U.S. objectives abroad. It had also permeated the political and cultural scene at home, as pursuit of internal subversion focused, as well, on real and alleged communists inside trade unions, academia and the entertainment industry.[1] The Cold War policies formed and executed at the highest levels of government, not only cast legitimacy on the existing anticommunist preoccupation of conservatives, but also effectively created a role for those movement organizations eager to collaborate in the anticommunist cause.

The anticommunist priority led conservative movement strategists to downplay the libertarian and traditionalist components of their three-dimensional ideology. Anticommunism was the tenet everyone on the Right could agree on; although, tactically, the anticommunist movement was not all of one mind. The most fervent movement players carried their anticommunist musings beyond the point of no return when they made wild charges of "communist subversion" against top government figures. Senator Joseph McCarthy himself set the pattern—

and met his own downfall—when he impugned military leaders as suspected Communist agents. Yet, as we will see in this chapter, McCarthy's demise was followed by the growth of a mass-based anticommunist movement, which endured, in part, because it was the beneficiary of a corporate-sponsored flood of anticommunist print and broadcast propaganda, directed at the U.S. public.

The widespread moblization of elite and mass-based anticommunist contingents helped consolidate public opinion in support of Cold War policies. But beyond ideology and moving into the realm of party politics, the unity of conservatives around the cause of anticommunism also made possible their growth into an influential faction of the Republican Party. That development, covered in our treatment of Barry Goldwater's 1964 presidential campaign in this chapter, paved the road for the New Right's forward march in the 1970s and beyond.

THE COLD WAR CONTEXT

Four short years after the end of World War II, the world was no more secure than before. In August 1949 the Soviet Union tested its first atomic bomb and ended the United States' monopoly over the new weapons of mass destruction. By the end of 1949, Chinese Communists had successfully defeated the U.S.-backed regime of Chiang Kai-shek. If China, with one quarter of the world's population, could "fall" to the Communists, it was not difficult to imagine that the rest of Asia, if not the rest of the developing world, might be next to "turn red."

By the late 1940s the Truman administration had launched a strategic program of intervention in Greece, Turkey, and the Mediterranean.[2] The 1947 National Security Act established the Central Intelligence Agency and the National Security Council as arms of the executive branch, and created the office of the Secretary of Defense to supervise the Departments of the Army, Navy, and Air Force.[3] In 1950, the National Security Council under Truman adopted a directive known as "NSC-68," which mandated a permanent peacetime military mobilization and a massive increase in military spending.[4] Aside from its role as liaison between the White House and the CIA, from 1951 to 1953 the National Security Council also coordinated the Psychological Strategy Board, which studied and recommended propaganda tactics aimed at the Soviet Union, combat troops on both sides of the Korean War, and international public opinion in general.[5]

Korea became the first testing ground for the foreign affairs establishment's debate about whether to "contain" or "rollback" Communist forces. Between 1950 and 1953, direct U.S. military intervention in the

Korean war cost more than 33,000 American lives, and the total number of Korean and Chinese casualties exceeded two million.[6] Heavy casualties on the U.S. side heightened conflict between President Truman and General Douglas MacArthur, commander of U.S. and United Nations forces in Korea. MacArthur was a popular war hero who had commanded U.S. occupation forces in Japan after World War II. While Truman wanted to limit the scope of the Korean conflict and fight purported Soviet expansionism through other means, MacArthur wanted to extend the Korean War into China. In the spring of 1951, when MacArthur disobeyed Truman's order to cease making unauthorized statements about the war, Truman fired the General and sparked heated public opposition.[7] From the standpoint of the White House, the dismissal signified Truman's determination to exert civilian control over the military. But among partisans of the Republican Right, the General's ouster fueled sentiment that liberal Democrats like Truman were ineffectual in fighting Communism, if not outright complicit in its spread.

By the time Senator Joseph McCarthy entered the center stage of U.S. politics, the groundwork for what would come to be known as "McCarthyism" had already been established. The Truman administration itself had in 1947 initiated loyalty checks for all federal employees and had encouraged the Justice Department to prosecute dozens of Communist Party leaders under the Smith Act.[8] A series of highly publicized spy cases exacerbated the Red Scare of the 1950s and lent credence to McCarthy's subversion-from-within thesis. In 1948 *Time* magazine editor Whittaker Chambers testified before the House Committee on Un-American Activities (HUAC) that Alger Hiss, a State Department official under President Roosevelt, had passed important documents to Soviet agents. Hiss was the only government official successfully prosecuted for pro-Communist activities. In 1950 Hiss was convicted and jailed, not for treason but for perjury, involving his connections to Communist Party members during the 1930s.[9]

Shortly thereafter, Ethel and Julius Rosenberg were tried and sentenced to death for conspiracy to transmit atomic bomb secrets to the Soviet Union during World War II. Public debate over the Rosenbergs' guilt or innocence persisted for the next two years, as the couple exhausted the appeals process and were finally executed in 1953. On the heels of the Hiss and Rosenberg cases, Congress investigated the Institute for Pacific Relations (IPR), the leading association of Western experts on China, for alleged connections to the People's Republic. The highly publicized disclosures of alleged Communist influence over the IPR's publications and recommendations to the State Department had the collateral effect of discrediting the institute's numerous liberal foundation backers.[10]

Senator Joseph McCarthy himself was more an exploiter than a creator of the political milieu in which he operated. Like-minded politicians at first benefited from having their enemies' reputations smeared by his infamous lists, investigative hearings, and skillful innuendo, and then they benefited from ostracizing him once his hunt for subversives had gone too far.[11]

Once McCarthy himself had faded from public prominence, pluralist social scientists could credibly neglect McCarthyism's roots in routine politics[12] and instead identify McCarthy's excesses as a function of what they called the "radical right."[13] In addressing McCarthyism, Daniel Bell, for example, acknowledged that McCarthy the man was less important than "the deeper-running social currents of a turbulent mid-century America."[14] Bell, and his colleagues who contributed to the influential anthology *The Radical Right*, fixed their analytical attention on the purported social base of the Senator's citizen supporters, and portrayed McCarthy's adherents as the political descendants of the anti-elite agrarian Populist movement of the late nineteenth century. By attributing McCarthy's support to the same small business class who had supported "left-wing" populism in earlier decades,[15] pluralist social scientists were able to propound a concept of "extremism" as something that crosses partisan lines and supersedes policy goals and implications.[16]

But when political scientist Michael Rogin studied the actual base of support for both populism and McCarthyism, he found that the two movements did not share the same constituency at all. Instead, at the elite level, McCarthy's support came from Republican Party, business, and military leaders. At the mass level, Republican Party affiliation was the strongest correlative factor. To the extent that McCarthy enjoyed a mass following, his appeal was based on widespread anticommunism and particular concern about the Korean war.[17]

Aside from Senator McCarthy's base of support, the ideology of McCarthy*ism* set the stage for the rise of movement organizations that took governmental preoccupation with "national security" to its logical extension. As it grew, the anticommunist movement of the 1950s forged mutually beneficial links with Republican Party leaders and elected officials. The movement developed a diverse array of lobbies, research institutes, media outlets, and, most importantly, an organizational apparatus that accomodated both elite and mass participants.

The division of labor between the elite and mass-based anticommunists enabled the movement to enjoy the broadest possible appeal. Chronologically, the emergence of centralized, elite anticommunist groups predated the rise of more decentralized groups of average citizens. In terms of tactics, the divide between elite and mass-based organizations helps explain how movement groups with similar goals and ideology can, nevertheless, frame their agendas so as to express, variably, a supportive or an oppositional stance toward the state. The distinction between elite and mass, system-supporters and opponents, also helps explain some of the varying responses anticommunist activists received from government officials.

ELITE ANTICOMMUNIST MOVEMENT ORGANIZATIONS

The China Lobby

Among the numerous anticommunist organizations of the 1950s and 1960s, those most focused on international affairs were dominated by elite activists. Compared with their grassroots counterparts, these foreign affairs lobbyists enjoyed disproportionate access to government officials and large, expensive media outlets.

Elite opponents of the Truman administration's containment policies turned the "loss of China" into a rallying cry for hard-line anticommunism. Throughout the Cold War years, many anticommunist groups could trace their organizational lineages to the "China Lobby." The term originated as a reference to Chinese agents of the Kuomintang, who during the 1940s sought to counteract U.S. leftists' attacks on Chiang Kai-shek's government.[18] Once the Chinese Communists had formally seized power over the mainland and had driven Chiang Kai-shek's army onto the island of Formosa, the China Lobby shifted its strategy toward prevention of any kind of international diplomatic recognition of the People's Republic.

Some of the China Lobby groups were directly associated with Chiang's government-in-exile. Most were non-Chinese who supported Chiang out of loyalty to the anticommunist cause.[19] Among these, the most influential organizations were those coordinated by public relations expert Marvin Liebman, whose New York City offices served as headquarters for dozens of anticommunist organizations throughout the 1950s and 1960s.[20]

Liebman became a colorful and ubiquitous character on the Right. But he started his political career, in New York in the 1930s, as a young, Jewish, closeted homosexual and a gadfly of the Left. He worked with the Young Communist League before he was drafted during World War II. He was swiftly thrown out of the military when his higher-ups discovered a love letter he had written to another man.[21] Liebman then became an ardent fundraiser for a number of Zionist organizations before he went to work for Harold Oram, a New York City public relations man. Oram's clients included the International Rescue Committee

(IRC), a project with a dual purpose. The IRC offered humanitarian aid to refugees from Eastern bloc countries and also used the refugees' plight as grist for the anticommunist propaganda mill. Liebman parlayed his work for the IRC into a similar project for refugees fleeing Communist China in the 1950s. He organized a group called Aid Refugee Chinese Intellectuals (ARCI), which received logistical assistance from the State Department and some of its money from the Central Intelligence Agency. In his 1992 autobiography, Liebman recounted that the CIA had used ARCI as a front for its intelligence gathering work in Hong Kong, a haven for Chinese refugees.[22] Beginning in the 1950s, Liebman also advised William F. Buckley, Jr. on how to raise funds for *National Review* and came to see Buckley as his political mentor.[23]

More than in any other project, Liebman's devotion to the anticommunist cause took form in his Committee for One Million (later renamed the Committee *of* One Million). Liebman waged an exhaustive campaign to influence elected officials and the general public through the carefully targeted use of newspaper advertisements, radio broadcasts, and distribution of books and pamphlets. The Committee was not an oppositional movement organization. It did not set out to change, but rather to intensify, prevailing public opinion and administration policy. The Committee sought to ensure President Eisenhower's commitment to non-recognition of the People's Republic of China, to exert similar pressure on United Nations members considering diplomatic recognition and trade ties with the PRC, and to strengthen negative public opinion regarding Communist China and its international allies.

In its efforts, the Committee for One Million garnered bipartisan support from Republican and Democratic politicians eager to exploit the China issue. Beginning in September 1953, the Committee's first goal was to collect one million individual signatures on a petition to President Eisenhower, urging opposition to United Nations recognition of the People's Republic of China. The Committee's intitial list of sponsors included former President Herbert Hoover, former Secretary of the Navy and New Jersey Governor Charles Edison, and former U.S. Ambassador to Japan Joseph C. Grew. Among members of Congress, initial signators included Representatives Walter H. Judd (R-MN) and John W. McCormack (D-MA) and Senators John Sparkman (D-AL) and H. Alexander Smith (R-NJ). George Meany, president of the AFL-CIO also signed on.[24]

Largely through solicitation via newspaper advertisements, by July 1954 the Committee for One Million had collected its one million signatures. The following month, the Committee closed its offices. But in February 1955 the Committee announced its intention to regroup as the Committee *of* One Million, "to publicly represent the opinion of the 1,037,000 American citizens who signed its Petition and the organizations and groups which endorsed its purposes."[25] The Committee continued its placement of anti-China newspaper advertisements and solicitation of new names for its petitions and mailing lists.[26]

By 1956 the Committee began publishing a monthly newsletter, with a circulation of 35,000, and enlisted leading Congressional Representatives to record endorsement spots, broadcast over 500 radio stations in the United States and Canada.[27] Also in 1956 the Committee lobbied business leaders in the National Association of Manufacturers and took credit when the Senate Committee on Interstate and Foreign Commerce decided to postpone indefinitely hearings on opening trade with China.[28]

In a confidential memorandum to his steering committee, Marvin Liebman warned that despite the U.S. delegation's repeated U.N. resolutions to block admission of the People's Republic, the number of nations in favor of its admission was growing. Liebman emphasized that what stood in the way of the eventual replacement of Taiwan's U.N. seat with a seat for China was that "many member nations . . . realize that the future of the UN rests in the full participation of the United States."[29] Liebman continued to boast that "the Committee of One Million has given our delegation the most potent weapon available in their fight—the pressure of a mobilized and articulate American opinion which is steadfast in its opposition to the admission of Communist China to the U.N."[30] In essence, the Committee's strategy was to create a volume of printed material and public proclamations sufficient to convince important policymakers that there was a consensus in the United States against international recognition of China.

Liebman later bragged that the Committee of One Million had more to do with perception than reality. "The perception that we were a powerful lobbying group speaking for one million Americans was far more important than the reality," Liebman wrote in his 1992 autobiography. "What it came down to was one individual—me—with a circle of influential allies who could get all these VIPs to sign the public statements we wrote . . . thus creating the illusion of an enormous people's movement."[31]

The illusion bore fruit. In 1958 the Committee claimed credit when the Japanese government cancelled a plan to enter a trade agreement with China. The Committee had published a statement, "An Appeal to Sanity," in a major Tokyo newspaper and distributed the statement in pamphlet form by the tens of thousands.[32] Also in 1958 the Committee published and circulated to U.N. delegates copies of Edward Hunter's *The Black Book on Red China*. The Committee translated and printed editions of the book in Korea, Taiwan, and Vietnam, and gave 300 copies to the United States Information Agency for its overseas literature distribution program.[33]

Following the Committee's success, Marvin Liebman started several spinoff groups. In 1957 Liebman started the American-Asian Educational Exchange as a tax-exempt outfit to engage in literature distribution, but not direct lobbying. By 1962 the Exchange had broadened its focus to include the "communist threat" to Africa, and changed its name to the American Afro-Asian Educational Exchange.[34] The exchange leadership overlapped significantly with that of the Committee of One Million: Representative Walter Judd served as chairperson and Senator Thomas Dodd, the Honorable Charles Edison, and Dr. Max Yergan served as vice-chairs. Also active were a number of prominent right-wing professors and intellectuals,[35] including Yale University political science Professor David Nelson Rowe. The Exchange distributed the anti-China writings of noted academics and Congressional leaders through a variety of channels, including the State Department, the AFL-CIO, *Harper's*, *National Review*, and *New Leader* magazines.[36] In one exchange publication, Professor Rowe acknowledged assistance from numerous ministries of the Taiwanese government.[37] By 1966, the Exchange claimed to have published and circulated 1.4 million pieces of anticommunist literature. The Exchange coordinated its activities with the Asian People's Anti-Communist League (APACL),[38] a consortium of anticommunist politicians. APACL would eventually merge with the World Anti-Communist League (WACL), founded in 1966 (see Chapters 6 and 9). The Exchange sent youth delegations to APACL conferences and, in the mid-1960s, was instrumental in involving William F. Buckley's Young Americans for Freedom in an APACL project to support the government of South Vietnam.[39] All told, the constellation of China Lobby groups provided a framework within which an, as yet, small number of right-wing activists collaborated with U.S. and foreign elites to fight communism on the Asian continent. The contacts and tactics established through the China Lobby would serve U.S. anticommunists well when they later expanded their numbers and applied what they learned to their foreign affairs projects of the 1970s and 1980s.

Captive Nations

One component of the U.S. strategy for victory in the Cold War was the mobilization of anticommunist East European exile and emigré groups, as well as their American supporters. In this endeavor, the leading set of government-sponsored "private" organizations were the National Committee for a Free Europe, the related Crusade for Freedom, and its beneficiary, Radio Free Europe. The National Committee was headed by "political warfare" specialist C. D. Jackson, who began his career as right-hand man to Henry Luce in his *Time–Life–Fortune* magazine publishing enterprise. During World War II, Jackson headed the United States Psychological Warfare Division and worked with General Dwight D. Eisenhower.[40] Under President Eisenhower, Jackson became a White House assistant on national security strategy.[41] From that position, Jackson became a leading advocate of corporate–government collaboration to influence public opinion through what he called "political warfare." The CIA-financed Radio Free Europe was considered the most important piece of this operation inside the Soviet sphere of influence, particularly in the wake of the 1956 Hungarian uprising and subsequent Soviet invasion.[42]

Politically oriented intelligence operations commonly rely on deceptive funding conduits, and Jackson's projects were no exception. Through Radio Free Europe, the National Committee for a Free Europe directed CIA funds to the Assembly of Captive European Nations (ACEN),[43] founded in 1954 for the purpose of coordinating media and lobbying activities of anticommunist East European nationalists. According to author Christopher Simpson, whose study of the U.S. government's recruitment of pro-Nazi East European emigrés relies heavily on declassified intelligence documents, "the ACEN became the showcase of the CIA's numerous exile projects inside the United States beginning in 1954."[44], Over time, the Assembly and an affiliated group called the Anti-Bolshevik Bloc of Nations (ABN) would become important vehicles through which the Republican Party would forge voter coalitions of East European emigré groups in the United States.[45] But during the 1950s and 1960s the Assembly and its support arm, the American Friends of the Captive Nations (AFCN), were the means through which elite activists sought to influence opinion among other elite decision makers, while disseminating anticommunist propaganda to the general public.

From the start, the AFCN was endorsed by some of the same anticommunist Congressional leaders who had sponsored the China Lobby's Committee of One Million.[46] At the same time that the China Lobby worked to keep the People's Republic out of the United Nations, the Captive Nations groups focused on pressuring the United Nations to enact anti-Soviet resolutions, especially after the 1956 Hungarian uprising.[47] In this respect, the Captive Nations groups functioned not as challengers to the Eisenhower and, later, Kennedy and Johnson administrations, but rather as system-supportive activists intent on maintaining the anti-Soviet consensus in the United States.

Throughout the 1950s and 1960s, the ACEN and the AFCN staffed an office in New York City across the street from the United Nations and maintained a steady public presence through letters to national newspapers and delegations that lobbied Congress. In 1959 President Eisenhower established a national "Captive Nations Week," enacted into federal law and celebrated with public rallies every July for years thereafter. Annually, the AFCN provided informational packets on Soviet misdeeds in Eastern Europe to hundreds of editorial writers, legislators, and church leaders.[48]

ACEN and AFCN meetings were routinely endorsed and attended by U.S. Senators and Repressentatives, State Department officials, and leaders of the AFL-CIO.[49] Through such endorsements, political elites lent legitimacy to the call by the Captive Nations groups for "liberation" of the East European countries, as opposed to the official U.S. doctrine of "containing" the Soviet Union by buttressing Western Europe militarily. A 1957 *ACEN News* article, "Does Liberation Mean War?" condemned the timidity of Western nations in failing to enact U.N. sanctions against the Soviet Union for its intervention in the 1956 Hungarian uprising, and in the closely timed rebellions and strikes in Poland and Czechoslovakia.[50] Advocates of "liberation" or "rollback" doctrine, like *National Review* contributor James Burnham, argued that a deadly nuclear confrontation was less, not more, likely if the Western allies would harden their anti-Soviet stance. Though ACEN, like the China Lobby, promoted "rollback," the doctrine was not mutually exclusive with "containment," particularly as U.S. policymakers sought justification for increased intervention in southeast Asia.[51]

The Military–Industrial Complex

While the China Lobby and Captive Nations groups remained prominent voices on foreign affairs, the American Security Council was the leading elite anticommunist organization of the 1950s. Founded by a group of former Federal Bureau of Investigation agents, the Council's original mission was to provide dues-paying corporations with politically sensitive information about prospective employees. ASC was started in Chicago in 1955 by ex-FBI agent William F. Carroll as the Mid-Western Research Library; in 1956 the name was changed to the American Security Council. From the 1950s through the 1980s, the Council was headed by former FBI agent John M. Fisher who had been a national security coordinator for the Sears Roebuck department store chain.[52] By 1958, the *New York Times* reported that the American Security Council had gathered files on more than one million supposedly "subversive" U.S. citizens and that the group was collecting names at a rate of 20,000 per month.[53] In 1961, the Council claimed that one of its major functions was "to maintain close liaison with the legislative and executive branches of government and the armed forces."[54] In a promotional brochure directed at the business community, the Council noted the superiority of its own intelligence gathering over that of the FBI, which by law "cannot divulge the information in its files except in a court of law or for the confidential use of another federal agency."[55] Thus, the ASC operated as a repressive agency, on a par with the FBI itself.

Among the American Security Council's original incorporators and file collectors were several right-wing activists who had actively opposed U.S. participation in World War II. These included Sears Roebuck Chairman General Robert E. Wood and publishing magnate William Regnery, both of the America First Committee; Harry Jung of the anti-Semitic American Vigilante Intelligence Federation; and John Trevor of the pro-Nazi American Coalition of Patriotic Societies.[56] These former advocates of a non-interventionist U.S. foreign policy now found a mission in the American Security Council's efforts to expose American leftists and deprive them of their livelihoods.

In addition to providing intelligence to large employers, the Council was also active in Cold War "education" aimed at the general public. Between 1955 and 1961, the ASC cosponsored an annual series of meetings called the National Military–Industrial Conferences, which brought Pentagon and National Security Council personnel together with executives from United Fruit, Standard Oil, Honeywell, U.S. Steel, Sears Roebuck and other corporations.[57]

At the 1958 National Military–Industrial Conference, the ASC launched the Institute for American Strategy for the purpose of inculcating elites and the public with anticommunist ideology.[58] Administration of the Institute was granted to Frank Barnett, U.S. Army Colonel William Kintner, and other "political warfare" advocates then stationed at the University of Pennsylvania's Foreign Policy Research Institute. Barnett was also research director for the Institute's key corporate benefactor, the Richardson Foundation (the charitable arm of Vick Chemical Company). In 1959 and 1960 the ostensibly private Institute for American Strategy held seminars for reserve officers at the National War College, under the auspices of the Joint Chiefs of Staff and the Secretary of Defense.[59] The manual for these seminars was the book *American Strategy for the Nuclear Age*, prepared by Foreign Policy Research Institute analysts Walter F. Hahn and John C. Neff. This book outlined an aggressive strategy of "protracted conflict" with the Soviets, involving the training of citizens and government leaders in "psychological warfare" schools. By 1961, the Institute for American Strategy had provided 10,000 copies of *American Strategy* to the National University Extension Association for distribution to public school libraries and citizen debate groups.[60]

Through the National Military–Industrial Conferences, regional meetings, National War College seminars and publications, the Institute began to assume the role of a military adjunct and a quasi-governmental propaganda agency. However, by 1961, Senator William J. Fulbright, Chair of the Senate Foreign Relations Committee, became alarmed by what he perceived to be a combination of right-wing and military encroachment on the formation of U.S. public opinion. (As will be discussed below, in early 1961 this same concern had surfaced following press revelations that Major General Edwin Walker was indoctrinating U.S. troops stationed in Western Europe using John Birch Society literature.) In the summer of 1961, Fulbright sent a personal memorandum on "propaganda activities of military personnel" to President Kennedy and Secretary of Defense Robert McNamara. Senator Strom Thurmond of South Carolina learned of the memo and demanded a copy, which then prompted Fulbright to enter the entire document into the *Congressional Record* on August 2, 1961.

In the memorandum, Senator Fulbright noted that a 1958 National Security Council directive indeed authorized the "use of military personnel and facilities to arouse the public to the menace of the cold war." Fulbright, however, objected to the use of *American Strategy for the Nuclear Age* as "by no means representative of the President's announced strategy" Fulbright's long memo read in part as follows:

> In at least 11 instances of what apparently are implementations of the National Security Council policy, the actual programs, closely identified with military personnel, made use of extremely radical, rightwing speakers and/or materials, with the probably net result of condemning foreign and domestic policies of the administration in the public mind.
> The content no doubt has varied from program to program, but running through all of them is a central theme that the primary, if not exclusive, danger to this country is internal Communist infiltration.
> The thesis of the nature of the Communist threat often is developed by equating social legislation with socialism, and the latter with communism. Much of the administration's domestic legislative program, including continuation of the graduated income tax, expansion of social security, federal aid to education, etc., under this philosophy, would be characterized as steps toward communism.
> This view of the Communist menace renders foreign aid, cultural exchanges, disarmament negotiations, and other international programs, as extremely wasteful, if not actually subversive.[61]

Fulbright proceeded to name dates, venues, and lists of speakers for a series of anticommunist "strategy seminars" at which the public had been instructed about communists within the government by Kintner, Barnett, and military personnel affiliated with the Institute for American Strategy.[62]

Here was a powerful Senator attempting to constrain a consortium of elite-based anticommunist organizations. Fulbright specifically named the Foreign Policy Research Institute, the Institute for American Strategy, the Richardson Foundation, and the National War College. The Senator's concern was not so much that the military was granting legitimacy to and aiding private organizations further to the right than the Kennedy administration; rather, he feared that a small number of corporate-backed private groups had assumed improper influence over the U.S. armed forces. At stake was nothing less than the question of whether the civilian, democratically elected administration would continue to control the military.

Fulbright's memorandum was attacked by grassroots anticommunist groups, including the by-then notorious John Birch Society. Senator Strom Thurmond responded to Fulbright by demanding an investigation of Defense Department "censorship" of military officers, and the John Birch Society supported such a move with a Congressional letter-writing campaign. Thurmond then held hearings in September of 1961, but to no avail.[63] Fulbright had already succeeded in tarnishing the reputation of the Birch Society and the military trainers affiliated with the Institute for American Strategy.

Despite the controversy, the American Security Council and the Institute for American Strategy continued their activities unabated. In fact, in 1962 the Council claimed credit for influencing the Kennedy administration's Cuba policy. In August 1961, the ASC's National Strategy Committee had received a letter from Assistant Secretary of State for Latin American Affairs Robert F. Woodward to the effect that key State Department officers were reading ASC's report recommending a cutoff of U.S. fuel to Cuba.[64] It would be impossible to prove a decisive role for the American Security Council in this aspect of the destructive economic embargo against Cuba. It is more plausible to suggest that, as with other elite-based foreign affairs lobbies, the Council pressured the administration in a direction toward which it was already inclined.

As was characteristic of system-supportive anticommunist groups, the American Security Council functioned as an asset to the Cold War state, largely by reinforcing anticommunist ideology. By 1962 the Council boasted of the success of its "Freedom University of the Air," a series of sixty-five half-hour television programs hosted by former ASC Field Director W. Cleon Skousen.[65] In 1964 former President Dwight Eisenhower, who, ironically, had warned of a "military–industrial complex" in his farewell presidential speech, inaugurated the "American Security Council Washington Report of the Air," over 500 radio stations. From Munich, the CIA's Radio Free Europe broadcast this program in six European languages. By November 1964 the program was added on the Mutual Broadcasting System's 535 stations, for a total number of stations greater than that of any other weekday news program.[66] With major financial backing from Patrick Frawley's Schick Safety Razor company, the Council's anticommunist radio programs reached an estimated 35 million people.[67]

While the American Security Council targeted mass public opinion, the Institute for American Strategy worked to influence public educators. In 1962 the National Governor's Conference, representing all fifty states, created a Committee on Cold War Education with the goal of coordinating anticommunist high school curricula. Through the office of Florida Governor Farris Bryant, who chaired this Committee, the Institute for American Strategy was enlisted to be the secretariat for the June 1963 National Governors Conference on Cold War Education held in Tampa, Florida. Speakers included representatives from Congress, the State Department, and the Organization of American States.[68] Governors Conference also invited the Institute to conduct two-week Cold War education courses for assistants to all fifty governors and to develop training courses for high school teachers and a curriculum guide.[69]

The Institute for American Strategy was also among many anticommunist organizations that tried unsuccessfully for several years to lobby the federal government to create a Freedom Academy.[70] The idea for a private-sector Freedom Academy originated in 1954 when a group of Orlando, Florida businessmen and political activists drafted a proposal and engaged the help of the Council Against Communist Aggression (CACA) along with Senators Paul Douglas of Illinois and Karl Mundt of South Dakota.[71] The purpose of such an academy would have been to enhance the federal government's use of psychological warfare against communist agents. In *American Strategy for the Nuclear Age*, Institute for American Strategy research director Frank Barnett advocated the creation of a "West Point of political warfare" for the training of Eastern bloc defectors.[72] A bill to create a Congressionally funded Freedom Commission made up of private citizens who would establish such a Freedom Academy was first introduced into Congress by Representative Syd Herlong of Florida in early 1959. Numerous similar bills were introduced and debated from 1959 through 1965. But despite widespread support from anticommunist organizations, and from some national security agency professionals, the bill was defeated, largely because the State Department opposed the creation of a new agency that would duplicate the work of its own Foreign Service program. Likewise, the Department of Defense and the U.S. Information Agency opposed the establishment of an academy that would have usurped some of their own functions.[73]

Throughout the Cold War era, the relationship between elite anticommunist organizations and government agencies was one of limited mutual support. Private sector propaganda campaigns were consistent with political warfare strategist C. D. Jackson's advocacy of corporate–

government collaboration in the fight against communism. Cold warriors inside the government, however, never gave up their prerogative to block the excesses of anticommunist movement groups. This pattern was particularly evident in the partially antagonistic relationships that developed between government officials and some of the Right's grassroots activists.

GRASSROOTS ANTICOMMUNIST ORGANIZATIONS

The John Birch Society, founded in 1958, was the prototypical right-wing activist group throughout the 1960s. The Society's pressure tactics, its top-secret membership lists and its all-encompassing conspiratorial worldview combined to make it a target of negative press and public ridicule. As a single organization, the Society developed a sizeable membership, but its influence was most likely due to its position within a larger constellation of mass-based anticommunist organizations and projects.

Numerous anticommunist groups predated the formation of the John Birch Society. The American Coalition of Patriotic Societies (ACPS), founded in 1927 to oppose foreign immigration, coordinated the activities of about one hundred long-standing fraternal and promilitary societies. By the mid-1950s, the ACPS had directed its membership toward opposing foreign aid, U.S. diplomatic ties with the Soviet Union, and admission of Communist China in the United Nations.[74] Moral Re-Armament, an organization that had grown out of the British Oxford Group of the 1930s, had by the late 1940s established a conference center and an active effort to recruit U.S. military officers, labor leaders, and rank-and-file unionists to its anticommunist cause.[75] Also in the late 1940s and early 1950s, numerous small anti-Semitic and racialist organizations active before and during World War II, shifted their sights to the seemingly related problems of domestic communism and civil rights legislation.[76] As we will see in Chapter 3, pro-civil rights Supreme Court actions, especially the 1954 decision mandating public school desegregation, sparked the formation of local segregationist Citizens' Councils throughout the South.

One early 1950s organization that drew both anticommunist and anti-civil rights activists was the Congress of Freedom, which claimed the United Nations threatened U.S. national security. Between 1953 and 1966, annual conferences held by the Congress drew hundreds of people, many of whom were leaders of their own organizations. One of the projects that unified these groups was the Liberty Amendment, a proposal drafted by Willis E. Stone's National Committee for Economic

Freedom, that would have amended the Constitution to repeal the federal income tax. Activists worked in their respective states to obtain endorsement of the proposal by their legislatures.[77] Though neither the United Nations nor the income tax were eliminated, the activism around these and other issues fostered some of the third-party efforts of the 1960s (see Chapter 3).

Before and after the formation of the John Birch Society, corporations played a major role in rallying the public to the anticommunist cause. One study of corporate anticommunist educational programs traced the trend to the 1947 Taft–Hartley Act which granted employers the right to distribute literature to counter labor union organizing. By 1963, corporations were spending an estimated $25 million per year on anticommunist literature distributed to consumers and to employees at the job site.[78] Sponsoring corporations included major firms such as Goodyear Tire, Minnesota Mining, Boeing Airplane Co., Jones & Laughlin Steel, and Texas Power & Light, as well as smaller companies that came to be associated with grassroots groups like the John Birch Society: Knott's Berry Farm, Dr. Ross Dog Food, Cherokee Textile Mills, Allen-Bradley Corporation, and others. Some corporations circulated print and audio–visual materials produced by the John Birch Society; other companies produced their own in-house literature. Coast Federal Savings and Loan Association in Los Angeles conducted one of the largest customer education programs, distributing millions of leaflets and booklets at a cost of about $250,000 a year.[79]

Coast Federal provided customers with a "Patriotic Program Log," listing radio and television schedules and corporate sponsors for leading anticommunist broadcasters: Paul Harvey, Billy James Hargis, Fulton Lewis, Jr., Reverend Carl McIntire, Dan Smoot, and Dean Manion.[80] By the early 1960s, the *Nation* magazine reported that there was a minimum of 6,600 corporate-financed anticommunist broadcasts, carried by more than 1,300 radio and television stations at a total annual budget of about $20 million. Broadcast themes included opposition to foreign aid, the United Nations, the Supreme Court, labor unions, medicare, and "forced integration." Leading sponsors included Texas oil billionaire H. L. Hunt and Howard J. Pew of Sun Oil.[81] The corporate sector's massive anticommunist propaganda campaigns created a favorable climate for the mobilization of activist groups like the John Birch Society.

The John Birch Society

At a time when the U.S. government was formally committed to fighting communism, yet appeared to many observers incapable of doing so, the John Birch Society gave its members an outlet to express their grievances and a compelling, explanatory world view that made sense of contemporary affairs. The Society's conspiracy theories cast even respectable public figures as the puppets of powerful "Insiders" lurking behind both communism and capitalism. The Society's bizarre ideology and aggressive use of massive letter writing campaigns led critics to characterize Birchists as "extremists" and supposedly antiestablishment "radicals." But while the Society positioned itself as oppositional in relation to elected administrations, its actual program was prototypically both right-wing and system-supportive. The Society supported those government agencies charged with *enforcing* law and order and global U.S. military supremacy while it opposed government efforts to regulate business, promote civil rights, and provide welfare services.

John Birch was a Baptist missionary and an air combat intelligence operative during World War II. Ten days after the war ended, Birch was killed by Chinese Communists, and thus earned folk hero status as the first casualty of "World War III." Among John Birch's admirers was Robert Welch, a retired candy manufacturer and former director of the National Association of Manufacturers.[82] Before he arrived at the idea of starting the John Birch Society, Welch began making a name for himself by distributing his own anticommunist writings. Among these was his 1954 manuscript called *The Politician*, in which Welch called President Eisenhower a conscious agent of the "communist conspiracy." (It was not until public exposure of *The Politician* in 1960 that Welch's conspiracy theories propelled the young John Birch Society into the limelight of controversy.) Welch inaugurated the Society in December 1958 when he invited a group of his business associates to spend two days listening to his theories and battle plans. The transcript of Welch's monologue was published as *The Blue Book*, which became required reading for new members of John Birch Society chapters starting in 1959.

The essence of Welch's doctrine was that Western societies faced an unprecedented, multi-faceted, and coordinated assault by secret conspirators:

> Communism is not a political party, nor a military organization, nor an ideological crusade, nor a rebirth of Russian imperialist ambition, though it comprises and uses all of these parts and pretenses. Communism, in its unmistakable present reality, is wholly a conspiracy, a gigantic conspiracy to enslave mankind; an increasingly successful conspiracy controlled by determined, cunning, and utterly ruthless gangsters, willing to use any means to achieve its end.
>
> As a result of this forty years of cumulative effort, the conspiracy is now incredibly well organized. . . . This octopus is so large that its

tentacles now reach into all of the legislative halls, all of the union labor meetings, a majority of the religious gatherings, and most of the schools of *the whole world*.[83]

Despite Welch's belief in a pervasive and unscrupulous "communist conspiracy," he did not promote violent or particularly undemocratic action to achieve victory. Instead, Welch urged Society members to increase the number of anticommunist radio programs and to establish "reading rooms" stocked with right-wing peridicals, including the Society's own *American Opinion*, the *Dan Smoot Report*, and William F. Buckley's *National Review*. (These "reading rooms" evolved into a chain of American Opinion bookstores.)

The chief tactic of the Birchists was the organization of massive letter-writing campaigns, directed from Society headquarters in Belmont, Massachusetts, through local chapters of ten to twenty people each. In an effort to mimic what he thought the Communists were doing, Welch also advocated the use of front groups not apparently linked to the Society. The idea was to form committees around very specific campaigns, that would quickly dissolve once the goal was met. In July 1959, for example, Birchists started a front called the Committee Against Summit Entanglements (C.A.S.E.) to stop a proposed exchange of visits between Soviet Premier Nikita Khruschev and President Eisenhower. In reality, C.A.S.E. did little more than publish newspaper ads which Welch later claimed led to Eisenhower's decision not to visit the Soviet Union.[84] The constant flurry of new petition gathering and letter writing projects helped maintain member interest and organizational cohesion.

Each month the Society's general circulation *American Opinion* magazine featured articles on exemplary patriots, whose noble life stories were contrasted with government officials the Society charged as virtually being traitors. In a separate monthly *Bulletin* sent to members only, Welch assigned specific tactics. Each *Bulletin* contained an "Agenda for the Month" that instructed members on what letters to write, what books to read and recommend to friends, and what chain stores to contact to protest the sale of products manufactured by "slave labor" in Eastern bloc countries. The *Bulletin* enabled chapters to concentrate their forces on a few targets and to give rank-and-file members a manageable number of tasks to accomplish. Each month, members were required to itemize their letters, postcards, and phone calls. Chapter leaders forwarded these "Members' Monthly Memos" to headquarters in Belmont, Massachusetts.[85] In this way, the Society maintained an explicitly hierarchical structure.

Welch assembled a National Council, including some of the eleven men at the 1958 founding meeting, to "show the stature and standing of the leadership of the Society"; to guide "the Founder," as Welch liked to call himself; and to select a successor to Welch after his death. The original Council consisted of three medical doctors, three lawyers, one retired General, one syndicated columnist, a priest, and seventeen executives of medium-sized corporations.[86] By 1961, a low estimate of the size of the Society placed rank-and-file membership at about 60,000, widely distributed throughout the country, but with particular centers of strength in Houston, Los Angeles, Nashville, Wichita, and Boston. Annual income from member dues was estimated at about $1.3 million.[87]

One detailed study of members' demographics and political attitudes found the Society's membership to be disproportionately young, upper middle class, well-educated (in technical fields more than in liberal arts), Protestant fundamentalist in religious orientation, and favorable toward the Republican Party. Membership was strongest in the southern and western regions of the country, in the relatively less populated states, and in areas characterized by recent population influxes. Over 50 percent of those sampled held high-status occupations and earned upper-middle-class incomes. The study suggested a relationship between the Protestant fundamentalism of Society members, with its emphasis on personal sin and responsibility, and their attraction to conspiracy theories, which tend to elevate the causal importance of the misdeeds of individuals over that of larger social forces. In terms of political attitudes, the study found Birchists to be advocates of an increased role for states' rights versus the authority of the federal government, of reduced government spending on social programs, of a tougher military policy to win decisively against communism (e.g., in Vietnam), and of less use of non-military foreign policy initiatives, such as the efforts of the United Nations. Birchists opposed medicare, social security, farm subsidies, pro-union legislation, disarmament, and foreign aid. They wanted a return to the gold standard and a reduction of government regulation over business.[88] In essence, the politics of Birchists were characteristically right-wing; they opposed government policies to distribute wealth and power more equitably, and they endorsed government policies to enforce traditional order at home and abroad.

The policy preferences of Birchists were consistent with those of other right-wing organizations, both elite and mass-based. Tactically, the Society's emphasis on letter-writing campaigns and literature distribution are hardly the kinds of activities that could be described as extremist or undemocratic. What may partially explain the public image of the Birchists as "extremists" was the Society's uncompromising conspiracy theory of world events, one that blamed domestic rather than foreign enemies for the spread of communism. Their reasoning went something like this: if communism was gaining influence all over the world, and if the United States was the most powerful nation on earth, but its leaders seemed unwilling or unable to stem the communist tide, then these very same leaders must be consciously or unwittingly collaborating with the "communist conspiracy."[89]

Why would such an indictment of U.S. leaders be attractive to the thousands of Society members? One scholar proposed that the national climate of anticommunism made the simplicity and rigidity of the Birchist worldview attractive precisely because it provided reinforcement for, rather than contradiction of, prevailing sentiments.[90] Other analysts suggested that Robert Welch's vision of a sort of undifferentiated ruling group of capitalist and communist Insiders helped explain apparent consistencies between American "liberals" and "conservatives." The same band of machiavellian Insiders controlled both Tweedledum and Tweedledee.[91] In essence, the Birchist worldview allowed adherents to hold typically right-wing policy preferences simultaneous with the belief that the Society's opponents, including many bona fide conservatives, were secretly part of the "communist conspiracy." Though the tactical repertoire of the Birchists deviated little from routine citizen lobbying, the Society earned the "extremist" label when it charged its political adversaries with outright treason.

Just as Senator Joseph McCarthy found himself opposed by state elites once his enemies list included leaders of the U.S. Army, likewise the John Birch Society met the limits of government tolerance when Robert Welch attacked former President Eisenhower's patriotism in *The Politician*. In 1961, Senator Milton R. Young (R-ND) read into the *Congressional Record* information pertaining to Welch's accusation that, while he was president, Eisenhower had secretly facilitated the "communist conspiracy."[92] Heated debate followed among elected officials. Society opponents argued that the group had gone beyond the bounds of decency and fair play; although supporters, including a number of legislators who acknowledged their own membership in the Society, argued the group's worthiness in the struggle against communism. Heightened press and Congressional attention prompted the Senate Internal Security Subcommittee to issue a statement, signed by Chairman James O. Eastland (D-MS) concluding that the John Birch Society was indeed a "patriotic organization." But other government officials took dimmer views. In March 1961, California Governor Edmund G. Brown ordered the state's Attorney General to investigate the John Birch Society, and California's Senate Un-American Activities Committee held a hearing on the Society's activities. On the federal level, Representative Francis E. Walter (D-PA) ordered an inquiry by the staff of the House Committee on Un-American Activities. Robert Welch himself urged the Senate Internal Security Subcommittee to investigate and give the Society a clean bill of health.[93]

The controversy surrounding Welch's charge against Eisenhower struck a nerve in a nation recently subjected to Senator Joseph McCarthy's disruptive charges of Communist subversion at the highest levels of government. If former President Eisenhower—a venerated World War II General and a leading figure in the Cold War—could be labeled a Communist, what government official could feel safe from the Birchists' smear tactics?

By 1961 the Society had also targeted Chief Justice Earl Warren in a letter-writing campaign aimed at removing him from the Supreme Court. Motivated by the charge of Society leaders that Warren had "voted 92 percent of the time in favor of Communists and subversives," rank-and-file members flooded their Congressional Representatives' offices with letters demanding Warren's ouster. The anti-Warren campaign attracted the interest of then-Attorney General Robert F. Kennedy, who reportedly considered the Society worthy of a federal investigation.[94]

No element of the John Birch Society's efforts at influence drew greater fire than the revelation, by the U.S. military newspaper *Overseas Weekly*, that a high-ranking Army officer was using Birch books and magazines to attempt to "indoctrinate" U.S. troops stationed in Europe. The Walker controversy broke several months before Senate Foreign Relations Committee chairman William Fulbright made public his controversial memo on the influence of elite right-wing groups on the National War College. That Major General Edwin A. Walker, a World War II and Korean War hero then commanding the Twenty-Fourth Infantry Division, could be extending the military's Cold War ideological training program for soldiers to include the John Birch Society's worldview was intolerable to many government leaders. Walker was denounced on the floor of the U.S. Senate when Senator William Proxmire (D-WI) called for the General's dismissal and said the incident showed that the fight against communism should be handled by "intelligent" people and not left to "morons." Days later, the Army relieved Walker of his command in Germany, and several months later Walker resigned.[95]

At the time of the Walker case, the *New York Times* noted that the General was operating within the mandates of a standing National Security Council policy calling for a full-scale Cold War mobilization at all levels of the government. The Defense Department had been ordered to educate troops on "national security" concerns; commanding officers were provided with literature and audio–visual material and required to report regularly on their training activities. According to the *New York Times*, Walker's "special warfare" training program was not the only one in which overzealous military personnel charged the U.S. government itself with communist subversion.[96]

Far from discouraging participation, negative publicity and denunciations from some elected officials seemed to heighten the popularity of the John Birch Society and similar groups. At the peak of controversy, the Society had organized between one and one hundred chapters in each of thirty-four states; Welch drew an audience of more than 6,000 people at a rally in Los Angeles.[97] The society's popularity was consistent with the spread of numerous business-backed grassroots anticommunist organizations.

Among these, Dr. Fred C. Schwarz's Christian Anti-Communism Crusade was the most succcessful. In October 1961, Schwarz's organization televised nationally a three-hour "Hollywood's Answer to Communism" rally at the Hollywood Bowl. Twelve thousand people attended, and an estimated total of four million viewers watched on television as John Wayne, James Stewart, Roy Rogers, and Dale Evans were joined on stage by Senator Thomas Dodd, Representative Walter Judd, and *Life* magazine publisher C. D. Jackson.[98]

Press coverage of this and other events distinguished Schwarz's Crusade from the John Birch Society on the basis of each group's *tactics*, rather than on the conspiratorial view of communism they shared. Whereas the Birchists used pressure tactics to demand the ouster of particular government leaders, the Crusade instead organized well-attended anticommunist training schools with distinguished faculty. Schwarz trained church leaders and military personnel to conduct their own anticommunist lectures and film-screenings.[99] Schwarz's anticommunist schools attracted participants similar to the membership of the John Birch Society: with better than average education and income; of disproportionately high-status professions; and highly identified with the Republican Party.[100]

By and large, these were not marginalized "extremists." Only a small proportion of the grassroots anticommunist movement was attracted to true fringe groups like Robert B. DePugh's paramilitary, survivalist Minutemen group. The Minutemen stockpiled weapons and trained for hypothetical "communist takeover" scenarios. Their numbers never grew beyond several thousand, but they did play a limited role in unifying some segments of the anticommunist movement with white supremacist organizations of the 1960s (discussed in Chapter 3).[101]

Overall, the response of government officials to the grassroots anticommunist movement was one of acquiescence. Unlike leftist organizations, which met various forms of strong and weak repression throughout the Cold War, groups like the John Birch Society were never seriously investigated. They experienced mild forms of public denunciation when their campaigns targeted respected figures. Though the grassroots anticommunists took an oppositional stance toward politicians deemed "soft" on communism, overall the Right reinforced prevailing state and corporate prerogatives during the Cold War era.

FROM MOVEMENT TO PARTY FACTION

Ultimately, neither the elite nor the mass-based wings of the anticommunist movement could fully pursue their agendas without contending for state power through electoral politics. By the late 1950s, the anticommunist movement sought to increase its influence within the Republican Party.

Until his death in 1953, Republican Senator Robert Taft of Ohio had been the leader of the party's right wing. Taft was a strong opponent of New Deal spending policies. He also upheld the Right's pre-World War II preference for non-interventionism in foreign affairs. In the context of the Cold War, Taft's prospects as a presidential contender grew dim, in part because it was part of his reputation that he would be unwilling to deploy massive state power to fight communism. While the Soviet Union helped install a Communist regime in Czechoslovakia, Taft fought in the Senate to reduce U.S. funding for post-war recovery projects in Europe. Taft also opposed military conscription; and he bucked his fellow Republicans' drive to weaken the Democrats' north–south unity through legislation to ban workplace racial discrimination. Taft voted, with southern Democrats, against the Fair Employment Practices bill.[102]

In view of Taft's weakening popularity with some Republicans, General Dwight D. Eisenhower presented himself as a candidate willing to run as either a Democrat or Republican. Initially, anticommunist activists gave Eisenhower only a lukewarm endorsement, but by 1952 they believed that Eisenhower would be able to beat incumbent President Truman. Taft's loss of the Republican presidential nomination to Eisenhower in 1952 was a disappointment to many Republicans, but Eisenhower's victory in 1952 and again in 1956 broke the Democrats' long hold on the White House.[103]

Prior to the formation of *National Review* in 1955, the *American Mercury* was the most widely circulated national magazine on the Right.[104] In a series of editorials, the *American Mercury* framed the 1952 election campaign in no uncertain anticommunist terms. The problem with President Truman, according to the *Mercury*, was his State Department chief Dean Acheson, whom the McCarthyite Right blamed for all manner of Communist misdeeds worldwide.[105] The 1952 election was the chance to defeat "communist subversion" once and for all.

Yet eight months after Eisenhower took office, the *American Mercury* indicted him for not fulfilling his campaign pledges to secure "an 'honorable' peace in Korea; a firmer policy toward Red imperialism; a balanced budget; and tax reductions, now." Instead, Eisenhower's policy was characterized as one of "Moderation, Compromise, and Caution."[106] Later, Eisenhower drew the enmity of the anticommunist Right for standing idly by during the infamous 1954 Army–McCarthy hearings. Senator McCarthy's reputation took a nosedive after he tried, unsuccessfully, to impugn the patriotism of the U.S. military itself. (It was after the Army–McCarthy hearings that the Senate voted formally to censure the Senator.) The *American Mercury* then blasted the Eisenhower White House for an alleged "Get McCarthy" drive, "touched off at the very crest of the Senator's popularity and public approval." Elite opposition to McCarthy's smear tactics, explained one *American Mercury* writer, "horrified literally millions of dedicated anti-Communist Republicans, who looked upon McCarthy as the very symbol of their own fight against the lowering Communist world threat."[107]

The electoral implications of the Right's anticommunism were significant. The *American Mercury* blamed McCarthy's White House and Congressional opponents for "a poisonous effect upon grass-roots enthusiasm among Republican workers in the 1954 campaign," and thereby causing Republicans to lose elections.[108] In his second term, Eisenhower's popularity on the Right dropped even further over the Bricker Amendment, among other issues. Ohio Republican Senator John Bricker had introduced a proposal to amend the Constitution so that Congress, not the executive branch, would wield ultimate authority over all foreign treaties. Eisenhower's opposition to the Bricker Amendment reinforced the view of right-wing activists that he and other Republican "moderates" were insufficiently distinguishable from New Deal Democrats.[109]

By 1960, the conservative movement remained without a national leader and lent only lukewarm support to Richard Nixon's presidential campaign against John F. Kennedy. *National Review* editorialized to the effect that Nixon was the lesser of two evils: "We are ready for either President Nixon or President Kennedy; our bomb shelters are in good order" wrote William F. Buckley, Jr.[110] After Nixon's defeat, however, *National Review* editor L. Brent Bozell analyzed what he called a "new strategic situation for the conservative movement."

> For eight years, the movement has necessarily been on the lead-strings of the Left. With Eisenhower Republicans in power, conservatives were, from every point of view, a captive faction. They could protest, but there was no requirement on anyone to listen. They could counsel, but could not develop any direction of their own. They could plot, but as long as the GOP—their natural vehicle to power—was still running and was in the opposition's hands, any direct bids for power were bound to fail. Worse still, they could not even build; for powerful forces among them fostered down-the-line support of the Republican leadership, as a lesser evil. Now the movement is provisionally emancipated. What it does and where it goes are essentially matters of its own choosing.[111]

Even though staunch anticommunist activists lacked true representation in a political party, their strength as a movement gave them the means to begin building a party faction. Even before 1960, the Right had already begun efforts to reconstitute the Republican Party, with the formation in 1958 of Americans for Constitutional Action (ACA). The ACA was an early effort to channel conservative movement support toward selected candidates. It was led by retired Admiral Ben Moreell who had formerly been the chairman of the board of the Jones and Laughlin Steel Corporation. The day after ACA's formation, Senator Karl Mundt (R-SD) inserted into the *Congressional Record* the group's press release, which claimed that ACA "could force back together the conservative coalition which for over 20 years successfully stopped the greatest excesses toward statism in this country."[112] Throughout the 1960s and 1970s, ACA published the "ACA Index" of Congressional members' voting records; through its local chapters, ACA representatives raised money and grassroots support for right-wing candidates.[113]

While ACA organized among older Republican conservatives, 1960 saw the formation of what would become the Right's most enduring organization of university students. Young Americans for Freedom (YAF) was born when ninety student activists from forty-four colleges gathered in September 1960 at the Sharon, Connecticut estate of William F. Buckley, Jr. There they formed regional chapters and drafted the often-quoted "Sharon Statement" proclaiming their opposition to government interference in the "market economy" and their commitment to "victory over, rather than coexistence with," the "menace" of "international Communism."[114] From the start, YAF's activist program focused on highly publicized rallies to honor right-wing politicians and celebrities. YAF's March 1962 rally in Madison Square Garden featured Senators John Tower (R-TX) and Barry Goldwater (R-AZ) and drew a crowd of 18,000 people.[115] Within its first two years, YAF started 310 chapters, and by 1962, thirty-eight members of Congress had joined YAF's National Advisory Board. Prominent figures like Senator Strom Thurmond and former FBI agent Herbert Philbrick wrote fundraising letters on YAF's behalf.[116] Unlike the Left's student movement of the early 1960s, YAF enjoyed extensive support from the older generation of activists. In turn, YAF members worked less on developing a new political ideology than on implementing that of their elders.

Along with YAF, one institution that was crucial in mobilizing anticommunist and libertarian Republicans was *Human Events*. Between 1954 and 1964, that weekly newspaper's circulation grew from 9,000 paid subscribers to over 140,000.[117] In the early 1960s, *Human Events* and Americans for Constitutional Action organized a series of Political Action Conferences in Washington, D.C. The conferences served to link YAF activists and a budding coalition of conservative Republicans, including Senators Barry Goldwater, John Tower, and Strom Thurmond, plus Representatives Walter Judd, Donald C. Bruce, John H. Rousselot,

John Ashbrook, and Bruce Alger.[118] (South Carolina Senator Strom Thurmond was among the first of the pro-segregation southern Democrats to switch to the Republican Party in support of Barry Goldwater's 1964 presidential campaign.)[119]

A Choice, Not an Echo: Barry Goldwater's Presidential Campaign

Beginning in 1961, a small group of conservative Republican activists began meeting to plan a presidential campaign for Barry Goldwater. In their respective memoirs, *National Review* publisher William F. Rusher and Republican strategist F. Clifton White chronicled the series of closed-door meetings in which a coalition of businessmen, state Republican Party chairmen, and leaders of the Young Republicans, many from the Sun Belt states, strategized to deprive "liberal" New York Governor Nelson Rockefeller of the 1964 Republican nomination. "One major factor influencing the conservative movement to seek control of the Republican Party in the early 1960s, rather than found a new party of its own," wrote Rusher, "was the sheer disarray of the GOP after Nixon's defeat by Kennedy."[120]

Goldwater initially rejected a run for the presidency. But no one could deny his popularity as de facto leader of the conservative movement. His 1960 book *Conscience of a Conservative*, ghostwritten by William Buckley's brother-in-law and *National Review* editor L. Brent Bozell, sold 700,000 copies by mid-1961.[121] Goldwater's base of support included both elite activists within the Republican Party and activists from the grassroots anticommunist movement.[122] In 1961, a poll of delegates from the 1960 Republican convention showed Goldwater to be their overwhelming favorite.[123] Once the 1964 primaries were underway, Goldwater, not Rockefeller, was able to tap a network of grassroots precinct workers. In Los Angeles county, 8,000 volunteers—many of them from the John Birch Society—canvassed 600,000 homes for Goldwater, while only 2,000 volunteers worked for Rockefeller.[124] At the nominating convention, Goldwater was nominated on the first vote.[125]

It was the Goldwater campaign that propelled actor Ronald Reagan into the political spotlight. As the host of television's "General Electric Theater," Reagan was a familiar figure. As volunteer coordinator for the Goldwater campaign in California, Reagan delivered his famous "Rendezvous with Destiny" speech, broadcast on national television on October 27, 1964. In the speech, Reagan rehearsed two of the essentials of the conservative movement's philosophy: military strength, reduced size of government, and reduced governmental control of the economy.

Reagan's theatrical performance caught the eye of conservative leaders who recognized his potential mass appeal.[126]

Strategically, Goldwater's candidacy allowed the Republican Right to expand its base of support, both demographically and in terms of salient issues. Central to the thinking of Goldwater strategists, even in the early 1960s, was the idea of winning southern voters who were upset about the civil rights issue. *National Review* editor William Rusher urged conservatives to consider the electoral vulnerability of the Democrats. Since the end of the Civil War, the Democratic Party had "run with the hares down South on the race issue, while riding with the hounds up North—nominating loudly integrationist presidential candidates while calmly raking in, on locally segregationist platforms, 95 percent of all Senate and House seats . . . south of the Mason–Dixon line."[127] Republicans could begin to turn the tables if they courted white voters opposed to the federal civil rights policies of the Democrats.

Candidate Goldwater had voted against the Johnson administration's 1964 Civil Rights Act—going against most of his fellow Republicans—not, he said, because he opposed civil rights in principle, but because he considered it "unconstitutional" to require states to desegregate public facilities.[128] Whatever his reason, Goldwater's opposition to civil rights legislation made him naturally attractive to segregationists who were, as we will see in Chapter 3, outraged by a series of federal government decisions to outlaw segregated public facilities. Along with his implicit appeal to segregationists, Goldwater was also attractive to right-wing proponents of military strength and opponents of New Deal economics. The Senator voted against the Limited Nuclear Test Ban Treaty in 1963 and favored a withdrawal of U.S. recognition of the Soviet Union. Goldwater also advocated a 10 percent yearly reduction in federal domestic spending programs. He favored an end to all federal farm subsidies, a ban on political activities by trade unions and industry-wide bargaining. He even voiced opposition to the graduated income tax as an artificial means for "enforcing equality among unequal men."[129]

Under candidate Goldwater in 1964, the Republicans drafted a party platform that was characteristically right-wing in its anti-distributive, pro-enforcer view of the ideal state. On policy issues, Goldwater aligned himself with *Human Events* and *National Review* writers. The latter magazine published an advisory "Program for a Goldwater Administration" in July 1964; this was the first time the conservative movement took seriously the possibility of directly influencing an administration.

Goldwater's campaign, however, was dogged by his public association with the John Birch Society and other elements of the so-called radical right. Goldwater backers did little to counter that impression. In fact, at the July party convention, Republican moderates were voted down on a proposed "anti-extremism" platform plank that singled out the Klan and the John Birch Society. Moderates were also defeated in their efforts to sustain their 1960 party platform's call for "vigorous enforcement" of existing civil rights statutes.[130] Instead, the party seemed to take a giant step to the right when Goldwater, in his acceptance speech, delivered his famous line, that "extremism in the defense of liberty is no vice."

The speech itself then became a campaign issue when Eisenhower declined to campaign for the ticket unless Goldwater would clarifiy his "extremism" remark. Goldwater met with Eisenhower and Nixon and about thirty Republican governors, and, in an effort to mend fences, Goldwater promised to consult with Eisenhower on key national security appointments. Goldwater pledged to support Social Security and civil rights legislation. He repudidated the KKK but refused to disassociate himself from the John Birch Society,[131] which by then had become an embarrassment to more respectable conservatives.

Before the 1964 campaign, Buckley had publicly criticized John Birch Society founder Robert Welch but joined Goldwater in supporting the group's rank-and-file membership.[132] During the campaign, Goldwater's image as an "extremist" was intensified with the publication and wide distribution of *Danger on the Right*, by the Anti-Defamation League of B'nai B'rith. Though generally factual, the book used a guilt-by-association technique to emphasize Goldwater's high approval rating with the John Birch Society and like-minded groups.[133] It was not until about a year after Goldwater's defeat that *National Review* published its own lengthy polemic against the John Birch Society because among other things, the group claimed that the U.S. war in Vietnam was just another part of the "communist conspiracy."[134] (See Chapter 6 for more on the John Birch Society's stance toward the war.)

Ultimately, Goldwater's image as an extremist was one of several factors that led to President Lyndon Johnson's unprecedented 61-percent landslide victory. Aside from his home state of Arizona, Goldwater carried only five Deep South states: Mississippi, Alabama, Louisiana, South Carolina, and Georgia. In Virginia, North Carolina, Tennessee, and Arkansas, Goldwater won a majority of the white vote, but Johnson benefited from relatively high black voter turnout.[135] Goldwater backers explained Johnson's win as inevitable, given public sympathy for the Democrats following the assassination of President Kennedy, Republican Party disunity, and Goldwater's image as a reactionary.[136]

Though Goldwater's candidacy was an electoral failure, it spelled the beginning of a new era in Republican Right organizing. Goldwater backers won control of the party in many states, particularly in the south and the west. The Right's growing strength in the Sun Belt region would pose an enduring challenge to the party's more liberal Eastern wing.[137] Goldwater's electoral success in the Deep South (mostly Democratic) states was not lost on Republican strategists who saw the mobilization of anti-civil rights constituencies as the key to eventually winning and controlling the White House. By 1968, segregationist Alabama Governor George Wallace's impressive third-party presidential challenge would lend further support to an emerging "southern strategy."[138]

Conservative movement activists themselves wasted no time mourning the loss of the White House in 1964. Five days after the election, a small group of movement leaders, including Representative Donald C. Bruce (R-IN), William F. Buckley, Jr., Representative John M. Ashbrook (R-OH), YAF Chairman Robert E. Bauman, and *National Review* contributor Frank Meyer met to regroup Goldwater forces. About a month later, they announced the formation of the American Conservative Union, with the aims of fundraising for right-wing candidates, "consolidating the over-all strength of the American conservative movement through unified leadership and action; . . . molding public opinion; . . . stimulating and directing responsible political action."[139]

Ultimately, the Goldwater campaign was a net gain for the anticommunist, libertarian and anti-civil rights activists of the conservative movement. They won access to the party's nominating procedures and broke the pattern of dominance by the Eastern-establishment in candidate selection. They demonstrated to Republican Party elites the organizing clout of grassroots citizen groups, and the potential salience of strong anticommunist and anti-civil rights campaign themes. Practically speaking, the Goldwater campaign was a training ground for a cohort of conservative youth, especially members of Young Americans for Freedom, who would form the New Right organizations of the 1970s and 1980s and who would eventually make common cause with a new constituency of evangelical Christians.

Thirty years after the original publication of Goldwater's *The Conscience of a Conservative*, one of the 1964 campaign's veteran activists wrote the introduction to a new edition of the book. Patrick Buchanan had by then become a conservative movement leader in his own right. He nostalgically recalled the 1964 campaign, likening it to "a first love, . . . an experience that will never recede from memory." But Buchanan's larger point was the Right's eventual vindication of the Goldwater defeat. Two decades later, Buchanan boasted, he and his comrades "took over the U.S. government, restored the nation's might and morale, gave her ten years of peace and prosperity unseen since the 1920s, and won the Cold War. Not bad, not bad at all."[140]

CHAPTER 3

• • •

Organized Resistance to Preserve Segregation

The conservative anticommunist movement made its initial forays into Republican politics at about the same time that the civil rights movement precipitated a major party realignment around the issue of race. Grassroots anticommunist activists mobilized strongly in the late 1950s and early 1960s. By then another right-wing movement was on the march in the form of the white segregationist Citizens' Councils. In response to federally mandated integration of public facilities, especially following the Supreme Court's 1954 ruling against separate-but-equal public schools, tens of thousands of mostly southern whites joined forces with their state and local elected officials to thwart the challenge to institutional racism.

The cause of "massive resistance" ultimately failed, but the mobilization of white racist sentiment had long-term political implications. As with many successful social movements, civil rights activism spawned a backlash. The Citizens' Councils, and the political elites who found them useful, represented the first organized wave of reaction to progress on race relations. The lesson of the segregationists' broad, though short-lived, campaigns was that racial divisiveness could pay dividends in electoral politics. That message resonated loudly within both political parties and among right-wing movement activists.

Like the conservative anticommunists, the segregationists held a mixed stance toward the state, opposing initiatives to redistribute power and wealth more equitably, while upholding the state's prerogative to preserve and enforce a traditional social order. The two movements diverged not only on their key organizing principles (anticommunism vs. segregationism) but also in their respective patterns of interaction with political elites. Elite anticommunist organizations tended to collaborate with government agencies while some grassroots anticommunist groups, notably the John Birch Society, were downright suspicious of the patriotism of their own government leaders.

The case of the segregationist movement was a bit different. Southern politicians and business elites largely facilitated the mobilization of what was also a veritable mass movement. We will see in this chapter how relations between the Citizens' Councils and the southern political establishment were mutually beneficial. The Councils' dependence on elite support may have sowed the seeds for the segregationist movement's eventual decline. The 1968 presidential campaign of segregationist Alabama Governor George Wallace, as we will see in Chapter 6, would prove to be the segregationists' last big hurrah. This chapter highlights some of the organized racist Right's earlier successes and defeats.

SOUTHERN POLITICS AT MID-CENTURY

From the late nineteenth century through the mid-twentieth century, Southern politics was characterized by near unanimous allegiance to the Democratic Party. Particularly in the "Black Belt" counties in which disenfranchised African Americans far outnumbered whites, Democratic Party cohesion in presidential and Congressional elections ensured the system of white privilege. In his pioneering work on the one-party South, social historian V. O. Key concluded that the unity of Southern Democrats at the national level, particularly in Congress, "was essential in order that the largest possible bloc could be mobilized to resist any national move toward interference with southern authority to deal with the race question as was desired locally."[1]

Moreover, the one-party unity of southern politicians suited the national Democratic Party just fine. In presidential elections from Reconstruction to the Depression era, the South voted more heavily Democratic than any other region in the country. (The one exception was the 1928 election when many southern voters favored Herbert Hoover over Democratic candidate Al Smith, a Catholic.) Southern allegiance to the Democrats derived not just from the party's tolerance of white supremacy, but also from the party's links to southern agricultural interests. The opposing Republicans were seen as representatives of (northern) industry, and the few southern blacks who voted tended to favor the party of Lincoln.[2] The South was a bastion of support for Roosevelt's New Deal policies, with the exception of pro-trade union legislation. In 1944, Roosevelt won 69 percent of southerners' votes, compared with leads of 55 percent in the western states, 52 percent in the Northeast, and 49 percent in the Midwest.[3] But 1944 was the last time the Democrats could rely on the solid South. At its 1948 convention, the Democrats nominated civil rights proponent Harry Truman and endorsed a strong civil rights platform plank. In anger, some southern delegates defected and later nominated South Carolina's then-Governor Strom Thurmond as the presidential candidate of the National States' Rights Party. (Thurmond would later switch to the Republican Party in order to support Barry Goldwater's 1964 campaign.)

Scholars attribute the Democrats' eventual adoption of a national civil rights agenda, despite the inevitable loss of support in the South, to a number of related factors. The gradual decline of labor-intensive cotton farming in the South encouraged a mass migration of black workers to the industrial North. Between 1910 and 1960, nearly five million African Americans migrated north, and that large-scale population shift had implications for electoral coalitions. Black voters had favored Republican candidates in seventeen straight presidential elections, but they voted overwhelmingly for Roosevelt in 1936. Once northern Democrats began to see black voters as a potentially permanent base of support, there was an incentive for the party to take seriously increasing demands of African Americans for civil rights.[4] After World War II, political opportunities for the nascent civil rights movement took form in a series of administration-led policy shifts. The Truman administration began the gradual desegregation of the armed forces and established a fair employment board within the Civil Service Commission. The Eisenhower administration continued the desegregation of the military and worked toward integration of public facilities in the District of Columbia.[5] New openings at the level of the federal government alone did not ensure the onset of black insurgency. The civil rights movement had at its disposal a pre-existing network of black colleges, churches, and voluntary associations. As the movement mobilized these resources, against the backdrop of a major party realignment and a willingness among national elites to consider civil rights demands, movement activists developed a crucial collective belief in the possibilities for profound social change.[6]

But the forces dedicated to preserving stark racial inequalities were likewise organized and able to rely on support from a segment of the elite, namely southern politicians. Prior to the mobilization of a massive, grassroots segregationist movement, in the form of the Citizens' Councils, the Ku Klux Klan was the most notorious of the racist Right. After the post-Civil War period known as Reconstruction, the Klan had reached its peak of recruitment and activism during the 1920s.

Then, at a 1944 "Klanvocation" in Georgia, leading Knights had agreed to formally disband, rather than pay a large Internal Revenue Service bill. But at the same gathering, the Knights decided to establish an unofficial alliance of local Georgia chapters, and Dr. Samuel J. Green was chosen to head the Association of Georgia Klans.[7] Following a lull during the remainder of World War II, Klan activity resumed. At a May 1946 ceremony on top of Georgia's Stone Mountain, 200 cross-burners pledged their fealty to Grand Dragon Samuel Green who proclaimed: "We are revived."[8] Reemergent Klan activity both in the South and in the states of California, New York, New Jersey, and Wisconsin was repressed by the enactment of various state and local laws prohibiting the wearing of masks in public, imposing fines and prison sentences on overt Klan organizers, and by the revocation of Klan groups' state charters. In 1946 U.S. Attorney General Tom C. Clark acknowledged that the FBI was monitoring the Klan, and in 1947 the Klan appeared on the Attorney General's list of "un-American" political groups.[9]

Despite mild repression by state agencies, during the late 1940s, Klan groups maintained tens of thousands of members, by modest estimates. Growth was impeded by perpetual infighting, splits, and mergers. The Association of Georgia Klans' Grand Dragon Samuel J. Green died in 1949 and was succeeded by Samuel W. Roper. Rival Klan groupings included the Federated Ku Klux Klans, based in Alabama; the Knights of the Ku Klux Klan, comprised of splinter groups from numerous states; and several smaller associations based in South Carolina, Alabama, Georgia, and Florida.[10] Klan tactics during this period included traditional cross-burning ceremonies and selected terrorism against black citizens and white "race-mixers." Klan groups, however, were not suited to attract the kind of resources or mass base needed to seriously challenge desegregation once it was ordered by the Supreme Court and legislated by Congress and the White House. Although the Klan would play an important role in intimidating civil rights activists of the 1950s and 1960s, "massive resistance" would require the development of organizations committed to more respectable tactics and facilitated, not repressed, by local elites.

"MASSIVE RESISTANCE" AGAINST INTEGRATION

In the context of a southern political class united four-square against integration, the Supreme Court ruled, in its landmark 1954 *Brown v. the Topeka Board of Education* case, that separate-but-equal public school facilities were unconstitutional. Though other important cases preceded *Brown*,[11] this ruling spelled the beginning of the end for legally sanctioned segregation, and marked a pivotal turn in favor of civil rights backers. In a second *Brown* case, heard in 1955, the Supreme Court ordered local school boards and federal district courts to oversee school desegregation in the South "with all deliberate speed." Chief Justice Earl

Warren lamented President Eisenhower's unwillingness to throw his public support behind this decision,[12] but neither did the Court itself specify a timetable for desegregation. It would be a full decade before the Kennedy–Johnson administration would succeed in passing the federal Civil Rights Act of 1964, which outlawed discrimination in all public accommodations, and made integration a slow but inevitable reality.

Even before the first *Brown* decision was handed down on May 17, 1954, a day segregationists dubbed "Black Monday," legislators in several southern states had initiated legal maneuvers to forestall school integration. The ability of politicians and activists to wage regional "massive resistance," however, did not mitigate the severity of the *Brown* decision. In its brief written opinion, the Court had extended itself beyond the question of whether separate facilities could ever be truly equal. Chief Justice Warren cited social scientific studies on segregation's detriment to the self-esteem of black children and argued that the negative impact "is greater when it has the sanction of law." Thus, the Court's opinion challenged the very foundation of racist ideology, which holds *inequality* between the races to be biologically inherent, and not determined by social circumstance. Though *Brown* implied, in a conceivably paternalistic way, that the achievement of black students depended on their attendance in white schools, the decision also assumed a limited responsibility for the state to enforce integration.

The Citizens' Councils

Soon after the *Brown* decision, four Deep South states banned public school desegregation within their borders and, in the event of concrete orders from the Supreme Court, made legislative provisions to abolish or cease funding to all or part of their public school systems. The Louisiana state legislature enacted a "local pupil assignment" law granting "police power" to sort individual students into schools, not by race but by achievement levels. The Georgia legislature passed a bill making it a felony for any state or local official to spend public money on an integrated school. North Carolina and Florida enacted laws undermining tenure protection for public school teachers whose views on integration deviated from community standards.[13]

But even before the legislatures of the southern states and educational commissions had time to draft their various legal responses, the *Brown* decision sparked one of the largest grassroots organizing campaigns in recent history. At its peak in 1956, the Association of Citizens' Councils claimed an estimated 250,000 members in Mississippi, Alabama, Louisiana, South Carolina, Texas, Florida, Arkansas, Tennessee, and Virginia. The significance of the Citizens' Councils went beyond sheer numbers and the years' worth of public outcry they made to forestall integration. The Citizens' Councils were influential by virtue of their close ties with powerful southern politicians and their ability to claim to speak for the entire white community.[14]

The man credited with inspiring the Citizens' Councils was Mississippi circuit court judge Tom Brady. Shortly after the *Brown* decision in May of 1954, Judge Brady delivered a fiery "Black Monday" address before a patriotic group, the Sons of the American Revolution. Encouraged by supporters, Brady then expanded the speech and published it as a ninety-page booklet. *Black Monday* was widely circulated as the Citizens' Councils' first handbook. In *Black Monday*, Brady opened bluntly with a purported history of "The Three Species of Man:"

> Why was it that the negro was unable and failed to evolve and develop? . . . Water does not rise above its source, and the negro could not by his inherent qualities rise above his environment as had the other races. His inheritance was wanting. The potential did not exist. This is neither right nor wrong; it is simply a stubborn biological fact.[15]

Following a litany of vulgar descriptions of "Negroes," Jews, and caucasians, Brady addressed the *Brown* decision itself. Brady claimed that the Supreme Court had effectively forced southerners to choose between "segregation or amalgamation"; the nation would only be saved if white citizens acted decisively to preserve the former against the latter. Brady then claimed that there was a "socialistic" conspiracy underlying the *Brown* decision. His plan of action called for: halting the "influx of Communist-minded immigrants," exposure of "communist" infiltration of the churches, and the election, not appointment, of future Supreme Court justices. If necessary, Brady proposed that there be the creation of a separate territorial state for blacks and the outright abolition of the public school system. Most immediately, Brady advocated the formation of resistance organizations in each of the southern states, to be coordinated by a national federation that would disseminate information and perhaps form a third political party. Finally, if all else failed, Brady urged southern whites to fire their black maids and, thereby, wage a crushing economic boycott on the entire African American community.[16]

Judge Tom Brady's call to arms attracted the attention of a Mississippi plantation manager, Robert B. Patterson. Along with several other prominent residents of Indianola, Mississippi, Patterson organized civic and business leaders, who with the help of the town's mayor and city attorney, sponsored a town hall meeting attended by about seventy-five people. They founded the first of the Citizens' Councils chapters in Indianola in July, 1954.[17]

Once started, Patterson and other Councilors traveled from county to county, repeating a successful formula for starting new chapters. They would get themselves invited to make a pro-segregation speech at a Rotary or Kiwanis club meeting, where they would meet local business and political leaders. Then they would meet with interested club members to plan a second and larger meeting, at which a temporary chairperson would be chosen and a steering committee formed by local business, labor, agricultural, and religious leaders. This meeting would be followed by a public rally to enlist large numbers of citizens. Council organizers would, meanwhile, send letters to county boards of supervisors, inviting them to help organize chapters in their areas. Included in some of the form letters Patterson used were pro-segregation reading lists that included stridently racist and anti-Semitic literature.[18]

The southern Democratic Party was strongest in counties overwhelmingly populated by disenfranchised blacks. So, too, the Citizens' Councils organized the most chapters in these same "Black Belt" areas, where the white minority was most fearful of integration.[19] Growth spurts for the Councils coincided with each new development on the school integration front, such as the Supreme Court's May 1955 implementation decree, and in response to the National Association for the Advancement of Colored People's (NAACP) petitions to local school boards.[20] Montgomery, Alabama became a bastion of Council organizing during the civil rights movement's bus boycott there in 1955 and 1956.[21] The membership and activism of the Citizens' Councils was strongest in Mississippi, followed by Alabama, Louisiana, Georgia, and South Carolina. In October, 1954, twenty Mississippi county chapters formed a statewide association and named Robert Patterson their leader. The Mississippi Council later started publishing a monthly newspaper edited by William J. Simmons.[22] By early 1956, there were enough statewide associations for the Councilors to follow Judge Brady's advice and form the national Citizens' Councils of America.[23]

Councilors were not interested in ousting their elected officials. Mostly, Citizens' Council activism took the form of education and propaganda: literature circulation, regional television and radio programs, and lots of public speaking events. With mixed results, Councilors sought influence within Southern Baptist churches. Amidst the flurry of segregationist activity, in 1956 two Southern Baptist colleges banned African Americans from admission. But while segregationist sentiment was strong among many parishioners, the leadership of the Southern Baptist Convention formally supported the Supreme Court's 1954 Brown decision.[24]

A persistent theme in Council literature was the importance of formal organizational membership in the Councils as opposed to collective action through churches and pre-existing political parties. The idea was to heighten the sense of urgency and potential influence by creating a new, large, and unified vehicle with enough name recognition to try to compete with the civil rights movement. "Organized aggression must be met with organized resistance," wrote Robert Patterson in a 1956 annual report of his Mississippi Association of Citizens' Councils.

The NAACP, CIO and other left-wing groups are well organized and highly financed. There are 40 million white Southerners and only 300 thousand members of the NAACP in the entire Nation. Forty million white Southerners, or a fraction thereof, if properly organized, can be a power in this Nation, but they must be thoroughly organized from the town and county level up. It must be an organization supported and controlled by the people and not by any politician or political party.

The fate of this Nation may rest in the hands of the Southern white people today. If we white Southerners submit to this unconstitutional judge-made law of nine political appointees, the malignant powers of mongrelization, communism and atheism will surely destroy this Nation from within. Racial intermarriage has already begun in the North and unless stopped will spread to the South.

Integration represents darkness, regimentation, totalitarianism, communism and destruction. Segregation represents the freedom to choose one's associates, Americanism, State sovereignty and the survival of the white race. These two ideologies are now engaged in mortal conflict and only one can survive.[25]

In this and other literature of the Citizens' Councils, the segregationists expressed a characteristically right-wing preoccupation with the communist threat, and a belief that the federal government was conspiring to implement some sort of "socialist" game plan. One brochure outlining the platform of the Citizens' Councils included in its preface this typically anti-statist position:

The wheel of federal oppression has many spokes. Beginning with a slow roll in the thirties, it gathered speed and power through the forties and fifties. It now threatens to wipe out the individual will to resist and to grind us to grist for a greedy, socialist-minded dictatorship in Washington.[26]

The brochure proceeded with an eight-point platform. The first three planks affirmed the integrity of the Constitution as it was originally drafted and opposed the Supreme Court's "irresponsible and revolutionary interpretations of this nation's most sacred document of law and justice." Proceeding, the platform included some of the essentials of right-wing ideology:

4. We think there is a need for a return to the *moral law* that requires us to think in terms of our *responsibilities* as well as in terms of our *rights*, and for halting the present trend of our national leadership toward *socialism*. We believe the teaching that people have a right to certain standards of food, clothing, housing, education, amusement, working hours, retirement provisions, and other bulwarks against hardships is wrong when the same teaching does not also present the responsibility of working to earn these rights.

5. We hold that people everywhere should work to become *self-supporting*, and should resist the growing tendency of the *federal government to foist "benefits"* upon a large segment of our populace at the price of federal control.

6. The Councils contend that the government's wild and reckless *foreign give-away* program has contributed toward the socialization of our country, that it has contributed little to saving other countries from socialism or communism, and that our *foreign spending* should be drastically curtailed. The bursting-at-the-seams federal budget, the overwhelmingly burdensome *national taxes*, and federal bureaucracy—all of which are so frightening a part of the national picture—move us to action.[27] (emphasis added)

Here the Councilors added salient concerns about economic distribution to their immediate focus on segregation. The emphasis on "a return to the moral law," and the seventh plank of the platform, below, conveyed the Right's characteristic concern with preserving traditionally unequal social relations against inroads by agents of change.

7. The Councils believe that the *sovereignty of the states* and the *individual rights* of the people are in grave danger from organized groups whose aims and purposes are *contrary to the American way of life* under which this country grew to a position of world leadership unequalled in history. We believe that such threats should be exposed and our people awakened against their treachery.[28] (emphasis added)

Assets of Southern Elites

Following a peak of recruitment and public rallies during the 1950s, the Citizens' Councils remained active throughout the 1960s and only ceased publishing *The Citizen* magazine as late as 1985. During their heyday, the Councils left behind an abundant historical record, indicating several

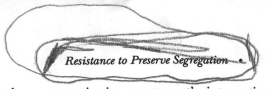

patterns in the segregationist movement's interaction with political elites. The Councils supported those southern elites who were most staunchly pro-segregation and most vocal in fighting against federal enforcement of civil rights. In turn, these elites responded by aiding and abetting the grassroots segregationists with vital resources. Together, grassroots segregationists and elected officials worked to repress the black-led civil rights movement. The Citizens' Councils functioned essentially as agents of a racist southern state apparatus. Through economic repression and physical attacks, some Councilors intimidated potential black voters, thereby weakening the civil rights movement's base of support and stalling the expansion of black political rights.

At each step in the battle to save segregation, Councilors turned out voter support for leading segregationist politicians. In 1954, the Councils claimed responsibility for the passage of two of the Mississippi legislature's anti-civil rights measures.[29] The first was a November 1954 ballot measure on voter qualifications, aimed at restricting black voters. The measure required that voters prove their ability to read and write by producing, in their own handwriting, a "reasonable" interpretation of the state constitution. A similar amendment had failed to pass in a 1952 election. But in November 1954, the restrictive voting bill passed overwhelmingly, and the Citizens' Councils claimed credit.[30] The following month voters approved, by a two-to-one margin, the legislature's proposal to abolish the public school system in the event of imminent federally enforced school integration. Again, the Councils claimed to be decisive in mobilizing voters to ratify the legislature's bill. In both cases, the pro-segregation bills were strongly approved in counties where the Councilors had organized heavily. But these were the same "Black Belt" counties characterized by minority white populations, few black voters, and traditionally solid support for segregationist Democratic politicians.[31]

Regardless of whether the school abolition and voter restriction bills would have passed without support from the Councils, segregationist legislators considered their role pivotal to the success of the measures. Aside from backing elites in various states' campaigns against integration, the Councilors also backed segregationist Democrats in Congress. In the first issue of their four-page monthly newspaper, *The Citizens' Council*, the Councils endorsed a resolution of "interposition" proposed by Mississippi Senator James Eastland, Representative John Bell Williams, and Judge Tom Brady. Interposition was the doctrine that a state has the legal right to nullify a federal law.

In December 1955, Senator Eastland addressed a statewide Citizens' Council convention in Jackson, Mississippi and proposed an idea to help the segregationist movement succeed. At the meeting, Eastland called for the creation of a southern regional commission, to be funded by taxpayer dollars, for publicity campaigns against integrationist "political pressure groups," which, Eastland said, ran "from the blood red of the Communist Party to the almost equally red of the National Council of Churches of Christ in the U.S.A."[32] Eastland's plan took form in what one critic of the segregationists called a "regional propaganda center." At a subsequent meeting in Memphis, Council delegates from twelve southern states announced the formation of the Federation for Constitutional Government. Founding members included Senators James Eastland and Strom Thurmond, Georgia Governor Marvin Griffin, nine former southern governors, six southern Congressional Representatives, and prominent Councilors. The Federation's stated purpose was to "coordinate the activities of all the resistance movements across the South."[33]

The Mississippi legislature followed Senator Eastland's proposal by creating a State Sovereignty Commission to

> do and perform any and all acts and things deemed necessary and proper to protect the sovereignty of the state of Mississippi and her sister states from encroachment thereon by the Federal government or any branch, department, or agency thereof.[34]

Mississippi Governor James Coleman was named chair of the Commission. Speaker of the Mississippi State House Walter Sillers announced the Commission's intention to cooperate with the Citizens' Councils, which he described as "the greatest forces we have in this battle to save the white race from amalgamation, mongrelization, and destruction."[35]

Here were political elites acting to facilitate the work of an ostensibly grassroots citizens' movement. Yet factions within Mississippi's political establishment viewed the State Sovereignty Commission variously. Governor Coleman saw it as a means to "pacify racial hysteria in the state," while some legislators saw it as a vehicle for "aggressively cementing racial orthodoxy at home and cooperating with Citizens' Councils' propaganda efforts abroad."[36] Under Governor Coleman, the Commission spent tens of thousands of dollars hosting northern journalists and distributing to the national press such pamphlets as "All Mississippi Asks Is Fairness and a Chance to Present Its Side of the Case." In 1960, with the inauguration of more staunchly segregationist Governor Ross R. Barnett, the Commission began making monthly contributions to the Citizens' Councils, reportedly up to $200,000.[37] Outside of Mississippi, similar state commissions were formed. Georgia's Education Commission, Louisiana's Rainach Committee, and the Virginia Commission on

Constitutional Government all engaged in media and lobbying activities during the late 1950s and early 1960s. The propaganda these agencies distributed was designed to discredit prominent civil rights groups such as the NAACP.[38]

While the state-funded sovereignty commissions produced their own public relations material, segregationist politicians also helped the Citizens' Councils produce their own. In 1957 the Councils started a television and radio series based on fifteen-minute interviews with politicians and other prominent figures. By 1962, about a quarter of the U.S. Congress had been interviewed. The programs were sent free of charge to hundreds of stations, and the Councilors' production expenses were vastly reduced because supportive Representatives invited activists to use the Congressional recording studios, meaning that a single program cost less than $55 to produce.[39] Through this Congressional resource, the Councils' propaganda was effectively subsidized by U.S. taxpayers.

In the early 1960s, southern elites promoted another key piece of segregationist movement propaganda, Carleton Putnam's book *Race and Reason: A Yankee View*. Putnam was a northern airline executive and white supremacist whose pro-segregation letters to the editors of newspapers had gained him a following throughout the South. Supporters formed the Putnam Letter Committee, and, from headquarters in New York City, they bought space in northern newspapers to publish Putnam's original open letter to President Eisenhower protesting the *Brown* decision. The Citizens' Councils distributed thousands of reprints of this "Putnam Letter,"[40] but Putnam himself could not keep up with all the correspondence he received. As a general response, he drafted *Race and Reason*, which graphically advocated second-class citizenship for black people.[41]

In July 1961, the Louisiana State Board of Education adopted a resolution making *Race and Reason* a textbook for "selected" high school and college students.[42] Mississippi Governor Ross R. Barnett proclaimed October 26, 1961 to be "Race and Reason Day" and urged the state's citizens to observe the occasion by reading and discussing the book, by "calling the book to the attention of friends and relatives in the North, . . . and by participating in appropriate public functions."[43] On the night of "Race and Reason Day," the Jackson, Mississippi Citizens' Councils honored Carleton Putnam at a banquet attended by 500 prominent segregationists. Mississippi Representative John Bell Williams chaired the dinner committee which included more than a hundred pillars of the Mississippi establishment: state legislators, attorneys, judges, and small business owners.[44] At a time when the cause of preserving legal segregation was losing strength, such an event served to maintain commitment among the organized racist Right.

Throughout the years of "massive resistance," Councilors and segregationist politicians displayed their mutual support for each other ideologically and through electoral politics. In the realm of partisan politics, numerous legislators openly aligned themselves with the Councils. One prominent exception was Mississippi Governor James Coleman, who refused to become a member. Coleman clashed with the Councils when he would not pursue calls to outlaw the NAACP, when he supported the donation of state land for an integrated Veterans Administration Hospital, and when he promoted racial moderates as delegates to the 1956 Democratic national convention.[45]

Overall, however, segregationist activists had little reason to try and reconstitute state governments or the South's Congressional delegation. Because regional elites maintained a pro-segregation consensus in the wake of the *Brown* decision, movement activists were not compelled toward a major third-party effort. Rhetorical and material support from regional elites enabled activists to position themselves as *challengers* in relation to the federal government and civil rights countermovement, but *system-supporters* in relation to the southern power structure.

Another noticeable element in relations between activists and politicians was the latter's drive to preserve their hegemony over the South. Regional elites did not direct resources toward movement groups until they came into direct conflict with elites at the federal level. The formation of state sovereignty commissions enabled elites to direct resources to politically useful Councilors while maintaining their own prerogative to initiate and implement policy.

Together, segregationist politicians and Councilors worked, ultimately unsuccessfully, to repress the civil rights movement. Repression took both "strong" and "mild" forms. Strong repression included physical attacks and economic retaliation against blacks who promoted integration or registered to vote.[46] One Alabama Councilor boasted of plans "to make it difficult, if not impossible, for any Negro who advocates desegregation to find and hold a job, get credit or renew a mortgage."[47] In one case of apparent retaliation against a politically assertive black neighbor, the Jackson, Mississippi chapter circulated a "confidential communique" itemizing the activities of a black integrationist. Coincidentally or not, within a week, the man's home was vandalized and he was asked to withdraw his money from the bank.[48]

Though particular Councilors were considered responsible for specific physical attacks on black people, escalated violence was also attributed to Ku Klux Klan groups, which flourished in the years following the *Brown* decision. Klan scholar Wyn Craig Wade concluded that the effect of the Councilors' recruitment of "respectable" segregationists "was not so much eliminating the Klan but leaving it nothing but the violence-prone dregs of Southern white society."[49] Between 1955 and 1959, an Atlanta-based civil rights organization reported 530 cases of suspected Klan violence in eleven southern states. Following the success of the Montgomery bus boycott, Klansmen bombed four black churches.[50]

During the civil rights era, Klan groups diverged from the Citizens' Councils in two key respects. First, the Klan groups' base of support was strongest among urban (skilled and unskilled) workers and marginal small businessmen, while the more rurally based Councilors tended to be middle-class businessmen who were also active in Kiwanis, Rotary, and Lions clubs.[51] Second, whereas the Councils constituted a "resistance movement" by virtue of their advance and decline in response to civil rights countermovement activity, Klan groups did not reach their peak until late 1956, 1957, and early 1958, chronologically after the South's "massive resistance" to school integration had begun to subside.[52]

For tactical and public relations purposes, the Citizens' Councils avoided open associations with Klansmen. In Alabama, for example, a power struggle developed when the state's Councils came under the control of one Asa "Ace" Carter, who was also the leader of Alabama's Original Ku Klux Klan of the Confederacy, among the most violent of the Klan groups. Carter's flagrant anti-Semitism and his reputation for violence against fellow white supremacists caused the region-wide Association of Citizens' Councils to form a state branch separate from Carter's Alabama Citizens' Councils.[53] Carter's notoriety soared following a 1957 incident in which one of his Klaverns, as part of an "initiation" rite, abducted a young black man, castrated him with razor blades and poured turpentine over his wounds.[54] Carter himself escaped prosecution for the atrocity, and later became a top aide to Governor George Wallace.[55]

Through violence and economic pressure, segregationists waged this type of vicious repression against actual, or potential, civil rights advocates. At the same time, the Councils engaged in milder forms of repression, in the form of smear campaigns against the National Association for the Advancement of Colored People (NAACP). The tactic was to link even the most prestigious wings of the civil rights movement to an "international communist conspiracy." Even before the Supreme Court handed down its 1954 *Brown* decision, Senator James Eastland of Mississipi charged that the "Supreme Court has been influenced and infiltrated by Reds."[56] Following Eastland's lead, Councilors later broadened the "conspiracy" to identify the NAACP as a leading agent of communism. To develop the theme, Council propagandists cited texts in which known Communists had advocated integration or had endorsed civil rights organizations. For example, one southern Louisiana Citizens' Council pamphlet, under the headline "Proof That Integration Is Part of the Communist Conspiracy," arrayed a series of quotes as follows:

> Editor-Publisher David Lawrence reported in his newspaper column (Times-Picayune, Nov. 12, 1958) that Prof. Allen Nevins, long-time professor of American history at Columbia University, two-time Pulitzer prize winner, is emphatically in favor of desegregation and calls upon the Southern people to face reality, as he tells them that intermarriage between the races in the coming years is "inevitable."
>
> Three years ago an NAACP official said precisely the same thing, that "intermarriage will be the natural consequence of integration."
>
> William Z. Foster, present head of the Communist Party in America, declared in his book entitled TOWARD SOVIET AMERICA: "The American Soviet will of course abolish all restrictions upon racial intermarriage. . . . The revolution will only hasten this process of integration, already proceeding throughout the world with increasing tempo." In some Negro circles, it has become a standard wisecrack that "The Kremlin proposes and the NAACP disposes."[57]

Just as the role of Councilors in specific acts of economic and physical retaliation would be hard to document, the results of such anticommunist smear campaigns would be difficult to assess. The anticommunist message, however, may have helped Councilors convince their supporters of the urgency of the anti-integrationist cause.

No Radicals

Both the Cold War and civil rights eras formed the backdrop for the mobilization of the Citizens' Councils. In the 1950s and 1960s, the prevailing scholarly view of the John Birch Society, the Klan, and the Councils was that they were part of a single species, a "radical right" operating ostensibly outside the bounds of legitimate democratic norms.[58] But if one were to apply pluralist scholars' definitions of "radical" and "extremist" tactics—"going beyond the limits of the normative procedures which define the democratic political process"[59]—then the Klan would qualify but most Birchists and Councilors would not. Both the John Birch Society and the Councils used a combination of grassroots lobbying and educational tactics, most of which were within the bounds of the democratic process. Apart from their tactics, though, Birchists, Councilors, and Klansmen did share a conspiracist worldview, which attributed complex social ills to a small, secretive, and powerful clique.[60] This cognitive approach may make a movement unattractive to mainstream political forces, but it does not necessarily make a movement "extreme" or undemocratic.

Furthermore, these three organizations, despite a shared cognitive style, differed in several respects: their social base, their precise tactics, and their significance within broader processes of social change. As was previously mentioned, the Klan and Citizens' Councils, though both based in the South and committed to racial inequality, drew followings from different strata of the class and political structure. The Councilors deliberately recruited from the ranks of upper-middle-class business leaders and local political officeholders. This type of membership led naturally to the Councils' greater resource base and a corresponding tactical repertoire: funded by state agencies like the sovereignty commissions, the Councils could emphasize mass propaganda and lobbying campaigns over physical intimidation. Klansmen had fewer resources and less access to political elites. Combined with their tradition of secrecy and violence, Klansmen's lower social status and their exclusion from elite decision-making circles made it predictable that the Klans of the 1950s and 1960s would rely primarily on tried-and-true terrorist tactics. The more resourceful Councilors were able to expand both their ideological and tactical repertoire, and they did just that. The Citizens' Councils mixed their belief in biologically determined white supremacy with the prevailing anticommunist consensus. They knew how to influence state legislatures, and with their objective of stopping integration, they were likely to be more successful than the Klan.

The Councils also pursued a more focused agenda than the Klan. Whereas the former mobilized around specific ballot and legislative measures to deprive black people of electoral power and access to public facilities, the Klan was an outright terror squad with little political focus. The Councils represented a timebound resistance movement.[61] Klansmen participated in the resistance movement, too, but their trajectory both predated and outlived the immediate issues of integration and voting rights. The Klan was not a resistance movement per se. In its "second era" of the 1920s, it was a mass political reform movement; by the late 1960s, it would degenerate into a small, violent subset of the larger white supremacist movement.

Nor were the segregationists thoroughly comparable to mass-based anticommunist groups like the John Birch Society. Both attracted a middle-class, educated following. Unlike the Councils, however, the Birch Society attracted few supporters among elected officials, no doubt because most political elites viewed the Birchists with derision. As we saw in Chapter 2, anticommunist elites had more options in choosing which movement organizations to facilitate and which to mildly repress. For southerners committed to preserving segregation, a coalition of political elites and respectable movement activists was the best, if not the only, option.

Where segregationism was a resistance movement, the John Birch Society was more reformist in its objectives. Birchists shared in the anticommunist consensus pervasive throughout society. They objected to what they perceived to be the ineffectual, if not treasonous, tactics employed by state elites in pursuit of the "red menace." In contrast, Councilors were less suspicious of their elected officials, but together, elite and mass segregationists deviated from a growing national consensus favoring a modicum of civil rights protections for racial minorities.

Despite differences among them, the John Birch Society, the Klan, and the Citizens' Councils would, over time, converge ideologically in a tenuous coalition behind George Wallace's presidential campaign. As a resistance movement, segregationism ultimately failed to stop legally mandated integration. The segregationists might have retreated altogether, but that was unlikely given their large numbers and high commitment. Instead, much of the movement adjusted to failure. Small numbers of segregationists, perhaps those already associated with the Klan, maintained a terrorist wing among white supremacists. The Citizens' Councils, though, eventually reduced in numerical and political strength, broadened their issue agenda to include opposition to the 1964 Civil Rights Act and concern with foreign policy issues like the Vietnam war and the national liberation struggles in southern Africa.[62]

PARTISANSHIP, COMPROMISE, AND PROGRESS IN CIVIL RIGHTS

The rise and decline of "massive resistance" was accompanied by a mixed set of political opportunities for civil rights forces. At one level, the Eisenhower and Kennedy–Johnson administrations sought to channel the momentum of the civil rights movement in an orderly direction, toward integration and voter registration. Under each administration, nevertheless, the FBI also repressed the civil rights movement through combined tactics of surveillance and covert disruption and by routinely turning a blind eye toward white supremacist violence.[63] Right-wing activists viewed even limited federal civil rights action with alarm. The days of legally sanctioned racial segregation were numbered.

Among the most heated of the civil rights battles, the 1957 school integration crisis in Little Rock, Arkansas came to symbolize southern intransigence on civil rights.[64] In the weeks before Little Rock's Central High School was scheduled to open and admit nine black students for the first time, rumors of looming violence spread. The Arkansas Citizens' Councils pressured Governor Orval Faubus to resist the Eisenhower administration and the Supreme Court.[65] A federal district court ordered integration to proceed, and on September 4, 1957, the nine black students braved a racist mob outside the high school, only to be turned back by Arkansas National Guardsmen. Three weeks later, in a dramatic display of federal power versus "states' rights," President Eisenhower sent 1,000 federal troops to Little Rock to escort the black students past the white mobs. Once admitted, the students were attacked physically and verbally by white teenagers. The Little Rock school board requested that integration be postponed, and the ensuing legal battle made its way to the Supreme Court, which ruled against the school board. Governor Faubus responded by closing all Little Rock high schools for an entire school year. For his stand, he was reelected for another four terms.[66]

The Little Rock school crisis solidified the popularity of other segregationist southern politicians, too, as three state legislatures passed resolutions condemning Eisenhower's dispatch of federal troops to Arkansas.[67] Southern political elites, however, were unable to prevent the slow but steady march of a slate of Congressional civil rights bills. A 1957 Civil Rights Act created a federal Civil Rights Commission with subpoena power, a civil rights division within the Justice Department, and empowered federal prosecutors, with or without the consent of victims, to use injunctions against anyone who blocked African Americans from voting.[68] Southern election officials, thereafter, could face imprisonment if they denied ballots to black voters. The bill passed overwhelmingly in both houses of Congress, but not before Senator Strom Thurmond (D-SC) held forth on the Senate floor continuously for twenty-four hours, and broke the record for the longest filibuster in U.S. history.[69]

Passage of the 1957 law paved the way for subsequent legislation.[70] The law also shifted the terrain of conflict over civil rights from small, local school districts to the larger realm of electoral politics. Senator Paul Douglas (D-IL) expressed the view that "if this [voting] right is guaranteed, then many other abuses which are now practiced upon the disenfranchised will be self-correcting."[71]

Two years after its passage, however, the 1957 Civil Rights Act had not added a single southern black voter to the electoral rolls. The new Civil Rights Commission's main accomplishment was the exposure of how pervasive voting rights violations were. As the 1960 election season unfolded, Congressional civil rights backers passed another civil rights bill, which President Eisenhower signed in May 1960. The Civil Rights Act of 1960 authorized federal courts to appoint voting referees to help blacks register. The bill also authorized the Justice Department to bring suit against discriminatory voting officials. Civil rights promoters, including the NAACP, criticized the 1960 bill because it focused narrowly on voting rights and required lengthy court proceedings before the federal government would appoint voter referees.

Nevertheless, the passage of modest civil rights bills in 1957 and 1960 began a process whereby the federal government would intervene to distribute political power more equitably across racial lines. That redistribution would require the creation of new federal agencies, legally empowered to break the hegemony of segregationist politicians in the South. The expansion of the distributive power of the state was, of course, anathema to the Right on philosophical grounds. But it was advantageous to civil rights forces, and it also carried implications for a coming realignment in the two-party electoral system.

While the 1960 Civil Rights Act underwent debate, both the national Democratic and Republican parties adopted civil rights planks in their presidential campaign platforms.[72] That caused some southern Democrats to refuse to endorse the Kennedy–Johnson presidential ticket.[73] But the Republican Party, then dominated by "moderate" presidential candidate Richard Nixon and "liberal" New York Governor Nelson Rockefeller, was no more attractive to segregationists. Not until Senator Barry Goldwater's 1964 campaign and Congress' passage of the landmark 1964 Civil Rights Act would large numbers of southern Democrats switch parties.

The 1964 Act's most sweeping provision was its public accomodations section, which overturned nearly a century of legally sanctioned segregation.[74] President Lyndon Johnson signed the bill into law on July 2, 1964. Two weeks later the Republican Party convened and nominated Barry Goldwater, the only Republican Senator who voted against the Civil Rights Act—not, he said, because he opposed integration but because he opposed the expansion of federal government power. As we saw in Chapter 2, though, Goldwater's capture of several Deep South states gave the Republicans a new toehold in the region.

Meanwhile, the Democratic Party faced its own dilemmas during the summer 1964 presidential campaign. During the party convention, three civil rights activists, one black and two white, remained missing somewhere in the back roads of Mississippi. They were among thousands of young people who had braved the wrath of southern segregationists that summer in a campaign to register new African American voters. James Chaney, Andrew Goodman, and Michael Schwerner were killed by white supremacists. Their mutiliated bodies were not recovered until after the Democratic convention. Outside the convention, civil rights activists demanded a speedier search for the three young activists. Inside the convention the Mississippi Freedom Democratic Party demanded that the party seat its racially integrated delegation in place of Mississippi's all-white party regulars. In a symbolic compromise, Johnson offered the civil rights delegation two at-large seats and picked as his vice-presidential running mate Minnesota Senator Hubert Humphrey, who was a known civil rights supporter.

This was a time when civil rights marches and riots in major cities were wracking the country. Johnson knew he needed to act decisively and, once elected, he encouraged Congressional passage of the 1965 Voting Rights Act. This bill outlawed "states' rights" to impose literacy tests and poll taxes, and authorized federal examiners to be sent to the South to register black voters and monitor poll access during elections.[75]

THE TRANSFORMATION
OF THE SEGREGATIONIST MOVEMENT

As a resistance organization focused initially on school segregation, the Citizens' Councils began to decline in the late 1950s.[76] Still, other racist Right groups, let alone the anticommunist movement, organized apace. George Wallace's 1968 presidential campaign would help unify some of the key players in both movements. But one important organization, the Liberty Lobby, played an earlier and more enduring role in unifying the grassroots Right. In 1957, the Lobby's forerunner, Liberty and Property, published its *First National Directory of "Rightist" Groups*, a listing of about 900 organizations, large and small, throughout the country.[77]

Founded in 1958 by Willis Carto, the Liberty Lobby emerged out of a long tradition of explicitly anti-Jewish conspiracy theorizing among a group of white supremacist intellectuals.[78] Little is known about Carto's personal background, but aside from his attraction to esoteric racialist tomes like Francis Parker Yockey's *Imperium*, Carto was also committed to mass-based organizing. He was an early participant in the Congress of Freedom, which drew racist and grassroots anticommunist activists together for a series of high-profile national conventions. In San Francisco in 1955, Carto organized the Congress of Freedom's conference against U.S. participation in the United Nations.[79]

That same year, Carto also began publishing a monthly newsletter, *Right*, which promoted the activities of a wide range of right-wing groups. (Carto, for example, heralded the establishment of William F. Buckley's *National Review* in 1955; years later Carto and Buckley would sue each other for libel.) Early issues of *Right* focused on the potential of small and obscure right-wing parties.[80] These included the American Woman's Party, founded by Blanche Winters in 1952; the Christian Party in Georgia, led by Klansmen J. B. Stoner and Edward Fields; the Texas-based Constitution Party; the Federal "Evergreen" Party in Chicago; the Greenback Party in Indiana; Kent and Phoebe Courtney's "Interim Committee for a New Party," chaired by Lieutenant General P. A. del Valle; the National Renaissance Party; the Nationalist Conservative Party; and the Nationalist Party.[81] *Right* also reported admiringly on the

Citizens' Councils.[82] Carto used the newsletter to try to synthesize the thinking of grassroots anticommunist groups with theories of white supremacy. Carto's rhetorical approach was to frame the problems of Soviet "expansionism" and anti-colonial national liberation movements as racial, not political and economic, in their origins and implications.

> The greatest hoax of the age is that Russia is a Communist nation. Using this canard, Russia has been able to enlist the active support of hundreds of thousands to her national cause in all lands. What a wry joke the masterminds in the Kremlin have played upon them!
>
> More, by masquerading as "Communist," the Russians have been able to play upon the pro-marxist sympathies of the dumb liberals, and so Russia's most unspeakable crimes against humanity, as well as her international network of subversion, have been excused or aided by these articulate fools.
>
> No, the battle is not between "Communism" and marxist liberalism. It is between East and West: between European and Oriental values, mores, ideals and ways of living. *It is actually between the white and the colored world, of which Russia is the Lord.*[83] (emphasis added)

Besides stressing white supremacy, Carto also promoted a conspiratorial analysis of world events. He drew his readers' attention, for example, to the purported role of U.S. elites in the spread of anti-Western, "communist" subversion.

> Internationally, "Communism" serves the same purpose of dividing the West against itself because it prevents the trotskyite eggheads from recognizing and uniting against the real foreign threat: the rise of the colored world. And it serves as a rationalization and camoflage [*sic*] for the fanatical anti-Western and anti-White drive of the nations of Central Asia and Africa.
>
> This is why American-style communism (Trotskyism) and all other forms of liberalism must be recognized and exterminated for what they really are: forms of treason.[84]

This type of conspiracy thinking made the Liberty Lobby a likely ally of the John Birch Society. But throughout the 1960s and 1970s, Willis Carto and Robert Welch would compete for followers, and their respective organizations would conflict on whether racial equality or communism posed the greatest threat to the republic. (Welch saw the civil rights movement as a "communist plot," but the John Birch Society did not officially peddle theories of racial biological determinism.)[85]

Carto launched the Liberty Lobby in Washington, D.C. in 1958 to serve "as a contact for patriots with their Washington representatives, . . .

set up a research department, and . . . operate a news service."[86] Invited to serve on Carto's first advisory board were some of the racist and anticommunist movements' leading lights, including Citizens' Councils founder Judge Tom Brady.[87]

During its five years of publication, *Right* focused increasingly on racial matters and downplayed the threat of communism, per se. *Right* promoted the writings of Roger Pearson, an obscure British eugenicist anthropologist who would become an influential leader of the World Anti-Communist League in the 1970s.[88] Carto also promoted the Klan-linked National States Rights Party and its print organ, the *Thunderbolt*.[89] *Right* circulated precisedly at the time when the mass-based anticommunist movement was on the rise, and at a time when conservative intellectuals had elevated the anticommunist preoccupation above rightists' concern with preserving traditional order. In that context, the stark racialist content of Willis Carto's newsletter evidenced the Liberty Lobby's goal of keeping biological determinism alive and well on the Right.

Electoral Politics

The racist Right's ill-fated efforts at forming a third party during the 1950s and 1960s served, nevertheless, as a base of support for George Wallace's 1968 presidential campaign. Perhaps the most promising of the third-party efforts was the Texas-based Constitution Party, which convened in 1952 and announced a campaign to win electoral college votes for General Douglas MacArthur for President and Senator Harry Byrd (D-VA) for Vice-President.[90] By 1956, the Constitution Party had affiliates in New York, Colorado, Pennsylvania, California, and Illinois.[91] At a 1956 "National States' Rights Conference," the Constitution Party adopted a platform that advocated a limited federal government, reduced taxes, and U.S. "independence" in foreign affairs. The platform emphasized that the Democrats and Republicans were "no longer two different political parties, but . . . mere contending factions of a single party campaigning for a single objective—namely, to possess and control the instruments of consolidated power afforded by the tyrant socialist state."[92] For President, in 1956, the Constitution Party nominated T. Coleman Andrews, who had been Eisenhower's Internal Revenue Service commissioner; California Congressmember Thomas H. Werdel was picked as Andrews' running mate. Endorsing the ticket was a slate of prominent anticommunist activists, including Clarence Manion, Bonner Fellers, Charles Edison, George E. Stratemeyer, and Dan Smoot.[93] Then in 1960 the party drafted retired Marine Corps Brigadier General Merritt B. Curtis for president, and campaign manager Curtis B. Dall, a former son-in-law of Franklin D. Roosevelt for vice-president.[94] Dall would become a leading Liberty Lobby activist in the 1960s.

The Constitution Party appealed to both an anticommunist and racist, anti-Semitic constituency. The National States' Rights Party (NSRP) was more narrowly based in the South and among the Ku Klux Klan and paramilitary wings of the racist Right. The NSRP was founded in Georgia in 1956 by Klansman J. B. Stoner,[95] who was convicted for the 1958 bombing of a black church in Alabama.[96] Klan historian Wyn Craig Wade described the NSRP as "neo-Nazi"; its insignia was the Third Reich symbol of a thunderbolt.[97] The NSRP's 1962 "Convention Report" highlighted the participation of James Warner (who would become an important preacher of Identity Christianity in the 1970s), Minutemen leader Robert DePugh, and Admiral John G. Crommelin, whom the NSRP had named as a vice-presidential candidate in 1960 when the party tried unsuccessfully to draft Arkansas Governor Orval Faubus for president.[98] J. B. Stoner's assistant in the NSRP was a young Edward Fields, who for the next three decades would remain a leading Klansman and editor of the *Thunderbolt*, renamed *The Truth at Last* in the 1980s.

The evidence is inconclusive as to whether the Constitution Party, the National States' Rights Party, let alone more obscure groups, could have grown from groups merely calling themselves "parties" into successful electoral vehicles. Instead, segregationist activists had their first national electoral breakthrough handed to them when Alabama Governor George C. Wallace decided to enter three presidential primaries in nothern states in 1964. Wallace had gained national notoriety in 1963, when he vowed during his inaugural address, to uphold "segregation now, segregation tomorrow, segregation forever." In June 1963, a few weeks after Birmingham's police chief "Bull" Connor had unleashed fire hoses and attack dogs on civil rights protesters, Wallace personally tried to block two African American students from entering the University of Alabama. After alerting the national press corps to his intended obstruction of a federal court integration order, Wallace set up a public address system and waited for President Kennedy to federalize the Alabama National Guard, which ordered him to step aside and allow the two students to register. Wallace was flooded with letters of support, financial donations, and invitations to speak from around the country.[99]

Wallace entered three northern state primary races with the stated intention of rallying opposition to the 1964 Civil Rights Act, then pending in Congress.[100] His campaign theme was not segregationism per se, but the idea that each state should do as it pleased on racial matters.[101]

In a campaign speech against the Civil Rights Act, Wallace neatly blended segregationist code words with the theme of the communist specter.

> We are faced with the astounding spectacle, for the first time in a civilized nation, of high officials calling for the passage of a so-called civil rights bill for fear of threat of mob violence. . . . This bill takes a long step toward transferring private property to public domain under a central government. . . . Under any name, it will create a dictatorship the likes of which we or our fathers have not witnessed. . . . It will make government master and God over man. . . . There are those who would amalgamate us into a unit of the one, subservient to a powerful central government, with laws designed to equalize us into the common denominator necessary for a slave people. . . . If victory for freedom is impossible, then surrender to communism is inevitable and we can begin fitting the yokes of slavery to the necks of our children even now as the riots and mobs lap at the streets of these United States.[102]

Electoral support for Wallace in the Wisconsin, Indiana, and Maryland primaries surprised observers at the time. In Wisconsin, Wallace won more than a third of the Democratic vote and nearly a quarter of the total. In Indiana, his vote tallies were almost as high. In Maryland, Wallace nearly won the state primary, with 42.7 percent of the total vote.[103]

The Maryland primary, which came last, was accompanied by press coverage of the "extremist" groups active on Wallace's behalf; these included the National States' Rights Party and Gerald L. K. Smith's California-based Christian Nationalist Crusade.[104] These groups were too small and inconsequential to have mobilized wide support for Wallace, but their presence on the scene signaled the salience of racist politics in the North. When political scientist Michael Rogin studied the base of Wallace's support in the 1964 primaries, he found that Wallace did especially well in white neighborhoods where voters' prejudices correlated with proximity to African Americans. The Wallace vote was a protest vote, but, Rogin concluded, it "was a reminder that the possibility of a mass-based racist movement was not completely remote."[105]

The Wallace vote in the North was one factor in the Republicans' decision to nominate Barry Goldwater in 1964.[106] Goldwater's strong showing in Republican primaries coincided with his opposition to the Civil Rights Act. But his nomination owed more to the strength of the anticommunist conservative movement inside the GOP than to segregationists' natural appreciation of his stance on civil rights. Within days of Goldwater's nomination, Wallace announced his own withdrawal from the race. He had planned on running in sixteen (mostly southern) states,[107] and some of these would go to Goldwater. Wallace himself would not endorse the Republican nominee out of loyalty to Democratic candidates in Alabama.[108] Some members of the Constitution Party, which had backed Wallace, left to form Independent Americans for Goldwater.[109]

Goldwater's landslide defeat meant that another four years would have to pass before right-wing political strategists could test a race-based "southern strategy." Wallace spent the next four years polishing his image,[110] and when he was unable to change Alabama's law prohibiting a second gubernatorial term, he persuaded his wife Lurleen to run for governor in 1966. She won, and her political appointments solidified Wallace's policies and base of support in Alabama,[111] and allowed husband George to concentrate on building the American Independent Party (AIP) for the 1968 campaign. Heading AIP organizing in California was William K. Shearer, the leader of the California Citizens' Council. Shearer had successfully organized passage of a 1964 ballot proposition nullifying California's open housing laws.[112]

SEGREGATIONISM'S LEGACY

As we will see in Chapter 6, factions of the segregationist movement survived in part by coalescing with the anti-elite wing of the anticommunist movement. The Wallace campaigns and subsequent third-party efforts allowed segregationist and anticommunist activists to make common cause through national organizations like the John Birch Society and the Liberty Lobby. These groups would manage to weather campaign losses and internecine conflict and maintain a base of thousands of supporters during the 1970s, despite the ascendance of the better funded and more professional New Right movement groups.

The segregationist Right was, to a certain extent, destined to decline because its central organizing principle—biologically determined white supremacy—did not enjoy the kind of broad popular support that anticommunism did. Political elites were able to make hay with widespread antagonisms over the unequal distribution of wealth and power between the races. But crude biological determinism was something else, and those that held tightly to such tenets were a minority on the Right.

Yet to posit the eventual decline of the organized, mass-based racist right is to raise the more crucial question of the movement's legacy. The Citizens' Councils failed to preserve legally sanctioned segregation of public facilities. But their intense activism galvanized a large sector of the electorate and thus created an unprecedented opportunity for Republican party organizers. As early as 1968, presidential candidate

Richard Nixon benefited from the backlash against civil rights. Over the next two and a half decades, the Republicans would link opposition to welfare, affirmative action, and street crime all to negative images of African Americans and their struggle for social equality. That linkage would prove to be a winning formula, for both Republicans and Democrats, from the 1988 "Willie Horton" television spots on behalf of George Bush to Arkansas Governor Bill Clinton's high-profile 1992 campaign stop to authorize the execution of a mentally retarded black prisoner. From the continuing salience of racist campaign appeals to the civil rights movement's inability to press equality to its most needed economic dimension, racist politics owes its longevity in part to the persistence of the organized racist Right.

CHAPTER 4

Historical Antecedents of the Christian Right

By the end of the twentieth century, the Christian Right was the most influential of right-wing movements. Its phenomenal influence perplexed outside observers who wondered how a seemingly fractious and inexperienced cast of characters had managed to win election to thousands of local offices all over the United States. Lost in the 1990s controversies over the rise of the Christian Right was a recognition that the politically conservative evangelical movement was decades in the making.[1]

In the first half of the twentieth century, evangelicalism was a *prepolitical* movement,[2] although one that constituted a large sector of North American Protestantism. From the mid-1940s through the 1960s, evangelicals took action to protect and promote their own interests, especially in winning access to the nation's broadcast airwaves. Unlike the anticommunist and segregationist movements of the same era, the evangelical movement was not yet directly linked to state policymaking, nor to a quest for state power. This was the time, though, when millions of American Christians followed the "positive thinking" teachings of Norman Vincent Peale, through his *Guideposts* magazine.[3] It was the time when huge crowds came to hear Billy Graham preach the gospel. In this early period, the culture of evangelicalism was more prominent than its politics. But in this cultural milieu, the theological emphases on personal salvation, individual achievement, obedience to higher authority and adherence to the national preoccupation with fighting communism, were all conducive to evangelicals' eventual political awakening.

Not until the 1970s would evangelical leaders begin to take the pursuit of political power seriously. By then, the movement would enjoy a rich network of organizational resources, including inter-denominational "parachurch" ministries[4] and an unparalleled religious broadcasting industry. This chapter examines the evangelical institution building and ideological campaigns that served as a backdrop to the rise of the Christian Right.

THE ROOTS OF POLITICAL EVANGELICALISM

Throughout its history, the evangelical movement has proven resilient in the face of a hostile secular public. As we will see in Chapter 10, the television preacher scandals of the 1980s did not deter grassroots Christian Right activists. On the contrary, the fall from grace of some of the movement's media celebrities may have contributed to the movement's decentralization and increased political activity.[5] In place of a few prominent figures, countless lesser known and more locally accountable leaders gained influence once some of the big names receded from view.

Decades before the secular media would mock the television preachers mercilessly, public scorn toward fundamentalists reached an all-time high following the 1925 trial of John Scopes, the Tennessee school teacher who violated that state's ban on teaching Darwinism.[6] Fundamentalism became a disreputable term, associated with anti-modernism, anti-intellectualism, and bigotry. During those same Depression years, fundamentalists established important training schools, including the Dallas Theological Seminary and Bob Jones University.[7] At the same time, fundamentalists and so-called modernist Protestants engaged in a series of denominational feuds. In 1933 a group of fundamentalists was expelled from the Presbyterian Church U.S.A. Among the renegades, Reverend Carl McIntire formed the Bible Presbyterian Church and became the most prominent leader of the separatist branch of the fundamentalist movement.[8]

McIntire and, later, his Cold War protégés Fred Schwarz, Billy James Hargis, and Edgar Bundy maintained limited contacts with some of the zealously anti-Semitic and racist Right organizations mentioned in Chapter 1. The Old Christian Right of the Depression and World War II eras was dominated by William Dudley Pelley's pro-Nazi Silver Shirts, Gerald L. K. Smith's Christian Nationalist Crusade, and Gerald B. Winrod's Defenders of the Christian Faith.[9] Of the three, Winrod was the one with the strongest ties to the fundamentalist movement proper.[10] However, none of the three played major roles in the denominational debates of the 1930s and 1940s over fundamentalism, nor did they work to spread a particularly religious message. Instead, their greater organizational emphasis on hatred toward Jews and communists locates them more accurately within the milieu of the racist Right and the anti-elite sector of the anticommunist movement.

Fundamentalism itself endured longer than some secular observers predicted. George Marsden, an historian of evangelicalism, attributes the popularity of classics like Richard Hofstadter's *Anti-Intellectualism in American Life* and *The Paranoid Style in American Politics* to the prevailing view of secular intellectuals that fundamentalism was some sort of "a side effect of the passing of an old order that . . . would die away when the cultural transformation was complete and the social causes removed."[11]

Historian Ernest R. Sandeen, however, provided a more complex view when he explained fundamentalism's survival by distinguishing between the fundamentalist movement and the "fundamentalist controversy" over the teaching of evolution in public schools. Conflict with a modernist society could account for the controversy over a public policy issue, but the belief system itself endured because of its doctrinal millenarianism. Sandeen traced the origins of the "dispensationalism" of evangelicals, a doctrine with deep implications for the later politics of the Christian Right. Among several strands of belief woven into fundamentalist doctrine, one of the most influential was the dispensationalism preached beginning in the late nineteenth century by Irish theologian John Nelson Darby. Dispensationalists divide worldly history into distinct epochs, the last one to culminate with the rapture of Christian believers into heaven, followed immediately by an apocalyptic tribulation, a battle of Armageddon between the forces of good and evil, culminating in Christ's return to rule on earth, with believers, for one thousand years.[12] This doctrine came to be known as "pre-millenialism," because it posited that the rapture, tribulation, and Armageddon would all occur *before* Christ's thousand-year reign, not after, as the "post-millenialists" believed. Premillenialists studied the Bible and attempted to correlate its prophecies with with world events, such as the 1948 establishment of the state of Israel, which, for many believers, marked the beginning of the last forty-year generation before Christ was expected to return.[13]

Irrespective of their various theological views on the coming "end-times," early twentieth-century evangelicals preferred to remain aloof from, if not hostile toward, the affairs of the world. Sociologist James Davison Hunter describes the period between the two world wars as a time when U.S. fundamentalists, in particular, "entrenched" themselves as a "cognitive minority" and invoked the Depression as evidence of God's vindictive punishment on an apostate America.[14]

Pessimistic times reinforced the conviction of fundamentalists' that the mainline denominations had gone astray. In opposition to modernist Protestantism, fundamentalist splinter churches flourished, as did pentecostal churches. Taken together, the "independent church movement" emphasized morality, personal salvation, and withdrawal from modernist denominations.[15] In 1941, for instance, Reverend Carl McIntire organized a separatist organization for churches and denominations willing to renounce affiliation with the Federal Council of Churches, which had coordinated ecumenical work among Protestants since 1908. McIntire's American Council of Christian Churches (ACCC) described itself as "militantly pro-Gospel and anti-modernist."[16]

Resource Mobilization and Ideological Consolidation

From the 1940s through the 1960s, evangelicals engaged in prepolitical activity that followed two general patterns. First, they formed parachurch ministries and lobbied against government obstacles to their propagation of the gospel. Second, at the ideological level, they played a role in the Cold War, through publicly accusing liberal church representatives of being communist sympathizers, or worse. Organizations established in the 1940s for primarily religious purposes facilitated the evangelical movement's mobilization along both these paths.

Beginning in 1941, Carl McIntire's American Council of Christian Churches (ACCC) successfully petitioned the Federal Communications Commission to divide radio air time allotted for Protestants between fundamentalists and the mainline Federal Council of Churches.[17] Then came the National Association of Evangelicals (NAE), formed in 1942, which shared the American Council's doctrine of biblical literalism but rejected McIntire's sectarian exclusion of all but the most rigid fundamentalist churches. NAE adopted an inclusivist membership policy, allowing pentecostal churches (scorned by McIntire and the fundamentalists) as well as churches still tied to the Federal Council of Churches.[18] A year after its formation in Chicago, NAE opened an office in Washington, D.C., and hired a full-time director to help missionaries stationed abroad and to secure better evangelical representation within the chaplaincy of the armed forces.[19]

NAE's growth soon far exceeded that of the ACCC. By the mid-1940s, NAE membership included adherents from twenty-two denominations and an additional one hundred individual churches, representing a total base of over one million American evangelicals. By comparison, the fundamentalist American Council, which excluded pentecostals, peaked at an estimated 200,000 members.[20] The Assemblies of God was the largest pentecostal denomination; altogether, pentecostals constituted about one third of the NAE's membership by the late 1950s.[21]

Of the two evangelical bodies, the National Association of Evangelicals would prove to be more influential in the eventual growth of the Christian Right. During the late 1940s and 1950s however, McIntire's Council captured more secular press attention as the Council vociferously opposed the growing ecumenical tendency among mainline Protestants. From the 1950s through the 1980s, fundamentalists would wage bitter anticommunist smear campaigns against the mainline Christian churches. For instance, in 1948 the ecumenical "modernists" formed the World Council of Churches in Amsterdam and its U.S. branch, the National Council of Churches in 1950. Every year, McIntire's group held a protest counterconvention in whatever city the ecumenicists chose for their meeting.[22] The fundamentalists considered the World Council of Churches to be insufficiently anticommunist and saw the mainliners' acceptance of the United Nations as proof that the two bodies were linked in a "communist conspiracy."

The National Association of Evangelicals waged its own rhetorical attacks on the World Council of Churches, but directed more of its activist resources toward securing access to the federally regulated radio airwaves. After the war, NAE took an interest in three other specific policy issues. In public opposition to U.S. diplomatic relations with the Vatican, NAE tempered its anti-Catholicism and instead invoked the principle of church–state separation.[23] In 1945 NAE urged readers of its *United Evangelical Action* to lobby against a $3 million aid to public schools bill in the Senate, on the grounds that it would "centralize control in Washington, capture our educational processes and proceed to educate the rising generations along 'liberal' lines."[24] In 1949, *United Evangelical Action* urged NAE members to oppose the Truman administration's Fair Employment Practices legislation, which was intended to reduce racial discrimination, on the grounds that evangelical organizations might be forced to hire non-believers.[25] Seen in retrospect, these lobbying campaigns foreshadowed some of the later concerns of the Christian Right.

In the 1950s, NAE began passing political resolutions at its national conventions. In 1951, it endorsed the combat role of the United States in Korea, commended President Truman's resolve not to send a U.S. envoy to the Vatican, and, under the heading "Christian Race Principles," advocated evangelization "among the members of every race and nationality at home and abroad."[26] In a 1954 convention resolution, NAE urged the State Department to persuade the government of Colombia, then writing a new constitution, to overrule the Catholic hierarchy's obstruction of "religious freedom."[27] By 1961, NAE's convention resolutions centered on "the means of combatting communism" and the preservation of tax-exempt status for religious institutions. NAE also urged President Kennedy to oppose admission of "Red China" to the United Nations.[28]

NAE took ideological positions consistent with the national anti-communist consensus, and in that sense the early evangelical movement was *system-supportive*. However, in their relationships with government agencies on questions of the right to proselytize, evangelicals positioned themselves as *challengers*, opposed to the state. Tactically, NAE wisely chose not to wage aggressive anti-government campaigns in its efforts to secure access to broadcast airwaves. Instead, NAE and other evangelicals worked proactively to develop independent religious broadcasting and missionary industries.

Prior to World War II, fundamentalist broadcasters enjoyed at least as much radio access as the mainline broadcasters.[29] Evangelicals understood the implications when, in 1944, the Mutual Broadcasting System abandoned its unrestricted sale of commercial time to religious broadcasters. The newly formed National Association of Evangelicals quickly assembled 150 radio preachers and formed an affiliate, the National Religious Broadcasters (NRB). NRB hired a Washington, D.C. communications attorney, began lobbying the Federal Communications Commission (FCC) and the networks, and initially won a small allotment of free air time for evangelical broadcasters.

In 1956 NRB began its annual conventions in Washington, D.C., which for decades thereafter featured a Congressional prayer breakfast and a luncheon honoring FCC officials.[30]

In 1957 President Eisenhower initiated the White House tradition of sending greetings (and some years the president himself) to the annual NRB convention. Eisenhower commended the broadcasters in a telegram read before NRB's closing panel discussion, "Religious Broadcasting and the Menace of World Communism." The discussion was moderated by John Broger, who served both as deputy director of the U.S. Office of Armed Forces Information and Education and as an executive committee member of the National Religious Broadcasters.[31]

Evangelical broadcasters proceeded to learn the ropes of "beltway" lobbying, and their efforts appeared to pay off in 1960, when the Federal Communications Commission announced a dramatic policy change. No longer would the federal government distinguish between "sustaining time programs," using free allotted air time, and "commercially sponsored programs" in evaluating licensed television and radio stations' performance in the public interest. Nor would the rules restricting the amount of commercial time permitted per program hour apply to paying religious broadcasters.[32]

These policy changes had enormous implications for the growth of the media resources of evangelicals. Local network affiliate stations were encouraged to accumulate profits by selling "religious" air time to the highest bidders, not to broadcasters most representative of the local religious community. An up-and-coming band of televangelists was now free to devote any amount of program time to fundraising. Over time, the staid mainline religious broadcasters were unable to compete with the more flamboyant NRB producers. The opportunity to begin to monopolize religious television and radio tied evangelicals' media success to the production of captivating programming, an example of which was the political talk show format pioneered by Pat Robertson's Christian Broadcasting Network, beginning in the early 1960s. As the content of such shows began to become more worldly, religious broadcasting eventually became the single most important resource in the mobilization of the Christian Right.[33]

The establishment of parachurch missions also laid the groundwork for later evangelical political activity. The more resourceful of the mainline denominations crowded the foreign mission field; evangelicals tended to concentrate on intensifying the religious zeal of the already converted, especially within the United States itself. Perhaps the most successful of these efforts was Youth for Christ, which proselytized North American youth, and trained and deployed evangelicals to lead post-World War II foreign shortwave radio missions and major overseas relief efforts.[34]

One itinerant Youth for Christ minister won larger followings than any other. Billy Graham began his traveling ministry in the late 1940s and might have remained unknown had he not drawn the attention of two media magnates, William Randolph Hearst and Henry Luce. In 1949 Hearst sent a telegram to his editors: "Puff Graham," which they dutifully did in Hearst-controlled newspapers, magazines, and films. Graham's vocal anticommunism landed him a promotional 1954 cover story in Henry Luce's *Time* magazine.[35] Apart from these corporate media boosts, Graham's own popularity drew thousands to hear him preach in major cities, from Los Angeles to New York.[36] With a growing following for Graham's message came greater opportunities for the evangelical movement to develop more resources.

Evangelical publications were important in this regard, as television had not yet become the dominant medium. Two of the most important national evangelical publications of the 1950s were *Christian Economics* and *Christianity Today*, both directed primarily at clergy. *Christian Economics* was a weekly four-page tabloid sent free to more than 175,000 Protestant clergymen. It was started in 1950 by Howard Kershner's Christian Freedom Foundation, with an initial $50,000 grant from Sun

Oil executive Howard Pew.[37] In the mid-1970s, the Christian Freedom Foundation would use its tax-exempt status to help launch one of the earliest Christian Right voter education projects.[38] But in the 1950s, Kershner's Foundation aimed primarily at inculcating clergy with a philosophy of anticommunism and libertarian economics. In that respect, *Christian Economics* was an evangelical version of 1950s "fusionist" publications *National Review* and *Human Events*, discussed in Chapter 1. In fact, *Human Events* editor Frank C. Hanighen was a frequent contributor to *Christian Economics*.

The Christian Freedom Foundation's consulting economist and front-page columnist Percy L. Greaves had ties to the secular Right. Greaves was a former researcher for Senator Owen R. Brewster of Maine and Representative Fred A. Hartley[39] (cosponsor of the anti-unionist Taft–Hartley Act). Greaves was an initial advisory board member of the racist and anti-Semitic Liberty Lobby[40] (discussed in Chapters 3 and 6) and a founder of the Constitution Party, which was formed in 1952 in opposition to the presidential nomination of General Eisenhower.[41] Greaves used his column to promote specific policy issues, such as the Bricker Amendment,[42] which would have restricted executive branch power to make foreign treaties. Most of Greaves' columns dwelled on the supremacy of capitalism at a time when Protestants in the World Council of Churches were questioning the system's injustices. Typical of Greaves' writings was a 1953 column, "Economic Equality":

> Today many people in both low and high places advocate what they call "more equality." By this they mean a "more equal" distribution of wealth and income in terms of money, or more specifically, dollars. They sincerely believe that this is a Christian objective which will furnish more total satisfaction than the economic inequalities which have existed, do exist and will continue to exist if our present ways of living are not altered considerably.
>
> The rich have more than they need or can use in a desireable manner. The poor are in constant need of the bare necessities of civilized life. Wouldn't it be better for everyone if the government, our monopoly organ of force, took the superfluous dollars from those with more than a certain specified wealth or income and distributed these dollars to those with less than a certain specified wealth or income?
>
> Many who seek economic equality as a desired goal believe that it will raise the standards of the poorest people. They are mistaken. Actually, the inequality of a free capitalist economy is a great boon to the relatively poor.
>
> The desire of many for the redistribution of wealth is nothing more than unchristian covetousness and economic ignorance. All men are better served if we permit our more able, industrious and intelligent

brothers to share their above average production with us through lower market prices. Low income people receive what they do, only because others have become rich by increasing total wealth which they must share with consumers.[43]

Greaves' early rendition of an economic view, later derided as "trickle down" economics, could have been written by the libertarian Foundation for Economic Education (FEE), discussed in Chapter 1.[44] Evangelicals rejected an evolutionary theory of human origins, but social darwinism was an acceptable justification for opposing state intervention to redistribute wealth.

Founded in 1956 and published through the 1990s, *Christianity Today* also advocated free-market economics, but within a broader editorial repertoire. The bimonthly magazine was founded by Billy Graham, his father-in-law L. Nelson Bell, and theologian Carl F. Henry. In his opening editorial, Henry wrote that the mission of *Christianity Today* would be to "apply the biblical revelation to the contemporary social crisis, by presenting the implications of the total Gospel message for every area of life."[45] Purporting to speak for the tens of thousands of evangelicals drawn to his rallies, in the same first issue Billy Graham said he was not "advocating bibliolatry,"[46] a clear negative reference to the Biblical literalism of the fundamentalists. The second issue's feature article by Senator William F. Knowland, against the admission of Red China into the United Nations, left not doubt about the magazine's anticommunist leanings.[47]

On the heels of the 1956 presidential election, *Christianity Today* polled a "random sampling of ministers from all states," found eight-to-one support for Eisenhower, and clergy preoccupation with foreign policy, not with issues of morality. Among ministers who had voted for Eisenhower in 1952, but who favored neither party in 1956, the *Christianity Today* survey found that "the bulk of the disappointment over President Eisenhower's first term concerned the failure to reverse the trend to socialism, and the failure to curtail the huge foreign aid program and to reduce taxes at home."[48] In other words, these respondents expressed a characteristically right-wing stance: support for government action against "socialism," and opposition to the state's redistribution of wealth. The *Christianity Today* article concluded with a caveat that "the stark fact of disagreement on leading social issues is a reminder that official agencies only at great risk constitute themselves pressure lobbies for specific politico-economic objectives."[49]

Thereafter, the magazine published strong editorials, such as its own in favor of racial integration,[50] but rarely took positions on specific policy proposals. *Christianity Today* published anticommunist polemics by Billy

Graham,[51] and a series of feature articles by FBI Director J. Edgar Hoover. With titles like "Communist Propaganda and the Christian Pulpit," Hoover's hyperbolic essays seemed tailored to ministers looking for Sunday sermon material:

> The Communists are today spraying the world with ideological and propaganda missiles designed to create a deadly radioactive cloud of Marxism-Leninism.
>
> The deadliest of these Communist missiles—whose warheads are exceptionally heavy—are being directed against the Christian pulpit. Communist gunners, with special ideological training and schooled in atheistic perversity, are "sighting in" the clergy—hoping to shatter, immobilize, and confuse this powerful form of idealism, morality, and civic virtue.[52]

Preoccupation with communism during the late 1950s and early 1960s positioned mainstream evangelicals not as challengers but as supporters of a national anticommunist consensus. The public legitimacy granted to the evangelical movement's commitment to anticommunist ideology by President Eisenhower and J. Edgar Hoover was an important resource in its development.

THE EARLY CHRISTIAN RIGHT AND McCARTHYISM

The concern of evangelicals with communism predated the mobilization of the secular, mass-based anticommunist groups discussed in Chapter 2. Both before and during the Cold War period, organized evangelicals functioned as watchdogs and vocal critics of the patriotism of liberal churches, thereby intensifying the climate of anticommunism in which right-wing movements, religious and secular, flourished.

One of the earliest forerunners of the Christian Right was the Church League of America, also known as the National Laymen's Council, which was formed in 1937 in opposition to New Deal policies. Unlike *Christianity Today* and other evangelical publications, the Church League's weekly *News and Views* bulletin for clergy and laypersons focused not on the gospel but on what it called "radical and revolutionary activities in certain social fields like those of religion, education, labor, public service, and politics."[53] In 1940, as the United States deliberated over how to participate in World War II, the Church League proclaimed communism a greater threat than fascism.

We must not for one moment minimize the perils of Fascism—nor the growing strength of the Nazi program in this country. As Germany and Italy expand their prestige and power in Europe it is reflected here in more open and active performance on the part of their sympathizers and agents.

But communism is greatly the more dangerous alien force at work here—for three reasons especially: (1) Communism had the advantage of nearly 20 years' start in its propagation program; (2) Communism gets its converts from all classes of people while Nazism is restricted almost entirely to Germans (and only a percentage of them); and (3) Communism is linked inseparably with certain brands of 'liberalism' graduating downwards from parlor pinks to revolutionary Socialists— which creates a substantial under-structure; and this adds greatly to the strength of the main *subversive* stem.

There is still another reason—and a highly important one—which is the sympathy—the aid—and the comfort that Communist forces have had from the administration in Washington since 1932. This is one of the blackest pages in American history.[54] (emphasis in original)

The internal subversion thesis and the view of liberalism as merely a soft form of communism provided the logic for Christian Rightists' attacks on reputable church bodies.

In 1947 the Church League distributed "The Smear Terror," a tract by associate John T. Flynn, who had led the isolationist America First Committee prior to U.S. entry into World War II. Flynn denounced the writers who had exposed some isolationists' links to pro-fascist groups and Nazis.[55] In 1949, Flynn published *The Road Ahead: America's Creeping Revolution*, in which he leveled his own anticommunist smear on the Federal Council of Churches.[56] *Reader's Digest* excerpted *The Road Ahead* in 1950, and by 1953 the book had sold almost a million copies.[57]

This was also the time when Senator Joseph McCarthy was riding high, and when subversion charges against liberal churches became a national controversy. In March of 1953 the National Council of Churches publicly denounced Representative Harold Velde (R-IL), chair of the House Committee on Un-American Activities (HUAC), for suggesting a possible investigation of communism in the churches; Velde dropped the idea due to outcry from fellow House members.[58] But several months later the popular anticommunist *American Mercury* magazine published "Reds and Our Churches," in which Senator Joseph McCarthy's aide J. B. Matthews charged that "the largest single group supporting the Communist apparatus in the United States today is composed of Protestant clergymen."[59] Matthews, who had been director of research for HUAC from 1938 to

1945, claimed that at least seven thousand Protestant ministers were Communist Party "members, fellow-travelers, espionage agents, party-line adherents, and unwitting dupes," and he named scores of "conspirators" over the space of several pages. Matthews' article hit the newsstands within days of his appointment to direct Senator McCarthy's Permanent Subcommittee on Investigations. In the heat of controversy, the Democratic Senators on that committee called for Matthews' ouster. McCarthy refused to fire his aide. President Eisenhower weighed in on the side of McCarthy's detractors, along with a coalition of mainline clergy, and Matthews decided to resign.[60]

During the Matthews incident, the National Association of Evangelicals took an equivocal public position. In one of its publications, NAE editorialized that it was "wholeheartedly in agreement" with President Eisenhower's repudiation of "irresponsible attacks" on "any group of citizens." But the same editorial buttressed Matthews' charges and claimed that "deliberate smears" against Matthews "make a splendid cover-up for the 'pinkos' in the Protestant clergy."[61] One year later, NAE went further and vented an expanded version of Matthews' thesis by publishing an article titled "The World Council of Communism."[62]

The Matthews incident was a piece of a larger power struggle between Joseph McCarthy's cohorts and the majority of political elites who opposed the Senator's tactics and his wide-ranging view of the communist "menace." Once McCarthy's power waned, red-baiting of liberal churches ceased as a tactic of government anticommunists but remained a central theme for right-wing evangelicals from the 1950s through the 1980s. During the Cold War, the American Council of Christian Laymen distributed a pamphlet, "How Red is the National Federal Council of Churches?"[63]

Billy James Hargis' Christian Crusade focused on lambasting the National and World Councils of Churches more than on any other single issue.[64] By the early 1960s, Hargis ran one of the largest of the anticommunist "ministries," with daily radio broadcasts on scores of stations.[65] Dr. Fred Schwarz's Christian Anti-Communism Crusade conducted large public rallies and training seminars.

At the height of mobilization of the mass-based anticommunist movement, the National Association of Evangelicals organized its own anticommunist programs for member churches, by then numbering forty-one denominations, serving a total constituency of ten million Protestants.[66] In 1961 *United Evangelical Action* published a monthly study guide series, "The Christian Answer to Communism," later published in book form, began distributing the popular John Birch Society film "Communism on the Map," and, jointly with Youth for Christ missionaries, held a Youth Leaders' Conference on Communism.[67]

APPROACHING PARTISAN POLITICS

During the Cold War era, right-wing evangelicals had their own religious and political motivations for waging anticommunist rhetorical campaigns against the liberal churches. Evangelical organizations, inadvertently or not, served state objectives by propagating a theologically adorned anticommunist ideology to millions of churchgoers. At that phase of the movement's development, evangelicalism constituted a system-supportive asset of the state. At the same time, the skills and resources evangelical leaders developed during the Cold War period facilitated the movement's later, more partisan, activism.

The prospect of a Roman Catholic president topped the concerns of evangelicals in 1960. In a private letter, Billy Graham warned Vice-President Richard Nixon in June 1960 that Democratic candidate John Kennedy was sure to "capture the Catholic vote." Graham urged Nixon to choose a popular Protestant running mate, and recommended Representative Walter Judd (R-MN).[68] Judd had been a missionary to China prior to serving in Congress, and he had also been a prominent figure in Marvin Liebman's China Lobby groups during the 1950s and 1960s.[69] Judd was allied with Nixon's opponents in the most staunchly anticommunist wing of the Republican Party, and Nixon had yet to recognize the imperative of courting the GOP's right wing. For his part, Kennedy pledged his commitment to separation of church and state. Specifically, he promised to oppose federal aid for parochial schools and to not appoint a U.S. envoy to the Vatican. Ministers polled by *Christianity Today* overwhelmingly favored Nixon over Kennedy.[70]

During Kennedy's campaign, Norman Vincent Peale and some of the evangelicals associated with *Christianity Today* united under the auspices of a National Association of Evangelicals committee called Citizens for Religious Freedom. They held a high-profile conference in Washington, D.C. in September 1960. Their goal was to promote the impression that Kennedy's candidacy represented a dangerous intrusion by the Roman Catholic Church into U.S. politics. They challenged Kennedy's patriotism by insinuating that as President he would be beholden to the Vatican. The Peale group's gambit was short-lived, though, as leaders of liberal Protestant churches, along with Jews and Catholics, viewed the attack on Kennedy as crude religious prejudice. Peale withdrew from the group and, without a nationally respected public leader, the campaign against Kennedy was blunted.[71]

Once elected, Kennedy assuaged the fears of evangelicals by bringing along cabinet officials (more, in fact, than Eisenhower had brought) to the annual prayer breakfast sponsored by an organization called International Christian Leadership.[72] Prior to his 1962 "crusade tour" through Latin America, Billy Graham was welcomed to a White House meeting with Kennedy, days before the President's own scheduled trip to South America. Kennedy told Graham, jokingly, "I'll be your John the Baptist."[73]

Amid cordial relations between evangelicals and the Kennedy ad-mininstration, a small group of business executives, led by Colorado real estate developer Gerri Von Frellick, launched the first electoral project of the Christian Right in 1962. It was called Christian Citizen, and its aim was to train Christians to work on campaigns and run for office. Because so little is known about the project, it has been neglected in previous studies of the Christian Right.[74] Behind the scenes, Von Frellick enlisted support from a prominent missionary, Bill Bright of Campus Crusade for Christ, and from Representative Walter Judd. Senator John Tower (R-TX), ABC news commentator Paul Harvey, and at least two members of the House of Representatives agreed to speak at Christian Citizen's inaugural banquet. Howard Kershner of the Christian Freedom Foundation offered advertising space in his *Christian Economics*.[75] Right from the start, Von Frellick claimed to have recruited 2,000 Christians who were organized into study committees in seventeen states.[76]

Christian Citizen maintained a low profile during the 1960s, and more than a decade would pass before the onset of large-scale electoral mobilization among evangelicals. In the interim, evangelicals expressed little response to the Supreme Court's 1962 and 1963 decisions restricting prayer in public schools. In a pair of decisions, the Court ruled first against the state of New York's use of a non-denominational prayer in public schools and, secondly, against devotional Bible reading and recitation of the Lord's Prayer in schools in two other states.[77] Though evangelicals generally opposed the decisions, *Christianity Today* reported and editorialized on these Supreme Court cases to a far lesser extent than would have been expected given the later salience of the school prayer issue to the Christian Right.[78]

In 1964 Republican presidential candidate Barry Goldwater ran on a platform advocating a constitutional amendment to override the Supreme Court ban on public school prayer. Yet Goldwater enjoyed no significant support from evangelical leaders.[79] To the extent that evangelical rightists backed Goldwater, they did so either as individual Republicans or as participants in the anticommunist conservative movement, not as part of a self-conscious Christian Right.

That post-war evangelicals were not mobilized within party politics may account for the general neglect by researchers of the movement at this phase. Except for the Supreme Court's restrictions on school prayer, the political context of the late 1940s to mid-1960s was not a particularly antagonistic one for evangelical Christians. They positioned themselves as challengers in relation to liberal, ecumenical church associations. But the political ideology of evangelicals was compatible with society's prevalent anticommunism. Though the early evangelical movement was not yet state-linked, the system-supportive role played by Christian cold warriors earned legitimacy for the movement's incipient organizations. The successful establishment of evangelical movement resources at this early phase would make the Christian Right an attractive ally for the New Right of the 1970s and would facilitate the Christian Right's own political development as a social policy challenger beginning in the 1970s and as a contender for Republican Party power in the 1980s and 1990s.

PART II

• • •

THE RISE OF THE NEW RIGHT, 1965–1979

CHAPTER 5

Breaking the Impasse

NEW POLITICAL AND
ORGANIZATIONAL OPPORTUNITIES
FOR THE CONSERVATIVE MOVEMENT

During the time following Barry Goldwater's failed presidential campaign through the 1980 election of Ronald Reagan, the conservative movement[1] flourished, and for two major reasons. One was the movement's strategy of working both within the Republican Party and, as opponents of the status quo, through autonomous organizations. The movement endorsed the 1968 nomination of Richard Nixon, who represented a break with the party's "liberal" wing but whose policies, especially on foreign affairs, ultimately disappointed right-wing activists.

A second strength of the movement was its persistent anticommunism. During the 1950s, the Right was preoccupied with both international and domestic communism. During the period considered in this chapter, the domestic Cold War had receded in intensity. The Vietnam war took center stage, and conservatives focused on the failure of the Johnson and Nixon administrations to defeat Vietnamese liberation armies on the battlefield. During the mid-1960s and 1970s, conservatives also gave increasing attention to the "threat" from progressive forces in Latin America. *National Review* and its affiliates participated in the propaganda campaign surrounding U.S. destabilization of Chile from 1970 to 1973. Following Nixon's diplomatic opening to China, the anticommunist movement retrenched its strategic commitment to global "rollback." New Right organizations promoted a buildup of the U.S. military arsenal and defeat for U.S. weapons treaties with the Soviet Union. The Carter administration's purported "surrender" of Panama's canal fueled the New Right's preoccupation with Central America, which would reach a peak during the 1980s.

Throughout the period of time considered in this chapter, the conservative movement was oppositional in that it was, tactically, more anticommunist than the administrations in power, but system-supportive in that it endorsed the prevailing strategic doctrine of U.S. military supremacy over the rest of the world. In contradiction to conservatives' professed goals of limiting government intervention in the capitalist economy and of opposing government attempts to achieve racial and gender equality, the movement was not anti-statist on questions of how to fight communism. At no time did the conservative movement oppose the deployment of state agencies, from the Pentagon to the FBI and CIA, to subvert and repress independent leftist political action at home and abroad. This chapter will trace both the conservative movement's increased influence in electoral politics and the execution of the movement's anticommunist agenda, in variable incidents of conflict and collaboration with state agencies.

By the early 1970s, two important developments impacted the right-wing organizations treated in this chapter. First came a split within the Young Americans for Freedom, resulting in the rise of a separate libertarian movement, which launched its own political party in 1972. Around the same time, the conservative movement proper experienced phenomenal growth in available resources, part of a newly advantageous political context. This chapter explains the mobilization of what came to be called the New Right as the result of (1) the movement's increased corporate resources, (2) the successful development of multiple-type organizations, and (3) an expanded issues agenda for a constituency with potential to grow in numbers and influence.

The emergence of the New Right was a logical consequence of the activism that grew from the 1950s fusionist coalition. New Right leaders were veterans of the Young Americans for Freedom, the 1964 Goldwater campaign, and, in a few cases, the John Birch Society. New Right ideology and issue content represented a reassertion of the old fusionist constellation of militarism, libertarian economics, and traditionalism on questions of race, gender relations, and law and order.

Goldwater's 1964 electoral success in the South had pointed to the utility of a backlash against civil rights in building a larger Republican voter base. In 1968, conservative movement leaders looked askance at the racists and segregationists surrounding presidential candidate George Wallace. However, by the mid-1970s, some New Right strategists were eager to embrace both Wallace himself and the range of issues he had used to build a following. Ultimately, though, the conservative movement focused primarily on pro-family issues and anticommunist militarism. New Right leaders nurtured the incipient Christian Right and laid the groundwork for Ronald Reagan's successful appeal on issues of "family values" and "patriotism."

PARTISAN ACTIVISM IN THE AFTERMATH OF THE GOLDWATER CAMPAIGN

Two national organizations and two movement publications dominated the coordination and education of conservative activists during the post-1964 period. One of these organizations was the American Conservative Union (ACU), started by Goldwater promoters in December 1964. Like the elite sector of the early Cold War anticommunist groups treated in Chapter 2, the ACU included numerous members of Congress. Along with its youth counterpart, Young Americans for Freedom (YAF), ACU continued its efforts to gain influence in the Republican Party and in the Nixon administration. Leadership of both ACU and YAF overlapped with the list of editors and contributors to the weekly *Human Events* and biweekly *National Review* publications. Together, in the 1960s, YAF, ACU, *Human Events*, and *National Review* issued position statements and sponsored conferences. But it was not until the 1970s, with the advent of computerized direct mail and accessible publishing technology that the New Right spawned dozens of single-issue pressure groups, most with their own newsletters.

The Right's post-mortem analyses of Barry Goldwater's 1964 defeat were pivotal to the conservative movement's continued growth as a Republican faction. The 1964 debacle prompted the question of whether the movement should make a priority of national elections or of educational work. In one post-campaign analysis, libertarian economics professor Benjamin A. Rogge argued that Goldwater's defeat meant that "conservatism as a potent political force will be dead."[2] Writing for the libertarians' theoretical journal *New Individualist Review*, Rogge attributed the Goldwater debacle to his supporters' "impractical and tragic" takeover of the Republican convention without first educating the population on the virtues of conservative philosophy. "The lesson," he wrote, "would seem to be that the real function of conservatism in America is not to try to win elections but to try to win converts. The real battle is, as always, a battle of ideas."[3]

Rogge's was a minority opinion among conservatives, who pointed to Goldwater's relative success in the South and remained convinced that the mere nomination of a "conservative" candidate over the "liberal" Nelson Rockefeller marked an irreversible step forward.[4] In a rejoinder to Rogge, Goldwater campaign strategist (and *National Review* publisher)

William Rusher disputed the notion that "ideas" must precede political action, and stressed the Goldwater campaign's role in increasing the size of the conservative movement. "Despite the disappointment naturally engendered in Senator Goldwater's defeat, conservatives are vastly better organized and infinitely more experienced in the ways of practical politics than they have ever been before," Rusher wrote.[5]

In a *National Review* forum on Goldwater's failed race, future President George Bush urged conservatives to remain faithful to the Republican Party. Ronald Reagan concurred and suggested that Goldwater's twenty six million "diehard party faithfuls" look to "the millions of so-called Republican defectors—those people who didn't really want LBJ, but who were scared of what they thought we represented."[6] Reagan's own prominence during the 1964 campaign won the politically inexperienced movie actor a national corps of admirers. The weekly *Human Events* newspaper promoted Reagan's 1966 race to become governor of California, not only because Reagan promised to implement conservative policies, but also, according to one analysis, because as governor Reagan would be able to steer California's 1968 presidential nominating delegation to the right.[7]

After 1964, conservatives wasted no time in planning their strategy for 1968. Frank Meyer, the Right's leading fusionist thinker, urged readers of his *National Review* column not to hope for an "ideal conservative candidate," but rather for one that would simply "owe his victory to conservatives." Meyer preferred Reagan on philosophical grounds, but considered Richard Nixon an acceptable second choice. "The solider the support for Reagan at the Republican convention," Meyer wrote, "the greater the possibility that he may be nominated—but also the certainty that any liberal candidate can be vetoed; the assurance that, if Nixon is nominated, he will owe it to conservative support; and the guarantee that conservative control of the Republican Party will be consolidated."[8]

After 1964, Nixon began courting allies within the conservative movement as well as among the GOP establishment. In 1966 Nixon invited directors of the American Conservative Union, Young Americans for Freedom, Americans for Constitutional Action, and the Free Society Association (the latter, Goldwater's own post-campaign group) to several discussion meetings, including one held at Barry Goldwater's apartment. At one meeting, Nixon reportedly impressed movement leaders with his calls for increased U.S. military aggression in Vietnam."[9] Also in 1966, Nixon hired YAF activist Patrick J. Buchanan, then a young editorial writer for the *St. Louis Globe-Democrat*, to serve as a speechwriter and liaison with the conservative movement.[10] It was this job that sped Buchanan's rise as a prominent right-wing spokesperson.

With Buchanan's help, conservatives came to view Nixon as a safe bet for defeating Lyndon Johnson or his successor in 1968. The Right feared another four years of the Democrats' domestic policy programs would widen and permanently entrench state power at the federal level. In 1965, *Human Events* had applauded Johnson's invasion of the Dominican Republic[11] but had denounced the administration's supposedly "radical" legislative program, which included:

> rent subsidies for middle-income families; Medicare for the elderly financed by a compulsory payroll tax; . . . a "voting rights" bill that is crudely political in focusing only on states that supported Senator Goldwater; elimination of silver in some coins and the removal of the gold backing for Federal Reserve deposits; direct federal aid to local schools; repeal of the laws allowing each state to decide for itself whether workers should be compelled to join labor unions; never-ending "subsidies" which bring the noose of federal control ever tighter around business, agriculture and education—all these measures and many more.
>   The Johnson revolution is truly staggering—and we don't attempt to minimize it.[12]

With an eye toward 1968, *Human Events* devoted close attention to the 1966 mid-term elections and claimed partial credit for a slew of rightist victories. Reagan defeated California Governor Edmund G. Brown by nearly one million votes, and the Republicans gained ten previously held Democratic governorships. Texas Republican Senator John Tower was reelected by a 57 percent margin, and helped elect Texas' first two Republican Representatives. Of the Republicans' forty-seven-seat gain in the House of Representatives in 1966, *Human Events* claimed a majority of them were "staunch conservatives," including prominent Goldwater backers.[13]

During the 1968 primary campaign and Republican convention, Ronald Reagan enjoyed support from YAF leaders, but majority conservative support went to Richard Nixon, who was endorsed by Barry Goldwater.[14] Southern Republicans also backed Nixon over Reagan, in large part because of the leadership of South Carolina's Senator Strom Thurmond, who had gained national prominence for his segregationist stance (see Chapter 3). *National Review* publisher William Rusher explained Thurmond's enthusiasm for Nixon in hardball political terms. Given the unlikely prospects of any Republican defeating George Wallace in the Deep South, the GOP needed a relatively moderate candidate who could carry northern states where Reagan stood little chance.[15] *Human Events* analyzed Nixon's nomination as a victory for the more "conservative" midwestern, western, and southern states, over the party's "liberal" northeast establishment.[16] The paper endorsed the 1968 Nixon–Agnew ticket as "the best vehicle for implementing the conservative philosophy and saving this country from the ills that beset it."[17]

Both *National Review* and *Human Events* editorialized against presidential candidate George Wallace, urging conservatives not to split the right-wing vote and not to ignore Wallace's record as a "big spender" who welcomed federal aid programs as long as they were not tied to school desegregation.[18] *Human Events* criticized Wallace's "failure to forthrightly repudiate extremist elements" like the Klansmen who worked in the Wallace campaign.[19]

The Nixon versus Wallace question distinguished rightists faithful to the Republican Party from those aligned with the more grassroots-based anticommunist groups, namely the John Birch Society. Both the Liberty Lobby and the John Birch Society suspected Nixon's anticommunist credentials from his days as vice-president under Eisenhower. In a pair of juxtaposed articles in 1968, the Birch Society's monthly *American Opinion* magazine subtly portrayed Nixon as a possible agent of establishment conspirators, while promoting George Wallace as an unabashed segregationist and "the only candidate in the race who is genuinely, outspokenly anti-Communist."[20]

Nixon won the election, but conservatives read Wallace's capture of five southern states and more than nine million popular votes as a sign that the country was headed toward the right and would be a factor the Nixon administration would have to contend with. "It is ridiculous to talk about these nine million as if they are all Ku Kluxers, illiterates and foaming racists," *National Review* editorialized.

> The Wallace voters are not alone in demanding that better order should prevail in the streets, that lawbreakers should not be coddled, that local communities should not be overwhelmed by a meddling federal bureaucracy, and that a necessary special consideration for the nation's poorer and more unfortunate citizens should not mean submission to blackmail at the expense of the responsible majority.[21]

Shortly after the election, Nixon campaign strategist Kevin Phillips published *The Emerging Republican Majority*, a much celebrated call for Republicans to pursue a "southern strategy" based on a realignment of national voting patterns and issue concerns. Phillips documented the Republicans' increasing electoral strength in the South and the new economic centers of suburban Sun Belt cities linked to the military and oil industries. Phillips emphasized the saliency of regional class and ideological concerns that Republicans might parlay into a permanent winning coalition.[22] In an interview for *Human Events*, Phillips argued that new Republican voters were not generally to be found concentrated in the northeast, nor among the already Republican upper class. New Republican voters were neither classic economic conservatives nor particularly staunch anticommunists, according to Phillips.

Instead, what you have here is a social conservatism, I think, in the sense that the role of government in taxing the many for the benefit of the few—whether they be rich or poor—has gone too far. You've got a resentment of the expanding role of government in everyday life, a resentment of the attempts of certain aspects of the liberal community to make government into an all-powerful social planning establishment and regulatory body. I think that's what's engendering a resentment.[23]

Phillips' reference to "social conservatism" was suggestive of the electoral implications of racial issues, though within a larger construct of "government intrusion."

Prior to Nixon's inauguration, the American Conservative Union issued a report claiming that the combined Nixon–Wallace vote represented "the outright repudiation of the Johnson–Humphrey policies" and urged Nixon to "remake the Republican Party as the majority party."[24] Nixon's transition team contacted ACU, YAF, *National Review*, and *Human Events* to solicit the names of hundreds of right-wing activists as prospective Nixon appointees. Among those Nixon chose were Senator Thurmond's aide and ACU board member Harry S. Dent, appointed deputy counsel; Maurice Stans, appointed Secretary of Commerce; and Robert Finch, named Secretary of Health, Education and Welfare.[25] Nixon hired Carol Bauman, a YAF co-founder and Goldwater campaign staffer, as a White House researcher. YAF and ACU activist Tom Huston was appointed deputy to Patrick Buchanan, who became Nixon's Special Assistant.[26]

Despite these high-profile appointments, Nixon quickly came under fire from some of the same conservative leaders who had endorsed him. At issue was the administration's proposed welfare reform legislation, the Family Assistance Plan, which the Right viewed as a "socialistic" plan intended to double the number of welfare recipients.[27] The Family Assistance Plan would have provided a minimum income level for all families with dependent children and specifically would have included families in which fathers remained in the household, held a job, yet were still unable to earn a family wage.[28] The plan outraged conservatives, and Nixon's approval rating on domestic issues plummeted.[29] The Right's disdain for Nixon's modestly redistributive welfare policies reflected the influence of the laissez-faire, libertarian economic strand of fusionist thinking. Ultimately, however, as will be discussed in the next section, it was Nixon's purported "softness" on communism that caused the greatest consternation among movement activists.

A year before Nixon would face reelection, and following Nixon's fateful overtures to China, leaders of the ACU, YAF, *National Review*, and *Human Events* drafted and released a statement, "We Suspend Our Support," applauding Nixon's "steadfastness" in Southeast Asia, while condemning his "failure" on the rest of his foreign and military policies.[30] Several weeks later, YAF convened 1,500 delegates from its membership of 68,000 and formally disavowed Nixon by holding a mock presidential convention and a mock nomination of Vice-President Spiro Agnew and Senator James Buckley (R-NY). Amid chants of "Dump Nixon," YAF members denounced administration policies on China, strategic nuclear weapons, welfare and wage–price controls and pledged to raise $750,000 to finance primary challenges to Nixon.[31]

Though they would eventually close ranks behind Nixon against Democrat George McGovern in 1972, conservatives successfully demonstrated their dissatisfaction with Nixon by backing ACU leader Representative John Ashbrook (R-OH) in three state primaries. In what one former Nixon campaign aide described as "one of the most effective political operations conservatives have ever undertaken,"[32] Ashbrook won about 10 percent of the vote in New Hampshire, Florida, and California, and conservatives claimed that minor threat moved Nixon to reverse his "leftward" drift.[33] (Ashbrook's successful challenge to an incumbent Republican president would, twenty years later, inspire Patrick Buchanan's primary race against President George Bush.)

Conservatives also claimed credit when Nixon began his second term by appointing Howard Phillips (no relation to Kevin Phillips) to direct the Office of Economic Opportunity (OEO). This agency was a creation of the Johnson administration's "war on poverty." Its mission was to disperse federal money to anti-poverty programs managed locally by community activists.[34] Howard Phillips had been an early leader of YAF and was among the most prominent right-wing activists to serve in the Nixon administration. Phillips had joined OEO in 1970 and had become convinced that the agency was nothing but a wasteful funding conduit for what he called "radical" leftist recipients. Under Phillips' direction, Nixon appointed several YAF and ACU activists for the purpose of eliminating numerous OEO programs.[35] Against intense opposition from liberal members of Congress, Phillips quickly launched a public relations campaign, eliminated OEO's ten regional offices, and defunded scores of anti-poverty programs before a federal court ruled his actions illegal because his appointment had not been confirmed by the Senate. Phillips then resigned from the administration.[36] But he continued to use the issue of federal anti-poverty programs to forge a coalition of New Right activists who melded anti-statist economic views with right-wing stances on busing, criminal justice, civil rights, abortion, and the like.[37] In the aftermath of the Watergate scandal, Howard Phillips would become an advocate of the conservative movement's third-party strategy, and a founder of key New Right organizations, which are discussed later in this chapter.

Once reelected, the Nixon administration soon became mired in the Watergate scandal's revelations, hearings, and Nixon's eventual resignation in 1974. During the early months of the scandal, conservatives were of mixed views as to whether Watergate amounted to much more than a bungled spy operation. As details of the cover-up emerged, some leading conservatives urged Nixon to resign honorably even before impeachment hearings were to be held.[38] After Nixon's departure from the White House, conservatives were infuriated when President Gerald Ford picked former New York Governor Nelson Rockefeller to be his Vice-President.[39] "Rocky" as the Right dubbed him, represented exactly the kind of "liberal" policies and GOP constituencies the conservative movement had been battling since the 1964 Goldwater campaign. His rise to the vice-presidency symbolized the seriousness of the Watergate setback and underscored the need of conservatives to build a movement both inside and outside the Republican Party.

THE PERSISTENCE
OF THE ANTICOMMUNIST PREOCCUPATION

At the time of the New Right's ascent, the conservative movement's anticommunism was not of the rigid variety promoted by the John Birch Society, which viewed elected officials as either wholesale enemies or allies. During the Nixon years, anticommunism served to maintain the conditional allegiance of conservatives to the administration. Conservatives found themselves opposing pivotal elements of Nixon's foreign and military policy. Specifically, they wanted to see a complete U.S. victory over rebel forces in Southeast Asia. They were loathe to accept the Nixon–Kissinger strategies of negotiated "phased withdrawal" and "Vietnamization," both of which were plans intended to reduce U.S. casualties while continuing the war. The Right opposed arms treaties with the Soviet Union, but supported the U.S. tactics of covert action that facilitated the 1973 military coup in Chile. Ultimately, it was Nixon's reversal of U.S. policy toward China that, more than anything, enraged conservatives who since the heyday of the China Lobby had committed themselves to the prevention of international recognition for the People's Republic of China.

The Right's early interest in Vietnam stemmed from the 1950s educational work of the China Lobby, treated in Chapter 2. Just as the Committee of One Million had successfully created a coalition of liberal and conservative anticommunists, the American Friends of Vietnam formed itself as a putatively bipartisan group in support of South Vietnamese President Ngo Dinh Diem.[40] By the 1960s, the avowedly right-wing anticommunist organizations generated the bulk of support for South Vietnam and the U.S. military role in the region. As early as 1961, Committee of One Million coordinator Marvin Liebman began sending YAF activists on "goodwill" tours of Vietnam and other Asian countries.[41]

After the 1964 Goldwater defeat, YAF had turned its activist energy to a number of non-electoral projects. YAF conducted a series of protests against major U.S. corporations (Firestone, American Motors, IBM) that were considering trade ties with Eastern bloc countries.[42] In 1966, YAF launched the International Youth Crusade for Freedom (later renamed World Youth Crusade for Freedom [WYCF]) to counter purported "communist" subversion on college campuses. YAF held pro-war rallies in numerous cities, and worked with the U.S. Marines in Operation Hand Clasp,[43] a counterinsurgency program that directed material aid to South Vietnamese refugees. China Lobby veterans Dr. Walter Judd and Professor David N. Rowe helped YAF leaders Tom Huston and David Keene recruit U.S. students for overseas meetings with member groups of the Asian People's Anti-Communist League (APACL).[44] Largely a propaganda front for the governments of Taiwan, South Korea, South Vietnam, and the Philippines, APACL would become the mainstay of the larger World Anti-Communist League (WACL). Formed in 1966, WACL would become a key player in the Reagan administration's "freedom fighter" operations, which are treated in Chapter 9.

The formation of this new network of international anticommunist associations came in response to emergent liberation movements in the developing world. The resilience of the Cuban revolution—in the face of countless U.S. efforts to overthrow it—inspired the commitment of 1960s revolutionaries to Che Guevara's vison of "two, three, many Vietnams." In 1966, Havana hosted a "Tricontinental Conference" of insurgent leaders from Asia, Africa, and Latin America, followed, in 1967, by a similar coordinating conference of the Latin American Solidarity Organization.[45]

Veterans of the Committee of One Million attempted to create a China Lobby type organization to address African politics, with a particular emphasis on Rhodesia (Zimbabwe). In 1965, Rhodesia declared its independence from Great Britain, and, soon after, the United Nations called for voluntary economic sanctions against the white minority-controlled government. In anticipation of the anti-colonial struggle there, *National Review* publisher William Rusher and African American journalist Dr. Max Yergan created the American African Affairs Association in an effort to develop conservative activist support for Rhodesia. The Association published a series of monographs alleging Cuban and "Red Chinese" subversion of independence-seeking African nations, and sent leading conservative figures on several highly publicized fact-finding missions to assess race relations and the impact of sanctions in Rhodesia.[46] Conservatives argued against the effectiveness of economic sanctions without military enforcement,[47] in much the same way they would later argue against international sanctions against South Africa's apartheid regime. A putative Rhodesia lobby—modeled on the old China Lobby—bore little policy significance during the late 1960s, but it set a precedent for intense right-wing activism against Angola, Mozambique, and the African National Congress during the 1980s.

Richard Nixon's first inauguration followed a shift in elite consensus thinking about the Vietnam war.[48] While mounting U.S. casualties and the unlikelihood of an outright U.S. military victory fueled the anti-war movement, conservatives expressed support for Nixon's war aims[49] but criticized the administration's bombing halts, negotiations with the North Vietnamese,[50] and, generally, the "incremental escalation" and "restrictions, both military and political, imposed by the government."[51] The leading right-wing publications did not lament the killing of hundreds of thousands of Vietnamese people nor did they generally acknowledge the domestic costs Nixon might face were he to follow the advice of those who urged greater savagery. *National Review* argued that "North Vietnam could be knocked out of the war quickly," if only Nixon would consider

> obliterating its cities and towns. If it be argued that only military targets are legitimate objects for bombing, the obvious answer is that as far as countries on the Asian mainland are concerned, the main—and sometimes the sole—military resource is population.[52]

The American Conservative Union publicly applauded Nixon's expansion of the war into Cambodia in 1970.[53] At the same time, the Young Americans for Freedom, boasting 51,000 members, supported their "Commander-in-Chief" with their "Tell it to Hanoi" campaign. Using tactics reminiscent of the Committee of One Million, YAF published newspaper advertisements in college newspapers, opened eight full-time regional campaign offices, and claimed to have collected more than a half million pro-war signatures on petitions YAF delivered to the North Vietnamese embassy in Paris.[54]

Reflecting a curious contradiction in rightist thinking, YAF promoted a war to sustain U.S. hegemony while simultaneously lobbying against the government's conscription of young men to fight in that war. Several prominent libertarian rightists were early bedfellows in the Left's anti-draft activities.[55] Generational self-interest exacerbated the antidraft tendency, and by 1969 YAF made a priority of legislative lobbying for an all-volunteer military.[56]

While the war raged, neither YAF nor its elder counterpart organizations seemed cognizant of how Vietnam fit into Nixon's larger foreign policy doctrine. In Nixon's "Grand Design," as historian Franz Schurmann termed it, management of the Vietnam war to a favorable conclusion was only one part of a plan to parlay the Sino-Soviet split into a reconstructed world order, in which both Communist superpowers would become less of a "threat" to the United States. Nixon's challenge was to achieve an "honorable," that is, victorious U.S. withdrawal from Vietnam and, simultaneously, a resolution to key domestic crises: massive social disruption from the anti-war movement; looming economic inflation; and bureaucratic in-fighting, both within military and civilian agencies.[57]

These were the imperatives of the state, but they were not wholly shared by the conservative movement, which had its own agenda. In July of 1971, Nixon announced his intention to visit the People's Republic of China (PRC) the following year. It was that announcement, and the prospects of normalized relations between the United States and mainland China, that prompted leaders of YAF, ACU, *Human Events*, and *National Review* to formally "suspend support" from the Nixon administration. The China issue figured prominently in conservatives' decision to back ACU leader Representative John Ashbrook (R-OH) in the 1972 primaries.

Before the election season, Nixon's diplomatic overtures paved the way for the United Nations to finally seat the People's Republic, not only in the General Assembly but also on the all-important Security Council. Conservatives viewed the "sell-out" of Taiwan with horror.[58] Major right-wing leaders had cut their activist teeth on the effort to keep "Red China" out of the United Nations. Once Taiwan was expelled from the United Nations, and the PRC was seated as the legitimate representative of the world's most populous nation, William F. Buckley called on Nixon to instruct UN Ambassador George Bush to cease voting in the General Assembly,[59] but to no avail. Buckley joined the U.S. press corps on Nixon's 1972 trip to Peking and reported back: "We have lost—irretrievably—any remaining sense of moral mission to the world."[60]

The response of conservatives to Nixon's dramatic reversal of U.S. policy toward China revealed much about the status of the state–movement relationship at that time. Movement activists were vocal in their condemnation of the Taiwan "sellout," yet they were unable to affect decision making. They ultimately saw little alternative but to support Nixon in his 1972 reelection bid against Senator George McGovern, who was likely the most left-wing candidate ever nominated by the Democratic Party.

The semi-oppositional stance of conservatives toward the Nixon administration held not only for Asia policy but also for Nixon's negotiation of the first Strategic Arms Limitation Treaty (SALT), the first phase of which was signed with the Soviet Union in 1972. Right-wing activists opposed the SALT talks because they believed the treaty would tilt the arms race in favor of the Soviets.[61] Not until the latter half of the Carter administration would conservatives wield strong influence in the SALT policymaking process. (The New Right made a priority of opposing SALT II.)

By 1970, however, the American Security Council began a long campaign to persuade the public that SALT posed a threat to U.S. nuclear capability. From the 1950s forward, the American Security Council (Chapter 2) was a cornerstone of the elite sector of the anticommunist movement. In particular, ASC's membership consisted of leading retired military and intelligence agency officers and, later, numerous members of Congress. ASC compiled voluminous files on U.S. "subversives," broadcast Cold War propaganda over hundreds of radio stations, and conducted training seminars for the Defense Department and public school educators.

In 1970, the American Security Council launched Operation Alert, described as "a massive nationwide voter education program" to alert the general public that the United States had become inferior to the Soviet Union in military strength. Operation Alert's first pamphlet on the "weapons gap" was mailed to about two million voters and three thousand civic organizations.[62] This phase of the campaign included ASC's placement of full-page advertisements in over one hundred newspapers and coincided with a major "weapons gap" speech by Vice-President Spiro Agnew shortly before the mid-term Congressional elections. After the fall 1970 elections, ASC claimed credit for strengthening national security sentiment within Congress.[63]

Nevertheless, the SALT I talks proceeded unabated. Shortly after his trip to Peking, Nixon traveled with Henry Kissinger to Moscow to sign two formal treaties. One was a five-year interim agreement limiting offensive long-range ballistic missiles; the other, the Anti-Ballistic Missile (ABM) treaty, limited each side to deploying no more than 200 anti-ballistic missiles.[64] Conservatives could do little but protest SALT I. Again, the timing of the treaties, shortly before the 1972 presidential election, constrained a movement dependent on and committed to Republican Party politics.

Meanwhile, the movement maintained its preoccupation with Third World communism, in the form of various movements and regimes. One of these was Chile's Popular Unity government, led by President Salvador Allende, who was elected into office in 1970, then deposed and killed in a 1973 U.S.-backed military coup. During its brief tenure, the Popular Unity government began to nationalize the large corporations that mined Chilean copper and kept Chilean workers in dire poverty. Along with major corporate media outlets in the United States, *National Review* waged a full court press against the Allende government.[65] While international lending agencies destabilized Chile's economy and the CIA fomented strikes, street violence, and rumor campaigns in the *El Mercurio* newspaper,[66] *National Review* elevated the threat of Chilean-style socialism to that of the superpower conflict. After the Chilean military stormed the presidential palace on September 11, 1973, killed Allende, and unleashed a vicious war of terror against "subversives" that lasted into the next decade, *National Review* explained the inordinate amount of attention it had devoted to Chilean affairs:

> *National Review* has given detailed, even extravagant coverage to the events in Chile during the past two years because we were convinced that the experience in Chile would deeply affect the progress of the Marxist movement throughout the world.
>
> The Allende experience will be important in the evolution of Marxist thought, and it has special meaning for the large Marxist parties in France and Italy. Allende believed he could bring about a Marxist revolution without abandoning democratic forms and without seizing control of the entire repressive apparatus of the state. It now looks as if the 'Chilean road' is no go, and the orthodox Communist expectation correct: A genuine Marxist revolution must be both violent and totalitarian in order to crush the inevitable opposition to it.
>
> Among other useful measures, the [Chilean] military government has begun to round up some two thousand Uruguayan and Brazilian terrorists and subversives given asylum by Allende. Events in Chile will thus have a beneficial spinoff effect elsewhere.[67]

Both before and after the Chilean coup had initiated "spin-offs" of repressive violence throughout South America, one frequent *National Review* contributor was Nena Ossa, a Chilean journalist. Ossa became an official in the post-Allende Chilean military junta and helped *National Review* associate Marvin Liebman establish the American Chilean Council, which conducted public relations projects on behalf of the military regime.[68] Drawing on his earlier experience with the China Lobby groups and the World Youth Crusade for Freedom's publicity tours to Asia, Liebman used the American Chilean Council to send right-wing activists and journalists on upbeat publicity trips to Chile.[69]

From the mid-1960s through the mid-1970s, the conservative movement's stance toward the administrations' foreign and military policies fit a consistent pattern. Conservatives quarreled with some of the tactics of the Vietnam war, and they strongly opposed Nixon's so-called "appeasement" moves toward diplomacy with China and arms treaties with the Soviet Union. Overall, however, conservatives were neither oppositional nor anti-statist. They were system-supportive allies of a national security state that maintained its prerogative to intervene in developing countries and to bolster that intervention with a nuclear arsenal matched only by the Soviet Union. To the extent that conservatives sought foreign policies more aggressive than those of the Nixon administration, they were capable of making their views known through their independent media outlets and by lobbying. Despite the growing influence of conservatives over Republican Party nominating processes, the movement did not yet wield significant power within decision-making agencies. But the persistence of the movement's anticommunist preoccupation foreshadowed the New Right's focus, in the 1970s and beyond, on the issues of arms control and Central America.

THE LIBERTARIAN MOVEMENT

While the New Right conservatives of the 1970s formed numerous issue-oriented organizations and pondered the idea of a third party, libertarianism coalesced as a movement unto itself. Prior to World War II, the Right's libertarianism had manifested in business-backed opposition to New Deal economic policy. After the war, leading libertarian thinkers founded long-lasting organizations, most notably the Foundation for Economic Education (FEE) and the Mont Pelerin Society, discussed in Chapter 1.

Throughout the 1950s and 1960s *National Review* and *Human Events* published occasional articles by libertarian authors. FEE and Mont Pelerin remained respectable venues through which conservatives who were primarily academics published and coordinated conferences. During the 1950s and 1960s, the libertarian strand in the conservative agenda was subsumed by Cold War anticommunism. The Right's libertarianism took form in the perennial concern of conservatives over the taxing and spending policies of both Democratic and Republican administrations. By the late 1960s, libertarians' agenda broadened, as numerous chapters of the Young Americans for Freedom formed a Libertarian Caucus to address issues of personal freedom such as military conscription and laws against smoking marijuana.

Among the large numbers of "baby boomers" attracted to political activism, most were drawn to movements of the Left. The civil rights, anti-war, women's, and ecology movements all flourished along with the counterculture's less political contingents of hippies and New Age spirituality seekers. While Nixon was unpopular on the Right, for reasons already delineated, the Watergate scandal raised anti-government cynicism to unprecedented heights across the political spectrum. By the late 1960s and early 1970s, libertarian thinking had become popular, not only among a large sector of YAF, but also among many politically unaffiliated, anti-establishment youth active in the leftist Students for a Democratic Society (SDS).

Libertarian movement leader, and one-time New York gubernatorial candidate, Jerome Tuccille traced the eruption of perennial tensions between traditionalists and libertarians on the Right to the 1958 publication of Ayn Rand's novel *Atlas Shrugged*. Rand became the intellectual leader of a philosophy she called "objectivism." In *Atlas Shrugged* and other best-selling novels, Rand defended unregulated capitalism, individualism, and reason, over and above "traditional" values of faith, altruism, and self-sacrifice. According to Tuccille, Rand's anti-Christian brand of libertarianism resonated with a minority YAF faction that opposed the draft, censorship, government taxation, laws against abortion and drug use, and state authority in general. Tuccille named the Right's young libertarians the heirs to pre-fusion era Old Rightists like Robert Taft, Albert Jay Nock, Frank Chodorov, and H. L. Mencken.[70]

The pivotal event in the formation of the 1970s libertarian movement was the 1969 convention of Young Americans for Freedom. A self-described "anarcho-libertarian" YAF contingent arrived with black flags, announced a counter-opening address featuring Barry Goldwater's former speechwriter Karl Hess, and circulated an open letter printed in Murray Rothbard's *Libertarian Forum* newsletter. Rothbard was then the libertarians' leading intellectual and, along with Hess, he had been actively recruiting libertarians within the New Left and among rightist dissidents. Rothbard called on conventioneers to defect from YAF, to "form your own organization, breathe the clean air of freedom, and then take your stand, proudly and squarely, not with the despotism of the power elite and government of the United States, but with the rising movement in opposition to that government."[71]

The YAF conference nearly turned into a riot when one of the anarchists seized a microphone and burned his draft card. Conservative YAF members started chanting "Kill the Commies!" and the Libertarian Caucus formed a human barrier to protect anarchists from violent conservatives. Later that night, while libertarians met to discuss future strategy, conservatives roamed the halls yelling "Kill the libertarians!" In the end, a sizeable portion of YAF's membership defected and joined forces with several left-leaning libertarian groups to form the Society for Individual Liberty.[72]

The early 1970s saw the formation of libertarian newsletters and discussion groups too numerous to list here.[73] Ultimately, the most successful of these publications was *Reason*, started as an eight-page mimeographed newsletter in 1968. In 1970 a group of California libertarians formed Reason Enterprises, purchased the newsletter and built it into a full-size magazine, with a circulation that reached 3,200 by 1972.[74]

While libertarian publications flourished along with the rest of the youth culture's underground press, Murray Rothbard remained the elder standard bearer for the libertarian movement.[75] In his often cited book *For a New Liberty*, Rothbard identified the "non-aggression axiom" as the core libertarian creed. He defined aggression as "the initiation of the use or threat of physical violence against the person or property of someone else." Thus broadly defined, freedom from aggression entails the individual's right to speak, publish, assemble, and engage in "victimless crimes," while modern warfare is "totally illegitimate."[76] Rothbard reviewed the "left–right" spectrum of libertarian thinking. He defined pro-statist positions as "right" and non-adherence to "free market capitalism or the rights of private property" as "left."[77] At what he called the "extreme right-wing fringe of the movement," Rothbard located Leonard Read's Foundation for Economic Education, which he criticized for moving "stateward" in its "stern injunctions for obedience to law-and-order." Read and FEE urged compliance with all laws, despotic or otherwise, and for that reason Rothbard noted that FEE "has virtually no influence on today's libertarian youth."[78] Rothbard also labeled Ayn Rand as a rightist because of her "implacable hostility to the New Left," her opposition to the Vietnam war on tactical grounds only, her "simplistic" anticommunism, and her adoration of big business.[79] What remained, then, as the "central mainstream of the libertarian movement," was the Society for Individual Liberty and those other groups adhering to a philosophy of "anarcho-capitalism," the rejection of superpatriotism, and its corresponding militarism.[80]

Rothbard argued against forging alliances with the New Left, in large part because some leftists endorsed assaults on private property.[81] Jerome Tuccille likewise urged libertarians to break ties with the Left's "new generation of crusading irrationalists, frustrated bomb-throwers and penis-hating feminists," and to take advantage of what he saw as a vacuum created by the New Left's internal fragmentation.[82] The incipient libertarian movement positioned itself as a radical alternative to disreputable New Left groups like the Weathermen, and because they were outspokenly anti-leftist, the libertarians enjoyed a spate of favorable press attention.[83]

In early 1972, former YAF member David Nolan announced the formation of the Libertarian Party.[84] The party's platform called for an

immediate reduction of both taxes and government spending; the elimination of wage/price controls and all governmental intervention in labor
relations; elimination of the Federal Reserve System and repeal of laws
prohibiting citizen ownership of gold; an end to censorship, busing,
conscription, and laws on sexual conduct and drug use; and an end to
U.S. involvement in international "programs, treaties, or organizations
which . . . surrender U.S. sovereignty to any foreign power."[85]

Throughout the 1970s, the Libertarian Party channelled activist
resources into campaigns for ballot access and largely symbolic local and
state electoral races. From the start, Murray Rothbard argued against the
wisdom of directing only a few thousand libertarian activists into a nearly
exclusive emphasis on electoral politics. When party leader David Nolan
argued that elections were not an end, but rather a means to educate the
public, Rothbard responded that, over time, an electorally unsuccessful
party would win no significant respect from average voters.[86] Nevertheless, numerous libertarian movement activists spent most of their time
either running for office or managing their colleagues' campaigns.[87] By
1976, when the party drafted Roger MacBride, many potential libertarian
voters instead backed Ronald Reagan in the primary elections.[88]

The libertarians found themselves hampered by their own limited
strategy. Movements intent on winning political power through elections
face two options. They can concentrate on placing candidates on the
ballot and convincing voters to abandon the relative certainty of the two
major parties. Or, conscious of the inevitability of short-term electoral
failure, partisan movements can use the electoral process to achieve
partial goals. The libertarians, for example, might have drafted ballot
initiatives to legalize marijuana, thus having a reason to build coalitions
with politically inclined members of the counterculture. Or they might
have worked on antitax ballot measures and made common cause with
right-wing tax protest groups.

At two ends of a tactical repertoire, some libertarians waged abstract
debates in theoretical journals, while others kept busy with nuts-and-bolts
electioneering. However, there was hardly any effort in the movement's
program to build coalitions, either with one or more factions of the two
major parties, or with sympathetic outsiders. The narrow electoralism of
the libertarians destined them to limited growth, though the movement
would manage to persist as a small, mostly intellectual current that would
continue to try to influence right-wing thinking on issues of economics,
military intervention, and environmentalism during the 1980s and
1990s.

Despite the limited influence of libertarians, conservative movement writers at *National Review* condemned their wayward counterparts,
particularly those associated with the Cato Institute. Founded in 1977,

with backing from Kansas oilman and Libertarian Party benefactor Charles Koch, the Cato Institute revived the libertarian quest to make common cause with some on the Left. Cato's sponsorship of *Inquiry* magazine, which published leading left-wing critics of the military–intelligence establishment, exacerbated the long-standing disdain of conservatives for anti-statists, left and right.[89] By the 1980s, Cato would abandon its links to leftist dissidents and join the network of right-wing think tanks based in Washington, D.C. and committed to business deregulation and a related concept they called "free market environmentalism."[90]

THE EMERGENCE OF THE NEW RIGHT

The New Right of the 1970s represented a reassertion of the old fusionist blend of anticommunism, traditionalism, and libertarianism. Separately, the libertarian movement appealed to conservatives who elevated laissez-faire economics and issues of personal freedom above the fight against communism and changing moral standards. But the libertarian movement also drew support from counterculture youth who advocated legalized abortion and drugs, civil rights for homosexuals, and, generally, decreased state enforcement of traditional reproductive, sexual, and personal behavior. This "libertinism" of the libertarian movement repelled older, traditional conservatives who were more inclined to want to join the fast-growing ranks of the evangelical movement. At the same time, some conservative strategists read the American Independent Party's nine-million vote tally for George Wallace in 1968 as a mandate for a new coalition between anticommunists and civil rights opponents.

During the 1970s, New Right leaders successfully forged their own variety of fusionism by linking supposed threats to U.S. military supremacy with a moralistic domestic policy agenda. Whereas the fusionism of the late 1940s and the 1950s subordinated moral traditionalism and economic libertarianism to the priority of defeating communism at all costs, the New Right brand of fusionism gave heightened priority to issues of moral traditionalism, without reducing the focus on anticommunism. The renewed salience of moral issues was a response to large social changes in the 1960s and 1970s, and it was also part of the process whereby new political activists from the evangelical subculture formed alliances with nominally secular conservatives.

New Right leaders continued the post-Goldwater campaign strategy of building influence within the established Republican Party. But they also directed increased resources toward *para-party* organizations that operated independently of the two-party system, with the eventual effect of moving the Republican Party further to the right. What was "new" about the New Right was that, by the 1970s, conservative movement leaders enjoyed a greatly enlarged resource base. New corporate money flowed into new and varied organizations, focused on an expanding set of policy issues and directed at a new and growing constituency.

What Was the New Right?

The "New Right" label has been applied in reference to anything and everything involving right-wing movements from the 1960s forward. Conservative activists themselves began to use the term "New Right" in the 1970s to describe several new aspects of their movement: the proliferation of new, well-funded organizations, many based in Washington, D.C., the movement's successful inroads within Republican Party politics, and the movement's incipient alliances with conservative evangelicals. The New Right attracted significant press attention for its sophisticated use of computerized mailings and the aggressiveness of its key personalities. The Heritage Foundation became widely known for its placement of opinion articles in major daily newspapers. Richard Viguerie grew rich and famous as the so-called "guru" of direct mail fundraising. But there was nothing particularly "new" about the New Right's ideology and strategic objectives. The movement's ascent came about through new political and organizational opportunities for conservatives active earlier in Cold War projects and the Goldwater campaign.

Several historical treatments trace the rise of the New Right.[91] The discussion which follows highlights the New Right's strategies both inside and outside the Republican Party, as well as some of the key elements of the 1970s political context that facilitated the movement's growing influence.

Third-Party Thinking

During the 1970s, conservative veterans of the Goldwater campaign gave serious thought to the formation of a third political party. But unlike the libertarians, who built a small party to the neglect of other movement strategies, conservatives kept their options open and used whatever third-party ideas they had to strengthen their issue-oriented activism. Throughout the 1970s, ACU and YAF continued to cosponsor the Conservative Political Action Conference (CPAC), an annual gathering of hundreds of activists started in the early 1960s by the *Human Events* newspaper (see Chapter 2).

At the 1974 CPAC, conservatives debated whether Nixon ought to resign the presidency.[92] By 1975, the CPAC agenda was more profound.

Many delegates came with the objective of declaring a formal break with the Republican Party. Others favored a less hasty approach and expressed hopes of drafting Ronald Reagan for the 1976 Republican presidential campaign.[93] The conference ended with the adoption of a compromise resolution and the formation of a Committee on Conservative Alternatives, charged with exploring the possible creation of a new political party. This committee included YAF chair Ronald Docksai and ACU chair M. Stanton Evans, both on record as supporting a third-party plan, plus a number of elected officials who were noncommittal: Representatives John Ashbrook (R-OH), Robert Bauman (R-MD), Steve Symms (R-ID), Senator Jesse Helms (R-NC), and Governor Meldrim Thomson (R-NH).[94]

The committee represented more of a symbolic gesture than an actual effort to launch a new party. But third-party thinking gained prominence among conservatives with the appearance of *National Review* publisher William Rusher's landmark 1975 book *The Making of the New Majority Party*. Rusher advocated the organization of a new "major" party, one "consisting of a nationwide coalition of interests and capable of capturing both the Presidency and the Congress."[95] Rusher predicted that, given the constraints of the two-party system, a new "Independence Party" would eventually either replace one of the two parties, or, alternatively, its issues and voters would be coopted by one of the two major parties.[96] Unlike the libertarians, who wanted *their* candidates to win offices on purist ideological platforms, Rusher's idea was not to add more parties to the electoral ballot, but rather to successfully win full representation for its issues and voters within an established party. Recognizing the historical tendency of U.S. parties' periodic realignments and transformations, Rusher urged conservatives to consider the new salient categories of economic and ideological cleavage. He divided political constituencies between "producers" and

> a new class of liberal verbalists, centered in the federal and state bureaucracies, the principal media, the major foundations and research institutions, and the nationwide educational establishment.
>
> Liberals are obssessed with the need to rectify, by federal intervention, the injustices historically perpetrated by whites against the black population of the country, as well as other wrongs allegedly committed against a whole series of newly-discovered and acutely self-conscious "minorities," ranging from homosexuals and American Indians to Spanish-speaking citizens, flower people, prison inmates and women.[97]

Conservatives, Rusher posited, were those who opposed using "federal largesse" for "forced integration of the public schools" but favored school prayer; liberals opposed the Pentagon and the CIA but favored arms control treaties and detente. Rusher called for conservatives to forge a "Great Coalition" between the Republican Party's usual base of economic conservatives and social conservatives found among the lower-middle-class and Catholic immigrant communities (Irish, Italian, East European).[98]

The concept of a "new majority party" involved shifting the Right's class appeal downward, precisely at a time when an inflationary economy spelled an eventual decline in economic prospects for a majority of the U.S. middle class. The idea of recruiting new supporters from the middle and working classes signaled a departure from the traditional association of Republicans with the upper class. It was an idea that mainstream Republicans themselves would adopt in the 1980 presidential campaign to elect Ronald Reagan.[99] In practice, though, third-party advocates inside the conservative movement cast their drive to organize middle-class discontent in terms more political than economic.[100]

By mid-1975, New Right fundraiser Richard Viguerie's new *Conservative Digest* magazine tailored its message to right-wing Republicans, "conservative Democrats,"[101] and, generally, a readership willing to consider an electoral coalition dominated by issues of "social conservatism" and staunch anticommunism. By 1975, Ronald Reagan's advisors formed a preliminary committee to work on his presidential candidacy.[102] *Conservative Digest* published articles promoting both the third-party plan and ideas about drafting right-wing candidates to run on the Republican ticket in 1976. The magazine polled movement leaders, who generally favored a Reagan–Wallace ticket, which ACU Chairman M. Stanton Evans termed "the symbolic constituency of the conservative majority; Reagan representing the Republican conservatives, and Wallace the blue collar Democrats."[103]

In 1976, New Right leaders drew national press attention when they attempted to usurp control of the American Independent Party (AIP). Formed as the electoral vehicle for Wallace's 1968 race, by 1976 AIP still maintained ballot status in more than thirty states. Richard Viguerie had raised seven million dollars for George Wallace's 1976 presidential bid, and he tried to use his ownership of the Wallace donor list as leverage over the party. Viguerie, Howard Phillips, and Paul Weyrich attended AIP's 1976 national convention and tried unsuccessfully to get delegates to endorse a presidential candidacy for anticommunist activist Robert Morris, with Viguerie as Morris' vice-presidential nominee. In the end, the New Rightists were unable to convince AIP not to nominate former Georgia Governor Lester Maddox, an avowed segregationist. The incident revealed, however, that Viguerie and company were willing and eager to take over a party led by veterans of the racist Citizens' Councils.[104]

The failed effort to control the American Independent Party was not decisive for the New Right because by then the movement had already established an array of electoral and non-electoral organizations.

A New Context, New Resources

By the 1970s, the conservative movement had yet to reshape the Republican Party. As we will see in Chapter 6, the mass-based anticommunist and racist Right groups were in disarray, and the Christian Right had yet to mobilize massively. Nevertheless, key aspects of a changing political context were advantageous for the conservative strategists who had been active since the Goldwater campaign. Increased availability of *corporate funding*, accelerated *organizational* development, and the mobilization of new constituencies behind an expanded *issues* agenda were the most relevant to the rise of the New Right.

These factors were interrelated. Corporate resources facilitated a group of already seasoned political activists, who had spent years thinking about ways to arouse constituencies using concrete policy issues. The political and economic context of the 1970s, presented tailor-made issues for resourceful conservative movement strategists. The 1960s and 1970s spawned growing societal acceptance of new cultural values promoted by the anti-war, women's, and civil rights movements. As we will see in Chapter 7, the onset of legally sanctioned abortion, gay rights protections in a handful of places, and a proposed Equal Rights Amendment for women all had the collateral effect of arousing and mobilizing the New Right's evangelical allies. On the international scene, the 1970s saw the end of the Vietnam war, revolutionary civil wars from Angola to Nicaragua, and economic inflation exacerbated by the Middle East oil crisis.

Among all these factors, shifts in the U.S. and world economies were crucial. Two international economic trends underway since World War II, globalization and concentration, became politically salient by the 1970s. Before World War II, only 100 to 200 U.S. corporations invested directly abroad; nor did the foreign subsidiaries of these businesses bring in the lion's share of profits. However, by 1965, more than 3,000 U.S.-based multinational corporations controlled approximately 23,000 subsidiaries. The larger corporations came to rely disproportionately on their interests overseas, where they were able to pay lower wages and extract a higher rate of profit. At the same time, fewer than 200 corporations came to control three-quarters of the total assets held by U.S. corporations abroad. Increased globalization and concentration corresponded to increasing monopolization inside the United States as well.[105] Exorbitant military expenditures during the Vietnam war had a strong inflationary impact on the U.S. economy. The war-induced boom increased prices of U.S. goods, while a loss of capital interest in exports led to a permanent loss of some overseas markets.[106]

A number of political analysts, including Thomas Ferguson and Joel Rogers, have traced a "right turn" among U.S. business and political elites to the seventeen-month recession, between November 1973 and March 1975, which they describe as "by far the longest and deepest economic downturn the United States had experienced since the great Depression."[107] The recession had its roots in the long-term decline of the position of U.S. capitalists in the world economy. By the mid-1970s, though, business leaders were eager to take preemptive action, both economically, by seeking to squeeze labor with wage cuts, and ideologically, by funding a slew of "free market" policy think tanks.[108]

Several key international developments contributed to the panic of business elites. In 1973 the Organization of Petroleum Exporting Countries (OPEC) raised oil prices and sent shockwaves through the world economy. Ferguson and Rogers argue, further, that the collapse of detente between the United States and the Soviet Union in the 1970s was driven by elites from both superpowers: the Soviets sought to build their military technology, while the United States sought new investment opportunities in the developing countries.[109]

But it was in the periphery of the world capitalist system where political turmoil raged. In Latin America, the decade of the 1970s saw increased violence and repression by military dictatorships against civilian populations. Revolutionary movements were on the march in Latin America, the Caribbean, southern Africa, and the Philippines. Some of these movements enjoyed military and political support from the Soviet bloc, but they were also indigenous responses to intolerable conditions. After losing the Vietnam war, the U.S. political class grew committed to defeating purported Soviet "aggression" on other Third World battle grounds. This would require another round of massive military spending, one which the Reagan administration would enthusiastically promote in the 1980s.

The 1970s was a time during which business leaders began to operate, more than previously, as a cohesive political force. The boards of directors of major U.S. and British corporations became increasingly interlocked, and corporate officers increased their donations to political projects.[110] With a heightened political and class consciousness, capitalists recognized the utility of right-wing institutions. They poured millions of dollars into political action committees, advocacy advertising, and think tanks.[111]

This increased corporate mobilization signaled changes not only in relations between the capitalist class and the state but also in relations between the state and social movements. Capitalists funded right-wing movement organizations in order to indirectly affect state policy. For the movement beneficiaries of corporate largesse, increased resources meant new opportunities to influence political elites, to shape the nature of state power. Right-wing organizations could lobby more persuasively once they wielded the resources to elect new officeholders and remove uncooperative incumbents. The mobilization of corporate conservatism meant a changing three-way relationship between the capitalist class, the state, and the New Right social movement.

Just as the capitalist class changed its strategy for influencing policy, so was it likely that state institutions would change under combined pressure from the New Right and its corporate backers. If corporate funders had been interested solely (or even primarily) in domestic tax and regulatory policies, they might have backed the fledgling libertarian movement but they generally did not. Instead, it is plausible that at least some capitalists understood the value of a movement that advocated a combined program of economic libertarianism, traditional "law and order" morality, and militarist anticommunism. That fusionist combination is amenable to capitalists' pursuit of favorable climates for investment and the repression of labor, both domestically and internationally.

Beginning even before the Watergate scandal forced Nixon's resignation, corporations and their affiliated charitable foundations directed funds two ways: into *electoral politics* via political action committees (PACs) and into *ideological politics* via think tanks and other types of organizations to be discussed shortly. Mere funding of selected candidates was not as attractive a strategy as attempting to influence pre-electoral terms of debate.

The archetypical right-wing funding conduit was the Coors beer company.[112] Chief executive Joseph Coors poured millions of dollars into dozens of evangelical and New Right organizations and established a pattern for other corporate funders: the Scaife, Smith Richardson, Olin, and Noble foundations; the Kraft, Nabisco, and Amway corporations, to name just a few.[113] Reported dollar amounts can be found in various sources.[114] What caught the attention of observers was the phenomenal and rapid expansion of rightist groups' financial coffers. *Congressional Quarterly* reported that during the 1972 Congressional elections, right-wing organizations raised $250,000. By 1976, with the addition of major New Right PACs, the figure rose to an estimated $3.5 million. Allowing for the New Right groups' large overhead costs, the net total spent on Congressional campaigns in that election was still a million dollars. The National Conservative Political Action Committee (NCPAC) and the Committee for the Survival of a Free Congress (CSFC) each raised over a million dollars, compared to about $100,000 raised by the American

Conservative Union's Conservative Victory Fund.[115] The New Right PACs, with their looser ties to the Republican Party establishment, were apparently more attractive, both to major corporate donors and to recipients of the new groups' slick direct mail appeals.

Increased corporate funding to New Right organizations gave an unprecedented strategic flexibility to conservative movement leaders, who were no longer limited to the role of outside agitators. Money raised by New Right PACs meant better prospects for conservative-backed candidates.[116] Money directed to non-electoral organizations meant greater capability to mobilize movement constituents during and *between* campaign seasons. Increased corporate resources and the diverse issues agenda of the New Right allowed for the creation of dozens of new organizations and the revitalization of old ones.

The political awakening of the evangelical movement, to be treated separately in Chapter 7, enlivened and expanded the New Right's organizational infrastructure. Nominally secular groups, old and new, were of several varieties, including: (1) para-party formations (e.g., the existing American Conservative Union and Young Americans for Freedom); (2) electoral vehicles, including political action committees; (3) think tanks; and (4) issue-oriented lobbies, many of which overlapped with the Christian Right.[117] Each type served specific functions. The first two types were closely related: para-party organizations facilitated candidate selection and provided networks for elected officials and activists; electoral vehicles raised money and trained candidates. Think tanks conducted background research and worked to frame terms of debates even before issue conflicts arose. Issue lobbies sought to educate large constituencies, often using think tank materials; and pressured candidates and elected officials, often in tandem with electoral vehicles.

Each of the organization types involved dynamic and changing relationships between specific groups. For example, the Committee for the Survival of a Free Congress started as an election vehicle but, by the 1980s, had evolved into a think tank as well. Two think tanks, the Heritage Foundation and the Free Congress Foundation, helped start and coordinate numerous issue lobbies. Each of these produced their own publications, thereby enhancing the educational clout of the major conservative movement periodicals, *National Review, Human Events*, and *Conservative Digest*. During the 1980s, New Right think tanks and issue lobbies coalesced into an extra-governmental, extra-legal foreign policymaking apparatus that facilitated Reagan administration covert operations.

The larger the network of New Right groups and projects grew, the more complex the inter-organizational relations became. Such a pattern is to be expected for the case of any major social movement and is not peculiar to the Right.

What was unique to the New Right was the movement's ability to add a growing bloc of elected officeholders to its organizational resources.[118] Corporate backing alone cannot account for the Right's success. Because the conservative movement, unlike the libertarian movement, maintained a dual insider–outsider relationship with the Republican Party from the Goldwater campaign forward, conservatives became influential in the party's nomination and election processes. ACU and YAF activists raised money for the party and turned out votes. Right-wing influence grew as the party's southern strategy facilitated the election of civil rights opponents, most notably Senators Strom Thurmond (R-SC) and Jesse Helms (R-NC), both veterans of the segregationist movement. Increased funding and activist resources helped elect right-wing candidates who, in turn, used their prestige to help New Right groups gain legitimacy and, thus, raise even more money. Over time, the New Right-backed Congressional bloc became a coordinated *party faction*, one that would help usher in the Reagan revolution of 1980. Ultimately, though the New Right focused heavily on electoral politics, its success was tied to its campaigns around highly charged issues.

Issue-Driven Mobilization

In its New Right phase, the conservative movement devoted increased attention to fusionism's traditional morality component. New Right leaders made common cause with Christian Right activists on the issues of abortion, gay rights, and the Equal Rights Amendment (ERA). At the same time, the conservative movement remained focused on the anti-communist part of its agenda, and opposed Carter administration policies, especially on sanctions against Rhodesia, the Panama Canal treaty, and the SALT II treaty with the Soviet Union.

On issues of traditional morality, nominally secular New Right leaders supported their evangelical counterparts, both by ventilating the concerns of the emerging Christian Right and, in some cases, by providing logistical assistance. Conservative movement publications reported regularly on efforts to stop the ERA and civil rights for gay people.[119] Both issues involved the question of whether state agencies should intervene to prevent discrimination based on traditional morality. Phyllis Schlafly started the Eagle Forum to unite activists against abortion, pornography, gay rights and the ERA.[120] With the exception of abortion, the "pro-family" issues were subject to compromise and remained contested throughout the 1970s and 1980s.

Abortion was a different kind of moral issue: one was either for "choice" or against "murder." By the time the New Right was highly mobilized, the Supreme Court had already ruled on abortion's constitutionality. Senator James Buckley (brother of William F. Buckley) introduced the first anti-abortion "Human Life Amendment to the Constitution,"[121] and New Right leaders quickly grasped abortion's enormous symbolic value as a movement-defining issue. Paul Weyrich helped anti-abortion leaders Paul and Judie Brown start the American Life Lobby and use it to target electoral campaigns.[122] At one of the Browns' political workshops, direct mail expert Richard Viguerie described the hypothetical case of a man who becomes so profoundly disturbed by abortion imagery that he joins a political group for the first time in his life and gradually becomes active on a host of family issues.[123] (At a 1979 meeting with Jerry Falwell, it was New Right leaders Paul Weyrich, Richard Viguerie, and Howard Phillips who suggested that the Baptist preacher start the Moral Majority,[124] and these same strategists promoted the Moral Majority among nominally secular New Rightists.)[125]

Similarly, New Right campaigns on specific foreign affairs questions intensified the movement's general commitment to militarism. President Carter's foreign policy decisions infuriated conservatives, who had earlier denounced Nixon's Secretary of State Henry Kissinger.[126] The Right blamed Kissinger, though not solely, for U.S. compliance with an international boycott of white minority-ruled Rhodesia (Zimbabwe).[127]

Still, Carter was the first post-Vietnam war president, and his administration faced a new generation of nationalist Third World leaders from one region of the southern hemisphere to the next. Developments in southern Africa spelled the beginning of the end for white minority rule. Oil-rich Angola's 1975 revolution required the assistance of Cuban troops to defend against South African aggression. Meanwhile, the Right made unsuccessful attempts to thwart the independence struggle in Rhodesia–Zimbabwe.[128] Among other activities, seventeen conservative movement journalists lobbied the Carter administration against closure of the Rhodesian Information Office, a propaganda agency based in Washington, D.C.[129] Carter's State Department ordered the office to close in compliance with a UN resolution prohibiting the transfer of Rhodesian assets within the territory of UN member nations.[130]

Closer to home, the Carter administration favored treaties granting Panama control over its canal zone. After Nixon's Taiwan "sell-out," no other foreign policy initiative caused such opposition from the conservative movement. Against the Panama Canal treaties, New Right Congressmembers and activist groups rallied together as a united front.

The American Conservative Union mobilized citizen opposition to the canal treaties through newspaper advertisements and a television "documentary" featuring appearances by Republican Senators Jake Garn, Jesse Helms, Paul Laxalt, and Strom Thurmond.[131] As the treaty negotiations neared conclusion, this same group of Senators, plus others and a team of retired military officers, traveled together on a nationwide Panama Canal Truth Squad speaking tour, in coordination with eight New Right groups: the Committee for the Survival of a Free Congress, the American Security Council, Conservative Caucus, Young Republicans, the National Conservative Political Action Committee (NCPAC), the National Defense Council, Citizens for the Republic, and the American Conservative Union.[132] Speakers urged their audiences to lobby against the Carter–Torrijos canal treaties and used the campaign to solidify their reputations as hard-line anticommunists.[133]

Perhaps no one gained more mileage from the canal issue than presidential aspirant Ronald Reagan, who joined the Truth Squad tour, testified against the treaties before a Senate committee, and debated the treaties' merits on live television with William F. Buckley.[134]

Ultimately, both houses of Congress passed the Carter–Torrijos treaties, granting Panama control of the canal by the year 2000. (This was before the U.S. invasion of Panama in 1989 changed the plan.) Conservatives endured yet another foreign policy defeat, but they had made important advances in their ability to coordinate multiple organizations as well as a party faction that represented them. While debate on the canal treaties continued, the pending second phase of Strategic Arms Limitation Talks (SALT) gave anticommunist activists another chance to flex their muscles.

As in the campaign against the canal treaties, the American Conservative Union produced a half-hour anti-SALT television program, which was aired on more than 200 stations across the country.[135] More significant for the movement's long-term trajectory, in 1978, the American Security Council expanded its Operation Alert program into the Coalition for Peace Through Strength, comprised of dozens of activist groups and hundreds of business and political leaders. The Coalition's initial objective was to prevent passage of a SALT II treaty. In the process of waging that campaign, the coalition also rallied supporters against the growing anti-nuclear movement and against the "Marxist threat" in Central America.[136] While military leaders and neoconservative intellectuals in the Committee on the Present Danger targeted elite thinking on SALT, the Coalition aimed at mass audiences through the Right's well-honed use of newspaper advertisements, speaking tours, and radio appearances.[137]

The Coalition's most celebrated anti-SALT activity was its production of the film *The SALT Syndrome*, featuring interviews with prominent military leaders on U.S. vulnerability to the Soviets' nuclear arsenal.[138] *The SALT Syndrome* aired on television more than 600 times in 1979 and was considered such a strong influence on public opinion that the Carter administration issued a detailed rebuttal of the film.[139] Apart from New

Right influence in Congress, by the time the SALT II treaty made its way to the Senate in 1979, numerous factors conspired to derail its ratification. These included U.S. intelligence reports of a Soviet "combat brigade" in Cuba; the Iranian students' seizure of U.S. embassy hostages in November, 1979; and the Soviet invasion of Afghanistan a few weeks later.[140] The Coalition for Peace Through Strength could not claim sole credit for defeating SALT II, but the Coalition's successful networking set a precedent for the anticommunist movement's well-coordinated "freedom fighter" campaigns of the 1980s.

THE BEGINNING OF THE REAGAN ERA

The issues that preoccupied the New Right of the 1970s reflected the persistent ideology of conservatives: anticommunism and traditional morality. The conservative movement consistently opposed government actions that would have changed traditional gender relations or redistributed power to subordinate groups, namely women and homosexuals. Conservatives supported a strong state role in the international realm. That pro-enforcer stance took form in calls for continued U.S. dominance over Latin America and perpetuation of the nuclear arms race against the Soviet Union.

Conservative movement ideology and objectives developed in tandem. As activists pursued concrete pieces of the movement's issues agenda, their ideological commitments were reinforced. At the 1978 Conservative Political Action Conference (CPAC), sponsored by the American Conservative Union, Young Americans for Freedom, *National Review*, and *Human Events*, plus a half dozen New Right groups, Ronald Reagan gave the banquet's keynote address. Reagan denounced Carter's foreign policy, and gave specific emphasis to the SALT talks and Soviet influence in Africa.[141] *Human Events* concluded that the leading concern of New Right activists was "the failure of the Carter Administration to come to grips with the burgeoning Soviet menace," and a poll of CPAC participants named Reagan the movement's top presidential choice.[142]

By the end of the 1970s, the conservative movement had risen to a high point in its long history. Millions of corporate dollars now flowed into a varied organizational network led by strategists committed to an agenda with potentially wide voter appeal. From Goldwater's defeat through the start of Reagan's 1980 presidential campaign, the conservative movement had solidified its role within the Republican Party. Surely, increased corporate resources gave the New Right advantages no other political movement enjoyed. But conservative strategists also deserve credit for their astute appreciation of two non-economic resources: the salience of race and traditional morality issues, and the Republican Party's potential reliance on an anti-civil rights, "pro-family" constituency.

The libertarian movement lacked three of the New Right's major assets: massive corporate resources, a broad and potentially appealing issues agenda, and leverage within an already established party. Combined with its tendency toward ideological purism and its narrow electoral focus, the libertarian movement was destined to wield marginal influence. However, one result of the Libertarian Party's 1970s mobilization was to preserve a strong voice for the libertarian component of fusionist ideology and objectives. By the time Ronald Reagan ran for president in 1980, his promoters stressed an anti-taxation, pro-business message along with anticommunist and pro-family themes.

From the Goldwater campaign failure to the onset of the Reagan era, the transformation of the conservative movement sheds light on some of the ways in which social movements interact with state institutions. Compared to the thoroughly anti-statist libertarian movement, the New Right maintained a mixed, though consistent, stance on the state's proper role in society. New Rightists opposed statist moves to increase social equality by redistributing wealth and power via legislation or by the funding of new agencies. However, unlike the libertarians, conservatives supported the state in its role as enforcer of "law and order," traditional morality, and U.S. hegemony abroad. Whereas libertarians wanted to eliminate state institutions, conservatives sought, instead, to control and transform them. By virtue of their acceptance of state prerogatives, conservatives were willing to make compromises within the Republican Party. That willingness made the New Right, more than the small libertarian movement, an attractive ally of business and elected officials. Corporate resources allowed movement activists to begin to reshape the political establishment, first within Congress, then in the White House. By the 1980s, the New Right would partially achieve its policy objectives. During that decade, the Reagan administration and its supporters would loosen the boundary between state and social movement.

CHAPTER 6

• • •

The Americanist Movement
and the Persistence
of Racist Nationalism

Nearly ten million voters chose presidential candidate George Wallace •
in 1968, in an election that made a lasting impression on both conservative movement and Republican Party strategists. Among the Wallace
voters, most were not activists; a small proportion came from the
organized racist and mass-based anticommunist movements. These Wallace supporters coalesced in 1968 and again in 1972 around the fractious
American and American Independent parties. But neither before nor
after the 1972 assassination attempt that left candidate Wallace disabled
did these parties ever surmount their incessant factionalism. What did
survive third-party failure was a core of self-described Americanist
organizations with ideological orientations and political opportunities
distinct from those of the New Right.

Before and after the Wallace campaigns, thousands of people remained active in the John Birch Society and the Liberty Lobby, the two
often overlapping fixtures of the mass-based anticommunist and anti-
civil rights movements of the 1960s. Members of these two groups
formed the backbone of the various short-lived American and American
Independent parties. Both Birchists and Lobbyists called themselves
Americanists, a term that implies notions about who or what is properly
considered "American," and how "America" ought to relate to the rest
of the world.[1]

The Liberty Lobby, treated at length in this chapter, also identified
itself with the conceptually problematic "populist" label. In common
parlance, populism refers to the proto-leftist American farmers' movement of the late nineteenth century. The Liberty Lobby appropriated the

140

term and promoted its version of populism strongly as part of the racist Right's overtures to farmers disaffected by the early 1980s farm crisis (see Chapter 11). In the 1970s, the Lobby claimed the populist mantle as part of a conscious effort to distinguish itself from New Right competitors. Populism, Americanist style, encompassed the tenets of patriotism, support of racial and other forms of social inequality, and the promotion of policies to benefit a strong middle class. All of these organizing principles related to questions of the state's role in society. Americanists supported the enforcement of U.S. military might abroad, though with stipulations: they were suspicious about the patriotism of established policymakers and tended to believe that elites were conspiring against the nation's true best interests. Wallace voters were white and from the middle and lower middle classes. Americanists purported to represent these class interests by opposing state policies to effect racial and class equality and by condemning a federal tax system disproportionately burdensome on wage earners and small business owners.

Populism was a euphemism for the Americanists' particular brand of nationalism. While New Right conservatives had broken with the Old Right's isolationism and xenophobia, right-wing populists perpetuated precisely these tendencies. In the late 1980s and 1990s, as we will see in Chapter 12, Patrick Buchanan would try to revive the Old Right, pre-World War II tradition of America First nationalism, and he would face stiff criticism from New Right and neoconservative proponents of an internationalist and interventionist "new world order." Prior to the late 1980s, however, populist nationalism was something promoted mainly by Americanists outside the mainstream of U.S. conservatism, namely the John Birch Society and the Liberty Lobby.

Where these two camps broke ranks was around questions of biologically based racism. As was discussed in Chapter 3, Willis Carto formed the Liberty Lobby with the idea of fusing the segregationist and grassroots anticommunist organizations of the Cold War era. An admirer of Germany's Third Reich, Carto viewed the struggle between the United States and the Soviet Union in racial terms, and he drew many of his supporters from the white Citizens' Councils and the Ku Klux Klan. The John Birch Society, on the other hand, had an overlapping base of support but, as an organization, did not endorse or promote theories of racial biological determinism. Nor did the Birch Society make formal coalition with explicitly racist or anti-Semitic groups. From the 1960s forward, the relationship between the Liberty Lobby and the John Birch Society fluctuated between one of symbiosis and antagonism.[2] Members of both organizations supported the 1972 presidential candidacy of southern California Representative John Schmitz.

Still, Americanists held fewer antagonisms among themselves than they did with New Right conservatives. The most obvious dividing line was the Americanists' inclusion of blatant racists and anti-Semites. Within the New Right, the presence of outright neo-Nazi activists was exceptional, not routine. Strategically, New Right conservatives remained focused on anticommunism and gradually came to emphasize the traditional morality agenda of born-again Christians, while Americanists gave race issues continued explicit emphasis.

Where conservatives defined their oppositional activism in terms of political conflict, both with fellow Republicans and libertarians, Americanists relied more on conspiracist interpretations of events and institutions they opposed. Americanists grew increasingly alienated from mainstream politics. But despite the failure of Americanists to achieve policy objectives or wield influence within a major party, the movement remained relatively intact because its ideology offered adherents a reliable explanation of political events and trends. Americanists were more avowedly anti-statist than were New Right conservatives, and that difference set some parameters for the future development of Americanists. The New Right won support from political and economic elites beginning in the 1970s. The same time period saw the growth of an Americanist sub-movement of "Christian patriots," whose fiercely antagonistic "Identity" religion and tax evasion tactics made them increasingly alienated from mainstream political institutions and set the stage for the violent resurgence of the racist Right during the 1980s.

THE WALLACE CAMPAIGNS

Several aspects of the Wallace presidential campaigns attracted the greatest scholarly and press attention. Most obvious was the support Wallace drew, and would not rebuke, from disreputable groups like the Ku Klux Klan, Citizens' Councils, and the John Birch Society. Scholarly analyses focused first on the significance of Wallace's large vote totals: the class, ethnic, and regional bases of support for Wallace; second, on the candidate's use of key polarizing campaign themes; and third, on the ramifications of Wallace's popularity for the future prospects of Republicans and Democrats.

Largely neglected in the sizeable literature on the Wallace campaigns was the role of Wallace's third-party alternative in the consolidation of a fractious, but long-lasting coalition of racist and grassroots anticommunist groups. Electoral activism, though unsuccessful, left a legacy for the Americanist movement of the 1970s, because, over time, electoral failure drove the racist Right further toward separatism and violence.

Wallace's 1968 presidential race, like his 1964 state primary cam-paigns, was largely a top-down operation. As early as 1965, Wallace encouraged support from the racist Right.[3] Between 1964 and 1968, Wallace was a frequent speaker at Citizens' Councils gatherings, and he benefited from their promotion of his candidacy.[4] California Citizens' Council leader William K. Shearer coordinated Wallace's state ballot qualification campaign,[5] and ran California's American Independent Party even into the 1990s. By 1968, members of the John Birch Society were as prominent as Citizens' Council activists within the Wallace campaign. In California, the Birch Society and the Citizens' Council together registered 100,000 voters for the American Independent Party. Aside from sheer numbers, the Birch Society activists brought skills in telephone canvassing, petition gathering and staffing of local offices, especially outside the South.[6] Unflattering press reports on "radical right" campaign personnel may account for Wallace's decision not to hold a national convention or encourage local candidates.[7] Despite negative press and opposition from prominent southern politicians, like Senator Strom Thurmond of South Carolina, Wallace received close to ten million popular votes (about 13.5 percent of the total) and won five southern states.

Analyses of typical Wallace voters supported historian V. O. Key's classic hypothesis on the endurance of racist white voting patterns in areas with the largest black populations.[8] On the issues of the Vietnam war, civil rights, and urban disorders, Wallace voters favored the most hawkish, most segregationist, and most punitive policy options. In contrast with other southerners, Wallace voters were most likely to name the federal government as "responsible for the trouble in the country."[9] The typical non-southern Wallace voter was male, in his twenties, an unskilled worker with a high school education who opposed civil rights policies and held negative attitudes toward blacks and the federal government. Wallace voters came disproportionately from the ranks of white workers who felt economically disadvantaged, compared to blacks and to white collar workers, especially professionals.[10] Compulsory school busing to achieve racial integration was an issue that galvanized Wallace voters perhaps more than anything else. Busing was opposed by some parents who, in principle, favored school integration. But Wallace voters tended to oppose busing and favor segregation.[11]

The large voter turnout for Wallace in 1968 fit the pattern of what political scientist Walter Dean Burnham called a "critical realignment" in U.S. electoral politics.[12] Burnham saw Wallace's ten million voters as a sign of the U.S. public's susceptibility to "a cryptofacist or neofascist movement dedicated to the preservation of the petit-bourgeois 'little man' against the personalized conspirators—symbols for many of the

large social forces at work—who are threatening both his material interests and his 'way of life.'"[13]

In previous eras, third-party movements had declined when one of
the major parties absorbed their adherents and some of their doctrine.[14]
That was precisely what Republican strategist Kevin Phillips and *National
Review* publisher William Rusher advocated after 1968. They called for
the Republicans to undercut Wallace's base of support by using race
issues to recruit from the historically Democratic South.

Realignments between the major political parties shape the prospects for political movements, even those considered outside the mainstream. Third party-oriented movements face two possible outcomes.
They can either pursue power and become new leaders inside a major
party, or they can find themselves left on the side lines while established
political actors coopt their agenda. Both the Christian Right and conservative movements pursued power inside the Republican Party and
eventually became dominant factions. The Americanist movement went
the second route. Most of the ten million Wallace voters were absorbed
into the two-party system (or into non-voting) in 1972 and thereafter.

Presumably, those Wallace voters most active in the 1968 campaign
were those most likely to remain in the Americanist movement. One
study of the motivations of blue collar Wallace campaign workers in a
suburban Michigan district found that they fell into two ideological
subgroups. Members of the category of "racial reactionaries" were
mostly southern-born white supremacists, opposed to civil rights and
concerned about "law and order." A second category of "ultraconservatives" shared these concerns but differed from the racialists on issues of
social welfare policy. Consistent with the positions of the John Birch
Society, the "ultraconservatives" opposed increased Social Security and
Medicare benefits, income taxes, increased government spending, and
foreign aid.[15] The different priorities of the "racial reactionaries" and the
"ultraconservatives" may have contributed to the American Independent
Party's internecine conflicts after 1968, though the issues of race and
communism did not neatly divide the various AIP factions.

It is plausible that third parties, both of the right and left, attract
followers less willing to compromise than established party activists.
Following the 1968 election, various factions of the AIP elevated their
own versions of an ideological party above the pursuit of real political
power, let alone the achievement of tangible policy objectives. Whereas
politician and candidate George Wallace used broad issue positions to
attract as wide a following as possible, party activists were sectarian, to
say the least and, without Wallace as a candidate, the Americanists'
electoral appeal took a nosedive. After 1968's total of nearly ten million
votes, the 1972 ticket of John Schmitz and Tom Anderson captured only

about one million votes; in 1976 Lester Maddox won only 170,000 votes. During the decade after 1968, the Wallace party's electoral fortunes plummeted, and factionalism became the name of the game.

In 1969, Wallace campaign workers split into two national groups. Wallace endorsed a group that included several prominent Birch Society activists and close Wallace aides, and established itself as the American Party, under the leadership of T. Coleman Andrews. The American Party emphasized anticommunism and called for the United States to win the war in Vietnam, withdraw from the United Nations, stop all disarmament activities, press for the "liberation" of Cuba and Communist China, impeach "Communist members" of the Supreme Court, repeal the federal income tax, and abolish the Federal Reserve Board.[16]

Under the leadership of California AIP founder William K. Shearer, a separate National Committee of the Autonomous State Parties united various state parties registered as AIP, American, Independent, Conservative, and Constitutional. Some of these small parties had been around since the 1950s, when Liberty Lobby leader Willis Carto had tried to unite them under one banner (see Chapter 3). Shearer's group included activists who had opposed Wallace's domination over the 1968 campaign and who also opposed Wallace's "liberal" social security and farm policies. Both groups included veterans of violent racist groups, and each charged the other with harboring unsavory "extremists."[17]

After the 1969 split, one would need a scorecard to follow the numerous faction fights and mergers.[18] Both national groups opposed federal intervention into schools, and favored increased police suppression of domestic disorder and U.S. military victory in Vietnam. In 1972, the Shearer and Andrews groups united briefly under the American Party banner.[19] Following an attempt on his life that left him partially paralyzed, Wallace declined the American Party's presidential nomination. The party then nominated John Schmitz, an Orange County, California Representative and an avowed John Birch Society member. Schmitz's running mate Tom Anderson was an original Birch Society Council member and a long-time contributor to the Society's *American Opinion* magazine. Their campaign amounted to little but a publicity boost for the Birch Society, as Schmitz regaled reporters with his conspiracy theories of history and raised funds by selling the classic book *None Dare Call It Conspiracy*, for which Schmitz wrote the introduction.[20]

After Schmitz's poor showing in the November race, Tom Anderson was elected chair of the American Party and soon after announced that the American Party would not back a Wallace candidacy in 1976. Anderson and his bitter opponent, California AIP leader William Shearer, resumed the feud between the two parties.

The period between 1972 and 1976 was marked by the conservative movement's strategic thinking on the need to forge a third party. The American Party held its 1976 convention (and nominated Tom Anderson), before the Democrats held theirs, ensuring that Wallace would have no third-party alternative once his candidacy was rejected by the Democrats.[21] As was discussed in Chapter 5, the American Independent Party rejected a takeover effort by New Right leaders Richard Viguerie, Howard Phillips, and Paul Weyrich. Over the objections of the New Right leaders, AIP nominated former Georgia governor Lester Maddox, a notorious segregationist. Maddox won only 170,000 votes for AIP, while Tom Anderson received 160,000 votes for the American Party.[22]

Whereas George Wallace's 1968 showing contributed to the commitment of Republican Party and conservative movement activists to a "southern strategy," the Americanists' subsequent third-party efforts were relatively uninfluential. Consistently, the Americanists were less adept than their conservative movement counterparts at making tactical alliances with ideological antagonists. On behalf of the American Party, Tom Anderson tried to recruit allies at the 1975 Conservative Political Action Conference, sponsored by Young Americans for Freedom and the American Conservative Union. Despite the conservatives' thorough dissatisfaction with the Republican Party under Nixon and Ford, they were unwilling to include Anderson's self-described contingent of "American Party people, Birchers, Liberty Lobbyists, radicals, and rednecks," who were forced to hold their own separate sessions.[23] Conservatives, by and large, were loyal to the Republican Party, and despite the fondness of New Right leaders for George Wallace, they were unwilling to ally with rank-and-file racists and conspiracists. Having developed greater resources and political acumen, conservatives had grown from a movement to a strong party faction. They did not need the Americanists, who pursued divisive and minor party goals and remained a relatively weak movement.

Remarkably, the onset of the New Right did not result in obsolescence for the Liberty Lobby and the John Birch Society, though the latter lost some prominent personnel to conservative movement projects.[24] Studies of Wallace voters suggested a downwardly mobile class base, and by the 1980s, a resurgent racist Right would attract displaced farmers and anxious job seekers. Yet the membership of the Citizens' Councils and the John Birch Society was known to consist of small businessmen and middle-class professionals, meaning that class alone does not explain why Americanists were not thoroughly integrated into the conservative movement of the 1970s. Instead, what accounts for the persistence of the Americanist movement, following numerous electoral defeats, is a set of ideological views, and some issue objectives, that deviated from those of the New Right.

AMERICANIST IDEOLOGY AND ACTIVISM

Despite the failure of the Americanists on the electoral front, their fervent ideological commitment kept them from total obsolescence. The Citizens' Councils and the John Birch Society had dominated grassroots right-wing activism during the 1950s and 1960s, respectively. By the mid-1960s, remnants of these groups transformed into an enduring coalition, under the rubric of the Liberty Lobby, which Willis Carto formed in the late 1950s with the goal of unifying mass-based right-wing groups (see Chapter 3). While the Wallaceite parties floundered through factionalism, and the Citizens' Councils and Birch Society declined in the face of permanent civil rights progress and diminished domestic McCarthyism,[25] the Liberty Lobby's significance for the racist and anticommunist Right grew.

Despite the Citizens Councils' close ties with southern politicians during the 1950s and 1960s, they had failed to prevent passage of key civil rights legislation. Most white southerners eventually accepted token integration,[26] and what remained of the old segregationist resistance movement needed a new lease on life. Leaders of the Citizens' Councils joined the 1968 Wallace presidential race and continued to organize for his 1972 campaign.[27] Once Wallace's prospects dimmed, some Councilors remained active in the Liberty Lobby and the Americanist parties, while others concentrated on establishing all-white private schools.[28]

Two political realities of the 1960s, the Vietnam war and the civil rights movement, caused shifts in the John Birch Society's strategy. From its inception, the Society had focused primarily on domestic communism. (President Eisenhower himself was considered a "dupe," if not an agent of the "conspiracy.") But President Johnson's escalation of the U.S. war in Southeast Asia produced a puzzling contradiction for adherents to Birchism. The war was popular with conservative movement leaders like William F. Buckley. The Birchists saw the war as a communist trick. In fact, in its 1965 *American Opinion* magazine "Scorecard" on freedom, the Society claimed the degree of "Communist influence or control of the United States" to be in the 60 to 80 percent range.[29]

Birchists faced a problem of logic: how could the war in Vietnam really be about fighting communism if the U.S. government itself was dominated by communist subversives? In an apparent effort to resolve the contradiction, founder Robert Welch used the Society's monthly membership *Bulletin* to craft a convoluted conspiracist interpretation of events. According to Welch, the war was a carefully managed fraud to convince the U.S. public of President Johnson's anticommunist goals. Eventually China would be drawn into the combat, so that the United States would be justified in allying with China's alleged enemy, but true friend, the Soviet Union.[30] By this pseudologic, Welch arrived at the slogan "Get US Out!" which had been the Society's position regarding the United Nations. In any event, Welch's anti-war stance was a central bone of contention in the *National Review*'s October 1965 attack on the John Birch Society. Soon after, Welch modified his position into a pair of rhetorical questions: if the United States is not winning the war, why not? and if the United States government will not do what is necessary to win, what are U.S. troops fighting for? This hawkish line on the war had a dual function. It brought the Society's position on the war closer to that of the rest of the U.S. Right. At the same time, Welch's hints of a conspiracy gave Birchists an explanation for why the United States suffered great casualties and was unable (or unwilling?) to win. In other words, Welch's revised position allowed Birchists to espouse characteristic right-wing militarism while remaining more oppositional than the "respectable conservatives," who were less prone to protest the government's conduct of the war.[31]

Conspiracism was central to Americanist thinking on civil rights matters as well. Buckley and other conservatives initially opposed federal civil rights initiatives on "states' rights" grounds, while wholesale racists opposed integration on the grounds of biological determinism. Before Goldwater's 1964 defeat, but escalating thereafter, the John Birch Society promoted a third view, that racial conflict and the civil rights movement were really one more part of the "conspiracy" to disrupt and weaken American society.[32] Beginning in 1965, Robert Welch directed Birch chapters to form hundreds of local Truth About Civil Turmoil or TACT committees. The TACT groups conducted the usual Birch Society meetings and letters-to-the-editor campaigns on the theme that the civil rights movement was all red.[33]

The "communist conspiracy" theory provided the initial framework for Birchists' interpretation of the civil rights movement. Corresponding to the decline of widespread domestic McCarthyism, Welch expanded the scope of the "conspiracy" to a generations-old plot by "Insiders" that employed all sorts of socialists and liberals, including even leading figures of the capitalist establishment. The expansion of Birchist conspiracism was a key factor in the coalition that developed between the Birch Society and the Liberty Lobby.

Activists from these two organizations came together around the 1968 Wallace campaign and the subsequent Americanist party efforts. Both organizations weathered the party infighting of the 1970s. But the Birch Society remained committed to educational tactics only, while the Lobby emphasized both publishing and grassroots legislative lobbying, and welcomed the collaboration of other organizations and elected officials.

In the 1980s, Liberty Lobbyists would earn reputations as promoters of holocaust revisionism[34] and for the electoral career of Klansman David Duke. During the late 1960s and 1970s, however, the Lobby focused, among other issues, on opposing United States–Soviet consular treaties, school busing to achieve racial integration, and income taxes. As with the Birch Society, the Lobby's agenda was consistent with right-wing support for militarism and traditionally unjust race relations, and opposition to the state's redistribution of wealth and expansion of civil rights.

As was the case of the conservative movement, Americanist ideology and activism developed in tandem. However, it was primarily ideological factors that separated Birch Society and Liberty Lobby Americanists from New Right conservatives. The two camps shared some policy objectives, but differed profoundly in their world views and tactics.

The Birch Society, more so than the Liberty Lobby, referred most consistently to its ideology as Americanism.[35] Liberty Lobby founder Willis Carto promoted the alternative term "populism," encompassing patriotism and conspiracism, plus the kind of racialism the Birch Society explicitly disavowed.[36]

Carto's use of the term "populism" was misleading because it attempted to link his racist right-wing movement to the progressive, left-leaning farmers' movement of the late nineteenth century. Such a misuse of the "populist" label was not new. During the 1950s and 1960s, anti-left academics like Seymour Martin Lipset and Daniel Bell promoted the view that right-wing McCarthyism enjoyed the same base of support as the earlier Populist movement. Political scientist Michael Rogin's 1967 book *The Intellectuals and McCarthy: The Radical Specter* refuted Lipset, Bell, and company's weakly documented portrayal of the early Populists as racist, anti-Semitic, nativist, and even fascist because they supported state intervention in the economy.[37] Nor, Rogin found, was Cold War-era McCarthyism a genuine fascist movement; it was relatively free of anti-Semitism, lacked an economic program, and did not challenge local elites.[38] Most of McCarthy's supporters were traditional conservative Republicans and elites.

But for Willis Carto, "populism" was a strategic concept, one that encompassed both the issues agenda of the Wallaceite movement and the mode of thinking that distinguished Americanists from their New Right counterparts. As we will see in Chapter 11, Carto would eventually found a racist right-wing Populist Party, which helped launch the electoral career of Klansman David Duke.

The Liberty Lobby's "populism" blended racism and anti-Semitism, anticommunism, and a conspiracist interpretation of history. Carto himself was an intellectual disciple of Francis Parker Yockey, the World War II era Nazi sympathizer who authored *Imperium*, the 1949 classic still popular in pro-fascist circles. *Imperium* is a tribute to Germany's Third Reich and a call to recreate its brand of authoritarian "socialism" and "cultural vitalism" as a defense against the "parasitic" nature of "culture distorting" Jews. Yockey did not promote race as a biological category but rather as the collective character of a society, similar to the Nazi concept of "volk." *Imperium* was a classic piece of anti-Jewish propaganda, linking Jews to banking, national indebtedness, and conspiracies behind racial conflict in American society. Yockey denounced U.S. collaboration with the Soviet Union against "Europe," a term he used interchangeably with the Nazis' wartime imperium.[39] Carto met Yockey shortly before the latter committed suicide while in jail on charges of passport fraud. Then in 1962, Carto wrote an introduction to a new edition of *Imperium* and distributed it through his own Noontide Press.[40] Yockey's influence was evident in the intensifying anti-Semitism in Carto's *Right* newsletter, published between 1955 and 1960, particularly in Carto's adoption of the term "culture-distorter" and his conflation of racism and anticommunism (see Chapter 3.)

A core group of Liberty Lobby organizers revered *Imperium* and similar works. But, for mass consumption, Carto distilled the precepts of his ideology under the "populist" label. Carto's most concise rendition of "populism" appeared in his introduction to a collection of articles reprinted from Liberty Lobby's weekly *Spotlight* newspaper in 1980. This *Profiles in Populism* series included admiring short biographies of Presidents Thomas Jefferson and Andrew Jackson, and Senator of the Progressive Party Robert LaFollette, as well as the anti-Semitic industrialist Henry Ford, radio preacher Charles Coughlin, America First leader Charles Lindbergh, and others. In the introduction to *Profiles*, Carto noted that "populism" was not restricted to agrarian society. More importantly, "populism" meant the following: political and economic nationalism over internationalism; opposition to "a global government secretly controlled by a financial elite"; "racial integrity," not integration; acceptance of "hereditary differences in intelligence and ability" between races or ethnic groups; anti-socialist "belief in private property" and "the inequality of human gifts"; and development of a "strong middle class through the free-enterprise system," distinct from "monopoly finance capitalism."[41]

The Liberty Lobby's "populist" tenets of nationalism, conspiracism, biological racism, and "free enterprise" anticommunism pervaded the organization's numerous publications from the 1960s to the 1990s. With the notable exception of biological racism, the "populist" credo appeared also in John Birch Society literature during the same period. As mentioned previously, the Birch Society disavowed biological determinism and, instead, interpreted racial conflict as part of a socially disruptive "communist" or "Insider" conspiracy. Both "Americanism" and "populism" were consistent with the definition of "right-wing" used in this book. Both the Liberty Lobby and the John Birch Society favored state action to *enforce* order and existing relations between classes and social groups, and opposed state action to *distribute* wealth and power more equitably.

Conspiracy thinking, more than anything else, was what separated Americanists from New Right conservatives. Historian Richard Hofstadter, in his treatment of the American right wing, had identified a "paranoid style." By "paranoid," Hofstadter did not mean to analyze the psychology of individual movement adherents, but rather to characterize a mode of thinking about history and current affairs. Within the narrow range of groups he included as part of the U.S. Right, Hofstadter reduced the essentials of right-wing thought to: a narrative on a sustained conspiracy to undermine capitalism, and the belief that top government agencies plus all the major civil institutions are thoroughly infiltrated by communists,[42] or, conceivably, any other designated enemy. According to Hofstadter, the peddlers of the "paranoid style" begin political analysis with some commonly known facts, but then they string these facts into implausible and illogical causal "explanations."[43] Conspiracism relies on the premise that power relations are vastly different than their surface appearance. Ever greater degrees of conspiracy and deception must then be invoked to "explain" events about which little tangible evidence exists. Because significant events and transactions often *are* revealed to be the work of secret, even deceptive, elites, the vast fields of government policy and finance are ripe for conspiracist interpretations.

During the 1960s, both New Right conservatives and Americanists opposed passage of a United States–Soviet consular treaty, as part of a step toward the reduction of Cold War hostilities. Yet conservatives and Americanists diverged in their interpretations of the causes and implications of the treaty's passage. What the Liberty Lobby called the "Soviet Spy Treaty" allowed for each country to maintain functioning embassies on the other's territory. *Human Events* opposed the treaty as an unwarranted capitulation to the Soviets, and the newspaper's columnists attributed passage to bipartisan compromise and Senate Minority Leader Everett Dirksen's disappointing collaboration with a Democratic president.[44] In contrast, the Liberty Lobby cast Dirksen as an exceptionally powerful conspirator, and argued that his "real motivation" was not a thaw in the Cold War, but

> a vast increase in trade with the Communist enemy, behind the backs of our American fighting men in Vietnam. . . . When it is seen that the East–West trade drive is led by the Wall Street interests which make up

the Eastern Establishment of the Republican Party, the performance of the Party in the Consular Treaty battle becomes a great deal clearer. American trade with the Soviet bloc will be controlled by the Rockefeller interests, in partnership with Cyrus Eaton, a multi-millionaire who is a close friend of top Soviet leaders, and a member of innumerable Communist fronts.[45]

Conservatives sought to deprive Rockefeller and his supporters of Republican Party dominance, and they conflicted with the "eastern establishment" on significant policy matters. Liberty Lobby outdid the conservatives by calling Nelson Rockefeller a witting "agent for the Soviet Union."[46]

Organizational Development

From the mid-1960s through the mid-1970s, the racist Right's Ku Klux Klan organizations suffered the most serious declines in their history. The "third-era" Klan of the 1950s and early 1960s continued to terrorize civil rights activists after passage of the 1964 Civil Rights Act. However, the FBI estimated a drop in Klan membership from a peak of 40,000 in 1965 to 14,000 in 1968. In the next two years, that number was reduced by about half, and by 1974, Klan membership was at an all time low of about 1,500.[47] The Klan's decline was attributed to the combined effects of FBI counterintelligence operations, House Un-American Activities Committee (HUAC) investigations of Klan leaders and the diversion of southern Klan resources to the Wallace presidential campaigns.[48] Beginning in the late 1970s, David Duke and others would revive Klan membership through electoral campaigns and a new and improved public image.

Several years before the Wallace campaigns catalyzed the Americanist movement, the Liberty Lobby established itself as a coordinator for the movement's legislative lobbying at the national level. Over time, the Liberty Lobby endured as the movement's leading umbrella organization. Despite its dubious record of success in achieving policy objectives, the Lobby used specific legislative issues and a series of associated front groups to inculcate supporters in Carto's brand of "populism" and to demonstrate clout on Capitol Hill.

By the early 1960s, Liberty Lobby's Washington, D.C. staff had issued positions against legislation for civil rights commissions, federal aid to education, and foreign aid, and in favor of bills to withdraw the United States from the United Nations and to abolish the Arms Control and Disarmament Agency.[49] The Lobby established working relations with a number of supportive Congress members, and organized groups of citizens to travel to Washington to demonstrate against the pending 1964 Civil Rights Act and to attend training sessions on pressure group tactics. At a 1963 School of Politics for 200 activists, the Liberty Lobby hosted a panel of Congress members it called the Government Educational Foundation.[50]

In 1964 Carto hired William B. Hicks, a former staff member of the conservative newsweekly *Human Events*, as the Lobby's executive director. During the Goldwater campaign, the Lobby distributed twenty million pieces of anti-Johnson literature.[51] In the process, circulation of the Lobby's monthly *Liberty Letter* soared from 26,000 copies in 1964 to more than 90,000 in 1965, and 174,000 in 1966. *Liberty Letter* enjoyed a wider circulation than any political publication, including *National Review* and *Human Events*, which each published about 95,000 copies in 1966.[52]

No doubt, the Liberty Lobby's constituency base overlapped with that of the conservative movement. The featured speaker for the Lobby's well attended 1965 National Defense Seminar was Phyllis Schlafly, then vice-president of the National Federation of Republican Women and a leading critic of nuclear disarmament.[53] In 1967, the Lobby organized grassroots opposition to the U.S. consular treaty with the Soviet Union discussed above.[54] The treaty was ratified by the Senate over the objections of both the elite and mass-based anticommunist movements. But the Lobby proceeded to rally an Americanist coalition of activists and sympathetic members of Congress. In 1967, the Lobby expanded its Board of Policy to include hundreds of delegates who would, thereafter, meet annually to chart the Lobby's legislative agenda for the year ahead.[55] By 1971, the Lobby maintained a staff of forty and an annual budget of about one million dollars.[56]

Despite its small size relative to the growing New Right, Americanism appeared to deviate little from the mainstream conservative movement. Beneath the surface, however, a core of Liberty Lobby personnel pursued a different agenda.

During the early 1970s, the Liberty Lobby survived a spate of negative press on the prominence of Nazi sympathizers in its ranks. In 1969, Willis Carto renamed his Youth for Wallace front group as the National Youth Alliance (NYA), and made an unsuccessful attempt to form a pro-Nazi campus organization.[57] The leadership of NYA included Liberty Lobby and Birch Society veterans who were enamored of Third Reich rhetoric and paraphernalia.[58] During its short existence under Carto's tutelage, NYA's major activity was the promotion of Francis Parker Yockey's *Imperium* and an article by NYA leader Revilo P. Oliver, whose public espousal of anti-Semitism had forced him to resign from leadership of the John Birch Society.[59] Concurrent with the post-1968 conflicts inside the American Independent Party, NYA broke into several ineffective feuding factions, each accusing the other of harboring extremists.[60]

The presence of Nazi admirers among the Liberty Lobby's leadership was not novel. George Wallace had included Klansmen and Nazis in the top levels of his presidential campaign. Significantly, though, the use of a small front group to promote the most disreputable piece of "populist" ideology allowed the Liberty Lobby to survive damaging publicity about the National Youth Alliance. Rank-and-file Lobby activists could plausibly deny any sympathies for the extra-curricular activities of a small group of leaders. Outright neo-Nazi influence continued, but was diluted within the Lobby's broader public policy agenda and constituency.

Following Israel's 1967 "Six Day War" (and subsequent occupation of the West Bank and Gaza Strip), the Liberty Lobby's fixation on Israeli "control" over U.S. foreign policymaking obscured the distinction between anti-Zionism and bigotry toward Jews. During the 1970s, the conflation of "Zionist" opportunism and actual Jewish history became a central element in affiliates of the Liberty Lobby's promotion of "holocaust revisionism." Revisionists claimed "Zionists" lied about the extent of Nazi atrocities as part of a political conspiracy.[61]

Aside from conspiratorial interpretations of Middle Eastern affairs, three issues dominated the Liberty Lobby's agenda during the late 1960s and early 1970s: opposing international pressure against Rhodesia, domestic tax reform, and opposing compulsory public school busing to achieve racial integration. All fit under the "populist" rubric of nationalism, "racial integrity," and protection of middle-class interests. Of these three policy issues, Liberty Lobby's support for Rhodesia's white minority government emerged earliest and coincided most with the Cold War perspectives of anticommunist conservatives.[62] The Liberty Lobby spinoff Friends of Rhodesian Independence placed newspaper advertisements opposing international sanctions against Rhodesia and took U.S. activists on tours to southern Africa where they met with Rhodesian and South African officials.[63]

At the same time, the Liberty Lobby promoted its "tax equity" program and lobbied Congress for a reduction of the tax burden on the middle class. The Lobby's 1970 Board of Policy conference, held in Los Angeles, featured a Tax Rebellion Rally that drew 1,000 participants, including many leaders of tax protest groups. (Among them was Howard Jarvis, who would later draft California's 1978 Proposition 13 tax revolt initiative.) More than any other event or issue sponsored by the Liberty Lobby, the Tax Rebellion Rally attracted congratulatory telegrams from a long list of Congressional Representatives.[64]

Busing was an issue that spawned a full-fledged opposition move-ment, most of which was not formally connected to the organized racist Right. Boston was the site of pitched battles between anti-busing parents and authorities intent on integrating public schools.[65] The Liberty Lobby tried, unsuccessfully, to exert leadership over a far-flung network of parents' groups in Boston and elsewhere. Under the banners of Save Our Schools and Action Now, the Liberty Lobby started a network of affiliates aimed at coordinating grassroots lobbying for a "school choice" bill introduced by Boston's anti-busing Representative Louise Day Hicks (D-MA) and for a constitutional amendment prohibiting school busing orders by local jurisdictions.[66] In 1972, the Liberty Lobby claimed its production of a television spot contributed to California voters' approval, by a two-to-one margin, of a referendum against public school busing.[67] But the Lobby never reported the role of anti-busing efforts in any major expansion for the racist Right. In fact, public opinion against busing did not correlate neatly with racial prejudice in the general population.[68]

On all issue priorities, Americanists, unlike conservatives, acted largely outside of major party politics and never gained influence with more than a handful of elected officials. In 1973, the Liberty Lobby began a daily radio series broadcast on more than one hundred sta-tions.[69] At the same time, the Lobby appeared to have retreated from pressure politics when its Board of Policy convention took the form of a Survival Seminar. Speakers included Robert DePugh of the paramilitary Minutemen, tax protest leaders, and a gun expert from the National Association to Keep and Bear Arms. The 750 "patriots" in attendance were instructed on food storage, amateur radio, and other means to survive a "national catastrophe."[70] Americanism had retreated into survivalism.

Faced with unlikely success in legislative and electoral politics, the Americanists' countercultural tendencies gained increased salience. In the fluctuating peaks and valleys of a movement's development over time, maintenance of some minimal degree of activity enhances the prospects for future mobilization. To the extent that the Americanists remained active, even on a basis more ideological than partisan, that activity made possible the movement's resurgence during the late 1970s and early 1980s.

NEW RIGHT NEMESES

With limited resources and a political context not conducive to the kind of expanded mobilization the conservative New Right underwent in the 1970s, the Americanist movement nevertheless developed along two tracks. The Liberty Lobby directed its efforts toward legislative lobbying. At another level, the 1970s saw the emergence of numerous decentralized, grassroots organizations mobilized against taxes and within the framework of a religious mandate known as Identity Christianity.[71] Identity Christians formed the base of the Posse Comitatus and other paramilitary racist Right groups of the 1970s and 1980s. An outgrowth of the racist and anticommunist Right, this movement of self-described "Christian patriots" developed into a diverse and loose array of conspiracy-minded tax protesters, survivalists, and religiously motivated racists.[72] Most Christian patriots deviated strongly from New Right conservatives in ideology, strategy, and tactics.

While conservatives followed a course of resurgent militarism and nascent commitment to the traditional morality agenda of evangelical Christians, Americanists also endorsed the agenda of the anticommunist movement and the Christian Right. In its newspaper, the Liberty Lobby praised anti-gay rights activism, from Anita Bryant's vocal efforts in Florida to California's failed 1978 "Briggs initiative" that would have purged public schools of openly homosexual teachers.[73]

On the major international affairs issues of the 1970s, Americanists shared goals with conservatives but deviated in interpretation and tactics. Whereas conservatives opposed the United States' restoration of Panamanian sovereignty over the canal zone as a capitulation to the supposedly pro-communist Omar Torrijos, the Liberty Lobby reported the treaty process as a conspiracy by Carter administration-linked elites to gain financially from lax Panamanian business regulations.[74] While conservatives opposed the administration's compliance with international sanctions against Rhodesia, the Liberty Lobby gave enthusiastic publicity to some 400 U.S. mercenaries who waged war on black Zimbabweans, and eulogized one who died fighting for white minority rule in southern Africa.[75]

In the realm of foreign affairs, the racist Right and the conservative movement converged in one important organization, the World Anti-Communist League (WACL). WACL was founded in 1966 as an expansion of the Asian People's Anti-Communist League (APACL), a propaganda arm of the governments of Taiwan, South Korea, South Vietnam, and the Philippines. (APACL coordinated activities with United States China Lobby activists.) As we discuss in Chapter 9, during the 1980s WACL helped coordinate the Reagan–Bush administration's covert supply operations for the Nicaraguan Contras. WACL was organized into national affiliates, consisting of a WACL-approved representative organization from each participating country or region. Eastern Europe was represented by the Anti-Bolshevik Bloc of Nations, a consortium that included veterans of the Nazi-era collaborationist governments. Western

European chapters included the fascist Italian Social Movement (MSI) party. Dominating WACL's Latin American chapters were ultra-Catholic and anti-Semitic groups, and leaders of military death squads.[76]

Three organizations served successively as the U.S. representative of WACL, while an ongoing controversy brewed over WACL's pro-Nazi contingents.[77] In the early 1970s, the American Council for World Freedom (ACWF) ignored the British chapter's warnings about neo-Nazi influence in WACL. But conflict with the Latin American chapters led to ACWF's resignation and replacement by Roger Pearson's Council on the Americas.[78] Pearson was a British-born anthropologist with long ties to European neo-Nazi intellectuals and to New Right groups in the 1970s.[79] Willis Carto had taken an early interest in Pearson's writings and had recruited him to edit the Liberty Lobby's journal *Western Destiny*.[80] While Pearson was active with the conservative movement, he also used his position in WACL to recruit former German SS officers, Italian terrorists, and assorted European fascists into WACL. By 1978, when Pearson and the Liberty Lobby hosted WACL's annual conference in Washington, D.C., the organization was so thoroughly dominated by neo-Nazis and their admirers that the John Birch Society chose to make itself conspicuously absent.[81]

The collaboration of the Liberty Lobby personnel with neo-Nazi activists in WACL coincided with the Lobby's accelerated excursion into holocaust revisionism. In 1979, Carto founded the Institute for Historical Review (IHR)[82] for the purpose of propagating pseudoscholarly pronouncements on the "myth" of the Nazi holocaust. In a crude publicity stunt, the Institute offered $50,000 to any Holocaust survivor who could "prove" the Nazis' use of gas chambers.[83]

Through IHR and WACL, pro-Nazi the Liberty Lobby affiliates sought to influence media and policymakers. At the level of a grassroots constituency, the Lobby promoted the rejuvenated Ku Klux Klan led by David Duke. Among Klan leaders, Duke was particularly committed to spreading Nazi race doctrine.[84] An early issue of the *Spotlight* newspaper featured a cover story on Duke's unabashed Klan organizing and his first race for a Louisiana State Senate seat.[85] Subsequent *Spotlight* reporting promoted Duke's San Diego area "border watch" harassment of undocumented Mexican immigrants[86] and the electoral campaigns of Klan Grand Dragon Tom Metzger.[87]

While the Americanist movement of the late 1970s operated mostly outside electoral politics, an important exception was the "populist" tax revolt. In 1978, Howard Jarvis and Paul Gann succeeded in achieving passage of California's Proposition 13, which drained state budget coffers by reducing and restricting property taxes.[88] The Americanist movement was a minuscule part of the tax revolt's broad constituency.

But on the heels of Proposition 13, a network of groups of grassroots taxpayers mobilized in support of an ephemeral Congressional bill to gut federal income taxes. This effort was led by Willis Stone's Liberty Amendment Committee, a relic of the 1950s anticommunist movement, along with the Liberty Lobby and leaders of the racist Right's paramilitary wing.[89] Republican strategist Kevin Phillips, in his book *Post-Conservative America*, explained the failure of the proposals to cut income taxes. While property taxes are understood as a regressive burden on middle- and lower-middle-class people whose sole asset is their home, income tax reductions tend to disproportionately benefit upper income taxpayers,[90] who did not have a broad grassroots base.

Tax protest remained, however, a central issue for the Posse Comitatus and affiliated Identity churches. This underground, and often violent, wing of the racist Right is treated in greater depth in Chapter 11. But the 1970s were the formative years for the paramilitary Aryan Nations groups of the 1980s.

Identity Christianity is an arcane racist doctrine that came to attract much of the white supremacist movement by the 1980s. Identity's roots lie in British Israelism, a set of nineteenth-century teachings on the purported settlement of the Old Testament's "ten lost tribes" in the Nordic and Anglo-Saxon regions. Identity preachers in the United States extended this belief to claim, in various versions, that the white, European conquerors of North America are God's true "chosen people," that Jews are Satan's offspring and that people of color are a subhuman species. Identity rooted biological determinism in the folklore of the Old Testament and "manifest destiny." It was popularized in the 1940s by two racist preachers, Bertram Comparet and Wesley Swift, a Klansman. One of Swift's earliest followers was William Potter Gale, who recruited a following in central California. Another of Swift's disciples was Richard Butler, who started the Aryan Nations compound in Idaho in the 1970s.[91]

The Identity religious-racial dogma developed in tandem with a set of political views derived from the "posse comitatus" notion that the county is the only legitimate seat of government power. Essential to the Posse Comitatus' doctrine is the claim that the federal government has, over many decades, committed treason by enforcing the income tax amendment to the Constitution and by allowing a private Federal Reserve Board to manipulate interest rates to the advantage of Jewish conspirators.[92]

William Potter Gale in California and Mike Beach in Oregon formed the earliest branches of the Posse Comitatus during the late 1960s. Thereafter, autonomous chapters spread like fire across the Midwest and parts of the northwest. By 1976, Posse membership was estimated at 12,000 to 50,000, with perhaps ten to twelve times that number of non-member supporters.[93] What made both Posse Comitatus and Identity church participation so difficult to quantify and monitor was the groups' thoroughly decentralized, secretive, and transient nature. The movement's general lack of coordinated organization allowed each preacher and tax protest leader to pick and choose which tenets and tactics to emphasize. Consistently, however, Identity–Posse groups focused on informal newsletter and tape distribution, weapons training, and illegal means of tax evasion. The latter brought tax protesters into trouble with state and federal agencies. A small number of "patriots" joined the Aryan Nations' violent underground and committed dramatic acts of anti-government violence during the 1980s.

THE DECLINE OF THE AMERICANIST MOVEMENT

In opposition to the confirmation of Nelson Rockefeller as vice-president, a broad but not exhaustive set of American Party, Posse Comitatus, Identity Church, Ku Klux Klan, and John Birch Society chapter leaders circulated a joint petition to Congress in which they claimed their organizations represented 700,000 registered voters.[94] In 1975, Klan leaders David Duke and Tom Metzger jointly organized a conference with Identity preachers in southern California.[95] But, for the most part, these groups were unable to collaborate effectively toward the achievement of policy goals. They had been unsuccessful in sustaining a serious third-party effort after 1968. Yet they conceived of themselves as a collective entity, a movement that opposed not only the administration in power but also the more respectable New Right conservatives.

To the extent that the Americanist movement remained unified and active, shared ideology was the reason. Identity belief alone might have yielded another of many separatist, subcultural strains of fundamentalist Christianity. But tax protest was inherently a form of oppositional activism toward the state. The Posse Comitatus and the numerous like-minded tax protest groups of the 1970s and 1980s developed elaborate explanations as to why the government had no business collecting taxes. On the surface, the "patriots'" thorough alienation from and hostility toward the U.S. political system lent an appearance of "radicalism" greater than that of the New Right. "Patriots" hated the state in all its roles and manifestations, while conservatives maintained a classically mixed right-wing stance toward the state and were willing to make compromises with centrist Republicans. By their eagerness to collaborate with political and economic elites, conservatives, though seemingly less "radical," had a real chance to influence state policymaking. The Americanist movement, particularly its most militant Christian patriot sector, was ideologically anti-elite to an extent that precluded collaboration with agents of the state. In terms of an achievable agenda, the New Right conservatives outranked the likes of the Liberty Lobby and the Posse Comitatus. Rather than seeking political engagement with opponents, the Americanist movement moved further toward arcane and conspiracist forms of racist ideology combined with tactics of lawbreaking and violence. At a time of increasing political efficacy for the conservative movement, the divergent strategy of the Americanists set severe limits on the racist Right's course during its subsequent period of development.

CHAPTER 7

◆ ◆ ◆

Casting the First Stones

THE EARLY MOBILIZATION
OF THE CHRISTIAN RIGHT

In the first part of this book we saw that the early evangelical movement was not yet linked to state institutions and policymaking processes. During the Cold War era evangelicals focused on securing their access to the broadcast airwaves. During its next phase of development, in the 1970s, the evangelical movement experienced phenomenal growth and began to impact the political landscape. The political awakening of evangelicals came about in response to profound social changes, especially around issues of women's equality, reproductive choice, and homosexual civil rights. An emergent Christian Right forged a symbiotic relationship with the nominally secular conservative movement, whose leaders were then working to become a major faction of the Republican Party.

The major social issues of the 1970s caused right-wing evangelicals to feel threatened about their ability to promote the supremacy of the traditional nuclear family. Women's equality, abortion, and gay rights were all issues that crossed lines of economic class, and even race. Even on these issues (pertaining to moral beliefs and preferences) early Christian Right activism was not solely motivated by collective obedience to religious strictures. Also at stake was the drive of evangelical activists to exert their democratic rights to participate in the political process and to assume some measure of political power. These highly charged social issues all involved questions of welfare state spending, law enforcement and business regulation in discrimination cases.

These questions came to the fore as evangelicals continued to build a politically relevant resource base. Along with continued growth in the religious broadcasting industry was a growth in evangelical churches.

161

The late 1960s to the mid-1970s were years when thousands of young people became born-again "Jesus freaks." Mainline denominations saw their numbers drop, while theologically conservative churches grew. These churches would become the organizational bastions for the Christian Right's political mobilization. Astute leaders of the New Right understood the political utility of evangelical churches and Christian broadcasting networks.

A coalition between the older conservative movement and the newly aroused Christian Right was natural. The secular New Right represented a new phase in fusionism's blend of anticommunist militarism, moral traditionalism, and economic libertarianism. As moral issues rose to the top of the national agenda, and because evangelicals constituted a large segment of the population, it was no wonder that New Right leaders sought to foster the new Christian Right. Under the wing of politically experienced conservatives, newly active evangelicals formed their own electoral vehicles and joined the drive to send Ronald Reagan to the White House. Chapter 9 deals with the coalition of conservatives and evangelicals active in the 1980s. This chapter helps set the stage.

THE GROWTH OF THE EVANGELICAL MOVEMENT

Social movement theorists use the term resources to include a wide variety of movement assets.[1] Movement participants themselves are a resource, not only because large numbers mean influence, but because pre-existing organizations facilitate quick and efficient mobilization. Black churches, for example, were a key resource for the civil rights movement. Churches help develop communication and educational networks that are neither dependent on the mainstream media nor the public school system. Churches nurture two tiers of active participants: pastoral leaders with particular skills in writing and speaking, who can arrange events and insure completion of tasks, and large numbers of reliable, committed parishioners, who are skilled in tasks such as canvassing and small-scale fundraising.

Before the onset of the Christian Right proper, religious broadcasting networks constituted evangelicals' most significant resource. Following the Federal Communications Commission's 1960 ruling that encouraged networks to sell air time to religious broadcasters, programming came to be controlled by evangelical and fundamentalist "parachurch" organizations.[2] Unlike the mainline churches, these ministries could afford to spend their large budgets on equipment and air time; they were unfettered by denominational bureaucracies and the daily necessities of running a church.[3] Between 1967 and 1972, membership in the National

Religious Broadcasters quadrupled. While evangelical broadcasters purchased air time on network affiliate stations, they also began to accumulate fully owned and operated stations of their own.[4] Reverend Pat
Robertson started the trend in 1960 when his Virginia television station
became the first station licensed to air religious programming more than
50 percent of the time.[5] Robertson's stations were also the first to raise
money through telethons. By 1979, Robertson's Christian Broadcasting
Network grew to be a $50-million-a-year operation, with a national
audience of five million for the syndicated "700 Club" talk show.[6]

For a long time, church leaders worried that church attendance
would decline with the increase in the viewing of religious television.
Several reputable studies dispelled that fear, but debate persisted
throughout the 1980s over the actual size of religious television audiences.[7] Conflicting figures reflected the politically charged nature of the
debate. In 1980, Jerry Falwell claimed an unbelievable audience of fifty
million viewers for his television program alone.[8] The most reliable
studies of religious television viewing yielded estimates of about thirteen
million regular viewers during the 1980s.[9] Viewers of religious broadcasts were found to be somewhat older, disproportionately female, lower
than average in education and income, more rural and conservative than
the general population, and more likely to attend and donate to local
churches.[10]

The growth of the religious broadcasting industry coincided with
the growth of theologically conservative churches and the emergence of
evangelical Christianity as a significant cultural phenomenon. A series
of Gallup polls between 1976 and 1979 found, variably, that one-third to
one-fifth of the U.S. adult population reported having experienced a
"born again" conversion. In 1976, the year marking the bicentennial
anniversary of the United States, and the campaign of (Baptist) President
Jimmy Carter, evangelicals enjoyed favorable treatment by the mass
media. Gallup's findings prompted pundits to name 1976 the "year of
the evangelical."[11] In his surveys, George Gallup, Jr. (himself an evangelical Episcopalian), defined an "evangelical" as a person who "has had a
born again conversion, accepts Jesus as his or her personal Savior,
believes the Scriptures are the authority for all doctrine, and feels an
urgent duty to spread the faith."[12] The typical evangelical was found to
be a middle-aged white female southerner with a modest income and
only a high school education.[13] Gallup's 1979 survey, commissioned by
the evangelical *Christianity Today* magazine, found that African Americans, who comprise about 10 percent of the general population, represented 15 percent of all evangelicals. Among all evangelicals, 92 percent
were church members, 82 percent attended church weekly, and over a
third attended church twice or more per week.[14] Heavy church atten-

dance meant that evangelicals were in a sense pre-organized and available for mobilization around whichever projects and issues became salient.

Gallup's data indicated general widespread popularity for evangelicalism. But the 50 million adults who identified themselves as "born-again" were by no means all interested in politics. Nor were they uniform theologically. They tended to fall into three categories: fundamentalists, charismatics, and neo-evangelicals.[15] Each developed its own set of parachurch organizations and theological emphases, most of which is beyond the scope of this study.

Gallup's data, however, were consistent with the general religious trend of the 1960s and 1970s, the decline of the mainline denominational churches and the growth of non-ecumenical, theologically conservative churches.[16] In *Why Conservative Churches Are Growing*, National Council of Churches official Dean Kelley argued that thriving churches were not necessarily those that were "tolerant, reasonable, and relevant." Instead, churches prospered when they accomplished the "essential function of religion," which Kelley defined as "making life meaningful in ultimate terms." Strict churches that imposed discipline and demanded commitment performed this function best. Kelley concluded that ecumenical churches were losing members not because they addressed social welfare issues but because they did so while neglecting to emphasize worship, religious instruction, and proselytization.[17] Strict churches were also found to be those best able to retain existing members and members' children.[18] Yet the most politically oriented evangelical churches were also those that emphasized winning new disciples.

The evangelicals had fervent foreign missions, but Billy Graham was the first contemporary evangelical to plow the domestic mission field. While the National Association of Evangelicals cultivated established evangelical churches, Bill Bright's Campus Crusade for Christ later focused on college recruitment. The late 1960s and early 1970s saw an expansion in the number of independent ministries aimed at proselytizing youth. Part of the hippie counter-culture joined the "Jesus movement," and some joined forces with a group of older Pentecostal "shepherds" who sought to guide the new converts. Out of the "Jesus movement" milieu emerged a strict, even dictatorial, organizational style, known as "shepherding." Leaders of the "shepherding" sub-movement emphasized charismatic practices such as faith healing and glossolalia, or speaking in tongues. Abuse of power by some of the shepherds made them controversial among fellow evangelicals. Nevertheless, the shepherds became central activists within the Christian Right of the 1980s.[19]

One of the assets the shepherds brought to Christian Right political coalitions was their ties with leaders of the Catholic charismatic renewal movement. The Catholic Church's second Vatican Council during the

1960s encouraged new forms of worship and greater participation of the laity. Beginning in the 1960s, a growing number of Catholics began to engage in charismatic practices previously seen only among Protestant pentecostals. Some Catholic charismatics formed communes and pastoral ties to the Protestant shepherding movement.[20] During the 1980s, the Catholic shepherds were active within the broader Christian Right, particularly in the movement's projects in Central America.[21]

Though they represented a broad segment of the U.S. population during the 1970s, evangelicals did not yet constitute a true political movement. But to the extent that evangelicalism was cohesive ideologically and organizationally, it was a real and latent political force not to be dismissed. Evangelicals controlled more non-mainstream media resources than any other sector of society. By the 1970s, the content of some religious broadcasting was already political in nature.[22]

FAMILY ISSUES AND STATE POLICYMAKING

Conceivably, the evangelical movement could have continued to expand its resource base but remain politically uninvolved were it not for two factors that contributed to the Christian Right's political mobilization: (1) actual and proposed policy changes at the level of state policymaking and (2) tactical assistance and encouragement from the secular New Right.

Political scientist Rosalind Pollack Petchesky argued that what gave both the secular and religious New Right its "ideological legitimacy and organizational coherence" was "its focus on reproductive and sexual issues."

> If there was anything genuinely 'new' about the current right wing in the United States, it is its tendency to locate sexual, reproductive, and family issues at the center of its political program—not as manipulative rhetoric only, but as the substantive core of a politics geared, on a level that outdistances any previous right-wing movements in this country, to mobilizing a nationwide mass following.[23]

Both the economic trends and the international relations of the 1970s were outside the control of average people. It was in the realm of reproductive and family policy where issues could resonate both at the most personal, even visceral, level of gender relations, and, on questions of state power and constitutionality, at the level of Congress and the Supreme Court.

Three issues of the 1970s reflected the influence on state policy makers of the New Left's (broadly defined) counter-movement: the Equal Rights Amendment (ERA), legally sanctioned abortion, and gay rights initiatives. All three carried enormous symbolic weight. They represented no mere changes in legal code. Each in its own right, and as part of a package, raised questions about proper roles and responsibilities for women and men, parents and children. Beyond these sex-related issues, concerns about textbooks, curriculum, and school prayer, though not particularly related to the Left's counter-movement successes, also became central.

All of the issues that aroused evangelicals also raised questions about the state's role in regulating society. Consistent with right-wing ideology, "moral majority"-type activists opposed policies that would expand or *distribute* power to subordinate groups, namely women and homosexuals, and supported state *enforcement* of "traditional" or "moral" gender relations and personal behavior. Educational concerns revolved around perceived government intrusion into the realm of the sacred (nuclear) family and its ideological and biological prerogatives, which should be upheld over those of the state.

As an alliance, the New Right and Christian Right responded to the women's and gay rights movements not in abstraction, but rather in terms of concrete policies they proposed should be enacted in state and federal government agencies. Concrete issue campaigns brought New Right and Christian Right forces together, with mixed results in policy achievement, but to mutual advantage for the increasing influence of the movements in partisan politics. It was precisely around the issues of ERA, gay rights, localized school concerns, and, especially, abortion, that the early Christian Right became a partisan movement. During the 1970s, Christian Right activists had yet to become the kind of skilled Republican Party players they would become in the 1980s and 1990s. Instead, the pattern of early Christian Right activism was one of support for action initiated by right-wing elected officials, experienced conservative movement leaders and, on the abortion front, the Catholic church. Later, Christian Right strategists would form autonomous organizations of an explicitly political nature. The following discussion summarizes the interactive process by which mobilization of the Christian Right was inspired by key policy controversies of the 1970s and facilitated by conservative movement professionals.

The Threat to the Traditional Family

After several years of strong lobbying by the women's movement, the Senate overwhelmingly passed the Equal Rights Amendment in March 1972.[24] President Richard Nixon supported the drive to add a constitutional amendment guaranteeing equal legal protection for female citizens. Ratification by a majority of state legislatures was then necessary for the ERA to be added to the constitution. Thirty out of the necessary thirty-eight states ratified ERA by early 1973.[25]

But ERA advocates could not have predicted the battles that would eventually result in the amendment's defeat. Despite popular support for ERA,[26] state legislators took seriously the arguments and pressure from Phyllis Schlafly's Stop ERA organization. A year after Congress approved ERA, Schlafly had created a national network to oppose ratification state by state. During the Congressional debate on ERA, Senator Sam Ervin (R-NC) had emerged as a leading national opponent. Once ERA was passed, Ervin and Schlafly joined forces. Schlafly gave Ervin the addresses for pivotal state legislators and mailing lists for her own monthly newsletter (initially devoted to the anticommunist cause but after 1972 focused almost exclusively on ERA). Ervin gave Schlafly his Congressional franking privilege for mailing anti-ERA literature packets. His Senate office became a national clearinghouse for ERA opposition,[27] around the same time that he also chaired the Senate's investigative committee on the Watergate scandal.

Schlafly's nearly single-handed leadership of the Right's anti-ERA project established a tactical pattern for New Right activism. In 1975, Schlafly changed the name of Stop ERA to the Eagle Forum. She continued to direct her claimed membership of 50,000 to single-issue lobbying,[28] but she also coordinated with leaders of related campaigns. She enlisted direct mail entrepreneur Richard Viguerie for mass mailings in states where ERA ratification was contested, and in Florida she joined popular anti-gay activist Anita Bryant for a rally at which Schlafly, Bryant, and Senator Sam Ervin implored 1,500 anti-ratificationists to pledge electoral defeat for any pro-ERA legislators.[29] From her home in Illinois, Schlafly supervised aides monitoring each of that state's fifty-nine legislative districts.[30] Schlafly and associates did not represent a majority of mass public opinion, but their diligent pressure caught the feminist countermovement unprepared for the competition.

The ERA issue brought the new Christian Right into a tactical alliance with officials of the Mormon church. Evangelicals were then, and continued to be, unalterably opposed to the Mormon religion, viewing it as an heretical cult. Since its founding in the nineteenth century, the Church of Latter-Day Saints (LDS) had been, generally, a separatist movement. Early Mormons came into conflict with the federal government over the practice of polygamy, which the church eventually abandoned. Mormons were concentrated in Utah and other western states where church officials were not infrequently aligned with Mormon politicians.

The 1980 election of two right-wing Senators from Utah, Jake Garn and Orrin Hatch, and Idaho Representative George Hansen, exemplified the Mormon connection to right-wing politics. Years earlier, many Mormons had been active in the John Birch Society. LDS Apostle, and later Prophet, Ezra Taft Benson was a fixture in the Society. W. Cleon Skousen, a former Salt Lake City chief of police and a former agent of the FBI, authored *The Naked Communist*, which became a classic in Birchist circles. In 1971 Skousen opened the Freemen Institute, a Mormon-staffed political think tank that worked closely with the Birch Society through the latter's affiliated Western Goals Foundation. Headed by U.S. Representative and John Birch Society national chair Larry McDonald, Western Goals was publicly exposed in the 1980s as an illegal intelligence gathering operation.[31]

Mormon opposition to ERA was not so cut and dried. By the time LDS hierarchy began speaking out against ERA, most of the required number of state legislatures had already ratified it. In fact, Mormons in the legislatures of Utah and Nevada supported ratification before the church formally opposed it. Many Mormon legislators reversed their positions, which made LDS opposition seem all the more inappropriate.[32] It was not until late in the game, October of 1976, that the Mormon hierarchy issued its first formal anti-ERA statement.[33] Thereafter, despite the pro-ERA sentiments of many devout Mormons, the church used phone trees and other grassroots lobbying tactics to defeat ERA in several swing states. Mormons were a minority outside of Utah, yet they achieved disproportionate influence in defeating ERA in Nevada, Florida, Virginia, Georgia, and possibly Illinois and Missouri.[34]

The end result was that ERA ratification fell three states short of the thirty-eight required to amend the Constitution. The ERA struggle had been central in many elections of feminists to political office, as well as in the achievement of legislative reforms in the areas of marital property rights and job discrimination.[35] The fight against ERA was also a boon to the budding coalition between the New Right and the Christian Right.

From Congressional passage in 1972, to the ratification deadline in 1982, the ERA battle was the first issue to attract large numbers of right-wing *women* activists. A study of Texas anti-ERA activists found that many were women who were classically right-wing in their belief in a domestic "communist conspiracy," their fear of an expanding "big government," and their strong commitment to traditional religion. Consistent with other studies of right-wing activists, these women were well educated, middle to upper middle class and active in electoral politics.[36]

The most compelling arguments of ERA opponents was that full legal equality would require women's conscription into the military in potential combat situations. Feminists underestimated the negative symbolism of the women-in-foxholes theme.[37] More than one analyst highlighted the strident claims of ERA opponents about its proponents' intent to legislate unisex public restrooms. This rhetorical device raised the old segregationists' fear of integrated restrooms to even more fearful heights.[38]

Schlafly herself concentrated on legal and economic themes. Reminiscent of the old "states' rights" arguments against public school integration, Schlafly labeled ERA a "gigantic grab for power" by a federal government out to destroy the power of state legislatures to make laws on divorce, child custody, inheritance, welfare, and labor.[39] Her earliest, and most compelling, arguments revolved around ERA's threat to the economic security of (married) women. In her first newsletter against ERA, prior to its passage in Congress, Schlafly emphasized the draft issue and claimed the ERA would "abolish a woman's right to child support and alimony."

> Under present American laws, the man is always required to support his wife and each child he caused to be brought into the world. Why should women abandon these good laws—by trading them for something so nebulous and uncertain as the "discretion of the Court"?
>
> Passage of the Equal Rights Amendment would . . . deprive the American woman of many of the fundamental special privileges we now enjoy, and especially the greatest rights of all: (1) NOT to take a job, (2) to keep her baby, and (3) to be supported by her husband.[4]

Social critic Barbara Ehrenreich interpreted the intensity of the drive to defend these "special privileges" and "greatest rights" as a battle over "the legitimacy of women's claim on men's incomes," particularly at a time of rising divorce rates.[41]

Organized labor overcame its initial opposition to ERA, but Schlafly, herself an upper-middle-class attorney, claimed to represent working-class women's "right to reject heavy and dangerous work without penalty." Consistent with the New Right's anti-elitist appeals, Schlafly portrayed her opponents as enemies of the downtrodden: "It comes with exceedingly poor grace for a woman who sits at a comfortable desk to demand legislation which will deprive a woman who stands on her feet all day of the right to have a chair."[42]

Schlafly's contribution to the New Right was to help broaden its cross-class appeal, a move that was consistent with the call by New Right thinkers Kevin Phillips and William Rusher to forge a "new majority" party faction. Middle-class women performed the day-to-day activist tasks that defeated ERA. But Schlafly's ideological appeal was directed downward, and revolved around themes that were of most vital interest to working-class women.

As the anti-ratification campaign proceeded, Schlafly also advanced arguments of particular appeal to religious traditionalists. She claimed ERA would grant legal sanction to "homosexual marriages" and make it impossible for the Supreme Court to reverse its 1973 *Roe v. Wade* decision protecting legal abortion on privacy grounds.[43] Schlafly would eventually devote her greatest attention to the abortion issue. (In 1992, she led the Christian Right's successful effort to strengthen the Republican Party's anti-abortion platform plank.)

Initially, however, it was the National Conference of Catholic bishops that mobilized the anti-abortion sub-movement.[44] Outside the church, the anti-abortion movement started with the National Right to Life Committee (NRLC) founded by Catholics around the time of the *Roe v. Wade* decision. Protestant evangelicals joined "right-to-life" activism several years after their Catholic counterparts.[45] Weeks after the *Roe* ruling, Senator James Buckley (brother of *National Review*'s William F. Buckley) introduced the first constitutional amendment to outlaw abortion.[46] Among the earliest of the New Right-sponsored political action committees were the National Pro-Life Political Action Committee (NPL-PAC) and the Life Amendment Political Action Committee (LAPAC). The PACs came into conflict with the National Right to Life Committee over tactics and principles. All three organizations backed a constitutional amendment to ban abortion. But NRLC was willing to allow an exception for abortions to save the life of a mother, and the PACs opposed any such exceptions. LAPAC, under the leadership of Paul and Judie Brown, sought to build multi-issue coalitions with other New Right groups; NRLC would not broaden its agenda beyond abortion. The PACs were legally authorized to take direct political action; in 1978, they claimed credit for the electoral victories of New Right Senators Roger Jepsen and Gordon Humphrey over liberal Democratic incumbent Senators Dick Clark of Iowa and Thomas McIntyre of New Hampshire.[47]

Rivalry between the PACs and the NRLC led Paul and Judie Brown to forge closer ties with the multi-issue conservative movement of the mid-1970s. New Right strategist Paul Weyrich recruited the Browns to attend weekly meetings of his Coalitions for America network of 120 right-wing organizations. Eventually, Weyrich established an office for the Browns in the headquarters of his Committee for the Survival of a Free Congress, and the Browns changed their Life Amendment PAC to the American Life Lobby. With advice from Weyrich, and the computer mailing services of Richard Viguerie, by 1981, Judie Brown claimed 68,000 subscribers to her *ALL* newsletter and had established working liaisons with 4,000 groups nationwide.[48]

It was Weyrich who suggested that anti-abortionists shift their name from "pro-life" to "pro-family." Weyrich studied feminist pro-choice literature and realized that its arguments for federally funded abortions and child care raised the larger questions of the state's role in family matters across the board.[49] Richard Viguerie promoted the anti-abortion cause as an emotional means of mobilizing new political activists for a slate of related family issues.[50]

Opposition to civil rights for homosexuals was the most visceral of the "pro-family" issues. During the 1970s, anti-gay campaigns were few in number and localized, despite national media attention. Popular singer Anita Bryant became synonymous with the fight against gay rights when she led the successful 1977 effort to overturn Miami–Dade county's inclusion of homosexuals in the local anti-discrimination law. The following year, Bryant's "Save Our Children" group proceeded to work for passage of a California state initiative to ban open homosexuals from teaching in the public schools. California's Proposition 6, sponsored by State Representative John Briggs, was defeated by voters,[51] but the campaign there, and in Florida, consolidated an activist network opposed to gay rights. Christian Voice, a major Christian Right electoral vehicle of the 1980s, grew out of the 1970s anti-gay activism of a group of southern California ministers.[52]

Not until the late 1980s and 1990s, however, would the Christian Right make the prevention and reversal of gay rights initiatives a centerpiece of its activist program. By then, the Christian Right had become organizationally decentralized and locally focused. It was at the local and state level that gay rights organizations were somewhat successful in instituting civil rights protections, and it was at that level that the anti-gay countermovement responded to concrete legal measures.

Local politics was the most appropriate site for school concerns activism as well. During the 1980s, as is discussed in Chapter 10, centralized national Christian Right organizations promoted numerous unsuccessful school prayer bills in Congress. As Christian Right activists were elected to positions on school boards, city councils, and the like, they also challenged public school curricula at the local level.

A precedent for this type of activism was set during the 1974 school book protest in Kanawha county, West Virginia. There, groups of parents, business leaders, fundamentalist ministers, and even some Klansmen, waged a spontaneous and short-lived protest of cultural relativism in school textbooks.[53] Of the family issues, abortion and the ERA were the kind of sweeping policy matters that lent themselves to Christian Right activism in its early, centrally organized phase. School prayer was not on the national agenda until the Reagan administration and New Right members of Congress, who were elected in 1980, took office.

By then, the anti-abortion movement had already achieved one objective, the ban on federal funding for poor women's abortions, sponsored by Representative Henry Hyde (R-IL), and upheld by the Supreme Court. In 1979, a group of New Right Senators introduced the first version of the Family Protection Act, an expansive bill with dozens of provisions to restrict abortion and gay rights, blunt sex discrimination laws and provide tax advantages for "traditional" families where the wife stays home.[54]

Of all the "pro-family" issues, abortion was the one on which the 1973 Supreme Court decision had produced the most definitive policy change in favor of the feminist movement. Abortion naturally resonated as the most urgent of issues. The debate over legal abortion is about who decides when life begins: individual women, hegemonic churches, and/or state institutions. Beyond life-and-death questions, though, the abortion debate was also about the legitimacy of the welfare state, in terms of government funding for women's health care and government's protection of a woman's right to choose to have an abortion. In the view of political scientist Rosalind Petchesky, abortion was about women's liberation itself.

> It seems undeniable that a major goal of the conservative state's effort to contract if not dismantle social welfare is to discipline and punish women who try to survive, and be sexual, outside the bounds of the traditional family.
>
> While unarticulated, often even by feminists, the meanings resonating from abortion politics have more to do with compulsory heterosexuality, family structure, the relationship between men and women and parents and children, and women's employment than they do with the fetus. Thus the campaign against abortion in the courts, the legislatures, and through electoral politics is—in some ways that are more devastating than the defeat of the ERA—a challenge to the changes in women's conditions that are identified with the feminist movement.[55]

The Shift toward Partisan Organizing

Phyllis Schlafly, Paul Weyrich, Richard Viguerie, and others who assisted the early Christian Right were all veterans of the 1964 Goldwater campaign. They were steeped in the conservative movement's dual strategy of forming wide-ranging political organizations and activism based on more specific issues. As a decidedly political movement, the Christian Right began with nationally focused drives against abortion and ERA. At the same time, some evangelical leaders started electoral vehicles and initiated the Christian Right's gradual move from the terrain of ideological and pressure group politics into the mainstream of the Republican Party. This shift into partisan politics is what allowed the New Right–Christian Right coalition to win power and influence within the Reagan administration during the 1980s. In contrast, the American-ists' persistent sectarianism, and failure to negotiate the compromises inherent in partisan politics, destined that movement to marginality.

1976, the "Year of the Evangelical," marked the Christian Right's first serious foray into electoral politics. It was also in 1976 that *Sojourners*, a liberal evangelical magazine, exposed the quiet activities of a group of evangelical businessmen intent on mobilizing "born again" Christians for the 1976 elections and beyond.[56] Beginning in 1974, these businessmen, along with Representative John Conlan (R-AZ) and Campus Crusade for Christ president Bill Bright, had established Third Century Publishers and assumed legal control of the tax-exempt Christian Freedom Foundation, publishers of the "free market" *Christian Economics* magazine, discussed in Chapter 4. Third Century produced literature for newly politically active evan-gelicals. Conlan and Bright recruited regional directors to train local leaders of home study groups in "priority Congressional districts."[57] Bright's Campus Crusade was a mainstay of the youthful "Jesus freak" revival. (In the late 1960s, Bright deployed evangelists to the Univer-sity of California's Berkeley campus in an effort to help his friend Governor Ronald Reagan quell student protest.) In the 1970s, Bright sponsored the multi-million dollar "I Found It!" bumper sticker and billboard campaign as an evangelization gimmick.[58] When Bright opened a Christian Embassy in Washington, D.C. to proselytize government officials, evangelist Billy Graham publicly criticized Bright's entry into partisan politics. Bright denied his partisan inten-tions, even though he had organized a prayer breakfast for 1,000 delegates at the 1976 Republican National Convention, at which popular singer, and Reagan delegate, Pat Boone told the crowd, "God is working in the political process here."[59]

Once Reagan lost the nomination to incumbent President Gerald Ford, the Democrats benefited from Sunday school teacher Jimmy Carter's appeal to evangelical Christians. Though Carter lost support among both Protestants and Catholics for his opposition to a constitu-tional amendment banning abortion, the evangelical vote helped Carter significantly in 1976. Poll data on Carter's initial and declining backing from evangelicals showed that in 1976 Carter won 56 percent of the white Baptist vote against 43 percent for Ford. However, in 1980, Carter received only 34 percent of the white Baptist vote against Reagan's 56 percent, and white evangelicals accounted for two-thirds of Reagan's 10-point margin of victory.[60]

As opponents of the administration during the Carter years, evangelical leaders created the organizational apparatus needed to get out the vote in 1980 and thereafter. The mid-term elections of 1978 taught the early Christian Right a few lessons. In California, state Senator John Briggs, a self-described born-again Christian, sponsored a ballot initiative that would have required public schools to fire openly homosexual teachers. Briggs claimed the support of about 500 fundamentalist churches, several Baptist denominations and the (pentecostal) Assemblies of God. Reflecting on the loss of Proposition 6, Briggs' campaign manager said they had failed to mobilize churches until the campaign's last few weeks and months.[61] Elsewhere in the country, abortion assumed major importance in several 1978 elections. In Minnesota, governor Albert Quie won on an anti-abortion ticket, and anti-abortionists helped elect sympathetic U.S. Senators Rudy Boschwitz and David Durenberger. In Virginia, Jerry Falwell's support boosted Republican John Warner into the governor's seat.[62]

The potential political influence of evangelicals appeared like the proverbial handwriting on the wall in 1979, the year the Christian Right became organized openly and on a massive scale. Veterans of anti-gay campaigns in Florida and California merged to form Christian Voice, the organization that originated the "moral report cards" used to rate candidates on issues from abortion to Zimbabwe. Sixteen members of Congress (including Senators Orrin Hatch, Roger Jepsen, Gordon Humphrey, and James McClure) joined Christian Voice's Congressional advisory committee. Through direct mail fundraising, Christian Voice produced a mailing list of 130,000 "members" and a one million dollar budget its first year.[63]

In the spring of 1979, Paul Weyrich, Richard Viguerie, Ed McAteer (of the Conservative Caucus), and Robert Billings traveled to Lynchburg, Virginia to visit Jerry Falwell, then a virtually unknown Baptist preacher. These New Right leaders persuaded Falwell to use his large church, weekly television broadcast, and numerous clergy contacts as the base for a national network with a name like "moral majority." Falwell agreed with his New Right mentors' goal of influencing the 1980 Republican platform. Weyrich and associates helped Falwell select the Moral Majority's first board of directors, which included Charles Stanley of Atlanta's First Baptist Church, Greg Dixon of Indianapolis' Baptist Temple, James Kennedy of the Coral Ridge Presbyterian Church in Florida, and Tim LaHaye, who, along with his wife Beverly, directed a Washington, D.C.-based lobby, Family America.[64]

Within a year of its formation, the Moral Majority claimed 400,000 members and $1.5 million in contributions; in 1980 Falwell claimed to have registered three million new voters.[65] Both Christian Voice and the

Moral Majority registered as non-profit, non-tax-exempt corporations, in order to be eligible to lobby and engage in electoral campaigning.[66] The Moral Majority and Christian Voice were both established as explicitly non-sectarian organizations.

Falwell's network appealed more to Baptists than to pentecostals. The latter dominated the planning for "Washington for Jesus," a day-long prayer rally attended by 200,000 evangelicals in April 1980. The event was organized beginning in 1978 by Pat Robertson, his associate John Gimenez, Bill Bright of Campus Crusade, and Demos Shakarian of the Full Gospel Businessmen's Fellowship International.[67] The large and unprecedented attendance at "Washington for Jesus" was made possible by grassroots activists in 380 offices across the country, one in almost every Congressional district. The event was seen as a high-water mark in the drive for inter-denominational unity.[68]

Upon founding the Moral Majority, Paul Weyrich (himself a Catholic, as were Richard Viguerie, Phyllis Schlafly, William Buckley, and some other New Right conservatives) explained his cross-denominational thinking and the salience of "family" for the Christian Right.

> There was, in fact, a moral majority of sorts who were in power in this country for many years, into the early part of this century. But the Scopes trial and the revolt against Prohibition swept these fundamentalists, if you will, out of power, and they have been on the defensive ever since, until recent times.
>
> Television and the new breed of religious leader, exemplified by the Rev. Jerry Falwell and by Pat Robertson of the 700 Club, have given life and effectiveness to the Word of God. . . . Unlike many of their predecessors, these "electronic preachers" understand the linkage between the religious and moral issues and the politics of our time.
>
> Meanwhile, the Second Vatican Council has produced a whole new dimension which its modernist advocates did not intend. . . . It is true, of course, that since Vatican II the social gospel advocates in the Catholic and Protestant churches have been working ever more closely together. But the 'ecumaniacs' had not counted on a reverse coalition. Now however, the true-believing Gospel-oriented Catholics, having been told by the hierarchy that they should seek accommodation with their Protestant brethren, have taken to working with fundamentalist/evangelical Protestants in, for example, the right-to-life movement rather than with liberal Protestants in boycotting grapes with Cesar Chavez.
>
> This is no false unity based on papering over doctrinal differences. . . . Our very right to worship as we choose, to bring up families in some kind of moral order, to educate our children free from the interference of the state, to follow the commands of Holy Scripture and the church is at stake. These leaders have concluded it is better to argue about

denominational differences at another time. Right now, it is the agenda of those opposed to the Scriptures and the church which has brought us together.[69]

Viguerie concurred with Weyrich's understanding of a religious right coalition's power. In his editorial for *Conservative Digest*'s cover story on the Moral Majority, Viguerie stressed the sheer audience sizes and budgets for the top televangelists, and made note of their relative youth compared with liberal Christian political activists.

> During the 25 years that I've been active in politics, the major religious leaders in America have been liberals who were in bed politically with the Democratic Party.
> But most are now over the hill. With few exceptions, the religious leaders who led civil rights marches, Vietnam war rallies, ERA demonstrations and welfare protests are now in their 60s and 70s.
> Take heart, conservatives. Our movement is gaining strength rapidly, and the liberals are on the defensive and losing strength.[70]

In 1979, Pat Robertson, Jerry Falwell, and other Christian Right leaders promoted by *Conservative Digest*[71] flexed their muscles in a series of private meetings with Republican presidential hopefuls John Connally, Ronald Reagan, Howard Baker, and Philip Crane. Reagan was the Christian Right's favorite,[72] and because evangelicals had delivered millions of votes to Jimmy Carter, the preferences of the television preachers carried weight.

Beyond sheer numbers, the early Christian Right's evident tactical know-how and inter-denominational unity could not have escaped the attention of politicians. The evangelicals brought to their activism a religious fervor unmatched by any other political force. But, contrary to stereotypes of unsophisticated "fundamentalists," the Christian Right's new national organizations conducted legislative research and employed the latest direct mail technology right alongside their sophisticated New Right counterparts.

TOWARD POLITICAL POWER

The early Christian Right represents a case in which a mass base of constituents, aroused for its own reasons, was facilitated by the ties of its movement's leaders with New Right allies. The early Christian Right was successful because it developed along two tracks. Without abandoning their roots in the broad evangelical subculture, the movement's most skilled activists also began to make common cause with elites in the realm of electoral politics.

Large numbers of evangelical Christians voted for Jimmy Carter, but soon thereafter became receptive to the appeals of skilled New Right organizers. These professional activists seized on some of the decade's profound social changes, made salient through initiatives by the state, to arouse a large segment of the population concerned about the declining prestige of its belief system.

The evangelical subculture reached a peak in the numbers of adherents who began to see the world in a similar way. For an elite, of sorts, among the Christian Right and its New Right allies, what mattered most was the expanding and increasingly sophisticated resources (televangelism, direct mail, new national organizations) and the ways that these resources could be used to influence legislation and electoral politics. For most of the evangelicals who would join the new Christian Right, it was the drive to preserve their vision of a traditional order that caused them to turn their attention toward earthly affairs.

CHAPTER 8

The Neoconservatives

While veterans of the conservative movement facilitated the political mobilization of the Christian Right, a small group of neoconservatives also contributed to the growth and efficacy of an expanding New Right. The Christian Right grew out of a larger evangelical cultural milieu. Similarly, many neoconservatives had roots in the New York-based, mostly Jewish, intelligentsia. By the late 1970s, neoconservatism represented the transformation of a segment of Cold War liberalism into a new resource for the New Right and the future Reagan administration. Neoconservatism was never a social movement, per se. Instead, Irving Kristol—known as the "godfather" of neoconservatism—dubbed it a "persuasion" or a "mode of thought" inspired by "disillusionment with contemporary liberalism," favorable toward capitalism and traditional institutions, but also toward a "conservative welfare state" that "takes a degree of responsibility for helping to shape the preferences that the people exercise in a free market."[1]

More than any of the others treated in this book, the neoconservative movement was the one that went through the most profound shifts in its political allegiances from the 1940s to the 1990s. Prior to the 1970s, the neoconservatives considered themselves liberals and welcome constituents of the Democratic Party coalition. For that reason, I did not include a chapter on the neoconservatives in Part I of this book. This chapter, however, will review the neoconservatives' development from the post-World War II anticommunist campaigns forward. From the late 1940s through the 1960s, Cold War liberals consolidated their own ideological positions, as public policy changes and the shifting parameters of conflict between Democrats and Republicans made the former party increasingly less hospitable for the neoconservatives. Some left the Democratic fold never to come back; others returned for the Clinton–Gore 1992 presidential campaign.[2]

Among all the groups treated in this study, the neoconservatives fit least comfortably into a "right-wing" category. Previous studies of the neoconservatives have characterized them accurately as a group of intellectuals who, having emerged from the various sects of the anticommunist Left, became uneasy allies of the New Right and the Reagan administration.[3] Many among the first generation of neoconservatives shared common roots in New York literary circles.[4] A younger cohort, including some opponents of the New Left, also produced several important neoconservative leaders.[5] As I detail in this chapter, the diverse neoconservative camp included some who heartily aligned themselves with big business, New Right, and military leaders during the 1970s, while others balked at such alliances. Only during the 1980s would the Reagan administration's foreign policy agenda forge unprecedented unity among these disparate forces.

Despite differences among them, however, the neoconservatives came to represent a coherent segment of the political class. They were political, as opposed to academic, intellectuals. They worked primarily outside of university settings. They were more concerned with influencing public debate and elite policymaking than they were with producing knowledge for other intellectuals. The neoconservatives themselves were neither mass-based nor, despite the personal wealth of some, particularly elite. But they became beneficiaries of economic and political elites: funded by big business, influential within corporate-backed think tanks, and appointed to government agencies under the Reagan–Bush (and Clinton) administrations.[6]

During their early phase of development, the neoconservatives wielded little influence with political elites. Instead, neoconservatives operated primarily in the realm of ideology, through conferences, books, magazines, and newspaper columns, in efforts to influence political opinion. Later, the neoconservatives would wield limited influence within partisan politics. They would play their greatest role at the national administrative level, especially during the Reagan era and with regard to foreign policy.

In contrast with other movement tendencies discussed in this book, the neoconservatives never adopted certain right-wing tenets, such as the biological determinism of the racialist Right, nor the theologically adorned social darwinism of Christian Right libertarians (discussed in Chapter 4). Instead, neoconservatives grew most closely to resemble their contemporaries in the New Right of the 1970s. As discussed in Chapter 5, the New Right represented a reassertion of the "fusionist" triad of moral traditionalism, economic libertarianism, and militarist anticommunism. After World War II, conservatives had moved away from their isolationist roots and came to champion large-scale U.S. intervention in the Third World to defeat communism. In their respective foreign policy stances, New Rightists were concerned with *national* "security," while neoconservatives remained more *internationalist* in their agenda. The differences showed up in debates over U.S. commitments to allied "democracies," especially Israel. (After the "fall of communism," in the late 1980s, the split between nationalists and internationalists would come to threaten unity between conservatives and neoconservatives; this conflict will be analyzed in Chapter 12.)

This chapter traces the evolution of neoconservatism, both as a set of policy preferences, and as the tendency of an (eventually) influential group of elite-oriented intellectuals. During the Cold War period of the 1950s and early 1960s, would-be neoconservatives promoted their views as comfortable members of the Democratic mainstream, within the literary milieu of the Congress for Cultural Freedom. Upon exposure of the Congress' ties to the Central Intelligence Agency, and as Cold War liberals grew weary of the Vietnam war, early neoconservative thinkers turned their attention to domestic social policy. The persistent anticommunism of neoconservatives left them generally supportive of successive administrations. But what turned neoconservatives into critics of the status quo was their evolving critique of welfare state programs and their related animosity toward a "new class" of fellow intellectuals, countercultural youth and black power movement militants.

Neoconservatives would argue that their political opponents on the left—not they themselves—were the ones who changed: first by expanding the welfare state to create new advantages for particular political constituencies (namely black nationalists and their New Left allies) and second by incorporating a proto-elitist "New Class" into the ranks of the Democratic Party. The antipathy of neoconservatives toward a new generation of movement intellectuals and policy advocates had a cultural basis as well. The New Left was as much the cultural expression of the youth generation as it was a political tendency, and the older neoconservatives shared the New Rightists' disdain for the New Left's abandonment of "traditional family values." As veterans of the Old Left, the neoconservatives had experience with internecine battles among small bands of ideologues. By the late 1960s and early 1970s, however, the neoconservatives faced a New Left represented by formidable mass movements (civil rights, anti-war, women's liberation), which also had some influence inside the Democratic Party.

To whatever extent liberalism itself changed, the neoconservatives likewise moved toward the right. They adopted concerns about state policy shared by their New Right counterparts, including the concern that an encroaching state both threatens traditional institutions and reduces individual freedom. Central to neoconservative policy quandaries during the 1970s was the issue of social equality and the question of whether the state ought to ensure equality of results, or simply equality of opportunity. The drift of neoconservatives away from the liberal, if not socialist, preference for a large state role in equitably distributing wealth and power coincided with the rise of their grievances with the McGovern wing of the Democratic Party. Nixon's 1972 reelection and McGovern's embrace of "new class" constituents inspired neoconservatives to ally with disaffected leaders of organized labor in a coalition that was separate from the Democrats' dominant faction. By the late 1970s, that organizational break (combined with Jimmy Carter's intended relaxation of superpower tensions) drove neoconservatives further into an alliance with New Right anticommunists and leaders of a politically aroused "military–industrial complex."

The transformation of neoconservatives from New Deal Democrats into eventual participants in the Reagan revolution is the result of their changing ideological stances toward the state, combined with a new set of organizational opportunities and restraints. The Democratic Party became less hospitable to neoconservatives precisely at a time when the conservative New Right, flush with increased resources from the corporate sector, was seeking new allies in the fight to restore traditional morality at home, and to defeat communism abroad. The neoconservatives were not opposed to the New Right's moralist agenda. They were preoccupied with the anticommunist cause.

Underlying the incipient unity between neoconservatives and the New Right were latent fissures (over control of movement resources and philosophical matters) that would not break open in a destructive way until the late 1980s, with the demise of the unifying "communist threat." This chapter charts the path of those anticommunist liberals who became neoconservatives during the 1970s, and working partners of the New Right during the 1980s.

THE COLD WAR ROOTS OF NEOCONSERVATISM

Neoconservatism has been associated with a core group of standard bearers: Irving Kristol, Daniel Bell, Nathan Glazer, and Seymour Martin Lipset are among the best known. During the 1930s, these men were student radicals at the City College of New York (CCNY), where they honed their rhetorical skills through bitter ideological combat with members of the Communist Party. The anti-Communists owed their intellectual allegiance to *New International*, a Trotskyist theoretical journal and to *Partisan Review*, an avant-garde cultural magazine.[7] These prominent graduates of CCNY assumed academic posts at prestigious universities,[8] and by the 1950s some led the Cold War liberals' Congress for Cultural Freedom, to be discussed below.

In the interim, after World War II, the Communist movement remained a relevant political force even within the United States.[9] But as the Truman administration reversed the wartime alliance of the United States with the Soviet Union, and prosecuted U.S. Communists under the Smith Act, liberal organizations were compelled to take a stand on the question of Communists within their own ranks; debate raged during the 1950s.[10] Earlier, a series of events had strengthened the anti-Communist Left. In 1947, the left-leaning Americans for Democratic Action (ADA) was formed as a counter to the Progressive Citizens of America (PCA), led by 1948 presidential candidate Henry Wallace. Both groups supported the New Deal and the labor movement, but the ADA was staunchly anti-Soviet and denied membership to U.S. Communists, while the PCA advocated a "united Left" strategy. The prominence of Communists within major labor unions intensified the conflict, as did Truman's pledge of military and economic aid to Greece and Turkey, and the installation of a Communist government in Czechoslovakia in 1948. Truman's unexpected electoral victory strengthened his conservative wing of the Democratic Party, and did nothing to diminish its focus on Communism. Meanwhile, the 1949 Chinese Revolution set a precedent for national liberation movements in the Third World.

These closely timed events, followed by the pervasive influence of McCarthyism in the 1950s, elevated the Communist issue among the policy quandaries of Cold War liberals and obscured two other elements of liberalism's agenda: (1) the perpetuation (if not expansion) of New Deal social welfare policies and (2) the promotion of civil rights legislation to end racial segregation. Cold War liberalism was characterized by support for state intervention to *distribute* wealth and power to traditionally subordinate classes and (racial) status groups. Yet the centrality of anticommunism as the foundation of a post-war political consensus positioned liberals as supporters, too, of the United States as military and diplomatic *enforcer* of the "free" world. Supportive of the state's prerogatives, both as *distributor* and *enforcer*, Cold War liberalism was by no means characteristically "right wing."

In the Cold War context, liberals consolidated their ideological positions and activist resources through the electorally focused Americans for Democratic Action,[11] and through the labor movement, which, during the late 1940s and early 1950s, was regrouping at both the national and international federation levels.[12] Within academia, Sidney Hook and other Cold War liberals crafted intellectual arguments for administrators keen on purging Communists and other leftists from the universities.[13]

In contrast to the small network of Cold War liberal intellectuals, who would eventually be known as the neoconservatives, ADA and the labor movement were larger and more diverse. As a subset of the Cold War liberal forces, the early neoconservatives were more ideologically coherent than their counterparts in electoral politics and organized labor, although the intellectuals' objectives were also less specific. By definition, labor movements pursue concrete interests for their rank-and-file members, and para-party organizations form necessary heterogenous coalitions to elect candidates. The early neoconservative movement had the advantage of operating with a relative degree of autonomy, both from economic constraints on its members, and from the imperatives of electoral politics. That relative autonomy allowed neoconservative intellectuals to compromise less and foment longer.

The Congress for Cultural Freedom and *The End of Ideology*

In June of 1950, in Berlin among the ruins of the Third Reich, and amid news reports of North Korea's invasion of the south, anticommunist intellectuals gathered to declare their own war on "totalitarianism" of the right and left. They called themselves the Congress for Cultural Freedom, and the impetus for their formation was a pair of widely publicized international peace conferences, the first held in Poland in 1948, followed by the second in 1949 at New York's Waldorf-Astoria hotel. These conferences featured urgent polemical speeches by prominent artists, scientists, and literary figures, concerned about the superpower conflict and the threat of another world war. Critics condemned the conferences as a boon to pro-Soviet propaganda.[14] Anticommunist philosopher Sidney Hook was denied a speaking platform at the Waldorf and promptly organized Americans for Intellectual Freedom for a counter-conference a few blocks away at the Freedom House headquarters.[15] Hook's group changed its name to the American Committee for Cultural Freedom and joined in founding the Congress for Cultural Freedom (CCF) in 1950.

The Congress formed affiliates in Britain, France, India, Italy, Japan, Norway, the United States, and West Germany, and spent the next decade and a half coordinating conferences and publishing activities for the "free" world's intelligentsia. Among the most prominent members of the Congress were novelist Arthur Koestler, sociologists Edward Shils and Daniel Bell, Italian social democrat Ignazio Silone, and French journalist Raymond Aron. Irving Kristol, Melvin Lasky, and Stephen Spender edited CCF's *Encounter* magazine, which had funding from the CIA.[16] The U.S. affiliate of CCF was closely tied to three New York-based journals: *Partisan Review, The New Leader,* and *Commentary;*[17] the latter would remain a central publishing vehicle for the later neoconservatives.

The Congress' most lasting intellectual artifact was its members' promotion of the "end of ideology" thesis.[18] The term gained currency after Edward Shils used it to title a report for *Encounter* on the 1955 meeting of the Congress in Milan. Daniel Bell's 1960 book *The End of Ideology* popularized for a wide readership the Cold War liberals' notion that profound ideological conflicts were no longer relevant to contemporary problem solving. Instead, the "end-of-ideologists" believed that the 1960s would be a decade in which technical experts would tackle poverty and injustice, unencumbered by debates between socialist and capitalist camps.

The influence of the "end of ideology" advocates within academia and policymaking circles survived the *New York Times'* 1966 revelation that the Congress for Cultural Freedom was a sponsored project of the CIA. The *Times* exposed both the "dummy" foundations used to fund CCF and the Agency's deployment of Michael Josselon as CCF's executive director.[19] Rumors of CCF's role in the CIA's monitoring of, and overtures to, the "non-communist Left" had circulated for years. Pleading plausible ignorance, Irving Kristol said he would not have taken the job of *Encounter* editor had he known of the CIA sponsorship, not because he disapproved of such operations but because he was "exceedingly jealous of [his] reputation as an independent writer and thinker."[20]

The *Times'* reportage on the dissolution of the Congress for Cultural Freedom coincided with revelations that the CIA had also secretly sponsored an array of U.S. civic groups and foreign labor organizations, through the auspices of the AFL-CIO.[21] At the time of these exposures in 1966 and 1967, CIA sponsorship did not carry the kind of public relations liability it would later. After the Vietnam war and Senator Frank Church's mid-1970s hearings on CIA abuses, press coverage increased public understanding of the CIA's role in overthrowing governments from the 1950s forward. But in 1967, the Cold War liberals who fancied themselves free-wheeling intellectuals were just beginning to confront the undemocratic implications of their government's routine use of deception. Growing opposition to the Vietnam war divided Democratic hawks and doves and exacerbated the anticommunist intellectuals' quandary over the meaning of "liberalism."

In 1967, *Commentary* magazine published "Liberal Anti-Communism Revisited," a symposium in which prominent anticommunist intellectuals were asked for their views on the CIA's funding of domestic civic organizations and on the charge that liberal anticommunists bore responsibility for continuation of the Vietnam war. Essay contributors included Daniel Bell, Lewis Coser, Sidney Hook, Irving Howe, Stephen Spender, and Lionel and Diana Trilling. Most were unfazed by the exposure of liberal CIA fronts. Most rejected the idea that liberal anticommunists were responsible for U.S. war policies in Southeast Asia, though most had also come to see continuation of the Vietnam war as tactically unwise.[22]

THE DEVELOPMENT
OF NEOCONSERVATIVE THINKING

If, by 1967, some of the anticommunist liberals opposed the continuation of the Vietnam war, an overlapping group of would-be neoconservatives were similarly uneasy about the direction of many domestic social policies and the interest groups such policies represented. If anything, the history of the neoconservative movement is a history of the development of ideas and policy preferences.

The 1964 presidential election had sharpened divisions between Goldwater backers of the conservative movement and more moderate Republicans. In a similar vein, the direction of national policy, after 1965, met with mixed reviews from those Democrats who would eventually become neoconservatives. The changing political context of the late 1960s and early 1970s raised new questions (and exacerbated old ones) for liberal intellectuals. By 1970, Nathan Glazer posed the rhetorical question:

> How does a radical—a mild radical, it is true, but still someone who felt closer to radical than to liberal writers and politicians in the late 1950's—end up by early 1970 a conservative, a mild conservative, but still closer to those who now call themselves conservative than to those who call themselves liberals?[23]

Glazer and his colleagues, no doubt, each traveled a slightly different road to neoconservatism. But what unified the neoconservatives was an evolving critique of fellow liberals' view that, essentially, the state has a major role to play in effecting greater social equality. The concentration of prominent neoconservatives on the themes of racial and class equality reflected their past commitments to one or another Marxist sects, as well as their urgent concern with the profound changes underway in U.S. society.

The year 1965 saw the escalation of the Vietnam war and the beginning of major domestic opposition to it, the U.S. invasion of the

Dominican Republic, and the explosion of the Watts riots in the face of the Democrats' Great Society agenda. That same year, Irving Kristol and Daniel Bell founded *The Public Interest* as a forum for supposedly non-ideological debate on public policy problems.[24] Between 1965 and the end of Nixon's first term, the early neoconservatives' leading publications, *Commentary* and *The Public Interest*, directed their readers' attention to three major themes: analyses of liberal social welfare programs (including the War on Poverty and affirmative action), opposition to the New Left, and dissatisfaction with the direction of the Democratic Party's "New Politics" faction. Following the 1973 Arab–Israeli war and the 1975 defeat of the United States in Vietnam, the neoconservatives would revive their persistent militarism and anticommunism. But prior to that, the neoconservatives' domestic concerns were central to the steady transition of Cold War liberals from being part of the Democratic mainstream to joining the Republican coalition of the Reagan era.

Most of the neoconservatives developed their stance toward the state as observant critics operating outside the demands of daily policymaking. The most notable exception was Daniel Patrick Moynihan, whose name became synonymous with neoconservatives' controversial views on race.

Moynihan's study *The Negro Family: The Case for National Action*, later nicknamed "The Moynihan Report," formed the basis of a June 1965 commencement speech delivered by President Johnson at Howard University. As Johnson's Assistant Secretary of Labor, Moynihan was concerned with those barriers to racial equality that could not be overcome directly through civil rights legislation. Anti-segregation and voting rights laws alone, he argued, would not alleviate the historical conditions that would prevent black people from taking advantage of new opportunities. Centuries of slavery, and another century of an inferior position for black men in the wage system, had left a legacy of unstable black families. In his report, Moynihan linked the absence of a strong father figure in many black homes to a "tangle of pathology," beginning with high rates of juvenile delinquency, teen pregnancy, and "illegitimate" births, and leading to persistent poverty and welfare dependency.

The timing of Moynihan's report fueled the controversy surrounding it. In 1965, the civil rights movement was at a crossroads. Jim Crow segregation laws had been successfully attacked, but de facto segregation and racism remained. As African Americans' expectations rose, so too did unemployment rates for black workers. Six days after President Johnson signed the Voting Rights Act in August of 1965, rioting broke out in the Watts area of Los Angeles. The next phase of the African American insurgency would have to address economic deprivation, in urban areas well outside the South. It was precisely the non-legalistic aspects of racial inequality that Moynihan wanted the Johnson administration to address. But Moynihan's report, released also in August 1965, focused statistically on black "illegitimacy" rates, lending a moralistic tone to an analysis that seemed to blame victimized black families for their own plights. Newspaper accounts elevated the Moynihan report to the status of an explanation for the Watts riot.[25] Liberal critics, both black and white, charged Moynihan with fueling racist stereotypes of black promiscuity and focusing on blacks' purported behavioral patterns as a distraction from the unfinished job of dismantling legal discrimination.[26]

One of the report's more generous critics, Herbert Gans, acknowledged Moynihan's "insistence on equality of results."[27] But that concern with de facto, as opposed to merely potential, equality, raised for neoconservative thinkers the question of whether the ends really do justify the means. In the late 1960s, from an academic post in between administrative appointments, Moynihan himself became a leading critic of anti-poverty programs geared toward equality of results rather than equality of opportunity. Moynihan objected to what he saw as policymakers' disingenuousness about the real objectives of the Great Society programs. "In retrospect," he wrote, "it is possible to view the war on poverty as a device that enabled the federal government to launch a fairly wide range of programs designed primarily to aid Negro Americans without having to specify that such was their intent."[28] Moynihan supported anti-poverty programs, including those for the black community. The problem, as he saw it, was

> the proliferation of projects; the constant association of such projects with academic activists, and academic conceptions such as "disadvantage" and "culture"; the precipitous rise of dissatisfaction with the program in the Congress, followed by restrictions in funding; the attendant rise of Negro militancy and hostility, accompanied by increasing sophistication and fiercely asserted independence, but also a very strongly held conviction that power continues to reside in a concealed but ruthless and disciplined freemasonry of the white elite.[29]

As he honed his arguments in articles for *Commentary* and *Public Interest*, Moynihan's policy critique centered on the argument that social welfare programs exacerbate demands for group rights as opposed to individual rights. In 1969, Moynihan reported a nearly tenfold increase in the number of federally sponsored domestic programs between 1960 and 1968. He linked this increase causally to a concurrent decline of "social satisfaction" and pointed to two related tendencies: the erosion of "the sense of general community" and "the authority of existing relationships," simultaneous with the growth of "a powerful quest for specific community . . . in the form of ever more intensive assertions of racial and ethnic identities."[30] Moynihan's solution was for policymakers to direct political activity into the electoral process, especially at the local level, rather than in increased demands for services from the federal government.[31]

What began, for Moynihan and his fellow neoconservatives, as a critique of the ways in which federal social welfare programs were administered, developed into what Nathan Glazer termed "the limits of social policy" itself. Glazer defined "social policy" as "all those public policies which have developed in the past hundred years to protect families and individuals from the accidents of industrial and urban life, and which try to maintain a decent minimum of living conditions for all."[32] For every social problem, Glazer argued, the "liberal stance" is to seek a policy solution and to indict the existing political system for failing to address the problem earlier. Conservatives, in Glazer's terminology, seek a slower process of problem solving, while "radicals" are those who believe there are no specific solutions to specific problems, but rather only a wholesale solution in the form of thorough societal transformation. For Glazer, the trouble with social policy was twofold: it encourages a "breakdown" of traditional problem-solving institutions such as the family, the ethnic group, and the church. It also creates and feeds a "revolution of rising expectations" and a *demand for equality*; in political rights and political power, but also "a demand for equality in economic power, in social status, in authority in every sphere."[33] Lest social policy encourage people to depend more on government and less on "some traditional arrangement," Glazer concluded that "we can have only partial and less than wholly satisfying answers to the social problems in question." In other words, society would have to be content with some undetermined level of poverty, disenfranchisement, and other social ills because expanding social policy solutions would eventually do more harm than good.

By his avowed skepticism toward the benefits of social policy, Glazer answered his own question of how he had moved toward the conservative camp. Social theorist Albert Hirschmann, in his review of two centuries worth of what he called "reactionary rhetoric," identified the "jeopardy thesis" as the essential conservative argument against proposals for reform: one set of supposed benefits (in this case, protective laws and social services) threatens to jeopardize allegedly more valued "traditional" arrangements (family, church, and ethnic ties), while perversely creating new and greater problems for the future.[34]

Glazer's argument, and its acceptance among fellow former liberals, placed the new conservatives in a position consistent with right-wing philosophy of the inevitability, if not desirability, of social inequality. Irving Kristol expressed the neoconservative view bluntly. "A just and legitimate society," he wrote, "is one in which inequalities—of property, or station, or power—are generally perceived by the citizenry as necessary for the common good. I do not see that this definition has ever been improved on."[35] Kristol attributed the growing demand by Americans for social equality to "the animus toward the business class" on the part of a "new class" of professionals and intellectuals "engaged in a class struggle with the business community for status and power."[36] Kristol, the former socialist advocate for the "working class," left no doubt as to which side of the class struggle he had come to occupy.

Other liberals in transition framed their arguments against a leftist social policy agenda less in philosophical terms than in fears of the New Left. Earl Raab, coauthor with Seymour Martin Lipset of an influential book on right-wing movements, warned of anti-Jewish inclinations within the Black Power movement of the post-civil rights era.[37] Nathan Glazer went further, indicting leading Jewish intellectuals of the Left for their sympathies with the Black Panther Party.[38] In their persistent criticism of the New Left, neoconservatives conflated opposition to the Israeli government with anti-Jewish bigotry.[39] The latter was a real, but minor tendency on the Left, and certainly not one approved by Allen Ginsberg, Noam Chomsky, or other left-wing intellectuals disparaged in *Commentary*.

Aside from making dubious charges of New Left anti-Semitism, the neoconservatives crafted other indictments of the younger generation of political activists. Glazer disputed the New Left's inclination to view human beings as good by nature but corrupted by institutions, on the grounds that this view underlaid the New Left's pursuit of participatory democracy. "I cannot imagine," Glazer wrote, "how one can ever overcome the danger raised by a direct dependence on the people, permanently in session. For it inevitably means depending on that part of the people that is willing, for one reason or another, to stay permanently in session."[40] In other words, participatory democracy would be dangerous because one or more interest groups not already "permanently in session" might gain access to decision-making processes. In this same polemic, Glazer wrote that universities and other undemocratic institutions provoked the abandonment of democratic tactics by left-wing activists in favor of "confrontation, disruption, and provocation," particularly against the Vietnam war.[41]

Irving Kristol condemned the New Left because, in his view, it evidenced little interest in economics and, unlike the Old Left of the 1930s,

> implicitly reject[ed] both the bourgeois-liberal and the Old Left idea of the common good, and . . . therefore reject[ed] . . . the ideological presuppositions of modernity itself. This movement, which seeks to end

the sovereignty over our civilization of the common man, must begin by seeking the death of "economic man," because it is in the marketplace that this sovereignty is most firmly established. It thinks of itself as a "progressive" movement, whereas its import is regressive.[42]

Kristol proceeded to call the New Left "nihilistic." But he blamed "liberal capitalism" for failing to recognize this "enemy" and instead for seeing the "counterculture" as "just another splendid business opportunity."[43]

In his revealing essay "Capitalism, Socialism, and Nihilism," Kristol alluded to the conflict of the early neoconservatives, not so much with the New Left, which they scorned, but with a liberal elite deemed responsible for allowing the New Left to flourish. Kristol's critique of a rising "new class" dovetailed with the critique by that faction of the Democratic Party which viewed the party's 1972 presidential election as dominated by elitists (see below).

Some of the neoconservatives' brewing animosity toward a "liberal establishment" reflected small-scale internecine conflict within New York-based literary circles.[44] More fundamentally, however, after the 1968 defeat of presidential candidate Hubert Humphrey, neoconservative intellectuals expressed a dim view of their prospects for representation within the Democratic Party.

Penn Kemble, a youth leader of the old Socialist Party and a founder of the Coalition for a Democratic Majority (to be discussed below), identified the intra-party sources of Humphrey's defeat by Richard Nixon in 1968. Three elements of the New Deal coalition had failed to rally firmly behind Humphrey: southern Democrats, northern "machine" politicians like Chicago's Mayor Richard Daley, and "anti-war liberals." That left Humphrey with a base of support concentrated among organized labor and integrationist civil rights organizations. In the face of George Wallace's popular presidential campaigns, the Dixiecrats had concentrated on preserving local and Congressional offices, as had the Democrats' northern "machine" politicians. Anti-war liberals had opposed Humphrey bitterly during the primaries, and they withheld serious support after the convention. Kemble predicted that Humphrey's supporters in the African American community and the AFL-CIO—the latter had opposed a party plank calling for a halt to bombing in Vietnam—would not be strong enough to reconstruct the Democratic Party in 1972. Instead, Kemble observed an emerging schism between the party's "class" and "conscience" wings.[45] Blacks and labor unions constituted the "class" wing and represented large numbers. But the broadening influence of the "conscience" wing would exacerbate intra-party conflict by 1972. As we will discuss in the following section, George McGovern's presidential candidacy moved the neoconservatives, in tandem with an anticommunist, pro-organized labor party faction, to forge a coalitional realignment that would pave the way for Ronald Reagan's 1980 victory.

Between the mid-1960s and the mid-1970s, the early neoconservatives moved into ideological positions that were complementary to those of the conservative New Right. Neoconservatives maintained their pro-statist stance on issues of communism and U.S. foreign policy, even though some opposed the Vietnam war, tactically. Typical of the Right in general, they moved away from a pro-statist view on the question of the state's role in distributing wealth and power to subordinate groups. Their polemical writings on equality reflected their ideological vacillation over a period of about a decade.

The ideological transformation of neoconservatives after the mid-1960s revolved initially around issues of domestic policy: the pitfalls of the welfare state's expansion into the realm of race relations, and parochial concerns about real and latent anti-Semitism among Black Power movement activists and their New Left allies. At this phase, neoconservatives focused on questions of the state's role primarily in their own limited circulation journals. Except for Daniel P. Moynihan, the neoconservatives wielded little influence at an administrative level, and they were too few in number to constitute a veritable party faction. However, by the mid-1970s, neoconservatives and their allies would begin to challenge political elites on an electoral terrain. That shift occurred after the Democratic Party nominated its most left-wing candidate in the twentieth century and embraced some of the very same "new class" constituents that Kristol and Glazer feared. Neoconservative intellectuals then found themselves in league with a more centrist, though by then dissident, Democratic faction.

THE CONSOLIDATION OF NEOCONSERVATIVE ORGANIZATIONS

In the wake of George McGovern's 1972 presidential defeat, a committee of neoconservative intellectuals, university professors, Democratic politicians, and labor leaders announced the formation of the Coalition for a Democratic Majority (CDM). It was the first organized network of neoconservatives and their allies since the dissolution of the Congress for Cultural Freedom. The Coalition's stated purpose was to counter McGovern supporters in the party's left-leaning "New Politics" wing. "New Politics" was a catch phrase for the anti-war activists, women's liberationists, and other New Leftists not averse to working within the Democratic Party.

In full-page *New York Times* and *Washington Post* advertisements soliciting supporters, the Coalition issued its call, "Come Home, Democrats," a play on the McGovern campaign slogan, "Come Home, America."

> As Democrats we naturally cannot find it in our hearts to applaud the fact that the American electorate has turned its back on our party's candidate for the Presidency. Nevertheless, we do not view the results of this election as the expression of some sweeping new shift to the Republicans.[46]

The statement proceeded to blame Nixon's reelection on the Democrats' capitulation to "forces and ideas unrepresentative of traditional Democratic principles." Labeled the handiwork of "New Politics" party activists, these ideas included a non-interventionist foreign policy, affirmative action, the "idea that American society is sick and guilty," and "a cavalier attitude toward the tens of millions of Americans who are genuinely and correctly concerned about public safety and respect for law." The CDM statement expressed no view on economic policy. Instead, it was crafted to appeal subtly to public concerns about U.S. international prestige, legal correctives to racial discrimination, and that echelon of the citizenry—presumably the youthful New Left—that "has sneered at the greatness of America."[47] Coalition founders included Ben Wattenberg, a former aide to Senator Henry "Scoop" Jackson; Bayard Rustin, an African American labor and civil rights leader; *Commentary* co-editor Midge Decter; Representative Thomas Foley (D-WA); former Humphrey aide Max Kampelman; and political science professor Jeane Kirkpatrick.[48] Also prominent was Robert Keefe, a consultant to the AFL-CIO's Committee on Political Education (COPE) which helped pay for the newspaper advertisements.[49] Coalition spokesperson Ben Wattenberg identified the liberal Americans for Democratic Action (ADA) as the chief opponent of CDM and other conservative Democrats.[50] Whereas, in the 1950s, Cold War liberals had backed ADA and the anticommunist American Federation of Labor as bulwarks against domestic communism, two decades later, alliances had shifted. Neoconservatives, united with organized labor, now found themselves opposed to the dominant Democratic faction.

The Nixon–McGovern Campaign and Its Aftermath

Conservative Democrats' opposition to Senator George McGovern as a presidential candidate revolved around his "premature opposition" to the Vietnam war, his perceived allegiances to the New Left, and his spotty record of support for organized labor.[51] Beginning in 1969, McGovern's "New Politics" faction had changed the Democratic Party's convention rules to make the selection of delegates better reflect the racial and gender diversity of the electorate. Critics perceived the new rules as a quota system for blacks, women, and youth, against the interests of party stalwarts and labor officials. Supporters of Senator Henry "Scoop" Jackson (D-WA) charged McGovern with stacking the 1972 convention with affluent, educated liberals and discriminating against middle and lower class constituencies by reducing the number of labor officials.[52] While neoconservative writer Irving Kristol portrayed the New Left as part of an elitist "new class" hostile to ordinary working people, McGovern opponents likewise pressed the need "to wrest the party from the 'kids and kooks.'"[53]

In the weeks between the convention and Nixon's reelection victory, the AFL-CIO's refusal to endorse McGovern spurred debate among organized labor's and neoconservatives' allies in the Socialist Party-Democratic Socialist Federation (SP-DSF). The Socialist Party, known best for its past presidential tickets headed by Eugene Debs and Norman Thomas, had long since abandoned a third-party strategy. Instead, by the 1960s, it had become a relatively uninfluential electoral voice for the interests of organized labor and the integrationist wing of the civil rights movement. Its youth affiliate, the Young People's Socialist League (YPSL), was staunchly anticommunist and generally hostile toward the New Left.[54] After the McGovern campaign, the Socialist Party and YPSL would regroup as Social Democrats U.S.A. and work with the new Coalition for a Democratic Majority.

As with the Coalition, it was issues sparked by the McGovern campaign that influenced the social democrats' shift away from the Democratic mainstream. Following McGovern's nomination, the SP-DSF offered the candidacy a lukewarm endorsement but condemned the "New Politics" faction as elitist, anti-labor and "neo-isolationist" on foreign affairs.[55] Under the headline "Nixon is the Lesser Evil," the Socialist Party's biweekly *New America* published an open letter to McGovern by Sidney Hook, who charged McGovern with softness on communism.[56] At the other end of the social democratic spectrum, *Dissent* editor Irving Howe urged support for McGovern, on the grounds that his appeal to a strong anti-war constituency demonstrated a new vitality for the Democratic Party. "This new political force . . . has shown that housewives and graduate students can be as sharp in ward organization as cigar-smoking politicians," Howe wrote.[57] Michael Harrington, the left-leaning co-chair of the Socialist Party, warned of organized labor's political shortsightedness in not backing McGovern and his supporters.[58] Shortly before the election, Harrington resigned his position as co-chair to protest the attacks of his fellow social democrats on

McGovern and their failure to support unconditional U.S. withdrawal from Vietnam.[59] After the campaign, and outside of the Socialist Party, Harrington formed the organizing committee that grew into the left-leaning Democratic Socialists of America.[60] In an edited collection of essays critical of the neoconservatives, Irving Howe and sociology professor Lewis Coser made it clear that their brand of "democratic socialism" remained within a left tradition, while that of the neoconservatives did not.[61]

The split among social democrats was formalized in December 1972 at which time the Socialist Party regrouped, changed its name to Social Democrats, U.S.A. (SDUSA) and pledged a renewed commitment against "communist aggression."[62] Noting its support for the newly formed Coalition for a Democratic Majority, SDUSA members voted down a resolution for an immediate end to the Vietnam war and instead adopted a platform calling for increased support for Israel and "all democratic elements within anti-colonialist national liberation movements."[63] (The latter phrase foreshadowed the role SDUSA members would play, during the 1980s, as creators of the National Endowment for Democracy, a subagency of the State Department.)

Beyond issuing public statements during Nixon's brief second term, neoconservatives, represented by SDUSA and the Coalition for a Democratic Majority, exerted little public presence.[64] On foreign policy, neoconservatives positioned themselves, separately but similarly, to New Right conservatives, against Nixon regarding detente with the Soviet Union. In 1973, for example, an ad hoc "Committee for Detente With Freedom," co-chaired by AFL-CIO leaders Bayard Rustin and Albert Shanker, and sponsored by leaders of organized labor and the Jewish community, protested Nixon's proposed trade openings to the Soviets, timed with Leonid Brezhnev's visit to the United States.[65]

The Carter Years and the "Present Danger"

Neoconservatives and New Right activists would eventually join forces against the "national security" threat posed by the Soviet Union and Third World liberation movements. However, in the mid-1970s, while the conservatives' international concerns focused on Taiwan, Rhodesia, and Panama, the incipient neoconservative movement focused on Israel. The 1973 Arab–Israeli war and the OPEC oil embargo, followed by the 1975 United Nations resolution equating Zionism with racism, raised the Jewish community's fear for Israel's security. United Nations Ambassador Daniel Patrick Moynihan denounced the resolution.

But neoconservatives observed a reluctance on the part of the Nixon–Ford administrations to take strong pro-Israeli action. *Commentary* editor Norman Podhoretz linked increasing U.S. "evenhandedness" in the Israeli–Arab conflict to two national objectives: to insure U.S. access to Arab oil reserves and to avoid inciting superpower tensions by provoking Middle Eastern allies of the Soviet Union. Oil and detente, Podhoretz argued, seemed to "dictate" U.S. pressures on Israel "to make territorial and eventually other concessions involving the PLO."[66]

Precisely at a time when solid U.S. backing for Israel was not to be taken for granted, neoconservatives were seeking political allies both within, and outside of, the Democratic Party. In the context of the U.S. withdrawal from Vietnam—and the subsequent continuation of inter-regional warfare— neoconservatives' concern with Israel's security had two sources. First, and most obviously, a disproportionate number of neoconservatives were Jews who had lived through the Holocaust. Second, unlike some of their New Right counterparts, neoconservatives were less nationalistic and more cosmopolitan. Through the Congress for Cultural Freedom, neoconservatives had built ties with anticommunist intellectuals abroad. Likewise, Marvin Liebman, William F. Buckley, and other leaders of the Old Right's elite sector maintained contact with their foreign counterparts in the China Lobby and its spin-off organizations. But the conservative movement also had strong roots in a tradition of isolationism and even xenophobia. The New Right of the 1970s broadened its base and tried to attract nationalists from the George Wallace-inspired American Independent Party, many of whom shared the John Birch Society's objections to foreign aid of any sort. In general, the New Right conceived foreign policy questions in *nationalist* terms: what is in the best interests of the United States? Neoconservatives were more likely to view the struggle between "freedom" and "communism" as an *internationalist* problem. Within that framework, the geopolitical circumstances of Israel and other allies could be elevated to an importance on a par with U.S. "national security."

As opponents of the Carter administration, however, both nationalist New Rightists and internationalist neoconservatives focused on conflict between the United States and the Soviet Union. Though neoconservatives found Jimmy Carter less offensive then McGovern, most had backed Senator "Scoop" Jackson.[67] Coalition for a Democratic Majority (CDM) activist Joshua Muravchik praised the Democratic Party's move away from requiring demographic balance among convention delegates,[68] and several neoconservatives joined a "writers' committee for Carter" sponsored by *Partisan Review*.[69]

Closely timed with Carter's election, however, CDM members joined forces with a loose network of top ranking former government officials and retired military leaders. They called themselves the Committee on the Present Danger (CPD), and their goal, according to Jerry Sanders' definitive study of CPD, was "to resurrect a militarized doctrine of containment as the cornerstone of U.S. foreign policy."[70] CPD took its name from an earlier group of policy advisors who had helped the Truman and Eisenhower administrations implement containment militarism, as outlined in the Pentagon and State Department's joint National Security Memorandum No. 68 or NSC-68.[71] Sanders traces the birth of the second-generation Committee on the Present Danger to an anti-detente position paper circulated by the Coalition for a Democratic Majority (CDM) beginning in 1974. A series of meetings led veteran cold warriors Eugene Rostow, Paul Nitze, and Charles Tyroler II in 1976 to assemble a CPD executive committee and board of directors that read like a who's who of neoconservative writers and professors, "national security" agency veterans, and anticommunist labor leaders. Whereas the Coalition for a Democratic Majority represented the neoconservatives' first try at uniting with disaffected Democratic labor leaders and politicians, CPD assembled an even more prestigious and politically astute quorum of elites; it was virtually a Reagan "shadow cabinet."[72] (Five dozen of the CPD members would be awarded appointments within the Reagan administration.)[73]

In 1976, as Reagan pressed the "national security" theme in his primary challenges to Gerald Ford, the incumbent president authorized then-CIA Director George Bush to select a team of intelligence specialists outside government for an alternative assessment of Soviet military capabilities. Bush appointed Richard Pipes, Paul Nitze, and several other CPD leaders, and the so-called Team B produced estimates portraying the Soviet "threat" far more ominously than official CIA reports.[74]

Team B's anti-detente views made press headlines in early 1977, just as the CPD mobilized to block Carter's appointment of Paul Warnke to head the Arms Control and Disarmament Agency. Shortly after Carter's election, the Coalition for a Democratic Majority and the Committee on the Present Danger, together, had offered Carter a list of sixty prominent neoconservatives they sought to see appointed to major administration posts.[75] As it became evident that Carter wanted little to do with the neoconservatives, CDM activists Penn Kemble and Josh Muravchik circulated a memorandum in Congress castigating Paul Warnke for his opposition to the arms race and for his role as former adviser to George McGovern. Warnke's nomination was approved, but the campaign against him forged an Emergency Coalition Against Unilateral Disarmament that united CDM neoconservatives with a slate of New Right organizational leaders[76] and laid a basis for the unprecedented, and successful, coalitional activism against the SALT II treaty (discussed in Chapter 5). Together, the Committee on the Present Danger, the American Security Council's off-shoot Coalition for Peace Through Strength, and the American Conservative Union mobilized public opinion against SALT through television "documentaries," speakers' tours, and direct mail. SALT opponents outspent treaty advocates by a margin of fifteen to one.[77]

Ironically, the drive against Carter's national security policies brought neoconservatives together with old antagonists. During the 1950s and 1960s, Cold War liberals were the ones responsible for the prevailing doctrine of containment. On the Right, conservative movement anticommunists had urged a strategy of "rollback" or "liberation." In the aftermath of the Vietnam war, however, consensus among foreign policymaking elites was in short supply. For the emerging neoconservative–New Right alliance, "rollback" could wait: containment was preferable to Carter's evident goal of relaxing relations with the Soviet Union. Under pressure from right-wing movements, between 1977 and 1980, Carter abandoned his inaugural day goal of eliminating nuclear weapons and basing foreign policy on respect for human rights. Sanders attributes Carter's eventual promotion of resurgent Cold War militarism to a split within capitalist circles, and a conflict among foreign policymaking elites. Carter's Trilateral Commission allies and advocates of economic "managerialism" lost the upper hand to blatant militarists backed by a military–industrial complex. The 1979 Iranian revolution and Soviet invasion of Afghanistan legitimized a U.S. military buildup that was already on the drawing board.[78]

In the end, Carter presided over real increases in military spending, reinstatement of draft registration, sanctions on trade (including grain sales) and "technology transfers" to the Soviet Union, and pursuit of the MX missile plan.[79] In 1978, Carter threatened covert action against newly independent Angola[80] and, generally, weakened his own espoused respect for human rights and international law.

In a 1984 review of CPD's accomplishments, Max Kampelman broached a "tentative conclusion" on the militarists' influence:

> From 1977 to 1981, as reported by public opinion polls, there was a steady increase in public perception of growing Soviet military strength and the threat that this posed to the United States and its allies. At the same time, there was a simultaneous surge in popular support for an increased defense effort and a corresponding sharp drop in sentiment for a decreased effort. To what extent this was due to the efforts of the Committee is impossible to gauge. It could be merely a coincidence but our presumption is that it is not.[81]

Apart from their role in influencing mass opinion against the SALT treaty, neoconservatives' influence within elite circles was at least as significant. In 1979, prominent neoconservatives joined conservative movement leaders in an appeal to Congress to "defend Taiwan" and oppose Carter's intent to open diplomatic relations with China.[82] Neo-conservative intellectuals dominated the U.S. delegation of the July 1979 "Jerusalem Conference on International Terrorism." Hosted by the Israeli government, it was at this gathering of intelligence officers and political leaders from Israel and the NATO countries that a worldwide propaganda offensive against "international terrorism" was launched.[83]

Influential in the formulation of the "Reagan Doctrine" against "terrorism" was Jeane Kirkpatrick's famous 1979 *Commentary* article "Dictatorships and Double Standards." Kirkpatrick, the future United Nations ambassador, urged U.S. support for "authoritarian" regimes as distinct from "totalitarian" ones. The former abused the human rights of their citizens, but, she claimed, they were reliable allies and candidates for democratization. Conversely, the "totalitarian" ideology of "communist" nations made them resistant to reform pressures and, therefore, more dangerous.[84]

Prior to Reagan's 1980 election and the ascent of Kirkpatrick and many of her colleagues to administrative positions, the neoconservatives supplied the intellectual ammunition for a renewal of the Cold war. Neoconservatives' small numbers precluded their becoming major players in electoral politics. Instead, their public prestige, rhetorical skills, and organizational ties with national security elites compensated for their lack of a mass base.

As incipient allies of the New Right during the 1970s, neoconservatives had also become joint beneficiaries of the political mobilization of big business (see Chapter 5). Just as corporations sought partisan influence by pouring millions of dollars into New Right political action committees, they also financed the growth of "free enterprise" think tanks, university programs, and journals. These outposts were precisely the kind of institutional bailiwicks most hospitable to neoconservative intellectuals.

The rationale for this trend, which continued through the 1990s, was expressed in William Simon's 1978 bestseller *A Time for Truth*. Formerly Secretary of the Treasury under Nixon, Simon was impressed by Irving Kristol's case against a "new class" that "combines a morbid economic ignorance with a driving power and . . . combines hostility to democracy with the illusion that it speaks for the People."[85] Like Kristol, Simon blamed "capitalists themselves" for the threat of "economic tyranny" posed by "new class" statists:

> Throughout the last century the attachment of businessmen to free enterprise has weakened dramatically as they discovered they could demand—and receive—short-range advantages from the state. To a tragic degree, coercive regulation has been invited by businessmen who were

unwilling to face honest competition in the free market with its great risks and penalties, as well as its rewards, and by businessmen who have run to the government in search of regulatory favors, protective tariffs, and subsidies, as well as those monopolistic powers which only the state can grant.[86]

Simon called on business leaders to act in their own interests, not by drafting political candidates, but rather by funding

intellectual refuges for the non-egalitarian scholars and writers in our society who today work largely alone in the face of overwhelming indifference or hostility. They must be given grants, grants and more grants in exchange for books, books and more books.[87]

Simon identified two groups of worthy "nonegalitarians": the "laissez-faire purist" disciples of economists Frederick Hayek and Milton Friedman and the neoconservatives, most prominently, Irving Kristol, James Q. Wilson, Nathan Glazer, Daniel Bell, Michael Novak, and Sidney Hook.[88]

The liberals and laborites in this "neo-conservative" group are still interventionists to a degree that I myself do not endorse, but they have grasped the importance of capitalism, are battling some of the despotic aspects of egalitarianism, and can be counted as allies on certain crucial fronts of the struggle for individual liberty.[89]

Simon was not alone in his thinking. By the late 1970s, corporations and corporate foundations had revitalized the pre-existing American Enterprise Institute (AEI) and Hoover Institution, plus a slew of new "non-egalitarian" think tanks. During the 1970s, AEI grew dramatically. In 1977, about 200 corporations provided 25 percent of AEI's $5 million budget; by 1981, 600 corporate donors accounted for 40 percent of a $10 million budget.[90] AEI welcomed as resident scholars libertarian economist Milton Friedman, as well as neoconservative thinkers Seymour Martin Lipset, Ben Wattenberg, and Irving Kristol. AEI, Hoover, and corporate-funded university programs concentrated on "free market" research and advocacy.[91]

Complementing this focus on economics, in 1978, William Simon and Irving Kristol started the Institute for Educational Affairs (IEA) to channel corporate dollars to "free marketeers" across a range of disciplines. With initial grants of $100,000 each from the John M. Olin Foundation, the Scaife Family Trusts, the JM Foundation and the Smith-Richardson Foundation, IEA assembled a donor base of dozens of corporations, including Bechtel, Coca-Cola, Dow Chemical, Ford Motor

Company, General Electric, K-Mart, Mobil, and Nestle.[92] The idea was for corporations to donate directly to IEA, whose board of largely neoconservative intellectuals then dispensed grants to applicants.

Initially, IEA directed its corporate largesse primarily to university-based authors and private think tanks.[93] Later, in the early 1980s, IEA established a network of several dozen right-wing campus newspapers, the best known of which was the *Dartmouth Review*. The newspapers focused favorably on Reagan administration foreign policy, and disparagingly on diversification of university curricula, affirmative action, and other trends anathema to the Right.[94] Through the effort to influence trends within academia, neoconservatives and their corporate benefactors supplemented the direct foreign policy lobbying they had been conducting through the Committee on the Present Danger. By the late 1980s, once the Cold War had ended, neoconservatives were better positioned than others on the right to shift gears and focus on domestic issues like education. (In fact, IEA was a forerunner to the National Association of Scholars, the leading neoconservative promoter of the notion that liberal and leftist intellectuals use academia to impose a narrow ideology of "political correctness.")[95]

MOVING TOWARD REAGANISM

Commentary editor Norman Podhoretz's contribution to Ronald Reagan's 1980 presidential campaign was a slim volume appropriately titled *The Present Danger*. With his usual literary flair, Podhoretz offered catchy metaphors for the coming renewal of the Cold War. He coined the term "Findlandization" to paint a scary scenario of U.S. capitulation to Soviet "domination."[96] Counterpoised to an "anti-American" "culture of appeasement," Podhoretz introduced his fellow "neoconservatives" as "new nationalists" prepared for a "literally fateful struggle."[97] Podhoretz's tract was a piece of vintage hyperbole, but its linkage of military and culture themes recalled the heady mission of the Congress for Cultural Freedom.

Prior to Reagan's election, the neoconservatives were far from unanimous on the wisdom of allying with Republican conservatives. In a 1979 article for the Republican *Commonsense* magazine, Jeane Kirkpatrick doubted any widespread party switching by "traditional liberals," despite her view that Jimmy Carter was "only slightly less objectionable" than George McGovern. Kirkpatrick argued that Republicans stood to reap short-term electoral gains from her fellow disaffected Democratic voters. On two critical issues, Kirkpatrick saw irresolvable differences between her own Coalition for a Democratic Majority and what she termed the "new liberals." National security policy presented the most obvious conflict, but so too did "social and economic policies" related to debate on "quotas." Kirkpatrick foresaw the increasing saliency of affirmative action and related policies.

> The distribution of scarce resources on the basis of race or sex not only violates widely shared beliefs concerning just rewards, it violates the traditional relationships between state and society. It commits government to use coercion to impose new practices on a reluctant society. New liberals argue that this use of government's power serves the cause of social justice. Traditional liberals see it as an unwarranted use of regulatory power which progressively narrows the scope of individual freedom, undermines the society's most basic values, and intrudes government's heavy hand into many subjects remote from its appropriate concern—from school busing to boys' choirs; from hiring and firing to football.[98]

Kirkpatrick, still a Democrat, expressed a stance toward the role of the state not incompatible with conservative ideology. But other neoconservatives maintained substantive differences with the agenda of the New Right. Sidney Hook, for example, urged fellow Social Democrats to recognize that conservatives were intent on dismantling the welfare state and "abandoning the principle of equality of opportunity, and insisting that the only kind of equality which is compatible with a truly liberal society is one in which there is simply and only equality before the law."[99] On a basis more practical than philosophical, Social Democrats U.S.A. executive director Carl Gershman criticized the New Right's brand of anticommunism as "frequently strident and occasionally paranoid."[100] Gershman cited the campaign against the Panama Canal treaties as evidence of the New Right's interest in arousing public anger and fixating on military solutions to the "challenge of communism." Instead, Gershman wrote, "we must seek to compete with communism ideologically, and defeat it on ideological grounds, while we contain it militarily."[101]

Ultimately, according to neoconservative sociologist Robert Nisbet, few of the prominent intellectuals associated with *Commentary* and *The Public Interest* voted for Reagan in 1980.[102] Some of the same stylistic, tactical, and ideological differences that caused neoconservatives to resist a thorough alliance with Reagan and the New Right would deepen in the late 1980s, once the defeat of "communism" was at hand. (As we will see in Chapter 12, the end of Ronald Reagan's second term coincided with an outbreak of New Right–neoconservative factional conflict.)

At the outset of the Reagan era, the reluctance of neoconservatives to abandon the Democratic Party made little difference on electoral outcomes. A sizeable number of registered Democrats voted Republican in 1980,[103] but that was not to the credit of neoconservatives, who were few in number and uninfluential outside elite circles. Instead, the primary political influence of neoconservatives would develop *after* Reagan's election. Though some neoconservatives remained hesitant to ally themselves with the New Right, the Reagan administration's anti-communist agenda proved irresistible. As we will see in the next chapter, neoconservatives became useful assets for the new administration's foreign and economic policy objectives and, in the process, inevitable allies of the conservative New Right.

PART III

THE REAGAN ERA
AND BEYOND, 1980–1995

CHAPTER 9

Right-Wing Power in the 1980s

THE STATE-MOVEMENT CONVERGENCE

Conventional wisdom recalls conservative activists as wholehearted endorsers of the "Reagan revolution." In reality, the Right gave candidate and President Reagan qualified support that was contingent on the Reagan camp's commitment to a three-fold right-wing agenda on issues of the economy, foreign affairs and traditional morality. During the 1970s, the New Right and neoconservative movements had grown in organizational influence. This was due in large part to the political arousal of conservative economic elites. Richard Mellon Scaife alone spent $100 million on the Heritage Foundation and a slew of similar think tanks.[1] By the early 1980s, the "conservative labyrinth" spanned nine foundations, dozens of corporate backers and some seventy major organizations, in categories ranging from military lobbies, electoral vehicles, media watchdogs, and campus outreach.[2]

The growth of conservative movement resources meant two things in relation to the Reagan campaign and new presidency. First, here was a movement strong enough to have helped elect a growing block of Republican Congressmembers. The mobilization of New Right and Christian Right voter constituencies shifted the party's electoral strategy away from drafting "moderates" like Richard Nixon and Gerald Ford. Second, the New Right's power to influence the GOP's direction gave the movement, paradoxically, a degree of independence from the party and the presidency. The movement sector of the "Reagan revolution" was strong enough that it could protest administration policy decisions vociferously, without risking loss of access to the White House, in fact, without jeopardizing the state–movement alliance that endured under both the Reagan and Bush regimes. During Reagan's second term, for example, a coalition of New Right groups waged a hostile media campaign to oust State Department officials responsible for U.S. policy on southern Africa, even while the same group of activists collaborated in a covert State Department and White House "working group" on Central America.

The collaborative movement–state relationship between the Right and the Reagan White House reflected the unique opportunities and constraints each set of players faced. Government agencies and political parties must balance budgets and compromise with opponents. Movement organizations have the luxury of remaining truer to their principles. By definition, movement activists do not hold state power, and even under a like-minded regime, they are unlikely to be satisfied. Such was the case for the conservative movement under the Reagan–Bush administrations.

Despite their occasionally harsh rhetoric, however, the oppositional stance of conservatives toward the administration was more symbolic than punitively partisan. Most right-wing critics had no intention of abandoning Reagan's 1984 reelection campaign. In each of the areas of policy dissatisfaction, movement activists faced slightly different openings and obstacles in their path. Economic policy was the most difficult. A president simply must negotiate economic plans with Congress, and, to the dismay of many on the Right, Reagan made little headway in dismantling the welfare state.[3] On the "pro-family" issues, Reagan's symbolic endorsements mollified evangelical constituents for a while. More importantly, Reagan's judicial appointments laid the groundwork for future Christian Right successes through the court system.

More than in these two areas, foreign policy offered the greatest opportunities for a flourishing alliance between right-wing movements and the administration. On foreign policy, state elites were less divided than they were on the quality and degree of state intervention in the economy. By definition, the state controls warfare, from the "low intensity conflict" tactics of intelligence agencies to the production of "high intensity" nuclear weapons. State elites can more credibly shape public opinion on foreign and military affairs than on issues closer to the direct experience of citizens.

During the 1980s, it was foreign and military policy that captivated New Right and neoconservative activists above all else. The Christian Right actively campaigned against abortion and gay rights, but shared the New Right–neoconservative alliance's preoccupation with communism. In part, that preoccupation derived from the administration's own obsession with the Soviet "evil empire" and its purported Third World outposts. Progressive countermovements mobilized against the nuclear arms race, in solidarity with Central American refugees and revolutions, and against South African apartheid. In league with an administration determined to roll back communism once and for all, anticommunist movement veterans had their work cut out for them.

In collaboration with state agencies, right-wing movements participated in making foreign policy in three ways: (1) *ideologically*, by spreading propaganda on behalf of anticommunist "freedom fighters" and in favor of the U.S. military buildup; (2) on a *partisan* level, by lobbying the administration and Congress for exhorbitant military spending; and (3) at an *administrative* level through collaboration in the military and intelligence agencies' covert operations, including the distribution of "humanitarian" supplies to paramilitary forces. In the realm of foreign policy, right-wing movements continued their pattern of a mixed system-supportive and oppositional stance. Activists endorsed the most interventionist and militarist of the Reagan administration's efforts, and protested those instances when State Department officials, in particular, seemed too soft on communism.

The collaboration of right-wing movements with Reagan's foreign policymaking apparatus was no mere academic question. During the 1980s, the U.S. government used proxy armies to wage the East–West struggle on Third World battlefields, particularly in Central America and southern Africa. In Guatemala, El Salvador, Nicaragua, Angola, Mozambique, and South Africa, hundreds of thousands of people were killed. The scope of the atrocities committed by forces allied with the United States defies calculation. In all of these countries, U.S. right-wing movement activists enlisted on the side of anticommunist military and paramilitary forces, and therefore share responsibility for the death and destruction perpetrated by their fellow "freedom fighters."

On foreign affairs, certainly, but also in regard to the Reagan administration's (upwardly) redistributive domestic tax policies, the Right's small libertarian contingent was unfavorably impressed with the Reagan agenda. In 1980, Libertarian Party candidate Ed Clark won a mere one percent of the popular vote.[4] A year after Reagan's election, one libertarian commentator noted that "Reaganism is steeped so thoroughly in the rhetoric of liberty and the free market that he has momentarily eclipsed the libertarian movement."[5] Libertarians analyzed Reagan's electoral victory as nothing but a referendum on Carter's economic policies.[6] But what they feared most about the new administration was Reagan's intended escalation of the nuclear arms race and U.S. military intervention abroad.[7] *Libertarian Review* editor Milton Mueller explained the distance between libertarians and the conservative movement and the New Right by tracing Reagan's electoral victory and the policy agendas that resulted from it to a "neoconservative coalition," one in which former New Deal liberal intellectuals came to wield excessive influence over the Republican Party. Writing for fellow libertarians, Mueller argued that

> Once we understand the nature of the political coalition that brought the GOP to power, it is easy to see just how wide a gulf separates the libertarian movement from the neoconservatives. Reaganites are not mushy libertarians and libertarians are not hard-core Reaganites. Neoconservatism is a mandate to reconsolidate and retrench state power; it is the New Deal encrusted with a patina of folksy conservative philosophy. Libertarianism, on the other hand, is animated by a radical critique of the justice and efficacy of state power—all state power, whether it be wielded by commissars or businessmen.[8]

Mueller proceeded to identify the anti-libertarian policy of the early Reagan administration: support for import quotas, immigration control, nuclear power subsidies, draft registration, illegalization of marijuana, and political spying. Underlying these were the "essential elements of the neoconservative program: renewed militarism, social conservatism, and economic retrenchment."[9]

The opposition of libertarians to all three dimensions of the Reagan policy plan left them unable to resume old alliances with the conservatives. Instead, during the 1980s, libertarianism remained a relatively isolated intellectual current, as it had been since the 1969 Young Americans for Freedom split had compelled anti-war libertarians to forge their own political party (see Chapter 5). As we will see in Chapter 12, it was only when the end of the Cold War spurred faction fighting between New Rightists and neoconservatives that self-described "paleoconservatives" reasserted a libertarian influence within the broader conservative movement. Under Reagan, the libertarian element of the three-fold "fusionist" strategy took a back seat to anticommunist militarism and moral traditionalism, and anti-statist libertarian thinkers played little role in the Right's state–movement relationship. Instead, the evident pattern was one of collaboration between a strong state and those right-wing movements likewise committed to statist policies.

FROM MARGIN TO CENTER

Ronald Reagan's popularity with the conservative movement began with his televised 1964 "Rendezvous with Destiny" speech on behalf of Barry Goldwater. After losing the 1976 Republican Party nomination to incumbent president Gerald Ford, Reagan's status on the Right was diminished only briefly when New Right leader Richard

Viguerie and others backed Texas Governor John Connally in the 1980 primaries. Connally promoters feared Reagan might not easily defeat Jimmy Carter. More than that, they suspected Reagan's right-wing stances were more rhetorical than real.[10] Against the vocal wishes of the New Right and Christian Right leaders, Reagan chose "moderate" running mate George Bush to balance the ticket.[11] Bush agreed to meet with anti-abortion movement leaders and publicly reverse his pro-choice position in favor of the Republican platform plank calling for a constitutional amendment against abortion.[12] But these assurances aside, Bush remained suspect for his "eastern establishment ties" and his skepticism about supply-side economics.[13]

Once the campaign intensified, New Right and Christian Right activists worked to solidify the debt of gratitude the new administration would owe them. Corporate America threw its weight behind Reagan's candidacy.[14] But not since the 1964 Goldwater campaign had large numbers of movement activists mobilized so enthusiastically for an election. Nixon's 1968 and 1972 campaigns had attracted only tepid support from the Right, and conservatives had been even less enthusiastic about Ford in 1976. 1980 proved to be a testing ground, both for the network of fundraising and electoral vehicles the New Right had been building outside of the Republican Party since the early 1970s, and also for the coalition of new constituencies Reagan hoped to attract.

Conservative movement columnist Robert D. Novak commended the Republican convention for its departure from "labor-baiting" and its "conscious effort to win the allegiance of the blue-collar worker." Like other commentators, Novak was struck by the participation of hundreds of delegates from the Moral Majority. To Novak, these new political activists represented "possibly the first massive addition to Republican ranks since the coming of the New Deal."[15] Not only did evangelical Christians contribute significantly to Reagan's vote totals,[16] but New Right-assisted organizations Christian Voice and the Moral Majority took credit for routing a slate of veteran liberal Senators and Representatives. These included Senators George McGovern (D-SD), Frank Church (D-ID), Birch Bayh (D-IN) and John Culver (D-IA). Together with the evangelicals, Paul Weyrich's Committee for the Survival of a Free Congress and Howard Phillips' Conservative Caucus targeted key Congressional races and celebrated the expansion of a right-wing bloc in the U.S. Senate.[17] Of the more than $16 million candidates received from supposedly non-partisan political action committees in the 1980 elections, an estimated 81 percent was spent by right-wing PACs. Of these PACs, the largest was Senator Jesse Helms' Congressional Club, which spent $4.6 million, mostly on the Reagan campaign.[18]

Conservatives hailed Reagan's victory as the ultimate reversal of Barry Goldwater's stunning 1964 defeat. Howard Phillips of the Conservative Caucus called 1980 "the greatest victory for conservatism since the American Revolution." But Phillips also warned that unless Reagan were to successfully carry out the conservative movement's mandate of reducing taxes and "zero-funding for unessential non-defense programs and agencies," Reagan voters would blame their future economic woes on the president and—by extension—on his New Right backers.[19]

Social democrats read the 1980 election results as a popular protest of a bad economy and a rejection of the Democrats' McGovernite "new liberalism" on foreign policy and moral issues. They also viewed Reagan's victory as a foreboding threat to the trade union movement and to racial and gender equality.[20] Prominent neoconservatives moved further to the right with Reagan's election. *Commentary* editor Norman Podhoretz pronounced the election the "artificially delayed emergence of a new Republican majority."[21] For Podhoretz, Reagan's victory would mean the completion of tasks left unfinished when Nixon, having beaten McGovern's "new politics" Democrats, had been forced ignominiously out of office. Reagan would be the one to implement a three-fold conservative agenda:

> economic policy that will unleash the productive energies of an artificially hampered people and thereby foster growth; a program of rearmament that will make our defenses invulnerable; . . . [and] a legal structure that will encourage the revitalization of the values of "family, work, and neighborhood."[22]

No sooner were the ballots counted than the National Conservative Political Action Committee (NCPAC) publicized a list of twenty-one Senators targeted for defeat in 1982.[23] Most of these stood little chance of losing their seats, but the New Right's goal was to stress its own permanence as a Republican Party asset. Reagan was quick to acknowledge his debt to the conservative movement as a whole. In a March 1981 speech before the annual Conservative Political Action Conference, Reagan thanked his "fellow truth-seekers" at *National Review* and *Human Events*, and invoked the names of the movement's intellectual forefathers: Russell Kirk, Friedrich A. Hayek, Henry Hazlitt, Milton Friedman, James Burnham, Ludwig von Mises, and Frank Meyer.[24]

Meanwhile, the intellectual and activist successors to these fusionist era thinkers had already formulated a comprehensive blueprint for the incoming Reagan team. Beginning in 1980, the Heritage Foundation had assembled over 250 academicians, corporate executives, Congressional staff members, and others to produce a 3,000 page list of recommendations for the overhaul of virtually every known federal agency. Reagan transition team director Edwin Meese pledged to rely on the leading New Right think tank's *Mandate for Leadership*, which, among other things, advocated the elimination of the Departments of Education and Energy, tax cuts, and expanded resources for U.S. intelligence agencies.[25]

Beyond policy suggestions, the Heritage Foundation sought to implement its "people are policy" slogan by establishing for itself an advisory role in the recruitment of administration appointees. Heritage president Edwin Feulner headed the group within the Reagan transition team that dealt with foreign aid policy,[26] but conservatives balked at Reagan's recruitment of moderate Republicans like George Shultz, Caspar Weinberger, and Elizabeth Dole.[27] Early in 1981, *Human Events* published two double-page spreads with photographs and brief descriptions of more than sixty movement conservatives granted administrative posts.[28] Among these, the plums were those credited to Representative Jack Kemp's influence over Reagan's economic policy transition team. Having lost the vice-presidential nomination to George Bush, Kemp remained the New Right's Congressional standard bearer, and it was because of Kemp's advice that Reagan named Representative David Stockman (R-MI) to direct the Office of Management and Budget (OMB), and supply-side advocates Dr. Paul Craig Roberts, Dr. Norman Ture, and Steve Entin to serve in Treasury Department posts under Donald Regan.[29]

Though Kemp's hand in the selection of Reagan's economic team was seen by conservatives as their biggest step toward influencing government, economic policymaking would prove to be the biggest stumbling block for the New Right–Reagan administration alliance. A year into Reagan's first term, conservative movement leaders began convening summit meetings and issuing "report cards" to the effect that the "Reagan revolution" was failing.[30] The administration fielded complaints on all policy fronts, but taxes and the budgetary process became the greatest sources of antagonism between the White House and outside movement supporters. That was because Reagan's proposed tax and spending cuts, more than other policy initiatives, faced the greatest resistance from Congressional Democrats. As we will see further on in this chapter, the extent of elite unity helped determine the degree to which right-wing movements saw their policy preferences realized. "Reaganomics" remained the most contested set of policies, while on foreign affairs, Reagan and the New Right proceeded relatively unchallenged. On social issues—particularly those made a priority by the Christian Right (and discussed in Chapter 10)—Reagan's first-term actions were largely symbolic, and therefore elicited less resistance than supply-side economics.

"REAGANOMICS"
AND THE REDISTRIBUTION OF WEALTH

Supply-side economic theory predated the Reagan administration by several years. In 1977, Representative Jack Kemp and Senator William Roth (R-DE) introduced legislation to reduce tax rates by 30 percent. The Kemp–Roth bill was based on the supply-side tenet that large tax cuts would stimulate economic activity and thereby increase tax revenues over time.[31] The term "supply-side" came from its advocates' recognition that Keynesian economists emphasized the "demand" side of economic planning: the macroeconomic features of government spending, wages, and credit. According to this new theory, the supply-side of the equation includes productivity, investment, and microeconomic variables of individual incentives. If inflation resulted from excess demand, the supply-siders argued, then the solution was to increase supply by reducing capitalists' disincentives to invest and produce.[32] Neoconservative supply-sider Irving Kristol lauded the theory as "frankly reactionary" and a throw-back to Adam Smith's *The Wealth of Nations*.[33] It was Kristol who recruited *Wall Street Journal* columnist Jude Wanniski to write the first lengthy explanation of supply-side theory for the neoconservative journal *The Public Interest*.[34] In that article, Wanniski introduced economist Arthur Laffer's hypothesis that high tax rates deter taxable economic activity. The so-called "Laffer curve" became the supply-siders' visual device for showing that a 100 percent tax rate would yield no tax revenue. As one after another of the leading supply-siders joined forces, they found no more forceful advocate than Jack Kemp. By the mid-1970s, Kemp's Capitol Hill office had become an informal base camp for the supply-side "revolution."

As the keynote speaker for the 1980 Conservative Political Action Conference (CPAC), Kemp invoked California's Proposition 13 as evidence of a voter consensus on the need to cut taxes, and he endorsed Ronald Reagan as the only Republican presidential candidate committed to pervasive tax cuts.[35] Republicans rallied behind Reagan's campaign pledge to push the Kemp–Roth tax bill through Congress.[36] In eager anticipation of the Reagan tax cuts, the 600 conservative economists and other members of the elite Mont Pelerin Society held their fall 1980 conference at Reagan's favorite think tank, the Hoover Institution at Stanford University.[37] Timed closely with Reagan's inauguration, the publication of George Gilder's bestselling *Wealth and Poverty* lent a "moral" imperative to the supply-siders' calls for tax and spending cuts.[38]

Within days of Reagan's election victory, Kemp recommended Representative David Stockman to head the Office of Management and Budget (OMB). Stockman's job was to balance Reagan's proposed 30 percent tax rate cuts with a plan to remove about $40 billion from the demand-side of the budget. That meant gutting federal spending programs. But for Stockman, the feat proved impossible. About half of the federal budget was devoted to untouchable entitlement expenditures like Social Security. Another chunk went to the Pentagon, and the Reagan administration was committed to the largest peacetime military spending increases in U.S. history—to the tune of $1.6 trillion over the first five years. That left only a few federal spending programs subject to elimination. Stockman quickly learned that politics took precedence over supply-side economic theory when he proposed unsuccessfully to cut $752 million from the Export–Import Bank, which subsidizes major U.S. manufacturers (including Boeing, Lockheed, General Electric, and McDonnell Douglas), all of whom had secured a loyal Republican Congressional constituency.[39] The plan to balance investment-inducing tax cuts with reductions in federal spending was unrealistic, because "free market" rhetoric was no match for the mutually advantageous dependence of political and economic elites on actual state intervention in the economy.

Despite resistance to massive spending cuts, Congress reached a compromise on taxes, and in July 1981 passed a 25 percent tax rate reduction bill. The satisfaction of conservative activists was short-lived, however. Without massive spending cuts, the administration saw mounting deficits and a recession on its way. They quickly blunted the 1981 Economic Recovery Tax Act with a series of tax hikes in 1982, 1983, and 1984, including a payroll tax increase that flew directly in the face of supply-side theory.[40] When the tax increases began, Richard Viguerie organized an ad hoc committee of "Conservatives Opposed to the Tax Increase,"[41] but the protests of movement activists fell on deaf ears. Reaganite Senators and Representatives fared no better in combatting the tax increases proposed by moderate Republican Senator Robert Dole and approved by the Democrats. Reagan aides accused Jack Kemp of grandstanding on the tax issue as a ploy to launch his own 1984 presidential campaign.[42]

At the start of the Reagan administration's campaign to cut taxes in 1981, OMB Director David Stockman admitted to *Atlantic* magazine writer William Greider that the across-the-board 30 percent tax cut idea was really "a Trojan horse to bring down the top rate."[43] Tax cutting was the supply-siders' new twist on the old "trickle down" economic theory that a benefit for the rich is a benefit for all.

The ultimate effects of Reagan economic policies were indeed a boon to the wealthy. Though the tax cutters were never fully satisfied with their handiwork, the wealthiest 5 percent of the population gained phenomenally from the new tax laws. By 1983 the percentage of federal tax receipts derived from corporate income taxes dropped to an all time low of 6.2 percent, down from 12.5 percent in 1980, and the top rate of the capital gains tax was reduced from 28 to 20 percent. The tiny percentage of Americans who saw their incomes soar during the 1980s paid a greater amount of taxes but contributed a smaller relative share of total tax revenues.[44]

REAGAN FOREIGN POLICY AND THE PARTICIPATION OF RIGHT-WING MOVEMENTS

Early in Reagan's first term, the conservative movement issued vocal protests of administration policy on numerous scores. In the summer of 1981, a coalition of New Right groups opposed Reagan's nomination of Sandra Day O'Connor to the Supreme Court on the grounds that she was insufficiently "pro-life."[45] The cover story for *Conservative Digest*'s July 1982 issue, headlined "Has Reagan Deserted the Conservatives?", featured a laundry list of policy complaints, commentaries from a range of New Right and neoconservative leaders, and an open letter from 43 right-wing Congressmembers. Topping the *Conservative Digest* list of criticisms was the administration's proposed tax increases and failure to balance the budget. Beyond that, critics protested Reagan's failure to enact constitutional amendments on school prayer and abortion. On specific foreign policy issues, critics charged Reagan with weakness toward the Soviet bloc.[46]

Just as a coterie of right-wing thinkers had crafted the arguments for supply-side economic policy, a small group of anticommunist activists proposed guidelines for Reagan administration foreign policy before the 1980 election. Before and during Reagan's tenure, the relationship between state elites and supportive movement activists evidenced a greater degree of tactical collaboration on anticommunist militarism than on economic policy. Reaganite anticommunists enjoyed even greater state facilitation than their McCarthy-era predecessors.

Building on the momentum of its campaigns against the Carter administration's Panama Canal and SALT treaties (see Chapter 5), in 1979 the American Security Council (ASC) formed a Congressional Task Force for the purpose of lobbying on behalf of anticommunist governments in Central America.[47] The Task Force blamed Jimmy Carter for Nicaragua's overthrow of dictator Anastasio Somoza, and the Congressmembers on board ASC's Task Force pledged to back remaining anticommunist forces in Central America. Two advisers to the Reagan presidential campaign, former Defense Intelligence Agency director Daniel Graham and Major General John Singlaub (USA-Ret.), led a

December 1979 delegation of ASC activists to Guatemala. There they assured leaders of military death squads that "Mr. Reagan recognizes that a good deal of dirty work has to be done."[48] In 1980, the Reagan campaign accepted millions of dollars in contributions from Guatemalan businessmen and U.S. businessmen living in Guatemala. In turn, Guatemalan death squad leader Mario Sandoval Alarcon was invited to dance at Reagan's 1981 inaugural ball.[49]

Also during the 1980 presidential campaign, a group of anticommunist activists calling themselves the Committee of Santa Fe, drafted a policy blueprint, *A New Inter-American Policy for the Eighties*, which outlined the means to roll back communism in Latin America.[50] The report was published by the Council for Inter-American Security, a Washington, D.C.-based research and lobbying outfit formed in the 1970s to promote the agenda of South American military governments.[51] During the 1980s, the Council became a vehicle for the gathering of intelligence data about the U.S. Left.[52] Among its proposals, the Committee of Santa Fe's report called on the incoming administration to "begin to counter (not react against) liberation theology" and to recognize that human rights is "a culturally and politically relative concept" to be replaced by a "policy of political and ethical realism."[53] Extending beyond references to Guatemala and Nicaragua, the report called for U.S. policy to "recognize the integral linkage between internal subversion and external aggression."[54] This phrase was a chilling and obvious nod to the use of state terrorism to eliminate Central American "subversives." (One of the report's authors later took credit for specific pieces of Reagan policy in Latin America.)[55]

The December 1980 assassinations of four North American church women working in El Salvador propelled the civil war in that country to the top of the incoming Reagan administration's agenda. At issue was the question of continuing U.S. aid to the Salvadoran military. Policy making toward El Salvador was closely tied to the "loss" of nearby Nicaragua to the 1979 revolution led by the Sandinista National Liberation Front (FSLN). In January of 1981 Reagan's Secretary of State Alexander Haig announced that U.S. foreign policy would no longer be dictated by a concern for "human rights." Instead, the threat of "international terrorism" would take center stage.[56] A month later, the State Department released a "White Paper," which purported to link Nicaraguan "communists" with an arms flow to El Salvador.[57] The White Paper was later shown to be factually spurious, but not until after its claims had successfully framed official debate on Central America as a fight between "democracy" and "communism."[58] For Guatemala, where Jimmy Carter had banned U.S. military assistance on human rights grounds, the new administration was poised to resume funding.[59]

Within this context, neoconservatives—including many veterans of the Congress for Cultural Freedom—joined *Commentary* editor Midge Decter in announcing the formation of the Committee for the Free World. At a time when U.S. military aid made death squad killings in El Salvador a daily reality, the Committee's April 6, 1981 announcement in the *New York Times* opened with the headline: "We—a group of intellectuals and religious leaders—applaud American policy in El Salvador." Signatories included prominent neoconservative academics and activists; the gist of their statement was support for El Salvador's military government and condemnation of the guerrilla movement's liberal "apologists" in the United States.[60] Several days after the announcement appeared, Midge Decter received a congratulatory note from Reagan's first National Security adviser, Richard V. Allen.[61] Decter would receive similar accolades from administration officials throughout the 1980s, as the Committee coordinated propaganda and lobbying activities on behalf of various "freedom fighter" armies, until she declared her mission accomplished in 1990.[62]

Adding to the neoconservatives' ideological support for Reagan's Central American policy, the American Security Council (ASC) continued its use of television documentaries to mobilize grassroots lobbying. Beginning in early 1981, ASC spent a small fortune airing *Attack on the Americas*, a film that juxtaposed frightening footage of Central American violence and calm interviews with foreign policy experts like Jeane Kirkpatrick and Henry Kissinger.[63] Like Midge Decter's group of neoconservative intellectuals, ASC combined media activities with lobbying and fundraising for Central American paramilitary forces.

The Committee for the Free World and the American Security Council each represented two cooperative but distinct wings of the anticommunist movement. The Committee attracted a more elite-oriented base of writers and university professors. ASC, funded since the mid-1950s by large corporations, and led by retired military officers, built a Coalition for Peace Through Strength that linked 158 mass-based anticommunist organizations and about 240 Congressmembers.[64] During the 1970s campaign against Senate ratification of the SALT II treaty, the New Right and neoconservative wings of the anticommunist movement had gained collaborative experience. Midge Decter's position as a trustee of the Heritage Foundation was representative of unity among the disparate sectors of the anticommunist movement.[65] The neoconservative wing won influential administrative appointments while ASC's Coalition for Peace Through Strength concentrated on grassroots Congressional lobbying.

Anticommunist activists viewed Reagan's appointment of Jeane Kirkpatrick as United Nations ambassador to be an important step in the reversal of Jimmy Carter's attention to international human rights. *Human Events* observed the appointment as "a shrewd move by the President-elect to cement Republican ties to the conservative Democratic community."[66] Kirkpatrick was a leader of the neoconservatives' Coalition for a Democratic Majority. Her 1979 "Dictatorships and Double Standards" *Commentary* article, indicting U.S. weakness for the "loss" of the Shah's Iran and Somoza's Nicaragua, had demonstrated her skill at crafting simple arguments out of diverse and complex international affairs. Beyond that, Kirkpatrick shared the view of Reagan's advisers that Latin America was the pivotal battleground in the East–West conflict.[67] Like Kirkpatrick, Reagan's nominee for Assistant Secretary of State for Human Rights, Ernest Lefever, had published articles stating that friendly foreign dictators deserved U.S. support. Lefever directed the neoconservative Ethics and Public Policy Center, and this think tank had also accepted money from the Nestle Corporation, after Lefever had sided with the company against a church-sponsored boycott to protest Nestle's marketing of infant formula in the Third World. (Unsanitary conditions make formula use hazardous to children in underdeveloped countries.) Amid revelations of Lefever's ties to Nestle, the Senate rejected the Lefever nomination.[68] But fellow neoconservative activist (and son-in-law to Midge Decter) Elliott Abrams, was appointed as an Assistant Secretary of State.

Like Kirkpatrick, Abrams was eager to advance the anticommunist cause in Central America, and the two appointments gave New Rightists and neoconservatives tangible evidence of the administration's commitment to the two movements' shared goals. During Reagan's first term, right-wing foreign policy activists hoped to direct an expanded Pentagon budget into research and deployment of MX missiles and the "Strategic Defense Initiative" (SDI), secure military aid for El Salvador and Guatemala and combat negative press coverage of those governments' death squads, secure material and training for a growing army of Nicaraguan Contras, and repeal the Clark Amendment, whereby Congress had prohibited U.S. funding of a proxy army, the purpose of which was to overthrow the Angolan government. During Reagan's second term, all the major New Right organizations joined a Coalition for the Strategic Defense Initiative, also known as High Frontier.[69] Reagan and the New Right were committed to SDI, against the demands of the mass movement for a freeze on the arms race. Apart from the drive to outdo the Soviet Union in nuclear weaponry, fighting left-wing forces in Central America topped the Right's foreign affairs agenda.

Early on, the administration's backing of the Nicaraguan Contras became the focus of policymakers' limited debate on Central America. The much celebrated Boland Amendment—passed in December 1982 as a weak compromise to Representative Tom Harkin's proposal to cease U.S. funding for the Contras altogether—accomplished little. Named after Senator Edward Boland (D-MA), the amendment banned funding for the express purpose of *overthrowing* the Nicaraguan government. Anything short of that was acceptable, and no one could have doubted that both Democrats and Republicans sought to replace Nicaragua's government with one to their liking. With reports of new outrageous acts of CIA-inspired terrorism against Nicaragua (the mining of the harbors, the publication of an assassination manual, and murder and mayhem at schools and health clinics), Congressional critics made motions toward restricting Contra funding. For right-wing activists, the Boland Amendment then became a political football that threatened to deprive their President of a free hand to fight the Sandinistas. The periodic threat of an official aid cut-off kept New Rightists, neoconservatives and the Christian Right continually mobilized on behalf of the "freedom fighters."

As early as 1983, Reagan's assistant Faith Ryan Whittlesey convened an Outreach Working Group on Central America, through which White House personnel coordinated with private organizations on media, direct mail, and legislative lobbying activities. The sheer scope of the "outreach" project—documented on White House stationary in the correspondence files of one of the participants—was impressive.[70] More than fifty groups attended White House briefings on Central America. These included Christian Right organizations such as Jerry Falwell's Moral Majority, Pat Robertson's Freedom Council, and Maranatha Campus Ministries; the neoconservative Institute on Religion and Democracy, the Ethics and Public Policy Center, the Jewish Institute for National Security Affairs, the Anti-Defamation League of B'nai B'rith, and the semi-governmental American Institute for Free Labor Development (AIFLD); plus the New Right outfits Accuracy in Media, the Eagle Forum, the Heritage Foundation, the Conservative Caucus, Young Americans for Freedom, and the Richard Viguerie Company.[71]

At the meetings, the groups gave reports on their recent activities. Whittlesey's office then circulated summary reports listing precise dates on which each organization hosted speakers, appeared on television and radio, mailed fundraising appeals, and so on. The agenda sheet of a May 18, 1983 White House meeting included a line asking participants, "How else can the administration be helpful?" Attached was a list of administration officials involved with the working group. These included Roger Fontaine and Walt Raymond of the National Security Council, Constantine Menges of the Central Intelligence Agency, Otto Reich of the Agency for International Development, Fred Ikle and Nestor Sanchez of the Defense Department, and Elliot Abrams, Assistant Secretary of State for

Human Rights. The agenda for one of the White House Working Group's meetings listed as a goal the "undermining [of] opposition organizations" such as the U.S. Catholic Conference, by arranging visits between conservative Central American and U.S. religious leaders.[72]

Around the same time, the administration's Office of Public Diplomacy contracted with right-wing activists William Pascoe and Michael Waller to provide intelligence reports on the activities of citizen groups opposed to U.S. intervention in El Salvador. These included the leftist solidarity movement and mainstream church groups.[73] Intelligence gathering by the Office of Public Diplomacy coincided with FBI operations aimed also at the anti-intervention movement.[74]

In addition to the media and lobbying work coordinated through Faith Ryan Whittlesey's office, member organizations of the Central American Working Group, plus others, conducted direct fundraising and logistical tasks for the Nicaraguan Contras. At the center of the "private" aid network was the World Anti-Communist League (WACL).[75] WACL was formed in the late 1960s as an outgrowth of the Asian People's Anti-Communist League, a consortium of right-wing Asian government leaders. As was discussed in Chapter 6, by the 1970s WACL had become a meeting ground for U.S. rightists, European neo-Nazis, and Latin American death squad figures. In 1981, the rotating leadership of WACL went to (retired) Major General John Singlaub's U.S. chapter, the American Council for World Freedom (ACWF). Singlaub volunteered himself as a "private aid" coordinator for the Reagan administration. Through his worldwide WACL contacts, Singlaub offered military advisers to the Nicaraguan Contras, and brokered some of the administration's third-country, covert supply deals.[76]

The fatal September 1984 helicopter crash of two U.S. mercenaries on a supply mission over Nicaragua punctuated the role of the "private" Contra supply network. By then the leading Contra fundraisers in the United States fell into several categories: paramilitary mercenary outfits (*Soldier of Fortune* magazine, Civilian Military Assistance, the Air Commando Association), Christian Right "ministries" (Pat Robertson's Christian Broadcasting Network, the Catholic Knights of Malta), and the network of conservative movement political lobbies (American Security Council, Citizens for America, the Council for Inter-American Security, and numerous others).[77] As early as 1984, Pat Robertson had used his tax-exempt "religious" television broadcasts to raise a reported $3 million for the Contras' Fuerza Democratica Nicaraguense (FDN).[78] The Reverend Sun Myung Moon's Unification Church, through its various front groups, likewise became a mainstay of the Contra supply network. In 1985, in one project that made for strange political bedfellows, the Unification Church-owned *Washington Times* established the Nicaraguan

Freedom Fund with an initial $100,000 donation from Moonie leader Bo Hi Pak, and an additional $20,000 from Jeane Kirkpatrick. The fund's board members included neoconservative activists Michael Novak and Midge Decter.[79] At the height of the fundraising campaign, in the mid-1980s, journalist investigators wondered about the credibility of the supply network's claims of "private" donations estimated at $25 million.[80] Many of the fundraising groups welcomed media attention for their delivery of supplies and their meetings with Contra forces. No doubt, "private" supply missions were approved—if not arranged—by the field officers of U.S. intelligence agencies responsible for covert operations in the staging area of southern Honduras.[81] For public relations purposes, the "private" Contra benefactors had an interest in exaggerating their fundraising successes. As with any effective covert operation, the element of "plausible deniability" was key. Citizen Singlaub's "private" network performed the role of an overt lightening rod for much of the public criticism over continued Contra aid. Only after the Iran–Contra scandal began to unravel did the scope and size of the Contra funding operation begin to come to light.

The significance of the "private" aid effort resided in the administration's disposition to use domestic anticommunist groups as a countermovement to the church- and mass-based anti-intervention movement (and the broad sector of public opinion it represented), and to thwart what little anti-intervention resolve was to be found among members of Congress.

To lobby Congress, a group of neoconservatives and social democrats—including prominent figures in the Committee for the Free World—formed Friends of the Democratic Center in Central America (PRODEMCA).[82] Publicly, PRODEMCA presented itself as a bipartisan group of former government officials, academics, business, and labor leaders at a time when the Reagan administration was determined to sustain the Contra supply effort, by the many means necessary. Behind the scenes, through what was no more than a closet-sized office inside the headquarters of the neoconservative Institute on Religion and Democracy (IRD),[83] PRODEMCA served as a conduit for the National Endowment for Democracy's funding of Nicaragua's pro-Contra *La Prensa* newspaper,[84] and gathered intelligence on various Congressmembers' rationales for opposing "covert aid" to Contra combatants.[85] PRODEMCA president Penn Kemble was a participant in the illegal Contra supply operations conducted by Carl "Spitz" Channell and Richard Miller.[86] Once the Iran–Contra scandal broke, PRODEMCA quickly vanished from public view.

At all levels of activity, there were both ideological and organizational incentives for state–movement collaboration in Reagan's Central American operations. The administration was more committed than its most recent predecessors to rolling back "communism." Yet unlike the Truman, Eisenhower, and Kennedy administrations of the early Cold War era, Reagan foreign policymakers faced a broad-based, post-Vietnam war-era peace movement that actively resisted U.S. military intervention. That countermovement led state elites to rely, to a heightened degree, on right-wing movement supporters. For their part, anticommunist activists seized an opportunity to fight on the winning side of a policy debate. To the extent that the White House offered coordination, logistical assistance, and legitimacy, the lobbying and fundraising groups stood to gain greater efficiency and an expanded resource base.

For many among the Christian right, U.S. operations in Central America were a motivating introduction to foreign affairs activism. Following the 1982 coup d'etat that installed General Efrain Rios Montt as dictator of Guatemala, Pat Robertson and other Christian Right leaders lobbied successfully for the resumption of U.S. military aid to Guatemala.[87] In 1984 the Christian Broadcasting Network devoted extensive air time to live reports and interviews regarding elections in El Salvador. Pat Robertson's large television audience was repeatedly instructed on how to lobby Congress for military aid to El Salvador.

As the wars in Central America wore on, anticommunist activists sought to expand the "freedom fighter" project into southern Africa. However, on this front, the relationship between right-wing movements and the Reagan administration became more complicated.

At issue was the question of U.S. support for the Contras' southern African counterparts. Following public exposure of the CIA's efforts to defeat the Angolan government in the late 1970s, Congress had passed the Clark Amendment, which prohibited funding for Angolan rebel leader Jonas Savimbi's UNITA army. Following Reagan's election, the U.S. anticommunist movement sought repeal of the restrictive Clark Amendment.[88] But only with the heightened momentum of the international movement against South African apartheid did Savimbi's UNITA cause gain salience. Unlike Central America, southern Africa was less credibly portrayed as part of the United States' "backyard." The stark racism of the apartheid regime's regional domination likewise made a case for U.S. intervention less easily explained as a fight against communism. Some Reagan administration players simply preferred not to meddle on Pretoria's turf.

Then, in June of 1985, at Jonas Savimbi's Jamba, Angola headquarters, Contra supporter Lewis Lehrman convened "freedom fighter" leaders from Nicaragua, Angola, Afghanistan, and Laos for a summit meeting at which all present signed a unity pact.[89] Lehrman was the head of Citizens for America, one of the numerous Washington-based lobbies implicated in the State Department's covert Office of Public Diplomacy operations.[90] The highly publicized Jamba meeting occurred in the midst of a wide-ranging lobbying effort that led to Reagan's November 1985 endorsement of covert aid for Savimbi's army.[91] The goal of defeating the Angolan military—and the Cuban troops who volunteered to fight alongside them—was understood by all partisans as a crucial battle in the struggle against apartheid. As a "frontline" state, socialist Angola was a safe haven for South African and Namibian revolutionaries. The Jamba meeting coincided with a peak in the international campaign to pressure governments and corporations for sanctions against South Africa. Pretoria's U.S. supporters understood the stakes and their own potential role in preventing change.

When international efforts against apartheid had increased during the 1970s, Pretoria had responded with a sophisticated campaign of propaganda and political influence, aimed primarily at Western Europe and the United States. Upon exposure, the scandalous covert operations were named "Muldergate" after South African Information Minister Cornelius Mulder. Among the 160 to 180 secret media projects involved in "Muldergate," it was revealed that the South African government had purchased interests in several U.S. newspapers, including the Unification Church-owned *Washington Times*. Muldergate's activist beneficiaries included (would-be Reagan foreign policy advisor) Lieutenant General Daniel Graham; neoconservative Ernest Lefever, head of the Ethics and Public Policy Center; plus numerous Christian Right "ministries."[92]

A decade later, a slate of New Right groups linked a resumption of aid to Savimbi to a pressure campaign against the Reagan State Department. At the forefront was Howard Phillips' Conservative Caucus. Beginning in 1985, Phillips led a series of publicity tours to South Africa while he sponsored newspaper advertisements attacking Secretary of State George Shultz and Assistant Secretary of State for African Affairs Chester Crocker. Prominent New Right leaders joined Phillips in condemning the State Department for insufficiently backing UNITA in Angola and the RENAMO terrorists in Mozambique, as well as for supporting elections in Namibia. A dozen New Right groups called for Secretary Shultz's ouster.[93] But these tactics of opposition belied a more nuanced relationship between the administration and the U.S. anticommunist movement regarding southern Africa. Even as elements of the State Department remained leery of Jonas Savimbi, Reagan resumed covert assistance to UNITA fighters responsible for killing thousands of Angolan civilians. In Mozambique, the violence of the "freedom fighters'" was even more indiscriminate and bloody. A 1988 State Department report criticized RENAMO's routine practice of cutting off the limbs and facial features of Mozambican civilians.[94]

Some of the same New Right groups active in the supply network to the Nicaraguan Contras joined forces on behalf of UNITA and RENAMO. These included the World Anti-Communist League (WACL), *Soldier of Fortune* mercenary magazine, Howard Phillips' Conservative Caucus, Jack Wheeler's Freedom Research Foundation, Lewis Lehrman's Citizens for America, and many others.[95] Jerry Falwell spoke publicly on behalf of South African President P. W. Botha and pledged to work to defeat a proposed sanctions bill.[96] Christian Voice-member and publisher David Balsiger organized the RAMBO Coalition to coordinate Christian Right and New Right supporters of southern African "freedom fighters." The RAMBO Coalition held demonstrations against Chevron Oil Corporation's business dealings with Angola and distributed propaganda subsidized by the South African government to hundreds of thousands of U.S. readers.[97]

As in the case of the Central American "freedom fighter" projects, these "private" groups evaded government scrutiny on a variety of potential legal violations, including tax-exempt status, the Foreign Agents Registration Act, and the Neutrality Act. While U.S. intelligence agencies surveilled and disrupted law-abiding liberal and leftist foreign policy groups, the federal government turned an acquiescent eye toward all manner of anticommunist movement activity.

Only on sanctions against South Africa was the administration ultimately forced to act against the New Right's preferences. Amid demonstrations by respected civil rights leaders outside the South African embassy in late 1984, *Human Events* denounced thirty-five Republican Congressmembers who signed a letter warning Pretoria that they would support economic sanctions against South Africa unless urgent action was taken to end apartheid.[98] Once a bipartisan sanctions bill began making its way through Congress, Reagan committed himself to vetoing it. Right-wing activists were unsuccessful in lobbying against a pro-sanctions override vote.[99] As pressure from the African National Congress mounted, Pretoria moved to severely restrict foreign press coverage inside South Africa. Then, in 1986, U.S. evangelical broadcasters began a pro-South Africa publicity campaign, in collaboration with the South African government. Propaganda operations in support of South Africa, UNITA, and RENAMO continued unabated, despite the anticommunist movement's failure to prevent economic sanctions against South Africa.[100] Beginning in 1986, Major General John Singlaub's World Anti-Communist League (WACL), along with a host of Christian Right groups, also joined forces with the Philippine military, following the election that forced dictator Ferdinand Marcos from power. To bolster the new leadership of Corazon

Aquino, some U.S. organizations participated in the expansion of violent counterinsurgency programs directed at the civilian supporters of Filipino Communist rebels.[101]

The Iran–Contra Scandal

By the late 1980s, the U.S. Right's foreign affairs activism spanned three continents. From Central America to Asia to southern Africa, the Right's zealous backing for anticommunist "freedom fighters" was matched only by that of the Reagan officials who lied to Congress about the labyrinth of illegal dealings known loosely as the "Iran–Contra" scandal. In late 1986, following Nicaragua's capture of U.S. mercenary Eugene Hasenfus, and the initial foreign press revelations about illegal U.S. arms sales to Iran, conservative movement activists rallied swiftly behind their public relations damaged president. White House Communications Director Patrick Buchanan, speaking before a gathering of right-wing Cuban Americans, voiced the Right's prevailing view that "if Colonel [Oliver] North ripped off the Ayatollah for $30 million and sent the money down to help the Freedom Fighters, then God bless Colonel North."[102] Right-wing activists Carl "Spitz" Channell and Richard Miller, who ran an interlocking cluster of lobbying and fundraising projects on behalf of the Contras, were quickly indicted and silenced by their agreement to cooperate with Iran–Contra prosecutors. Channell and Miller were effective fall guys as revelations of their illegal activities obscured the full gamut of involvement by right-wing activists in Contra supply operations. As Congressional investigators prepared for the summer 1987 Iran–Contra scandal hearings, they scrupulously avoided the role of movement activists, and narrowly focused on *what* Reagan knew and *when* he knew it. Political elites effectively protected each other and their outside movement supporters.

As a result, right-wing "freedom fighter" activism continued unabated. Howard Phillips and other New Rightists continued to lead publicity tours to South Africa; U.S. mercenaries continued to fight alongside their Nicaraguan Contra counterparts; and U.S. conservatives continued to praise El Salvador's ARENA political party, which was linked to death squads.[103] As the 1988 elections approached, Congressional conservatives sought to bolster their reputations as unyielding "freedom fighters." In May 1987 Senator Robert Dole addressed a conference and endorsed the efforts of the Freedom Federation, described by *Human Events* as "a Washington-based united front of Cuban, Afghan, Vietnamese, Angolan and numerous other groups dedicated to freeing their homelands from rule by the Soviet Union or its proxies."[104] Congressmember Donald Lukens (R-OH) used his Capitol Hill office to launch a medical aid supply effort by "private citizens" for the Nicaraguan Contras; eight other Republican Congressmembers joined Lukens' "Action Fund."[105] Presidential hopeful Jack Kemp led fifty New Right leaders on "Mision Libertad," a publicity tour through Central America to demonstrate support for the Contras and right-wing government officials and to protest the Reagan administration's tepid endorsement of the Arias peace plan for the region.[106]

At the high-technology end of the militarist spectrum, New Right activists continued to promote Reagan's pet weapons program, the Strategic Defense Initiative (SDI).[107] While she was also running a "humanitarian" assistance project for the Contras, Christian Right leader Beverly LaHaye, for example, collected 500,000 petition signatures to lobby Congress to proceed with SDI's "nuclear shield" plan.[108] In late 1987, the American Security Council led a slate of New Right groups in protest of Reagan's signing a treaty with the Soviet Union banning intermediate range nuclear forces (INF).[109] Howard Phillips called Reagan a "useful idiot for Kremlin propaganda,"[110] but the President signed the INF treaty anyway.

Despite strained relations between the movement and the administration, the unfinished fight against communism held factions of the conservative movement in check. Democrats contributed to the Right's unity by failing to exploit the opportunity to prosecute Iran–Contra players. Democratic presidential candidate Michael Dukakis proved unable—or unwilling—to challenge image makers' portrayal of George Bush as the stronger of two weak contenders.

UNFINISHED BUSINESS AT THE END OF THE REAGAN ERA

By the late 1980s, beneath the facade of unity among right-wing movements were strategic fissures that would widen into major lines of conflict once Reagan left the White House and the Cold War came to an end. One early development that foreshadowed the intra-movement disunity of the 1990s (see Chapter 12) was the formation of the National Endowment for Democracy (NED) in 1983.

"The creation of the National Endowment for Democracy was part and parcel of the resurgence of intervention abroad and the development of low-intensity conflict doctrines," wrote William I. Robinson in his study of NED's interventionist role in Nicaragua.[111] NED was designed to assume some of the same operational tasks the CIA performed for decades: funding and coordination of foreign political parties, trade unions, media outlets, and business and civic groups amenable to U.S.

corporate interests. But NED projects were to be conducted overtly, so as to avoid the public relations liabilities that accompanied the CIA's track record of scandalous exposures.[112] Four agencies were established as the primary funding conduits for NED grants abroad: the AFL-CIO's Free Trade Union Institute, the U.S. Chamber of Commerce's Center for International Private Enterprise (CIPE) and the two parties' respective international arms, the National Democratic Institute for International Affairs (NDI) and the National Republican Institute for International Affairs (NRI).

From the start, NED drew its executive personnel from neoconservative ranks. NED President Carl Gershman was an aide to UN Ambassador Jeane Kirkpatrick and a former leader of Social Democrats, U.S.A.[113] Between 1984 and 1990, NED channeled about $152 million to pro-U.S. political and cultural institutions in 77 countries, mostly in Latin America and Eastern Europe.[114] Individual foreign projects were solicited from, and administered by, U.S. university departments and right-wing think tanks.[115] Through an elaborate and expensive campaign, NED claimed large responsibility for the Nicaraguan Sandinistas' 1990 electoral defeat. In that operation, NED-sponsored election propaganda played the proverbial role of "carrot" in tandem with the "stick" of continuing Contra violence.[116]

Though NED's grant-making patterns followed the Reagan and, later, Bush administrations' priorities, rather than the other way around, the neoconservatives—unlike others on the Right—effectively secured an entire federal agency from which to operate. During the Nicaragua election operation, NED found favor across the New Right–neoconservative spectrum.[117] But well after the collapse of the Soviet Union left rightists of Patrick Buchanan's stripe calling for a reduction in U.S. intervention abroad, NED remained an institutional vehicle through which neoconservatives continued to export U.S.-style "democracy." During the Bush years—and especially around the time of the Persian Gulf war—the charge made by conservatives that neoconservatives held excessive influence over U.S. foreign policymaking became the centerpiece of a feud between neoconservatives and their nemeses, the self-described "paleoconservatives." As we will see in Chapter 12, inherent philosophical differences between neoconservative internationalism, and a latent "America First" nationalism, became increasingly salient and threatened the Right's unity prior to Bush's reelection defeat.

Until the end of the Cold War was at hand, however, neoconservatives and New Right conservatives shared a generally supportive stance toward Reagan–Bush foreign policy. Exceptions arose when the administration—for reasons of its own limitations in the international arena—was restrained from following the consistently harder line of right-wing movements and, instead, implemented sanctions against South Africa, condemned RENAMO terrorist atrocities in Mozambique, and signed the INF treaty with the Soviet Union. None of these administration actions resulted in the unwillingness of right-wing activists to promote the Reagan doctrine in Central America. On that front, the degree of state–movement collaboration was unprecedented.

Apart from the state–movement alliance's impact in the foreign affairs realm, the reconstitution of the federal judiciary was the administration's most enduring legacy. On the Supreme Court, Reagan elevated William Rehnquist to Chief Justice and appointed Sandra Day O'Connor, Antonin Scalia, and Anthony Kennedy. Beyond that, Reagan appointed nearly half the judges serving in lower federal courts.[118] Reagan's judicial appointments would have long-term social issue implications but little immediate impact on the ability of right-wing movements to achieve policy objectives. In fact, the Right's domestic agenda—despite supply-side tax cuts for the rich—did not fare as well as the effort to roll back communism. On social spending programs, as well as on questions of moral traditionalism (abortion, school prayer, and the like), the Right and the administration faced a general public that showed no signs of a right turn.[119] Irrespective of mass public opinion on reproductive choice and church–state separation, the political clout of the Christian Right had a limited influence on the administration's family policies. As we will see in the next chapter, the obstacles to the Christian Right's achievement of its moral issues agenda did not stop the movement from expanding its repertoire of issues and tactics, nor from pursuing its drive toward influence within the Republican Party.

CHAPTER 10

Undaunted Allies

THE CHRISTIAN RIGHT IN THE 1980s

Politically active evangelical Christians held high hopes as the Reagan administration assumed office. By the late 1970s, the evangelical subculture had produced several nationally coordinated Christian Right organizations with help from the secular New Right. Together, in 1980, the New Right and the Christian Right represented the most influential movement on the U.S. political scene. However, as the new Reagan administration began to implement its agenda, economic and military policies took precedence over questions of moral traditionalism, and the Christian Right found itself, in a practical sense, without a champion in the White House. In Congress, where Christian Right voters had helped create a solid Republican Right bloc, Senators Jesse Helms and Orrin Hatch represented the Christian Right by introducing legislation against abortion and for school prayer. These efforts proved unsuccessful given the administration's weak support and the Democrats' hold on Congress.

Contrary to what might have been expected, legislative disappointments did not turn the Christian Right to adopt an oppositional stance toward the state. In part, that was because the Reagan administration offered enough symbolic gestures to keep the movement hopeful about future policy successes. In part, also, the Christian Right leaders' enlistment in the administration's foreign policy operations kept the movement in the Reagan camp. Throughout the 1980s, the Christian Right remained partially oppositional toward the political establishment on social policy questions but system-supportive regarding U.S. militarism and intervention abroad. Studies of the Christian Right have typically failed to address the movement's active involvement in propaganda, lobbying, and paramilitary activities on behalf of U.S.-allied "freedom fighter" armies during the second wave of the Cold War. In fact, "freedom fighter" activism absorbed a large part of the movement's attention during the 1980s, as evidenced in Christian Right publications, television broadcasts, and the content of movement events.[1]

As the Christian Right expanded its issue repertoire into the foreign affairs field during the early 1980s, the movement's organizational structure also began to change. Whereas the Christian Right of the late 1970s consisted of a few centralized national organizations (Moral Majority, Christian Voice), the 1980s saw the formation of numerous grassroots organizations, each with different purposes, though each offering leadership opportunities to a greater number of movement activists. Pat Robertson's 1988 presidential campaign was designed to encourage newly aroused evangelical voters to assume greater degrees of involvement in the political process. Despite Robertson's poor numerical showings in the primary races, his campaign did serve as a training ground for activists who became precinct coordinators, convention delegates, and Republican Party officials in their home states.

Despite the demonstrated strength of the evangelical constituency, by the time George Bush was elected president, the Christian Right had yet to achieve major policy changes on the priority issue of abortion. Beginning in the mid-1980s, the frustration level of anti-abortionists had driven some to bomb and vandalize women's health clinics, resulting in detrimental public relations for the movement as a whole. As the violence escalated, the most militant among the Christian Right's anti-abortion sub-movement started Operation Rescue as a direct action outlet for activists eager to directly confront women seeking abortions. This tactical innovation was highly significant for the Christian Right's continuous mobilization. The movement as a whole began as an effort to *reform* policymaking to conform to "moral majority" standards. Only after policy changes such as legally sanctioned abortion were widely accepted in society did the movement's *resistance* wing emerge.

In chapter 3 we analyzed the resistance strategies of the civil rights era Citizens' Councils and Ku Klux Klan, in contrast to the reformist John Birch Society. Adherents of the John Birch Society later joined with the segregationists to organize the 1968 presidential campaign of George Wallace (Chapter 6). But initially the mass sector of the anticommunist movement was not a resistance force because its ideology and objectives were not fundamentally oppositional in relation to the prevailing policy consensus in the United States against communism. Later, of course, as the New Right became the dominant right-wing movement on the scene, those Birch Society members allied with the racist Liberty Lobby and American Party became increasingly marginalized as Americanism gave way to survivalism. As we will see in Chapter 11, the survivalist wing of the racist Right degenerated further into an underground terrorist network, and its violence was met with repressive action by the state.

Resistance involves a militant, sustained effort to prevent pending change or to overturn existing policies seen as reversible. Reformist movements pursue modest goals within the parameters of a shared societal consensus, and they can more easily shift their strategic priorities, concentrating on the most feasible elements of their agenda. Thus, during the 1980s, the Christian Right collaborated with the Reagan foreign policy agenda at a time when the movement experienced difficulty achieving its domestic moral issues agenda. Yet movement adherents also remained committed to resisting designated evils like abortion and homosexuality.

This book's chapter on the segregationist movement (Chapter 3) suggested that a resistance movement cannot sustain, indefinitely, the intense activism of large numbers of participants against intractable or more powerful forces. Instead, a resistance movement can retreat entirely or it can evolve into either a reformist or (counter) revolutionary movement; the latter may include the use of violence. In the case of segregationist resistance, defenders of the status quo were simply overwhelmed by a growing societal consensus—spearheaded by a massive civil rights movement and sympathetic political elites—favoring formal integration. Though the segregationist movement involved as many as several hundred thousand people at its peak, the long-term possibilities for segregationist diehards were limited. Most moved on to other concerns. A small number of segregationists formed the nucleus of the Wallace presidential campaign and subsequent splinter parties. But as we saw in Chapter 6, they were never willing or able to contend for limited political power like an electorally-oriented reformist movement. Eclipsed by the New Right, they became increasingly marginalized.

The racist Right declined in large measure because its central organizing principle lost legitimacy. In the case of the Christian Right, the anti-abortion stance was justifiable in a way that segregation and white supremacy were not. The pro-life position was not without its contradictions. As pro-choice critics were quick to emphasize, anti-abortionists were generally not opposed to the death penalty. Nor were they vocal advocates for reliable contraception, pre-natal care, and social services for young children. Nevertheless, the abortion issue was fundamentally unique in that it begged life-and-death philosophical questions that cannot be solved in the realm of legal and public policy decision making. The abortion issue offered little room for compromise. If one's beliefs equated abortion with murder, then the imperative to act was urgent.

At the same time, legal abortion was sanctioned by the Supreme Court, and various states' medical services subsidized women's abortions. Abortion policy was suited to attempts by the Christian Right—and like-minded political elites—to make the issue a focus of the drive to restore the state's role as enforcer of traditional morality. The abortion issue was suited to both *reformist* and *resistance* tactics. Large numbers of Christian Right activists engaged in the modest tactics of voting and legislative lobbying. Smaller numbers carried the movement's belief that life begins at conception to its logical end and resorted to direct action, violent and otherwise, against abortion facilities. The onset of Operation Rescue in 1988 allowed for the expansion of the direct action wing at a time when the Robertson campaign likewise increased the movement's electoral activism.

Had the Christian Right not become an indispensable asset to (Republican) political elites, the Reagan and Bush administrations might have moved to repress the movement's violent wing. (The Reagan administration investigated and prosecuted the racist Right's violent echelon.) Relatively free from repression, the Christian Right's resistance wing did not became a serious liability. Instead, the two grew in tandem. Resistance and reformist strategic approaches proved not mutually exclusive as electorally-minded preachers (including Pat Robertson) endorsed and encouraged militant anti-abortionists. The Christian Right developed the potential to make or break elections and also to cause disruption outside the halls of power. Because the movement remained broader than an electoral force, it weathered legislative failures and flourished well after the Republicans' 1992 presidential defeat.

THE "PRO-FAMILY" AGENDA AND THE REAGAN ADMINISTRATION

The Christian Right began the 1980s with a resourceful organizational network in place and the potential to wield influence at the electoral level. Jerry Falwell's Moral Majority, founded in 1979, focused their efforts on registering an estimated two million new voters in time for the 1980 election.[2] But before the campaign season, beginning in 1979, the Carter administration handed the Christian Right an ideal organizing opportunity through the proposed White House Conference on Families. The administration's idea was to convene a series of public hearings in which delegates from each state would raise concerns on policy questions relevant to families, from federally funded child care to gay civil rights. Delegates were to be drawn both from pools of volunteers and from governors' lists of appointees. The newly aroused pro-family movement charged Carter program coordinators with stacking state delegations against evangelical Christians and with defining "families" to include unmarried and homosexual couples.[3] At one of the hearings, Connie Marshner, director of the Free Congress Foundation's Family Policy Division, led a walkout of sixty pro-family delegates.[4] The Moral Majority and the Free Congress Foundation held their own series of "family forums" to protest the Carter administration's endorsement of the Equal Rights Amendment, legalized abortion, and gay rights.[5]

In an interview about the pro-family movement for *Conservative Digest*, Free Congress Foundation strategist Paul Weyrich likened the significance of "family" issues for the Right in the 1980s to the role played by the Vietnam war in the mobilization of the New Left. He cited passage by Congress of the Equal Rights Amendment, the 1973 Supreme Court decision legalizing abortion, and the Internal Revenue Service's denial of tax exemptions to sectarian private schools as triggering events in bringing together evangelical Protestants and conservative Catholics, including large numbers who traditionally voted Democratic.[6]

As the 1980 presidential campaign got underway, *Conservative Digest* profiled the leading figures in the emerging "pro-family movement." These included a block of New Right Senators and Congressmembers, Washington, D.C.-based Christian Right lobbies, television preachers, and single-issue organizers like Phyllis Schlafly, Anita Bryant, and Judie Brown.[7] They were all encouraged when Senator Paul Laxalt (R-NV), with Connie Marshner's assistance, drafted the Family Protection Act, an encompassing piece of legislation with thirty-five major provisions. (The bill was debated in Congress in 1981 but never voted on, in part because of its omnibus nature.)[8] Heritage Foundation researcher Dr. Onalee McGraw disputed critics' charges that the Family Protection Act would increase government intrusion into people's personal lives. Instead, she argued, the bill's intention was to stop the state from using "federal funds and programs to effect changes in cultural, moral and familial values."

> Why are issues such as when human life begins, and the authority of the state to protect it, religious freedom, the sexual activity of minors, and pornography political issues in the first place? These issues became political because liberal ideologues insisted on using the mechanisms of the state to impose their own values and policy goals on American society[9]

Reagan's talk of "getting the government off people's backs" was, thus, assumed by the Christian Right to mean legislation to reinstate traditional morality. New Right politicians' rhetorical advocacy of the Family Protection Act laid a basis for the movement's expectation of big changes from a Republican administration.

On that assumption, Christian Right leaders choreographed several high-profile demonstrations of their electoral clout in 1980. The first was Washington for Jesus, an April 1980 day-long prayer rally in Washington, D.C. Organized by Pat Robertson, his friend John Gimenez, Bill Bright of Campus Crusade for Christ, and Demos Shakarian of the Full Gospel Businessmen's Fellowship, the event brought more than 200,000 charismatic and fundamentalist Christians together in an unprecedented display of inter-denominational unity. More than a demonstration, Washington for Jesus resulted in the establishment of 380 organizing offices in most Congressional districts in the United States.[10] Meanwhile, Religious Roundtable leader (and Moral Majority co-founder) Ed McAteer organized a series of public affairs briefings attended by about 40,000 Christian Right activists. The largest, held in Dallas in August 1980 and attended by about 15,000 ministers, featured candidate Ronald Reagan, who told the crowd of his plan to base policymaking on "traditional values."[11]

Reagan's active courting of the evangelical vote prompted Christian Voice strategist Colonel Doner to tell *Newsweek* magazine: "Christians gave Jimmy Carter his razor-thin margin of victory in 1976. We plan to reverse that in 1980."[12] Christian Voice alone raised about $500,000 for voter mobilization and the production of "moral report cards" that targeted thirty-five Senators and Congressmembers for defeat.[13] The combined efforts of Christian Voice, Moral Majority, and New Right electoral vehicles, like Conservative Caucus and the Free Congress Foundation, produced about two million new evangelical voters in 1980. That was a significant minority, given that Reagan was elected by only 26 percent of the electorate.[14] Pollster Louis Harris estimated that white evangelical voters accounted for two thirds of Reagan's 10-point margin over Jimmy Carter.[15] An ABC poll showed that 17 percent fewer white Protestants voted for Carter in 1980 than in 1976; traditional Democratic southern and border states swung to the Republicans; and for the second time in U.S. history (Nixon's 1972 victory was the first), a plurality of Catholics voted Republican.[16] The Christian Right was credited with electing Representative Robert Dornan (R-CA) and Senator Jeremiah Denton (R-AL). (Denton, a Catholic, was a former employee of Pat Robertson's Christian Broadcasting Network.) But Reagan's landslide coattails made it difficult to determine how many of the other new Senators and Congressmembers (mentioned in Chapter 9) owed their victories to the Christian Right.

Appointments and Disappointments

At the celebratory January 1981 convention of the National Religious Broadcasters, Jerry Falwell urged fellow television and radio preachers to be patient with the new administration regarding reinstating public school prayer and enacting a constitutional amendment outlawing abortion.[17] Reagan appointed several Christian Right activists to prominent administrative posts,[18] but showed little interest in moving swiftly on the movement's legislative agenda.

After Reagan's election, the Christian Right turned its attention to Congress. There the Republicans had won control of the Senate and thirty-three new seats in the House. Apart from conservatives' greater representation in Congress, there are several explanations for the Christian Right's focus on Congress. During the 1970s, the number of staff members for legislators and committees had grown, and that meant increased accessibility for lobbyists. The escalating costs of Congressional campaigns increased politicians' dependency on the money and ability of new interest groups to register new voters. In terms of movement tactics, the complexity of Congress lent itself to the Christian Right leaders' continuing need to keep their constituents posted. On any given legislative bill, direct mail and newsletter writers could tell the story of a Congressional committee's foot dragging, or they could report success as a bill moved up on the legislative calendar. In any event, Congressional action or inaction offered continual grist for fundraising appeals.[19]

But two major obstacles thwarted the Christian Right's success on Capitol Hill. The first was successful maneuvers by Democrats. They placed solid liberals on the pivotal House Judiciary Committee, where they could block proposals to amend the Constitution to allow school prayer or ban abortion. In the Senate, Democrats used the filibuster to obstruct Christian Right-backed legislation. At the same time, the movement faced a second obstacle in the priority given by the new administration to economic and military policies.[20] The Reaganites' tax cuts and social spending cuts, plus a proposed weapons buildup, simply preoccupied administration officials in their dealings with Congress.

Not until early 1982 did the administration begin to act on the Christian Right's issue agenda. Reagan endorsed a constitutional amendment to allow prayer in public schools, and he sent a generally supportive letter to "pro-life" leaders, encouraging them to unite behind one of two anti-abortion measures before Congress.[21] By 1982, however, Reagan's Christian Right backers were beginning to lose their patience. Falwell aide Ronald Godwin charged the administration with throwing symbolic bones to the "moral majoritarians" and expecting them to remain loyal.

It has become repetitively axiomatic at certain levels in the White House to (a) actually infer that gestures and symbolism are to Reagan's conservative grassroots supporters what beads and mirrors were to the savages of the new world; and that (b) members of Moral Majority and other pro-life, pro-family groups may gripe and bellyache but they have no choice but to support the Reagan administration.[22]

Without serious action from the White House, the Christian Right was left to rely on the impetus of key New Right Senators. Movement activists watched while two of their top agenda items, abortion and school prayer, failed to make their way through Congress.

Two anti-abortion measures were introduced in 1981. Senator Orrin Hatch (R-UT) sponsored a constitutional amendment that would have nullified the 1973 *Roe v. Wade* Supreme Court decision. Senator Jesse Helms (R-NC) introduced a "human life bill" to permanently prohibit taxpayer-funded abortions and to remove federal courts' power to overturn state anti-abortion laws. Anti-abortion leaders conflicted over which Senator's initiative to support. The Catholic bishops endorsed Hatch's wholesale amendment approach. New Right groups saw the Hatch amendment as foolhardy because it required an impossible two-thirds majority Congressional vote for starters, and they resented the amendment's failure to grant personhood to the fetus.[23] In September 1982, Helms' Senate opponents used the filibuster tactic to force a vote on the "human life bill," and after three tries, anti-abortion Senators failed to muster a majority to keep the bill afloat. Senator Hatch withdrew his proposed amendment, rather than subject it, too, to defeat.[24] Anti-abortionists' only early legislative accomplishment was passage of Senators Hatch and Denton's Adolescent Family Life Act, which funded programs to promote teenage chastity.[25]

On the school prayer front, the Christian Right's Congressional activism produced results more symbolic than substantive. In September 1981, Congress overwhelmingly passed a measure barring the Justice Department from blocking voluntary prayer in public schools; that was something the Justice Department was not, in fact, doing.[26] Yet the symbolic vote effectively tabled the prayer issue until May 1982 when Reagan himself proposed a constitutional amendment to return "voluntary" prayer to public schools. The Senate Judiciary Committee held three days of hearings at which Christian Right leaders testified, but the amendment languished in Senate committees.[27] Once again, Senator Hatch introduced a companion amendment that divided the Christian Right's Congressional supporters. Hatch tried to blunt controversy over organized religious indoctrination in public schools with a "silent prayer" amendment allowing students to observe a moment of silence and use school facilities for afterschool Bible study.[28] Christian Right leaders strongly opposed the notion of "silent prayer" and charged Hatch with dividing pro-prayer forces.[29] But by 1984, the Christian Right achieved limited success with passage of a streamlined "equal access" bill that allowed evangelicals to use public school facilities for extra-curricular proselytization.[30]

Ultimately the Christian Right witnessed a mixed bag of Congressional successes and failures during Reagan's first term. The multi-tentacled Family Protection Act never made its way out of committees, nor did proposed measures to restore organized school prayer and outlaw abortion. Pressure from the Christian Right did, however, result in Congress' maintenance of the ban on federal funding for poor women's abortions. The period after Reagan's reelection saw a noticeable decline in Congressional interest in the social issues. By 1986, when the Democrats regained control of the Senate, the Christian Right's prospects in Congress dimmed further.[31]

The frustration of the Christian Right's legislative agenda was followed by a two-part expansion of the movement's issue repertoire and tactics. First, beginning mid-way through Reagan's first term, Christian Right leaders enlisted in the administration's multi-faceted campaign to roll back communism, particularly in Central America. Second, the movement expanded on its 1980 voter registration and electoral successes by broadening the activist opportunities of its grassroots constituents. Organizations formed to deliver evangelical votes for Reagan's reelection and to promote Pat Robertson's 1988 presidential campaign gave increasing numbers of Christian Right activists the experience they would need to assume increasing control over the Republican Party by the late 1980s and 1990s.

There is no way to test whether these two dimensions of the Christian Right's transformation would have occurred had the movement's social issue agenda achieved greater success at the administrative and Congressional levels. Nor were these two sets of changes necessarily related, either in origin or in long-term impact on the movement. The Christian Right's collaborative relationship with the state on foreign policy matters stemmed from the administration's courting of prominent Christian Right figures; grassroots participants active on behalf of U.S. foreign policy objectives followed the cues of White House-connected national leaders like Pat Robertson and Jerry Falwell. While the administration treated the Christian Right's moral issues agenda with benign neglect, the leaders of national, centrally coordinated organizations maintained interest among constituents in part by joining the secular New Right's "freedom fighter" campaigns. At the same time, the growth of the Christian Right's grassroots apparatus followed naturally from the movement's initial role as a large, coherent voting block. Once people had gained experience conducting voter registration, their most logical tactical escalations were to participate in elections in other ways: as precinct coordinators, convention delegates, and eventually as candidates for local offices. Pat Robertson's 1988 presidential campaign was deliberately crafted as a grassroots organizing vehicle. Robertson himself refused to put his name on the ballot until three million supporters signed petitions and pledged $100 each.

As we will see in the next two sections of this chapter, the Christian Right's mobilization into the foreign policy realm and within an increasingly skilled and decentralized organizational structure had ramifications for the movement's value to political elites. Along the road to power, the Christian Right became both an asset of the state in the prosecution of paramilitary operations and an increasingly indispensable faction of a Republican Party intent on perpetuating its reign.

WITH THE "FREEDOM FIGHTERS"

As opponents of the mass movement against nuclear power and weapons, the Christian Right mobilized late in the game and without a lot of fanfare. The secular American Security Council's Coalition for Peace Through Strength (discussed in Chapters 5 and 9) drew its evangelical members' attention to campaigns for various new weapons systems. By 1983, the nuclear "freeze" movement reached a peak of activity, with millions of Americans demonstrating outside weapons laboratories, testing sites, and nuclear power plants. Liberal clergy led the way across much of the country, and that prompted Jerry Falwell to launch his own lonely crusade against the "freezeniks." Falwell used his weekly television show and Moral Majority mailing lists to raise funds for pro-nuclear newspaper advertisements and to sponsor a Peace Through Strength demonstration outside Congress.[32] Falwell also circulated a pamphlet, "Nuclear War and the Second Coming of Christ" linking the two events to belief in Christian salvation in a "pre-tribulation rapture," followed by a final "battle of Armageddon." This popular version of evangelical millenarianism caused observers to wonder what President Reagan meant when he told a 1983 National Association of Evangelicals gathering that the Soviet Union was an "evil empire." Most evangelicals were prepared to wait for, but not hasten, fulfillment of the Book of Revelations' prophecies.[33]

In no area of U.S. foreign and military policy did the Christian Right play a greater role than in the effort to defeat communism in Central America. The movement's first major effort involved lobbying and aid for the dictatorship of Guatemalan General Efrain Rios Montt, who assumed the presidency in a March 1982 coup d'etat. Rios Montt had been converted to Protestant pentecostalism after a group of young California "Jesus Freaks" brought their Gospel Outreach church to earthquake-ravaged Guatemala in 1976. Immediately following the 1982 coup, Pat Robertson interviewed Rios Montt on his "700 Club" television show and promised to send Rios Montt aid and missionaries. Weeks after the coup, a Gospel Outreach pastor came to the United States for a meeting between Reagan administration officials and Christian Right leaders. Shortly thereafter, the State Department held a special briefing for Christian Right groups, at which the administration endorsed International Love Lift, a project to supply the Guatemalan regime with humanitarian supplies and a public relations boost to counter its reputation as a leading human rights abuser. The same day that President Reagan lifted the ban on military aid to Guatemala, in January 1983, 350 U.S. evangelicals set sail in a boat carrying one million dollars' worth of food, clothing, medical supplies, and housing materials destined for Guatemalan refugee camps.[34]

By then, thousands of Guatemalans had been massacred and made homeless in one of the bloodiest counterinsurgency campaigns in Central America's history.[35] The target was Guatemala's civilian, mostly indigenous population, seen as the base of support for the Guatemalan guerrilla movement. Some Gospel Outreach members reportedly took part in the regime's espionage and torture–interrogation operations. Entire villages were annihilated, while Rios Montt's U.S. backers justified the "scorched earth" campaign in religious terms. In one interview, a Gospel Outreach pastor defended the killings:

> The Army doesn't massacre the Indians. It massacres demons, and the Indians are demon possessed; they are communists. We hold Brother Efrain Rios Montt like King David of the Old Testament. He is the king of the New Testament.[36]

By the time Rios Montt was himself deposed in August 1983 by another military coup, his North American Christian Right backers had joined the White House Working Group on Central America (see Chapter 9), through which the Reagan administration coordinated the media, lobbying, and "freedom fighter" supply operations of private groups.

One of the hallmarks of Reagan era foreign policy was the use of non-governmental organizations in the execution of what was euphemistically called "low intensity conflict" (LIC) strategy.[37] As outlined by military planners, LIC includes tactics ranging from proxy guerrilla warfare and economic sanctions against designated enemies, to the promotion of "humanitarian aid" and "psychological operations." It was in the latter two categories of LIC strategy that the New Right and Christian Right movements functioned as assets of state policymakers. Specifically, the Christian Right applied its notion of "spiritual warfare," or religious confrontation with evil, in three patterns of activity: (1) through propaganda aimed at domestic movement constituents and potential foreign allies of U.S.-sponsored armies, (2) through partisan lobbying on behalf of administration preferences, and (3) through direct distribution of materiel to militarily relevant groups abroad.

The war against Nicaragua became a laboratory for the administration's use of private organizations. In all three of the above patterns of state–movement collaboration, Christian Right leaders worked with Reagan State Department and intelligence agency officers. Central to the Christian Right's propaganda and lobbying efforts for the Nicaraguan Contras was the Institute on Religion and Democracy (IRD), formed by neoconservative church activists opposed to the foreign affairs liberalism of the National Council of Churches. IRD leaders Penn Kemble, David Jessup, Mary Temple, and Paul Seabury were veterans of Social Democrats U.S.A. and the neoconservative Coalition for a Democratic Majority (see Chapter 8). IRD was the organization chiefly responsible for propagating the State Department's claim that Nicaragua's Sandinista government persecuted Christians. Since most Nicaraguans are religious, it was not difficult to cast Contra supporters as Christian victims of "godless revolutionaries." But to make the charges stick, IRD had to discredit Nicaragua's own large and mostly pro-Sandinista Evangelical Committee for Aid and Development (CEPAD) as a haven for "communist" dupes. The persecution theme rang more credible coming from respectable IRD spokespersons like Michael Novak and Richard Neuhaus than from pulpit-pounders Jerry Falwell and Jimmy Swaggart.[38] One joint project between IRD and the Christian Broadcasting Network turned up on a list of pro-Contra projects funded covertly by National Security Council aide Lieutenant Colonel Oliver North, through Carl "Spitz" Channell's National Endowment for the Preservation of Liberty (NEPL).[39]

During its investigation of the Iran–Contra scandal, Congress neglected Oliver North's role in recruiting Christian Right activists for the multi-tentacled Contra aid network, discussed at some length in Chapter 9. U.S. taxpayers effectively subsidized private Christian Contra aid missions, such as the mission called Friends of the Americas, which shipped tons of supplies aboard U.S. military aircraft.[40] Reverend Phil Derstine, head of one of the largest Contra supply projects, was recruited by Oliver North to work directly with Contra leaders Adolfo Calero and Enrique Bermudez. In an interview, Derstine detailed his regular debriefings with U.S. intelligence agents.[41]

Elsewhere, Christian Right activists collaborated with U.S. and allied military forces. In El Salvador, U.S. evangelical groups conducted inspirational rallies for soldiers and, in turn, produced favorable media coverage of the U.S.-dependent Salvadoran military.[42] In the Philippines, following the 1986 election of Corazon Aquino, Christian Right missionary groups increased their politically targeted "humanitarian aid" work. The Unification Church and the Christian Anti-Communism Crusade, separately sponsored anticommunist and anti-union training forums for Filipino organizers of the paramilitary Alsa Masa vigilante groups.[43] Similarly, in southern Africa, U.S. evangelicals joined their South African counterparts in propaganda campaigns against the African National Congress and in sporadic supply efforts for regional paramilitary "freedom fighters."[44]

Theoretically, all of this activity is suggestive of how the working relationship between the state and (right-wing) movements affect the development of each. At least four implications are evident from the Christian Right's role as a foreign affairs asset of the Reagan administration. First is the state as agenda-setter for the movement's allocation of resources. Evangelical ministries have a long history in the foreign missionary business. Those most politically committed to the Reagan administration targeted their "humanitarian" supply efforts to anticommunist combatants and neighboring civilian communities. That meant that there would be aid to the Philippines, not East Timor, to Central American peasants, not Brazilian slum dwellers. In the Christian Right's lobbying and media priorities, too, state prerogatives established which "human rights" situations merited activists' attention.

Second (also with the state as agenda-setter), state policymakers saw it was in their interests to allow or facilitate direct foreign intervention by non-governmental organizations. One school of social movement theory explains mobilization as the result of the state's cessation or relaxation of repression. In the case of the Christian Right, though, a system-supportive movement enjoyed outright facilitation by state actors. This raises questions about how policy is formulated and conducted in a formally democratic system. Groups representing a minority of the U.S. citizenry were permitted to violate the Neutrality Act, the Foreign Agents' Registration Act and, in some cases, their own tax-exempt status in order to expedite administration policy objectives.

Third, the collaborative relationship changed the correlation of forces between movements, the state, and countermovements—for example, between interventionists and anti-interventionists, between pro-South Africa and anti-apartheid forces. The state weighed in on the side of movements amenable to a general consensus among political and economic elites: fighting communism justified extraordinary means. Right-wing organizations became an additional obstacle to leftist movements in the United States and abroad.

Fourth, as an asset of state policymakers, the Christian Right also increased its value to allied political actors, in this case the secular anticommunist movement and the Republican Party. It was useful for the secular Right to have leaders of a large constituency—legitimate by virtue of its "religious" motivations—ratify by their actions the foreign policy objectives of the administration in power. The secular New Right and a few key Congressmembers were committed to pursuing the moral issues agenda of the Christian Right. Shared foreign policy objectives further strengthened the inter-movement alliance to mutual advantage.

All of these dimensions of the state–movement relationship meant that the Christian Right never became fully oppositional toward political elites, despite failure to achieve domestic moral issue objectives. To an extent not previously considered in analyses of the Christian Right, the movement's collaboration in the conduct of U.S. foreign policy helped keep participants mobilized, not as outsiders, but as generally compatible allies of the administration and the Republican Party.

TACTICAL INNOVATION

The Christian Right's failure to legislate its moral issues agenda caused no diminution of the movement's growing sophistication. Movement strategists gradually moved away from an exclusive focus on making policy change at the federal level and, instead, dug their heels in for a long, multi-faceted struggle. By the early 1980s, but especially after Reagan's reelection, the Christian Right's tactical innovations included both increased use of direct action protests and violence against abortion clinics, and a shift toward the kind of local electoral activism that would involve larger numbers of newly mobilized evangelicals.

In 1982 a small group of anti-abortionists kidnapped a Michigan abortion doctor and his wife. That same year saw the onset of clinic bombings.[45] The number of attacks, ranging from bombings, arson, and vandalism to death threats and assaults on clinic workers, rose sharply between 1984 and 1986, and rose sharply again as Republicans lost control of the White House in 1992.[46] The majority of Christian Right participants steered clear of clinic violence, though some "pro-life" leaders were loathe to condemn clinic bombers as extremists.[47] For the most part, though, the Christian Right chose electoral politics over direct action. To have done otherwise would have jeopardized the movement's mutually advantageous relationship with the Republican Party. However, to the extent that the Christian Right developed both a militant direct action wing and a broader constituency more inclined to the compromises and constraints of electoral politics, the movement nurtured both *resistance* and *reformist* tendencies. These proved to be not mutually exclusive as, by the late 1980s and early 1990s, Operation Rescue-type "resistance" groups worked hand in hand with more "reformist" electoral organizations, such as Pat Robertson's Christian Coalition.

The Second Reagan Term

The Christian Right anticipated Reagan's reelection campaign as another opportunity to demonstrate the movement's influence. Likewise, the Reagan–Bush reelection committee welcomed evangelical support. Three Christian publishing houses affiliated with the National Religious Broadcasters produced mass-circulation books about Ronald Reagan.[48] The Moral Majority and the Free Congress Foundation sponsored Family Forum conventions, one in San Francisco and one in Dallas, to capture press attention in conjunction with the Democratic and Republican conventions.[49] The Reagan–Bush campaign assigned Reverend Tim LaHaye to coordinate Christian Right voter registration projects. Toward that end, in 1983, LaHaye had established the American Coalition for Traditional Values (ACTV), consisting of and largely funded by television preachers. Together with Christian Voice and the Moral Majority, ACTV received a one million dollar grant from White House fundraiser Joe Rodgers, for the purpose of registering new voters. Thousands of churches affiliated with the Christian Right, supervised by 350 field directors, delivered an estimated 200,000 new voters to the Republican Party in 1984.[50]

The theme of "religious persecution" was a staple in the Christian Right's 1984 organizing. The same group of television preachers leading Tim LaHaye's ACTV were also part of the Coalition for Religious Freedom, established by the Unification Church while cult leader Sun Myung Moon was imprisoned for tax fraud, perjury, and obstruction of justice. In 1984 and 1985, Moon's followers spent millions of dollars courting Christian ministers to support Moon as a "victim" of government prosecution. Some of the Coalition for Religious Freedom ministers tried to distance themselves from the Unification Church after unflattering press reports on Tim LaHaye's acceptance of "Moonie" money.[51] The heretical nature of Moon's teachings made the financial link a scandal, though one that would pale by comparison to the television preacher scandals of the late 1980s.

The infusion of Moon money into the Christian Right came at a time when the movement's organizational structure was changing. Out of the evangelical church milieu, in the late 1970s, the Christian Right had taken form in a few nationally headquartered, highly centralized organizations, most notably the Moral Majority and Christian Voice. By the mid-1980s, the structure expanded. New organizations with locally based affiliates gave more activists opportunities to become leaders in their own right.

That voter registration projects could not continue to deliver millions of new voters for each election was less significant than the mobilization of already aroused voters into greater degrees of political participation.

Christian Right leaders constructed several grassroots organizations, each with different purposes. Pat Robertson's Freedom Council was started in 1981, and promoted frequently on the "700 Club," for the stated purpose of educating viewers about threats to the "religious freedom" of Christians. The Freedom Council never became a decentralized organization—with semi-autonomous state chapters—as did Robertson's Christian Coalition, started in 1989. Instead, Robertson used the Freedom Council's tax-exempt educational status to build direct mail fundraising lists, and to cull precinct delegates for Michigan's early presidential campaign caucuses.[52]

Tim LaHaye's ACTV faded from public view but his wife Beverly's Concerned Women for America (CWA) soared after the LaHayes moved to Washington, D.C. in 1985. CWA was organized along two tracks, one a truly grassroots formation, the other a typical centralized lobbying operation. Beginning in San Diego in 1979, Mrs. LaHaye had organized "kitchen table activists" into "prayer chapters" of fifty women. Each chapter consisted of a leader and seven prayer chain leaders who contacted seven women on a phone tree whenever a piece of legislation warranted constituent phone calls and letters. CWA's monthly newsletters listed the names and phone numbers of new chapter leaders, plus summaries of legislative action to be taken. Through the initiative of chapter leaders, who had an interest in seeing their recruits start new chapters, CWA's membership grew by leaps and bounds, reaching a claimed total of 600,000 by 1992.[53] "Membership" implied only a small yearly dues and commitment to write a few letters, thus involving thousands of women not otherwise willing or able to commit to a social movement organization. Beverly LaHaye invoked CWA's large numbers routinely in the lobbying and legal affairs side of the organization's work. In 1987, LaHaye was chosen as a representative women's leader to testify at a Senate hearing on the qualifications of Judge Robert Bork, whom the Senate ultimately rejected as a Supreme Court nominee.[54] LaHaye's notoriety increased further when President Reagan himself addressed CWA's 1987 convention. Reagan thanked CWA for its grassroots support for Bork and for the Nicaraguan Contras.[55] During the mid- and late 1980s, CWA devoted considerable resources to propaganda and material aid for Contra forces based in Costa Rica.[56] At the same time, CWA provided attorneys to parents' groups in litigation to remove "secular humanist" books from public schools.[57] With its hand in virtually every issue, CWA remained one of the Christian Right's cornerstone organizations, capable of shifting its focus as political opportunities changed.

Where CWA's approach attracted unprofessional, though committed and useful, activists, the Coalition on Revival (COR) functioned as
a network of full-time Christian Right activists and ministers. COR was
designed to increase unity among theologically disparate camps of
evangelicals. It was at COR's 1986 conference that leading figures of the
Christian Right met and discussed the use of "stealth" candidacies in
local elections, one county at a time.[58] COR itself, however, never became
an electoral vehicle. It remained, instead, a forum through which prominent evangelical ministers debated politically relevant theological positions, namely "pre-" versus various forms of "post-" millenialism, and
controversial organizing styles such as the autocratic "shepherding"
system.[59] COR also promoted a broad view of political participation by
organizing itself into about two dozen working groups on everything
from home schooling to legal defense to an alternative "kingdom"
banking system.[60]

Similarly, the American Freedom Coalition (AFC), started in 1987
as a grassroots merger between Christian Voice and Unification Church
affiliates,[61] established topical "task forces" on economics, education, the
environment, "religious freedom," and "world freedom." Each of AFC's
state chapters elected to concentrate, variably, on local activism within
one of these spheres; while nationally, the organization raised funds
selling a videocassette about Reagan National Security Council aide
Oliver North.[62] Within the Right, controversy over AFC's financial
dependence on the Unification Church prevented it from becoming as
influential as it might have been.[63]

In any event, by the time Pat Robertson began his dark horse bid for
the 1988 Republican presidential nomination, the Christian Right's
grassroots constituency was well organized and ready to be mobilized.
But before the Robertson campaign began in earnest, the evangelical
world was hit with the most debilitating set of public relations debacles
since the Scopes trial. One after another, three of the most prominent
television preachers fell from grace before a mocking secular press and
public. First came Oral Roberts, who in early 1987 announced that God
would "call him home" unless he received $8 million in donations within
three months. Next came revelations that Jim Bakker of the PTL network
had been blackmailed by another television evangelist who knew of
Bakker's affair with church secretary Jessica Hahn. As PTL's long-standing financial discrepancies came to light and the scandal grew, in early
1988 Jimmy Swaggart appeared live on television to confess his adulter-
ous sins, also under threat of blackmail from a fellow televangelist.[64]

The television preacher scandals were significant in their irony. As
a movement resource, televangelism had contributed profoundly to the
Christian Right's mobilization and cohesion during the 1970s and 1980s.

At the same time, religious broadcasting had fostered an echelon of corrupt entrepreneurs whose crimes and misdemeanors reinforced an image of the Christian Right as a movement of hypocrites and scoundrels. The news media's focus on Roberts, Bakker, and Swaggart lent a false impression that the religious broadcasting industry was doomed. The industry did suffer short-term financial losses. Contributions to Pat Robertson's Christian Broadcasting Network declined by 30 percent over a two-year period, and audiences for the top television preachers decreased.[65] By the early 1990s, however, the industry had recuperated. Cable television continued to be a growing market for new and untarnished television ministries.[66] Yet the mainstream press focus on the television preacher scandals precluded widespread public awareness of the Christian Right's uninterrupted political mobilization.

Given a disdainful press and general public, Pat Robertson's 1988 presidential campaign was surprisingly successful. Robertson's candidacy was first promoted in the March 1985 issue of *The Saturday Evening Post*,[67] followed by an August 1985 *Conservative Digest*'s cover story in which Paul Weyrich lent his stamp of approval to the idea. "Robertson, more than anyone else on the scene," Weyrich said, "is likely to be the national conservative figure who could not only equal what Reagan has accomplished, but can exceed it."[68]

After that, Robertson allowed both friends and detractors to speculate about his intentions, while he continued to host his 90-minute weekday "700 Club" program. In September 1986, Robertson announced his plan to enter the primary races only if, within one year, three million voters each pledged $100. During that year, evangelical churches added more than three million pledge cards to Robertson's mailing lists. The churches became headquarters not only for Robertson's campaign but also for the Christian Right's successful takeover of Republican Party county committees in several states.[69] While on the campaign trail, Robertson urged his supporters to run for local offices themselves.[70]

Ultimately, Robertson spent about $27 million in the primary races. All told, Robertson garnered about one million votes, or about 9 percent of the total cast, and did better than Republican candidates Jack Kemp and Pierre DuPont. Robertson fared particularly well in caucus states, where Christian Right activists were able to dominate the Republican meetings.[71] Four years later, once George Bush's popularity on the Right had plummeted, fellow dark horse candidate Patrick Buchanan would win between 20 and 30 percent of the votes in the Republican primaries. In 1988, although Robertson's formal Republican convention delegates numbered only about 100, a Democratic polling firm found that a quarter of the delegates present were born-again Christians. Though most were committed to vote for Bush, 13 percent were actually Robertson campaign workers in their home states. After the convention, the Republican National Committee hired Robertson campaign manager Marc Nuttle as a consultant.[72]

Dominion Theology

After Robertson's defeat, Christian Right leaders deftly shifted their strategic focus from the national to the local levels of politics. Robertson's own Christian Coalition was largely responsible for the shift toward grassroots electoral organizing. But there were other reasons why the decline of the Christian Right was not in the realm of possibility. The movement's organizational strength was key. Also indispensable was the subtle motivating influence of dominion theology among evangelicals of various stripes.

Dominion theology took a number of forms. It was really more of a world view than a discrete set of tenets. Essentially, dominionism revolved around the idea that Christians, and Christians alone, are Biblically mandated to occupy all secular institutions until Christ returns.[73] By definition, dominionism precluded coalition or consensus-building between believers and non-believers. The most explicit rendition of dominion thinking was found in the teachings of a small group of Christian Reconstructionists, who gained influence among rank-and-file Christian Right activists during the 1980s and 1990s.[74]

An earlier source of dominion theology was an evangelical philosopher named Francis Schaeffer, who died of cancer in 1984. Schaeffer's 1981 book A Christian Manifesto sold 290,000 copies in its first year,[75] and remained one of the Christian Right's most important texts into the 1990s. The book's argument was simple: America began as a nation rooted in Biblical principles. But as society became more pluralistic, proponents of a new philosophy of secular humanism gradually came to dominate debate on policy issues. Since humanists place human progress, not God, at the center of their considerations, they pushed American culture in all manner of ungodly directions, the visible results of which included abortion and the secularization of the public schools. At the end of A Christian Manifesto, Schaeffer advocated the use by Christians of civil disobedience to restore Biblical morality,[76] which explains Schaeffer's popularity among activists. Operation Rescue leader Randall Terry credited Schaeffer as a major influence in his own life and among fellow "rescuers."[77] In the 1960s and 1970s, Schaeffer and his wife Edith ran a retreat center called L'Abri (Hebrew for "the shelter") in Switzerland. There young converts to Christ came to study with Schaeffer and learn how to apply his teachings to the political process back home. Schaeffer himself was a product of the internecine conflicts that split the

Presbyterian church between the 1930s and 1950s. Schaeffer was initially allied with the strident anticommunist leader Carl McIntire (see Chapter 4). Later Schaeffer joined an anti-McIntire faction that, after several name changes, merged into the Presbyterian Church in America.[78]

While Schaeffer struggled with cancer in the last years of his life, several of the younger men he had influenced joined the Coalition on Revival (COR), which was founded by Jay Grimstead with two major purposes. One was to unify politically active evangelical pastors who differed on important theological points, especially eschatology, or the study of the end-times. Most contemporary evangelicals were pre-millenialists who believed that Christ would return to earth *before* establishing a 1,000-year reign by believers. Grimstead and many COR members were post-millenialists who believed that their mandate was to establish God's kingdom on earth now; only after believers' millenial reign would Christ return.[79] COR's second purpose was to develop a series of working papers on how to apply dominion theology to Christian Right activism in more than a dozen spheres of social life, including education, economics, law, and even entertainment. Though COR's so-called "world view documents" were more theoretical than practical,[80] the idea was to encourage activists to try to "take dominion" over secular institutions.

This approach was consistent with the teachings of Christian Reconstructionists, a small number of whom were members of COR.[81] Reconstructionism was the most intellectually grounded, though esoteric, brand of dominion theology. Its leading proponent was Rousas John Rushdoony, a largely unknown figure within the Christian Right. Born in 1916, at a young age Rushdoony was strongly influenced by Westminster Theological Seminary professor Cornelius Van Til, a Dutch theologian who emphasized the inerrant authority of the Bible and the irreconcilability between believers and unbelievers.[82] Rushdoony founded the Chalcedon Foundation in California in the mid-1960s. One of the Foundation's early associates was Gary North who eventually married Rushdoony's daughter.[83] North had been active within the secular libertarian and anticommunist movements; he was an early contributor to the Foundation for Economic Education, and he had been strongly influenced by intellectuals of the Old Right, particularly the anti-statist Albert Jay Nock.[84]

Rushdoony and North eventually became estranged from each other. North started his own think tank, the Institute for Christian Economics, in Tyler, Texas. From California and Texas, Rushdoony, North, and fewer than a half dozen other Reconstructionists published countless books and journals advocating postmillennialism and "theonomy" or the application of God's law to all spheres of everyday life. North geared his writing for a more popular audience; his books were easily available in Christian book stores.[85] Rushdoony's writing was more turgid and also more controversial. It was Rushdoony's seminal 1973 tome *The Institutes of Biblical Law* that articulated the Reconstructionists' vision of a theocracy, one in which Old Testament law would be reinstated in modern society. Old Testament law classified a wide range of personal "sins" as punishable by the death penalty; these included murder, adultery, incest, homosexuality, witchcraft, incorrigible delinquency of youth, and even blasphemy.[86] In the Reconstructionists' vision of a millenial or "kingdom" society, there would be only local governments; there would be no central administrative state to collect property taxes, nor to provide education or other welfare services.[87]

The unabashed advocacy of a future theocracy insured a limited following for the most explicit of the Reconstructionists, who tended to be sectarian in their sharp criticism of evangelicals who disagreed with them for one reason or another. North, for example, published a series of attacks on proponents of the "pre-tribulation rapture" theology.[88] In one of his most important books, *Political Polytheism: The Myth of Pluralism*, North included a lengthy polemic against Francis Schaeffer, whom he blasted for not adhering to Mosaic law and for being too soft on liberals and humanists.[89] (North also charged Schaeffer with plagiarizing portions of *A Christian Manifesto* from Reconstructionist author David Chilton.)[90]

What was important about Reconstructionism and other expressions of dominion theology was not so much the eccentricities of its key advocates but rather the diffuse influence of the ideas that America was ordained as a Christian nation and that Christians, exclusively, were to rule and reign. Most activists in the Christian Right were not well versed in the arcane teachings of Rousas Rushdoony, nor were leading figures like Pat Robertson inclined to associate with advocates of an Old Testament theocracy.[91] But there was a wide following for softer forms of dominionism. Among the most popular of Christian Right ministries was one called WallBuilders, a lucrative book and tape sales operation, that promoted the claims that America's Founding Fathers were nearly all evangelical Christians, and that the only answer to rampant social problems was for Christians alone to run for elected office.[92]

Dominionist thinking revealed how far evangelicalism had come in the twentieth century. After the humiliating Scopes trials of the 1920s, fundamentalists had retreated into political obscurity. They had, after World War II, staked their claim to the nation's broadcast airwaves, and they had done their fair share of anticommunist red-baiting of fellow Christians during the Cold War era. By the end of the twentieth century, many evangelicals were no longer content to secure their rights to preach a gospel message. They sought to save not just lost souls but the engines of society itself.

The Bush Years

Eight years after Ronald Reagan had promised to implement a "moral majority" agenda, Christian Right activists remained cautiously optimistic about their prospects under the administration of George Bush. Eighty percent of evangelical voters backed Bush in 1988. Following the election, about 100 Christian Right leaders were invited to the White House for an in-depth exchange with Vice-President Dan Quayle and top Bush aides.[93] Antiabortion movement leaders were confident in the new president's intention to appoint Supreme Court Justices who would overturn *Roe v. Wade*.[94] They were disheartened when Bush nominated Louis Sullivan as secretary of Health and Human Services; Sullivan was known to support fetal tissue research. But prolifers were encouraged when, in January 1989, the Supreme Court agreed to hear arguments over a 1986 Missouri law restricting abortion.[95] The law became the basis for *Webster v. Reproductive Health Services*. The state law included a ban on the use of public funds, facilities, and employees in counseling or performing abortions. In July 1989, the Supreme Court upheld the Missouri law, effectively granting state legislatures wide latitude in blunting *Roe v. Wade*.[96] From the perspective of the Christian Right, the *Webster* decision underscored the value of grassroots, state-based anti-abortion activism, as opposed to earlier attempts to overturn *Roe* in one fell swoop.[97]

As is discussed in Chapter 12, the Bush administration never enjoyed its predecessor's popularity among right-wing activists. During the late 1980s, the Christian Right in particular conveyed its opposition to the status quo in two ways. One was through the continued pursuit of power within the Republican Party, though primarily at the local level following Pat Robertson's failed 1988 presidential bid. The other was through a variety of tactics (blockades, ballot initiatives, tried-and-true media campaigns) on a set of single "pro-family" concerns: abortion, gay rights, and federal funding for the arts. The movement's multiple issues and tactical repertoires were mutually reinforcing and allowed for different types of activists to make themselves useful.

In the summer of 1989, Jerry Falwell announced the disbanding of the Moral Majority.[98] By then, Pat Robertson was in the process of regrouping his 1988 campaign apparatus into the Christian Coalition. Robertson hired Ralph Reed, a former College Republicans organizer, to direct the new grassroots project. In an interview with *Christianity*

Today, Reed explained the Christian Coalition's emphasis on state and local politics.

> We believe that the Christian community in many ways missed the boat in the 1980s by focusing almost entirely on the White House and Congress when most of the issues that concern conservative Catholics and evangelicals are primarily determined in the city councils, school boards and state legislatures.[99]

With an initial membership of 25,000, the Christian Coalition wasted no time forming scores of chapters and fielding candidates for local offices (as discussed below). As part of its broad issue repertoire, Robertson's group also made itself central to the Christian Right's campaign to defund the National Endowment for the Arts.

Complementing the new Christian Coalition, after the 1988 election, Dr. James Dobson merged his Focus on the Family radio broadcast ministry (heard on 1,300 stations in 1989) with the Family Research Council, a Washington, D.C.-based think tank headed by Reagan domestic policy adviser Gary Bauer. Together, Focus on the Family and the Family Research Council organized Dobson's radio listeners into a network of semi-autonomous state-based think tanks, oriented toward grassroots lobbying of state legislatures.[100] On behalf of Focus on the Family's enormous following, Bauer filed a friend of the court brief and celebrated victory in the July 1989 *Webster* Supreme Court abortion case.[101]

By then Operation Rescue, too, had conducted several large blockades of abortion clinics across the country, and numerous smaller groups had turned their attention to conflicts within local school boards and city councils.[102] Not until the 1992 presidential campaign would the Christian Coalition assume a role as primary coordinator of the movement's grassroots electoral work.

Prior to that, between elections, issues of morality provoked continual skirmishes in what activists called a "cultural war." Opposition to abortion and gay rights remained the Christian Right's highest priorities as they had since the 1970s. Supplanting earlier efforts against the ERA and for the reinstatement of public school prayer, there emerged a new concern with the National Endowment for the Arts' funding of "obscene" art.

Abortion captured the lion's share of activist commitment. As the Reagan–Bush administrations appointed new Supreme Court justices and pushed closer the legal threat to *Roe v. Wade*, anti-abortionists in several states worked for laws to restrict access to abortion. The most significant was a Pennsylvania law, upheld partially by the Supreme Court

in 1992, that required women to receive state-published abortion information and wait twenty-four hours before going ahead with the proce-
dure. The law also required parental consent for minors who were
seeking abortions.[103]

Though *Roe v. Wade*'s days appeared numbered, the Christian
Right's most aggressive anti-abortion activists were not content to pursue
slow and uncertain legal avenues. By the mid-1980s, abortion clinics were
plagued with a wave of violence, including bombings, arsons, vandalism,
and death threats. Few perpetrators were investigated and prosecuted
by the Reagan–Bush administrations,[104] though there was evidence to
suggest that clinic violence was not just the work of a few isolated
criminals. *A Pro-Life Manifesto*, released in 1988 by a major Christian
publisher, expounded on the possibilities of using "armed aggression":

> If we are going to attempt to close abortion clinics and end abortion by
> the current strategy, then the only logical thing to do is to take that
> strategy to its ultimate conclusion, to take it all the way. We would take
> the Declaration of Independence at its word and, since we have at-
> tempted to change the laws to no effect, we would change the govern-
> ment. That means revolution.... It would mean serious armed aggres-
> sion against both the clinics and hospitals that perform abortions and
> the abortionists themselves.
>
> If armed aggression were the answer, it would have to be aggression
> that did not hesitate. It would have to be done on a large scale, and more
> than a few abortion clinics would have to be destroyed. To succeed, it
> would require the destruction of all hospitals or clinics that performed
> abortions. Heroes who would lay down their life for the cause would
> have to come forth. Armies would need to be organized. Companies
> producing abortifacients would have to be bombed and their employees
> terrorized. In short, we would have to be willing to plunge ourselves into
> civil war.[105]

Short of outright civil war, however, aggressive anti-abortionists were
prepared to escalate their tactics in other ways. Their handbook was
Joseph Scheidler's widely circulated *Closed: 99 Ways to Stop Abortion*, which
instructed activists in the means to harass clinic providers, pro-choice
groups, and women seeking abortions.[106]

Scheidler was an inspiration to Randall Terry, founder of Operation
Rescue (OR),[107] which made its debut in May 1988 with a week of clinic
blockades in New York City. As hundreds of anti-abortionists were
arrested at clinics nearby the 1988 Democratic Party convention in
Atlanta and elsewhere, some Christian Right leaders were hesistant about
the long-term public relations detriments of the civil disobedience
tactic.[108] Among the majority who used their pulpits and broadcast

outlets to endorse Operation Rescue were Jerry Falwell, Pat Robertson, James Dobson, Beverly LaHaye, and Cardinal John J. O'Connor. "I think every pro-life person should attend one of these," said Beverly LaHaye of Concerned Women for America. "This experience brings you face to face with how strong your convictions are."[109]

In turn, Operation Rescue leaders were careful not to claim tactical supremacy over fellow anti-abortionists using legal tactics. A letter to "rescuers" from OR's northern California branch explained:

> Our specific task is to save babies by placing our bodies between the innocent victim (the pre-born) being transported by another victim (the mother) and the executioner (the abortionist).
>
> We are part of a larger community of rescuers united by this common purpose with different but complementary callings. Crisis Pregnancy Centers, Birthrights, Heritage Homes, Post Abortion Syndrome counselors and many other ministries that offer compassion and alternatives to women allow us to say to the mother "we'll help you" with integrity. Right to Life, Concerned Women of America, Eagle Forum and others lobby to provide legislative relief that may one day make our actions unnecessary.
>
> A by-product of our rescues has been the elevation of the issue of abortion to the front pages, challenging both the church and secular community to act on their convictions. Many organizations have received new recruits both from previously uninvolved rescue participants and others challenged by them.[110]

If the anti-abortion movement as a whole was galvanized by the practice of civil disobedience, the mounting arrests also brought legal and financial headaches to OR headquarters. Randall Terry's Binghamton, New York office was closed in early 1990 when the U.S. Attorney's office seized OR's financial assets after Terry refused to pay a $50,000 settlement in a suit brought by the National Organization for Women.[111] By then, the rescue movement was truly a grassroots phenomenon. OR headquarters relocated to South Carolina and stopped soliciting funds that could wind up in the hands of suing plaintiffs. Instead, about 100 autonomous "rescue" organizations remained loosely connected, and OR spawned the Christian Defense Coalition to recruit "pro-life" attorneys to defend clinic blockaders in the courts.[112]

Politically, the militancy of the anti-abortion movement threatened to turn the abortion issue into a double-edged sword for the Republicans. Following the Supreme Court's *Webster* decision the 1990 elections produced mixed results for "pro-life" and "pro-choice" candidates, thereby intensifying the Republicans' quandary over the party's official anti-abortion stance. But before any consensus could be reached, the issue of gay civil rights likewise galvanized the Christian Right and threatened more moderate to liberal elements of the Republican coalition.

The growing AIDS epidemic exacerbated the Christian Right's hatred of homosexuals and maintained the issue of sexual "deviance" as a prevalent theme in the movement's propaganda.[113] Among other effects, the AIDS epidemic aroused awareness among gays and lesbians (and their heterosexual supporters) of the need to fight bigotry by securing basic legal protections against discrimination. Defeated in 1978, California's "Briggs initiative," which would have banned gay teachers from public schools, had encouraged the Christian Right's mobilization nationally. Absent protective federal legislation, gay civil rights activism in the 1980s began to focus on the drafting of local ordinances and state initiatives to eliminate anti-gay discrimination in employment, housing, and access to public facilities.[114] Not surprisingly, proposed gay rights laws met opposition from evangelicals, who were also increasingly active at the state and local levels by the late 1980s.[115]

In California, conflict centered around an assembly bill that would have added sexual orientation to the list of categories protected by the state's Fair Employment and Housing Act. Under fierce grassroots lobbying by the Christian Right, in 1991, Republican Governor Pete Wilson vetoed Assembly Bill 101, ostensibly on the grounds that it would have clogged the courts with increased litigation. A year later, Wilson ignored a formal resolution by the California Republican Party and signed a compromise bill that delegated job discrimination complaints to the state's labor commissioner. For that, the state's Christian Right targeted Wilson for defeat.[116]

Further north, the Oregon Citizens' Alliance (OCA) made its public debut with a 1988 Oregon ballot measure to rescind an executive order, by that state's governor, banning discrimination in state employment on the basis of sexual orientation.[117] By 1992, OCA sponsored Measure 9, a far-reaching ballot initiative that would have amended the state constitution to prohibit "sexual orientation" as a category of protection or inclusion by any state or local agency.[118] Oregon's Measure 9 was defeated, but Colorado voters approved a less stringent ballot measure that preemptively sought to ban any gay rights legislation in the state. Colorado's Amendment 2 was swiftly challenged in the courts and was ruled unconstitutional.[119]

The various ballot initiative campaigns developed a rhetorical theme of "no special rights" for homosexuals. The idea was to convince voters that gays and lesbians were demanding something beyond basic legal protections enjoyed by other groups of citizens. In an ironic inversion, the Christian Right sought "special" denial of rights to a group it saw demanding special excessive privileges.

As the Cold War came to an end and the Right, in general, made domestic policy issues a greater priority, the Christian Right's resurgent anti-gay activism took symbolic as well as electoral form. Closely linked to the fear of "special rights" for sexual deviants was the furor over the National Endowment for the Arts' grant-making practices. The controversy tapped a widely held view that publicly subsidized, sexually explicit art was an affront to "traditional family values," though the outbreak of anti-NEA resentment was anything but spontaneous.

Shortly after President Bush took office, a handful of Christian Right leaders and Congressional Representatives literally made a federal case over the NEA's funding of two controversial photographers. Andres Serrano's work *Piss Christ* displayed a crucifix immersed in a container of urine. To a sophisticated art critic, the image might have evoked multiple meanings; to the morally righteous, the work was pure blasphemy. Likewise, Robert Mapplethorpe's collection of homosexually explicit photographs was, intentionally or not, bound to offend plenty of plain folks. Though Serrano's and Mapplethorpe's photographs constituted a minority of the art works funded by the NEA, they came to symbolize the Christian Right's grievance. In April of 1989, Donald Wildmon of the American Family Association began circulating a letter to Congress, the media, and Christian organizations, framing *Piss Christ* within a pattern of "bias and bigotry against Christians."[120] Ambitious politicians saw a chance to make political points as defenders of "traditional" morality, at the expense of reasoned debate over the vitality of government support for the arts. Senators Alfonse D'Amato and Jesse Helms denounced the NEA on the Senate floor in May 1989. Days later Representative Richard Armey (R-TX) led 100 Congressmembers in a letter criticizing the NEA for its support of a Mapplethorpe exhibit. Into the ensuing fray, President Bush appointed John Frohnmayer, a moderate Republican lawyer and arts patron, to preside over the NEA during a two-year battle over its continuing funding by Congress. In 1990 Congress imposed an "indecency" restriction on NEA grant applicants, but the restriction was ruled unconstitutional in an artist's suit against the NEA.[121]

The federal government's continued subsidies of "obscene" art remained a contested issue for the Christian Right versus civil libertarians. Pat Robertson's Christian Coalition, eager for an irresistible recruitment issue, spent $200,000 on a *USA Today* advertisement against the NEA.[122] The political utility of the arts controversy was further punctuated in the 1992 New Hampshire primary when Republican challenger Patrick Buchanan crafted television advertisements against the incumbent president, using scenes from *Tongues Untied*, an award-winning NEA-funded documentary about black gay men. George Bush had no intention of losing the election over a homophobic campaign ad. After the New Hampshire primary, Bush demonstrated his resolve against the "pornographic" film by forcing the resignation of NEA director John Frohnmayer.[123]

THE ENDURANCE OF THE CHRISTIAN RIGHT

Local and national campaigns against abortion, gay civil rights, and objectionable public art were all driven by widespread and deep-seated resentment over the dominant culture's threats to "traditional family values." Beyond that, each of these purported abominations served Christian Right electoral designs by fanning the outrage of movement constituents. Liberal proponents of abortion choice, gay rights, and unfettered expression in the arts were not about to retreat. The Reagan–Bush administrations had failed to stem the tide of affronts to traditional morality. Nor had aggressive acts of civil disobedience succeeded in closing abortion clinics. That left Christian Right antagonists with the imperative to seek political power through elections.

Beginning in 1990, Pat Robertson's Christian Coalition became the nucleus for the Christian Right's local and state election campaigns.[124] The movement enjoyed its greatest success in California's San Diego county where, among 90 candidates for local school boards, city councils, and the water district, 60 won, in large part by not disclosing their allegiance to the Christian Right.[125] The use of "stealth" candidates in the so-called "San Diego surprise" became one model for the Christian Right's successful local campaigns in 1992.

As we will see in Chapter 12, the 1992 presidential campaign marked the Christian Right's successful transformation from outside to inside the Republican Party establishment. In 1980 Reagan campaigners and secular New Right activists eagerly courted the votes of politically aroused evangelicals. To do so, the New Right made a priority of "traditional family values" and nurtured new Christian Right organizations. Reagan himself led evangelicals to believe that he, not Sunday school teacher Jimmy Carter, would use state power to enforce a traditional moral order. Once such promises were not realized, and after the Christian Right had implicated itself in the counterinsurgency wars of the 1980s, the movement had developed a symbiotic relationship with the administration and, to a greater extent, with the Republican Party. George Bush was less prepared than Reagan to champion the Christian Right's causes. Whatever gains the movement enjoyed under his tenure were incidental. But what could not be taken for granted was the Christian Right's enduring capacity to make itself count: at the polling stations, outside abortion clinics, and in the minds of elected officials conscious of public opinion.

The Christian Right developed both reformist and resistance wings and a repertoire of issues based on some of society's major unresolved controversies. Combined with the large numbers evangelicals represented, these features enabled the movement to exert an influence not possible for the racist Right. Blatantly segregationist notions of white supremacy no longer held popular legitimacy, though by the early 1990s, more subtle versions of racist rhetoric would attract sizeable electoral followings for the Republican candidacies of David Duke and Patrick Buchanan. Both based their appeal on a combined message of traditional morality and white ethnic frustration. This was a potentially powerful mix, though, as the next chapter details, one around which the organized and explicitly racist Right remained too marginalized and fragmented to promote to its own advantage.

CHAPTER 11

• • •

The Racist Right
in the 1980s and 1990s

DIMINISHED INFLUENCE, RESURGENT VIOLENCE

The end of massive resistance to segregation and the breakup of political parties formed to back candidate George Wallace doomed the organized racist Right to marginal influence. To the extent that the movement persisted into the 1980s, it was in large part due to successful organizing efforts by the Liberty Lobby and a loose network of Posse Comitatus tax protesters and Christian Identity preachers.

Added to these movement players, the Ku Klux Klan experienced renewed growth during the 1970s. From an all-time low of a few thousand members at the end of the 1960s, membership in various Klan factions totaled about 11,500 by 1979. That year saw one group of Klansmen shoot a crowd of civil rights marchers in Alabama. Another Klan group killed five anti-Klan demonstrators in front of television cameras in Greensboro, North Carolina.[1] Ten years later, researchers estimated the size of the white supremacist movement at 10,000 to 20,000 hard core members and about ten times that many passive supporters. The larger figure, as high as 200,000, included the 100,000 subscribers to the Liberty Lobby's *Spotlight* newspapers and an estimated 30,000 adherents of Christian Identity churches.[2]

As Ronald Reagan assumed the presidency in 1981, the organized racist Right consisted of a stable number of participants but little potential for influence within the incoming administration. Evangelical Christians represented a mass constituency taken seriously by Reagan campaigners, and the Christian Right turned out to be useful to the Reagan administration's anticommunist foreign policy agenda. Moral traditionalism subsumed explicit racism as the overall Right's dominant concern in the realm of domestic social policy. The Reagan administra-

257

tion was perfectly willing to back policies (on welfare spending and civil rights laws, for example) with racist implications. But crude biological determinism was unpalatable to a party and government claiming to represent the majority. Political elites found the racist Right's enduring anti-Semitism particularly unsavory. For example, a minor scandal ensued when Warren Richardson, Reagan's nominee for a post in the Health and Human Services Department, was exposed in the press as a former attorney for the anti-Jewish Liberty Lobby. Richardson had a track record within more respectable New Right circles, but he was unable to shake charges of anti-Semitism and abandoned the nomination rather than cause the administration further embarrassment.[3]

In the early 1980s, though, perilous economic conditions spelled political opportunities for a resurgent racist Right. Reagan's economic program of increased military spending and tax rate cuts for the wealthy left predominantly midwestern manufacturing industries to deteriorate. Agriculture was also particularly hard hit, and some farmers became receptive to the Jewish banking conspiracy theories of the Posse Comitatus.

In this context, the racist Right's existing leadership pursued two courses of action. Some united under the violent Aryan Nations and tried to spark a race war against what they called the "Zionist occupational government." Others, under the banner of the Populist Party, tried to revive the old American Independent parties. Violent crimes by the Aryan Nations drew widespread press coverage. Little attention was paid to the racist Right's electoral organizing; the exception was David Duke's 1991 gubernatorial race.

Ultimately, neither the "ballots" nor the "bullets" strategy built broad support for the racist Right. The Populist Party repeated the crippling factionalism of its predecessor parties. In response to the Aryan Nations' spate of killings and armed robberies, the federal government prosecuted those directly involved and then tried, unsuccessfully, to convict a ring of racist Right leaders on sedition charges. Legal repression of the racist Right seemed to slow the advance of the movement's violent echelon, but not eliminate it entirely.

As the New Right and Christian Right gained influence within elite policymaking circles, the racist Right degenerated into a movement not merely oppositional, but thoroughly alienated from routine political processes. The movement became incapable of appealing to people and institutions outside its own ranks. It became increasingly irrelevant—except, of course, to the immediate targets of its violence.

David Duke was the notable exception to the organized racist Right's ineptitude. Duke was elected to the Louisiana state legislature in 1989 but his reputation as "former" leader of the Ku Klux Klan prevented his election to the governorship two years later. Publicly, political elites considered Duke's neo-Nazi associations beyond the pale. That did not stop the majority of Louisiana's white voters from responding to Duke's coded use of race-related policy issues: opposition to welfare programs, affirmative action, and other state-based means of redistributing power and wealth, namely, to African Americans. Duke's electoral career demonstrated the continuing salience of race-based political appeals. That lesson did not go unnoticed by a faction of the broader conservative movement eager to expand its own appeal around themes of "cultural nationalism."

THE FARM CRISIS AND THE RACIST RIGHT'S FORAY INTO ELECTORAL POLITICS

The backdrop to the racist Right's 1980s resurgence was a crisis in the U.S. agricultural economy, more severe than any since the 1920s.[4] In the 1970s, farmers were encouraged to expand their businesses. Then inflation drove interest rates up. Those farmers who could still pay their loans saw their land prices plummet between 1981 and 1987, while they read about Wall Street speculators becoming millionaires through insider trading and other crafty means of moving numbers on paper.[5] The magnitude of the farm crisis was staggering. In Minnesota, the average price of an acre of land fell from $1,947 in 1981 to $628 in 1987, amounting to a loss of paper wealth of between $20 and $40 billion for that state alone. The U.S. farm population dropped from nine million in 1975 to less than five million in 1987, as absentee investors assumed an ever greater percentage of farm ownership.[6] In Iowa, an estimated 30 percent of the farmers were threatened with the loss of their land.[7]

Individual farmers saw everything they had worked for fall into the hands of bankers who foreclosed on their property. In that context, the racist Right took advantage of a rare opportunity to spread their spurious conspiracy theories about Jewish control of the financial system.

Beginning in the 1970s, a loose network known as the Posse Comitatus (meaning "power of the county") had emerged in the West Coast and Midwest regions. A 1976 FBI estimate of seventy-eight Posse Comitatus chapters in twenty-three states placed total memberhip at between 12,000 and 15,000, with as many as ten to twelve times that number of peripheral supporters.[8] From California to Wisconsin, each Posse leader developed a slightly different style. Common to all was belief in white supremacist Identity Christianity (discussed in Chapter 6) and variations on a few "constitutionalist" themes: Jewish bankers manipulate and control the Federal Reserve Board, if not the whole U.S. financial system; the income tax amendment was never legally approved by Congress and, therefore, "sovereign citizens" need not pay taxes; the United States is a "republic," not a "democracy"; and the only lawful authority is the county sheriff and his appointed "posse" of adult men who reside in his jurisdiction.[9]

Through the Posse Comitatus' pre-existing network of Farm Belt groups, the Midwest became fertile ground for the spread of racist and anti-Jewish propaganda during the 1980s. Wisconsin Posse leader James Wickstrom circulated a pamphlet, "The American Farmer: 20th Century Slave," blaming Jews for the crisis in agriculture. Wickstrom and another Christian Identity minister, William Potter Gale, were frequent speakers on a daily Posse radio program broadcast from Kansas. Rick Elliott's National Agricultural Press Association (NAPA) published *The Primrose and Cattlemen's Gazette*, featuring bona fide agricultural news mixed with virulent anti-Semitic articles and advertisements for the Aryan Nations. Elliott recruited a claimed membership of 3,000 in thirty states before he was indicted for selling disreputable legal kits and absconding with supporters' money.[10] Both the Posse Comitatus and recruiters for Lyndon LaRouche's right-wing cult made efforts to gain control over the American Agricultural Movement (AAM), a leading farmers' lobby. Conflict within AAM over whether to ally with the racist and anti-Semitic Right led to a factional split in 1982, precisely at a time when farmers needed a coherent protest organization to make their voices heard in Washington. Had mainstream farmers not taken serious steps to educate AAM's rank-and-file about infiltration by the far Right, the extent of the damage might have been much worse.[11] One AAM faction sponsored guerrilla warfare training and classes on the making of pipe bombs; another faction advocating violence formed a Farmers' Liberation Army.[12]

North Dakota farmer Gordon Kahl was typical among the Posse Comitatus organizers of the rural Midwest. Kahl joined the Posse in 1974 and landed in prison after a 1976 television appearance in which he urged others to join him in not paying taxes. Once paroled, Kahl was ordered to stay away from Posse activities, but he continued to travel around the Midwest explaining to small audiences the Posse's theory that Jews were to blame for the farm crisis. For violating the terms of his probation, the federal government issued a warrant for Kahl's arrest. In February 1983, two federal marshals sent to capture him were killed in a shootout with Kahl, his son and a family friend. Kahl escaped and spent the next several months sheltered in a series of Posse members' homes. When the FBI finally located him at the ranch of an Arkansas couple, Kahl refused to surrender and instead died in a thirty-six-hour gun battle with federal agents.[13] The following year, Arthur Kirk, a Posse farmer active with Rick Elliott's National Agricultural Press Association, was killed in a gun fight with Nebraska state police when he refused to allow his farm to be repossessed.[14]

Kahl and Kirk became martyrs among the Posse and the broader racist Right. Their deaths exacerbated the conviction of fellow patriots that the existing federal government was wholly illegitimate and that a thorough break with "the system" was long overdue.

Toward the goal of unifying the racist Right into a coherent opposition, in 1980 Willis Carto published a series of articles on "populism" in the Liberty Lobby's weekly *Spotlight* newspaper. The series featured laudatory biographies of historical "populist" heroes, and, as was mentioned in Chapter 6, Carto republished the series in book form as *Profiles in Populism*. Carto defined "populism" as an amalgam of political and economic nationalism, a conspiracist view of history, commitment to "free enterprise" and a strong middle class, and a justification for racial prejudice.[15]

In fact, in regular usage, the Liberty Lobby applied the term "populist" as a euphemism for individuals and movements more accurately termed "neo-Nazi" or "fascist" (e.g., Klansman David Duke and French National Front leader Jean-Marie Le Pen).[16] The Farm Belt was receptive to some of the racist Right's organizers. Carto and other career racists hoped to use the "populist" label to pass themselves off as true-blue democrats. The same *Spotlight* pages wherein the Liberty Lobby projected itself as heir to historical populist role models also promoted the latest activities of unreconstructed anti-Semites and white supremacists. These included leading preachers of Identity Christianity;[17] the Liberty Lobby-affiliated Institute for Historical Review, with its claims that no Jews died in Hitler's gas chambers;[18] and the group of Ku Klux Klansmen on trial for the murder of five U.S. Communists at a 1979 anti-Klan rally in Greensboro, North Carolina.[19]

These were the kind of "populists" the Liberty Lobby sought to unite with the creation of the Populist Party in 1984. But by then, the Liberty Lobby faced competition over the use of the "populist" label from an old nemesis, Richard Viguerie. Along with fellow New Right leaders Paul Weyrich and Howard Phillips, Viguerie had tried unsuccessfully to gain control of the American Independent Party at its 1976 convention.

Soon after Reagan took office, the New Right became so thoroughly disgruntled with the administration's performance that Viguerie devoted the entire July 1982 issue of his *Conservative Digest* magazine to critiques from a spectrum of neoconservative, anticommunist, and Christian Right activists. From the Nixon years forward, Viguerie, Weyrich, and Phillips had toyed with the idea of launching a new third party. Toward reviving that idea, and in advance of Reagan's reelection campaign, Viguerie published a widely circulated book, *The Establishment versus the People.* In it, Viguerie took aim at "Big Business, Big Banks, Big Media, Big Unions, Big Government, and their allies." He criticized Reagan for failing to take tougher stands against the Communist bloc, for creating exorbitant federal deficits by not eliminating welfare spending, and for acting on behalf of elites in both major parties by increasing outlays to the National Endowment for the Arts and the Corporation for Public Broadcasting.[20]

Viguerie's multi-million dollar direct mail business gave him an advantage in promoting his version of "populism." But the Liberty Lobby portrayed Viguerie as a phony populist, "still echoing the same philosophy that he's been peddling for the last twenty years, . . . support [for] big business, free trade and internationalism, including military intervention in useless foreign wars."[21] A *Spotlight* review of Viguerie's book continued:

> A hallmark of Viguerie-style conservatism has been diligent avoidance of any controversy regarding racial issues, the money and banking question, the influence of internationalist outfits such as David Rockefeller's Trilateral Commission and the ever-growing power of political Zionism.
> Viguerie prefers to avoid noting that international Zionism has been perhaps the key force which led America into two bloody world wars and even now threatens to drag the world into a nuclear holocaust.[22]

In contrast, *Spotlight* reiterated, Willis Carto's "populism" stressed a nationalist, "America-first" foreign policy; "an awareness of the malign nature of international high finance" and the banking system; "a stand for producers, farmers and workers over money-lenders and speculators" and tariffs to protect U.S. jobs and industry; "a recognition of human differences" and the idea that "each race has the right to pursue its own destiny free from outside manipulation."[23]

These fundamental conceptual differences aside, Viguerie's appropriation of the populist mantle threatened to confuse potential recruits to the Populist Party, fostered by the Liberty Lobby. The Populist Party represented the racist Right's first concerted foray into electoral politics since the 1968 George Wallace presidential campaign and subsequent efforts by factions of the American Independent Party (AIP). Like the AIP, the Populist Party, too, proved incapable of sustaining unity among contentious racist Right stalwarts.

But in 1984, success seemed possible. With pressing deadlines to achieve ballot qualification status in as many states as possible, the party quickly assembled a team of state leaders. At the helm was the Populist Party's first national chairperson Robert Weems, a former Mississippi

Ku Klux Klan leader and head of *Spotlight*'s southern regional bureau.[24] "We don't think that it is communistic to belong to a union, or that it is reactionary to enact tariffs to protect American jobs and we intend to repeal the funny money Federal Reserve Act and abolish the income tax," Weems said upon announcing the party's formation in March 1984.[25] In addition, the party's platform called for a rejection of the Equal Rights Amendment and gay rights, an end to "forced racial busing" and illegal immigration, denial of voting rights to anyone on welfare more than one year; reduction of foreign aid, and a "national policy of nonintervention in foreign wars."[26]

Just as Klan and neo-Nazi activists had assumed leadership roles in the 1968 George Wallace campaign, the Populist Party likewise was organized by veterans of the racist Right. From the Posse Comitatus milieu came Keith Shive of the Farmers' Liberation Army and Joseph Birkenstock, the party's Wisconsin state chairperson. From the Klan came Ralph Forbes of Arkansas and A. J. Barker of North Carolina. Volunteering for the party's speaking bureau was Colonel Jack Mohr, the notoriously anti-Semitic Identity preacher and leader of the Christian Patriots Defense League.[27] Small, pre-existing racist third parties enabled the Populist Party to achieve quick ballot status in fourteen states. In California, for example, the American Independent Party, headed by Wallace organizer William K. Shearer, offered itself as the new party's official state representative, thus eliminating the Populists' need to collect thousands of voter signatures. In other states, outposts of the old Constitution and the Conservative Parties followed suit.[28] The Populists held their nominating convention in Nashville, Tennessee—where they emphasized that the area was the landmark site of Andrew Jackson's home, the Hermitage—and nominated Bob Richards and Maureen Salaman. Presidential candidate Bob Richards was the 1954 Olympic gold medal winner and "Wheaties" brand cereal spokesperson. Vice-presidential nominee Salaman was the president of the National Health Federation, author of popular health food books, and a *Spotlight* health writer.[29] Though neither had national reputations as racist activists, both heartily endorsed the Populists' platform and spoke at campaign stops organized by the racist Right.[30]

The Populists captured a meager 63,864 votes in the fourteen states where the party was on the ballot as a challenger to incumbent President Reagan. Compared with other small but better publicized third-party candidacies, however, the Populists fared well. The Libertarian Party, active since 1972, won only about 228,000 votes in 1984. Perennial candidate and cult leader Lyndon LaRouche won only about 79,000 votes, despite his expensive television campaign.[31]

Before the Populist Party had much of an opportunity to plan its next moves, factionalism set in, and two years after its formation the party was torn asunder. In a repeat of his performance within the Wallace campaign organization, California AIP leader William Shearer persuaded a majority of the Populists' executive committee to vote to oust Willis Carto. Shearer's faction registered a rival San Diego-based populist party with the Federal Election Commission.[32]

Carto's faction eventually regrouped under a younger group of populists, headquartered in Pittsburgh. In 1987, the Pittsburgh group nominated Representative George Hansen (R-ID) as its presidential candidate, but Hansen declined the offer.[33] By then, former Klansman David Duke had launched his bid for the 1988 Democratic presidential nomination. In its coverage of Duke's campaign, *Spotlight* consistently identified him as a "maverick populist."

In fact, from the time he attended Louisiana State University in the late 1960s, Duke was an avowed neo-Nazi.[34] He rose through the ranks of various neo-Nazi and Klan splinter groups, and eventually became Grand Wizard of the Louisiana Knights of the Ku Klux Klan in 1975.[35] Duke was among a generation of post-civil rights era Klansmen who advocated a more wholesome public image for their historically terrorist organizations. Duke in particular preferred an electoral strategy. His first campaign, for a Louisiana state Senate seat in 1975, never mentioned his role as Klan leader, but instead focused on arousing voters against taxes, gun control, mandatory school busing, reverse discrimination, and the welfare state. On that platform, Duke garnered about a third of the votes cast; the following year, he won 26 percent of the vote in a race for another state Senate seat. In 1980, Duke formally left the Klan and started his own National Association for the Advancement of White People (NAAWP). He claimed no lingering ties to the Klan even while he continued to advertise racist, anti-Semitic, and pro-Nazi literature through the NAAWP newsletter. In 1988, Duke waged a short-lived primary campaign for the Democratic presidential nomination. The Democrats refused to include him in party-sponsored debates. He received no government election matching funds and won only 22,000 votes in the few states where he ran.[36]

Before Duke formally abandoned his campaign as a Democrat, he agreed to run as the Populist Party's 1988 presidential nominee. Duke's original running mate was Lieutenant Colonel James "Bo" Gritz, the former Green Beret whose widely publicized prisoner-of-war "rescue missions" in Southeast Asia made him a role model for the "Rambo" movie character.[37] Gritz soon left the Duke ticket to run for a Congressional seat in his home state of Nevada; in his place the Populists matched Duke with an unknown medical doctor named Floyd Parker.[38] The Populist Party campaign raised $500,000, and Duke received about 150,000 votes.[39]

Without doubt, Duke's growing national notoriety contributed to his first electoral victory a few months later. In January 1989 Duke entered the race as a Republican for a seat in the Louisiana legislature and won by a small margin. After the election, an anti-racist coalition in New Orleans conducted a poll and found Duke's prototypical supporter to be a white Catholic male Democrat between the ages of thirty-five and forty-nine, with no college education and children enrolled in public school.[40] From his legislative district office, Duke continued to sell neo-Nazi literature.[41] His undying reputation as a Klansman left him unable to repeat his 1989 victory. In 1990 Duke ran unsuccessfully for the U.S. Senate. The following year he ran a heated campaign for the Louisiana governorship. That race attracted greater national press scrutiny than Duke's previous campaigns. The state's business community understood the stakes when anti-racist activists threatened an international boycott against Louisiana if Duke were elected governor. Louisiana's political establishment united against Duke and took steps to ensure high turnout—particularly among black voters—to defeat him. Duke lost the 1991 governor's election but won a majority of the state's white vote.[42]

As of the early 1990s, Duke's 1989 capture of a seat in Louisiana's legislature remained a unique electoral victory for the racist Right.[43] The Populist Party itself continued to flounder in its own factionalism. In 1991 Willis Carto's Liberty Lobby formed yet another electoral front, the Populist Action Committee, which lent its endorsement to right-wing candidates for local offices but withheld support for Bo Gritz's 1992 presidential campaign with the Populist Party.[44] The "populists" were crippled by their own sectarianism, while the stigma of outright Klan and neo-Nazi associations proved untenable from a public relations standpoint. Racist campaign themes and imagery were, nevertheless, appropriated by mainstream politicians—particularly within the Republican Party—who, unlike David Duke, were not tarnished by past leadership of terrorist organizations.

THE ARYAN NATIONS AND THE STRATEGY OF VIOLENCE

Before the Populist Party had exhausted its chances for success, at the opposite end of the tactical spectrum, those racist Right leaders most inclined toward violence also sought to unify disparate elements of their movement. Ultimately, the racist Right's decidedly violent echelon drew a predictably repressive response from state authorities. Like the Populist Party, the racist Right's paramilitary wing was dominated by Klansmen and Identity preachers of the Posse Comitatus. David Duke's closest associates overlapped with a new breed of avowedly Christian racist militants.[45]

A pivotal moment came in 1982 when a consortium of racist Right leaders came together as the Aryan Nations at an annual camp meeting held at Identity preacher Richard Butler's compound in Hayden Lake, Idaho. Butler was a sort of elder statesman among Identity preachers. While involved in anticommunist activities during the early 1960s, Butler met fellow World War II veteran William Potter Gale, who introduced him to Dr. Wesley Swift's Identity church in Lancaster, California. Swift had been a follower of Gerald L. K. Smith, the notorious racist who had inspired George Lincoln Rockwell to form the American Nazi Party. Swift preached an Americanized version of British Israelism, the doctrine that the ten lost tribes of Israel had migrated across the Caucasus Mountains and settled in the territories of Scandinavia and Western Europe. White Aryans, not European Jews, are, therefore, the true Israelites. Non-Caucasian races are explained by a "two-seed theory" to the effect that Eve bore a son to Adam and another to Satan. After Swift's death in 1970, Butler and Gale established separate Identity churches. Gale bought a ranch near Yosemite in California. Butler relocated to Idaho and began to sell family memberships in the Aryan Nations; by the early 1980s, Butler claimed 300 local members and 6,000 members across the country.[46]

Along with the rise of the Posse Comitatus in the 1970s, the Identity message became the unifying theological position for the resurgent racist Right. Starting in 1979, Butler sponsored an annual summer gathering of Identity preachers and leaders of various Klan and neo-Nazi groups. Butler's 1982 Aryan Nations Congress drew some of the racist Right's most notorious leaders: Michigan Klan leader Robert Miles who had served a six-year prison sentence for bombing school buses; J. B. Stoner of the National States Rights Party, who was eventually sentenced for a 1956 church bombing in Alabama; Louis Beam, leader of the Texas Klan and of a paramilitary training camp.[47]

Hayden Lake was a likely venue for the coalescing of the racist Right's violent wing. Identity Christianity not only unified the movement's diverse sects; it also provided a legitimating framework for advocates of violent tactics. Apart from its bedrock issue of white supremacy, Identity is a brand of post-tribulational or post-millenial Christianity. Among Bible-based sects, pre-millenialists believe Christians will be "raptured" into heaven before a "battle of Armageddon" and Christ's subsequent return to earth. Post-millenialists believe they will have to fight Christ's enemies during a period of "tribulation;" in this version of prophecy, Christ will return only after Christians establish their reign on earth. Ideologically, the post-millenial view is better suited to aggressive political strategies, including those involving violence. During the 1980s, leading Christian Right figures turned toward post-millenialism; a few went so far as to associate with Identity adherents.[48] Over time, Identity theology might have become a more common meeting ground for white supremacists and politically active evangelicals, had it not been for the Aryan Nations' development into a terrorist underground.

One influential item circulated at the 1982 Aryan Nations Congress was a racist fantasy novel, *The Turner Diaries.* In grisly detail, the book described a clandestine cell of white patriots, "the Order," who launch an apocalyptic urban race war—complete with armed robberies and numerous assassinations— against a Jewish-controlled government. *The Turner Diaries* left a vivid impression on Robert Mathews, a Seattle area lumberjack and member of the Aryan Nations. In 1983, Mathews recruited several other men from Butler's church to join him in creating a group modeled after "the Order." In early 1983 Mathews' group began a crime spree involving bank and armored car robberies and a counterfeiting operation. Their plan was to raise a war chest to turn the northwest region of the United States into a "last bastion" for the white race. Posse Comitatus martyr Gordon Kahl's 1983 death in the shootout with federal agents spurred Mathews' group to escalate the pace of their armed robberies. By June 1984, they successfully conspired to murder Alan Berg, a Denver radio talk show host known for his frequent on-air arguments with noted white supremacists.[49]

The following month, they recruited two Brinks security company employees to help them rob an armored truck carrying $3.6 million. With that kind of cash they were able to buy 110 acres of Idaho land for a future paramilitary camp and had extra to share with some of their favorite Klan and neo-Nazi leaders. At the scene of the Brinks heist, however, Robert Mathews dropped a pistol that the FBI traced to a mailbox registered under an Order member's real name. Meanwhile, an Order associate named Tom Martinez was arrested for passing some of the group's home-made counterfeit money in Philadelphia. Martinez plea bargained and agreed to become a government informant. Under the FBI's instruction, Martinez flew to Oregon to meet with Mathews and feign interest in joining the Order. Following them from their rendezvous point, the FBI succeeded in arresting Order member Gary Yarborough. Mathews escaped, but the FBI soon located him in Washington State where he died in a shootout with the federal agents sent to capture him.[50]

Eventually the FBI caught twenty-three Order members and associates and charged them with dozens of offenses, including the murder of Alan Berg. They were brought to trial in Seattle in 1985. Ten were convicted and given lengthy jail sentences.[51] That brought an end to one dramatic chapter in the racist Right's history of violence. But the Order was only one tentacle of a much larger organism.

The 1983 Gordon Kahl incident had heightened the IRS' interest in a far-flung collection of right-wing tax protesters, some prone to violence. While Richard Butler's Aryan Nations spawned the Order, followers of California Identity preacher William Gale likewise formed a secret paramilitary network, the Committee of the States, beginning in 1984.[52] As part of its wide-ranging investigation and crackdown on the white supremacist movement, the government arrested Gale and six members of the Committee of the States, plus four members of the allied Arizona Patriots, all in October 1986.[53] A year later, they were convicted for mailing death threats to IRS officers.

In the mean time, fifteen national white supremacist leaders were indicted for the Alan Berg murder and for conspiring to overthrow the U.S. government. Defendants included Robert Miles, Richard Butler, Louis Beam, Richard Scutari, and Bruce Pierce. One of their former comrades, Jim Ellison, became the star witness in the government's effort to prove key Aryan Nations leaders guilty of sedition. North Carolina Klan leader Glenn Miller likewise informed for the prosecution. In 1988, after a lengthy trial in Fort Smith, Arkansas, the defendants were all acquitted.[54]

By casting a wide net of potential culprits and by defining their alleged crimes beyond specific acts to an interconnected conspiracy, the government established a legal case that was difficult to prove. Nevertheless, evidence presented at the trial demonstrated that the Order was not an aberration but, rather, an integral part of a concerted movement strategy of violence. The trial process itself had the effect of destabilizing the tentative unity that had prevailed among Aryan Nations leaders. Throughout the trial and its aftermath, Michigan Klan leader Robert Miles filled his "From the Mountain" newsletter with incriminations against the few white supremacists who turned state's evidence and, more broadly, against those who failed to voice support for the defendants.[55]

The Seattle and Fort Smith trials signalled only partial setbacks for the violent echelon of the white supremacist movement. San Diego Klan leader Tom Metzger was among those not implicated in these two major prosecutions. By the late 1980s, Metzger had successfully pioneered two tactics in the promulgation of white supremacist thinking. First, Metzger took advantage of a new trend among cable television systems to allot one channel for amateur public access programs. Metzger's series of half hour "Race and Reason" interviews met public access criteria and could only be rejected at the expense of the First Amendment.[56]

Second, Metzger and his son John concentrated on recruiting young racist skinheads from the subcultural milieu of punk rock music. In

Portland one night in November 1988, a group of skinheads from Metzger's White Aryan Resistance (WAR) used a baseball bat to beat Mulageta Seraw, an Ethiopian man, to death. Three skinheads were sentenced for the crime. Then on behalf of Seraw's family, the Southern Poverty Law Center and the Anti-Defamation League sued Tom and John Metzger for $10 million, on the legal theory that their "vicarious liability" had caused the killing.[57] The idea was to win a settlement in such a way as to permanently bankrupt the Metzgers. Two years after the murder, a jury found the Metzgers guilty and awarded Seraw's family $12.5 million. The case was decided largely on the basis of testimony from Dave Mazzella, the WAR organizer whom the Metzgers had sent to Portland to organize violent skinheads. Mazzella's subsequent defection from WAR and continued participation with rival skinhead groups made his credibility less than sound, and civil libertarians worried about the means used to achieve legal victory over the Metzgers.[58] Beyond that, the judgment against the Metzgers did not put an end to racist skinhead violence.[59]

Violent acts perpetrated by adherents of racist and neo-Nazi groups coincided with a general rise in the phenomenon of hate crimes during the late 1980s.[60] For many years civil rights organizations had tried to cull reliable data on violence inspired by various forms of bigotry. In 1990 Congress passed a Hate Crimes Statistics Act under which the Justice Department is charged with collecting and reporting hate crime data submitted by local police departments.[61] Reliable totals remain difficult to come by, however, because reporting is voluntary and because of the problems in definitively categorizing isolated acts of violence as hate crimes. Among civil rights monitors, the general consensus has been that most hate crimes are committed by individuals not formally associated with organized racist groups, though such groups may have influenced some perpetrators. By degrees, but in a pervasive sense, U.S. society held a reservoir of support for race-based political appeals.

THE APPEAL OF RACIST POLITICS

Writing in the aftermath of the Fort Smith sedition trial acquittals, Klansman Robert Miles detailed the toll taken on the racist Right's fragile unity and concluded in his hyperbolic style:

> The Movement is dead . . . long live the Movement! And as kings pass on but their monarchy lives on, so it will be with this Movement. The Movement which we built and saw pass, will live on in other movements yet to be born. The Race will live on if it is sufficiently important to the ones about which it is concerned. The old is dead. It has passed with

time. It is now for a new wave, a new age, to be born. For those of us who were the leaders from a generation now dying, the hour is late. We can aid in the new birth but we must not delay such new birth from happening.

We have stood! We have fought! We won! One battle is not the entire war but the war is endless in our struggle as a Race to endure. FOR FAITH AND OUR FOLK![62]

Miles' post-mortem conveyed the avowedly racist Right leaders' recognition of their failure to mobilize a mass following. But as Miles himself hinted, the fading of old Klan leaders meant no end to race-based politics of a more conventional nature.

A year after the Fort Smith trial acquittals, "former" Klansman and neo-Nazi David Duke moved quickly from his Populist Party presidential campaign to his first electoral victory. Shortly after George Bush was inaugurated as president in 1989, Duke won a seat in the Louisiana legislature. Though Bush and Duke were worlds apart in their backgrounds and widely divergent on foreign affairs questions, they shared a common understanding of racial scare tactics.

Among all aspects of Bush's 1988 presidential campaign against Massachusetts Governor Michael Dukakis, none grabbed attention like the infamous "Willie Horton" television spots. Horton, a black man, was the convicted murderer who raped a white woman while out on the prison furlough program in Dukakis' home state. Horton personified the sins of liberalism: violence, disruption of family tranquility, wasted tax dollars, the Democrats' obeisance to black people, all rolled into a single symbol.

The Willie Horton spots made no claims about genetic racial differences, as the organized neo-Nazi movement would have done. Instead, Republican campaigners played the race card as one part of a right-wing message that also featured the American flag as a military symbol and Bush's famous "read my lips" pledge of "no new taxes." Once Bush was elected, he made a priority of waging war against non-compliant Third World regimes (Panama, Nicaragua, and, of course, Iraq). At home, Bush staged a War on Drugs that emphasized legal repression, targeting black and Latino communities disproportionately.

For his part, David Duke made a serious bid for a U.S. Senate seat in 1990, when he received most of the white vote in Louisiana. The next year he came close to becoming Louisiana's governor. Duke's race for the governorship was a major national news story in 1991, as it seemed emblematic of larger trends in U.S. politics. Duke was the beneficiary of Louisiana's peculiar run-off system in which the top two primary vote getters, regardless of party, face each other in the general election.

Division among Louisiana Republicans, in part surrounding incumbent Governor Buddy Roemer's pro-choice abortion stance, worked to Duke's advantage when the choice was between Duke and former Governor Edwin Edwards. Not only did Edwards have a personal reputation for illicit gambling, but he was also widely associated with the welfare and affirmative action policies of his term during the 1970s. Edwards' numerous mainstream political enemies rallied behind him against David Duke with the bumper sticker slogan "vote for the crook."[63]

Duke, who by then had literally undergone facial surgery to improve his image, steered clear of genetic race issues. He instructed readers of his National Association for the Advancement of White People (NAAWP) newsletter to "stay away from the 'n' word" in conversations with potential white supporters.[64] In his frequent direct mailings and media appearances, Duke hammered at themes publicly understood as coded race language: crime, "illegitimate" pregnancy among welfare recipients, "forced busing." In an appeal to the Christian Right, Duke also peppered his speeches and fundraising letters with references to Jesus and a "Christian nation."[65]

Despite high black voter turnout and an extravagant anti-Duke campaign by Louisiana's political and business establishment, Duke still netted 39 percent of the total vote and 55 percent of the white vote. Scholars who studied the David Duke electoral phenomenon explained the candidate's appeal in several ways. About half of Duke's supporters were found to favor segregation; some voters genuinely liked Duke's genetic racism and Klan past.[66] Others responded to Duke's overt message against welfare and affirmative action. These bits of symbolic racism locate racial inequality within the ideology of the American work ethic: blacks should demand less and work harder. This dimension of Duke's appeal was found to be particularly effective among white working-class and lower-middle-class voters concerned about declining economic prospects.[67]

Duke's class base of support seemed consistent with the classic explanation, developed by Seymour Lipset and other pluralist social scientists, of right-wing "extremism" as an expression of downwardly mobile people's status anxiety. Duke's supporters, though, were downwardly mobile not so much as a status group but as an economic class. Duke's electoral success is better explained as the result of voters' declining economic conditions. Among anti-Duke voters, there was an understanding that Louisiana's economic fate would worsen were Duke elected. The state was threatened with an international boycott of its tourist, real estate and other industries if voters elected a former Klansman as governor. That threat motivated Louisiana's political and business elites to oppose Duke, leaving the candidate with only an anti-elitist base of support. Duke's previous campaigns had not aroused strong opposition from elites, who were perfectly willing to admit the same "extremist" Duke into the polite corridors of state policymaking. Duke himself carried too much public relations baggage to ascend beyond the state legislature. His rhetoric against taxes, welfare, and affirmative action, however, was consistent with mainstream conservatism.

While the end of the Cold War brought no hoped for world peace and prosperity, the diminished international commitments of the United States elevated questions of race relations, "family values," and the domestic economy to higher levels of national priority. As we will see in Chapter 12, the foreign affairs President George Bush never enjoyed the enthusiasm of right-wing movement activists. The tail end of the Reagan–Bush era was accompanied by a realignment of various movement tendencies, marked by the ascension of a group of self-identified "paleoconservatives," who opposed U.S. military intervention abroad and welfare statism at home, who also championed the Christian Right's moral causes and the racist Right's concerns about illegal immigration and cultural nationalism. For paleoconservative thinkers, David Duke's 1991 near win was a watershed event. Samuel Francis, an editor for the paleoconservatives' *Chronicles* magazine, called it a "turning point in American history."

> Democrats and liberals have spent the last year whining that Duke represents the logical culmination of the conservative resurgence of Ronald Reagan, and conservatives, for the most part, have spent an equal amount of time denying it. The Democrats and liberals are, for once, dead right, though as usual they miss the point. Reagan conservatism, in its innermost meaning, had little to do with supply-side economics and spreading democracy. It had to do with the awakening of a people who face political, cultural, and economic dispossession who are slowly beginning to glimpse the fact of dispossession and what dispossession will mean for them and their descendants.
>
> There was a subtext to what Mr. Duke explicitly and formally said in his speeches and his campaign literature, and the subtext, communicated by the continued depiction of Mr. Duke in Nazi uniform and Klan hood by his enemies, is that the historic core of American civilization is under attack. Quotas, affirmative action, race norming, civil rights legislation, multiculturalism in schools and universities, welfare, busing, and unrestricted immigration from Third World countries are all symbols of that attack and of the racial cultural, and political dispossession they promise to inflict upon the white post-bourgeois middle classes.[68]

Francis minced no words about the implications of David Duke's message and popularity for "the mainstream of American conservatism in the

1990s." If the Right were to remain the dominant political force into the twenty-first century, it would have to make "cultural nationalism" the "center of public concern and public policy."[69]

Likewise, in his syndicated column, discussing the Louisiana gubernatorial race, Patrick Buchanan warned that the Republicans dismissed David Duke at their own peril.

> If his resume is Mr. Duke's handicap, what is his appeal? In his 15-point platform, he zeros in on issues that should be a wake-up call for all our Big Government Conservatives.
>
> Mr. Duke pledges to oppose any new tax increase. He wants to toss the able-bodied off welfare, stop payments to drug users and freeze benefits to welfare mothers who keep having children. He favors tougher penalties for crime and an end to "unjust affirmative action," i.e., all reverse discrimination, whether quotas or racial set-asides. He calls for freedom of choice for parents in sending children to public schools, and a track system inside schools where the brightest are advanced fastest. He opposes gun control, wants the United States to halt illegal immigration, and would slash foreign aid.
>
> The national press calls these positions "code words" for racism, but in the hard times in Louisiana, Mr. Duke's message comes across as Middle Class, meritocratic, populist and nationalist.[70]

In the year following the Persian Gulf War, Buchanan emerged as the leading "cultural nationalist," to fill the vacuum of incumbent President Bush's plummeting popularity. Buchanan endorsed Duke's political program just weeks before he adopted some of the same themes in his early 1992 New Hampshire primary campaign against Bush. Throughout the primary season, Buchanan won about a third of the Republican vote.

The popularity of Duke and, later, Buchanan, was reminiscent of George Wallace's anti-elitist and pro-segregationist appeal to nearly ten million voters in 1968. After that juncture, New Right strategists took the lessons of Wallace's message to heart. Their "southern strategy" was designed to co-opt the Americanist movement's positions—minus its crude biological determinism—and its base of support, to forge a "new majority" Republican Party. In the late 1960s and twenty years later, the explicitly racist Right movement remained internally fractured and unattractive to more than a hard core of stalwarts. Yet, in the wake of the organized racist Right's evident failures, the question of race, cast at times as "cultural nationalism," would continue to intrigue and inspire the broader conservative movement.

CHAPTER 12

❖ ❖ ❖

After Reagan, Rumbling
on the Right

With the exception of the avowedly racist Right movement, which continued to go its separate way during the 1980s, the onset of the Reagan era brought unity to the Right's disparate elements. New Right think tanks and electoral projects promoted a three-fold set of priorities: anticommunist militarism, supply-side economics, and "traditional family values." These were the concerns of Old Right conservative intellectuals from the immediate post-World War II period forward. Yet conservative intellectuals alone never would have seen their ideals manifested at the highest levels of state policymaking had not New Right political strategists, neoconservative intellectuals, and a mass-base of evangelical Christians mobilized during the 1970s. These relative newcomers to the conservative movement assumed positions of importance within corporate-funded think tanks and the Republican Party, and they were not particularly beholden to the fusionist era thinkers treated in Chapter 1.

Beginning in the mid-1980s, Christian Right strategists accommodated themselves to the disappointments of Reagan's failed social policy promises by building their movement into a grassroots constituency indispensable to the Republican Party. Around the same time, other dissatisfied elements of the tenuous Reagan coalition began analyzing the Right's future prospects. Reagan's personal popularity remained the most obvious and dominant feature of the right-wing political scene. Less obvious to the uninitiated were profound, simmering intra-movement conflicts that would not manifest fully until after the end of Reagan's tenure and the closely timed break-up of the Communist bloc.

Neoconservatives and their self-identified "paleoconservative" detractors became the central antagonists in what some observers called the "conservative crack-up" of the late 1980s and early 1990s. This chapter treats that conflict in depth. At one level, the conflict revolved around several key events, polarized charges of nativist anti-Semitism versus Zionism, and competition over administrative appointments and foundation grants. Underlying the specific grievances between groups of conservatives, brewed deep, and in some cases irresolvable, philosophical differences. The actual partisans in the neoconservative–paleoconservative conflict were relatively few compared to the larger number of right-wing movement activists who found themselves strategically uncertain once George Bush broke his "no new taxes" pledge and pursued other policies anathema to die-hard Reaganites.

But the paleoconservative–neoconservative conflict was the tip of a larger iceberg, and for that reason it attracted the attention of New Right activists who were not immediately involved. Questions of the state's proper role in society were central to the debate. Paleoconservatives espoused a quintessential right-wing view: the state should neither redress class inequalities nor broaden the civil rights and political representation of traditionally subordinate groups. Instead, the state should enforce a domestic moral order dominated by native-born Christian white men. Internationally, the state should protect economic advantages for its own business class—and go to war if necessary—but beyond that, the state should remain relatively neutral toward other nations.

Neoconservatives, with their roots in welfare state and Cold War liberalism, were miles apart from the paleoconservatives. Neoconservatives believed in the role of the United States as world leader: the defeat of Communism was a first step toward spreading American-style "democracy" around the world. At home, the state had an obligation to ensure a modicum of social welfare and tranquility, though not equality between classes and status groups. The neoconservatives were disproportionately Jewish and Catholic, and they took pride in the United States' immigrant past. They opposed multicultural trends in education but they were not convinced, as were the paleoconservatives, of a thoroughgoing threat posed by expanding the definition of what it means to be an "American."

These philosophical differences rose to the surface even before the Cold War ended, but their salience was heightened by the ultimate disappearance of Communism as an international force. Throughout the Cold War, U.S. rightists shared the view that the principal obligation of the United States was to defeat communism, in two senses of the term: as the actual political–economic practices of the socialist bloc countries and as a set of ideals espoused by revolutionaries around the world.

For decades, right-wing movements had challenged one administration after the next over civil rights legislation, the Vietnam war, taxes, abortion rights, and the like. But across the board, the legitimacy of the anticommunist struggle had wedded conservatives both to each other and to one or more echelons of the political elite. The rapid and unexpected collapse of the Communist bloc left the Right, generally, without an unquestionable vision of its own purpose. Absent the communist "threat," the Right was in internal conflict over the U.S. role in the "new world order." Iraq's invasion of Kuwait presented policymakers and movement activists with the first major post-Cold War crisis, and the Persian Gulf war exacerbated pre-existing conflicts among rightists. At the same time, the end of Communism elevated, by default, the salience of domestic policy matters, and the Right was less than unified on this front as well.

Only the Christian Right had developed a coherent, strategic view of problems demanding attention and a tactical repertoire that ensured the movement's limited success. From the 1970s forward, the Christian Right had galvanized a mass base of supporters and a varied network of organizations for both issue-oriented and electoral activism. During the 1980s, the Christian Right had enlisted in the Reagan administration's counterinsurgency wars in the Third World. The end of Communism enabled Christian Right activists to focus more exclusively on issues of greatest concern to a broad evangelical constituency: abortion, gay civil rights, the state's role in the production of public art and educational ideology, let alone the representation of Christians in elected office. The 1992 Republican Party convention and local electoral races signaled the Christian Right's maturation into a full-fledged faction of mainstream Republicanism. By the time President Clinton took office, the Christian Right enjoyed more clout than any other element of the post-Cold War Right. This chapter traces the denouement of the Right's long career as Cold War partisan, the quandaries and shifting alignments presented by the end of the Reagan era, and the persistence of the Christian Right's influence.

CRACKS IN THE FACADE OF RIGHT-WING UNITY

President Reagan's departure from the White House left neoconservatives, the New Right, and the Christian Right without a unanimously popular and unifying leader. Upon the election of George Bush, right-wing activists initially hoped Vice-President Dan Quayle would serve as a liaison between themselves and the new administration, though Quayle himself was less than enthused about playing such a role.[1] Bush enjoyed early approval from movement conservatives. They liked his endorsement of Reagan's Strategic Defense Initiative (SDI), capital gains tax cuts, and proposed tuition tax credits for parents of children enrolled in private schools.[2] They liked his appointments of Dick Cheney to head the Pentagon, Jack Kemp as Secretary of Housing and Urban Development, and William Bennett as "drug czar."[3] But among the differences between the Reagan and Bush presidencies, it was evident early on that Bush would engage in little outreach within conservative movement circles. Instead he surrounded himself with a tight coterie of policy advisors: James Baker, Brent Scowcroft, John Sununu, all of them fixtures of the Republican Party establishment. In his first year in office, Bush identified his reign with the War on Drugs and a related effort to orchestrate a coup against Panamanian military leader (and long-time CIA collaborator) Manuel Noriega. Eleven months after Bush's inauguration, the United States invaded Panama and killed an as yet unknown number of civilians in the process of apprehending Noriega—and insuring U.S. military control over the canal zone.

Neither the domestic War on Drugs nor the invasion of Panama involved right-wing movement activists. They concurred with these policies but they were, "out of the loop," to use Bush's own description of his professed innocence in the Iran–Contra affair.

Not until the Bush administration embarked on divisive domestic policy initiatives did it arouse the ire of right-wing movement activists. At issue were the perennial questions of the state's role as distributor of wealth and power. Bush's first fateful move came in 1990 when he reluctantly abandoned his 1988 campaign pledge, "read my lips: no new taxes."

For Bush, the problem was an intractable one. Whereas the Republicans had built their 1980s electoral constituency in part on the resentments of the tax-burdened middle class, the Democrats understood the Republicans' political liability to be their refusal to tax the rich. In the face of rising federal deficits, the Democratic-controlled Congress was simply unwilling to make huge cuts, Reaganomics style, in basic entitlement programs like Social Security and Medicare. That left the Bush administration over a barrel and forced to agree to increases in the top tax rate.

Right-wing activists were outraged. In a cover story for *National Review*, libertarian economist (and former assistant Treasury Secretary under Reagan) Paul Craig Roberts charged Bush with destroying his own credibility, turning the tide in favor of a progressive redistribution of the tax burden, encouraging state spending and thereby inviting increased deficits. "It is ironic," Roberts wrote, "that Reagan's successor, terrified by the ancient nemesis of the Republican Party—the budget deficit—has renewed the assault on economic liberty that the politics of opportunity had laid to rest."[4]

Aside from the 1990 tax hike, the only other issue that would draw across-the-board condemnation from right-wing activists was Bush's "surrender" to a 1990 civil rights bill that made it easier for employees to press charges of racial discrimination in job hiring.[5] By then, the animosity of right-wing movement activists toward Bush was a permanent condition. Though Republicans held their ground in the 1990 mid-term elections, activists outside the party were clear in their denunciation of the Bush administration. *Human Events* put it this way:

> President George Bush, always a weak supporter of conservative causes, is no longer a credible voice. The most solemn and vivid political promise ever made to the American people—no new taxes—has been shredded beyond repair.
>
> The President not only agreed to raise the top tax rate from 28 to 31 per cent, thus eviscerating a key component of the supply-side revolution, but then embraced a 10 per cent hike in the capgains tax for higher-bracket individuals, the very people whose investments are needed for economic growth.
>
> On the social issues, the President has not wholly betrayed the conservatives, but he has hardly been rock solid, either.
>
> Bush has, in effect, encouraged the homosexual agenda by increasing funds for potential AIDS cures out of all proportion to funds for other life-threatening diseases, inviting members of prominent gay activist groups to the White House and giving wholehearted support to the National Endowment for the Arts, a multi-million-dollar cornucopia for deviant artists eager to depict degrading homosexual practices.
>
> Unless they are willing to do so, conservatives will be unable to change the increasingly leftward drift of the Bush administration, and may well lose the ongoing battle to control the Republican party.[6]

As the Bush administration prepared the U.S. military and public opinion for the January 1991 war on Iraq, Richard Viguerie publicized the Right's disdain for the President with a December 1990 *New York Times* guest editorial. "George Bush and his minions are heading into a civil war with GOP conservatives that will leave the political fields covered with blood." In vintage populist style, Viguerie continued:

> Members of the Establishment—the folks who have sent our sons to die in no-win wars, who have bused kids across town to schools where prayer was almost the only activity not allowed—have now raised our taxes to pay for an increase in an already bloated budget. As their agent, Mr. Bush has done more harm to the GOP than any Democrat in a decade.[7]

Viguerie's missive was a confused one. In reality, the modest 1990 tax hike was intended to shift the tax burden upward toward "members of the establishment." While Viguerie blasted the President, he was simultaneously among the Right's most vocal endorsers of Bush's march toward the Persian Gulf war.

Where opposition to Bush's violation of his "no new taxes" campaign pledge unified right-wing activists, the U.S.-led war on Iraq would divide the Right like nothing before. Conflict over the proper role of the United States in what Bush called a New World Order contributed to right-wing activists' inability to challenge the Bush administration on the domestic policy front. More profoundly, the Right's disunity on foreign affairs reflected deep and debilitating fissures, particularly between two prominent sets of conservative movement thinkers.

The trouble began, paradoxically, during the mid-1980s, when conservatives had their man in the White House and the country was sailing in a policy direction generally in the Right's favor. Cold War II was in full swing, and supply-side economics was not yet discredited. On the traditional morality front, the Christian Right was disheartened by the Reagan administration's weak action, but the leaders of that movement were busy laying the groundwork for evangelicals' increasing their clout within the Republican Party.

It was among conservative and neoconservative intellectual cadres that conflicts first erupted onto the pages of the Right's most sophisticated journals of opinion: *National Review, Commentary,* and the more obscure *Intercollegiate Review.* Within movements, intellectuals are the professional activists who can see what strategic pitfalls lie ahead. They are also the ones most concerned with ideological correctness, most attentive when resources flow to heretics and competitors.

Anniversaries occasioned two provocative pieces of self-reflection by conservative intellectuals. In honor of its fortieth anniversary, *Commentary* magazine published a special symposium issue in which prominent neoconservatives, and a few liberals, commented on the question, "how has the United States met its major challenges since 1945?"[8] That was the year when *Commentary*'s founding editor, the late Elliot E. Cohen, had defined the magazine's mission in terms of the American Jewish Committee's immediate post-World War II concerns: how would the United States continue to prosper economically, face the quandaries posed by the onset of the nuclear age, and, beyond that, address the "kind of thinking and feeling" that had led to the "colossal latter-day massacre of innocents, whether Jews or other 'minorities.'"[9] Forty years later, of course, *Commentary*'s leading liberals-turned-neoconservatives were supporters of the nuclear arms race and advocates of the Reagan administration's proxy warfare, which resulted in "massacres of innocents" in Central America, Palestine, and elsewhere.

As successful and self-conscious players in the formulation of public policy, contributors to *Commentary*'s anniversary issue were celebratory in tone. The gist of their essays was that the United States had prospered as an industrial giant, eradicated the worst manifestations of racial prejudice, and had only to see the final demise of Communism before declaring global victory. The message echoed Daniel Bell's old *End of Ideology* thesis, to the effect that the planet was safe from the threat of profound conflicts in world view and only needed to continue tinkering with solutions to solveable problems. (In 1989 State Department official Francis Fukuyama would revive this theme with the publication of "The End of History" in the neoconservative journal *The National Interest*.) Among the *Commentary* contributors, Midge Decter complained that the United States' forty-year policy toward Communism had been inconsistent and not strong enough.[10] The liberal Sidney Hook wrote that "the danger of Soviet totalitarianism to the survival of the free world today is greater than the threat of Nazi totalitarianism was in the 30's."[11]

Among the neoconservatives, Irving Kristol's was the position closest to that of the New Right, in that he sought to emphasize moral traditionalism on a par with economic and foreign affairs concerns. Kristol applauded the United States' "extraordinary economic achievements," the worldwide decline of anti-Jewish prejudice, and the dismantling of Jim Crow segregation. But then Kristol turned his attention to the crisis of morality of the United States.

> All in all, then, in the past forty years Americans have lived through a period that any fair-minded historian would describe as one of significant economic and social progress, as these terms are conventionally used. The trouble, however, lies precisely in the conventional use of these terms. They are part of a "progressive" vocabulary that rests on hidden assumptions. The major assumption is—and always has been—that improvement in economic and social conditions, as statistically measured, will make people more contented, more law-abiding, even "happier." . . . Certainly no one—whether liberal or conservative—would have dared predict, forty years ago, that the improvement in our economic and social circumstances would be accompanied by a massive, harrowing increase in crime, drug addiction, family disintegration, sexual promiscuity and illegitimacy among teen-agers, rampant homosexuality, and widespread pornography. Something clearly has gone wrong.
>
> It is not mass democracy that makes modern societies less habitable than anticipated, it is secular, "progressive" liberalism—in its modern version, anyhow—that excacerbates our social problems, while creating a spiritual and moral void in which they proliferate as so many cancers. This secular liberalism is the religion of our elites—in academia, in our educational establishments, in our media, in our arts—but not the

religion of a majority of the American people. This majority finds itself imprisoned within a culture ... that disenfranchises its moral and religious sensibilities.[12]

Kristol's definition of the problem should have enhanced neoconservatives' reputation within the New Right. But Kristol's choice of words reflected a persistent neoconservative concern with authoritarianism of the Right. Kristol predicted that "unless a modern conservatism emerges that can successfully cope with the distressful human condition in America today ... we could easily be in for a very nasty right-wing explosion."[13] His choice of words hinted at neoconservatives' conflicts with those to their right.

On the heels of *Commentary*'s fortieth-anniversary issue, *National Review* celebrated its thirtieth year by publishing Joseph Sobran's lengthy manifesto, "Notes for the Reactionary of Tomorrow." Prepared well in advance of the *Commentary* symposium, Sobran's article targeted liberals, not communists, as the most slippery enemies of the true conservative. "Liberalism has come to stand for an obsession with the abnormal for its own sake—the minority, the dissident, the outsider, the deviant, and so on," Sobran wrote, under the subheading "Native Aliens."[14] Against the stereotype of rightists as racist and nativist, Sobran coined the term "alienism" and defined it as

a prejudice in favor of the alien, the marginal, the dispossessed, the eccentric, reaching an extreme in the attempt to "build a new society" by destroying the basic institutions of the native. The most terrible fulfillment of this principle is Communism.

Liberalism and Marxism are variant forms of Alienism; so are feminism and "gay liberation," for that matter. Liberalism does all it can to accommodate its sister ideologies without overtly endorsing them; and it is bound to insist that the real peril to humanity is always some form of Nativism. This accounts for its obsession with the Nazi period, its endless search for old Nazis, its wild alarm over the most eccentric expression of neo-Nazism, and above all its attempts to link its enemies with Nazism.[15]

Sobran made no specific mention of the Jewish neoconservatives. His point was to identify "liberalism" as the bête noire of *National Review* readers in the next phase of the conservative movement's development. The backdrop to Sobran's clarion call was a simmering resentment among self-termed "paleoconservatives" over the influence of neoconservatives, disproportionate to their actual numbers, within right-wing circles and within the Reagan administration itself. In paleoconservatives' eyes, neoconservatives were dressed-up liberals, still promoting Big Government as the solution to all problems.

The paleoconservatives were a group of staunch traditionalists—explicitly Christian—who advocated a non-interventionist foreign policy and the libertarian economic theories of Ludwig von Mises. Paleoconservatives were not in league with the Libertarian Party and its associated Cato Institute, neither of which endorsed "traditional" moral strictures. Instead, the paleoconservatives' organizational headquarters was the Illinois-based Rockford Institute, publisher of the paleos' monthly magazine *Chronicles of Culture*. While paleoconservatives overlapped with the mass-based Christian Right, the self-described paleoconservatives were mostly academics grounded in the ideas in Russell Kirk's 1953 book *The Conservative Mind*: adherence to notions of custom, "natural" social inequality, and the detriments of mass democracy.[16]

In 1981 paleoconservatives and neoconservatives locked horns over the Reagan administration's appointment of a chairperson for the National Endowment for the Humanities. The position went to neoconservative William J. Bennett (whom President Bush later named "drug czar") over M. E. Bradford, a University of Dallas English professor, who was preferred by the paleoconservatives. Bradford was known for his opposition to the 1964 Civil Rights Act and his support for presidential candidate George Wallace in 1968 and 1972. Bradford went on to become president of the Philadelphia Society, an annual gathering in which conservative intellectuals perpetuated the fusionist era debates over libertarianism and traditionalism.[17]

In advance of the Philadelphia Society's 1986 meeting, Bradford and others who traced their lineages to the Old Right published "The State of Conservatism: A Symposium" in the Intercollegiate Studies Institute's quarterly *Intercollegiate Review*. Echoing Joseph Sobran's *National Review* treatise against liberalism and in response to *Commentary*'s celebration of social progress, the paleoconservatives declared open season on the neoconservative influence and participation within the New Right. One after another of the *Intercollegiate Review* contributors blamed neoconservatives in large part for a crisis of coherence on the Right. Clyde Wilson, a University of South Carolina historian, defined the problem as one of allowing too much diversity under the mantle of conservatism:

First of all, we have simply been crowded out by overwhelming numbers. The offensives of radicalism have driven vast herds of liberals across the border into our territories. These refugees now speak in our name, but the language they speak is the same one they always spoke. . . . Our estate has been taken over by an impostor, just as we were about to inherit.[18]

Melvin Bradford cited the November 1985 *Commentary* issue as evidence that the neoconservatives thought "that the leftward drift of 1932–1968 was essentially a wholesome development and that the mistake came later, from radicals who wished to go too far." Neoconservatives, he wrote, held fast to the "achievements" of the New Deal, Fair Deal, and Great Society.

> These interlopers want to get their agenda defined as axiomatic by leaving no useful space to their right; and they want all the persuasive advantages that come, in a post-liberal era, of calling their view conservative regardless of its essentially statist, pacifist and coercively egalitarian implications.[19]

Having thrown down this gauntlet, Bradford's next move was to convene a debate between neoconservatives and their detractors at the April 1986 Philadelphia Society meeting. *National Review* editor Jeffrey Hart, reporting on the event under the headline "Gang Warfare in Chicago," considered the conflict to be overrated and urged readers to rally behind neoconservatives Norman Podhoretz, William Bennett, Irving Kristol, and Elliott Abrams.[20] But the speech made by University of Michigan historian Stephen Tonsor, "Why I Too Am Not a Neoconservative," stuck like glue. Condensed and reprinted in *National Review*, Tonsor's speech made no bones about conservatism's decidedly *Christian* basis.[21]

That prompted neoconservatives to bring one of their long-standing grievances out of the closet. After the Philadelphia Society meeting, Midge Decter circulated copies of a letter she had written to Joseph Sobran, denouncing him as "little more than a crude and naked anti-Semite."[22] In his syndicated newspaper columns, Sobran had increased his attacks on the state of Israel and Zionism; this the neoconservatives equated with anti-Semitism. Beyond that, in a column on Jewish reactions to the Pope's trip to a synagogue, Sobran had alleged a historical pattern of Jewish persecution of Christians.[23] Then in May 1986, Sobran wrote a column praising *Instauration* as

> an often brilliant magazine covering a beat nobody else will touch, and doing so with intelligence, wide-ranging observation and bitter wit. It is openly and almost unremittingly hostile to blacks, Jews, and Mexican and Oriental immigrants.[24]

Instauration was an obscure racist magazine featuring a news update section called "Primate Watch."[25]

Sobran's overt anti-Semitism, though apparently not his broader racism, was addressed by a *National Review* editorial conference and a published policy statement by William F. Buckley himself. Though Buckley denied that his associate editor was an anti-Semite, he nevertheless reprimanded Sobran, demanded that he cease writing about Israel and reiterated *National Review*'s intolerance for anti-Semitism. (In 1957, Buckley had banned from *National Review*'s pages anyone who also wrote for the anti-Semitic *American Mercury*.)[26]

The neoconservatives were mollified. But the neo–paleo feud persisted and came to a head in 1989. In a sort of symbolic truce, the Scaife Foundation had financed a New York City outpost for the paleoconservative Rockford Institute, under the leadership of neoconservative Lutheran minister Richard John Neuhaus.[27] While Neuhaus' Center for Religion and Society attracted corporate foundation grants denied to the parent Rockford Institute,[28] Neuhaus himself made no secret of his anger over Rockford's publication (in *Chronicles*) of articles denouncing the promotion by neoconservatives of "democratic globalism," plus what Neuhaus described as the Rockford editors' "anti-Semitic and nativist tendencies."[29] In a watershed May 1989 incident, reported on the front page of the *New York Times*, Rockford executives finally flew from Illinois to New York, where they locked down Neuhaus' Manhattan office, carted away furniture, and left Neuhaus with his personal belongings waiting for a taxi cab on Madison Avenue.[30]

Though the incident was comical at one level, conservatives viewed it as ominously symptomatic and serious.[31] Around the time of Neuhaus' firing, the paleoconservatives' intellectual leader Russell Kirk weighed in with a speech delivered at the Heritage Foundation. Kirk charged that some neoconservatives "mistook Tel Aviv for the capital of the United States."[32] This old "dual loyalty" refrain was a piece of a larger picture. The right-wing *Washington Times* newspaper accompanied reportage of the Kirk speech and Neuhaus firing with a sidebar summarizing the grievances between "paleocons" and "neocons." Paleocons not only charged neocons with tilting too much toward Israel in foreign policy but also with wielding excessive influence over the Reagan administration, caring little about the abortion issue, and controlling the New York publishing industry and influential right-wing magazines. Neocons said paleocons were anti-Semitic, anti-Catholic, and nativist, that they distrusted "democracy" and the efforts of the United States to promote "democracy" around the world.[33]

The significance of this split was exacerbated by its timing. President Bush had just entered the White House in 1989. That same year marked the beginning of the end for the Soviet empire. Without anticommunism as their raison d'etre, conservatives looked around for what else might possibly unify them.

New Right and Old Right activists achieved no consensus when they met at the end of 1989 under the auspices of the American Conservative

Union, the fusionist umbrella formed after Goldwater's defeat in 1964 (see Chapter 2). There New Right strategist Paul Weyrich urged the Right to maintain its anticommunist priority and take advantage of new opportunities to train anti-Soviet political operatives in Eastern Europe. Thomas Fleming, the paleoconservative editor of *Chronicles* magazine, argued to the contrary, that it was long past time for the Right to shift gears, deemphasize anticommunism and advocate a non-interventionist U.S. foreign policy.[34] Disunity prevailed again a few weeks later at a summit meeting of twenty conservative movement leaders convened by William F. Buckley[35] and again at the 1990 Conservative Political Action Conference.[36]

Nor were the neoconservatives themselves united in their thinking about their post-Cold War mission. In April 1990 the Committee for the Free World held its last major gathering.[37] Norman Podhoretz condemned the Bush administration for its failure to back the Lithuanian independence movement, while Jeane Kirkpatrick and Irving Kristol argued for the legitimacy of the United States to act in its own "self-interest" and wait for events to take their natural course.[38]

Neoconservatives were, nevertheless, less far apart from each other than they were from the paleoconservatives, whose most vocal critic in the foreign affairs field was none other than Patrick Buchanan. Months before he distinguished himself as the leading right-wing critic of the U.S. role in the Persian Gulf war, Buchanan sounded an alarm against any post-Cold War push to foist "democracy" on the rest of the world. In a guest article for the neoconservative journal *The National Interest*, "America First—and Second, and Third," Buchanan lumped the Israeli lobby and neoconservative Ben Wattenberg together with Jesse Jackson and TransAfrica's Randall Robinson:

> Each substitutes an extra-national ideal for the national interest; each sees our national purpose in another continent or country; each treats our Republic as a means to some larger end. "National purpose" has become a vessel, emptied of original content, into which ideologues of all shades and hues are invited to pour their own causes, their own victims.
>
> With the Cold War ending, we should look, too, with a cold eye on the internationalist set, never at a loss for new ideas to divert U.S. wealth and power into crusades and causes having little or nothing to do with the true national interest of the United States.[39]

Buchanan's dispatch foreshadowed a debate that would intensify after Iraq's August 1990 invasion of Kuwait and the Bush administration's headlong march toward war against Iraq.

By then, nearly all that unified warring conservative movement factions was a common preoccupation with the trend toward multiculturalism in higher education. A number of the leading paleoconservatives were themselves humanities professors, and the Rockford Institute published a special issue of *Chronicles* under the heading "Vandals in the Academy." But the organizational initiative to fight academic "political correctness" came from the neoconservative-dominated National Association of Scholars (NAS).[40] Formed in 1988, NAS recruited hundreds of professors disaffected by universities' policies of affirmative action and expansion of the curriculum into areas like women's and ethnic studies. Harkening back to the neoconservatives' earlier fears of an excessively influential New Class, NAS promoted the notion that a powerful core of leftist intellectuals were using the universities as a base camp for the "politically correct" indoctrination of college sudents. This theme attracted the attention of magazine and newspaper columnists, and by 1991 the anti-PC media campaign took on a life of its own.[41]

Conservative movement unity around questions of higher education might have helped heal festering wounds. Before that issue assumed national proportions, however, the Persian Gulf war fueled the Right's foreign policy debates and muted everything else by comparison.

The New World Order

Almost from the moment President Bush drew his infamous "line in the sand" and ordered Iraqi President Sadaam Hussein to retreat from Kuwait, opinion shapers entered their own war of words over the United States' first major post-Cold War military intervention. On the Right, paleoconservatives and neoconservatives squared off behind two of their most vocal advocates, syndicated columnist Patrick Buchanan versus the *New York Times'* A. M. Rosenthal, respectively. Their fight began in September 1990 when Buchanan appeared on a television talk show and remarked that the only two groups favoring war in the Middle East were "the Israeli Defense Ministry and its amen corner in the United States." Rosenthal shot back with a *Times* column charging Buchanan with anti-Semitism for ascribing "alien loyalties" to American Jews. Buchanan then used his syndicated column to charge Rosenthal with having made a "contract hit" on him "in collusion with" the Anti-Defamation League of B'nai B'rith. The Buchanan–Rosenthal fight then became a news story in itself,[42] and threatened to obscure the substance of disagreements among political elites over a response to the Gulf crisis.

The Bush administration's drive toward a UN-supported military assault on Iraq found support from the *New York Times'* Rosenthal and William Safire and, generally, from neoconservative media pundits.[43] Ben

Wattenberg of the American Enterprise Institute used his column to call Buchanan a "chicken hawk" on the Persian Gulf and to describe himself as a "neo-manifest destinarian."[44] The editors of *Human Events* positioned themselves as cautious endorsers of the Bush administration's war plans.[45] *National Review* editorialized similarly and allowed senior editor Joseph Sobran space to present the anti-war position.[46] In *Commentary*, Norman Podhoretz promoted warfare in the Persian Gulf as a means for the United States to avoid being "permanently debellicized and forever unmanned by the idea . . . that nothing is worth fighting and dying for."[47]

Apart from media pundits, among the leaders of conservative movement organizations, the Right split into two apparent camps. Philip Nicolaides, a long-time conservative movement activist and former deputy director of Voice of America radio, formed a short-lived Committee to Avert the Mideast Holocaust, which distributed anti-war position papers and ran announcements in *Human Events*. The Committee included paleoconservatives Joseph Sobran and Llewellyn Rockwell plus several prominent libertarians: economics professor Murray Rothbard, William A. Niskanen of the Cato Institute, and former Texas Congressmember (and the Libertarian Party's 1988 presidential candidate) Ron Paul.[48] The Committee's limited financial resources left it no match for its rival, the Coalition for America at Risk. This pro-war outfit was led by Sam Zakhem, the former U.S. ambassador to Bahrain, and two John Birch Society veterans, William Kennedy and Scott Stanley. The Coalition spent an estimated $10 million on pro-war newspaper and television advertisements and claimed to have received more than 1,000 daily literature requests from the general public between October 1990 and the start of the Gulf war.[49] The Coalition's "emergency action kits," endorsed by leading New Right figures, included "talking points for radio call-in shows" and a petition of support to be sent to President Bush.[50] Before the war, Coalition leader William Kennedy was exposed as a registered agent of the Kuwaiti government who reportedly helped manage Kuwait's flight capital after the Iraqi invasion. A year after the Gulf war, Zakhem, Kennedy, and Stanley were indicted for failing to report millions of dollars they received from Kuwait as part of a propaganda campaign to sway public opinion in favor of war.[51]

Here was a case where right-wing activists feigned roles as ordinary citizens when they were really paid agents of the Kuwaiti state, acting on behalf of the Bush administration's war for domestic support. The pro-war Right helped turn the tide of public opinion away from a negotiated resolution to Iraq's occupation of Kuwait and in favor of full-scale war.[52] All told, aerial bombardment by the United States and its allies destroyed Iraq's civilian and military infrastructure, at the cost of between 100,000 and 200,000 Iraqi lives.[53]

While the bombs were exploding, Patrick Buchanan temporarily muted his dissent, rallied behind U.S. war aims, and urged readers of his private newsletter to do the same.

> For the moment, friends, we remain deep in the bomb shelters. As the President's popularity has soared, talk of a challenge to him by conservatives has gone as dead as that big communications center in Baghdad.
> It was the natural and right thing to do, when the guns started, to support U.S. armed forces until victory is attained; and that includes our Commander-in-Chief. Whatever one thought of Franklin Roosevelt, and the manner with which he maneuvered us toward war, after Pearl Harbor the debate was over.
> But, when this war ends, we ought to be first to sound the "All clear!" to reopen the debate over just where America is headed. For with U.S. troops now in Israel manning the Patriots, and a vast U.S. army in the Gulf, we are acquiring permanent commitments in the most explosive region on earth. We don't need any new commitments. We have too many old ones right now.[54]

Once Operation Desert Storm came to an end, Buchanan and other right-wing analysts resumed debate and remained divided roughly along the same lines as before the war. There were those who argued a "quagmire" thesis, to the effect that the war had been too costly, both to the deficit-ridden U.S. economy and to the long-term stability of the Middle East region. Others advanced an "opportunity" thesis, emphasizing the war's public relations boon to the Pentagon and the Bush presidency.[55] The "quagmire" proponents were the minority faction. They included Buchanan, the Committee to Avert a Mideast Holocaust, and the libertarian Cato Institute. Neoconservatives and pro-Pentagon think tanks like the Heritage Foundation were among those who analyzed the Gulf war as an opportunity for resurgent U.S. militarism.[56] Still, the ideological dividing lines were not clear. Heritage Foundation vice-president Burton Pines leaned toward the anti-interventionist end of the spectrum. "For a conservative," Pines wrote in the neoconservative journal *National Interest*,

> the only legitimate goal of American foreign policy is the creation of a world environment in which America is left alone and at peace, in which America can trade and raise its living standards, in which Americans can expand their options and enrich their lives.[57]

Ultimately, the infighting that persisted through the Gulf war and its aftermath left the conservative movement intact but weakened in its ability to influence the course of the Bush administration. As Bush's reelection campaign approached, the Christian Right was in a better position than its secular counterparts to mobilize a following and make an impact on the Republican Party platform.

CONSERVATIVE MOVEMENT QUANDARIES

At the height of the United States' military assault on Iraq, the Conservative Political Action Conference (CPAC) convened under the title "Where Do Conservatives Go From Here?" CPAC was the annual gathering cosponsored since the 1960s by the American Conservative Union, Young Americans for Freedom, *Human Events*, and *National Review*, in addition to several dozen other New Right outfits. According to *Human Events'* reportage of the event, many of the 800 participants felt compelled to muffle their opposition to George Bush out of respect for his leadership of the war against Iraq. The speeches and panel discussions reinforced conservatives' "continued emphasis on the liberating potential of the free market, on the critical need to maintain a strong defense, and on the enriching and stabilizing potential of traditional Western moral values."[58]

One highlight of the February 1991 CPAC was a three-way debate on the conservative movement's proper stance toward the Republican Party and the Bush administration. Heritage Foundation vice-president Burton Pines advocated a partial rebellion, through the drafting of Congressional candidates to the right of Bush. Conservative Caucus leader Howard Phillips acknowledged that his own views were unrepresentative of the New Right—and then unveiled his plan to break permanently from the Republicans with his newly formed United States Taxpayers Alliance (USTA) party. Donald Devine, the former director of the Office of Personnel Management under Reagan, jokingly played the role of "moderate" and called on movement activists to remain committed, for better or worse, to the mainstream of the Republican Party.[59] Neither Pines, Phillips, nor Devine offered the CPAC audience a concrete plan for wielding greater influence over the incumbent president and party.

Ten years after the launch of the "Reagan revolution," the New Right could rest on its organizational and policy accomplishments, but with little forward vision of the next steps to be taken. A mid-1991 interview with Heritage Foundation president Edwin J. Feulner was telling. Under the cover headline "Conservatism's Growing Pains" in the think tank's quarterly *Policy Review*, Feulner focused on past achievements: influential input into the Reagan administration's military buildup, anticommunist proxy wars, and supply-side tax cuts, accompanied by the Heritage Foundation's own successful growth. From 1977 to 1990, the think tank's annual income rose from $800,000 to $18.1 million, mostly from large corporate donors but also from Heritage's 175,000 individual members and its "resource bank" of 1,600 scholars and 400 organizations world-wide.[60]

Still, Feulner lamented conservatives' debilitating post-Cold War factionalism at length. He made a particular point of defending his much criticized neoconservative allies, and he wondered aloud about the longevity of the old fusionist era coalition between social, economic, and foreign policy conservatives. "Conservatism is going to have to involve coalitions between people who don't always agree with each other if it is going to be a broader-based movement and become a governing majority for the future," Feulner concluded.[61]

But as the 1992 campaign season approached, it was not the secular and coalitional New Right but, rather, politically active evangelicals who represented the most coherent right-wing movement on the scene. The embarassing television preacher scandals, followed by Pat Robertson's failed 1988 presidential bid, had left the general public unaware of the Christian Right's determined political strengths and aspirations. While the paleoconservative–neoconservative feud boiled over in 1989, Pat Robertson regrouped his campaign apparatus into a new Christian Coalition, which then grew by leaps and bounds during the Bush years. While the break-up of the Communist bloc exacerbated secular conservatives' inter-movement disputes, the renewed importance of domestic issues in U.S. politics was tailor-made for the Christian Right's focus on traditional morality. For the Christian Right, the strategic lesson of the 1980s was to keep one figurative foot inside formal Republican Party circles and another planted firmly within evangelical churches.

That lesson was reinforced in 1990 when the Bush administration abruptly fired presidential aide Douglas Wead, whose job was to serve as a liaison to evangelical Christians. Wead, a staunch advocate for the Christian Right, had antagonized a higher ranking Bush aide by protesting the inclusion of homosexual activists at a White House signing of a bill to extend civil rights protections to the disabled, including people with AIDS.[62] Wead was replaced by Leigh Ann Metzger, a former legislative director of Phyllis Schlafly's Eagle Forum.[63] But Wead's dismissal registered as a stark affront to Christian Right leaders who had never particularly liked George Bush anyway. In October 1990 Robert Dugan of the National Association of Evangelicals led a group of Christian Right activists to meet with Bush. They told him they felt betrayed by a series of policy decisions: his inclusion of gay rights activists at two presidential bill-signing ceremonies; his opposition to restricting federally funded arts content; his failure to act forcefully against abortion; and the lack of evangelical representation on the White House staff.[64]

By then, though, the Christian Right had already embarked on a 1990s strategy combining issue-based and electoral activism. Focus on the Family announced that the 1990s would be the "the Civil War decade." Focus identified abortion and gay rights as the Christian Right's two most important national battlegrounds.[65] Pat Robertson's Christian Coalition made its organizational debut with a $500,000 advertising campaign against the National Endowment for the Arts.[66] At the street level, Operation Rescue reached the peak of its disruptive capability in Witchita, Kansas during the summer of 1991. There Operation Rescue protestors from around the country converged and successfully blockaded women's health clinics, with the assistance of local pastors and with the endorsement of Kansas' anti-abortion governor Joan Finney.[67] That same summer the Christian Right concentrated also on building Senate support for Supreme Court nominee Judge Clarence Thomas, whose own membership in a Virginia charismatic church assured anti-abortionists of his "pro-life" commitments. The California-based Traditional Values Coalition coordinated pro-Thomas rallies by conservative black clergy,[68] before Anita Hill's allegations of sexual harassment came to dominate the Senate's deliberations and divide the black community. While Hill's charges propelled the confirmation hearings to the status of a national referendum on sexual harassment, grassroots Christian Right activists lobbied hard for Thomas. Christian Coalition, along with Concerned Women for America and other national groups, delivered an estimated 100,000 petitions, letters, and phone calls to Senators on behalf of Judge Thomas.[69]

The Thomas–Hill hearings were but one more opportunity for the Christian Coalition to flex its political muscles. In November 1991, Robertson's cadre took Virginia by surprise when they worked behind the scenes to elect Republicans to state offices. Having assumed leadership roles in the Virginia Republican Party following the 1988 presidential race, Robertson backers delivered votes by, first, telephone polling thousands of registered voters on salient issues and, then, giving second calls to voters whose views matched the Christian Coalition's.[70] Voter identification and other grassroots tactics were the focus of the Christian Coalition's November 1991 national Road to Victory conference, held at the Virginia Beach headquarters of Robertson's Christian Broadcasting Network and Regent University. There 800 state and local Christian Coalition leaders (out of about 150,000 total members) learned how to become GOP convention delegates and, eventually, members of the Republican National Committee.[71]

Underlying the tactics promoted by the Christian Coalition was the theory that low voter turnout is the key to winning. Since only about 60 percent of all eligible voters are registered to vote, and only about half of those actually do vote, slightly more than 15 percent of the electorate can determine election outcomes. The Road to Victory conference concluded on the night of David Duke's run-off gubernatorial race in Louisiana, and many of the Christian Coalition delegates watched the television newscasts with visible sadness at Duke's defeat.[72]

Duke campaign supporter Reverend Billy McCormack played a dual role as the Christian Coalition's Lousiana state director (and a close Robertson associate). Duke's seeming popularity with the Christian Right pointed ominously to a potential fusion between the evangelicals and the organized racist Right. But that potential was undercut once Patrick Buchanan's 1992 presidential primary campaign offered right-wing movement activists an alternative far more more palatable than Duke himself. For their part, Christian Coalition leaders Pat Robertson and Ralph Reed gave mixed signals. The Christian Coalition itself endorsed neither Buchanan nor Bush, though Robertson personally announced his support for Bush during the Georgia primary.[73]

Buchanan and Perot

Patrick Buchanan's August 17, 1992 speech before the Republican Party convention in Houston struck a chord among his friends and detractors alike. Television audiences unfamiliar with Buchanan's rhetoric—he had been a speech writer for Nixon and Reagan—were surprised by his hyperbole. But the speech was vintage Buchanan, and there were no real surprises. Buchanan thanked the three million Americans who had voted for him and threw his unequivocal support behind George Bush. He then used the rest of his time to sound the themes of a "cultural war" and to lambaste the Democratic convention as "that giant masquerade ball up at Madison Square garden, where 20,000 radicals and liberals came dressed up as moderates and centrists in the greatest single exhibition of cross-dressing in American political history."[74]

Buchanan's speech and another delivered by Pat Robertson were widely interpreted as a clarion call against the Democrats' endorsement of civil rights for homosexuals. But the symbolism ran deeper than the content of the speeches. Buchanan's performance recalled the onset of the New Right: the 1964 convention and nomination of Barry Goldwater, then considered an "extremist" by the mainstream of the party. Buchanan and his activist generation paved the way for Ronald Reagan, whose 1992 convention appearance reminded conservatives of their recent past. Pat Robertson and Marilyn and Dan Quayle foreshadowed the party's future domination by a new echelon, the Christian Right.

The 1992 convention culminated many months' worth of shifting alignments within right-wing movement and Republican Party circles.

Barry Goldwater, once considered an "extremist," was among a handful of Republican politicians who were appalled by their party's adoption of a strict anti-abortion plank.[75] A group of neoconservatives chose the opening day of the Houston convention to announce, in a *New York Times* advertisement, their endorsement of Bill Clinton.[76] Some of the neoconservatives had never left the Democratic Party; others had switched to the GOP and had now come full circle.

By then, also, independent presidential candidate H. Ross Perot had galvanized a huge following among disgruntled voters across party lines. Perot's significance as a political leader would endure, though in ways unknown. During the campaign Perot's impact was to sharpen visible differences between Clinton and Bush. Buchanan's impact was to solidify the Republicans' hard right wing.

Initially, it looked like Buchanan would run for president on behalf of Howard Phillips' small, upstart U.S. Taxpayers Alliance (USTA) party. Phillips tried unsuccessfully to persuade Buchanan to lead a revolt against the Republicans.[77] That both Buchanan and David Duke chose to run as Republicans reflected the prevailing view of right-wing activists that the GOP was a vehicle worth trying to influence, not reject. Buchanan announced his candidacy in time for the early New Hampshire primary and explained why in a letter to his supporters.

> Quite simply, our country is careening off course. And neither Mr. Bush nor his advisors have the foggiest notion how to steer her back.
>
> Mr. Bush's all-consuming passion lies in some gauzy New World Order he has never quite been able to define or explain. To advance this dreamy idea, he flies all over the world shoveling out foreign aid as though this were 1951, not 1991.
>
> Again, the problem is not Mr. Bush's motives. It is his ideas, or rather his lack of them. Mr. Bush is an Ivy League globalist wedded to such institutions as the UN and World Bank, when we Americans have got to start looking out for America first.[78]

In his first speech in New Hampshire, Buchanan addressed the three dimensions of right-wing ideology. He called for tax cuts and a reduction of the welfare state, an America First foreign policy, and a return to "Judeo-Christian values" as the solution to domestic social problems.[79] Buchanan's image as a protectionist, isolationist, and nativist likewise covered the Right's characteristic triple concern with economics, foreign affairs, and social order.

New Hampshire was an ideal launching pad. Not only had the state been particularly hard hit by economic recession, but former governor John Sununu's unpopularity reflected poorly on his boss, President

Bush.[80] Buchanan used the New Hampshire primary as a podium to press Bush to make a capital gains tax cut,[81] which he did. Buchanan surprised political pundits when he won 37 percent of the New Hampshire Republican vote, despite mainstream media's emphasis on his reputation as an anti-Semite.[82]

National Review had given its tactical endorsement to the Buchanan campaign, but only after William F. Buckley devoted the December 30, 1991 issue to a lengthy analysis of anti-Jewish themes in the writings of Buchanan and Joseph Sobran.[83] (*Human Events*, on the other hand, turned itself into a virtual house organ for Buchanan's campaign.) In his essay, Buckley distinguished between anti-Zionism and anti-Semitism and then offered verbal evidence to indict Buchanan and Sobran on both counts. Buckley also recalled, and in a sense repented for, his father's anti-Semitism and his own childish envy when, on the eve of the Holocaust, his older siblings were allowed out one night to burn a cross outside a Jewish resort. All of this reminiscence was Buckley's way of reiterating contemporary conservatism's historic break with the Right's traditional anti-Semitism. In the context of Buchanan's campaign, *National Review* delivered a clear message that anti-Semitism—but not racism in all its forms—was permanently unwelcome among respectable conservatives.

But as Buchanan continued to capture between a quarter and a third of Republican primary votes, his opponents on the Right grew concerned. American Conservative Union chairperson David Keene refused to lend his endorsement.[84] William J. Bennett described Buchanan publicly as one who "flirts" with fascism, and Charles Krauthammer used his *Washington Post* column to remind readers of Buchanan's professed admiration for Spain's fascist dictator Francisco Franco and, later, for Chilean dictator Augusto Pinochet.[85] Bennett's animosity toward Buchanan reportedly prompted Paul Weyrich to blame Bennett for not running himself against Bush.[86] Among Jewish neoconservatives, Norman Podhoretz argued that Buchanan's primary showings were merely a protest vote. What really worried Podhoretz was the enthusiasm of conservative activists for Buchanan.[87]

Podhoretz identified Buchanan's most important critics as William Bennett, Jack Kemp, Senator Phil Gramm, and Representative Vin Weber. After Bush's defeat, Bennett, Kemp, and Weber, plus Jeane Kirkpatrick, would form Empower America as a faction intent on leading opposition to Clinton without ceding ground to Ross Perot.

The "Perot phenomenon" was the real wild card in the 1992 campaign. Following Perot's appearance on the "Larry King" cable television show, volunteers rapidly assembled a campaign apparatus, though their hero would commit himself neither to the candidacy nor to firm policy positions. The national press emphasized Perot's billionaire quirkiness and his penchant for free-lance intelligence operations. Some conservative movement activists voiced distrust for Perot,[88] but his mass following made him irresistible to others. After Buchanan ended his primary challenge to Bush, *National Review* editors praised Perot for destabilizing the Republican mainstream, but wrote that "in the final analysis, we will grit our teeth and vote for Mr. Bush."[89] Libertarian Party candidate Andre Marrou opposed Perot's candidacy, while two libertarian leaders active in Patrick Buchanan's campaign, Murray Rothbard and Lew Rockwell, voiced tentative support for Perot.[90]

From the racist Right, the Liberty Lobby took a cautious but generally pro-Perot stance and seemed intent on hitching itself, opportunistically, to Perot's coat tails. In a *Spotlight* editorial, the Liberty Lobby objected to Perot's call for a federal investigation of the Rodney King's beating by police and urged Perot to steer clear of campaign advisors linked to the Council on Foreign Relations.[91] But *Spotlight* published numerous pro-Perot letters from readers, and the newspaper sold "Perot for President" bumper stickers with Liberty Lobby's address and toll-free phone number on the bottom in small print.

Had Perot transformed himself from an enigmatic electoral showman into a bona fide right-wing movement leader, he would have had to appeal to the mass-based Christian Right. A June 1992 call-in poll of Pat Robertson's "700 Club" viewers yielded a surprising 47 percent vote for Perot and 50 percent vote for Bush. (Buchanan had by then dropped out of the race.) Ralph Reed of Robertson's Christian Coalition explained the result as a "protest vote" and predicted that the evangelical audience would back Bush in the real election. An informal poll of Christian Right activists, also in June, found solid support for Bush and strong opposition to Perot for his pro-choice views and his wife's position on a Planned Parenthood advisory board.[92] Perot was denounced at the June 1992 National Right to Life convention.[93] Operation Rescue founder Randall Terry vowed to mobilize anti-abortionists to "become Ross Perot's worst nightmare."[94]

Lacking a base of support within an ideologically coherent social movement—right or left—Perot appealed, instead, to the diverse constituency of "middle American" voters both Clinton and Bush needed to win. In 1992, the "Perot phenomenon" was more an anti-incumbent mood than a defined political tendency. Despite his 19 percent share of the November 1992 vote, Perot's following did not represent a coherent social movement like the Christian Right. A social movement entails independently generated resources, a well-conceived ideology and set of policy objectives, and dense networks of individuals and organizations with some sort of long-term commitment to each other, and to shared principles and goals. Perot's following bore the potential to coalesce as a social movement, but that would take time.

Election 1992 Post-Mortems

Apart from the Democrats, Christian Right activists were winners in 1992. Conventional wisdom blamed Bush's defeat largely on voters' economic fears but partly on the Republicans' overly zealous embrace of the Christian Right's "family values" theme. That view was shared by some neoconservatives.[95] Others indicted Bush for having run as a "moderate."[96]

But no one could argue with the Christian Right's success as a faction inside the Republican Party. An estimated 47 percent of the delegates at the 1992 party convention were self-described born-again Christians,[97] and the Christian Right had its way in drafting the party platform. Over the preferences of candidate Bush himself, the platform called for a constitutional amendment to ban abortion (with no exceptions). Other planks included opposition to any civil rights laws for homosexuals, a call for the government to ban the sale of pornography and for condemnation of public funding for "obscene" art, endorsement of home schooling and school prayer, and opposition to contraception being made available in schools.[98]

After the convention, the movement's long-term plan to elect its partisans one city council seat at a time paid off. The liberal monitoring group People for the American Way studied 500 state and local races and reported victories for 40 percent of the candidates backed by the Christian Right. In California, thirteen out of twenty-two Christian Right-backed Congressional candidates, and sixteen out of twenty-nine state assembly candidates, were elected or reelected.[99] Tactically, the key was the movement's distribution of millions of voter guides. These were newsprint tabloids or two-sided flyers listing "yes" or "no" positions of the Christian Right's preferred candidates and their opponents on heated issues like abortion, gay rights, tax increases, term limits, private school vouchers, and the death penalty. Pat Robertson's Christian Coalition alone sent 40 million voter guides to 100,000 churches and to members in all fifty states.[100] Strategically, the Christian Right made good on its perception that low voter turnout is an inherent advantage to the well-coordinated efforts of low-profile minority candidates. The paleoconservative–neoconservative feud and the controversy over Patrick Buchanan's candidacy had been largely irrelevant to the Christian Right, which, instead, had spent years developing its grassroots electoral capability in conjunction with issue-based activism.

As of the early 1990s, opposition to legal abortion and gay rights remained the movement's two greatest issue priorities. At least as significant as the Christian Right's 1992 electoral victories were the results of two anti-gay rights efforts, in Oregon and Colorado. The Oregon Citizens' Alliance (OCA) arose in the late 1980s with the specific mission of fighting gay civil rights.[101] By 1992, OCA placed on the statewide ballot Measure 9, which would have mandated a change in Oregon's constitution to forbid state agencies and schools from allowing any program construed to "promote, encourage, or facilitate homosexuality, pedophilia, sadism, or masochism."[102] Measure 9 was narrowly defeated by voters. But it did well in several Oregon counties, and in mid-1993 local elections, OCA succeeded in passing six county measures banning civil rights protections on the basis of sexual orientation.[103] For the November 1992 general election, the Christian Right group Colorado for Family Values ran a ballot measure that did not mandate Measure 9's draconian changes in the state constitution but that did preemptively ban any local jurisdictions from enacting protective civil rights ordinances. Colorado's Amendment 2 was approved by voters, but faced a swift legal challenge. About a year after voters approved Amendment 2, a Colorado judge ruled it unconstitutional.[104]

Public debate over anti-gay ordinances in Oregon, Colorado, and other states where Christian Right groups hoped to place ballot initiatives coincided with a nationwide controversy over President Clinton's promise to lift the ban on openly homosexual military personnel. That prospect in 1993 galvanized massive direct mail fundraising campaigns by Christian Right organizations;[105] the proposal was also opposed by the military's Joint Chiefs of Staff. Under pressure from military brass and key Congressional leaders, Clinton abandoned his promise to lift the ban, thus implicitly acknowledging the influence of the Christian Right. Without the movement's promotion of anti-gay sentiments—pervasive in American culture—discrimination against homosexuals would have diminished and civil rights protections could have been extended to one more traditionally persecuted sector of society. Instead, opposition to gay rights intensified as a central theme of right-wing movements and representative Republican Party leaders.

In the immediate aftermath of Clinton's election, Republican Party and conservative movement strategists dwelled on the question of whether the Christian Right was an asset or a liability. Christian Coalition director Ralph Reed argued that Bush would have fared far worse without the Christian Right: evangelical Christians and voters with incomes over $200,000 a year were the only two demographic groups Bush carried solidly.[106] Both Reed and Jerry Falwell predicted resurgent evangelical activism under the Clinton administration.[107] The highlight of a post-election Republican governors' meeting was a controversy over Mississippi Governor Kirk Fordice's insistence on calling the United States a "Christian nation."[108] At a post-election strategy session sponsored by the Heritage Foundation, Paul Weyrich warned activists and outgoing Bush administration political appointees that they would never regain power at the national level without catering to grassroots supporters and making a priority of "moral authority" over economic policy.[109] Significantly, the first issue of Weyrich's political strategy newsletter to appear after the election featured a call for the Right to recruit Ross Perot's supporters.[110]

No immediate effort was made to do so, but three competing camps emerged to assert themselves as representative of mainstream conservatism. Former California Congressmember Tom Campbell formed the Republican Majority Coalition to represent moderate, pro-choice Republicans.[111] Patrick Buchanan and a small group of paleoconservatives announced plans to start their own think tank. In the spring of 1993, Buchanan's American Cause Foundation held its founding conference.[112] Buchanan opened with a speech on "Winning the Culture War," in which he told his audience of 400 that "we traditionalists and conservatives have only just begun to fight; and we look upon this gathering as the Boston Tea Party of the cultural counter-revolution."[113]

In competition with Buchanan's paleoconservatives, the strongest faction emerged under the name Empower America, formed by four pillars of the Reagan revolution: former Congressmember and Housing Secretary Jack Kemp, former "drug czar" William Bennett, Congressmember Vin Weber, and former UN Ambassador Jeane Kirkpatrick. Kemp had built his national name recognition as a leading advocate of supply-side tax cuts. Bennett had a reputation as protector of traditional morality, having served at the National Institute for the Humanities and, later, as "drug czar." Kirkpatrick represented conservatism's anticommunist and militarist tendency. All had opposed Buchanan's presidential candidacy, yet they sounded themes similar to Buchanan's as opponents of the new Clinton administration. A few weeks after the inauguration, William Bennett released a study called an "Index of Leading Social Indicators" in which he documented "social decomposition" through statistics on rising crime, divorce, and teen pregnancy rates; he advocated building more prisons and a voucher plan for parental choice in selecting schools for their children.[114] Jeane Kirkpatrick joined the "cultural war" by calling President Clinton and his wife Hillary "cultural revolutionaries" for their liberal views on gay rights and abortion.[115] By mid-1993, Empower America had received more press attention and had conducted more direct mail fundraising than Patrick Buchanan's American Cause Foundation.[116]

Yet all three new factional groupings were oriented toward elite, Republican Party circles. At the grassroots level, only the Christian Right proceeded to organize and train its supporters in the tactics of direct action protest, citizen lobbying, and electoral campaigning. Only the Christian Right had both a dense grassroots organizational network and receptive ears among key Republican Senators and Congressmembers. Without elite ties, the Christian Right would not have assumed the status of an influential movement. With elite ties alone, the movement could not have remained the most formidable right-wing movement at the end of the Reagan era and into the 1990s.

THE CLINTON YEARS

The sheer numbers of evangelicals made it unlikely that the Republicans would abandon them as a core constituency. A group of political scientists who studied the 1992 election results arrived at several important findings. Exit polls revealed that voters identifying themselves as "fundamentalist" or "born-again" constituted 17 percent of the electorate in 1992.[117] About 60 percent of all evangelical voters and 70 percent of regular churchgoers voted for Bush; evangelicals provided more than a quarter of Bush's 1992 base of support.[118] Not only were evangelicals Bush's strongest ethnoreligious voting bloc, but evangelicals were also the most conservative group of voters on a range of economic and domestic policy matters, apart from the usual "pro-family" stances against abortion and homosexuality and favoring school prayer.[119] The Christian Right was in sync with the Republican mainstream.

As the Republican National Committee (RNC) looked toward its next chance to capture the presidency, the party lacked a frontrunning candidate, but there was no doubt about the continuing salience of the "family values" agenda. In 1993 RNC surveyed party donors, elected officials, and grassroots activists. True to form, about 63 percent responded that the federal government is "primarily an adversary to be avoided rather than a postive force for helping people," and an overwhelming 92 percent said they favored cuts in capital gains taxes. On the social issues, 72 percent favored school choice vouchers; 92 percent favored voluntary prayer in public schools; 93 percent opposed the "teaching of homosexuality as an acceptable lifestyle in public schools, 84 percent opposed federal funding of abortion, although only 58 percent identified their position as 'pro-life.'"[120]

Despite the Christian Right's generally compatible and mutually dependent relationship with the Republican Party, the movement needed to live down its public image as a band of extremists, just as the 1960s Goldwaterites had to struggle to achieve respectability. The summer after Clinton's election, Christian Coalition executive director Ralph Reed published a widely read article, "Casting a Wider Net," in the

Heritage Foundation's quarterly *Policy Review*. Reed called for the Christian Right to broaden its base by granting as much priority to economic issues such as taxes, college scholarships, and higher wages as to the movement's moral agenda.[121] Around the same time, Reed told the popular *Charisma* magazine that he regretted having fostered the impression that he was running "stealth" candidates; in 1991 Reed had told reporters that he operated like an invisible guerrilla warrior.[122] Then in 1994, the Coalition spent over a million dollars on a grassroots lobbying campaign against health care reform legislation.[123] Denying the Clinton administration a clear victory on health care reform was one of the Republicans' chief goals.

Along with Reed's image as a Republican team player, the Christian Coalition announced its intention to recruit people of color into its ranks, to no longer "concede the minority community to the political left."[124] The Coalition commissioned a poll showing that African Americans and Latinos tend to hold conservative views on social issues like abortion, gay rights, crime, welfare, and affirmative action; the organization announced it would begin advertising on minority-owned radio stations and sending its literature to black and Latino churches.[125] This move by the Christian Coalition toward greater racial inclusiveness, though more rhetorical than real, coincided with a more pervasive drive by evangelicals to promote "racial reconciliation" within historically segregated churches and denominations.[126]

For Christian Right political activists, racial reconciliation was part of an effort to make the movement appear more mainstream. The Democrats, however, were determined to tar Christian Right candidates as "radicals" and "extremists," somehow not connected to the existing two-party system. Virginia's highly polarized 1993 election was a testing ground for the Democrats' ill-fated attempt to win by smearing Christian Right candidates. First-time candidate Michael Farris, a home-schooling activist and former attorney for Concerned Women for America, was pilloried by the Democrats as an "extremist." Farris lost his race for lieutenant governor but managed to raise a million dollars and win 46 percent of the vote.[127] (Thereafter Farris remained a major power broker in Virginia politics; in 1994 his supporters helped win the Republican nomination for Senate candidate Oliver North.)[128] Despite Farris' loss, Virginia Governor George Allen and Attorney General James S. Gilmore, both moderate Republicans, won largely because of support from right-wing evangelicals.[129] In return, Governor Allen appointed prominent anti-abortion activists to his transition team and nominated Family Research Council Vice-President Kay Cole James as Virginia's secretary of health.[130]

The Democrats' tactics seemed to backfire in Virginia. Christian Right activists charged liberals with "religious bigotry," and their sense of persecution seemed to fuel commitment to grassroots electoral activity, particularly aimed at school boards.[131] This was an arena where the Christian Right enjoyed several advantages. School board races suited the movement's locally focused grassroots organizational structure in the 1990s. Without having to spend a fortune, first-time candidates were able to channel the fears of their local church-based supporters about sex education, homosexuality, and multiculturalism into some winnable fights. One national Christian Right organization, Citizens for Excellence in Education, claimed in 1993 to have won control over some 2,000 school boards by helping to elect nearly 5,000 new school board members.[132]

In New York City in 1993, the Christian Coalition won majorities in a few of the city's several dozen districts by joining forces with the Catholic diocese in a campaign against a gay-positive, multicultural curriculum program called *Children of the Rainbow*.[133] In several parts of the country, school boards become irreconciliably polarized when Christian Right activists won slim majorities. In Vista, California, three right-wing activists dominated a five-person board and voted to mandate the teaching of creationism and a religiously oriented sex education program promoting abstinence.[134] In a central Florida school district, the Christian Right's three-member majority voted in 1994 to amend the district's multicultural curriculum with the requirement that teachers instill in students the notion that the United States' form of government, its capitalist economic system, and "other basic values" make it "superior to other foreign or historic cultures."

The idea of U.S. superiority drew a storm of controversy,[135] but the significance of this and other incidents was the relative ease with which the Christian Right had begun to take dominion over secular state institutions. The Christian Coalition's Ralph Reed told the *Human Events* newspaper that the Florida school board controversy was a watershed event. "Instead of focusing on winning the White House," Reed said,

> we're developing a farm team of future officeholders by running people for school boards, city councils and state legislatures. . . . Now we're seeing those institutions that are closest to people's lives and have the greatest impact on them in the hands of conservative people of faith.[136]

That was only partially true: a few months after the controversy over the America First school curriculum, voters in Lake County, Florida threw the Christian Right school board members out of office,[137] proving that it was easier to win short-term office than to maintain power indefinitely.

The Right found it even more difficult to win wholesale victories on hotly contested issues. Opposition to civil rights protections for gays and lesbians rose to the top of the Christian Right's issue agenda in the 1990s, yet the movement met with mixed results. Following a court ruling against Colorado's 1992 voter approved anti-gay rights amendment, similar ballot initiatives were attempted in about a dozen states. Using the false rhetorical claim that homosexuals sought "special rights" above and beyond those accorded to other citizens, the Christian Right found an issue that appealed to large numbers of voters beyond the movement's own cadre. In 1993 voters in Cincinnati, Ohio and Lewiston, Maine repealed city ordinances outlawing discrimination based on sexual orientation.[138] In 1994 voters in Austin, Texas repealed, by a two-to-one margin, that city's policy of granting insurance benefits to all "domestic partners" of city employees.[139] Also in 1994, Christian Right activists in ten states tried to place anti-gay rights measures on their statewide ballots. Only in Idaho and Oregon did anti-gay rights groups gather enough signatures to qualify ballot measures.[140]

Despite the mixed success of the anti-gay rights ballot measures, the issue itself remained salient. The National Gay and Lesbian Task Force culled data from several surveys and found the U.S. public to be divided on the necessity of protective legal measures for homosexuals. Most Americans opposed outright discrimination, but most also thought homosexuality was immoral and unacceptable,[141] meaning that a sizeable segment of the population was receptive to the Christian Right's anti-gay propaganda. The 1990s saw the growth of a cottage industry in the production of anti-gay newsletters, books, and, especially, videotapes.[142] The first and most infamous video in the genre was *The Gay Agenda*, produced by a previously unknown southern California couple, Ty and Jeanette Beeson from the Antelope Valley Springs of Life church. Produced largely with graphic footage taken at gay rights marches, the video was widely circulated during the 1993 debate on the proposed lifting of the ban on openly gay military personnel.[143]

The proliferation of anti-gay propaganda and organizing efforts maintained a hostile and threatening environment for openly gay and lesbian people, especially in rural areas. Brenda and Wanda Henson, a lesbian couple who purchased land to build a retreat center in rural Mississippi, were subjected to terrorist attacks by their neighbors. It turned out that some of the people who tried to drive the Hensons off their land took organizing advice from the American Family Association, a national anti-gay, anti-pornography outfit.[144]

On the abortion front, the Christian Right was plagued by a series of setbacks, all of which exacerbated tensions between the directly harrassing and the legal–legislative wings of the anti-abortion movement.[145] Around the time of President Clinton's election, Randall Terry and other Operation Rescue leaders encouraged their supporters to target doctors, as the weak link in the availability of legal abortion. "No Place to Hide" was a terror campaign against abortion clinic workers and their families. In countless cases, militant anti-abortionists issued death threats and used quasi-legal means to obtain abortionists' home addresses, their itineraries, and even to ascertain their children's whereabouts, all with the intent of shrinking the supply of abortion doctors.[146]

Violence against clinics escalated with Clinton's election.[147] In March 1993, abortion doctor David Gunn was assassinated by anti-abortion activist Michael Griffin. Months later, Rachelle Shannon, an Oregon woman who had edited an underground newsletter written by a man serving prison time for firebombing an Ohio clinic, tried but failed to murder another abortion doctor in Kansas.[148] The execution of abortion doctors was supported by a handful of "ministries," including the monthly *Life Advocate* magazine, a mimeographed *Prayer and Action Weekly News* newsletter, and a loose network of activists who signed a statement circulated by a Reverend Paul Hill, defending Michael Griffin's use of lethal force against doctors.[149] In July of 1994 Hill himself shot and killed an abortion doctor and one of the doctor's escorts at a Pensacola, Florida clinic.[150]

After each shooting, moderate anti-abortion leaders tried to assure the general public that the attacks were not representative of the movement at large.[151] True or not, government repression of the movement's violent wing was already in motion. In January of 1994 the Supreme Court issued a ruling with perilous consequences for anti-abortionists and, for that matter, any other group of dissident demonstrators. The National Organization for Women (NOW) had sued Joseph Scheidler on the grounds that his Pro-Life Action League constituted a criminal conspiracy to close abortion clinics. The Supreme Court ruled that, indeed, NOW could use the Racketeer Influenced and Corrupt Organizations (RICO) Act, established in the 1970s to prosecute profit-making enterprises like the Mafia. The RICO ruling opened the possibility that activists only loosely connected to those causing clinic damage could be held legally liable.[152]

Next came a Texas jury decision ordering Operation Rescue and associates to pay more than a million dollars in punitive damages to a Houston Planned Parenthood clinic that was targeted during the 1992 Republican National Convention. Defendants vowed they would not pay one cent.[153] Meanwhile, Congress passed and President Clinton signed the Freedom of Access to Clinic Entrances (FACE) Act, which added federal civil and criminal penalties to the crimes of blockading or vandalizing clinics. Anti-abortion groups immediately sued the federal government on the grounds that FACE violated First Amendment rights to protest.[154] A month after Clinton signed the FACE Act, the Supreme Court ruled in *Madsen v. Women's Health Center*, sustaining a lower court injunction barring anti-abortionists from demonstrating closer than thirty-six feet from a clinic. Jay Sekulow of the American Center for Law and Justice, a Christian Right legal firm, called the ruling a "devastating blow for the pro-life movement."[155]

Years' worth of clinic harassment had finally yielded restrictive decisions by the Supreme Court, Congress, and the executive branch. In effect, state agencies moved to repress the militant wing of the anti-abortion movement, to the advantage of women in need of abortions and political supporters of reproductive choice. Apart from the anti-abortionists, no other group in society had been allowed to wreak havoc on the targets of its protests. Under the Democratic administration, setbacks in the legal and legislative realm pushed the anti-abortion movement to a crossroads: some members would continue to advocate violence while others would have to reevaluate some of their tactics.

Meanwhile the Christian Right's electoral activists scored victories in several states in 1994. In Virginia, the movement succeeded in winning the Republican Senatorial nomination for former Marine Lieutenant Colonel Oliver North. In Texas, the Christian Coalition's 60,000 members took dominion and elected former Reagan official Tom Pauken to head the state GOP.

Oliver North would ultimately lose his Senate campaign. But by November of 1994 the Christian Right would help bring the Republican Party to power in both houses of Congress. (Post-election analyses revealed that nationwide about a third of those who voted in the 1994 elections were self-identified born-again Christians. Among the 600 national, state, and local candidates backed by Christian Right activists, about 60 percent won their races.)[156]

Historically, the party in control of the White House fared poorly in mid-term Congressional elections, and in early 1994 the Democrats knew they stood to lose a large number of seats. President Clinton had been plagued by scandals surrounding his finances and allegations of sexual misconduct. With each new revelation in the press, the Christian Right trumpeted the scandals through its own religious broadcasting outlets and through lucrative sales of anti-Clinton video tapes.[156]

By June of 1994 the heat between the Right and the Democratic establishment reached a boiling point. The Democrats, who had no loyal mass movement in their corner, launched an attack on the Christian Right. Vic Fazio (D-CA), chair of the Democratic Congressional Campaign Committee, convened a press conference to lambast the Republicans for courting what he called the "firebreathing Christian radical right." Republicans and movement leaders called Fazio a religious bigot, and all forty-four Republican Senators signed a letter calling on President Clinton to repudiate "Christian bashing."[157] Later that same week, eighty-seven Republican House members called for the resignation of Surgeon

General Joycelyn Elders who had given a speech denouncing the Christian Right.[158] Clinton responded by going on the offensive. In a phone interview with a St. Louis radio station, Clinton blasted right-wing radio and television broadcasters, naming Jerry Falwell and Rush Limbaugh in particular, as the source of a "constant, unremitting drumbeat of negativism and cynicism."[159]

Secular right-wing commentators rallied reliably to defend the Christian Right.[160] *National Review* treated the Democrats' attack as sour grapes election-year politicking.[161] *Human Events* editorialized on behalf of the Christian Right as one of the Republicans' greatest assets. "They are," concluded one article on the controversy, "the key to obtaining majority party status and, for that very reason, Democratic vilification of religious conservatives is likely to increase, not diminish, over the coming months and years."[162]

But the effectiveness of the Democrats' strategy was dubious. Even after a heightened campaign against the Christian Right in the mainstream media, a national poll conducted by the *Los Angeles Times* showed that a minority of respondents feared that "conservative Christians have too much political power." Only one in five respondents said the involvement of the Christian Right would make them less likely to vote Republican, and that sentiment was strongest among partisan Democrats who were least likely to switch parties anyway.[163]

The Democrats' campaign against the Christian Right coincided with the efforts of well-heeled interest groups: Planned Parenthood, the Anti-Defamation League of B'nai B'rith, the Human Rights Campaign Fund, and others. These groups fostered an intellectually dishonest portrayal of a "radical right" somehow disconnected from routine two-party electoral politics. Through their publications and press briefings, the interest groups characterized the Christian Right as an undifferentiated crew of fanatics who were winning political power through wholly illegitimate means. The idea was to downplay the Christian Right's status as a veritable mass movement, let alone one that had developed over two decades with backing from political elites and agencies.

For the Right, the most disconcerting piece of interest group propaganda came in the form of a book released in June 1994 by the Anti-Defamation League (ADL). Fresh from a public relations debacle over the 1993 press revelations of its role in spying on leftists and Arab-Americans,[164] ADL compiled facts from previously published books and articles and wove them together in its characteristic guilt-by-association style. The Right accused ADL of doing its own bit of defamation.[165] A group of prominent Jewish neoconservatives published a *New York Times* advertisement calling on fellow Jews to reject ADL's view of the Christian Right as a threat to "tolerance and pluralism in

America."[166] The Christian Coalition responded to ADL with a 29-page rebuttal.[167] Pat Robertson had been an avid booster of the Israeli government, and he consistently conflated anti-Zionism with anti-Semitism. Robertson was beside himself over the rupture of his long-standing alliance with ADL.[168] He, ADL, and neoconservatives had all worked together when the agenda was fighting communism by fueling wars in Central America (see Chapter 9). Now former allies were at odds with each other over basic civil rights issues but not over the fundamentally unjust and unequal distribution of wealth and power in the United States and all over the world.

The controversy over the "radical right" reflected a split among sectors of the political establishment. Some wanted to work with the Christian Right while others opposed it and feared it. Yet the propaganda of liberal groups about "radicals" and "extremists" served to distract public awareness from the organic relationships between right-wing movements and political elites. The term "radical right" was a smear against right-wing opponents of liberalism and, implicitly, also against radicals of the progressive Left. This was no surprise. Historically, U.S. liberals had been as diligent as the Right when it came to hunting subversives during the Cold War and waging wars of aggression against leftists in the Third World.

It was within the Cold War context of the 1950s and 1960s that liberal social scientists of the "pluralist" school developed a mystique around "radical" and "extremist" social movements. The scholarly work of pluralists influenced the thinking of non-academic opinion shapers in media and politics, so that each successive mobilization of a mass movement was treated as an aberration on the political landscape.

Only after the Christian Right passed through its phase of collaboration with the U.S. military and foreign policymakers and grew into a grassroots movement focused on domestic policy issues did the liberal establishment see a threat from a "radical right." Then opponents of the Christian Right focused narrowly on the most arguably extreme elements of the movement while neglecting the substantial popular base of support for the movement's reactive policy agenda.

There was nothing particularly "radical" about a movement that opposed things like national health care reform while supporting status quo inequalities between rich and poor, black and white, men and women. But opponents' constant repetition of the "radical right" slogan took the place of reasoned presentation and debate on what the Christian Right was really all about. Absent that sort of national discussion, the Right had only to dismiss its detractors and forge ahead on the roads to dominion.

CHAPTER 13

• • •

Epilogue

At the start of the Cold War era, a small group of conservative intellectuals sought to build a strong movement based on their bedrock principles of economic libertarianism, moral traditionalism, and anticommunism. At the time, the forerunners of the New Right could not have foreseen the extent to which their ideas and policy preferences would galvanize untold thousands of activists over the course of many decades.

Right-wing movements in the first half of the twentieth century were characteristically focused on themes of xenophobia and isolationism. The term "nativism" referred to the Right's drive to maintain supremacist status for white, native-born Americans. After World War II, nativist tendencies would subside and right-wing politics would come to be dominated, instead, by policy concerns in the realms of economics, moral order, and foreign affairs. All but the avowedly racist Right dropped tenets of crude biological determinism and, thereby, expanded their ability to attract wide societal support.

Beginning in the 1970s, the Heritage Foundation took its motto, "ideas have consequences," from the title of fusionist era thinker Richard M. Weaver's book on modernity's threat to "Western civilization." But it was not just *ideas* that yielded success for the conservative movement. Throughout the second half of the twentieth century, U.S. politics were advantageous to movements of the Right on a number of scores. The pervasive anticommunist imperative created a context within which right-wing activists found themselves opposed to both Democratic and Republican administrations' precise means of fighting communism but still system-supportive toward elites' resolve to do so.

Anticommunism endured as the most compelling and unifying organizing principle for the Right. It also affected other, even conflicting, drives. Each aspect and phase of the trajectories of right-wing movements set the stage for future possibilities. As part of the United States' project of asserting a hegemonic role in post-World War II international affairs, one sector of the political elite perceived the wisdom of dismantling the long-standing system of legal racial segregation. The Democrats had dominated federal policymaking in no small part because the southern states maintained a solid segregationist Democratic delegation in Congress. Northern Democrats saw political advantages in responding to pressures from the civil rights movement and in recruiting new voters from among the large numbers of African Americans who migrated northward after the war. Against the backdrop of partisan realignment and in the context of the Cold War, crucial Supreme Court decisions against segregation had the effect of arousing "massive resistance" from southern politicians and a network of semi-autonomous Citizens' Councils.

The arousal of the segregationist movement coincided with the mobilization of mass-based anticommunist groups. These groups came after the heyday of Senator Joseph McCarthy himself, and they perpetuated McCarthy's influence long after his death. Conservative movement thinkers grouped around William F. Buckley's *National Review* exerted little influence over grassroots right-wing movements. But these and others interested in capturing power inside the Republican Party were the beneficiaries of large-scale anticommunist and segregationist activism.

Barry Goldwater's 1964 presidential nomination was a turning point in this regard. A small coterie of conservative activists drafted the Goldwater candidacy. After that, his campaign attracted support from the John Birch Society and similar-minded groups around anticommunism and opposition to civil rights legislation. Four years later, George Wallace's candidacy strengthened the hand of those conservative movement and party activists eager to use race and law-and-order themes to drive the Republicans' class base downward. Thus, the right-wing movements of the 1950s and 1960s paved the road for the New Right's ascent in the 1970s. Along the way, it was crucial for movement strategists to maintain ties both within state policymakers' circles and among large citizen constituencies.

As segregationism eventually faded as a dominant organizing principle for all but a small movement of Christian Identity tax protestors, the values and priorities of a much larger evangelical subculture came to the fore. The New Right consolidated a second wave of fusionism between anticommunist and moral traditionalist activists. Veterans of the Goldwater campaign brought with them corporate backing and the skills of partisan organizing. Evangelicals brought ideological commitment and a strong church-based infrastructure. Together with articulate, elite-linked neoconservative intellectuals, the New Right coalition shifted the national policy agenda rightward.

It would be difficult to identify precisely the impact of right-wing movements on specific pieces of state policymaking. Throughout this book, we have seen that right-wing movements often acted in such a way as to reinforce policy orientations already determined by one or more sector of the political elite. On some issues outside the state's immediate prerogatives, the Right took the initiative and wielded influence equal to or greater than that of other social movements.

Anticommunism was the classic case in which the Right was, overall, system-supportive but also vigilant against elites deemed insufficiently committed to the cause. From the Vietnam war to the Reagan-era "freedom fighter" projects, the Right pushed the most intransigent pro-war positions, thereby ensuring the United States' responsibility in killing hundreds of thousands of people and destroying the hopes for self-determination of millions more. By lobbying for weapons systems and against arms treaties, the Right helped line the pockets of military corporations, at the expense of all the domestic social programs that went unfunded, and with the effect of continuing an arms race that left the Soviet Union ultimately bankrupt and defeated.

Anticommunism was, moreover, the rubric under which the state supported right-wing movements. The relationship was mutually beneficial. While a succession of Cold War administrations repressed American leftists, the same regimes encouraged right-wing movement activity. From political elites' collaboration with the China Lobby and the American Security Council in the 1950s and 1960s to the Reagan administration's covert coordination of the "private" Contra aid network, the Right owes its strength and longevity in part to the power of the state. No honest understanding of the Right's history can neglect the crucial role of state and, more generally, elite facilitation.

On specific elements of U.S. economic policy, again, the impact of right-wing movements is difficult to discern. In part, that is because in this realm movement activists themselves wield less influence than do the capitalists who directly bankroll political campaigns and lobby officeholders over tax and regulatory policies. The role of right-wing movement activism, from the 1950s tracts published by the Foundation for Economic Education to the promotion of 1980s supply-side theory, has been to sustain ideological arguments that make a system based on sharp class inequalities seem, somehow, just. For their role in sustaining capitalism's legitimacy, right-wing organizations have enjoyed a virtually bottomless pit of corporate largesse. That resource has given the Right the wherewithal to participate significantly in electoral politics.

In the area of domestic social policy, the legacy of right-wing movements is immeasurable but difficult to deny. On race matters in the United States, one can only imagine how much progress *might* have been made absent the longevity of the racist Right. Though ultimately unsuccessful in its goals, the segregationist movement's strength left an enduring mark on partisan politics as the Republicans and eventually the Democrats, too, made themes of racial division central to their campaigns. The indirect effect of the organized racist Right was to leave policymaking stalled at the phase of ending formal segregation, and to hinder the redress of continuing and pervasive racial injustice.

Then in the 1990s, attacks by policymakers on welfare dependency and street crime were joined by a new crop of popular books and articles on genetically based differences in intelligence and attendant class inequalities. There was a renewed appetite among some of the white public for racially charged and biological determinist pseudo-scholarship, and that trend threatened to derail any principled policy debate over how best to reduce poverty and violence.

Earlier, and continuing into the 1990s, the Christian Right deterred progress on civil rights for women and homosexuals. Prior to the mobilization of the "pro-family" movement in the 1970s, the Equal Rights Amendment was expected to win full ratification. That victory would have freed feminists to pursue gender equality in other forms. Instead, activists' twenty-year struggle to preserve women's right to safe and legal abortion strained women's movement resources while the Christian Right mobilized on a slate of related family affairs. Without the Christian Right's promulgation of anti-homosexual attitudes, there might have been a societal consensus for early public education campaigns to stop the spread of AIDS. Instead, the disease became a political hot potato. Gay rights advocates were forced to spread themselves thin on both AIDS activism and on controversial initiatives to grant civil rights protections to homosexuals.

In the end, the right-wing movements' effect on the body politic can be thought of more in terms of "what might have been" than in terms of what has actually transpired. This is, ultimately, what hegemony is all about: the power to make our present circumstances appear to us as inevitable, the power to prevent the kinds of social change that we now can only imagine.

The Christian Coalition's 1994 Road to Victory conference offered a glimpse into some of the Right's coming opportunities and quandaries.

Five years after its founding, this, the single largest Christian Right organization was still growing, adding hundreds of new local chapters every year. The leading Republican presidential hopefuls were all men who could count. They heard the Coalition's claim of one million members and, two years in advance, they hastened to make the conference one of their earliest campaign stops. By far the most popular was former Vice-President Dan Quayle who brought the house down. The three thousand conventioneers assembled in the Washington Hilton Hotel ballroom lept to their feet and cheered wildly while Quayle urged them to cede not one inch in the culture war for "family values." At a workshop the next day, Republican National Committee spokesperson Leigh Ann Metzger told activists that "despite press reports, the Republican Party has a welcome mat out for the Christian Coalition."

That was because by the 1990s the Christian Right represented the largest and most influential grassroots movement on the political scene. Not since the 1960s anti-war and civil rights movements had tens of thousands of average citizens taken it upon themselves to change public policy, one city council seat at a time, one ballot measure at a time. There was nothing comparable on the left. Nor even in the recent history of the American right wing had there been such a reservoir of activist commitment and know-how. Almost to a person, the convention delegates were either already local Republican Party or elected officeholders; or they were active in one of the Coalition's 1,100 chapters or with other groups like Concerned Women for America, Focus on the Family, or the National Right to Life Committee.

The movement was on the march, but there were some foreseeable obstacles in its path. Not least of these was a looming fight inside the Republican Party over keeping the restrictive 1992 anti-abortion platform plank. Phyllis Schlafly came to the Christian Coalition gathering with a plan for how to head off a divisive conflict. She proposed new language that would replace the strident call for a constitutional "human life" amendment with a simple "pro-life" statement, leaving the means of outlawing abortion to specific candidates and legislators. But that was not likely to sit well with some anti-abortion activists. Even while the Coalition was still meeting in Washington, D.C., Operation Rescue founder Randall Terry blasted fellow Christians on the opinion page of the *Washington Post*. Terry took aim at Coalition leaders who had already gone out on a limb and endorsed several pro-choice Republican Senators. Terry warned his brethren that unless they would repent for such unholy alliances, "God Himself will fight against them with the sword of His mouth, and spew out their lukewarm agenda as a rebuke and a sign."

Controversy over abortion politics was temporarily overshadowed by the results of the 1994 mid-term Congressional elections. The Republicans were swept to power in both houses of Congress for the first time in forty years. Many of those elected to Congress and to state governments for the first time were seasoned Christian Right activists. More broadly, the Republican Party as a whole reaped the fruits of two decades' worth of Christian Right organizing. Despite low voter turnout by the full eligible electorate, on election day about 30 percent of those who voted were evangelical Christians and among these, about 69 percent voted Republican. Though right-wing Christians represented only an estimated 9 or 10 percent of the population, their disproportionate electoral participation made them a force to be reckoned with.

They developed their clout wisely. Soon after the inauguration of the new Congress, the Christian Coalition pledged to spend more than one million dollars lobbying for welfare cuts and other legislative proposals in the Republicans' "Contract with America." In exchange for Christian Right commitment to Republican economic policies, the party would owe the movement support in backing public school prayer and opposing abortion and gay rights. Despite many obstacles to unity, together the Christian Right and the Republican Party hoped, by 1996, to throw the Democrats out of the White House and to enforce a new era of moral righteousness and economic severity, with a vengeance.

Notes

NOTES TO INTRODUCTION

1. On the political process model, see Charles Tilly, *From Mobilization to Revolution* (Reading, MA: Addison-Wesley, 1978); Frances Fox Piven and Richard A. Cloward, *Poor People's Movements* (New York: Vintage Books, 1977); and Doug McAdam, *Political Process and the Development of Black Insurgency, 1930–1970* (Chicago: University of Chicago Press, 1982).

   On social movements theory generally see, among other useful treatments, Aldon D. Morris and Carol McClung Mueller, eds., *Frontiers in Social Movement Theory* (New Haven, CT: Yale University Press, 1992).

   To date, the most cogent rendition of political process theory is Sidney Tarrow, *Power in Movement: Social Movements, Collective Action and Politics* (New York: Cambridge University Press, 1994).

2. On the difficulty of applying the "conservative" label to the right wing, see William B. Hixson, Jr., *Search for the American Right Wing: An Analysis of the Social Science Record, 1955–1987* (Princeton University Press, 1992), p. xvii. Hixson writes that "it is a good rule not to grant final authority over the use of words to those whose interests are served by them." Rightists call themselves "conservatives," but they are not truly conservative in seeking just to preserve things as they are.

3. See, esp., Daniel Bell, ed., *The Radical Right* (New York: Anchor Books, 1964); and Seymour Martin Lipset and Earl Raab, *The Politics of Unreason: Right-Wing Extremism in America, 1790–1970* (New York: Harper and Row, 1970).

   In Bell's highly influential collection, Cold War-era right-wing activists were portrayed as anti-elite populists. Using empirical data on Senator Joseph McCarthy's actual base of support, Michael Paul Rogin refuted this image in *The Intellectuals and McCarthy: The Radical Specter* (Cambridge, MA: MIT Press, 1967).

   Lipset and Raab continued to promote the notion of a politically deviant and "extremist" "radical right" in their later work. By defining "extremism," both of the Left and the Right as "going beyond the limits of normative procedures which define the democratic political process," they narrowed the boundaries of legitimate social movement activists to those who engage in electoral politics and who do not disrupt business as usual. Historically, profound and rapid social change comes about when social movements no longer ratify the status quo, when they use tactics that both challenge public perceptions and force elites to cede power.

4. Noam Chomsky, *Year 501: The Conquest Continues* (Boston: South End Press, 1993), p. 106.
5. Joel Kovel, *Red Hunting in the Promised Land: Anticommunism and the Making of America* (New York: Basic Books, 1994), pp. xi–xii, 1–13.

NOTES TO CHAPTER 1

1. On rightist opposition to the New Deal, see, e.g., Michael W. Miles, *The Odyssey of the American Right* (New York: Oxford University Press, 1980). On the history of isolationism among conservatives, see Selig Adler, *The Isolationist Impulse: Its Twentieth Century Reaction* (New York: Abelard-Schuman, 1957); Manfred Jonas, *Isolationism in America, 1935–1941* (Chicago: Imprint Publications, 1990); Ronald Radosh, *Prophets on the Right: Profiles of Conservative Critics of American Globalism* (New York: Simon and Schuster, 1975); and Justus D. Doenecke *Not to the Swift: The Old Isolationists in the Cold War Era* (Lewisburg, PA: Bucknell University Press, 1979).
2. See George H. Nash, *The Conservative Intellectual Movement in America Since 1945* (New York: Basic Books, 1979), esp. pp. 84–130.
3. On the process of post-war party realignment, through which African Americans came to be a crucial Democratic bloc and Republicans gained new constituents among disaffected former southern Democrats, see, e.g., Alexander P. Lamis, *The Two-Party South* (New York: Oxford University Press, 1990); Paul Allen Beck, "Partisan Dealignment in the Postwar South," *American Political Science Review*, Vol. 71, 1977, pp. 477–496; and Raymond Wolfinger and Robert B. Arsenau, "Partisan Change in the South, 1952–1976," in Louis Maisel and Joseph Cooper, eds., *Political Parties: Development and Decay* (Beverly Hills, CA: Sage Publications, 1978).
4. On the long-term effects of the Republican Party's strategic use of anti-civil rights sentiment, see, e.g., Thomas Byrne Edsall and Mary Edsall, *Chain Reaction: the Impact of Race, Rights, and Taxes on American Politics* (New York: Norton, 1991).
5. See, e.g., David H. Bennett, *The Party of Fear: From Nativist Movements to the New Right in American History* (New York: Vintage Books, 1990), pp. 208–214 and passim.
6. Ibid., p. 248.
7. Ibid.
8. David M. Chalmers, *Hooded Americanism: The History of the Ku Klux Klan* (New York: New Viewpoints, 1965), p. 322.
9. Bennett, op cit., p. 210, cites a figure of one million Klan members during the 1920s. Chalmers, pp. 332–333, reports Klan membership at not more than 10,000 by 1949.

10. Wyn Craig Wade, *The Fiery Cross: The Ku Klux Klan in America* (New York: Simon and Schuster, 1987), p. 275.

11. Ibid., pp. 299–303; see also, Wilma Dykeman and James Stokeley, "The Klan Tries a Comeback," *Commentary*, January 1960, pp. 45–51.

12. On Coughlin, see for example, Geoffrey S. Smith, *To Save a Nation: American Countersubversives, the New Deal, and the Coming of World War II* (New York: Basic Books, 1973); and Alan Brinkley, *Voices of Protest: Huey Long, Father Coughlin, and the Great Depression* (New York: Alfred A. Knopf, 1982).

13. Bennett, op cit., p. 244.

14. For the history of Long, Smith, and the milieu in which they operated, see Brinkley, op cit; Bennett, op cit., pp. 251–253; Leo P. Ribuffo, *The Old Christian Right: The Protestant Far Right from the Great Depression to the Cold War* (Philadelphia: Temple University Press, 1983); and Glen Jeansonne, *Gerald L. K. Smith: Minister of Hate* (New Haven, CT: Yale University Press, 1988).

15. Morris Schonbach, *Native American Fascism During the 1930s and 1940s: A Study of Its Roots, Its Growth and Its Decline* (New York: Garland Publishing, 1985).

16. Ibid., pp. 234–235.

17. Ibid., pp. 245–247.

18. See George Wolfskill, *The Revolt of the Conservatives: A History of the American Liberty League, 1934–40* (Boston: Houghton Mifflin, 1962); and Frederick Rudolph, "The American Liberty League, 1934–40," *American Historical Review*, vol. LVI, no. 1, October 1950, pp. 19–33.

19. Ibid., p. 23.

20. Miles, op cit., p. 32.

21. Sumner Gerard, letter to supporters, May 1954, Committee for Constitutional Government, Reel 29, Right-Wing Collection of the University of Iowa.

22. See Committee for Constitutional Government (CCG) annual reports, pamphlets, newsletters, and speech reprints, Reel 29, Right-Wing Collection of the University of Iowa. In 1950, the CCG and several other groups were subpoenaed by the House of Representatives' Lobby Investigating Committee. The CCG was asked to provide financial records that would determine violations of the lobbying legislation requiring contributors of $500 and over to be named. See "Rumely on the Spot," *Newsweek*, July 10, 1950, p. 30 and "Rightists Under Attack," *New Republic*, June 19, 1950, p. 9.

23. Ibid. See, e.g., Sumner Gerard, trustee, Committee for Constitutional Government, "Mid-Year Report, 1954," regarding the Committee's support for the Reed–Dirksen Amendment to limit the power of Congress to tax.

24. Ibid. On the Bricker Amendment, see, e.g. Sherman Adams, *Firsthand Report: The Story of the Eisenhower Administration* (New York: Harper & Bros., 1961), pp. 105–109.

25. See Justus D. Doenecke, ed., *In Danger Undaunted: The Anti-Interventionist Movement of 1940–1941 as Revealed in the Papers of the America First Committee* (Stanford, CA: Hoover Institution Press, 1990), pp. 1–78.

    Among the founders was General Robert E. Wood, Chairman of the Board of the Sears, Roebuck chain. Wood had been an early backer of the New Deal; he broke with President Roosevelt over the Wagner National Labor Relations Act and the administration's drive toward war. Another major founder was

William H. Regnery, a Chicago textile manufacturer and president of Western Shade Cloth Company. Initially, Wood and Regnery underwrote the AFC. Eight businessmen alone supplied over $100,000. These included Regnery; Harold L. Stuart, a Chicago investment banker; and H. Smith Richardson of Vick Chemical Company of New York.

26. Justus D. Doenecke, ed., *In Danger Undaunted: The Anti-Interventionist Movement of 1940–1941 as Revealed in the Papers of the America First Committee* (Stanford, CA: Hoover Institution Press, 1990), p. 6.

27. Justus D. Doenecke, *Not to the Swift: The Old Isolationists in the Cold War Era* (Lewisburg, KY: Bucknell University Press, 1979), p. 12.

28. Ibid.

29. Lindbergh quoted in Wayne S. Cole, *Charles A. Lindbergh and the Battle Against American Intervention in World War II* (New York: Harcourt Brace Jovanovich, 1974), p. 87.

30. Doenecke, *Not to the Swift*, op cit., p. 20.

31. Lindbergh, quoted in Cole, pp. 171–172.

32. The anti-Semitism charge against isolationist groups, including the America First Committee, remains controversial. Doenecke, in *Not to the Swift*, p. 20, emphasizes that the ranks of pre-war isolationists included a tiny minority of professional anti-Semites, including fundamentalist preachers Gerald L. K. Smith and Gerald Winrod, lobbyist Merwin K. Hart and radio broadcaster Upton Close. Jonas, op cit., pp. 253–256, writes that the America First Committee attracted "considerable numbers" of anti-Semites but that the leadership took measures to blunt their impact.

33. Doenecke, *Not to the Swift*, op cit., p. 40.

34. See, e.g., Norman Thomas, "When Cruelty Becomes Pleasureable," *Human Events*, September 26, 1945, in which Thomas condemned the United States' use of atomic bombs on Japan.

35. Felix Morley, William Henry Chamberlin, Frank C. Hanighen, "Human Events: A Statement of Policy," March 1, 1944, published in Frank C. Hanighen and Felix Morley, eds., *A Year of Human Events: A Weekly Analysis for the American Citizen*, vol. 1 (Washington, DC: Human Events, 1945), pp. x–xi. This volume is a collection of the first year's worth of *Human Events* articles.

36. Felix Morley, "Pointing Towards Imperialism," Feb. 23, 1944, published in the above-cited collection.

37. Felix Morley, "The Proposed Security Organization," October 18, 1944, published in the above-cited collection.

38. William Henry Chamberlin, "Russia Moves West," October 25, 1944, published in the above-cited collection.

39. See Henry Chamberlin, "The Course of Soviet Expansion," *Human Events*, February 6, 1946 and William Chamberlin, "Shifting American Alignments," *Human Events*, May 22, 1946.

40. Edna Lonigan, "The End of the Beginning," *Human Events*, January 1, 1947.

41. Frank Hanighen, "Not Merely Gossip: A Supplement to *Human Events*," January 8, 1947.

42. Friedrich A. Hayek, *The Road to Serfdom* (University of Chicago Press, 1944), p. 56.

43. Nash, op cit., p. 7–8.
44. Ibid., 22–24.
45. William A. Rusher, *The Rise of the Right* (New York: William Morrow, 1984) pp. 33–35 for a brief history of *The Freeman*'s incarnations, the last of which reduced the journal's impact and contributed to the formation of the *National Review* magazine in 1955.
46. Leonard Read, "Notes from FEE," April 15, 1954, Reel 88, Right-Wing Collection, University of Iowa.
47. "Notes from FEE," March 2, 1956, Reel 88.
48. Nash, op cit., p. 24.
49. "Notes from FEE," May 21, 1956, Reel 88.
50. "Notes from FEE," September 4, 1956, Reel 88.
51. FEE, list of trustees, 1955–1956, Reel 88.
52. Leonard Read, "Notes from FEE," October 1, 1954, p. 1, Reel 88.
53. The Mont Pelerin Society archive collection at Stanford University's Hoover Institution contains the attendance lists, conference agendas, and publications of the Society.
54. Milton Friedman, quoted in Nash, op cit., p. 26.
55. Nash, op cit., p. 27.
56. Russell Kirk, "The Mt. Pelerin Society," *National Review*, October 21, 1961, p. 270.
57. The best available sources on fusionism are Nash, pp. 131–185 and Jerome L. Himmelstein, *To the Right: The Transformation of American Conservatism* (Berkeley, CA: University of California Press, 1990), pp. 28–62.
58. Russell Kirk, *The Conservative Mind: From Burke to Eliot* (Chicago: Regnery Books, [1953] 1987), pp. 3–11.
59. Here I have not done justice to Leo Strauss' philosophy. See Robert Devigne, *Recasting Conservatism: Oakeshott, Strauss, and the Response to Postmodernism* (New Haven, CT: Yale University Press, 1994); and Nash, op cit., pp. 50–53 and passim.

    For rightists' rendition of Strauss' influence, see, e.g., Irving Kristol, *Reflections of a Neoconservative* (New York: Basic Books, 1983), p. 76; a symposium, "The Achievement of Leo Strauss," *National Review*, December 7, 1973, pp. 1347–1357; Allan Bloom, "Leo Strauss," *Political Theory*, November 1974, pp. 372–392; Milton Himmelfarb, "On Leo Strauss," *Commentary*, August 1974, pp. 60–66; Dinesh D'Souza, "The Legacy of Leo Strauss," *Policy Review*, Spring 1987, pp. 36–43.
60. Nash, op cit., p. 30.
61. See John B. Judis, *William F. Buckley, Jr.: Patron Saint of the Conservatives* (New York: Simon and Schuster, 1988) pp. 92–98.
62. Frank Chodorov, founding statement of the Intercollegiate Society of Individualists, 1953, published as an advertisement in *National Review*, January 31, 1959, pp. 488–489.
63. See "The ISI Story as of 1961," in Henry Regnery Collection, Box 34, file: Intercollegiate Society of Individualists, Hoover Institution Archives, Stanford University.
64. See the masthead of the ISI publication *The Intercollegiate Review*, Vol. 1, No. 1,

January 1965. ISI business manager and foreign correspondent Edwin J. Feulner, Jr. later became the head of the Heritage Foundation. Among the initial editorial advisory board members, Richard V. Allen became a Nixon aide and later President Reagan's National Security Advisory. Philip M. Crane of Bradley University went on to become a member of Congress. M. Stanton Evans became a Young Americans for Freedom activist and a prominent syndicated columnist.

65. Nash, op cit., p. 159.
66. Frank Meyer, "Freedom, Tradition, Conservatism," *Modern Age*, Fall 1960, p. 356. Meyer stated this argument in numerous writings; this article was among the most concise.
67. Ibid.
68. Nash, pp. 178–179. It was *National Review* publisher William Rusher, himself a "devout fusionist," who coined term "strategic integration."
69. See Judis, op cit., pp. 114–161 and passim.
70. Buckley, Jr., "Publisher's Statement," *National Review*, November 19, 1955, p. 5.
71. "The Magazine's Credenda," *National Review*, November 19, 1955, p. 6.
72. Ibid.
73. William Henry Chamberlin, "A New Nationalism," *National Review*, August 25, 1956, p. 15.
74. James Burnham, "Liberation: What Next?" *National Review*, January 19, 1957, pp. 59–71.
75. Frank S. Meyer, "'New Ideas' or Old Truth," *National Review*, February 2, 1957, pp. 107–198.
76. William S. Schlamm, "Neutralizaton: What Next?" *National Review*, January 26, 1957, pp. 81–84.
77. "Should Conservatives Vote for Eisenhower–Nixon?" *National Review*, October 20, 1956, pp. 12–15.
78. "Why the South Must Prevail," *National Review*, August 24, 1957, pp. 148–149.
79. See James T. Patterson, *Congressional Conservatism and the New Deal: The Growth of the Conservative Coalition in Congress, 1933–1939* (Lexington, KY: University of Kentucky Press, 1967).
80. On these four leading former leftist intellectuals, see esp. John Diggins, *Up From Communism: Conservative Odysseys in American Intellectual History* (New York: Columbia University Press, 1994).

NOTES TO CHAPTER 2

1. The literature on Cold War-era anticommunism is vast. See, e.g., David Caute, *The Great Fear: The Anti-Communist Purge Under Truman and Eisenhower* (New York: Simon and Schuster, 1978), Ellen W. Schrecker, *No Ivory Tower: McCarthyism and the Universities* (New York: Oxford University Press, 1986); and Cedric Belfrage, *The American Inquisition, 1945–1960: A Profile of the "McCarthy Era"* (New York: Thunder's Mouth Press, 1989.)

2. See Richard M. Freeland, *The Truman Doctrine and the Origins of McCarthyism: Foreign Policy, Domestic Politics, and Internal Security, 1946–1948* (New York: New York University Press, 1985).

3. Saul Landau, *The Dangerous Doctrine: National Security and U.S. Foreign Policy* (Boulder, CO: Westview Press, 1988), p. 7.

4. NSC-68 has been the subject of debate among policy analysts. At issue is whether the document, classified until 1977, promoted "containment" or "rollback" of Soviet bloc forces as the primary U.S. strategic doctrine. See, esp. Jerry Sanders, *Peddlers of Crisis: The Committee on the Present Danger and the Politics of Containment* (Boston: South End Press, 1983), pp. 23–50 and also Thomas Bodenheimer and Robert Gould, *Rollback! Right-Wing Power in U.S. Foreign Policy* (Boston: South End Press, 1989), pp. 23–24; Landau, op cit., pp. 50–51.

5. See the *New York Times*, December 10–15, 1951 for a six-part series on the Psychological Strategy Board and U.S. government propaganda operations. Projects included the "Voice of America" shortwave radio broadcasts, stateside "psychological warfare" training schools for U.S. military personnel, and a State Department pamphlet series, including "An Outline of American History," coauthored by Columbia University Professor Richard Hofstadter. On psychological warfare, generally, see Christopher Simpson, *Science of Coercion: Communication Research and Psychological Warfare, 1945–1960* (New York: Oxford University Press, 1994) and Michael McClintock, *Instruments of Statecraft: U.S. Guerrilla Warfare, Counter-Insurgency, and Counter-Terrorism, 1940–1990* (New York: Pantheon, 1992

6. Landau, op cit., p. 62.

7. For an in-depth treatment, see John W. Spanier, *The Truman–MacArthur Controversy and the Korean War*, (Cambridge: The Belknap Press of Harvard University Press, 1959). For a summary of the Truman-MacArthur controversy, see J. Ronald Oakley, *God's Country: America in the Fifties* (New York: Dembner Books, 1986), pp. 79–93. Oakley reports, p. 88, that the White House received over 27,000 letters and telegrams within the first twelve days of the firing, and that public opinion ran twenty to one against Truman.

8. Oakley, op cit., p. 51.

9. Oakley, pp. 51–53; Richard M. Fried, *Nightmare in Red: The McCarthy Era in Perspective* (New York: Oxford University Press, 1990), pp. 17–23.

10. Ross Y. Koen, *The China Lobby in American Politics* (New York: Harper & Row, 1974), pp. 132–159 and passim.

11. See esp. Robert Griffith, *The Politics of Fear: Joseph R. McCarthy and the Senate* (Amherst: University of Massachusetts Press, 1987).

12. Ibid., pp. ix–xi.

13. Daniel Bell, ed., *The Radical Right* (New York: Anchor Books, 1964).

14. Ibid., p. 47.

15. See, e.g., Seymour Martin Lipset, *Political Man: The Social Bases of Politics* (New York: Anchor Books, 1963), pp. 169–173.

16. See also, Seymour Martin Lipset and Earl Raab, *The Politics of Unreason: Right-Wing Extremism in America, 1790–1970*, (New York: Harper Torchbooks, 1970).

17. See Michael Paul Rogin, *The Intellectuals and McCarthy: The Radical Specter* (Cambridge, MA: MIT Press, 1967).

18. Three excellent sources on the China Lobby are: Ross Y. Koen, *The China Lobby in American Politics* (New York: Harper & Row, 1974); Stanley D. Bachrack, *The Committee of One Million: "China Lobby" Politics, 1953–1971* (New York: Columbia University Press, 1976); and a two-part series on the China Lobby in *The Reporter*, April 15, 1992 and April 29, 1952. Bachrack, p. 5, notes that the Communist Party of New York State, in January 1949, called for a Congressional investigation of Chiang's network of agents in the United States.

19. Koen, op cit., 29.

20. The Marvin Liebman Collection at Stanford University's Hoover Institution Archives includes 149 boxes of materials from the dozens of organizations he coordinated or advised.

21. Marvin Liebman, *Coming Out Conservative: An Autobiography* (San Francisco: Chronicle Books, 1992), pp. 33–47.

22. Ibid., pp. 92–93.

23. John B. Judis, *William F. Buckley, Jr.: Patron Saint of the Conservatives* (New York: Simon and Schuster, 1988), pp. 189–191.

24. "The Committee of One Million Against the Admission of Red China to the United Nations," 1965, Box 121, Stanley Hornbeck Collection, Hoover Institution Archives, Stanford University.

25. Ibid., p. 4.

26. See, e.g., The Committee of One Million advertisement, *New York Times*, April 12, 1955, p. 19.

27. "The Committee of One Million Against the Admission of Red China to the United Nations," op cit., p. 5.

28. Ibid., p. 7. See also Reel 29, Right-Wing Collection of the University of Iowa, for the Committee's July 16, 1957 news release, "Business Leaders Oppose Trade with Red China: 176 Call on President to Maintain Embargo." The release includes the list of business leader signators.

29. Committee of One Million, Confidential Memorandum, dated November 1956, p. 7, Right-Wing Collection of the University of Iowa, Reel 29.

30. Ibid.

31. Liebman, op cit., p. 111.

32. Committee of One Million, Confidential Memorandum, op cit., p. 8.

33. Ibid. See also Edward Hunter, *The Black Book on Red China* (New York: The Bookmailer, 1958). The book includes a listing of the Committee of One Million's officers and a description of the group's work. Edward Hunter was reportedly a CIA propagandist who specialized in journalistic accounts of Chinese and Korean "brainwashing" programs. See John Marks, *The Search for the Manchurian Candidate: The CIA and Mind Control* (New York: McGraw Hill, 1980), pp. 125–128.

34. "The American Afro-Asian Educational Exchange," report dated 1966, Box 5, File AAAEE, Stanley Hornbeck Collection Hoover Institution Archives, Stanford University.

35. See "Free Afro-Asia," no. 1, the newsletter of the American Afro-Asian

Educational Exchange, Inc., Reel 12, Right-Wing Collection of the University of Iowa.

36. "The American Afro-Asian Educational Exchange," report dated 1966, Box 5, file AAAEE, Stanley Hornbeck Collection, Hoover Institution Archives, Stanford University.

37. David Nelson Rowe, "Free Afro-Asia," published by the American Afro-Asian Educational Exchange, Inc., acknowledgments page, February 1, 1963, Reel 12, Right-Wing Collection of the University of Iowa. Professor Rowe would later become an important leader of the U.S. chapter of the World Anti-Communist League. See John Anderson and Scott Lee Anderson, *Inside the League* (New York: Dodd, Mead, 1986), pp. 53, 85, and passim.

38. "The American Afro-Asian Educational Exchange," 1966, op cit.

39. Ibid. The group was called the International Youth Crusade for Freedom in Vietnam.

40. Blanche Wiessen Cook, "First Comes the Lie: C. D. Jackson and Political Warfare," *Radical History Review, 31*, 1984, p. 46.

41. Ibid., p. 52.

42. Ibid., pp. 50, 64. On the relationship between Radio Free Europe/Radio Liberty, the National Committee for a Free Europe, the CIA, and U.S. operations to recruit pro-Nazi Eastern European exiles and emigrés, see esp. Christopher Simpson, *Blowback: The First Full Account of America's Recruitment of Nazis, and Its Disastrous Effect on Our Domestic and Foreign Policy* (New York: Weidenfeld and Nicolson, 1988), pp. 125–136 and passim.

43. Ibid., p. 267.

44. Ibid. Simpson cites a 1972 Congressional Research Study which acknowledged that ACEN had been funded by the CIA.

45. See Russ Bellant, *Old Nazis, the New Right, and the Republican Party* (Boston: South End Press, 1991).

46. "Outline of Purpose, American Friends of the Captive Nations," Box 5, file: American Friends of the Captive Nations, Christopher Emmet Collection, Hoover Institution Archives, Stanford University. Emmet was the chairman of the American Friends of the Captive Nations. Initial Congressional supporters included Senator Paul H. Douglas, Senator John F. Kennedy, Representative Walter Judd, Senator Karl E. Mundt.

47. For full details on the activities of the Assembly of Captive Nations directed toward the United Nations, see the *ACEN News*, the Assembly's newsletter, from the 1950s to the 1970s, Reel 1, Right-Wing Collection of the University of Iowa.

48. *ACEN News*, July–September 1960, pp. 6–7, Reel 1, Right-Wing Collection of the University of Iowa.

49. See ibid.

50. "Does Liberation Mean War?" *ACEN News*, June–August, 1957, p. 3.

51. In 1960 ACEN honored Captive Nations and China Lobby supporter Senator Thomas Dodd (D-CT) with a testimonial dinner. Dodd later joined ACEN chair Vaclovas Sigzikauskas at a May 1961 Asian People's Anti-Communist League conference in Manila, Philippines, where Dodd pledged that the United States was "prepared to fight" Communism in Southeast Asia. See "Senator Dodd Honored by ACEN at Testimonial Dinner," *ACEN News*, November 1960, p. 9;

and "ACEN Chairman at APACL Conference in Manila—May 2–5, 1961," *ACEN News*, April–May, 1961, p. 23; both articles on Right-Wing Collection of the University of Iowa, Reel 1.

52. See *Group Research Report*, Directory, 1962–1970, special report dated May 25, 1962.

53. "Group Lists Data on 'Subversives,'" *New York Times*, July 10, 1958, p. 56.

54. ASC, quoted in *Group Research Report*, Directory 1962–1970, special report dated May 25, 1962. ASC claimed that "During 1960, eight government agencies and two Congressional committees obtained information from the Council's Research and Information Center on a regular basis."

55. Updated American Security Council brochure, Reel 13, Right-Wing Collection of the University of Iowa.

56. Bellant, op cit., pp. 31–33.

57. Ibid., p. 33.

58. Harold C. Relyea, "The American Security Council," *Nation*, January 24, 1972, p. 115. The Institute for American Security's board of advisors overlapped with the leadership of the American Security Council.

59. Gene M. Lyons and Louis Morton, "Schools for Strategy," *Bulletin of Atomic Scientists*, March 1961, pp. 103–106.

60. Ibid., p. 103.

61. "Memorandum Submitted to Department of Defense on Propaganda Activities of Military Personnel," *Congressional Record*, August 2, 1961, p. 14433.

62. Ibid., pp. 14434–14436.

63. On the right-wing response to the Fulbright memorandum, see J. Allen Broyles, *The John Birch Society: Anatomy of a Protest* (Boston: Beacon Press, 1964), pp. 104–106; and Seymour Martin Lipset and Earl Raab, *The Politics of Unreason: Right-Wing Extremism in America, 1790-1970* (New York: Harper & Row, 1970), pp. 314–315.

64. American Security Council, "Council Notes," October 23, 1962, Reel 13, Right-Wing Collection of the University of Iowa.

65. American Security Council, "Council Notes," November 27, 1962, Reel 13, Right-Wing Collection of the University of Iowa.

66. American Security Council, "Council Notes," October 26, 1964, Reel 13, Right-Wing Collection of the University of Iowa. ASC reported that most local station sponsors were not ASC member companies. Those that were included Motorola, Inc.; Bourns, Inc.; and the Albuquerque Sand and Gravel Company.

67. *Group Research Report*, September 15, 1964, p. 67.

68. Institute for American Strategy, "Progress Memo: 1963 Conference on Cold War Education," Box 33, file: Institute for American Strategy, Henry Regnery Collection, Hoover Institution Archives, Stanford University.

69. Institute for American Strategy, "1964 Program into Home Stretch," Box 33, file: Institute for American Strategy, Henry Regnery Collection, Hoover Institution Archives, Stanford University.

70. Letter from John M. Fisher to Henry Regnery, June 16, 1965; Box 33, file: Institute for American Strategy, Henry Regnery Collection, Hoover Institution Archives, Stanford University. In this letter, IAS President Fisher refers to a fundraising proposal for a private freedom academy. Fisher writes that Profes-

sor James D. Atkinson, who headed the Psychological Warfare School conducted by the Defense Department at Georgetown University, "is working for us full time this summer." Also working full time for the Institute, Fisher writes, was Major General Edward M. Lansdale, USAF (Ret.), the "father of counterinsurgency." Fisher notes that Lansdale was the key advisor to Philippines President Ramon Magsaysay and, later, to President Diem in South Vietnam.

71. Undated memorandum, Box 14, file: "Freedom Academy, 1959–82," Marx Lewis Collection, Hoover Institution Archives, Stanford University.

72. Frank Rockwell Barnett, "What is to Be Done?" in Walter F. Hahn and John C. Neff, eds., *American Strategy for the Nuclear Age* (New York: Anchor Books, 1960), pp. 447–448.

73. See "Freedom Commission and Freedom Academy," House of Representatives Report No. 1050, December 15, 1967, for a history of the bill's unsuccessful passage through Congress and the Senate. For more history on the failed Freedom Academy bill, see "The Story of the Council Against Communist Aggression: 20 Years on Active Duty, 1950–1970," Box 226, file: Council Against Communist Aggression, 1963–1980, Walter H. Judd Collection, Hoover Institution Archives, Stanford University.

74. See organizational membership lists, brochures, and policy platforms of the American Coalition of Patriotic Societies, Reel 5, Right-Wing Collection of the University of Iowa.

75. Space limitations preclude a thorough discussion of this under-researched organization and its role in the aftermath of World War II and the beginning of the Cold War. See, generally, *Group Research Report*, special report dated November 23, 1966. For conference details and statements by U.S. military and labor leaders, see *New York Times* dispatches, dated July 29, 1947; September 1, 1947; September 6, 1947; September 7, 1947; September 8, 1947; November 23, 1947; and November 26, 1947. For MRA's descriptions of its role within anticommunist labor unions in the United States and abroad, see Right-Wing Collection of the University of Iowa, Reel 78. For MRA's reports of its work with foreign political leaders during the Cold War, see "MRA Information Service," Reel 75, Right-Wing Collection of the University of Iowa. "MRA Information Service," vol. 1, no. 1, June 1952, reports that Radio Free Europe broadcast MRA programs "across the Iron Curtain."

76. For a thorough treatment of racist and anti-Semitic organizations active from a time span including the World War II years and the aftermath, see, esp. Arnold Forster, *A Measure of Freedom* (New York: Doubleday, 1950).

77. On the Congress of Freedom, see the summary report in *Group Research Directory*, 1962–1970. See also Reel 36, Right-Wing Collection of the University of Iowa, for Congress for Freedom ephemera, including the published conference proceedings from the group's April 1955 San Francisco conference, "The Truth About the United Nations." One of the leaders of the Congress of Freedom, and Chairman of the 1955 San Francisco conference, was Willis Carto, founder of the Liberty Lobby in 1958. See also Gene Marine, "The U.N. Haters," *Nation*, May 14, 1955, pp. 419–421. On the "Liberty Amendment," see, e.g., Willis E. Stone's *American Progress* magazine, Reel 7, Right-Wing Collection of the University of Iowa.

78. Alan F. Westin, "Anti-Communism and the Corporations," *Commentary*, December 1963, pp. 479–487.

79. Ibid.

80. See "Patriotic Program Log" and other Coast Federal Savings brochures and newsletters, Reel 36, Right-Wing Collection of the University of Iowa.

81. See Fred J. Cook, "Hate Clubs of the Air," *Nation*, May 25, 1964, pp. 523–527.

82. On John Birch, see, e.g., "Who Was John Birch?" *Time*, April 14, 1961, p. 29. On Welch's background and his admiration of John Birch, see Broyles, op cit., pp. 22–43.

83. The Blue Book of the John Birch Society (Belmont, MA: Western Islands, 1959), pp. 21, 60.

84. Broyles, op cit., p. 103.

85. Alan F. Westin, "The John Birch Society: Fundamentalism on the Right," *Commentary*, August 1961, p. 99.

86. See *The Blue Book of the John Birch Society*, op cit., 169–172. Of the original twenty-six members of the John Birch Society National Council, those best known or who continued as important right-wing activists were Thomas J. Anderson, publisher of "Straight Talk" editorials and a leader in the American Independent Party; A. Clifford Barker, who remained a prominent Birch leader; Clarence E. Manion, former dean of Notre Dame Law School and director of the "Manion Forum" radio and television program; Lawrence P. McDonald, M.D., who represented Georgia in the House of Representatives until his death aboard KAL-007 in September 1983. Broyles, op cit., pp. 48–50 identifies new Council members as of 1964. These included Fred C. Koch, president of Rock Island Oil and Refining Company. The Koch fortune, administered by Koch's son Charles Koch, later became a major resource for the libertarian movement of the 1970s and 1980s.

87. Westin, op cit., p. 93. See also, "Birch Group Lists Units in 34 States," *New York Times*, April 12, 1961, which cites a Birch Society member's claim of 1000,000 members by 1961.

88. See Fred W. Grupp, Jr., "The Political Perspectives of Birch Society Members," in Robert A. Schoenberger, ed., *The American Right Wing: Readings in Political Behavior* (Holt, Rinehart & Winston, 1969), pp. 83–118. Grupp's study was conducted with the approval of the John Birch Society Council, which normally maintained intense secrecy about membership. Surveys were mailed to a geographically distributed sample, with a mildly endorsing cover letter signed by Robert Welch. Of the 650 responses Grupp received, a disproportionate number (21 percent) indicated that they were chapter leaders or other John Birch Society officials.

89. Broyles, op cit., p. 143.

90. Ibid., p. 151.

91. Seymour Martin Lipset and Earl Raab, *The Politics of Unreason: Right-Wing Extremism in America, 1790–1970* (New York: Harper & Row, 1970) pp. 250–257.

92. "Senator Scores Group Calling Eisenhower a Red," *New York Times*, March 9, 1961.

93. Representative John Rousselot (R-CA) was named as a John Birch Society member and said he welcomed a Congressional investigation to clear the group's name. "Rousselot a Member," *New York Times*, April 1, 1961. On other elected officials' responses, see "John Birch Society is Held 'Patriotic,'" *New York Times*, March 21, 1961; "Birch Group Stirs Dispute on Coast," *New York Times*, March 26, 1961; "Inquiry is Sought on Birch Society," *New York Times*, March 31, 1961; and "Birch Group Head Asks U.S. Inquiry," *New York Times*, April 2, 1961.

94. "Birch Unit Pushes Drive on Warren," *New York Times*, April 1, 1961.

95. On the Walker affair, see "Birch Unit Ideas Put to U.S. Troops," *New York Times*, April 14, 1961; "General Walker Denies Charge of Link to John Birch Society," *New York Times*, April 15, 1961, p. 22; "Walker is Relieved of Command While Army Checks Birch Ties," *New York Times*, April 18, 1961, p. 1; and "Walker Resigns from the Army," *New York Times*, November 3, 1961, pp. 1, 22.

96. "Right-Wing Officers Worrying Pentagon," *New York Times*, June 18, 1961, pp. 1, 56.

97. "Birch Group Lists Units in 34 States," op cit., and "6,000 Hear Welch in Coast Address," *New York Times*, April 12, 1961.

98. See "Right-Wing Groups Multiplying Appeals in Southern California," *New York Times*, October 29, 1961, and Fred J. Cook, "The Ultras," *Nation*, June 30, 1962, p. 576.

    On business backing for anticommunist organizations, see "Aid to Right Wing Laid to Big Firms," *New York Times*, September 20, 1964, pp. 1, 73. The Anti-Defamation League of B'nai B'rith reported an annual budget of about $14 million for groups including the John Birch Society, Christian Anti-Communism Crusade, Billy James Hargis' Christian Crusade, Church League of America, Kent and Phoebe Courtney's Conservative Society, and Willis Stone's Liberty Amendment Committee. Heavy contributors included U.S. Steel, Republic Steel, Gulf Oil, and Humble Oil and Refining Company, as well as the Allen-Bradley Foundation, the Donner Foundation, and others.

99. Ibid. Schwarz's faculty included former FBI agent Herbert Philbrick; Richard Arens, then staff director for the House Un-American Activities Committee; and Professor Anthony Bouscaren of LeMoyne College.

    The May 19, 1964 issue of *National Review* advertised a June 15–19, 1964 Christian Anti-Communism Crusade school in Washington, D.C. Faculty included Philbrick and Bouscaren, plus Yale political science professor David N. Rowe; Serafino Romualdi, then executive director of the American Institute for Free Labor Development; Georgetown political science professor James D. Atkinson; Charles Lowry, president of the Foundation for Religious Action in the Social and Civil Order; and Serafin Menocal, identified as a former top executive in Cuba's Power and Light company. See also "Anti-Red Dispute Grips Illinois," *New York Times*, May 21, 1961, p. 54, and "TV: Christian Anti-Communism Crusade Here," *New York Times*, November 3, 1961. Schwarz's main benefactor was Patrick Frawley of Schick Safety Razor Company and Technicolor Corporation.

100. Raymond E. Wolfinger et al., "America's Radical Right: Politics and Ideology,"

in David E. Apter, ed., *Ideology and Discontent* (New York: Free Press, 1964).

101. On the Minutemen, see esp. J. Harry Jones, Jr., *The Minutemen* (New York: Doubleday, 1968); William W. Turner, *Power on the Right* (Berkeley: Ramparts Press, 1971), pp. 63–90; and "Minutemen Guerrilla Unit Found to be Small and Loosely Knit," *New York Times*, November 12, 1961, pp. 1, 76.

102. On Taft's track record in the immediate post-World War II period, see for example Kenneth Crawford, "Taft the Presidential Candidate," *The American Mercury*, June 1948, pp. 647–653.

103. On Taft versus Eisenhower, see David W. Reinhard, *The Republican Right Since 1945* (Lexington: University Press of Kentucky, 1983), pp. 75–96.

104. On the history of the *American Mercury*, see for example, John B. Judis, *William F. Buckley, Jr.: Patron Saint of the Conservatives* (New York: Simon and Schuster, 1988), pp. 103, 112, 173–174. In the 1950s the *American Mercury* had a circulation of about 90,000 and published articles by Buckley and other eventual contributors to *National Review*. A change in the magazine's editorial directorship, in 1952, led to the *Mercury*'s turn toward anti-Semitic content under editor Russell Maguire. In January of 1959, Maguire published an anti-Semitic editorial. Buckley then circulated a memo to *National Review* writers to the effect that he would not allow on his magazine's masthead any writer who also appeared on the *Mercury*'s masthead. The *American Mercury* eventually faded into obscurity as *National Review* became more prominent.

105. See the following *American Mercury* articles: editorial, "In The Mercury's Opinion," March 1952; "Freedom's Case Against Dean Acheson," April 1952; "In The Mercury's Opinion," June 1952; and "In The Mercury's Opinion," September 1952.

106. Patrick McMahon, "Third Party Coming?" *American Mercury*, August 1953, p. 42. McMahon was the *American Mercury*'s Washington, D.C. editor.

107. Harold Lord Varney, "Is the Republican Party Committing Suicide?" *American Mercury*, July 1954, p. 8.

108. Harold Lord Varney, "Eisenhower Midway," *American Mercury*, March 1955, p. 15.

109. Reinhard, op cit., pp. 116–117.

110. "National Review and the 1960 Elections," *National Review*, October 22, 1960, p. 234.

111. Bozell, "The Challenge to Conservatives, II," *National Review*, January 4, 1961, p. 12.

112. *Congressional Record*, August 4, 1958, p. 14558. See "Group to Defend Free Enterprise," *New York Times*, August 5, 1958, and *Group Research Report*, special July 20, 1962 report on ACA.

113. *Group Research Report* on ACA, op cit. "Group of Conservatives Assigns Secret Aides to 46 Candidates," *New York Times*, October 22, 1962.

    See also ACA materials, Reel 13, Right-Wing Collection of the University of Iowa. In one brochure ACA reports that in 1960 it assisted 180 Senatorial and Congressional candidates and that 74 percent of these won; in 1962 73 percent of ACA-endorsed candidates won. ACA did not claim that its assistance alone accounted for candidates' victory.

114. For the full Sharon Statement, see *National Review*, September 24, 1960, p. 173, and the accompanying article by William F. Buckley, Jr.
115. "18,000 Rightists Rally at Garden," *New York Times*, March 8, 1962, pp. 1, 22; "Notes from the YAF Rally," *National Review*, March 27, 1962, pp. 190–191
116. See YAF Executive Secretary Richard A. Viguerie's letter to YAF supporters, September 1962, plus fundraising letters, convention materials, and newsletters, Reel 154, Right-Wing Collection of the University of Iowa.

    YAF's National Advisory Board included Congressional members: Representatives John M. Ashbrook, Donald C. Bruce, Robert H. Michel, and John H. Rousselot; and Senators Barry M. Goldwater, Strom Thurmond, and John G. Tower. Non-Congressional members included Professor Anthony T. Bouscaren, L. Brent Bozell, William F. Buckley, Jr., Frank Chodorov, Ralph de Toledano, Lev Dobriansky, M. Stanton Evans, Russell Kirk, Frank Meyer, Ludwig von Mises, Ronald Reagan, William Rusher, and John Wayne.
117. See obituary for *Human Events* president James L. Wick, *Human Events*, November 21, 1964, p. 3.
118. See reports on the Political Action Conferences in *Human Events* for the following dates: December 29, 1960; July 28, 1961; January 20, 1962; May 26, 1962; December 22, 1962; December 29, 1962; January 26, 1963; July 6, 1963.

    The *Human Events* conferences eventually developed into the Conservative Political Action Conference (CPAC) held annually from the 1960s to the 1990s.
119. Senator Strom Thurmond, "Why I am a Republican for Goldwater," *Human Events*, September 26, 1964, p. 15.
120. William A. Rusher, *The Rise of the Right* (New York: William Morrow, 1984), p. 98. See also F. Clifton White, *Suite 3505: The Story of the Draft Goldwater Movement* (New Rochelle, NY: Arlington House, 1967), and Robert D. Novak, *The Agony of the G.O.P. 1964* (New York: Macmillan, 1965).
121. Reinhard, op cit., p. 161.
122. Even before the John Birch Society was formally organized, the second issue of Robert Welch's *American Opinion* featured a promotional biography of Barry Goldwater. See "A Fighter from Phoenix," *American Opinion*, March 1958.
123. Reinhard, op cit., p. 159.
124. Nicol C. Rae, *The Decline and Fall of the Liberal Republicans: From 1952 to the Present* (New York: Oxford University Press, 1989), p. 57.
125. Rusher, op cit., p. 166.
126. *Human Events* published the text of Reagan's speech, after Barry Goldwater's defeat, in its November 28, 1964 issue, with a photo caption noting Reagan's recent switch to the Republican Party. See also, Rusher, op cit., pp. 173–174, regarding the Goldwater campaign as the start of Reagan's political career.
127. William A. Rusher, "Crossroads for the GOP," *National Review*, February 12, 1963, p. 111.

    On the southern and western demographic base of the GOP's Goldwater wing, see Rae, op cit., pp. 49–58.
128. Henry J. Taylor, "Barry's 'No' Vote is Setback for LBJ," *Human Events*, July 4, 1964, p. 1. See also Representative Louis C. Wyman, "Civil Rights Bill: Blatantly Unconstitutional," *Human Events*, February 29, 1964, p. 9. On

right-wing activist support for Goldwater's vote against civil rights bills, see "ACA Newsletter," August 10, 1964, Reel 1, Right-Wing Collection of the Universiy of Iowa.

129. Reinhard, op cit., pp. 162–163.

130. Ibid., p. 194.

131. Ibid., pp. 196–199.

132. "The Question of Robert Welch," *National Review*, February 13, 1962, pp. 83–88, and "Goldwater and the John Birch Society," *National Review*, November 19, 1963, p. 430.

133. Arnold Forster and Benjamin R. Epstein, *Danger on the Right* (New York: Random House, 1964), pp. 20–21, 152–155, and passim. See also William F. Buckley, Jr., "The Vile Campaign," *National Review*, October 6, 1964, pp. 853–858.

134. See "The John Birch Society and the Conservative Movement," *National Review*, October 19, 1965, pp. 914–929, esp. p. 920.

135. Theodore H. White, *The Making of the President, 1964*, (New York: Atheneum, 1965), p. 380.

136. Reinhard, op cit., pp. 206–207.

137. Ibid., pp. 206–208.

138. See Kevin Phillips, *The Emerging Republican Majority* (New Rochelle, NY: Arlington House, 1969), *inter alia*, for demographic data on the 1964 Johnson versus Goldwater campaign. Phillips' study begins and ends with an analysis of how Republicans could utilize the "Wallace factor" and extend the Republicans' base of support from Richard Nixon's 1968 victory forward.

139. See letter from the Law Offices of Robb, Porter, Kistler, and Parkinson to Representative Donald C. Bruce, December 4, 1964, regarding the legal and tax status of the American Conservative Union, Box 6, file: American Conservative Union, Stanley Hornbeck Collection, Hoover Institution Archives, Stanford University.

   See also, "American Conservative Union, Confidential Preliminary Report," Box 6, file: American Conservative Union, Stanley Hornbeck Collection, Hoover Institution Archives, Stanford University.

   Among the original founders of ACU listed were Representative John Ashbrook, Robert E. Bauman, L. Brent Bozell, Representative Donald C. Bruce, William F. Buckley, Jr., John Chamberlain, Lee Edwards, Dr. John A. Howard, Howard Kershner, James Jackson Kilpatrick, General Thomas J. Lane, Frank Meyer, Admiral Ben Moreell, Dr. Stefan Possony, Henry Regnery, William Rusher, Ralph de Toledano.

140. Patrick J. Buchanan, "Introduction," in Barry Goldwater, *The Conscience of a Conservative* (Washington, DC: Regnery Gateway, 1990), pp. x–xxi.

NOTES TO CHAPTER 3

1. V. O. Key, Jr., *Southern Politics in State and Nation* (Knoxville: University of Tennessee Press [1949] 1986), p. 9.

2. See Everett Carl Ladd, Jr., and Charles D. Hadley, *Transformations of the*

American Party System: Political Coalitions from the New Deal to the 1970s (New York: Norton, 1978), esp. pp. 31–87.

3. Ibid., pp. 129–135.

4. Doug McAdam, *Political Process and the Development of Black Insurgency, 1930–1970* (University of Chicago Press, 1982), p. 82. See also, generally, pp. 77–86.

    For a thorough history of the southern Democratic Party and its influence on the rest of the political system, see especially Nicol C. Rae, *Southern Democrats,* (New York: Oxford University Press, 1994).

5. Ibid., pp. 84–86. For an in-depth treatment of Eisenhower's record on civil rights, see Robert Fredrick Burk, *The Eisenhower Administration and Black Civil Rights* (Knoxville: University of Tennessee Press, 1984).

6. Political context, indigenous resources, and collective attribution are the three major factors that McAdam, op cit., uses in his political process explanation of the black-led civil rights movement.

7. Arnold S. Rice, *The Ku Klux Klan in American Politics* (Washington, DC: Public Affairs Press, 1962), p. 108.

8. Ibid., pp. 108–109.

9. Ibid., pp. 110–114. See also Wyn Craig Wade, *The Fiery Cross: The Ku Klux Klan in America* (New York: Simon and Schuster, 1987), pp. 279–280.

10. Rice, op cit., pp. 115–118.

11. See, e.g., G. Theodore Mitau, *Decade of Decision: The Supreme Court and the Constitutional Revolution 1954–1964* (New York: Charles Scribner's Sons, 1967), pp. 51–57.

12. J. Harvie Wilkinson III, *From Brown to Bakke: The Supreme Court and School Integration: 1954–1978* (New York: Oxford University Press, 1979), p. 24.

    See also Numan Bartley, *The Rise of Massive Resistance: Race and Politics in the South During the 1950s* (Baton Rouge: Louisiana State University Press, 1969), pp. 61–66 regarding Eisenhower's general support for desegregation, but hesitance to use the power of federal government in matters of "states' rights."

13. See ibid., pp. 67–81 for detail on specific states' legislative responses.

14. Ibid., p. 84 and passim.

15. Tom P. Brady, *Black Monday* (Winona, MS: Association of Citizens' Councils, 1955), p. 2.

16. Ibid., p. 84.

17. Neil R. McMillen, *The Citizens' Council: Organized Resistance to the Second Reconstruction, 1954–64* (Urbana: University of Illinois Press, 1971), pp. 18–19.

18. Ibid., pp. 20–22. On Patterson's and the Councils' recommendation of racist and anti-Semitic literature, see also John Bartlow Martin, *The Deep South Says "Never"* (New York: Ballantine Books, 1957), p. 15.

19. Bartley, op cit., pp. 84–85; McMillen, op cit., pp. 27–28.

20. McMillen, op cit., pp. 28–29.

21. Bartley, op cit., p. 90.

22. Ibid., pp. 85–86.

23. Ibid., p. 124.

24. Andrew Michael Manis, *Southern Civil Religions in Conflict: Black and White Baptists and Civil Rights, 1947–1957* (Athens: University of Georgia Press), 1987, pp. 24–26.

25. Robert B. Patterson, "Second Annual Report," August 1956, Association of Citizens' Councils, p. 2, Reel 9, Right-Wing Collection of the University of Iowa.
26. "The Citizens' Councils . . . Their Platform," undated brochure distributed by the Association of Citizens' Councils of Louisiana, Reel 9, Right-Wing Collection of the University of Iowa.
27. Ibid.
28. Ibid.
29. See "Second Annual Report," August 1956, Association of Citizens' Councils of Mississippi, Reel 9, Right-Wing Collection of the University of Iowa.
30. Hodding Carter III, *The South Strikes Back* (New York: Doubleday, 1959), p. 41.
31. See Ibid., p. 46. Because the bills were strongly approved in counties already known as bastions of segregationism, Hodding Carter, a prominent southern critic of segregation, was highly skeptical of the Councils' self-proclaimed role.
32. Eastland, quoted in Carter, op cit., p. 61.
33. Ibid., p. 62.
34. Ibid., p. 63.
35. Quoted in ibid.
36. Bartley, op cit., p. 180.
37. Ibid., p. 181.
38. Ibid., pp. 182–189.
39. McMillen, op cit., p. 38.
40. W. J. Simmons, "The Reason for 'Race and Reason,'" *The Citizen*, November 1961, pp. 5–6.
41. See Carleton Putnam, *Race and Reason: A Yankee View* (Washington, DC: Public Affairs Press, 1961) for the story of his letter-writing campaigns and for his biological determinist views. Three "biological scientists" wrote the introduction to *Race and Reason*.
42. "'Race and Reason' to Be Studied in Louisiana Schools," of the July 25, 1961 Louisiana State Board of Education resolution, published in *The Citizen*, November 1961, p. 34.
43. Governor Ross R. Barnett, October 26, 1961 proclamation, reproduced in *The Citizen*, November 1961, p. 4.
    The entire November 1961 issue of *The Citizen* was devoted to honoring Carleton Putnam, his letter-writing campaign, and his book *Race and Reason*.
44. The complete list was published in *The Citizen*, November 1961, pp. 42–45. See the rest of the issue for descriptions of the banquet.
45. McMillen, op cit., pp. 322–325.
46. On the Councils' economic retaliation tactics, see Carter, op cit., pp. 114–115 and passim; Martin, op cit., pp. 20, 25–26 and passim.
47. Quoted in Martin, ibid., p. 24.
48. Carter, op cit., p. 122.
49. Wade, op cit., p. 300.
50. Ibid., pp. 300–302.
51. James W. Vander Zanden, *Race Relations in Transition: The Segregation Crisis in the South* (New York: Random House, 1965), pp. 26–44.
52. Ibid., p. 41.

53. The complicated story is told in McMillen, op cit., pp. 47–58. See also Martin, op cit., pp. 116–123 regarding Ace Carter's racist and anti-Semitic activities.
54. The story is told in Wade, op cit., p. 303, and James Graham Cook, *The Segregationists* (New York: Appleton-Century-Crofts, 1962), pp. 140–144.
55. Wade, op cit., p. 303.
56. Quoted in Carter, op cit., p. 51.
57. From "The Citizens' Council is Your Protection Against Integrated Schools, Mongrelization and Red Tyranny," undated South Louisiana Citizens' Council ephemera, Reel 127, Right-Wing Collection of the University of Iowa.
58. Daniel Bell, ed., *The Radical Right* (New York: Doubleday, 1963) is the classic collection of pluralist scholars' essays on McCarthy era "radical right" groups.
    See also Seymour Martin Lipset, *Political Man* (New York: Doubleday, 1963), especially his chapter on "Working-Class Authoritarianism," p. 87, where he points to "southern workers' support of the White Citizens' Councils" but does not address the actual elite base of the Councils.
59. Seymour Martin Lipset and Earl Raab, *The Politics of Unreason: Right-Wing Extremism in America, 1790–1970* (New York: Harper & Row, 1970) pp. 4–7.
60. See ibid., pp. 14–17 and passim, for a cogent analysis of the conspiracist mind-set of the movements chronicled.
61. On segregationism as a resistance movement, and comparing the Klan with the Citizens' Councils, see James W. Vander Zanden, "A Note on the Theory of Social Movements," *Sociology and Social Research*, XLIV (September–October, 1959), pp. 3–7. See also James W. Vander Zanden, *Race Relations in Transition*, op cit., pp. 84–99.
62. See, e.g., the following articles in *The Citizen*: "Is It 'Civil Rights' or Federal Tyranny?" April 1964, p. 5; "Official Council Statements On The 'Civil Rights Act,'" July–August, 1964, pp. 6–9; William J. Simmons, "Report on a Trip to Southern Africa," July–August, 1966, pp. 4–5, with an accompanying interview with Rhodesian Prime Minister Ian Smith in the same issue; William K. Shearer, "Is U.S. Involvement in Vietnam Necessary?" March 1967, pp. 4–5.
    One frequent contributor to *The Citizen* during the 1960s was Jesse Helms, who was a broadcast journalist and editorial writer in Raleigh, North Carolina long before he first ran for office. Helms wrote extensively for *The Citizen*, against the civil rights movement and in favor of the southern "way of life." See, e.g., "Why Do They Lie About the South?" March 1962; and "The Stacked Deck and Blackmail Power," April 1968.
63. See Kenneth O'Reilly, *"Racial Matters": The FBI's Secret File on Black America, 1960–1972* (New York: The Free Press, 1989).
64. Bartley, op cit., pp. 251–252, notes that white Arkansans were not as staunchly pro-segregationist as their counterparts in the Deep South. In November 1956 almost half of Little Rock's voters opposed a Citizens' Council-sponsored constitutional amendment nullifying the *Brown* decision. When the city's token desegregation plan of March 1957 was challenged in school board elections, racial moderates defeated staunch segregationist candidates.
65. See Ibid., pp. 252–265, for details on all the maneuvering that precipitated the Little Rock crisis. Bartley disputes one conventional view, that Governor Faubus unilaterally provoked the crisis for cynical political advantage. Instead, Bartley portrays

the crisis as the result of an "accumulation of failures" by state and local leaders who did not prepare a concrete plan for orderly desegregation.

66. Wilkinson, op cit., pp. 94–95.

67. See Bartley, op cit., pp. 270–278.

68. See James L. Sundquist, *Politics and Policy: The Eisenhower, Kennedy, and Johnson Years* (Washington, DC: Brookings Institution, 1968), pp. 221–238, for detailed analysis of the politics and events leading to passage of the 1957 Civil Rights Act.

69. See the following *New York Times* reports: "House Passes Rights Bill, Senators Rule Out a Delay," August 28, 1957, pp. 1, 55; "Thurmond Talks Hours on Rights," August 29, 1957, p. 1; "Senate Votes Rights Bill and Sends it to President, Thurmond Talks 24 Hours," August 30, 1957, p. 1; "Congress Closes as House Passes Aid and F.B.I. Bills," August 31, 1957, p. 1.

70. On implementation of the 1957 Civil Rights Act's creation of the Civil Rights Commission and the Justice Department's own investigative division, see Robert Fredrick Burk, *The Eisenhower Administration and Black Civil Rights* (Knoxville: University of Tennessee Press, 1984) pp. 228–270.

71. Douglas quoted in Sundquist, op cit., p. 235.

72. See the following *New York Times* reports: "Strongest Plank on Rights Voted Over Threat of Fight," July 12, 1960, pp. 1, 22; "Nixon–Rockefeller Plank on Rights Sets Off Fight," July 25, 1960, pp. 1, 15; "Rockefeller Ready to Fight on Floor for Rights Plank," July 25, 1960, pp. 1, 16; "Republican Platform Approves Strengthened Plank on Civil Rights," July 27, 1960, p. 18.

73. "Democrats Face A Fight for South," *New York Times*, July 24, 1960, p. 42.

74. See Hugh Davis Graham, *Civil Rights and the Presidency: Race and Gender in American Politics, 1960–1972* (New York: Oxford University Press, 1992), pp. 67–86.

75. On the long-term results of the Voting Rights Act, see for example Lani Guinier, *The Tyranny of the Majority: Fundamental Fairness in Representative Democracy* (New York: Free Press, 1994), esp. Chapter 3, "The Triumph of Tokenism," pp. 41–70.

76. Bartley, op cit., pp. 83–84.

77. *First National Directory of "Rightist" Groups, Publications and Some Individuals in the United States (and Some Foreign Countries)* (San Francisco: Liberty and Property, 1957).

   The number of listings is inflated by the inclusion of several dozen "Congressmen who vote reliably anti-communist and nationalist but unreliably on government spending and/or 'civil rights'"; and by the duplication of organizations and their publications. For example, the Church League of America and its organ, *News and Views* are listed separately, as are Liberty and Property and *Right*.

   For an earlier, useful source that describes some of the post-World War II right-wing groups not covered in Willis Carto's 1957 *Directory*, see Arnold Forster, *A Measure of Freedom: An Anti-Defamation League Report* (New York: Doubleday, 1950).

78. See, esp., Frank P. Mintz, *The Liberty Lobby and the American Right: Race, Conspiracy, and Culture* (Westport, CT: Greenwood Press, 1985).

79. See Congress of Freedom, 1955 convention materials, which includes Willis Carto listed as the chairman of the Convention Committee, Reel 36, Right-Wing Collection of the University of Iowa.

    On the Congress of Freedom, see esp. *Group Research Directory, 1962–1970* Section 1, Organizational Report, dated May 26, 1966. On the 1955 convention, see Gene Marine, "The U.N. Haters," *Nation*, May 14, 1955. For details on other meetings of the Congress, see, e.g., *Group Research Report*, April 28, 1966, p. 31, and May 15, 1968, p. 33.

80. See, e.g., *Right*, no. 1, October 1955, and no. 3, December 1955. A complete collection of *Right* is available on Reel 103, Right-Wing Collection of the University of Iowa.

81. *Right*, December 1955, pp. 2–3.

82. *Right*, October 1955, p. 3; January 1956, p. 3; June 1958, p. 1.

83. "The Right Line," *Right*, March 1956, p. 1.

84. "The Right Line," *Right*, May 1956, p. 1.

85. The complex relationship between the Liberty Lobby and the John Birch Society is treated in Mintz, op cit., pp. 141–162. Mintz calls the relationship "symbiotic."

86. *Right*, August 1957, p. 1.

87. Ibid. The other leaders, from the Citizens' Councils, *Christian Economics* magazine, We the People, the Liberty Amendment Committee, and other organizations were Mary D. Cain, Ralph Courtney, Lieutenant General P. A. del Valle, Robert B. Dresser, Harry T. Everingham, W. L. Foster, George B. Fowler, Percy Greaves, Dr. Bela Hubbard, Honorable J. Bracken Lee, Paul O. Peters, Robert B. Snowden, Willis E. Stone, Lieutenant General George E. Stratemeyer, and Edwin L. Wiegand.

88. See *Right*, December 1957, p. 6, promoting Pearson's *Northern World* journal and his article "The Analysis of Blood Groups as an Aid to the Study of History." Also, see *Right*, February 1958, p. 4. The June 1959 issue of *Right* led with an article on Roger Pearson's tour of the United States.

    On Pearson and WACL, see esp. Scott Anderson and Jon Lee Anderson, *Inside the League* (New York: Dodd, Mead, 1986), pp. 92–103.

    For background on Pearson's eugenicist work, see Stefan Kuhl, *The Nazi Connection: Eugenics, American Racism, and German National Socialism* (New York: Oxford University Press, 1994), pp. 3–11.

89. *Right*, July 1958, p. 1.

90. On the Constitution Party's founding and immediate internal faction fighting, see Arnold Forster and Benjamin R. Epstein, *Cross-Currents* (New York: Doubleday, 1956), pp. 54–90. Forster and Epstein, researchers for the Anti-Defamation League of B'nai B'rith, covered the Constitution Party's 1952 Chicago conference and identified veteran racist and anti-Semitic activists in leadership roles: Merwin K. Hart, Upton Close, Kenneth Goff, George Foster, W. Henry MacFarland, Jr., and Allen Zoll.

    See also these two brief *New York Times* articles: "New Party Formed to Back MacArthur," September 1, 1952, p. 8; and "Two Leaders Quit Party Over 'Anti-Semitism,'" September 2, 1952, p. 17.

91. Constitution Party, 1956 brochure, Reel 36, Right-Wing Collection of the University of Iowa.
92. "Declaration of Principles of the National States' Rights Conference," Constitution Party, September 14–15, 1956, Reel 36, Right-Wing Collection of the University of Iowa.
93. Constitution Party, 1956 campaign brochure, Reel 36, Right-Wing Collection of the University of Iowa.
94. "Campaign Note," *New York Times*, July 26, 1960, p. 19.
    The "newspaper of record" did not report election results for the Constitution Party in 1952, 1956, or 1990.
95. For sketchy details on the National States' Rights Party's origins, see ephemera, Reel 89, Right-Wing Collection of the University of Iowa.
96. Wade, op cit., p. 302. Stoner was indicted for the 1958 bombing of the Bethel Baptist Church in 1977 and convicted in 1990.
97. Ibid., p. 325.
98. "Sixth Annual National States' Rights Party Convention Report," Montgomery, Alabama, September 1–2, 1962, Reel 89, Right-Wing Collection of the University of Iowa.
99. Wallace's infamous "stand in the schoolhouse door" is detailed in Jody Carlson, *George C. Wallace and the Politics of Powerlessness: The Wallace Campaigns for the Presidency, 1964–1976* (New Brunswick, NJ: Transaction Books, 1981), pp. 24–26.
100. "Wallace Considers Primaries in North," *New York Times*, January 11, 1964, p. 11, and "Wallace Faces Wisconsin Fight," *New York Times*, May 8, 1964, p. 76.
101. Carlson, op cit., pp. 29–100.
102. Wallace, 1964 speech, quoted in ibid., p. 100.
103. Ibid., pp. 30–36.
104. " 'Hate' Groups Back Wallace Bid," *New York Times*, May 14, 1964, p. 27.
105. Michael Rogin, "Politics, Emotion, and the Wallace Vote," *British Journal of Sociology*, 20 (March 1969), p. 41.
106. One right-wing group, the National Conservative Council, which included John Birch Society leader Tom Anderson, threatened to form a third party and draft Wallace for president if the Republicans failed to nominate Goldwater. See "Rightists Warn of Third Party Step," *New York Times*, July 9, 1964, p. 18.
107. "Wallace Drops Presidency Bid, Denies Any Deals," *New York Times*, July 20, 1964, pp. 1, 12.
108. Carlson, op cit., p. 43.
109. "Right-Wing Party Favors Wallace," *New York Times*, July 19, 1964. Those who left the Constitution Party to join the Goldwater campaign included Kent and Phoebe Courtney, New Orleans publishers of the *Independent American* newspaper.
110. "Wallace Seeking Statesman Image," *New York Times*, September 6, 1965.
111. Carlson, op cit., pp. 69–71.
112. "Wallace Group on Coast Opens Campaign for 1968," *New York Times*, June 21, 1967, p. 28. "Proposition 14" was declared unconstitutional by the Supreme Court in 1967.

Shearer was an occasional contributor to *The Citizen*. See, e.g., "California Voters Win Big Victory in Battle Against Mixed Housing!" *The Citizen*, November 1964, pp. 8–12.

NOTES TO CHAPTER 4

1. In this book, the term *evangelical* is used to describe a range of conservative Christians. Many evangelicals are also *fundamentalists*, but the latter term has a pejorative connotation and, in common parlance, is often used inaccurately. Pentecostal or "charismatic" Christians do not typically identify themselves as "fundamentalists." *Fundamentalist* is used herein only in reference to individuals and groups who themselves use that term.

   For definitions of *evangelicalism*, see, e.g., James Davison Hunter, *American Evangelicalism: Conservative Religion and the Quandary of Modernity* (New Brunswick, NJ: Rutgers University Press, 1983), p. 7:

   > It may best be understood as a religiocultural phenomenon unique to North America, though clearly related in intimate ways to other forms of theologically conservative Protestantism in other times and places. The world view of Evangelicalism is deeply rooted in the theological tradition of the Reformation, in northern European Puritanism, and later in American Puritanism and the First and Second Great Awakenings in North America.... At the doctrinal core, contemporary Evangelicals can be identified by their adherence to (1) the belief that the Bible is the inerrant Word of God, (2) the belief in the divinity of Christ, and (3) the belief in the efficacy of Christ's life, death, and physical resurrection for the salvation of the human soul. Behaviorally, Evangelicals are typically characterized by an individuated and experiential orientation toward spiritual salvation and religiosity in general and by the conviction of the necessity of actively attempting to proselytize all non-believers to the tenets of the Evangelical belief system.

   Cf. Louis Gasper, *The Fundamentalist Movement* (The Hague, The Netherlands: Mouton, 1963), p. 13. Gasper defines *fundamentalism* as a movement

   > which arose in opposition to liberalism, reemphasizing the inerrancy of the Scriptures, separation and Biblical miracles, especially the Virgin Birth, the physical Resurrection of Christ, and the Substitutionary Atonement. In this respect, therefore, it represents a conservative reaction against the teachings of the modernists who declared that historic Protestant theology was incompatible with modern scientific discoveries and religious knowledge.

2. For Michael Rogin's use of the term *prepolitical*, see "Political Repression in the United States," in *Ronald Reagan the Movie, and Other Episodes in Political Demonology* (Berkeley: University of California Press, 1988), pp. 44–80. Rogin develops the *prepolitical* concept in order to account for "countersubversive" repression at a point prior to active dissent.

   The term *prepolitical* is used in this chapter in a manner complementary to Rogin's usage. Whereas Rogin uses *prepolitical* in reference to those "private" and cultural practices that effectively suppress potential opposition, I use *prepolitical* to refer to the way similar phenomena, i.e., religious activities, can account for the eventual mobilization of a system-supportive movement that attempts to repress other movements and to blunt processes of social change.

3. See Carol V. R. George, *God's Salesman: Norman Vincent Peale and the Power of Positive Thinking* (New York: Oxford University Press, 1993).

4. The term "parachurch" is not my own. It is a term used frequently by evangelicals in reference to what they call "ministries," or organizations that are not actually churches but serve to support church work. "Parachurch ministries" include a gamut of missionary, media and even research projects.

5. On the Christian Right's strategic transformation from large national campaigns during the early 1980s to more decentralized, local activism beginning in the late 1980s, see esp. Matthew C. Moen, *The Transformation of the Christian Right* (Tuscaloosa: University of Alabama Press, 1992).

6. On the Scopes trial, see, e.g., George M. Marsden, *Fundamentalism and American Culture: The Shaping of Twentieth Century Evangelicalism, 1870–1925*, (New York: Oxford University Press, 1980), pp. 184–195.

7. Ibid., pp. 189–94. See also Joel A. Carpenter, "Fundamentalist Institutions and the Rise of Evangelical Protestantism, 1929–1942," *Church History*, March 1980, pp. 62–75. Carpenter discusses the formation of numerous evangelical colleges, missions boards, and youth groups. Among the most prominent are Youth for Christ, the Slavic Gospel Association, Wycliffe Bible Translators, Moody Bible Institute, Bible Institute of Los Angeles (BIOLA), and others.

8. Gasper, op cit., pp. 15–17.

9. See Leo P. Ribuffo, *The Old Christian Right: The Protestant Far Right from the Great Depression to the Cold War* (Philadelphia: Temple University Press, 1983); and Glen Jeansonne, *Gerald L. K. Smith: Minister of Hate* (New Haven: CT: Yale University Press, 1988.) A useful contemporary study of the Christian Right during the 1940s and 1950s is Ralph Lord Roy, *Apostles of Discord* (Boston: Beacon Press, 1953).

On McIntire et al.'s contacts with anti-Semitic Christian groups, see Roy, pp. 199, 208–209, and passim. Harvey Springer, an executive officer of McIntire's International Council of Christian Churches, also worked with Gerald L. K. Smith and Gerald Winrod. Both Smith and Winrod backed McIntire's organizations.

10. Ribuffo, op cit., p. 87. In 1926, Winrod addressed the World Christian Fundamentals Association and was given a leadership position in that body. In 1935, the Bible Institute of Los Angeles (BIOLA) awarded Winrod an honorary doctorate of divinity.

11. Marsden, op cit., p. 199.

12. Ernest R. Sandeen, *The Roots of Fundamentalism: British and American Millenarianism, 1800–1930* (Chicago: University of Chicago Press, 1970), pp. 59–80 and passim.

13. See Timothy P. Weber, *Living in the Shadow of the Second Coming: American Premillennialism, 1875–1982* (Grand Rapids, MI: Zondervan, 1983); and Paul

Boyer, *When Time Shall Be No More: Prophecy Belief in Modern American Culture* (Cambridge, MA: The Belknap Press of Harvard University Press, 1992).

14. James Davison Hunter, *American Evangelicalism: Conservative Religion and the Quandary of Modernity* (New Brunswick, NJ: Rutgers University Press, 1983), p. 39.

15. Ibid., pp. 40–41.

16. Gasper, op cit., p. 23.

17. Ibid., p. 24.

18. See the National Association of Evangelicals' publication *United Evangelical Action*, no. 1, August 1, 1942 for NAE's doctrinal statement. NAE accepted only those churches that believed in the Bible as the "infallible Word of God," the trinity, the deity of Christ, the necessity of Holy Spirit regeneration, the resurrection of the "saved," and the "spiritual unity of believers."

19. On NAE's Washington, D.C. office, see *United Evangelical Action*, September 10, 1943, p. 1. On NAE's lobbying for representation among the U.S. armed forces' chaplaincy, see Gasper, op cit., pp. 25–29.

20. Ibid. pp. 30–34. Gasper qualifies this figure as tentative, because the American Council counted separately full-fledged "constituent" members and "auxiliary" members who still belonged to churches affiliated with the Federal Council of Churches. The accuracy of the American Council's reporting was also questionable.

21. Gasper, pp. 38–29, provides charts listing denominations included in both NAE and ACCC. For NAE, the 1956 denomination list includes numerical breakdowns; adding together the memberships of denominations with the names "pentecostal" and/or "holiness" yields a figure of about .5 million, or one-third of the total 1.5 million of all the denominations combined.

22. On the first World Council of Churches meeting and McIntire's counterconvention, see "Bells to Herald Church Assembly" and "Bible Body Lashes at World Council," *New York Times*, August 21, 1948, p. 16.

    The *Times* did not report that McIntire's International Council received major financial backing from Sun Oil owner J. Howard Pew. See Roy, op cit., pp. 302–304.

23. See, e.g., James DeForest Murch, "The Roosevelt Formula for a Vatican Envoy," *United Evangelical Action*, February 1, 1946, p. 3; and "America's Vatican Envoy Must Be Recalled Now," *United Evangelical Action*, March 15, 1946, p. 5.

24. George W. Robnett, "Our Schools in Danger of Centralized and Subversive Controls," *United Evangelical Action*, October 1, 1945, p. 6. Robnett was editor of *News and Views*, published by the National Laymen's Council of the Church League of America.

25. Glenwood Blackmore, "What's Wrong with FEPC?" *United Evangelical Action*, September 15, 1949, pp. 5–6. See also, *United Evangelical Action*'s editorial against the legislation, "Threats to Freedom," October 1, 1949, p. 11.

26. "NAE Convention Resolutions," *United Evangelical Action*, May 1, 1951, p. 6. Regarding "race principles," NAE took no position on civil rights issues per se.

27. "NAE Convention Resolutions," *United Evangelical Action*, June 1, 1954, p. 13.

28. "Text of Resolutions," *United Evangelical Action*, June 1961, pp. 21, 23.

29. See, e.g., Quentin J. Schultze, "The Wireless Gospel," *Christianity Today*, January

15, 1988, pp. 18–23. As early as 1930, fundamentalist broadcasters accounted for 246 of the 290 weekly fifteen-minute segments of Christian radio programming in Chicago alone. In 1939, Charles E. Fuller's "Old Fashioned Revival Hour" had the largest prime-time distribution of any radio program in the United States, with air time on 60 percent of all the licensed radio stations in the country, and a weekly audience estimated at twenty million.

30. See Jeffrey K. Hadden and Anson Shupe, *Televangelism: Power and Politics on God's Frontier* (New York: Henry Holt, 1988), pp. 47–50.

31. See "NRB Sees Great Gains in Radio–TV Cooperation," *United Evangelical Action*, March 1, 1957, p. 4. Eisenhower's telegram read, in part,

> In the world-wide competition for the allegiance of the minds of men, your presentation of truth and loyalty can be most effective. Through your broadcasts to the people of our country and abroad, the message you preach helps to inforce [*sic*] the spiritual stamina needed by mankind everywhere.

> Present at the panel discussion were leading Armed Forces chaplains, the deputy chief of the Education Division of Eisenhower's International Cooperation Administration; and the "religious adviser" for the "Voice of America," the U.S. government's shortwave radio propaganda project.

> *United Evangelical Action*'s report of administration officials' participation in the anticommunist panel at the 1957 convention includes the following cryptic passage: "Valuable 'behind the scenes' information was revealed concerning the encouragement the United States government is giving to every American agency engaged in the moral and religious amelioration of world problems."

32. Peter G. Horsfield, *Religious Television: The American Experience* (White Plains, NY: Longman, 1984), pp. 13–14.

33. I argued this point in Sara Diamond, *Spiritual Warfare: The Politics of the Christian Right* (Boston: South End Press, 1989).

34. Ibid., pp. 10–12.

35. Ben Bagdikian, *The Media Monopoly*, 2nd ed. (New York: Beacon Press, 1987), pp. 42–43. See "The New Evangelist," *Time*, October 25, 1954.

36. See, e.g., "Billy Graham Crusade Takes on the Big City," *New York Times*, May 19, 1957, p. E11.

37. Roy, op cit., pp. 294, 304

38. Diamond, op cit., p. 50.

39. Roy, op cit., 295.

40. *Right*, August 1957, p. 1., Reel 103, Right-Wing Collection of the University of Iowa.

41. Roy, op cit., p. 296.

42. Percy L. Greaves, Jr., "The Bricker Amendment," *Christian Economics*, January 26, 1954, pp. 1–2.

43. Percy L. Greaves, Jr., "Economic Equality," *Christian Economics*, January 27, 1953, pp. 1–2.

44. One Foundation for Economic Education (FEE) staff member, Congregational minister Russell J. Clinchy, was also a director of the Christian Freedom

Foundation, and a frequent contributor to *Christian Economics*. See Roy, op cit., p. 299.

45. "Why 'Christianity Today'?" *Christianity Today*, October 15, 1956, p. 20.

46. Billy Graham, "Biblical Authority in Evangelism," *Christianity Today*, October 15, 1956, p. 6.

47. William F. Knowland, "Admit Red China?" *Christianity Today*, October 29, 1956, pp. 10–11.

48. "Where Do We Go From Here?" *Christianity Today*, November 12, 1956, p. 18.

49. Ibid.

50. "The Church and the Race Problem," *Christianity Today*, March 18, 1957, pp. 20–22.

51. See, e.g., Billy Graham, "Facing the Anti-God Colossus," *Christianity Today*, December 21, 1962, pp. 6–8. In this article, in the wake of the "Cuban missile crisis," Graham reported on a trip to Latin America, and claimed that "Castro's agents are busy everywhere, and in some places such as Venezuela and Guatemala they have resorted to terrorism."

52. See J. Edgar Hoover's three-part series, "Red Goals and Christian Ideals," "Communist Propaganda and the Christian Pulpit," and "Soviet Rule or Christian Renewal," *Christianity Today*, October 10, 24, and November 7, 1960. See also J. Edgar Hoover, "Christianity Encounters Communism," *Christianity Today*, December 21, 1962.

    The November 7, 1960 issue of *Christianity Today* included a lengthy list of anticommunist books, compiled by Herbert Philbrick.

53. "A Statement of Policy," *News and Views*, July 1942, p. 3, Reel 86, Right-Wing Collection of the University of Iowa.

54. "Communism's Iron Grip on the U.S.A.," *News and Views*, August 17, 1940, pp. 1–2, Reel 86, Right-Wing Collection of the University of Iowa.

55. John T. Flynn, *The Smear Terror*, self-published in 1947; printed in entirety in the Church League's *News and Views*, no. 172 (supplement), Reel 86, Right-Wing Collection of the University of Iowa. The pamphlet was also serialized in the Chicago *Tribune* beginning on January 12, 1947.

56. John T. Flynn, *The Road Ahead: America's Creeping Revolution* (New York: Devin-Adair, 1949), pp. 106–119.

57. Roy, op cit., p. 232. Roy reported that more than 725,000 copies of *The Road Ahead* were distributed through the Committee for Constitutional Government, the anti-New Deal organization discussed herein in Chapter 1.

    The date of the *Reader's Digest* condensation of *The Road Ahead* was February, 1950.

58. See "Churchmen Assail Congress' Abuses in School Red Hunt," *New York Times*, March 12, 1953, pp. 1, 13; and "Red Inquiry Group Assails Chairman," *New York Times*, March 11, 1953, p. 12.

    Carl McIntire's fundamentalist American Council of Christian Churches circulated a petition requesting that Congress investigate "the infiltration of Communists into religious organizations," *New York Times*, March 14, 1953, p. 8.

59. J.B. Matthews, "Reds and Our Churches," *American Mercury*, July 1953, p. 3.

60. See page-one dispatches in the *New York Times* for July 3, 4, 8, and 10, 1953.

61. *United Evangelical Action*, August 15, 1953, p. 5.

62. *United Evangelical Action*, August 1, 1954, pp. 3–5.
63. For a description of this pamphlet, see "Deception Used by National Council in Vain Effort to Whitewash its 'Joiners,'" *Challenge*, November 1953, published by the American Council of Christian Laymen, Reel 19, Right-Wing Collection of the University of Iowa.
64. See miscellaneous issues of Hargis' *Christian Crusade* newsletter, Reel 22, Right-Wing Collection of the University of Iowa.
65. "Evangelicals and the Right-Wing Renascence," *Christianity Today*, December 22, 1961, p. 25.
66. "NAE Reaffirms Strong Anti-Communist Stand," *Christianity Today*, May 9, 1960, p. 30.
67. On NAE's anticommunism programs, see *United Evangelical Action*, June 1961, p. 22; the July 1961 advertisement for the film "Communism on the Map"; and August 1961, p. 22 regarding the Youth Conference.
68. Billy Graham, letter to Richard Nixon, June 21, 1960, Box 30, file: Billy Graham, 1950–1973, Walter Judd Collection, Hoover Institution Archives, Stanford University.
69. For a promotional biography of Judd, see Lee Edwards, *Missionary for Freedom: The Life and Times of Walter Judd* (New York: Paragon House, 1990). Judd died in 1994. "Walter H. Judd, 95, Missionary to China and U.S. Representative," *New York Times*, February 15, 1994, p. A17.
70. "Pre-Election Review of the 'Religious Issue,'" *Christianity Today*, October 24, 1960, p. 25.
71. George, op cit., pp. 200–208.
72. "Prayer Breakfast Offers Gospel to New Frontier," *Christianity Today*, February 27, 1961, p. 31.
73. "Southern Travelers," *Christianity Today*, January 5, 1962, p. 32.
74. While conducting research for *Spiritual Warfare*, I had yet to discover the existence of Christian Citizen. Previous histories of the Christian Right, including *Spiritual Warfare*, trace the movement's growth spurt of the 1970s and 1980s to the 1974 formation of Third Century Publishers by Campus Crusade leader Bill Bright, Representative John Conlan (R-AZ), and evangelical businessmen Arthur De Moss and Richard De Vos. As discussed in *Spiritual Warfare*, pp. 49–51, Third Century led to the formation of other Christian Right organizations active in the mid-1970s.
75. Bill Bright, letter to Walter Judd, December 8, 1961, and Gerri Von Frellick, letter to Walter Judd, January 15, 1962, Box 241, file: Christian Citizen, Walter Judd Collection, Hoover Institution Archives, Stanford University.
76. "Devout Prepared for Office," *Arizona Republic*, February 1, 1962, pp. 1, 11. See also "Christian Group Aims at Politics," *New York Times*, February 1, 1962, p. 23.
77. For details on the two Supreme Court cases, see Edward Keynes and Randall K. Miller, *The Court vs. Congress: Prayer, Busing, and Abortion* (Durham, NC: Duke University Press, 1989), pp. 174–205; and Rodney K. Smith, *Public Prayer and the Constitution: A Case Study in Constitutional Interpretation* (Wilmington, DE: Scholarly Resources, 1987), pp. 171–190.
78. See, e.g., the following *Christianity Today* articles: "Court Weighs Religious

Exercises," March 15, 1963, p. 31; "The Meaning of the Supreme Court Decision," July 5, 1963; pp. 29–30; "Response to the Bible-Prayer Ban," July 5, 1963, p. 47; and "What About the Becker Amendment?" June 19, 1964, pp. 20–22.

On the importance of the school prayer issue in the Christian Right's legislative activism during the 1980s, see Matthew C. Moen, *The Christian Right and Congress* (Tuscaloosa: University of Alabama Press, 1989), pp. 101–103 and passim.

79. "The GOP Ticket: The Religious Factors," *Christianity Today*, July 31, 1964, p. 39.

NOTES TO CHAPTER 5

1. I use the term "conservative" advisedly. This is the term used by the activists and organizations treated in this chapter, and I use it in contrast to the Americanists, treated in the next chapter. However, as I noted in the Introduction, the term "conservative" is problematic because it implies reticence toward change which has not always been the case among self-described conservatives. On this point, see Hixson, Jr., *Search for the American Right Wing: An Analysis of the Social Science Record, 1955–1987* (Princeton, NJ: Princeton University Press, 1992), p. xvii.
2. Benjamin A. Rogge, "Note on the Election," *New Individualist Review*, Spring 1965, p. 28.
3. Ibid., p. 29.
4. See, e.g., "Goldwater's Southern Strategy," *Human Events*, May 29, 1965, p. 5; and M. Stanton Evans, "The Vital Arithmetic of Conservative Victory," *Human Events*, May 28, 1966, pp. 8–9.
5. "The 1964 Election, Rusher on Goldwater," *New Individualist Review*, Summer 1965, pp. 39–40.
6. "The Republican Party and the Conservative Movement," *National Review*, December 1, 1964. Bush's and Reagan's commentaries appeared on pages 1053 and 1055 respectively.
7. "Reagan Triumph Blueprint for Conservatives," *Human Events*, June 18, 1966, p. 1. See also, esp. the following *Human Events* analyses: "Reagan: GOP Hope?" July 3, 1965, p. 4; Lee Edwards, "Why Californians Look to Ronald Reagan," February 19, 1966, pp. 7–10; and Barry Goldwater, "Reagan's Calif. Victory Vindicates 1964 Platform," June 18, 1966, p. 9.
8. Frank S. Meyer, "Thinking Aloud about 1968," *National Review*, June 13, 1967, p. 640.
9. "Major Groups Form Alliance: Goldwater, Nixon, Meet with ACU Leaders," *ACU Report*, September 1966, p. 1. Reel 155, Right-Wing Collection of the University of Iowa.
10. See William A. Rusher, *The Rise of the Right* (New York: William Morrow, 1984), pp. 197–201, on Buchanan's role in diplomatically resolving a feud between Nixon and the "Buckleyites."

11. "The Bosch Threat," *Human Events*, May 15, 1965, p. 4. Alongside a cartoon of President Johnson saying, "Extremism in the defense of liberty is no vice," *Human Events* described the Dominican invasion as a "bold counter-stroke necessary to head off a Castro-style takeover of the island."

      Months after the invasion, however, hard-line anticommunist leaders were displeased with Johnson's inaction against ousted Dominican President Juan Bosch's return to Santo Domingo, and with Johnson's announcement that he would formulate a treaty recognizing Panama's sovereignty over its canal. See James Jackson Kilpatrick, "Johnson is Playing a Losing Game in Latin America," and Holmes Alexander, "How the Fulbright Doctrine Helps the Reds," *Human Events*, October 16, 1965, p. 8.

12. "Conservatives Can Defeat the 'Great Society,'" *Human Events*, August 7, 1965, p. 1.

13. See "LBJ Suffers Stunning Setback," *Human Events*, November 19, 1966, pp. 1, 3 for winners' names and vote margins.

14. William A. Rusher, "What Happened at Miami Beach," *National Review*, December 3, 1968, pp. 1206–1231. Rusher identified as Reagan backers Robert Bauman and Alan MacKay of YAF. Tom Huston of YAF supported Nixon as did Senator John Tower and Peter O'Donnell, both of Texas; Senator Strom Thurmond and Roger Milliken, both of South Carolina; and right-wing financial patron Jeremiah Milbank.

15. Ibid., p. 1209.

16. M. Stanton Evans, "The Meaning of Miami," *Human Events*, August 24, 1968, p. 8.

17. "Nixon–Agnew: A Winning Ticket?" *Human Events*, August 17, 1968, p. 1.

18. See, e.g., Barry Goldwater, "Don't Waste a Vote on Wallace," *National Review*, October 22, 1968, pp. 1060–1079; "And Anyway Is Wallace a Conservative?" *National Review*, October 22, 1968, pp. 1048–1049; "A Vote for Wallace Is . . ." *National Review*, November 5, 1968, p. 1098; and "Should Conservatives Vote for Wallace?" *Human Events*, October 19, 1968, p. 7.

19. "A Close Look at Wallace's Words and Actions," *Human Events*, October 19, 1968, p. 9.

20. See Gary Allen, "Mr. Nixon: A Hard Look at the Candidate," and Susan L. M. Huck, "Mr. Wallace: A Hard Look at the Candidate," both in *American Opinion*, September, 1968. The quote on Wallace is on page 39. Gary Allen's political profile of Richard Nixon highlighted the apparent contradiction between Nixon's red-baiting in 1950 of his Senate campaign opponent, Helen Gahagan Douglas, and his later collaboration in Eisenhower's public criticism of Senator Joseph McCarthy's excesses. Allen also stressed Nixon's attendance at Martin Luther King, Jr.'s funeral and his "alliance with the revolutionary black power fanatics of the Congress of Racial Equality" (p. 21).

21. "The Power of George Wallace," *National Review*, November 19, 1968, p. 1153. See also M. Stanton Evans, "Why the GOP Must Move Right," *Human Events*, November 23, 1968, p. 1.

22. Kevin P. Phillips, *The Emerging Republican Majority* (New Rochelle, NY: Arlington House, 1969).

23. "'The Emerging Republican Majority': An Interview with Author Kevin Phillips," *Human Events*, August 16, 1969, p. 8.

24. "ACU Reports on the Nixon Administration—The Conservative Mandate for Change," *ACU Report*, January 1969, p. 1. The report was drafted by Dr. Philip M. Crane, an ACU board member from Illinois who was elected to the House of Representatives in November 1969.

25. "ACU Leader Named to White House Staff," *ACU Report*, January 1969, p. 1; "Conservatives Join Nixon Talent Hunt," *ACU Report*, January 1969, p. 3.

26. "ACU Leaders Named to White House Staff," *ACU Report*, March 1969, p. 4.

As a Nixon aide, Tom Huston in 1970 originated the infamous "Huston Plan," whereby the administration increased its intelligence gathering on U.S. anti-war groups through illegal covert operations. On Tom Huston and the "Huston Plan," see Frank Donner, *The Age of Surveillance* (New York: Vintage Books, 1981), pp. 155–156 and passim.

27. See, e.g., "American Dream or Republican Nightmare," *Battle Line* (ACU), August 1969; Henry Hazlitt, "Welfarism Out of Control," *National Review*, September 9, 1969, p. 903; "ACU, Human Events Fight Welfare Bill," and Representative John M. Ashbrook, "The Welfare Bill—Worthy of Defeat," *ACU Report*, March 1970, pp. 1–2. The point-persons for Nixon's contested welfare policies were HEW Secretary Robert Finch, initially recommended by ACU, and Daniel Patrick Moynihan, a holdover from the Kennedy administration.

28. See Vincent J. Burke and Vee Burke, *Nixon's Good Deed: Welfare Reform* (New York: Columbia University Press, 1974) for a thorough history of Nixon's Family Assistance Plan, from its inception through its defeat.

29. See "Conservative, GOP Leaders Rate the Nixon Administration," *Battle Line*, November 1969; "Nixon After One Year," *Human Events*, January 24, 1970, p. 1; "Nixon Moves to the Left," *Battle Line*, July 1970; and "A Hard Look at Nixon's Performance," *Human Events*, July 17, 1971, p. 1.

30. "We Suspend Our Support," was published in at least three places: the *National Review* issue of August 10, 1971; the *Human Events* issue of August 7, 1971, and ACU's *Battle Line*, August 1971. The signers were Jeffrey Bell and John L. Jones of ACU; William F. Buckley Jr., James Burnham, Frank Meyer, and William Rusher of *National Review*; Allan H. Ryskind and Thomas S. Winter of *Human Events*; Randall C. Teague of YAF; J. Daniel Mahoney, chair of the New York State Conservative Party; Neil McCaffrey of the Conservative Book Club; and Anthony Harrigan of the Southern States Industrial Council.

The statement noted that the signers continued their "personal admiration" for Richard Nixon and did not plan to "encourage formal political opposition" to him.

31. "YAF Rebuffs President Nixon," *Human Events*, September 18, 1971, p. 8.

32. Jeffrey Bell, "The State of Conservatism," *Human Events*, February 24, 1973, p. 9.

33. See ibid., and William F. Buckley, Jr., "Why John Ashbrook?" *National Review*, July 21, 1972, p. 814. Bell specifically attributed Nixon's abandonment of support for a Child Development bill, a value-added tax, and a version of the Family Assistance Plan to the Ashbrook campaign's focus on welfare and tax issues and "to the literally millions of pieces of direct mail the Ashbrook campaign sent to registered Republicans around the country."

34. See Burke and Burke, op cit., pp. 14–21.
35. On Phillips' appointment to direct OEO, see "Conservative Likely to Get OEO Post," *Human Events*, January 27, 1973, p. 4. On other appointments, see "Serious Shakedown at OEO," *Human Events*, February 17, 1973, p. 5. Nixon named David R. Jones, former executive director of YAF, to be Phillips' principal assistant. Also appointed as aides were Alvin Arnett; Ronald Fuller; Daniel F. Joy, former editor of YAF's *New Guard* magazine; J. Laurence McCarty, former ACU treasurer; John E. Schrote; and Randall C. Teague, former executive director of YAF and former ACU board member.
36. "OEO Rescued from the Abyss," *Human Events*, July 7, 1973, p. 6. On Phillips' campaign against OEO programs, see "Another Hoax from OEO's Old Guard," *Human Events*, February 24, 1973, pp. 1, 6; and "Scandal Stories Illustrate Why OEO Must Be Junked," *Human Events*, March 24, 1973, pp. 1, 5. The method of Phillips' attack was to expose the dollar amounts of specific programs, then to identify local administrators' liberal and leftist affiliations, plus their alleged misuse of funds for non-program-related items.

    In "Nixon Can Abolish OEO This Week," *Human Events*, June 29, 1974, p. 16, Phillips blamed OEO's funding of "pro-impeachment groups like the American Civil Liberties Union, the National Lawyers Guild, the AFL-CIO," and so on for exacerbating Nixon's Watergate troubles.
37. See, e.g., "Phillips' Memo to Conservative Lawmakers," *Human Events*, November 3, 1973, p. 3; and the following *Human Events* articles by Howard Phillips: "Will Nixon Redeem Anti-Abortion Pledge?" January 26, 1974, p. 10; "Some Lessons for the Next President," April 27, 1974, pp. 33–35; "A New Political Strategy for Conservatives," October 19, 1974, p. 9.
38. Senator James L. Buckley (R-NY) recommended Nixon's resignation before the Senate Caucus Room, March 19, 1974. His statement appeared in *National Review*, April 12, 1974, pp. 413–415; and was followed by William F. Buckley, Jr., "The Resignation Proposal," *National Review*, April 26, 1974, p. 498.

    "Reflections on the Resignation," *National Review*, August 30, 1974, pp. 954–959 details the timing of the move by some leading conservatives to endorse resignation.
39. See, e.g., "Rockefeller Choice Anathema to Conservatives," *Human Events*, August 31, 1974, p. 3.
40. See Robert Scheer and Warren Hinckle, "The 'Vietnam Lobby,'" *Ramparts*, July 1965, pp. 16–24. Scheer and Hinckle reported on the role of the liberal anticommunist *New Leader* magazine, under the editorship of Sol Levitas, and the International Rescue Committee in the formation of the American Friends of Vietnam.

    For a list of participants, see American Friends of Vietnam, meeting minutes and the letterhead of the memo accompanying Chairperson Wesley R. Fishel's letter to *Ramparts* editors, Box 22, Colonel Charles Bohannan Collection, Hoover Institution Archives, Stanford University. Fishel found some inconsequential factual errors in the Scheer–Hinckle article. The American Friends of Vietnam board included Gilbert Jonas, Frank Trager, Colonel Charles Bohannan, Leo Cherne, Christopher Emmet, Roger Hilsman, Harold Oram, and others.

Evidence suggests the American Friends of Vietnam was involved in a White House covert operation. See "White House, Memo for the Record, August 4, 1965," declassified White House document, published as Record No. 2191, *Declassified Document Collection* (Woodbridge, CT: Research Publications, 1985). On page 2 of this document, White House Executive Secretary Chester L. Cooper is reported to have said that

> We have an instrument for public information on Vietnam in the shape of the "American Friends of Vietnam." While we have been careful to keep our hand fairly hidden, we have, in fact, spent a lot of time on it and have been able to find them some money. Unfortunately, the raising of money is very difficult and the group does not have available sufficient funds to send their top man, Mr. Fishel, to Vietnam.

41. Marvin Liebman, letter of January 18, 1961, to the New York-based Chinese News Service, Box 5, file: American-Asian Educational Exchange, letters to foundations and embassies, Marvin Liebman Collection, Hoover Institution Archives, Stanford University.

    Liebman proposed bringing fifty to sixty YAF members on a "Frontiers of Freedom" tour to Vietnam, the Philippines, Hong Kong, and Taiwan for "substantial and important propaganda impact." Liebman suggested that Civil Air Transport

> would be the ideal airline to handle this part of the trip. . . . It would be of great help, of course, if the Chinese Government could help subsidize part of the Asian transportation. . . . I am sure that the Governments of Free China, Korea, Viet Nam, and the Philippines will make arrangements to receive these young Americans at Government expense.

    By then, Civil Air Transport was the CIA's first proprietary airline. See William Blum, *The CIA: A Forgotten History* (London: Zed Books, 1986), p. 17.

42. See "Big Conservative Win," *Human Events*, May 8, 1965, p. 4, for YAF's successful campaign to get Firestone Tire and Rubber Company to terminate negotiations for a rubber plant in Rumania; "YAF Scores Again," *Human Events*, February 4, 1967, p. 4, on YAF pressuring American Motors not to negotiate a trade deal with the Soviet Union; and "YAF Pickets IBM," *Human Events*, December 16, 1967, p. 14, regarding YAF picketing IBM offices to protest IBM sales to Eastern European countries.

43. Irene Corbally Kuhn, "YAF Spearheads Rallies For Freedom in Viet Nam," *Human Events*, January 22, 1966, p. 12.

44. See *WYCF Report*, vol. 1, no. 1, July 1966; and Tom Charles Huston, memorandum of November 18, 1966, Box 255, file: World Youth Crusade for Freedom, 1966–1969, Walter Judd Collection, Hoover Institution Archives, Stanford University. Huston's internal memo includes details on meetings leading up to the formation of the WYCF, an itemized breakdown of the group's first-year budget of about $135,000, and a letterhead listing the advisory council, which included William F. Buckley, Jr., James Burnham, Barry Goldwater, Walter Judd, Frank Meyer, Richard Nixon, Stefan Possony, William Rusher, Clifton White, and others.

45. Both events were reported with alarm in "Communists Plan New Revolutionary Activity Around the Globe," *Human Events*, February 5, 1966, p. 6; and Paul D. Bethel, "New Havana Meeting Spells Trouble for U.S.," *Human Events*, July 22, 1967, p. 8.

46. On the activities of the American-African Affairs Association, see e.g., William A. Rusher and Max Yergan, memorandum of May 20, 1966, Box 1, file: American Business Contacts, Marvin Liebman Collection, Hoover Institution Archives, Stanford University; and miscellaneous American-African Affairs Association pamphlets, Reel 12, Right-Wing Collection of the University of Iowa. These sources list the Association's officers, directors, and members, who overlapped significantly with the membership of Marvin Liebman's American Afro-Asian Educational Exchange and the American Conservative Union. Prominent names included: L. Brent Bozell, John Chamberlain, Philip M. Crane, Ralph de Toledano, John Dos Passos, Henry Hazlitt, Walter Judd, Dr. Russell Kirk, Major General Thomas A. Lane, Frank Meyer, Henry Regnery, and Professor David N. Rowe.

    By 1968, the Association claimed 3,800 financial contributors and expenditures of $68,904; expenditures for 1969 totaled $108,800, but the Association reported a failure to enlist support from U.S. corporations and foundations.

    The Association's 1967 fact-finding mission trip to Rhodesia was reported by participants James Jackson Kilpatrick, Rene Albert Wormser, and Walter Darnell Jacobs in "Rhodesia: A Case History," *National Review*, May 16, 1967.

47. See, e.g., James Burnham, "Do Sanctions Work?" *National Review*, November 14, 1967, p. 1254.

48. On this point, see, e.g., Gabriel Kolko, *Anatomy of a War* (New York: Pantheon, 1985), pp. 341–355 and passim; Daniel C. Hallin, *The "Uncensored War": The Media and Vietnam* (Berkeley: University of California Press, 1989). Hallin correlated a shift in media coverage of the war with the 1968 Tet offensive and a subsequent decline in U.S. elite support for the war.

49. Conservatives adopted Vice-President Spiro Agnew's image of a "silent majority" in favor of the war and sponsored a string of rallies across the country on Veterans' Day, 1969. See James Jackson Kilpatrick, "A Time to Bear Witness," *Human Events*, November 15, 1969, p. 1; and "The 'Silent Majority' Speaks Out on Veterans' Day," *Human Events*, November 22, 1969, p. 9.

50. General Thomas A. Lane, "Why Nixon Should Abandon Kissinger's Plan," *Human Events*, August 9, 1969, p 9.

51. "What Now in Vietnam?" *National Review*, May 6, 1969, p. 418.

52. "Vietnam: The Political Crunch," *National Review*, November 4, 1969, p. 1101.

53. "Nixon Needs Country's Support," *Human Events*, May 9, 1970, p. 1.

54. See "Tell it to Hanoi" campaign advertisement, *Human Events*, May 30, 1970; and miscellaneous YAF literature, Reel 154, Right-Wing Collection of the University of Iowa. The latter source includes an undated "Tell it to Hanoi" campaign news tabloid reporting Vice-President Agnew's, Representative Donald Lukens', and Sam Steiger's praise for YAF, and details of YAF's counterdemonstrations against college peace groups.

55. See James Burnham, "The Antidraft Movement," *National Review*, June 13, 1967, p. 629.

Libertarian economics professor Milton Friedman; Karl Hess, a Goldwater speech writer; and James Powell, editor of the libertarian journal *New Individualist Review*, joined pacifist and civil rights activists in forming the Council for a Volunteer Military in 1967. Burnham blasted "right-wing libertarianism" for its "isolationism" and "anti-U.S." position.

56. See YAF Executive Director Randall C. Teague's September 29, 1969, "Statement on the Draft," printed in *New Guard*, November 1969, pp. 6–7; and Ronald B. Dear, "Young America's Freedom Offensive, a 1969 Report," *New Guard*, January 1970, pp. 13–14. Under the latter article, YAF published an advertisement for its "Volunteer Military Legislative Action Kit."

57. See Franz Schurmann, *The Foreign Politics of Richard Nixon: The Grand Design* (Berkeley, CA: Institute of International Studies, 1987), esp. Chapter 2, pp. 47–93.

58. See, for example, "The Betrayal of Taiwan: What It Would Mean," *Human Events*, July 31, 1971, p. 3; and "Red China to the UN," *National Review*, Oct 8, 1971, p. 1097.

59. William F. Buckley, Jr., "The End of the United Nations?" *National Review*, November 19, 1971, p. 1317.

60. William F. Buckley, "Veni, Vidi, Victus," *National Review*, March 17, 1972, p. 258.

61. See, e.g., "Is 'Era of Negotiation' Coming to an End?" *Human Events*, October 24, 1970, p. 1; and "A Hard Look at Nixon's Performance," *Human Events*, July 17, 1971, p. 5.

62. American Security Council, *Washington Report*, September 28, 1970.

63. "Operation Alert—Interim Report," *Washington Report*, November 16, 1970.

64. On the results of SALT I see, e.g., Dan Caldwell, *The Dynamics of Domestic Politics and Arms Control: The SALT II Treaty Ratification Debate* (Columbia: University of South Carolina Press, 1991), pp. 31–35.

It was Senator Henry Jackson (D-WA), not a leading conservative member of Congress, who successfully attached an amendment to the Interim Agreement before it was approved by the Senate. The Jackson amendment stipulated that any subsequent arms agreement should not limit the United States to levels inferior to the Soviet Union.

65. Among numerous *National Review* articles and columns on Chile, see, e.g.: Nena Ossa, "Chile's Che Guevara?" March 23, 1971; "Chilean Notes," November 5, 1971, p. 1219; "Chilean Notes," November 19, 1971, p. 1283; Nena Ossa, "The End of the Line," March 16, 1973, pp. 308–309; M. J. Sobran, Jr., "Looking Back on What Happened," April 13, 1973, pp. 413–414; Nena Ossa, "What Now?" April 13, 1973, p. 417; Nena Ossa, "Never a Dull Moment," August 3, 1973, p. 841; James Burnham, "The Canonization of Salvador Allende," October 12, 1973, p. 1103.

66. See, generally, Blum, op cit., pp. 232–243; Les Evans, ed., *Disaster in Chile: Allende's Strategy and Why it Failed* (New York: Pathfinder Press, 1974); Samuel Chavkin, *The Murder of Chile: Eyewitness Accounts of the Coup, the Terror, and the Resistance Today* (New York: Everest House, 1982).

On the press campaign against the Allende government, see also Fred S. Landis, *Psychological Warfare and Media Operations in Chile, 1970–73*, unpublished doctoral dissertation, University of Illinois, Urbana, 1975. (Landis conducted research in Chile during the 1973 coup and its immediate aftermath, and served as a consultant for Senator Frank Church's Subcommittee on CIA Covert Action in Chile.)

National Review's editorial preoccupation with Chile under the Popular Unity government ought to be seen in the context of CIA supported media projects, both domestic and foreign. See "Report on CIA Chilean Task Force Activities, 15 September to 3 November 1970," declassified CIA document, published as Record No. 1226 of the *Declassified Documents Collection* (Woodbridge, Connecticut: Research Publications, 1988). In this seventeen-page document, the CIA boasts of its worldwide media operations against Chile and claims "726 articles, broadcasts, editorials, and similar items" in a six-week period to be the "direct result of agent activity" (p. 10). *National Review* is not mentioned by name, but further on the same page, the CIA claims to have given "special intelligence and 'inside' briefings' . . . to U.S. journalists. . . . Particularly noteworthy in this connection was the *Time* cover story which owed a great deal to written materials and briefings provided by CIA." Salvador Allende was the subject of *Time*'s October 19, 1970 cover story, "Marxist Threat in the Americas." The article was published during the six week period covered by the CIA report.

67. "Allende Out," *National Review*, September 28, 1973, p. 1040.

68. See Donald Freed, with Fred Landis, *Death in Washington: The Murder of Orlando Letelier* (Westport, Connecticut: Lawrence Hill & Co., 1980), p. 157–161 and passim. According to Freed and Landis, in 1978 the U.S. Justice Department filed suit against the American Chilean Council for its violation of the Foreign Agents' Registration Act.

69. Marvin Liebman's American Chilean Council correspondence is scattered among the various disorganized boxes of his collection at the Hoover Institution Archives, Stanford University.

See, e.g., Marvin Liebman, September 8, 1975 letter to C. Robert Devine, vice-president of *Reader's Digest*, Box 111, file: Marvin Liebman Collection, Hoover Institution Archives, Stanford University. In this letter, Liebman reviews for Devine a recent meeting between the *Digest* and the American Chilean Council, including details about trips planned for Senatorial aides and proposals for the *Digest* to help cover costs. Liebman writes that

> The ACC is an informally organized ad hoc effort to counteract the anti-Chilean propaganda campaign. . . . The initial financing for the work of the ACC came originally from private Chilean contributions which were transmitted to us by the Consejo Chileno Norteamericano.

At the end of this letter, Liebman tells Devine that he has reported on his meeting with *Reader's Digest* to Ambassador Spruille Braden, who was the "Chairman pro-tem" of the Council.

In another illustrative letter, from Marvin Liebman to Dr. William Schneider, c/o office of Senator James L. Buckley, January 28, 1976, Box 117, file: Marvin Liebman Collection, Hoover Institution Archives, Stanford University, Liebman instructs the Senator's aide on what to look for during a forthcoming trip to Chile and urges Schneider to "plug the American-Chilean

Council to anyone you see and tell them what an absolutely spectacular job we're doing for Chile in the United States."

The letterhead of Liebman's American Chilean Council includes the following, listed as "founding members": Professor James D. Atkinson, Murray Baron, Professor A. T. Bouscaren, Ralph de Toledano, Lev Dobriansky, Ronald Docksai, Walter Judd, David Keene, Anthony Kubeck, Eugene Lyons, Stefan Possony, David N. Rowe. This group was among those prominent in the China Lobby groups.

70. Jerome Tuccille, *Radical Libertarianism: A Right Wing Alternative* (Indianapolis, IN: Bobbs-Merrill, 1970), pp. 4–10.

71. Rothbard quoted in ibid., p. 99.

72. Ibid., pp. 106–108.

73. See, e.g., Dale Haviland, *Libertarian Directory 1972*, self-published, Brighton, Michigan, 1972, for a catalog of dozens of libertarian groups and newsletters, spanning a spectrum from objectivist, anarcho-capitalist, anarchist, laissez-faire, classical liberal, and conservative.

74. See "Reason Magazine: History and Aims," a one-page description prefacing the microfilmed collection of *Reason*, 1968–1972, Hoover Institution library. Also on that reel of microfilm is "A Message from the Publisher of Reason," January 1971, which announces *Reason's* new ownership. Reason Enterprises included Lynn Kinsky, Manuel Klausner, Tibor Machan, Robert Poole, Jr., Marilyn Walther, and James Weigl.

75. On Rothbard's role among intellectual rightists, see George H. Nash, *The Conservative Intellectual Movement in America Since 1945* (New York: Basic Books, 1979), pp. 3313–3318 and passim.

76. Murray N. Rothbard, *For A New Liberty* (New York: Macmillan, 1973), pp. 8–9.

77. Ibid., pp. 12–20.

78. Ibid., pp. 13–15.

79. Ibid., pp. 15–17.

80. Ibid., p. 18.

81. "Farewell to the Left," *Libertarian Forum*, May 1, 1970.

82. Jerome Tuccille, "The New Libertarianism," *The Libertarian Forum*, June 1, 1970, pp. 2–3.

83. See, e.g., the cover story, Stan Lehr and Louis Rossetto, Jr., "The New Right Credo-Libertarianism," *New York Times Magazine*, January 10, 1971. The article publicized the split between libertarians and conservatives, and prompted a negative syndicated column by William F. Buckley. Jerome Tuccille answered Buckley in "A Split in the Right Wing," *New York Times*, January 28, 1971. The *Times'* op-ed page editors apparently found the feud so interesting that they offered the antagonists more space: Murray Rothbard, "The New Libertarian Creed," February 9, 1971, p. 39; William F. Buckley, Jr., "The Conservative Reply," February 16, 1971, p. 33.

The various columns rehashed the well-known points of contention between libertarianism and fusionism. But Rothbard claimed the press attention as a net gain for the libertarians. See his "Take Off," *The Libertarian Forum*, February 1971, pp. 1, 8; and "Take Off II," *The Libertarian Forum*, March 1971, pp. 1–2.

84. See "New Party Makes A Debut in Denver," *New York Times*, February 6, 1972,

p. 47. Nolan's membership in YAF comes from Karen Lehrman, "Libertarian Free-for-All," *In These Times*, September 14–20, 1988, p. 12.

John Hospers, a University of Southern California philosophy professor, was the Libertarian Party's first presidential candidate. ("A Party is Formed By 'Libertarians,'" *New York Times*, July 5, 1972, p. 24.) He received one electoral college vote when Roger MacBride, a Virginia Republican elector, voted for him. ("Electors Affirm Nixon's Victory," *New York Times*, December 19, 1972, p. 17.) MacBride was later drafted as the Libertarian Party's 1976 presidential candidate.

85. Libertarian party, platform brochure, inserted into *Reason* magazine, October 1973.

86. See "The Party," *The Libertarian Forum*, March 1972, p. 1; and "The Party Once More," *The Libertarian Forum*, May 1972, p. 3.

87. *Reason* magazine reported regularly on various races. Among the most successful, Fran Youngstein of New York City's Free Libertarian party, received 8,000 of 1.7 million votes cast for mayor. See *Reason*, January 1974, p. 32.

88. "Frontlines," *Reason*, February 1976, p. 68.

89. See the following *National Review* articles, Ernest Van den Haag, "Libertarians and Conservatives," June 8, 1979, pp. 725–739; Lawrence V. Cott, "Cato Institute and the Invisible Finger," June 8, 1979, pp. 740–742; "Has the Libertarian Movement Gone Kooky? A Spirited Exchange," August 3, 1979, pp. 967–986.

90. See, e.g., Sara Diamond, "Free Market Environmentalism," *Z Magazine*, December 1991, pp. 52–56.

91. See, especially, Alan Crawford, *Thunder on the Right: The "New Right" and the Politics of Resentment* (New York: Pantheon, 1980); and John S. Saloma III, *Ominous Politics: The New Conservative Labyrinth* (New York: Hill & Wang, 1984). From the perspective of participants themselves, see Richard Viguerie, *The New Right: We're Ready to Lead* (Falls Church, VA: The Viguerie Co., 1981); and *The New Right at Harvard* (Vienna, VA: Conservative Caucus, 1983). The latter includes reflections on New Right issues and developments by Howard Phillips, Paul Weyrich, Brigadier General Albion Knight (Ret.), John Lofton, Richard Viguerie, and Morton Blackwell, from a 1981 lecture series held at Harvard.

92. Daniel Oliver, "What Conservatives Are Telling Each Other," *National Review*, March 1, 1974, pp. 256–73.

93. David S. Broder, "Conservatives Put Off Bid on Third Party," *Washington Post*, February 17, 1975, p. 1, 16.

94. See "Reagan Key to Conservative Hopes," *Human Events*, March 1, 1975, pp. 1–18 about the conference; p. 5, for the "Text of Resolution"; and the list of signers. The Committee consisted of the following: Representative John Ashbrook, Representative Robert Bauman, Ronald Docksai of YAF, M. Stanton Evans of ACU, Senator Jesse Helms, Eli Howell (former assistant to Governor George Wallace), State Senator Cyril Joly from Maine, James Lyon of the Republican Finance Committee, J. Daniel Mahoney of the New York Conservative party, William Rusher of *National Review*, Phyllis Schlafly, Representative Steve Symms of Idaho, Governor Meldrim Thomson of New Hampshire, former Reagan gubernatorial aide Robert Walker, and *Human Events* editor Thomas Winter.

95. William A. Rusher, "A New Party: Eventually, Why Not Now?" *National Review*, May 23, 1975, p. 550, excerpted from William A. Rusher, *The Making of the New Majority Party* (New York: Sheed and Ward, 1975).

96. Rusher, "A New Party," op cit.

97. Ibid., pp. 550–551.

98. Ibid., p. 553.

99. See Thomas Byrne Edsall and Mary Edsall, *Chain Reaction: The Impact of Race, Rights, and Taxes on American Politics* (New York: Norton, 1991).

100. See, e.g., the following *Conservative Digest* articles on the idea of recruiting among middle- and working-class conservative Democrats: Richard Viguerie's "From the Publisher," August 1975, p. 1; Viguerie, "Let's Get Union Members to Support Conservatives," August 1977, p. 56; Louis Jenkins, "Let's Organize Conservative Democrats," October 1977, p. 2; Representative Philip Crane, "The Blue Collar Constituency Is Really Conservative," April 1978, p. 6.

101. See, e.g., Richard Viguerie's "From the Publisher" column, *Conservative Digest*, August 1975. The monthly magazine was started in May 1975.

102. "Reagan Moves Closer to Presidential Bid," *Human Events*, July 19, 1975, p. 1.

103. Evans, quoted in "Conservative Leaders and That 'Dream Ticket,'" *Conservative Digest*, June 1975, which polled leaders on the question: "Would you support a 1976 Presidential ticket which included Ronald Reagan and George Wallace?" Those favoring the ticket included Senator Jesse Helms, Wallace aide Eli Howell, William Rusher, Howard Phillips, and Paul Weyrich.

 In July 1975, *Conservative Digest* published an exclusive interview with George Wallace. See also Kevin Phillips, "Reagan and Wallace: Shaping the Right Deal for America," *Conservative Digest*, July 1975, pp. 30–31; Dr. Melvin Bradford, "Full Speed Ahead—With Wallace," *Conservative Digest*, October 1975; and Patrick Buchanan, "Wallace: the Most Influential Outsider," *Conservative Digest*, August 1976, p. 24. Buchanan called Wallace "the authentic voice of the Forgotten American, the angry white working man, North and South, heard raucously and continuously since 1964."

 In "What Is Your Dream Ticket for 1976?" *Conservative Digest*, August 1975, Reagan was mentioned most often as a presidential candidate, followed by Senator Helms and Governor Meldrim Thomson. For vice-presidential candidate, conservatives polled mentioned Representative Phil Crane most often, followed by Senator James McClure (R-ID), former Treasury Secretary John Connally of Texas, and Governor George Wallace.

104. "Maddox a Favorite as Third Party Meets in Chicago," *Washington Post*, August 27, 1976, p. 3 and "Newcomers' Hopes Are Scuttled at Third Party Session," *Washington Post*, August 29, 1976, p. 3. AIP chair William K. Shearer was a founding leader of the Citizens' Council in California. Among those considered for the AIP presidential nomination was Representative John R. Rarick (D-LA), a founder of the Louisiana Citizens' Councils.

105. Joyce Kolko, *America and the Crisis of World Capitalism* (Boston: Beacon Press, 1974), pp. 29–30.

106. Ibid., p. 57.

107. Thomas Ferguson and Joel Rogers, *Right Turn: The Decline of the Democrats and the Future of American Politics* (New York: Hill & Wang, 1986), p. 78.
108. Ibid., pp. 86–87.
109. Ibid., pp. 94–100.
110. Michael Unseem, *The Inner Circle: Large Corporations and the Rise of Business Political Activity in the U.S. and U.K. (New York: Oxford University Press, 1984).*
111. On increased corporate mobilization see Frances Fox Piven and Richard A. Cloward, *The New Class War: Reagan's Attack on the Welfare State and Its Consequences* (New York: Pantheon, 1985); Thomas B. Edsall, *The New Politics of Inequality* (New York: Norton, 1984); Thomas Ferguson and Joel Rogers, *Right Turn: The Decline of the Democrats and the Future of American Politics* (New York: Hill & Wang, 1986); Joseph G. Peschek, *Policy-Planning Organizations: Elite Agendas and America's Rightward Turn* (Philadelphia: Temple University Press, 1987).

　　See also J. Craig Jenkins and Teri Shumate, "Cowboy Capitalists and the Rise of the 'New Right': An analysis of Contributors to Conservative Policy Formation Organizations," *Social Problems*, vol. 33, no. 2, December 1985, pp. 130–145.
112. See, esp., Russ Bellant, *The Coors Connection* (Boston: South End Press, 1991) and a four-part investigative series on Coors' funding and organizing of New Right groups, *Washington Post*, May 4–7, 1975.
113. See, e.g., John S. Saloma III, *Ominous Politics* (New York: Hill & Wang, 1984), pp. 24–37, 63–80; and Val Burris, "Business Support for the New Right: A Consumer's Guide to the Most Reactionary American Corporations," *Socialist Review*, January–February 1987, pp. 33–63.
114. See Ibid., and, among other sources, Dan Morgan, "Conservatives: A Well-Financed Network" *Washington Post*, January 4, 1981; Karen Rothmeyer, "Citizen Scaife," *Columbia Journalism Review*, July–August, 1981, pp. 41–50.
115. "'New Right' Plans Move to Change Congress," *Congressional Quarterly*, October 23, 1976, pp. 3027–3031. Precise PAC figures appear on page 3029.
116. See ibid., p. 3028, for a list of the ten Congressional incumbent and ten Congressional challenger races backed by fundraiser Richard Viguerie. Incumbents included Representative John Ashbrook (R-OH), Senator James L. Buckley (R-NY), Representative Charles Grassley (R-IA). Challengers included Senate candidate Orrin Hatch (R-UT), and House candidates Robert K. Dornan (R-CA), Mickey Edwards (R-OK), and Robert J. Casey (R-PA).
117. Without attempting to list all of the New Right's organizations by name, here are the most well known, by type:

   1. Para-party organizations: American Conservative Union, Young Americans for Freedom
   2. Electoral vehicles: Citizens for the Republic, Conservative Caucus, Committee for the Survival of a Free Congress (later renamed Free Congress Foundation), National Conservative Political Action Committee (NCPAC)

3. Think tanks: American Enterprise Institute, Center for Strategic and International Studies, Heritage Foundation, Hoover Institution, Institute for Contemporary Studies

4. Issue lobbies: Accuracy in Media, American Security Council, Council for Inter-American Security, Eagle Forum, Gun Owners of America, National Defense Council, National Right-to-Life Committee

118. These included Representatives Phil Crane, Robert Bauman, and Robert Dornan, and Senators James Buckley, Orrin Hatch, and Jesse Helms. Many others entered Congress on Ronald Reagan's coattails in 1980. See the following *Conservative Digest* articles: "Terry Dolan: Conservative Point Man," January 1979, pp. 26–27; Sanford Ungar, "New Right Senators: They're Getting Results," March 1979, pp. 26–28; Morton C. Blackwell, "Inside the Crane Campaign," July 1979, pp. 4–5; and "Jesse Helms' Brainy Brain Trust," October 1979, pp. 34–35.

119. See, e.g., Phyllis Schlafly, "Are You Paying for Women's Lib and the ERA?" *Human Events*, February 23, 1974, pp. 12, 20; "Where Next?" an interview with the communications director for Anita Bryant's campaign to repeal an anti-discrimination measure in Florida, *Conservative Digest*, August 1977, pp. 11–13.

120. Paul Scott, "Schlafly Forms New Group to Defend Family," *Human Events*, September 6, 1975, p. 4.

121. "James Buckley: Life Amendment," *National Review*, June 22, 1973, pp. 667–670. Though such an amendment had little chance of passage, it functioned as a rallying point for the New Right Congressional leaders who supported it. See, for example, "Thousands Protest on Anniversary of Abortion Decree," *Human Events*, February 8, 1975, p. 23. Senators Buckley and Helms, Representative Robert Bauman (R-MD), and others gave speeches supporting the Human Life Amendment before an estimated crowd of 50,000.

122. Connie Paige, *The Right to Lifers* (New York: Summit Books, 1983), p. 150. See also Andrew H. Merton, *Enemies of Choice: the Right-to-Life Movement and its Threat to Abortion* (Boston: Beacon Press, 1981), p. 164. Weyrich was an adviser to Paul and Judie Brown's Life Amendment Political Action Committee (LAPAC), a spin-off of the original National Right to Life Committee.

123. Paige, op cit., pp. 151–152.

124. Dinesh D'Souza, *Falwell: Before the Millenium* (Chicago: Regnery Gateway, 1984), pp. 109–112.

125. See, e.g., "Mobilizing the Moral Majority," *Conservative Digest*, August 1979, pp. 14–17, which featured flattering brief biographies of Christian Right leaders; Paul Weyrich, "Building the Moral Majority," *Conservative Digest*, August 1979, pp. 18–19.

126. See, e.g., "Four More Years of Kissinger?" *Human Events*, August 21, 1976, p. 1. The unsigned article blamed "Kissinger foreign policy" for a litany of foreign affairs problems:

> Indochina is gone, because we tended to "trust" the Russians. Angola is now a Marxist-Leninist state, because we tended to "trust" the Soviets. . . .

A Soviet-supported Cuba rips apart detente by invading Angola and promoting guerrilla warfare against the U.S. Commonwealth of Puerto Rico. . . . Meanwhile, the Cubans are doing it again by moving into Mozambique—and there is still no effort by Ford to retaliate. We have become so pusillanimous under Kissinger that the United States, 200 million strong, would rather yield its rights over the Panama Canal than to risk a confrontation with a country having one two-hundredth of the population.

127. See, e.g., "Sidelights on Kissinger's Speech on Rhodesia," *Human Events*, May 8, 1976, pp. 4–5; and Roger Freeman, "Why Does the U.S. Government Want to Destroy Rhodesia?" *Human Events*, June 26, 1976, p. 8.

128. For example, in August 1978, Senators Jesse Helms (R-NC) and John Danforth (R-MO) tried to pass an amendment to lift trade sanctions imposed on Rhodesia pending its move to majority rule. Supporters of the Helms–Danforth amendment included the conservative Senate block: Howard Baker, Robert Dole, Jake Garn, Barry Goldwater, Orrin Hatch, Jesse Helms, Paul Laxalt, Strom Thurmond, and John Tower. See "The Killing of Rhodesia," *Human Events*, August 5, 1978, p. 1.

129. See "Conservative Forum," *Human Events*, June 18, 1977, p. 18; and M. Stanton Evans, "Crackdown on Rhodesian Info Office Protested," *Human Events*, October 22, 1977, p. 13.

The seventeen journalists who wrote to President Carter included William Rusher, Patrick Buchanan, M. Stanton Evans, James J. Kilpatrick, Thomas Winter (editor of *Human Events*), John Chamberlain, John Lofton, Ralph de Toledano, and Alan Crawford.

130. See "Conservative Forum," *Human Events*, January 14, 1978, p. 18.

131. See the "Conservative Forum" columns in *Human Events*: June 18, 1977, p. 18; November 19, 1977, p. 18; January 7, 1978, p. 2.

132. See " 'Truth Squad' Battles Carter on Canal Treaties," *Human Events*, January 21, 1978, pp. 1, 4. Participants included: Senators Laxalt, Dole, Hatch, Garn, Helms, Thurmond, Tower, and Domenici; Representatives Mickey Edwards, Larry McDonald, George Hansen, Phil Crane, Bob Bauman, and John Rousselot; Admiral Thomas Moore, former head of the Joint Chiefs of Staff; Lieutenant General Daniel Graham, former director of the Defense Intelligence Agency; Admiral John McCain, former commander-in-chief of the Pacific. Also on the tour was future presidential candidate Ronald Reagan.

See *Conservative Digest*, March 1978 for tour photos and captions.

See also the American Security Council's *Washington Report*, January 1978. ASC contributed $5,000 to pay for the "Truth Squad" 's chartered plane. This ASC newsletter also reports the anti-treaty activities of the following groups: the American Legion, Veterans of Foreign Wars, Reserve Officers Association, the Council for Inter-American Security, Young Americans for Freedom, and the Heritage Foundation.

133. New Right fundraiser Richard Viguerie considered the canal treaties a "no-loss" issue: even if the treaties were ratified, conservatives could mobilize public opposition in the coming election campaigns. On the role of New Right

pressure groups in the activism for and against treaty ratification, see George D. Moffett III, *The Limits of Victory: The Ratification of the Panama Canal Treaties* (Cornell University Press, 1985), pp. 166–180.

134. See "Reagan Waging Major Effort to Defeat Canal Treaties," *Human Events*, September 3, 1977, p. 1; "Conservative Forum," *Human Events*, January 14, 1978, p. 18; Ronald Reagan, "Canal Treaties Contain Fatal Flaws," *Human Events*, March 11, 1978, p. 8. (During the 1970s, Ronald Reagan's byline appeared on numerous *Human Events* opinion articles.)

135. Dan Caldwell, *The Dynamics of Domestic Politics and Arms Control: The SALT II Treaty Ratification Debate* (Columbia: University of South Carolina Press, 1991), p. 105.

136. See the following issues of the American Security Council's *Washington Report*: "Coalition for Peace Through Strength," October 1978; "The Anti-Defense Lobby," December 1978; "An Analysis of SALT II," May 1979; and "The Marxist Threat to Central America," August 1979.

137. On the division of labor between the Committee on the Present Danger and the Coalition for Peace Through Strength, see Caldwell, op cit., pp. 101–106.

138. "Major Film on SALT Released Nationwide by Coalition," *The Coalition Insider* (Report of the Coalition for Peace Through Strength), September 1979. The newsletter also included instructions for getting the film on local television stations.

139. Caldwell, op cit., p. 105.

140. See Caldwell, pp. 153–176 for analysis of how these international events impacted domestic debate on SALT II.

141. "1978 Conservative Political Action Conference Highlights," *Human Events*, April 1, 1978, pp. 8–15.

142. Ibid., p. 15.

NOTES TO CHAPTER 6

1. In my extensive reading of "Americanist" literature published by the American Independent Party, the John Birch Society, the Liberty Lobby, and its affiliates, I have not yet found a concise definition of the frequently used terms "Americanist" and "Americanism." One of my motivations for using "Americanist" in this chapter's title is the term's use from the 1960s to the 1990s. From the mid-1980s through 1995, I monitored the weekly radio talk show "One Man's View of Americanism," hosted by John Katz, a longtime John Birch Society and American Independent Party activist in central California. The program aired on AM stations KTRB-Modesto and (later) on KPLA-River Bank. (KPLA was purchased in 1993 by Crawford Broadcasting and renamed KCBC.) The program's content included frequent readings from John Birch Society publications, guest interviews with Birch Society personnel, leaders of major Christian Right, anti-immigrant, and pro-gun organizations. Katz made weekly promotions for the American Pistol and Rifle Association (APRA), a group intersecting with the "Posse Comitatus" sub-movement. Listeners called the

program from a signal area ranging from Sacramento, west to San Franciso, and as far south as Bakersfield.

2. On the historical relationship between the Liberty Lobby and the John Birch Society, see Frank Mintz, *The Liberty Lobby and the American Right: Race, Conspiracy, and Culture* (Westport, CT: Greenwood Press, 1985), pp. 141–162.

3. In November 1965, Wallace conducted the first reported meeting to plan his 1968 presidential campaign. Included were Ned Touchstone, editor of the publication of the Louisiana Citizens' Councils; Judge John Rarick, a founder of the Louisiana Citizens' Council; and Richard Cotten, an anti-Semitic radio broadcaster. See Philip Crass, *The Wallace Factor* (New York: Mason Charter, 1976), p. 85.

    See also "Wallace Accepts Support of Klan," *New York Times*, October 1, 1967.

4. See, e.g., George Wallace speeches published in *The Citizen*, March 1965, June 1965; "Wallace '68" buttons and bumper stickers advertised in *The Citizen*, July/August 1967.

5. Jeffrey M. Elliot, "Exclusive Interview with William K. Shearer, American Indpendent Party," *Community College Social Science Quarterly*, vol. IV, no. 1, Fall 1973, p. 2, Box 21 (Right-Wing), file 21:12, Social Protest Collection, Bancroft Library, University of California, Berkeley.

6. See "Rightists Strong in Wallace Drive," and "Wallace Drive in New England Gains," *New York Times*, September 29, 1968, p. 75; and "Right-Wing Extremists Provide Vital Manpower for Third Party Drive," *Wall Street Journal*, October 24, 1968, p. 1.

    These articles name specific Wallace campaigners' precise affiliations with the John Birch Society, Citizens' Councils, Liberty Lobby, Constitution Party, and other right-wing groups.

7. Seymour Martin Lipset and Earl Raab, *The Politics of Unreason: Right-Wing Extremism in America, 1790–1970* (New York: Harper & Row, 1970), p. 355.

8. William B. Hixson, Jr., *Search for the American Right-Wing* (Princeton, NJ: Princeton University Press, 1992), pp. 124–128. Hixson summarizes the findings of Gerald C. Wright, Jr., who tested Key's hypothesis, called the "contextual effect." Wright refined the Key hypothesis by showing differences between the Deep South and the Upper South. Whereas white supremacy was more pervasive in the political culture of the Deep South, in the Upper South, electorally significant attitudes were more likely to vary depending on the size of the black population. See Gerald C. Wright, Jr. "Contextual Models of Electoral Behavior: The Southern Wallace Vote," *American Political Science Review*, vol. LXXI, June 1977, pp. 497–508.

9. Hixson, op cit., pp. 133–136.

10. Ibid., pp. 141–143.

11. Jody Carlson, *George C. Wallace and the Politics of Powerlessness* (New Brunswick, NJ: Transaction Books, 1981) pp. 160–164.

12. Walter Dean Burnham, *Critical Elections and the Mainsprings of American Politics* (New York: Norton, 1970), p. 10:

    Eras of critical realignment are marked by short, sharp reorganizations of the mass coalitional bases of the major parties which occur at periodic intervals on the national level; are often preceded by major third-party revolts which reveal the incapacity of "politics as usual" to integrate . . . emergent political demand; are closely associated with abnormal stress in the socioeconomic system; are marked by ideological polarizations and issue-distances between the major parties; . . . and have durable consequences as constituent acts which determine the outer boundaries of policy in general, though not necessarily of policies in detail.

13. Ibid., p. 189.
14. Ibid., p. 191.
15. James Lewis Canfield, *A Case of Third Party Activism: The George Wallace Campaign Worker and the American Independent Party* (Lanham, MD: University Press of America, 1984), pp. 77–78.
16. "American Party Tells Major Objectives," *The Dixon Line-Reason*, June 1969, p. 15. This was a newsletter published in southern California by Dixon Gayer, a critic and monitor of the Right.
17. Seymour Martin Lipset and Earl Raab, "The Wallace Whitelash," *Trans-Action*, December 1969, pp. 24–25.
18. Canfield, op cit., pp. 85–96, provides a useful summary.
19. For a list of the various state parties that united, and their respective chairpersons, see "National Platform of the American Independent Party," 1972, Box 21, file 12, Social Protest Collection, Bancroft Library, University of California, Berkeley.
20. Stephan Lesher, "John Schmitz is No George Wallace . . ." *New York Times Magazine*, November 5, 1972, p. 29; See also "Schmitz Details Theory on Plots," *New York Times*, August 6, 1972. The 1972 editions of *None Dare Call It Conspiracy*
21. Canfield, op cit., p. 93.
22. Ibid., pp. 94–95.
23. Tom Anderson, "Self Described 'Responsible Conservatives' Meet, Eat, and Retreat," *Liberty Bell*, May 1975, p. 6, Reel 69, Right-Wing Collection of the University of Iowa.
24. Numbers of actual activists are not available, but the Liberty Lobby appeared to fare better than the Birch Society, as indicated by the Lobby's steady maintenance of *Spotlight* newspaper circulation over 100,000. In 1985, the Birch Society consolidated its weekly *Review of the News* and monthly *American Opinion* into the biweekly *New American* magazine with a subscription base in the tens of thousands.

During the 1980s, Richard Viguerie's monthly *Conservative Digest* was edited by numerous John Birch Society figures. See the magazine's masthead for the names Scott Stanley, Jr., William R. Kennedy, Jr., John Rees, Larry Abraham, Gary Allen, Medford Evans, Susan Huck, Alan Stang, and others.

In *The Coors Connection* (Boston: South End Press, 1991), pp. 43–46, author Russ Bellant makes the important point that the New Right's leading coordinating body for funding and strategy, the Council for National Policy, included Birch Society veterans Nelson Bunker Hunt and A. Clifford Barker.

On the relationship between the Liberty Lobby and the Birch Society, see Frank Mintz, op cit., pp. 141–162. Mintz notes that under the leadership of Representative Larry P. McDonald (D-GA) during the late 1970s, the John Birch Society moved toward greater respectability through associations with the

Moral Majority, the Conservative Caucus, and the Free Congress Foundation. McDonald was targeted by *Spotlight for his pro-Israel views.*

25. On the decline of the John Birch Society, see Richard Stone, "Many Top Aides Quit Right-Wing Group, Say Funds, Members Decline," *Wall Street Journal,* September, 29, 1967, pp. 1, 16. Though membership lists and numbers were never a matter of public record, by 1967 the Society's membership was estimated at 30,000, down from about two or three times that figure a few years earlier.

26. Numan V. Bartley, *The Rise of Massive Resistance: Race and Politics in the South During the 1950's* (Baton Rouge: Louisiana State University Press, 1969), pp. 342–343.

27. Wallace was the keynote speaker at the Citizens' Councils of America's 14th Annual Leadership Conference, August 1969 in Jackson, Mississippi, along with Governors Ross Barnett and Lester Maddox, and Representative John Rarick (D-LA). See *The Citizen,* July/August 1969. The following year, Wallace was again the Councils' keynote conference speaker, in Atlanta, advertised in *The Citizen,* September 1970.

28. See William J. Simmons, "How to Organize a Private School," *The Citizen,* January 1970.

29. "Communist Influence," *American Opinion,* July-August, 1965, p. 59.

30. See Stephen Earl Bennett, "Modes of Resolution of a 'Belief Dilemma' in the Ideology of the John Birch Society," *Journal of Politics,* vol. 33, no. 3, August 1971, pp. 734–772. Bennett distilled Welch's argument from various issues of the monthly *John Birch Society Bulletin,* circa 1965.

31. For other examples of the Birch Society's stance on the Vietnam war, see, the following *American Opinion* articles: Hilaire du Berrier, "Asia: The Continent is Nearly Lost," July–August 1964, pp. 17–30; Earl Lively, Jr., "Limited War: The War We Are Supposed to Lose," October 1964, pp. 25–32; E. Merrill Root, "Vietnam: A Letter to Our Soldiers There," February 1966, pp. 31–40; and Wallis W. Wood, "It's Treason: Aid and Comfort to the Vietcong," May 1968, pp. 1–14.

32. See, e.g., the following *American Opinion* articles: Jim Slick, "King of Slick," November 1963, pp. 1–11; Jere Real, "Mr. March: Bayard Rustin and 'Civil Rights,'" May 1964, pp. 11–17; Scott Stanley, Jr., "Revolution: The Assault on Selma," May 1965, pp. 1–10; and Alan Stang, "The King and His Communists," October 1965, pp. 1–14.

    Stang authored the Birch Society's widely distributed book *It's Very Simple,* which linked U.S. race problems and the civil rights movement to a purported "communist" plot.

33. Benjamin R. Epstein and Arnold Forster, *The Radical Right: Report on the John Birch Society and Its Allies* (New York: Random House, 1966), pp. 95–106.

34. On holocaust revisionism, see especially Deborah Lipstadt, *Denying the Holocaust: The Growing Assault on Truth and Memory* (New York: The Free Press, 1993).

    This book has useful and accurate information about right-wing revisionists. But Lipstadt does a serious disservice by conflating anti-Zionism with anti-Semitism. She reports as if accurate the disinformation story that eminent linguist Noam Chomsky endorsed a revisionist book. Chomsky wrote a statement supporting Roberto Faurisson's right to free speech, but Chomsky did not endorse Faurisson's book nor his pseudoscholarship.

35. The term is used throughout John Birch Society literature. For an example of early usage, see *American Opinion*, May 1960, p. 47, which includes Robert Welch's pamphlet "The New Americanism" on a publications list. See *American Opinion*, November 1962, p. 58, for a bumper sticker advertisement, including one with the slogan "Americanism is the only 'ism' for Me!"

36. Frank Mintz, op cit., pp. 141–162 analyzes the relationship between the Lobby and the Society and notes that while Robert Welch himself would not endorse explicit racism and anti-Semitism, many of the Society's members and some of its chief ideologists did.

37. Michael Rogin, *The Intellectuals and McCarthy: The Radical Specter* (Cambridge, MA: MIT Press, 1967, pp. 173–7.

38. Ibid., pp. 212–215.

39. The best critical reading of Yockey's *Imperium* and the philosophical influences that underpinned it is to be found in Frank Mintz, op cit., pp. 24–31.

40. Ibid., p. 79. See also, Paul Valentine, "Power Base for Hard Right," *Washington Post*, May 16, 1971, p. 8, for an in-depth profile of Willis Carto. *Imperium* is featured on page 2 of the 1992 Noontide Press catalog.

41. Willis A. Carto, ed., *Profiles in Populism* (Greenwich, CT: Flag Press: 1982), pp. ix–xvi.

42. Richard Hofstadter, *The Paranoid Style in American Politics and Other Essays* (New York: Vintage Books, 1967), pp. 25–26.

43. Ibid., pp. 36–37.

44. See, e.g., Ralph De Toledano, "A Dubious Dirksen Victory," *Human Events*, March 18, 1967, p. 5; and "Consular Vote," *Human Events*, March 25, 1967, p. 3.

45. *Liberty Lowdown*, April 1967, p. 2, Reel 69, Right-Wing Collection of the University of Iowa. For more of the Liberty Lobby's conspiracy theory on the consular treaty, see also *Liberty Lowdown*, February and March 1967.

46. *Liberty Lowdown*, April 1968, p. 1.

47. Wyn Craig Wade, *The Fiery Cross: The Ku Klux Klan in America* (New York: Simon and Schuster, 1987), pp. 364–7.

48. Ibid., pp. 354–365.

49. See *Liberty Letter*, May 1963, Reel 69, Right-Wing Collection of the University of Iowa.

All subsequent *Liberty Letter* citations come from this same microfilm reel.

50. *Liberty Letter*, August 1963 and October 1963. The "faculty" for the Government Education Foundation included Senators E. Y. Berry (R-SD), William E. Brock (R-TN), John Dowdy (D-TX), James B. Utt (R-CA), Albert W. Watson (D-SC), and an aide to Texas Senator John Tower.

See also *Liberty Letter*, April 1964 and June 1964 regarding the Lobby's May 1964 "Project America" training session, cosponsored by the Government Education Foundation and the Lobby spinoff Americans for National Security. Speakers included Representatives Don Brotzman (R-CO), Clarence Brown (R-OH), Del Clawson (R-CA), Joe Waggoner (LA), and Senator John Tower's aide Tom Cole.

In April 1964 the Lobby organized a group of northern opponents of the Civil Rights Act to travel to Washington and receive a briefing by Senator Sam Ervin (D-NC).

51. William W. Turner, *Power on the Right* (Berkeley, CA: Ramparts Press, 1971), p. 153.

52. Robert Walters, "Surprising Strength Shown by Liberty Lobby," (Washington, D.C.) *Evening Star*, March 10, 1967, p. A4.

53. *Liberty Letter*, June 1965 and August 65. Over 200 "patriots" attended the seminar, jointly sponsored by Liberty Lobby, Americans for National Security, and the Government Educational Foundation.

54. Walters, op cit., The *Evening Star* reported the Liberty Lobby's role in generating thousands of constituent letters to Senators and its expenditure of thousands of dollars for the placement of newspaper advertisements against the treaty.

55. On the Liberty Lobby's first National Board of Policy convention of January 1967, see *Liberty Letter*, February 1967 and April 1967. Over 300 delegates formed issues committees and agreed to lobby against a proposed guaranteed annual income, for an immediate U.S. withdrawal from Vietnam, against federal urban renewal programs, and against federal regulation of health food sales. Speakers included Representatives George V. Hansen (R-ID), James A. McClure (R-ID), John Rarick (D-LA), James B. Utt (R-CA), and California State Senator John G. Schmitz. Around the time of the convention, Liberty Lobby invited its member–subscribers to attend dozens of coordinating meetings held in cities around the country.

   See Mintz, op cit., pp. 90–92. In 1967 the Lobby claimed 10,000 "Board of Policy" members out of the 170,000 claimed subscribers to *Liberty Letter*.

56. Paul W. Valentine, "Power Base for Hard Right," *Washington Post*, May 16, 1971, p. 8.

57. See National Youth Alliance ephemera, Reel 89, Right-Wing Collection of the University of Iowa. In particular, a "Memorandum" dated January 5, 1969, from NYA Executive Secretary Lou Andrews to "All State Chairmen," described two regional leadership conferences held in late 1968. One was held in Atlanta and included participation by Governor Lester Maddox; the other was held in New Orleans and was joined by Representative John Rarick (D-LA). The memorandum discusses the goal of forming chapters on college and high school campuses and reports "promises of help" from Maddox, Rarick, Liberty Lobby director Colonel Curtis Dall, and novelist Taylor Caldwell.

   See also "New Youth Group," *Liberty Letter*, February 1969, p. 3, which mentions "leadership organizational conferences in various cities." The NYA's stated goals were to stop drug use, "oppose black power, to restore law and order on campuses by eliminating the subversive SDS, and to keep America out of further overseas wars."

58. Turner, op cit., p. 163. NYA director Louis T. Byers was a former Birch Society coordinator who had joined the Liberty Lobby payroll. The NYA advisory board included Revilo P. Oliver, Admiral John Crommelin, Lieutenent General Pedro del Valle (Ret.), Austin App, and Richard Cotten.

   Turner, pp. 145–146, reports on a 1969 NYA meeting replete with Nazi room decorations and German marching music. The same story is told in C.

H. Simonds, "The Strange Story of Willis Carto," *National Review*, September 10, 1971, p. 986.

59. Revilo P. Oliver, "After Fifty Years," included in NYA collection, Reel 89, Right-Wing Collection of the University of Iowa. The article is prefaced by a version of the well-known story of Oliver's departure from the John Birch Society National Council.

On Oliver, generally, see Mintz, op cit., pp. 163-80.

Oliver resigned from the Birch Society in 1966 amid controversy over a speech he gave, "Conspiracy or Degeneracy," at the annual Rally for God, Family and Country held in Boston by the Birch Society. In that speech, Oliver said that "vaporizing" Jews was a "beatific vision." Turner, op cit., p. 26.

According to NYA's account, after ending his role in the Birch Society, Oliver remained on the board of Americans for National Security (a Liberty Lobby project) and a director of the Congress of Freedom.

60. The various accounts differ on precise details. See Simonds, op cit., pp. 985-987; Turner, op cit., pp. 162-164; the previously cited Paul Valentine *Washington Post* article of May 16, 1971.

61. On the development of anti-Jewish "historical revisionism" by the Liberty Lobby et al., See, e.g., Mintz, op cit., pp. 107-126. See, generally, Lipstadt, op cit.

62. Following Great Britain's relinquishing of colonial control over Rhodesia in 1965, Liberty Lobby viewed Rhodesia as

> key to the West's entire precarious position in the Afro-Asian world. If Rhodesia fails, both South Africa and Portuguese Africa will soon follow. . . . Then the entire African Continent would be in anti-Western hands and Europe would be completely outflanked and isolated from all water-borne intercourse with the Far East. ("Rhodesia—The Gathering Storm," *Liberty Lowdown*, December 1965, p. 2.)

63. *Liberty Letter*, September and December 1969, January 1972. See also the Fall 1969 issue of the Friends of Rhodesian Independence newsletter, Reel 69, Right-Wing Collection of the University of Iowa.

64. "Liberty Lobby Charts Future Gains at Giant L.A. Rally," *Liberty Letter*, May 1970.

Speakers at the event included Representatives Otto E. Passman (D-LA), Bob Price (R-TX), and John R. Rarick (D-LA).

65. See, generally, Ronald P. Formisano, *Boston Against Busing: Race, Class, and Ethnicity in the 1960s and 1970s* (Chapel Hill: University of North Carolina Press, 1991).

66. On the Lobby's anti-busing activism, see the following issues of *Liberty Letter*: April 1970, p. 2; December 1970, p. 3; "Forced Integration Threatens Public Schools," July 1971; "Forced Busing—An Un-American Outrage," November 1971; and "Busing Amendment Hot," January 1972.

67. *Liberty Letter*, December 1972, p. 4.

68. Jonathan Kelley, "The Politics of School Busing," *Public Opinion Quarterly*, Spring 1974, pp. 23-39. Anti-busing motivations were found to be mixed among the general public; among college graduates, anti-busing opinion was closely linked to racial prejudice.

69. Les Brown, "Liberty Lobby Series on Mutual is Scored by A.D.L.," *New York Times*, July 9, 1974, p. 75.

70. "Liberty Lobby Holds Survival Strategy '73 Seminar, Board of Policy Convention," *Liberty Letter*, December 1973.

71. See, esp., Michael Barkun, *Religion and the Racist Right: The Origins of the Christian Identity Movement* (Chapel Hill: University of North Carolina Press, 1994).

72. For a particularly useful typology of Christian Patriot tendencies and specific organizations, see James A. Aho, *The Politics of Righteousness: Idaho Christian Patriotism* (Seattle: University of Washington Press, 1990), pp. 13–21. Aho's diagram on p. 19 has three overlapping circles representing: (1) Christian Constitutionalists, (2) Identity Christians, and (3) Issues-oriented patriots. These categories break down further, and most of the organizations Aho lists are national rather than exclusively Idahoan.

73. See, e.g., the following *Spotlight* articles: "Anita Bryant Back on TV After Exile for Fighting Homosexual Rights Law," May 23, 1977, p. 11; "Support for Anita Bryant Morality Crusade Grows," August 1, 1977, pp. 12–13; "Sex Deviates and Their Political Backers Are in Full Retreat," September 18, 1978, pp. 4–5; and "Perverts Waging Strong Fight for 'Rights' in California," October 30, 1978, p. 8.

74. See, e.g., the following *Spotlight* articles: "Secret Deals Found in Canal Treaty Package," September 19, 1977, pp. 4–5; and "Spotlight to Charter Plane," March 20, 1978, p. 8.

75. "Youth Killed Fighting Black Reds Feared for Future of West," *National Spotlight*, September 17, 1975, p. 15.

76. See Scott Anderson and Jon Lee Anderson, *Inside the League* (New York: Dodd, Mead, 1986) for a thorough treatment of WACL's constituent member organizations.

77. First was the American Council for World Freedom (ACWF), from 1970 to 1975, led by prominent conservative activists Walter Judd, Lev Dobriansky, Lee Edwards, Reed Irvine, and John Fisher. Next was the Council on American Affairs, led by Roger Pearson, a pro-Nazi anthropologist. During the 1980s, the U.S. WACL chapter was the U.S. Council for World Freedom, headed by Major General John Singlaub (Ret.). Singlaub was the Reagan–Bush National Security Council's designated coordinator of "private" fundraising for illegal terrorist operations in Central America. See Russ Bellant, *Old Nazis, the New Right, and the Republican Party* (Boston: South End Press, 1991), pp. 65–67.

78. Two collections at the Hoover Institution Archives contain internal memoranda and correspondence on the WACL controversy over pro-Nazi member groups. See, esp. Geoffrey Stewart-Smith's Foreign Affairs Circle (British WACL chapter) memorandum, "Background Material for Evaluation," March 1974, Box 226, file: WACL, General, 1974–82, Walter Judd Collection, Hoover Institution Archives, Stanford University. Stewart-Smith's lengthy report identifies the pro-Nazi activities and affiliations of numerous WACL member groups and individuals. That same file contains a March 1, 1974 memorandum by American Council for World Freedom (ACWF) leader Thomas Lane and a March 15,

1974 ACWF memo dismissing the evidence provided by Geoffrey Stewart-Smith.

See also the WACL documents in Box 129 of the Stefan Possony Collection of the Hoover Institution Archives. Possony's collection includes WACL conference materials, plus, inter alia, a December 19, 1974 "Memorandum" to the ACWF Committee from Fred Schlafly and Lee Edwards regarding the fascist tendencies of WACL's Brazilian and Mexican affiliates.

79. Kuhl, op cit., Bellant, *Old Nazis, the New Right, and the Republican Party*, op cit., pp. 60–64. Pearson was an advocate of eugenics, the notion that human racial stock can be improved through selective breeding. Pearson was a member of the editorial board of *Policy Review*, the quarterly journal of the Heritage Foundation, until after the *Washington Post* reported on the numerous neo-Nazi groups present at the 1978 WACL conference, which Pearson sponsored. Pearson remained on the board of the American Security Council's American Foreign Policy Institute, and Pearson's Council on American Affairs was a member group of the ASC's Coalition for Peace Through Strength during the 1980s.

80. Bellant, *Old Nazis*, op cit., p. 60.

81. Paul W. Valentine, "The Fascist Specter Behind the World Anti-Red League," *Washington Post*, May 28, 1978, pp. C1–C2.

82. Lipstadt, op cit., pp. 137–156.

83. Ibid. See also Lewis Brandon (director of the IHR), "$50,000 Reward for 'Holocaust' Proof Unclaimed," *Spotlight*, June 9, 1980, p. 16. Dr. Arthur R. Butz, an electrical engineering professor at Northwest University was a major figure in the Liberty Lobby's promotion of holocaust revisionism. See, e.g., these *Spotlight* articles: "A Model of Scholarship and Research . . . Deserves Hearing," June 27, 1977, pp. 12–13; "Author Says '6 Million' Hoax Thrives on Herd Instinct," May 1, 1978, p. 4; and Dr. Arthur R. Butz, "The Extermination Allegation Entails Dramatic Impossibilities," May 8, 1978, pp. 14–16.

84. Lance Hill, "Nazi Race Doctrine," in Douglas Rose, ed., *The Emergence of David Duke and the Politics of Race* (Chapel Hill: University of North Carolina, 1992), pp. 94–111.

85. "Klan No Longer 'Invisible Empire'; Issues Aired Publicly," *National Spotlight*, October 31, 1975, p. 3. On the cover photo was a photo of a burning cross. Duke was shown in Klan uniform and was identified as the director of the Knights of the Ku Klux Klan.

86. "Klan Patrols Border to Stop Illegal Aliens," *Spotlight*, November 7, 1977, pp. 12–13.

87. "Klan Leader Runs Strong in California," *Spotlight*, July 10, 1978, p. 14; "Klansman May Ride Grass-Roots Issues Into Congress," *Spotlight*, April 21, 1980, pp. 8–9. Metzger ran first for a San Diego County supervisor's seat and then for the Democratic nomination for California's 43rd district Congressional election in 1980.

88. See, generally, Robert Kuttner, *Revolt of the Haves: Tax Rebellions and Hard Times* (New York: Simon and Schuster, 1980).

89. Robert M. Bartell, "Tax Fighters Plot 'Yes on 23' Drive," *Spotlight*, October 2, 1978, p. 3. Organizations participating included: the Liberty Lobby, American

Pistol and Rifle Association, Christian Patriots Defense League, We the People, Tax Strike News, and Liberty Amendment Committee.

90. Kevin P. Phillips, *Post-Conservative America: People, Politics, & Ideology in a Time of Crisis* (New York: Vintage Books, 1983), pp. 126–127.

91. For greater detail, see Barkun, op cit.

92. The best sources of primary Posse–Identity documents I found were William Potter Gale's *Identity* newsletter of the early and mid-1970s, Reel 61, Right-Wing Collection of the University of Iowa; and Rick Norton's *Christian Vanguard* newsletter of the same time period, Reel 23, Right-Wing Collection of the University of Iowa.

93. James Ridgeway, *Blood in the Face* (New York: Thunder's Mouth Press, 1990), p. 114.

On Mike Beach's Oregon Posse Comitatus, see "Founder of Posse Comitatus Decries Radicals, Lives Quietly," *The Oregonian,* June 23, 1985, p. B1.

94. "Petition to the Congress of the United States of America from 700,000 Registered Votes," Reel 78, Right-Wing Collection of the University of Iowa. The seventy signatories included leaders of the following outfits: various chapters of the Posse Comitatus, John Birch Society, American Party, Christian Sons of Liberty, Knights of the Ku Klux Klan (David Duke), National Association to Keep and Bear Arms, New Christian Crusade Church (Identity), National Alliance (William Pierce), Minutemen (Robert DePugh), and Liberty Lobby.

95. "Victory in Los Angeles," *Christian Vanguard* (newsletter of the New Christian Crusade Church in Louisiana), March–April 1975, pp. 1–3, Reel 23, Right-Wing Collection of the University of Iowa. The New Christian Crusade was founded by James K. Warner and led also by Reverend Rick Norton.

NOTES TO CHAPTER 7

1. John D. McCarthy and Mayer N. Zald, "Resource Mobilization and Social Movements: A Partial Theory," *American Journal of Sociology,* vol. 82, May 1977, pp. 1212–1239.

2. I introduced "parachurch" in Chapter 4 as the term used by evangelicals themselves to describe organizations or "ministries" that perform functions complementary to those of actual churches. Typically "parachurch ministries" are sustained financially by members of more than one church.

3. Jeffrey K. Hadden and Anson Shupe, *Televangelism: Power and Politics on God's Frontier* (New York: Henry Holt, 1988), p. 52.

4. Dr. Benjamin L. Armstrong, "NRB on the March," *Religious Broadcasting,* Spring 1972. As NRB's executive secretary, Armstrong reported an increase from 107 members in 1967 to 443 in 1972. Of these, 262 were program producers, 153 were Christian station owner-operators, and twenty-eight were associate members of NRB.

5. "Decade of the Tube," *Christianity Today,* March 17, 1972, pp. 40–41.

6. Russ Williams, "Heavenly Message, Earthly Designs," *Sojourners*, September 1979, pp. 17–22.
7. In Sara Diamond, *Spiritual Warfare: The Politics of the Christian Right* (Boston: South End Press, 1989), pp. 36–38, I discussed the audience size debate, including the partisan role played by sociologist Jeffrey Hadden, who evidenced his own interest in endorsing audience estimates larger in 1985 than in 1981.
8. Hadden and Shupe, op cit., p. 146.
9. Ibid., pp. 142–159. Hadden and Shupe analyze studies commissioned jointly by groups represented by the National Council of Churches and NRB in 1980. The Annenberg School of Communication and the Gallup Polling Company were hired to study audience size and viewer demographics. Results were released in 1984 and summarized in William Fore, "Religion and Television: Report on the Research," *Christian Century*, July 18–25, 1984. Unfortunately, Annenberg and Gallup did not use uniform methodology. Using different measures of viewing frequency and duration, they produced conflicting results. Annenberg reported a non-duplicated audience of 13.3 million weekly viewers, or about 6.2 percent of the viewing public. Gallup reported 70 million people responding that they had watched religious television in the past one-month period.

    Hadden and Shupe (p. 151) warned that quantitative data obscures variations between programs of different frequency and length as well as factors such as how much attention viewers pay to programs they "watch." Nevertheless, Hadden and Shupe endorsed a Nielsen company survey commissioned by Pat Robertson's Christian Broadcasting Network, which showed surprisingly large audiences of about 67 million monthly viewers of one or more of the top ten syndicated broadcasts.
10. Fore, op cit.
11. See, e.g., Kenneth L. Woodward, "Born Again! The Year of the Evangelicals," *Newsweek*, October 25, 1976; and "Back to That Oldtime Religion," *Time*, December 6, 1977.
12. "Who Are the Evangelicals?" *Christianity Today*, January 27, 1978, p. 42.
13. Ibid.
14. "The Christianity Today–Gallup Poll: An Overview," *Christianity Today*, December 21, 1979, p. 18.
15. Richard Quebedeaux, *The Worldly Evangelicals* (San Francisco: Harper & Row, 1978), p. 7.
16. For some precise figures, see Matthew C. Moen, *The Christian Right and Congress* (Tuscaloosa: University of Alabama Press, 1989), p. 22. During the 1970s, the Southern Baptist Convention grew by 14 percent; the Church of God (pentecostal) by 32 percent; the Assemblies of God (pentecostal) by 18 percent. In contrast, the Disciples of Christ declined by 23 percent; the Episcopal Church by 17 percent; the United Methodist Church by 11 percent, and the United Presbyterian Church by 22 percent.
17. Dean M. Kelley, *Why Conservative Churches Are Growing* (New York: Harper & Row, 1972); and Dean M. Kelley, "Why Conservative Churches Are Still Growing," *Journal for the Scientific Study of Religion*, June 1978, pp. 165–172.
18. Reginald W. Bibbly and Merlin B. Brinkerhoff, "The Circulation of the Saints:

A Study of People Who Join Conservative Churches," *Journal for the Scientific Study of Religion*, September 1973, pp. 273–283.

19. For details on the politics of the "shepherding" movement, see Diamond, op cit., Chapter 4, and my earlier article on the subject, "Shepherding," *Covert Action Information Bulletin*, Spring 1987, pp. 18–31. Both treatments cite the primary and secondary sources I used in studying "shepherding."

20. Diamond, *Spiritual Warfare*, op cit., Chapter 4

21. See, esp. Russ Bellant, "Word of God Network Wants to Save the World," *National Catholic Reporter*, November 18, 1988.

22. Pat Robertson's "700 Club" talk show was an ideal format for political propaganda. See Russ Williams, op cit., p. 18 for the political issues covered and the guests hosted by Robertson during the 1970s. See Diamond, *Spiritual Warfare*, op cit., pp. 14–19 and passim for CBN's political content during the 1980s.

23. Rosalind Pollack Petchesky, "Antiabortion, Antifeminism, and the Rise of the New Right," *Feminist Studies*, Summer 1981, p. 207. See also Petchesky, *Abortion and Woman's Choice: The State, Sexuality, and Reproductive Freedom* (Boston: Northeastern University Press, 1990).

24. See, e.g., Flora Davis, *Moving the Mountain: The Women's Movement In America Since 1960* (New York: Simon & Schuster, 1991), pp. 121–136. The text of ERA reads as follows:

   1. Equality of rights under the law shall not be denied or abridged by the United States or by any state on account of sex.
   2. The Congress shall have the power to enforce, by appropriate legislation, the provisions of this article.
   3. This amendment shall take effect two years after the date of ratification.

25. Donald G. Mathews and Jane Sherron De Hart, *Sex, Gender, and the Politics of ERA* (New York: Oxford University Press, 1990), pp. 44–57; Davis, op cit., p. 387.

26. Ibid., p. 389, reports that in 1975, 63 percent of men, compared with 54 percent of women polled, backed ERA. Davis cites "58% in Gallup Poll Favor Equal Rights," *New York Times*, April 10, 1975, p. 45.

27. Mathews and De Hart, op cit., pp. 50–51.

28. The 50,000 membership figure comes from "The New Activists," *Newsweek*, November 7, 1977, p. 41.

29. Mathews and De Hart, op cit., p. 87.

30. "The New Activists," op cit.

31. Anson Shupe and John Heinerman, "Mormonism and the New Christian Right: An Emerging Coalition?" *Review of Religious Research*, vol. 27, no. 2, December 1985, pp. 146–157. See also O. Kendall White, Jr., "A Review and Commentary on the Prospects of a Mormon New Christian Right Coalition," *Review of Religious Research*, vol. 28, no. 2, December 1986, pp. 180–188.

   Ezra Taft Benson died in 1994 at the age of 94. "Saints Preserve Us," *Time*, June 13, 1994, pp. 65–66.

32. Armand L. Mauss, *The Angel and the Beehive: The Mormon Struggle with Assimilation* (Urbana: University of Illinois Press, 1994), p. 117.

33. O. Kendall White, Jr. "Mormonism and the Equal Rights Amendment," *Journal of Church and State*, 1989, p. 251.
34. Ibid., p. 258.
35. Davis, op cit., pp. 400–401 and passim.
36. David W. Brady and Kent L. Tedin, "Ladies in Pink: Religion and Political Ideology in the Anti-ERA Movement," *Social Science Quarterly*, March 1976, pp. 564–575.
37. Jane J. Mansbridge, *Why We Lost the ERA* (Chicago: University of Chicago Press, 1986), pp. 67–89.
38. Ibid., pp. 90–117; Mathews and De Hart, op cit., p. 165; Pamela Johnston Conover and Virginia Gray, *Feminism and the New Right* (New York: Praeger, 1983), p. 85.
39. *The Phyllis Schlafly Report*, May 1973, p. 1, Reel 92, Right-Wing Collection of the University of Iowa.
40. *The Phyllis Schlafly Report*, February, 1972, pp. 2–3, Reel 92, Right-Wing Collection of the University of Iowa.
41. Barbara Ehrenreich, *The Hearts of Men: American Dreams and the Flight From Commitment* (New York: Anchor Books, 1983), p. 146.
42. *The Phyllis Schlafly Report*, July 1973, p. 1, Reel 92, Right-Wing Collection of the University of Iowa.
43. *The Phyllis Schlafly Report*, September 1974 and December 1974, Reel 92, Right-Wing Collection of the University of Iowa.
44. See, esp., Andrew H. Merton, *Enemies of Choice: The Right-to-Life Movement and its Threat to Abortion* (Boston: Beacon Press, 1981), pp. 91–116.
45. Ibid., pp. 126–133.
46. "The Abortion Front: End of the 'Phony War,'" *National Review*, March 2, 1973, pp. 249–250.
47. Merton, op cit., pp. 159–164.
48. Connie Paige, *The Right to Lifers* (New York: Summit Books, 1983), pp. 149–150.
49. Ibid., pp. 135–136.
50. Ibid., p. 151.
51. See, e.g., Joseph R. Gusfield, "Political Ceremony in California," *The Nation*, December 9, 1978, pp. 633–635.
52. "Christian Voice Gains Visibility Following Realignment of New Right," *Christianity Today*, November 7, 1986, p. 47. See also Perry Deane Young, *God's Bullies: Native Reflections on Preachers and Politics* (New York: Holt, Rinehart, & Winston, 1982), pp. 37, 101 for the political backgrounds of Christian Voice founders Gary Jarmin, Colonel Doner, Richard Zone, and Robert Grant.
53. Ann L. Page and Donald A. Clelland, "The Kanawha County Textbook Controversy: A Study of the Politics of Life Style Concern," *Social Forces*, September 1978, pp. 265–281.
54. "Is Morality All Right?" *Christianity Today*, November 2, 1979, p. 76. The Family Protection Act's provisions included a return of voluntary prayer to public schools, tax equity for married couples, tax deductibility for wives' housework, restriction of the food stamp program, an end to compulsory coeducational school sports programs, a ban on government funding to organizations that

"promote" homosexuality, and required parental consent for minors seeking treatment for pregnancy or venereal disease.

55. Petchesky, *Abortion and Woman's Choice*, op cit., pp. 251–252.

56. Jim Wallis and Wes Michaelson, "The Plan to Save America," *Sojourners*, April 1976. See also Kenneth L. Woodward, "Politics From the Pulpit," *Newsweek*, September 6, 1976, pp. 49–50.

57. "Field Directors Manual," Christian Freedom Foundation, Box 241, file: Christian Freedom Foundation, Walter Judd Collection, Hoover Institution Archives, Stanford University. The file also includes meeting minutes, the board of directors list, and some correspondence related to the transfer of Christian Freedom Foundation into the hands of the businessmen.

   The manual describes the "objectives of district field operations" as the education of "born again" Christians through "study groups in the neighborhoods," voter registration of Christians, participation of Christians in elections, and the development of "broad based financial support of small monthly contributors for the movement."

   The Board of Directors of the Christian Freedom Foundation, Inc. consisted of Chairman Richard M. DeVos, president of Amway Corporation; Vice-Chairman Arthur DeMoss, president of National Liberty Corporation; Secretary–Treasurer John G. Talcott, Jr., Ocean Spray Cranberry Company Executive; Claude Brown, president of Brown Trucking Corporation; Walter Gastile (in the insurance business); Dr. Howard E. Kershner, publisher of *Christian Economics*; W. Robert Stover, president of Western Temporary Personnel; Dr. Walter H. Judd (former U.S. Representative); and Jerry Hagee, John Snowberger, Ethan Jackson, and Dalton G. Seago, Jr.

58. On the history of Bright's Campus Crusade for Christ, see Diamond, *Spiritual Warfare*, pp. 51–54.

59. Woodward, op cit.; "Graham: Bright Future," *Christianity Today*, September 24, 1976, p. 56; and "God and the GOP in Kansas City," *Christianity Today*, September 10, 1976.

60. Kevin P. Phillips, *Post-Conservative America* (New York: Vintage Books, 1983), p. 91.

61. "Religion at the Polls: Strength and Conflict," *Christianity Today*, December 1, 1978, p. 40.

62. Ibid., p. 41.

63. "Is Morality All Right?" *Christianity Today*, November 2, 1979, p. 77.

64. For the story of Moral Majority's founding, see ibid., p. 78; and Dinesh D'Souza *Falwell, Before the Millennium* (Chicago: Regnery Gateway, 1984), pp. 109–112.

65. Figures cited in William B. Hixson, Jr., *Search for the American Right Wing* (Princeton, NJ: Princeton University Press, 1992), p. 237.

66. "Is Morality All Right?" op cit., p. 76.

67. On all of these people and their organizations, see Diamond, *Spiritual Warfare*, op cit.

68. "Washington for Jesus: Revival Fervor and Political Disclaimers," *Christianity Today*, May 23, 1980, pp. 46–47.

69. Paul Weyrich, "Building the Moral Majority," *Conservative Digest*, August 1979, p. 18.

70. Richard A. Viguerie, "Born-Again Christians: A New Political Force," *Conservative Digest*, August 1979, p. 48.
71. "Mobilizing the Moral Majority," *Conservative Digest*, August 1979, pp. 14–17, profiled Jerry Falwell, Moral Majority executive director Robert Billings, Greg Dixon, Ed McAteer, Pat Robertson, televangelist James Robison and Southern Baptist Convention president Adrian Rogers.
72. "Is Morality All Right?" op cit., p. 81.

NOTES TO CHAPTER 8

1. Irving Kristol, "Confessions of a True, Self-Confessed–Perhaps the Only–"'Neoconservative,'" in Kristol, *Reflections of a Neoconservative* (New York: Basic Books, 1983), pp. 75–76. Kristol notes that

   > it is most misleading to think of [neoconservatism] as any kind of "movement." It holds no meetings, has no organizational form, has no specific programmatic goals, and when two neoconservatives meet they are more likely to argue with one another than to confer or conspire.

2. Gary Dorrien, *The Neoconservative Mind: Politics, Culture, and the War of Ideology* (Philadelphia: Temple University Press, 1993), pp. 389–390 names leading neoconservatives who backed the 1992 Clinton–Gore ticket, and those who remained in the Republican camp.

3. The two definitive studies of neoconservatism are Peter Steinfels, *The Neoconservatives* (New York: Simon and Schuster, 1979) and Gary Dorrien's above-cited recent contribution. Both are excellent intellectual histories. Dorrien's focuses on the intellectual development of Irving Kristol, Norman Podhoretz, Michael Novak, and Peter Berger. Curiously, however, he neglects the role of the neoconservatives in the operational end of Reagan–Bush foreign policy during the 1980s.

4. See Alan M. Wald, *The New York Intellectuals: The Rise and Decline of the Anti-Stalinist Left from the 1930s to the 1980s* (Chapel Hill: University of North Carolina Press, 1987); Alexander Bloom, *Prodigal Sons: The New York Intellectuals and Their World* (New York: Oxford University Press, 1986); and Terry A. Cooney, *The Rise of the New York Intellectuals: Partisan Review and Its Circle* (Madison: University of Wisconsin Press, 1988.)

   The term "New York intellectuals" was associated with a cohort of writers and critics, including: Philip Rahv (*Partisan Review* editor), Mary McCarthy, Lionel Trilling, Dwight McDonald, Sidney Hook, and Hannah Arendt. These writers influenced the political thinking of would-be neoconservatives, such as Norman Podhoretz and Irving Kristol.

5. The younger generation of neoconservatives included Joshua Muravchik, Carl Gershman, Penn Kemble, and Elliot Abrams. The first three were active with the Socialist Party-affiliated Young People's Socialist League and the SP's successor, Social Democrats, U.S.A., discussed later on in this chapter. Elliot Abrams, son-in-law of Midge Decter and Norman Podhoretz, was, like Mu-

ravchik, Gershman, and Kemble, a supporter of Democratic presidential candidate Hubert Humphrey.

6. On corporate funding for neoconservatives within think tanks, see, e.g., Joseph G. Peschek, *Policy-Planning Organizations: Elite Agendas and America's Rightward Turn* (Philadelphia: Temple University Press, 1987).
7. Irving Kristol, "Memoirs of a Trotskyist," op cit., pp. 11–12.
8. Ibid., p. 10.
9. Harvey Klehr and John Earl Haynes, *The American Communist Movement* (New York: Twayne Publishers, 1992), pp. 96–147.
10. Liberals debated the domestic "communism" question heatedly in numerous issues of *Commentary* and *The New Leader*. From *Commentary*, see, e.g., Sidney Hook, "Academic Integrity and Academic Freedom," October 1949; Irving Kristol, "'Civil Liberties,' 1952—A Study in Confusion," March 1952; and Alan F. Westin, "Our Freedom—and the Rights of Communists," July 1952. From *The New Leader*, see Lucy S. Dawidowicz, "Liberals and the CP Line on McCarthyism," April 21, 1952; Senator Hubert H. Humphrey, "Should the Government Control Communist Unions," June 2, 1952; and J. C. Rich and Joseph L. Rauh, Jr., "Should Liberals Support the Smith Act?" June 23, 1952.
11. See Mary Sperling McAuliffe, *Crisis on the Left: Cold War Politics and American Liberals, 1947–1954* (Amherst: University of Massachusetts Press, 1978), pp. 5–21.
12. See Ann Fagan Ginger and David Christiano, eds., *The Cold War Against Labor* (Berkeley, CA: Meiklejohn Civil Liberties Institute, 1987).
13. The definitive work on academic McCarthyism in general, and Sidney Hook's role in particular, is Ellen W. Schrecker, *No Ivory Tower: McCarthyism and the Universities* (New York: Oxford University Press, 1986).
14. See, e.g., Sidney Hook, "Report on the International Day Against Dictatorship and War," *Partisan Review*, July 1949, pp. 722–732; Freda Kirchwey, "Battle of the Waldorf," *The Nation*, April 2, 1949, pp. 377–378; Sidney Hook, "Letter to the Editor," *The Nation*, April 30, 1949, p. 511; and Joseph P. Lash, "Weekend at the Waldorf," *New Republic*, April 18, 1949, pp. 10–14.
15. Job L. Dittberner, *The End of Ideology and American Social Thought: 1930–1960* (UMI Research Press, 1979), pp. 106–108.
16. For a thoroughly favorable treatment of the Congress for Cultural Freedom, see Peter Coleman, *The Liberal Conspiracy: The Congress for Cultural Freedom and the Struggle for the Mind of Postwar Europe* (New York: Free Press, 1989). Coleman edited *Quadrant*, the journal of CCF's Australian branch. See also Dorrien, op cit., p. 85 on CIA funding of *Encounter*.
17. Dittberner, op cit., p. 120.
18. Ibid., p. 103. Dittberner notes that the earliest use of the term "end of ideology" was by historian H. Stuart Hughes in 1951 and by Raymond Aron in *The Opium of the Intellectuals*, 1955. Cf. Seymour Martin Lipset, "Ideology and No End," *Encounter*, December 1972, p. 17. Lipset cites H. Stuart Hughes, "The End of Political Ideology," *Measure*, Spring 1951.
19. For a succinct rendition of the exposure of CCF's CIA sponsorship, complete with press citations, see Christopher Lasch, *The Agony of the American Left* (New York: Penguin, 1969), pp. 64–111.

20. Irving Kristol, "Memoirs of a Cold Warrior," *New York Times Magazine*, February 11, 1968; reprinted in Kristol, op cit., pp. 14–24.
21. See *New York Times* reports for April 27, 1966 and May 10, 1966. See also Thomas W. Braden, "I'm Glad the CIA Is 'Immoral,'" *Saturday Evening Post*, May 20, 1967. CIA officer Braden proudly detailed some of the CIA's covert funding of U.S. organizations.
22. "Liberal Anti-Communism Revisited, A Symposium," *Commentary*, September 1967, pp. 31–79. Irving Howe, on p. 52, called the Congress for Cultural Freedom unrepresentative of the anticommunist Left, but also criticized as "indefensible" the intellectuals' connections with the CIA.

    Dorrien, op cit., p. 161, discusses Norman Podhoretz's opposition to the Vietnam war for tactical, not moral, reasons.
23. Nathan Glazer, "On Being Deradicalized," *Commentary*, October 1970, p. 74.
24. Daniel Bell and Irving Kristol, "What is the Public Interest?" *Public Interest*, no. 1, Fall 1965, pp. 3–5.
25. Lee Rainwater and William L. Yancey, *The Moynihan Report and the Politics of Controversy* (Cambridge, MA: MIT Press, 1967), p. 194.
26. See, e.g., William Ryan, "Savage Discovery: The Moynihan Report," *The Nation*, November 22, 1965, reprinted in Rainwater and Yancey, op cit., pp. 457–466.
27. Herbert J. Gans, "The Negro Family: Reflections on the Moynihan Report," *Commonweal*, October 15, 1985, expanded in Rainwater and Yancey, op cit., p. 456.
28. Daniel Patrick Moynihan, "The Professors and the Poor," *Commentary*, August 1968, p. 23.
29. Ibid., p. 19.
30. Daniel P. Moynihan, "Toward a national urban policy," *Public Interest*, Fall, 1969, p. 5.
31. Ibid., pp. 16–17.
32. Nathan Glazer, "The Limits of Social Policy," *Commentary*, September 1971, p. 51.
33. Ibid., p. 53.
34. Albert O. Hirschmann, *The Rhetoric of Reaction: Perversity, Futility, Jeopardy* (Cambridge, MA: The Belknap Press of Harvard University Press, 1991).
35. Irving Kristol, "About Equality," *Commentary*, November 1972, p. 42, reprinted in Irving Kristol, *Two Cheers for Capitalism* (New York: Basic Books, 1978), paperback edition, p. 162.
36. Kristol, "About Equality," op cit., p. 43.
37. Earl Raab, "The Black Revolution and the Jewish Question," *Commentary*, January 1969.
38. Nathan Glazer, "Blacks, Jews and the Intellectuals," *Commentary*, April, 1969, p. 35.
39. See, e.g., Nathan Glazer, "Revolutionism and the Jews: The Role of the Intellectuals," *Commentary*, February 1971, pp. 55–61. This article of Glazer's, along with several others in the same issue, attracted a favorable editorial from William F. Buckley's *National Review*. See "Come On In, the Water's Fine," *National Review*, March 9, 1971, pp. 249–250. *National Review* lauded *Commentary* editor Norman Podhoretz for his "explicit disavowal of Jewish participation

in The Movement" and his labeling of "Jewish support for revolutionary groups such as the Al Fatah as 'Jewish antisemitism.'" Tellingly, Buckley appreciated Glazer's article because it "says about the Jewish intellectual establishment in America what no non-Jew could say without being thought prejudiced."

40. Nathan Glazer, "The New Left and Its Limits," *Commentary*, July 1968, p. 36.
41. Ibid., p. 37.
42. Irving Kristol, "Capitalism, Socialism, and Nihilism," *The Public Interest*, Spring, 1973, p. 9. This essay was republished in Kristol, *Two Cheers for Capitalism*, op cit.
43. Ibid., p. 12.
44. See Dennis H. Wrong, "The Case of the 'New York Review,'" *Commentary*, November 1970, pp. 49–63; and Merle Miller, "Why Norman and Jason Aren't Talking," *New York Times Magazine*, March 26, 1972, pp. 34–111.
45. Penn Kemble, "The Democrats After 1968," *Commentary*, January 1969, pp. 35–41.
46. "Come Home, Democrats," *New York Times*, December 7, 1972, p. 14; *Washington Post*, December 7, 1972, p. A6.
47. Ibid.
48. Ibid. The Coalition for a Democratic Majority's initial list of about seventy sponsors included the following: Daniel Bell, Reinhard Bendix, Zbigniew Brzezinski, Nathan Glazer, Seymour Martin Lipset, Michael Novak, Richard Pipes, Norman Podhoretz, Nelson Polsby, Eugene Rostow, Paul Seabury, and Albert Shanker.

   Of the original CDM activists, a number received appointments in the Reagan administration: Richard Schifter was an assistant secretary of state; Max Kampelman became an arms negotiator; Jeane Kirkpatrick was UN ambassador. Others joined right-wing think tanks: Ben Wattenberg, Michael Novak, and Jeane Kirkpatrick joined the American Enterprise Institute. Zbigniew Brzezinski assumed a leadership role at the Center for Strategic and International Studies.
49. "Democrats Form Group to Halt Defections," *Los Angeles Times*, December 7, 1992, p. 11.
50. "Democratic Group Forms a Coalition Against 'New Left,'" *Washington Post*, December 7, 1992, p. 13.
51. The "premature opposition" charge comes from Walter Goodman, "McGovern the Radical," *The New Leader*, Sept. 4, 1972, p. 14. See also, from the same issue, Gus Tyler, "Saving the Party," pp. 7–9; and Carl Gershman and Steven Kelman, "Two Views: Labor's Stand on McGovern," September 4, 1972, pp. 10–13.

   The phrase "premature opposition" was a play on the earlier label, "premature anti-fascist," applied as a red-baiting epithet to Communists and other anti-fascist leftists of the 1930s and 1940s. Later, anti-fascists used the term about themselves, with pride.
52. Penn Kemble and Joshua Muravchik, "The New Politics and the Democrats," *Commentary*, December 1972, p. 83.
53. Tyler, op cit., p. 8.
54. See the Socialist Party's bi-weekly newspaper *New America* from 1960 forward. During the early 1960s, editorial emphasis was given to critiques of John Birch

Society-type groups, to support for civil rights legislation; and to opposition to the Cuban revolution. During the late 1960s, *New America* featured mixed views on the Vietnam war and frequent negative reportage on the anti-war movement.

On the history of the Socialist Party, see Paul Buhle's entry in Mari Jo Buhle, Paul Buhle and Dan Georgakas, eds., *Encyclopedia of the American Left* (Urbana: University of Illinois Press, 1992), pp. 716–723.

55. "SP-DSF: 1972 Elections," *New America*, September 30, 1972, p. 2.

56. Sidney Hook, "An Open Letter to George McGovern," *New America*, September 30, 1972, pp. 4–5.

57. Irving Howe, "A New Political Force is Arising in U.S.A.," *New America*, September 30, 1972, p. 4, reprinted from the Fall 1972 issue of *Dissent*.

58. Michael Harrington, "On AFL-CIO Neutrality," *New America*, September 30, 1972, p. 5.

59. "Harrington Quits His Post: SP-SDF Disputes His Criticism," *New America*, October 25, 1972, p. 6.

60. Buhle, op cit., pp. 722–723.

61. Lewis A. Coser and Irving Howe, *The New Conservatives: A Critique from the Left* (New York: Quadrangle, 1973).

62. Arch Puddington, "Building a Social Democratic Movement in the United States," *New America*, December 31, 1972, pp. 1, 7. See also two *New York Times* dispatches: "Socialist Party Now the Social Democrats, U.S.A.," December 31, 1972; and "'Firmness' Urged on Communists," January 1, 1973.

63. Puddington, op cit., p. 7.

64. See various reports in *New America*, e.g., "CDM Hits Nixonomics," March 20, 1973; "Representative Democracy," August 30, 1973, p. 4; and "The New American Social Democratic Movement," October 31, 1974.

65. "Social Democrats, Liberals, Unionists Demand Detente with Freedom for Assistance to U.S.S.R.," statement of the Committee for Detente with Freedom, printed in *New America*, May 31, 1973. Signatories included Carl Gershman, Sidney Hook, Penn Kemble, Joshua Muravchik, Richard Perle, Earl Raab, and Ben Wattenberg.

66. Norman Podhoretz, "The Abandonment of Israel," *Commentary*, July 1976, p. 25.

67. Sidney Blumenthal, *The Rise of the Counter-Establishment: From Conservative Ideology to Political Power* (New York: Harper and Row), 1986, p. 128; Seymour Martin Lipset, "Neoconservatism: Myth and Reality," *Society*, July–August 1988, p. 34.

68. Josh Muravchik, "Democrats to the Center," *New Leader*, November 24, 1975, pp. 5–6.

69. "Writers for Carter," *Partisan Review*, vol. XLIV, no. 1, 1977, pp. 105–706. The list included Daniel Bell, Midge Decter, and Seymour Martin Lipset.

70. Jerry W. Sanders, *Peddlers of Crisis: The Committee on the Present Danger and the Politics of Containment* (Boston: South End Press, 1983), p. 8.

71. Ibid., pp. 23–70.

72. Ibid., pp. 150–160. Sanders includes the list of CPD's original membership. The executive committee consisted of Eugene Rostow, Paul Nitze, Henry Fowler, Lane Kirkland, David Packard, Charles Walker, Max Kampelman, Richard V.

Allen, Edmund Gullion, Rita Hauser, Charles Burton Marshall, Richard Pipes, John Roche, Dean Rusk, Richard Whalen, Admiral Elmo Zumwalt, Jr., (U.S.N.-Ret.), and Charles Tyroler II.

Several dozen additional members served on CPD's board of directors. Among them, prominent neoconservatives included Nathan Glazer, Jeane Kirkpatrick, Seymour Martin Lipset, Midge Decter, Norman Podhoretz, Richard Schifter, and Paul Seabury (deceased).

Other well-known figures included William J. Casey, Reagan's CIA director; Ray S. Cline, former CIA deputy director; William Colby, former CIA director; J. Peter Grace, chair of W. R. Grace Co.; Ernest LeFever, of the Ethics and Public Policy Center; Jay Lovestone, prominent AFL-CIO consultant; Richard Mellon Scaife, whose Scaife Foundation was a key funding source for the New Right; and Edward Teller, nuclear scientist.

73. For the names and precise positions, see "Members of the Board of Directors Appointed to the Reagan Administration," in Charles Tyroler II, ed., *Alerting America: The Papers of the Committee on the Present Danger* (Washington, DC: Pergamon-Brassey's International Defense Publishers, 1984), pp. ix–70i.

74. Sanders, op cit., pp. 197–704.

75. Dorrien, op cit., p. 170. The list included Jeane Kirkpatrick, Max Kampelman, Nathan Glazer, and Richard Perle. Of those on the list, Carter appointed only Peter Rosenblatt.

76. Sanders, op cit., pp. 204–708; "Groups Favoring Strong Defense Making Gains in Public Acceptance," *New York Times*, April 4, 1977, p. 50.

77. "Anti-SALT Lobbyists Outspend Pros 15 to 1," *Christian Science Monitor*, March 23, 1979, p. 1, 7.

78. Sanders, op cit., pp. 239–241.

79. Andrew Kopkind, "The Return of Cold War Liberalism," *The Nation*, April 23, 1983, p. 509.

80. Sanders, op cit., p. 252.

81. Max M. Kampelman, "Introduction," *Alerting America*, op cit., p. x

82. See "Conservatives and Liberals United to Defend Taiwan," advertisement in *Human Events*, February 17, 1979. Neoconservative signatories included Sidney Hook, Jeane Kirkpatrick, Seymour Martin Lipset, Michael Novak, Richard Pipes, Bayard Rustin, Ben Wattenberg, and AFL-CIO leaders Sol Chaiken and Albert Shanker. Veteran conservative movement signers included John Chamberlain, Ray Cline, Representative Phil Crane (R-IL), Milton Friedman, William Kintner, Stefan Possony, William Rusher, and Thomas S. Winter.

83. See esp., Philip Paull, *"International Terrorism": The Propaganda War*, San Francisco State University, unpublished MA thesis, 1982. Paull details the media outlets and "journalists" involved in the campaign, their working relationships with U.S. and foreign intelligence agencies, and the role of U.S. neoconservatives in the "terrorism" project. See pp. 105–806 for the list of U.S. participants, including George Bush, Ray S. Cline, Senator John Danforth, Midge Decter, Henry Jackson, Major General George J. Keegan, Jr., Representative Jack Kemp, Lane Kirkland, Professor Richard E. Pipes, Norman Podhoretz, Bayard Rustin, Claire Sterling, Edward Teller, Ben Wattenberg, and George F. Will.

84. Jeane Kirkpatrick, "Dictatorships and Double Standards," *Commentary*, November 1979, pp. 34–45.

85. William E. Simon, *A Time For Truth* (New York: Reader's Digest Press, 1978), p. 195.

86. Ibid., pp. 195–196.

87. Ibid., p. 231.

88. Ibid., pp. 224–225.

89. Ibid., p. 227.

90. Peschek, op cit., pp. 28–29.

91. Peter H. Stone, "The Counter-Intelligentsia," *Village Voice*, October 22, 1979, p. 14.

92. Institute for Educational Affairs, 1980 Annual Report.

93. One source for the meeting minutes and summaries of grant applications of the Institute for Educational Affairs is the John Bunzel Collection, Hoover Institution Archives, Stanford University.

94. See, e.g., Sara Diamond, "Readin', Writin', and Repressin'," *Z Magazine*, February 1991; and Sara Diamond, "Endowing the Right-Wing Academic Agenda," *Covert Action Information Bulletin*, Fall 1991.

95. Ibid.

96. Norman Podhoretz, *The Present Danger* (New York: Simon and Schuster, 1980), pp. 58–90.

97. Ibid., pp. 79–89. Dorrien, op cit., p. 170 notes that Podhoretz wrote "The Culture of Appeasement" essay during President Jimmy Carter's first year in office; Dorrien implies that Podhoretz was motivated by Carter's refusal to appoint neoconservatives to his administration.

98. Jeane Kirkpatrick, "Why We Don't Become Republicans," *Commonsense*, vol. 2, no. 3, Fall 1979, p. 30.

99. Sidney Hook, "Social Democracy Means Human Freedom: A Response to the Conservatives," *New America*, January 1979, p. 7.

100. Carl Gershman, "Why the Right is Dead Wrong," *New America*, July–August 1980, p. 6.

101. Ibid., p. 7.

102. Robert Nisbet, "The Conservative Renaissance in Perspective," *The Public Interest*, Fall 1985, p. 137.

103. See, e.g., Walter Dean Burnham, "The 1980 Earthquake: Realignment, Reaction, or What?" in Thomas Ferguson and Joel Rogers, eds., *The Hidden Election* (New York: Pantheon, 1981), p. 104. Burnham reports that Reagan won the votes of 28 percent of self-identified Democrats, while Carter won the votes of only 12 percent of self-identified Republicans.

NOTES TO CHAPTER 9

1. Karen Rothmyer, "Citizen Scaife," *Columbia Journalism Review*, July–August 1981, p. 41. Rothmyer's $100 million figure included Scaife contributions from 1979 to 1981. Her article details the recipients.

2. John S. Saloma III, *Ominous Politics: The New Conservative Labyrinth* (New York: Hill and Wang, 1984), p. 4.
3. This is the thesis of Frances Fox Piven and Richard A. Cloward, *The New Class War: Reagan's Attack on the Welfare State and Its Consequences* (New York: Pantheon, 1985).
4. Roy A. Childs, Jr., and Jeff Riggenbach, "The Lesser of Two Frights," *Libertarian Review*, December 1980, pp. 4–5.
5. Milton Mueller, "The Neoconservative in the White House," *Libertarian Review*, November–December 1981, p. 13.
6. Childs and Riggenbach, op cit.
7. Roy A. Childs, Jr., "The Landslide Before the Storm," *Libertarian Review*, January 1981, pp. 13–19; Jeffrey Rogers Hummel, "The Arms Race: Billions for Security," *Libertarian Review*, May 1981, pp. 8–17; Roy A. Childs, Jr., "El Salvador: The Myth of Progressive Reform," *Libertarian Review*, June 1981, pp. 30–35.
8. Mueller, op cit., p. 13.
9. Ibid.
10. See the following articles in the February 1980 issue of *Conservative Digest*: Paul Weyrich, "John Connally's Tough Campaign Decision," p. 19; Richard Viguerie, "John Connally for President," p. 48; George Fowler, "John Connally: A Man for the Times," pp. 10–11.
11. F. Clifton White and William J. Gill, *Why Reagan Won: A Narrative History of the Conservative Movement 1964–1981*, (Chicago: Regnery Gateway, 1981), pp. 3–7; Paul Weyrich, "George Bush Choice Raises Troublesome Questions," *Conservative Digest*, August 1980, p. 10.
12. "Bush Meets With Right-To-Lifers; Abortion Question Important," *Conservative Digest*, September 1980, p. 46.
13. "The Trouble With George Bush," *Human Events*, February 9, 1980, pp. 1, 8.
14. On corporate support for Ronald Reagan in 1980, see e.g., Thomas Ferguson and Joel Rogers, "The Reagan Victory: Corporate Coalitions in the 1980 Campaign," in Ferguson and Rogers, eds., *The Hidden Election* (New York: Pantheon, 1981), pp. 3–64. Ferguson and Rogers note on page 52 that while the heads of most major manufacturing corporations backed Reagan, investment bankers feared the economic implications of Reagan's proposed military buildup.
15. Robert D. Novak, "Reagan's New Coalition," *National Review*, August 22, 1980, p. 1023.
16. Kevin P. Phillips, *Post-Conservative America*, (New York: Vintage, 1981), p. 191.
17. "Victory at Last!" *Human Events*, November 15, 1980, pp. 1, 23; Paul Weyrich, "Election Proves Conservatives Don't Have to Abandon Their Principles to Be Victorious," *Conservative Digest*, November 1980, pp. 2–5; "Key Senate Chairmanships Won By Conservatives" and "Brief Sketches of New GOP Lawmakers," *Human Events*, November 15, 1980, pp. 3–22. Newly elected Senators and Representatives included Senators Jeremiah Denton (R-AL), Steve Symms (R-ID), Chuck Grassley (R-IA), Dan Quayle (R-IN), Bob Kasten (R-WI), Al D'Amato (R-NY), Don Nickles (R-OK), Paula Hawkins (R-FL), and Representative Vin Weber (R-MN). Important leadership of the Senate Judiciary

Committee and its Constitution subcommittee moved from Senators Ted Kennedy and Birch Bayh, respectively, to Senators Strom Thurmond (R-SC), and Orrin Hatch (R-UT).

18. Jane Stone, "Have Calumny, Will Travel," *The Nation*, October 10, 1981.

19. Howard Phillips, "Election is Biggest Win For Conservatives Since the American Revolution," *Conservative Digest*, November 1980, pp. 5–6.

20. Arch Puddington, "Hard Times Ahead After the Debacle," *New America*, November 1980, pp. 1, 9; Bayard Rustin, "Reaganomics Won't Solve Black Plight," *New America*, November 1980, p. 1.

21. Norman Podhoretz, "The New American Majority," *Commentary*, January 1981, p. 27.

22. Ibid., p. 25.

23. "NCPAC Names 1982 Targets," *Conservative Digest*, December 1980, pp. 3–5. These targets included Lloyd Bentsen (D-TX), Robert C. Byrd (D-WV), Dennis DeConcini (D-AZ), Henry Jackson (D-WA), Edward M. Kennedy (D-MA), Howard Metzenbaum (D-OH), George Mitchell (D-ME), Daniel Patrick Moynihan (D-NY), and Lowell Weicker (R-CT).

24. "A Tribute to the Conservative Movement," *National Review*, April 17, 1981, p. 402.

25. Charles L. Heatherly, ed., *Mandate for Leadership* (Washington, DC: The Heritage Foundation, 1981); Andrew C. Seamans, "Heritage Study Sets Firm Foundation for Reagan," *Human Events*, January 10, 1981, pp. 10, 16–17.

26. "Reagan Needs Conservatives to Select Key Personnel, *Human Events*, December 13, 1980, p. 1.

27. "Mixed Reviews for Reagan Transition Team," *Human Events*, November 22, 1980, p. 1; "George Bush for Secretary of State?" *Human Events*, November 22, 1980, pp. 3–4; "Caspar Weinberger: Reagan's Budget Watcher," *Human Events*, November 22, 1980, p. 4.

28. "Conservatives in the Reagan Administration," *Human Events*, February 28, 1981, pp. 10–11; "More Conservatives in the Reagan Administration," *Human Events*, April 4, 1981, pp. 10–11. These appointees included Ed Rollins, Lee Atwater, Richard V. Allen, Martin Anderson, James L. Buckley, Paul Craig Roberts, William Schneider, Norman B. Ture, Annelise G. Anderson, Doug Bandow, Elliot Abrams, Angela Buchanan, Richard Pipes, Carol Bauman, Morton C. Blackwell, Roger Fontaine, and C. Everett Koop.

29. "Kemp Places Key People in Administration," *Human Events*, January 24, 1981, p. 3.

30. See e.g., "Heritage's Report Card on Reagan Presidency," *Human Events*, 5, 1981, pp. 3–5; and "Conservative Leaders Find Administration Officials Undermining Reagan Mandate," *Human Events*, January 30, 1982, pp. 17–18.

31. On the first introduction of the Kemp–Roth tax cut bill see Paul Craig Roberts, *The Supply-Side Revolution: An Insider's Account of Policymaking in Washington* (Cambridge, MA: Harvard University Press, 1984), pp. 7–33.

32. On supply-side theory generally, see e.g., Roberts, op cit.; Sidney Blumenthal, *The Rise of the Counter-Establishment* (New York: Harper and Row, 1986), pp. 166–209; and Tom Bethell, "The Death of Keynes: Supply-Side Economic," *National Review*, 31, 1980, pp. 1560–1566.

33. Irving Kristol, "Ideology and Supply-Side Economics," *Commentary*, April 1981, pp. 50–51.

34. Blumenthal, op cit., p. 182. Jude Wanniski, "The Mundell–Laffer Hypothesis–A New View of the World Economy," *The Public Interest*, Spring 1975.

35. Representative Jack Kemp, "A Conservative Agenda for the 1980s," *Human Events*, February 23, 1980, pp. 10–11.

36. "The Reagan, GOP Tax-Cut Strategy," *Human Events*, July 5, 1980, p. 3.

37. For a brief report on the 1980 Mont Pelerin Society meeting, see John Chamberlain, "Robber Governments," *National Review*, November 28, 1980, pp. 1449–1450.

38. George Gilder, *Wealth and Poverty* (New York: Basic Books, 1981). See also "George Gilder's Wealth and Poverty: A Symposium," *National Review*, April 17, 1981, including reviews by Irving Kristol, Jay Parker, John Chamberlain, and Alan Reynolds.

39. William Greider, "The Education of David Stockman," *The Atlantic Monthly*, 1981, p. 34. For Stockman's memoir on his tenure as OMB Director, see David A. Stockman, *The Triumph of Politics: How the Reagan Revolution Failed* (New York: Harper & Row, 1986).

40. Michael Schaller, *Reckoning with Reagan: America and Its President in the 1980s* (New York: Oxford University Press, 1992), p. 47.

41. See the list of 200 New Right and Christian Right organizational leaders in "Conservatives Form Committee Against Tax Hike," *Conservative Digest*, August 1982, p. 37.

42. See the following from coverage by *Human Events* of the tax hike controversy: M. Stanton Evans, "The Largest Tax Increase in History," July 31, 1982, p. 1; "Top Reaganites Battle GOP Tax Hike," August 14, 1982, p. 3; "Civil War Rages Over GOP Tax Hike," August 21, 1982, p. 1; M. Stanton Evans, "It's Still the Biggest Tax Hike," August 21, 1982, p. 3; and M. Stanton Evans, "Is Reagan Changing Partners?" August 28, 1982, p. 1.

43. Greider, op cit., pp. 46–47.

44. Kevin Phillips, *The Politics of Rich and Poor* (New York: Harper Perennial, 1990), pp. 76–82. See also Kevin Phillips, *Boiling Point: Republicans, Democrats, and the Decline of Middle-Class Prosperity* (New York: Random House, 1993), esp. pp. 107–128.

45. "Justice Memo Raises Questions on O'Connor," *Human Events*, July 18, 1981, p. 5; "O'Connor Choice Breaks Reagan Promise, Made in Haste and Harms His Coalition," *Conservative Digest*, August 1981, p. 3. Page 17 of the same *Conservative Digest* issue lists the New Right and Christian Right groups that opposed O'Connor.

46. "Has Reagan Deserted the Conservatives?" *Conservative Digest*, July 1982. The entire issue was devoted to lists of issues, complaints, and statements by prominent New Right, neoconservative, Christian Right, and economic conservative leaders.

47. American Security Council's *Washington Report*, August 1979.

48. Holly Sklar, *Washington's War on Nicaragua* (Boston: South End Press, 1988), pp. 82–83. Sklar cites the Council on Hemispheric Affairs report of Allan Nairn, summarized in Nairn's "Reagan's Administration Links With Guate-

mala's Terrorist Government," *Covert Action Information Bulletin*, April 1981, pp. 16–21. Nairn, p. 21, quoted Reagan military adviser General Gordon Sumner (Ret.), in August 1980, defending the Guatemalan death squads: "there is really no other choice."

49. Sklar, op cit., p. 83.
50. Committee of Santa Fe, *A New Inter-American Policy for the Eighties* (Washington, DC: Council for Inter-American Security, 1980). The committee included Roger Fontaine, a Latin America adviser on Reagan's National Security Council who later went to work for the Unification Church-owned *Washington Times*; Council president Lynn Francis Bouchey; General Gordon Sumner, referred to in note 48 above; and David C. Journal of the Institute for Foreign Policy Analysis at Tufts University.
51. L. Francis Bouchey's Foreign Agents Registration Act application to the Justice Department, dated 1976, is included in Box 111, Marvin Liebman Collection, Hoover Institution Archives, Stanford University. Bouchey worked for Liebman's American Chilean Council (ACC), treated in Chapter 5. After working for ACC, Bouchey founded the Council for Inter-American Security in the late 1970s, and continued to lobby, officially or unofficially, in the interests of the Chilean and Argentine juntas. See Bouchey's own collection at the Hoover Institution Archives for miscellaneous correspondence and travel itineraries related to his South American lobbying work.
52. Ross Gelbspan, *Break-ins, Death Threats and the FBI: The Covert War Against the Central America Movement* (Boston: South End Press, 1991), pp. 76–77.
53. Committee of Santa Fe, op cit., p. 20.
54. Ibid., p. 17.
55. "How CIS Battles the Left on Central America," an interview with L. Francis Bouchey, *Human Events*, July 23, 1988, pp. 12–14. Bouchey claimed credit for recommending the establishment of "Radio Marti" aimed against Cuba and for the business investment plan known as the Caribbean Basin Initiative.

    See L. Francis Bouchey's Council for Inter-American Security collection at the Hoover Institution Archives, Stanford University. Several boxes consist of stacks of mimeographed forms on which Bouchey hand-recorded casualty counts (deaths and injuries) from various fire fights between military and guerrilla forces in El Salvador.
56. Edward Herman and Gerry O'Sullivan, *The Terrorism Industry: The Experts and Institutions that Shape Our View of Terror* (New York: Pantheon, 1989), p. 22 and passim.
57. Sklar, op cit., pp. 67–69.
58. On the El Salvador "White Paper," see e.g., Jonathan Kwitny, *Endless Enemies: The Making of an Unfriendly World* (New York: Penguin, 1984), pp. 359–71.
59. Susanne Jonas, *The Battle for Guatemala: Rebels, Death Squads, and U.S. Power* (Boulder, CO: Westview Press, 1991), pp. 198–199.
60. The Committee for the Free World, *New York Times* advertisement, April 6, 1981, Midge Decter, executive director. The lengthy signatories' list included Edward Banfield, Arnold Beichman, William J. Bennett, Robert H. Bork, John H. Bunzel, Ray S. Cline, James S. Coleman, Edwin J. Feulner, Chester E. Finn, James Finn, Roy Godson, Paul Henze, Paul Hollander, Sidney Hook, Penn

Kemble, Michael Ledeen, Guenter Lewy, Joshua Muravchik, Norman Podhoretz, Arch Puddington, Eugene V. Rostow, Bayard Rustin, Paul Seabury, Philip Siegelman, Lewis Tambs, W. Scott Thompson, and Ben Wattenberg.

For a list of the Committee for the Free World's membership as of January 1981, see Midge Decter's Committee for the Free World collection, Box 25, Hoover Institution Archives, Stanford University.

61. Richard V. Allen to Midge Decter, April 9, 1981, Committee for the Free World Collection, Hoover Institution Archives, Stanford University.

62. See the various alphabetically arranged correspondence files in Decter's collection at the Hoover Institution Archives.

On the closure of the Committee for the Free World at the end of 1990, see the small announcement in "Cease Fire," *San Francisco Chronicle*, December 28, 1990.

63. For background on *Attack on the Americas*, see David L. Aasen, "Coming Distractions," *The Nation*, February 28, 1981, pp. 246–248.

64. On the Coalition for Peace Through Strength, see Russ Bellant, *Old Nazis, the New Right, and the Republican Party* (Boston: South End Press, 1991), pp. 39–46.

65. See Midge Decter's Committee for the Free World Collection at the Hoover Institution Archives, particularly her correspondence files, for evidence of mutually supportive working relationships between neoconservative and New Right anticommunist activists.

66. "Reagan Signals Shift in U.S.-Third World Policy," *Human Events*, January 3, 1981, p. 3.

67. Kirkpatrick's November 1979 "Dictatorships and Double Standards" *Commentary* article is frequently cited. At least as revealing is Jeane Kirkpatrick, "U.S. Security and Latin America," *Commentary*, January 1981, pp. 29–40. In this article, Kirkpatrick severely distorts the history of the region, especially the role of the United States in Nicaragua. On page 36, she charges the Carter administration with deliberately bringing down the Somoza dictatorship. The main point of her article is that U.S. policy on Latin America must abandon universalist assumptions about human rights and recognize "the realities of culture, character, geography, economics, and history" (p. 40), that make each nation's circumstances a unique challenge to U.S. "security."

68. On the Lefever controversy, see e.g., the following *Human Events* reports: "Possible Lefever Choice Alarms *Post*," February 14, 1981, p. 4; "Battle Heats Up Over Lefever Nomination," April 19, 1981; "Lefever Nomination Comes to a Boil," May 30, 1981, pp. 1, 8.

In *Spiritual Warfare*, p. 150, I briefly discussed Lefever's role in the Nestle boycott in the context of his published attacks on the World Council of Churches. See also the Ernest Lefever Collection, Hoover Institution Archives.

69. *High Frontier Newsletter*, November–December 1985, pp. 7–8, listed about 150 organizations in the coalition. *High Frontier Newsletter*, author's collection.

70. Box 8, Council for Inter-American Security Collection, Hoover Institution Archives, Stanford University, includes Lynn Francis Bouchey's copies of participant lists and meeting minutes from the White House Central American Working Group.

71. Ibid.
72. See the May 31, 1983 meeting agenda, Box 8, Council for Inter-American Security collection, Hoover Institution Archives, Stanford University.
73. Memorandum, to Larry Tracy and Otto Reich, from William Pascoe and Michael Waller, dated June 14, 1984, titled "Research and Monitoring Projects," Box 2, Council for Inter-American Security Collection, Hoover Institution Archives, Stanford University. Pascoe and Waller noted that "under a personal services contract, we will prepare reports on the topics listed below and will keep the Ambassador for Public Diplomacy briefed on the activities of FMLN support groups. In addition, we will maintain a calendar of their future plans." The topics listed included a survey of the World Front in Solidarity with the People of El Salvador; a review of a Central America study prepared by the Institute for Policy Studies, and a study of "pro-revolutionary clerics and missionary personnel" in "the Central American Church Connection."

Pascoe was a Heritage Foundation policy analyst. Waller was an investigator for the Council for Inter-American Security.

For a summary of the Office of Public Diplomacy's role in the Iran-contra scandal, see Robert Parry and Peter Kornbluh, "Iran–Contra's Untold Story," *Foreign Policy*, Fall 1988, pp. 3–30.
74. Gelbspan, op cit.; Sklar, op cit., pp. 350–355.
75. See esp. Scott Anderson and Jon Lee Anderson, *Inside the League* (New York: Dodd, Mead, 1986); Joe Conason and Murray Waas, "The Old Right's New Crusade," *Village Voice*, October 22, 1985, pp. 19–22; Fred Clarkson, "Behind the Supply Lines," *Covert Action Information Bulletin*, Winter 1986, pp. 50–56.
76. Sklar, op cit., pp. 235–36.
77. In 1985, Congress' Arms Control and Foreign Policy Caucus investigated the private funding network and published a report, "Who Are the Contras?," April 18, 1985. There were numerous press accounts of the private organizations involved. See, e.g., John Dillon and Jon Lee Anderson, "Who's Behind the Aid to Nicaraguan Rebels Increases, Raising Prickly Legal Questions," *Wall Street Journal*, September 14, 1984, p. 30; "Knights of Malta Help Channel," *Washington Post*, December 27, 1984; and "Private Groups Step Up Aid to 'Contras,'" *Washington Post*, May 3, 1985.
78. Sara Diamond, *Spiritual Warfare*, op cit., p. 171.
79. Sklar, op cit., p. 241. The co-chairs of the Nicaraguan Freedom Fund board were Michael Novak and William Simon. Simon was the former Nixon administration Treasury Department official who later became a prime funder of neoconservative projects, ass head of the John Olin Foundation (see Chapter 9).
80. "Nicaragua Rebels Reported to Raise Up to $25 Million," *New York Times*, August 13, 1985, p. 1. Sklar, op cit., p. 236, notes that Singlaub's claim to have raised $25 million was highly inflated. According to figures reported by the Iran–Contra committees, Singlaub actually raised $279,612 in 1985 and a similar amount in 1986.
81. In February 1987, at the National Religious Broadcasters' convention in Washington, D.C., I interviewed Reverend Phil Derstine, whose Gospel Crusade Inc.

was part of Lieutenant Colonel Oliver North's "private" Contra supply network. Under questioning, Derstine said that following his various missions into Honduras, he was routinely debriefed at the airport by U.S. State Department and CIA officials. See Sara Diamond, "Oliver North's Religious Side—How 'Born Again' Colonel Set Up Contra's Christian Donors," February 24, 1987, syndicated by Pacific News Service, San Francisco.

82. An advertisement in the *New York Times*, June 2, 1985, p. 24C, listed PRODEMCA members, including the following: Zbigniew Brzezinski (Center for Strategic and International Studies), William C. Doherty, Jr. (American Institute for Free Labor Development), Mark Falcoff (American Enterprise Institute), Rita Freedman (Social Democrats, U.S.A.), Professor Sidney Hook, Professor Samuel P. Huntington, Penn Kemble (Coalition for a Democratic Majority), Clark Kerr (University of California), Jeane Kirkpatrick (former UN Ambassador), Professor Seymour Martin Lipset, Jorge L. Mas (Cuban American National Foundation), Michael Novak (American Enterprise Institute), Martin Peretz (*New Republic*), Norman Podhoretz, Edmund Robb (Institute on Religion and Democracy), Albert Shanker (AFL-CIO), John Silber (Boston University), Ben Wattenberg (CDM), and Allen Weinstein (Center for Democracy).

83. In February 1986, I visited the Washington, D.C. address PRODEMCA listed on its letterhead stationery and found it to be a one-desk, closet-sized office inside the larger offices of the Institute on Religion and Democracy.

84. Sklar, p. 240.

85. Box 7, file: PRODEMCA, Committee for the Free World Collection, Hoover Institution Archives, Stanford University, includes Midge Decter's list of Congressmembers who were pro- and anti-Contra aid, plus a survey form, with PRODEMCA's mailing address on the bottom, "Congressional Opinion on Aid to Nicaraguan Resistance." The PRODEMCA survey asked Congressmembers and/or their legislative aides for the reasons they supported or (especially) opposed, Contra aid. The survey asked respondents what type of information they would be amenable to, and whether they would be interested in meeting with Contra leader Arturo Cruz (who was overtly on the CIA payroll.)

86. "State Department and Intelligence Community Involvement in Domestic Activities Related to the Iran/Contra Affair," Sept. 7, 1988 Staff Report, Committee on Foreign Affairs, U.S. House of Representatives, p. 27.

At one point during the Iran–Contra operations, Kemble and Bruce Cameron took charge of (Oliver North aide) Rob Owen's front organization, the Institute for Democracy and Education in America (IDEA). Kemble was also a leader of the Institute on Religion and Democracy (IRD), which worked with Otto Reich in the State Department's Office of Public Diplomacy and received money from Miller's International Business Communications. At the PRODEMCA offices, Kemble hosted legislative strategy sessions, including at least one with State Department official Robert Kagan, prior to the 1986 Congressional votes on Contra aid.

87. See Diamond, *Spiritual Warfare*, op cit., pp. 164–168.

88. "Clark Amendment Repeal Could Wreck Soviet Plans," *Human Events*, October 10, 1981, pp. 1, 10.

89. "Four Rebel Units Sign Anti-Soviet Pact," *New York Times*, June 6, 1985, p. 16.
90. Sklar, op cit., p. 246.
91. "Right-Wing Groups Join in Capitol Hill Crusade to Help Savimbi's Anti-Communists in Angola," *Wall Street Journal*, November 25, 1985, p. 52. Central to the lobbying for UNITA were the Cuban American National Foundation and Representative Claude Pepper (D-FL); the College Republican National Committee's spin-off American Republican Foundation, Neal Blair's Free the Eagle, and Howard Phillips' Conservative Caucus. UNITA hired the high-powered Washington lobbying firm of Black, Manafort, Stone, and Kelly.
92. On the "Muldergate" operations, see Murray Waas, "Destructive Engagement: Apartheid's 'Target U.S.' Campaign," *The National Reporter* (formerly *Counterspy*), Winter 1985; Karen Rothmyer, "The South African Lobby," *The Nation*, April 19, 1980, pp. 455–458; and Diamond, *Spiritual Warfare*, op cit., pp. 192–197.
93. "Why is Chester Crocker Trying to Sell 20 Million Black Africans into Communist Slavery?" advertisement, *Conservative Digest*, May 1985, p. 18. Sponsors listed were Howard Phillips, Conservative Caucus; Paul Weyrich, Coalitions for America; Richard Viguerie, *Conservative Digest*; Major General John K. Singlaub, U.S. Council for World Freedom; F. Andy Messing, National Defense Council; Joan L. Heuter, National Association of Pro America; Larry Pratt, Gun Owners of America; Jack Abramoff, USA Foundation; Colleen Morrow, College Republican National Committee; Dr. Joseph Churba, Center for International Security; Phillip Abbott Luce, Americans for a Sound Foreign Policy; Robert Dolan, Young Americans For Freedom; Carl Olson, Conservative Caucus; Rhonda Stahlman, Conservative Alliance; Myron Wasytyk, National Captive Nations Committee; and Donald McAlvany, Council on Southern Africa.

    On the campaigns against Shultz and Crocker, see also, "Conservatives Target Shultz for Removal," *Conservative Digest*, August 1985, pp. 26–27, which described a coalition including the above-named activists plus Morton Blackwell; Ron Godwin of the Moral Majority, Ted Pantaleo of Christian Broadcasting Network; Howard Phillips, "Replace Chester Crocker," *Conservative Digest*, November 1985, pp. 69–72; "Rightists Mount Drive to Induce Shultz to Resign," *New York Times*, July 28, 1985, p. 1.
94. *Summary of Mozambican Refugee Accounts of Principally Conflict-Related Experience in Mozambique*, submitted to Ambassador Jonathan Moore, Director, Bureau for Refugee Programs and Dr. Chester Crocker, Assistant Secretary of African Affairs by Robert Garsony, U.S. Department of State, Washington, D.C., April 1988; "U.S. Asserts Mozambicans Fled From Rebels' Brutality," *New York Times*, April 21, 1988, p. 4.
95. "Rightists in U.S. Aid Mozambique Rebels," *New York Times*, May 22, 1988, p. 1. A more lengthy list of U.S. backers of UNITA and RENAMO was appended to: Prexy Nesbitt, (U.S. consultant for the Mozambican government), "Terminators, Crusaders and Gladiators: Western Support for Renamo and Unita," December 1988, unpublished paper, author's collection.
96. "Falwell Launches Campaign to Aid South Africa," *Human Events*, August 31, 1985, pp. 5–6.

97. On the Restore a More Benevolent Order (RAMBO) Coalition, see Diamond, *Spiritual Warfare*, pp. 196–97; In a 1987 phone interview, David Balsiger told me the South African government paid for the mailing of his South Africa: Nation on Trial magazine. See also Pippa Green, "Apartheid and the religious right," *Christianity and Crisis*, October 12, 1987, p. 327. RAMBO Coalition activist phone lists, press releases, and magazines, author's collection.

98. "Why Did Conservatives Join Anti-South African Brigade?" *Human Events*, 29, 1984, pp. 1, 17.

99. "Anti-Sanctions Pressure Picking Up Steam," *Human Events*, September 7, 1985, pp. 4, 8; "President Courageously Proclaims His 'No Sanctions' Policy," *Human Events*, August 2, 1986, pp. 1, 8; "Dole Key to Blocking South African Sanctions," *Human Events*, August 9, 1987, p. 3; "Lugar Hands Reagan Stunning Sanctions Defeat," *Human Events*, October 11, 1986, p. 3.

100. See Diamond, *Spiritual Warfare*, op cit., pp. 193–97, for details.

101. See ibid.,, pp. 181–191, for details. For the context in which U.S. right-wing groups participated in counterinsurgency operations in the Philippines see e.g., Lawyers' Committee for Human Rights, *Vigilantes in the Philippines: A Threat to Democratic Rule* (New York: author, 1988) and Enrique Delacruz, et al., eds. *Death Squads in the Philippines*, (San Francisco: Alliance for Philippine Concerns, 1987).

102. "Conservatives Strongly Defend Embattled President," *Human Events*, December 20, 1986, p. 17.

103. See, e.g., the advertisement for Howard Phillips' and Donald McAlvany's "South Africa '87" annual geopolitical-financial tour, in *Insight* magazine, September 21, 1987, p. 39. On mercenary activity in Central America, see, e.g., "Lonely War on the Southern Front," *Insight*, June 15, 1987, pp. 34–36. On U.S. right-wing support for ARENA, see, e.g., Deroy Murdock, "ARENA: Strong Second Party Emerging in El Salvador," *Human Events*, August 22, 1987, pp. 10–11.

   On one of Howard Phillips' and Donald McAlvany's "geopolitical financial tours" of South Africa, McAlvany reportedly urged South Africa's business community to take action against Archbishop Desmond Tutu. "The least you can do is remove the idiot's passport and not let him travel over to our country, and somebody might want to even shoot him," McAlvany said. See David Corn and Jefferson Morley, "Beltway Bandits," *The Nation*, September 26, 1988, p. 228.

104. "Conservative Forum," *Human Events*, May 9, 1987, p. 18.

105. "Conservative Forum," *Human Events*, October 31, 1987, pp. 22–23.

106. Thomas McArdle, "Kemp Leads a 'Mision Libertad' to Central America," *Human Events*, September 26, 1987, pp. 10–12. Howard Phillips and Richard Viguerie helped fund the trip. Participants included Colonel Sam Dickens of the American Security Council, television commentator Bruce Herschensohn, *Washington Times* Vice-President Ron Godwin, Contra leader Adolfo Calero, Christian Right broadcaster Marlin Maddoux, Christian Right activist Tim LaHaye, Council for Inter-American Security President Lyn Francis Bouchey, and Midge Decter of the Committee for the Free World.

107. See, e.g., Gregory Fossedal and Lewis Lehrman, "The Strategic Defense Initiative is Workable," *Human Events*, March 28, 1987, pp. 10–11.
108. "Conservative Forum," *Human Events*, May 9, 1987, p. 18.
109. "Conservatives Scramble to Set Up a Campaign Against the Missile Treaty," *New York Times*, November 27, 1987, p. 9.
110. "Conservatives Hit Reagan on Treaty," *Los Angeles Times*, December 5, 1987, pp. 1, 12.
111. William I. Robinson, *A Faustian Bargain: U.S. Intervention in the Nicaraguan Elections and American Foreign Policy in the Post-Cold War Era* (Boulder, CO: Westview Press, 1992), p. 14.
112. Ibid., pp. 15–17. See also *National Endowment for Democracy: A Foreign Policy Branch Gone Awry* (Washington, DC and Albuquerque, NM: Council on Hemispheric Affairs and Inter-Hemispheric Education Resource Center, 1990).

      NED was the outgrowth of the U.S. Information Agency-funded American Political Foundation, a bipartisan coalition of labor, business, academic, and political leaders. APF recommended that the Reagan administration establish an agency for the promotion of "democracy" abroad. With White House approval and State Department funding, APF became the nucleus of "Project Democracy," formally incorporated as NED by Congress in 1983. NED was organized as a publicly funded agency with a private citizens' board of directors. Initially, Project Democracy was attached to the National Security Council, under the supervision of Walter Raymond, Jr., a CIA propaganda specialist, who also directed the previously mentioned Office of Public Diplomacy. Raymond was also one of the administration officials active in Faith Ryan Whittlesey's White House Working Group on Central America, through which Raymond and others coordinated pro-Contra projects with the New Right, neoconservative, and Christian Right organizations.
113. Other prominent neoconservatives in NED leadership roles included AFL-CIO president Lane Kirkland, who had also been active with the Committee on the Present Danger; John Richardson, a former president of the CIA-co-ordinated Radio Free Europe; and Allen Weinstein of the Coalition for a Democratic Majority. Weinstein's own Washington, D.C. think tank, the Center for Democracy, was a principal player in NED's Nicaragua elections operation.
114. Holly Sklar and Chip Berlet, "NED, CIA and the Orwellian Democracy Project," *Covert Action Information Bulletin*, Winter 1991–1992, pp. 12–13.
115. See NED annual reports. In 1990 and 1991, as a correspondent for the (New York) *Guardian* newspaper, I wrote a series of articles on NED's collaboration with right-wing think tanks in the conduct of propaganda projects abroad. See, e.g., "Contra Funders Aid Soviet Right," *Guardian*, September 26, 1990; "U.S. Sends Central America Free (Market) Books," *Guardian*, January 9, 1991; and "What Will U.S. Send Cuba Next?" *Guardian*, May 1, 1991.
116. Robinson, op cit. is the definitive study of the role of NED and other U.S. agencies in Nicaragua's 1990 election.
117. The August–September 1989 issue of *The Freedom Fighter* newsletter (author's collection), e.g., urged anticommunist activists to consider the importance of

non-military aid to "resistance movements," and praised NED as "the best existing channel for such aid." *The Freedom Fighter* was published by the Freedom League and the Freedom Research Foundation, both non-neoconservative affiliates of the World Anti-Communist League (WACL).

118. Dilys M. Hill and Phil Williams, "The Reagan Legacy," in Dilys M. Hill, Raymond A. Moore, Phil Williams, eds., *The Reagan Presidency: An Incomplete Revolution?* (New York: St. Martin's Press, 1990), p. 235.

119. Thomas Ferguson and Joel Rogers, "The Myth of America's Turn to the Right," *The Atlantic*, May 1986, pp. 43–53. Ferguson and Rogers summarize opinion poll data showing the mass public to have remained liberal on domestic social issues despite a significant turn toward support for military spending. This finding is consistent with my earlier comment that the foreign affairs realm is one where, because citizens lack direct experience, state elites hold greater potential to shape public opinion.

NOTES TO CHAPTER 10

1. Because I have written extensively about the Christian Right's 1980s foreign affairs activism, I am not here citing precise publications, direct mail campaigns, broadcasts, events, etc. See Diamond, *Spiritual Warfare: The Politics of the Christian Right* (Boston: South End Press, 1989), and sources cited therein.

2. Matthew C. Moen, *The Transformation of the Christian Right* (Tuscaloosa: University of Alabama Press, 1992), p. 7.

3. JoAnn Gasper, "The White House Conference on Families," *Conservative Digest*, January 1980, p. 23; JoAnn Gasper, "White House Conference on Families: Stacking the Deck," *Conservative Digest*, May–June 1980, p. 31; "The White House Feud on the Family," *Christianity Today*, May 2, 1980, pp. 47–50.

4. "White House Conference Endorses Radical Program," *Human Events*, June 21, 1980, p. 8.

5. "The White House Feud on the Family," *Christianity Today*, May 2, 1980, pp. 47–50.

6. "The Pro-Family Movement," *Conservative Digest*, May–June 1980, pp. 14–15.

7. Ibid., pp. 16–24. *Conservative Digest* profiled the following New Right Senators: Jake Garn (R-UT), Orrin Hatch (R-UT), Jesse Helms (R-NC), Gordon Humphrey (R-NH), and Paul Laxalt (R-NV). On the House side, the New Right block included John Ashbrook (R-OH), Bob Bauman (R-MD) and Phil Crane (R-IL), Bob Dornan (R-CA), Henry Hyde (R-IL), and Larry McDonald (D-GA). Under "the Washington Connection," *Conservative Digest* listed Bob Baldwin, executive director of Citizens for Educational Reform; Bill Billings, executive director of the National Christian Action Coalition; his father Robert Billings, executive director of Jerry Falwell's Moral Majority; JoAnn Gasper, editor of *The Right Woman* newsletter; Connie Marshner of the Free Congress Foundation; Howard Phillips' Conservative Caucus; and Kathy Teague, executive director of the American Legislative Exchange Council.

8. Pamela Abbott and Claire Wallace, *The Family and the New Right* (London: Pluto

Press, 1992), pp. 102–103; Matthew C. Moen, *The Christian Right and Congress* (Tuscaloosa: University of Alabama Press, 1989), pp. 108, 153.

Connie Marshner's role in helping Laxalt comes from "Connie Marshner: Pro-Family Dynamo," *Conservative Digest*, May–June 1980, p. 26.

9. "The Family Protection Act: Symbol and Substance," *Moral Majority Report*, November 23, 1981, pp. 4–5.

10. On "Washington for Jesus," see Diamond, op cit., p. 61; and "Washington for Jesus: Revival Fervor and Political Disclaimers," *Christianity Today*, May 23, 1980.

11. Richard Viguerie, *The New Right: We're Ready to Lead* (Falls Church, VA: The Viguerie Company, 1981), p. 175; "Reagan Strongly Backs Traditional Values Based on Religious View of Morality," *Conservative Digest*, September 1980, pp. 20–21.

12. Doner quoted in "A Tide of Born-Again Politics," *Newsweek*, September 15, 1980, p. 29.

13. "Evangelical Group Plans November 2 Political Appeal at Churches," *Washington Post*, October 5, 1980.

14. James K. Guth, "The New Christian Right," in Robert C. Liebman and Robert Wuthnow, eds., *The New Christian Right: Mobilization and Legitimation* (New York: Aldine, 1983), p. 37.

15. Kevin P. Phillips, *Post-Conservative America: People, Politics and Ideology in a Time of Crisis* (New York: Vintage, 1982), p. 191.

16. "The Religious Right: How Much Credit Can It Take For Electoral Landslide?" *Christianity Today*, December 12, 1980, p. 53.

17. "Evangelical Leaders Hail Election And Ask Continuation of Efforts," *New York Times*, January 28, 1981.

18. Diamond, op cit., pp. 63–64. Morton Blackwell was named as the president's religious affairs adviser. Anti-abortion activist C. Everett Koop was appointed deputy assistant secretary of the Department of Health and Human Services and was later promoted to Surgeon General. James Watt was named Secretary of the Interior, and Robert Billings (Moral Majority's executive director) was given a top post in the Department of Education.

19. Moen, *The Transformation*, op cit., pp. 89–91.

20. Ibid., pp. 93–94.

21. "Reagan Starts Action on Issues Supported By New Right Groups," *Washington Post*, May 8, 1992, p. A2.

22. Godwin, "Symbols Wear Thin," *Moral Majority Report*, August 1982, p. 3.

23. Michele McKeegan, *Abortion Politics: Mutiny in the Ranks of the Right* (New York: Free Press, 1992), p. 43.

24. Douglas Johnson, "Filibuster Kills Pro-Life Bill," *Moral Majority Report*, October 1982, pp. 6–7.

25. McKeegan, op cit., p. 45.

26. Matthew C. Moen, *The Christian Right*, op cit., p. 97.

27. Ibid., pp. 102–103.

28. "Historic Amendment," *Moral Majority Report*, May 24, 1982, p. 3; "Two Prayer Amendments Sent to Senate Floor," *Moral Majority Report*, August 1983, p. 5.

29. Dick Dingman, "Conservatives Oppose Silent Prayer Amendment," *Moral Majority Report*, September 1983, p. 4.

30. Moen, *The Christian Right*, op cit., pp. 112–120; Moen, *The Transformation*, op cit., p. 96, notes that the "equal access" legislation "bred considerable litigation for the remainder of the 1980s, culminating in a Supreme Court decision upholding the constitutionality of the Equal Access Act in June 1990."

31. Moen, *The Transformation*, pp. 94–100 reviews how the Christian Right fared in Congress during the early 1980s.

32. Russell Chandler, "Falwell Sets His Sights on 'Freezeniks,'" *Los Angeles Times*, April 2, 1983; "An Open Letter from Jerry Falwell on the Nuclear Freeze," advertisement in *The Washington Times*, March 4, 1983; Robert E. Baldwin, "Peace Through Strength," *Moral Majority Report*, April 1983, pp. 2–3.

33. On the varieties of Christian Right adherents' eschatology, and Ronald Reagan's apparent belief in the "pre-tribulation rapture" version, see Diamond, op cit., pp. 130–139. Evidence of Reagan's own views is outlined in Lawrence Jones, "Reagan's Religion," *Journal of American Culture*, vol. 8, 1985, pp. 59–70.

34. Donna Eberwine, "To Rios Montt, With Love Lift," *The Nation*, February 26, 1983.

35. Susanne Jonas, *The Battle for Guatemala: Rebels, Death Squads, and U.S. Power* (Boulder, CO: Westview Press, 1991), pp. 145–154.

36. *Sectas y religiosidad en America Latina*, published by the Instituto Latinoamericano de Estudios Transnacionales, Santiago, Chile, October 1984, author's translation into English. Gospel outreach pastor quoted on p. 23.

     For further details on the role of U.S. evangelicals in Guatemala, see Diamond, op cit., pp. 164–169.

37. See, e.g., Michael T. Klare and Peter Kornbluh, *Low Intensity Warfare: Counterinsurgency, Proinsurgency, and Antiterrorism in the Eighties* (New York: Pantheon, 1988).

38. On the Institute on Religion and Democracy (IRD), see Diamond, op cit., pp. 148–157; Cynthia Brown, "The Right's Religious Red Alert," *The Nation*, March 12, 1983; "Anticommunism Binds IRD to White House," *Christianity and Crisis*, November 28, 1984, pp. 115; "U.S. State Department Joins Religious Groups to Consider Human Rights Questions," *Christianity Today*, June 14, 1985, pp. 64–66; "IRD Backs Out of Trip to Nicaragua," *Sojourners*, August–September 1985, p. 12.

39. Diamond, op cit., p. 155; Report of the Congressional Committees Investigating the Iran-Contra Affair, Senate Report No. 100–216, p. 646.

40. Diamond, op cit., p. 174.

41. Ibid., pp. 172–173. I interviewed Phil Derstine on February 2, 1987.

42. Ibid., pp. 176–177. See also Sara Diamond, "Covert Crusade for Salvador," (New York) *Guardian*, June 6, 1990, pp. 1, 8.

43. Diamond, *Spiritual Warfare*, op cit., pp. 181–191, and sources cited. The Philippines Council of Churches conducted extensive research on U.S. right-wing activity. See also Howard Goldenthal, "The Religious Right in the Philippines," *Covert Action Information Bulletin*, Winter 1987, pp. 21–24.

44. Diamond, *Spiritual Warfare*, op cit., pp. 192–200; Paul Gifford, *The Religious Right in Southern Africa* (London: Pluto Press, 1991), Jeffrey Marishane, "The Religious Right and Low-Intensity Conflict in Southern Africa," in Jan P.

Nederveen Pieterse, ed., *Christianity and Hegemony: Religion and Politics on the Frontiers of Social Change* (Oxford, England: Berg, 1992), pp. 59–120.

45. McKeegan, op cit., pp. 111–112.
46. "Incidents of Violence and Disruption Against Abortion Providers, 1993," a statistical memorandum, dated April 16, 1993, provided by the the National Abortion Federation, 1436 U Street, N.W. Suite 103, Washington, D.C. 20009. The NAF is the professional association of abortion providers.
47. McKeegan, op cit., pp. 112–113.
48. Diamond, *Spiritual Warfare*, op cit., p. 65. One of these, *Abortion and the Conscience of the Nation*, published by Thomas Nelson Books, was an expansion of an anti-abortion article, ostensibly written by Reagan himself.
49. Ibid., pp. 65–66.
50. Ibid., p. 66; *Group Research Report*, September 1984; "Some Christian Leaders Want Further Political Activism," *Christianity Today*, November 9, 1984, p. 46.
51. Diamond, *Spiritual Warfare*, op cit., pp. 69–70, and sources cited, p. 253.
52. Ibid., p. 74.
53. "Not NOW, Dear," *Washington Post*, September 26, 1992, pp. D1, D6.
54. Diamond, *Spiritual Warfare*, op cit., p. 109; Concerned Women for America newsletter, December 1987–January 1988, p. 21.
55. "Beverly LaHaye and the Hymn of the Right," *Washington Post*, September 26, 1987.
56. Diamond, *Spiritual Warfare*, op cit., pp 109–110.
57. Ibid., pp. 86–87.
58. Ibid., pp. 128–129.
59. On COR's role as a forum for evangelical theological debate, see the following *Christianity Today* articles: "The Theonomic Urge," April 21, 1989, pp. 38–40, and "Is Christ or Satan Ruler of This World?," March 5, 1990, pp. 42–44. On the cultlike organizational style known as "shepherding," see Diamond, *Spiritual Warfare*, op cit., pp. 111–127; and, on shepherding's decline, see "An Idea Whose Time Has Gone?" *Christianity Today*, March 19, 1990, pp. 38–42.
60. Fred Clarkson, "Hard COR," *Church and State*, January 1991, p. 11.
61. Diamond, *Spiritual Warfare*, op cit., pp. 78–79, and sources cited.
62. American Freedom Coalition's *American Freedom Journal*, monthly, 1987 to 1988, author's collection. The centerfold of each issue featured reports from each region, detailing each state's recent activities. These included hosting public speeches by prominent figures on the Right, literature distribution, and locally-oriented electoral training seminars.
    See also John Judis, "Rev. Moon's Rising Political Influence," *U.S News and World Report*, March 27, 1989, p. 28. The Moon organization's foreign policy arm CAUSA participated in Oliver North's covert funding operation for the Nicaraguan Contras. See Louis Trager, "Evidence Points toward North Tie to Rev. Moon," *San Francisco Examiner*, July 20, 1987.
63. Most Christian Right activists considered it beyond the pale to accept funding from Rev. Moon's Unification Church. The Church's financial and organizing influence over AFC became widely known among right-wing activists through the circulation of a self-published book by a former AFC leader. David G. Racer,

Jr., *Not For Sale: The Rev. Sun Myung Moon and One Man's Freedom*, 1989, Tiny Press, P.O. Box 6446, St. Paul, Minnesota 55106.

64. Diamond, *Spiritual Warfare*, op cit., pp. 28–35, summarizes the scandals surrounding Oral Roberts, Jim Bakker, and Jimmy Swaggart. In 1987 and 1988, the daily newspapers covered every detail of the unfolding scandals.

65. "Surviving the Slump," *Christianity Today*, February 3, 1989, pp. 32–34. See page 33 for a table summarizing Arbitron's audience size figures. Between February 1986 and July 1988, the number of viewing households for Jimmy Swaggart's ministry plummeted from 2,298,000 to 836,000; Oral Roberts' audience went from 1,269,000 to 561,000 households; Jerry Falwell's from 708,000 to 284,000 households; and Pat Robertson's from 527,000 to 191,000 households.

66. *The Directory of Religious Broadcasting*, 15th International Edition, 1992–1993, (Parsippany, NJ: National Religious Broadcasters, 1992). Overall, the religious broadcasting industry remained stable during the late 1980s and 1990s, with a few areas of flux. The table on page 20 summarizes data on numbers of part-time and full-time Christian radio and television systems and cable systems. Between 1986 and 1991, the number of full-time Christian television stations grew from 58 to 104; the number of cable television systems during the same period grew from 466 to 1,006. The number of television and film program producers dropped from 411 to 348.

67. Cory SerVaas, M.D., and Maynard Good Stoddard, "CBN's Pat Robertson: White House Next?" *The Saturday Evening Post*, March 1985. Dr. SerVaas, at the time, had a regular medical "update" feature on Robertson's "700 Club" program.

68. "What They Say About Pat Robertson," *Conservative Digest*, August 1985, p. 10.

69. Diamond, *Spiritual Warfare*, op cit., p. 75.

70. "Robertson Exhorts Followers to Run for Local Offices," *Los Angeles Times*, March 7, 1988, p. 14.

71. Moen, *The Transformation*, op cit., pp. 110–111. In Hawaii, a caucus state, Robertson won 81.3 percent of the vote. He also won the state caucuses in Alaska and Washington and came in second in caucus states Minnesota and Arizona. In regular primaries, Robertson won 21 percent of the vote in Oklahoma, 19.6 percent in South Dakota, 19.1 percent in South Carolina, 18.9 percent in Arkansas, and 18.3 percent in Louisiana.

72. Diamond, *Spiritual Warfare*, op cit., p. 80.

73. Bruce Barron, *Heaven on Earth: The Social and Political Agendas of Dominion Theology* (Grand Rapids, MI: Zondervan, 1992), p. 14.

74. On Reconstructionism, generally, see Barron, op cit.; David A. Rausch and Douglas E. Chismar, "The New Puritans and Their Theonomic Paradise," *Christian Century*, August 3–10, 1983, pp. 712–715; Rodney Clapp, "Democracy as Heresy," *Christianity Today*, February 20, 1987, pp. 17–23; Rob Boston, "Thy Kingdom Come," *Church and State*, September 1988, pp. 6–12; Anson Shupe, "Prophets of a Biblical America," *Wall Street Journal*, April 12, 1989; Randy Frame, "The Theonomic Urge," *Christianity Today*, April 21, 1989, pp. 38–40; and Frederick Clarkson, "Christian Reconstructionism," a two-part series published in Spring 1994 by *The Public Eye*, Political Research Associates, 678 Massachusetts Ave., Suite 702, Cambridge, Massachusetts 02139. For a concise treatment by Reconstructionists see

Gary North and Gary DeMar, *Christian Reconstructionism: What It Is, What It Isn't* (Tyler, TX: Institute for Christian Economics, 1991.

75. "Guru of Fundamentalism," *Newsweek*, November 1, 1982, p. 88. See also "Mission to Intellectuals," *Time*, January 11, 1960, pp. 62–64

76. Francis A. Schaeffer, *A Christian Manifesto* (Westchester, IL: Crossway Books, 1981).

77. Garry Wills, *Under God: Religion and American Politics* (New York: Simon and Schuster, 1990), p. 324.

78. Vernon C. Grounds, "An Evangelical Thinker Who Left His Mark," *Christianity Today*, June 15, 1994.

79. On pre-millenialism and post-millenialism, see Paul Boyer, *When Time Shall be No More: Prophecy Belief in Modern American Culture* (Cambridge, MA: Harvard University Press, 1992). On the Coalition on Revival, see Diamond, *Spiritual Warfare*, op cit., p. 138 and passim; Frederick Clarkson, "HardCOR," *Church and State*, January 1991.

80. Randy Frame, "Plan Calls for Doing Away with Public Schools, IRS," *Christianity Today*, November 19, 1990, pp. 57–58.

81. "COR stays put for now," *The Freedom Writer*, June 1994; newsletter published by the Institute for First Amendment Studies, P.O. Box 589, Great Barrington, Massachusetts, 01230. Newsletter editor Skipp Porteous reported the departure of Reconstructionist leader R.J. Rushdoony from COR. That left Gary DeMar and David Chilton as the only two avowed Reconstructionists on COR's board as of 1994.

82. Barron, op cit., pp. 37–41.

83. Ibid., p. 40.

84. North told me this in a March 2, 1988 phone interview.

85. Two of North's most widely circulated titles were *Backward Christian Soldiers: An Action Manual for Christian Reconstruction* (Tyler, TX: Institute for Christian Economics, 1984); and *Conspiracy: A Biblical World View* (Fort Worth, TX: Dominion Press, 1986). The latter book invoked and elaborated on the conspiracist interpretations of history promoted by John Birch Society authors, with a Biblical literalist overlay.

86. Rob Boston, "Thy Kingdom Come," *Church and State*, September 1988, p. 9.

87. Rodney Clapp, "Democracy as Heresy," *Christianity Today*, February 20, 1987, pp. 19–20.

88. For example, North's Institute for Christian Economics published Gary DeMar, *The Reduction of Christianity* and *The Legacy of Hatred Continues: A Response to Hal Lindsey's "The Road to Holocaust."*

89. Gary North, *Political Polytheism: The Myth of Pluralism* (Tyler, TX: Institute for Christian Economics, 1989), pp. 165–220.

90. Ibid, p. 194.

91. Robertson's relationship to Reconstructionism was less than clear. Robertson himself did not endorse Reconstructionism. But some of the professors at his Regent University, including Joseph Kickasola and Herbert Titus, were Reconstructionists, and the University generally promoted a "constitutionalist" version of dominion theology, one which emphasized the biblical foundations of the American political and legal system. See Barron, op cit., pp. 53–66.

92. On WallBuilders, Inc., see Rob Boston, "Sects, Lies and Videotape," *Church and State*, April 1993, pp. 8–12; and Sara Diamond, "School Days, Rule Days," *Z Magazine*, October 1994.

93. "Evangelicals Still Not Sure About Bush," *Christianity Today*, January 15, 1990, p. 44.

94. "Abortion Foes, Claiming Momentum With Bush's Election, Set Sights on High Court," *New York Times*, November 14, 1988.

95. "Promises to Keep," *Christianity Today*, February 3, 1989, pp. 44–45.

96. "Supreme Court, 5–4, Narrowing Roe v. Wade, Upholds Sharp State Limits on Abortions," *New York Times*, July 4, 1989, pp. 1, 8.

97. "On Both Sides, Advocates Predict a 50-State Battle," *New York Times*, July 4, 1989, pp. 1, 9.

98. Don Lattin, "Jerry Falwell Decides to End Moral Majority," *San Francisco Chronicle*, June 12, 1989, pp. 1, 20.

99. "Robertson Regroups 'Invisible Army' into New Coalition," *Christianity Today*, April 23, 1990, p. 35.

100. "Evangelical Broadcaster Seeks 'Pro-Family' Lobby," *Los Angeles Times*, March 4, 1989, part II, p. 7; "Why Psychologist Without a Pulpit Is Called Religious Right's New Star," *New York Times*, June 5, 1990, p. 10.

101. "Conservative Forum" *Human Events*, April 22, 1989, p. 23; July 3, 1989 Family Research Council letter to supporters, author's collection.

102. "Religious Right Drops High-Profile Tactics, Works on Local Level," *Wall Street Journal*, September 26, 1989, pp. 1, 15.

103. McKeegan, op cit., p. 145. Other restrictive anti-abortion laws were passed in Guam, Utah, and Louisiana.

104. See Dallas A. Blanchard, and Terry J. Prewitt, *Religious Violence and Abortion: the Gideon Project* (Gainesville: University Press of Florida, 1993), for a detailed treatment of a case in which four Pensacola anti-abortionists were prosecuted for a series of Christmas 1984 clinic bombings. Their trial became a *cause celebre* for the anti-abortion movement.

105. Klasen, *A Pro-Life Manifesto* (Westchester, IL: Crossway Books, 1988), pp. 20–21.

106. Scheidler, *Closed: 99 Ways to Stop Abortion* (Westchester, IL: Crossway Books, 1985).

107. Susan Faludi, "Where Did Randy Go Wrong?" *Mother Jones*, November 1989, p. 61.

108. Diamond, *Spiritual Warfare*, op cit., p. 92.

109. Endorsers listed and Beverly LaHaye quoted in *Operation Rescue News Brief*, December 1988, Binghamton, New York, pp. 1–2, author's collection.

110. Operation Rescue, May 19, 1989 letter to supporters, author's collection.

111. "Holy Week Rescues Show Movement Still Active," *Christianity Today*, August 29, 1991, p. 48.

112. Ibid.; "Time to Face the Consequences," *Christianity Today*, September 10, 1990, p. 51. I confirmed the Christian Defense Coalition's purpose, to coordinate "pro-life" attorneys, in an October 1992 phone interview with OR and CDC spokesperson Reverend Patrick Mahoney.

113. Diamond, *Spiritual Warfare*, op cit., pp. 101–104.

114. Margaret Cruikshank, *The Gay and Lesbian Liberation Movement* (New York: Routledge, 1992), pp. 77–79.

115. "Religious Right Rallies for Gay-rights Battles," *Christianity Today*, July 22, 1991, pp. 38–39.

116. George Skelton, "Wilson Signs Bill on Gay Job Rights Legislation," *Los Angeles Times*, September 26, 1992, p. 1.

117. Steve Gardiner, *Rolling Back Civil Rights: The Oregon Citizens' Alliance at Religious War*, a 1992 report published by the Coalition for Human Dignity, Portland, Oregon, pp. 22–24.

118. Ibid., p. 44.

119. "Colorado Can't Ban Gay Rights Measures," *San Francisco Chronicle*, December 15, 1993, p. 1, 18.

120. Reverend Donald Wildmon's April 5, 1989 letter is reproduced in Richard Bolton, ed., *Culture Wars: Documents from the Recent Controversies in the Arts* (New York: New Press, 1992), p. 27. Bolton's collection includes a thorough chronology of events in the NEA controversy.

121. John Frohnmayer, *Leaving Town Alive: Confessions of an Arts Warrior* (New York: Houghton Mifflin, 1993), pp. 256–258.

122. Ibid., pp. 175–176. The NEA issue was, of course, featured in early issues of *Christian American*, the newsletter Robertson's Christian Coalition mailed to prospective donors and members.

123. Frohnmayer, op cit., begins with his memoir with his February 1992 "resignation" and details the events leading up to it.

124. *Christian American* newsletters, author's collection. The Fall 1990 issue reported the Christian Coalition's role in defeating a gay rights initiative in Florida's Broward County. The Winter 1990 issue reported Christian Coalition's distribution of four million voter guides in key states where "pro-life" candidates won or retained governorships and Senate seats.

   See also Frederick Clarkson, "The Christian Coalition: On the Road to Victory?" *Church and State*, January 1992, pp. 4–7.

125. Frederick Clarkson, "California Dreamin'," *Church and State*, October 1991, pp. 4–6.

NOTES TO CHAPTER 11

1. The figure of 11,500 Klan members in 1979 comes from *When Hate Groups Come to Town: A Handbook of Effective Community Responses* (Atlanta: Center for Democratic Renewal (CDR), 1992), p. 7. CDR is the United States' leading and most reliable monitor of the organized racist Right.

2. Elinor Langer, "The American Neo-Nazi Movement Today," *The Nation*, July 16–23, 1990, p. 85. Langer based her figures on the estimates of three leading monitors of white supremacist movement activity: the Center for Democratic Renewal, the Southern Poverty Law Center, and the Anti-Defamation League of B'nai B'rith.

3. Warren Richardson's short-lived Health and Human Services nomination and

his previous employment as Liberty Lobby counsel was reported in detail in the *Washington Post*. See dispatches for the following dates in 1981: April 17, April 22, April 24, April 25, and April 26.

4. Kevin Phillips, *The Politics of Rich and Poor* (New York: Harper Collins, 1990), p. 192.

5. David H. Bennett, *The Party of Fear* (Chapel Hill: University of North Carolina Press, 1988), pp. 354–355.

6. Phillips, op cit., pp. 192–194.

7. Bennett, op cit., p. 354.

8. James Ridgeway, *Blood in the Face* (New York: Thunder's Mouth Press, 1990), p. 115.

9. For a summary on the Posse Comitatus, see James Coates, *Armed and Dangerous: The Rise of the Survivalist Right* (New York: Hill and Wang, 1987), pp. 104–122.

10. For details on the activities of James Wickstrom, Rick Elliott, and others, see Leonard Zeskind, "Background Report on Racist and Anti-Semitic Organizational Intervention in the Farm Protest Movement," Center for Democratic Renewal, Atlanta, Georgia, 1985; Wayne King, "Right-Wing Extremists Seek to Recruit Farmers," *New York Times*, September 20, 1985; and Coates, op cit.

11. For details on anti-racist organizing in the Farm Belt, see the Center for Democratic Renewal's *When Hate Groups Come to Town*, op cit., pp. 118–127.

12. "Bureaucracy Grows in America," *Spotlight*, March 21, 1983, p. 5.

13. The whole story is told in James Corcoran, *Bitter Harvest: Gordon Kahl and the Posse Comitatus, Murder in the Heartland* (New York: Penguin, 1990).

14. Coates, op cit., pp. 120–122.

15. Willis A. Carto, ed., *Profiles in Populism* (Old Greenwich, CT: Flag Press, 1982). Throughout the 1980s, *Profiles in Populism* was promoted frequently and sold through the Liberty Lobby's *Spotlight*.

16. For *Spotlight*'s application of the "populist" label to Jean Marie LePen and David Duke, see, e.g., "French Populist Leading in Polls," *Spotlight*, February 29, 1988, p. 6; "Drive for Matching Funds by David Duke Campaign," *Spotlight*, December 7, 1987, p. 6. In *Spotlight* reportage, Duke was routinely identified as "the maverick populist."

    The connection between populism and fascism recalls the analysis of populism produced by pluralist social scientists of the 1950s. See Michael Paul Rogin, *The Intellectuals and McCarthy: The Radical Specter* (Cambridge, MA: MIT Press, 1967). Rogin notes (p. 212) that Victor Ferkiss, in particular, linked American populism to fascism "because both movements favored government intervention in the economy to preserve capitalism. By this token, the New Deal was also fascist."

17. See, e.g., "Christian Pastors Praise Spotlight's Trilateral Exposes," *Spotlight*, April 14, 1980, p. 12, plus regularly published advertisements for Pastors Sheldon Emry, Bertrand Comparet, and others.

18. *Spotlight* published frequent Institute for Historical Review advertisements such as "The Hoax of the Twentieth Century," *Spotlight Supplement*, March 2, 1981, p. B3, and detailed reports on IHR conferences such as "Revisionists Hold Conference Despite Harassments and Threats," *Spotlight*, Dec, 14, 1981, pp. 16–17.

19. *Spotlight* published regular news reports, flattering to the Klansmen on trial. See, e.g., "Government Role in Killings Probed," March 14, 1983; "'Asheville Six' Conviction Overturned," June 6, 1983; "Government Will Try Again For Asheville Six Conviction," August 8, 1983; "Informer Involvement Downplayed at Shootout Trial in North Carolina," April 30, 1984.

20. Richard A. Viguerie, *The Establishment vs. the People* (Chicago: Regnery Gateway, 1983), pp. 3–11 and passim.

21. "New Right Wants 'Populist' Mantle," *Spotlight*, January 2–9, 1984, p. 4.

22. Ibid.

23. Ibid.

24. Weems' Klan background was detailed in a 1984 report by Leonard Zeskind, "It's Not Populism—America's New Populist Party: A Fraud by Racists and Anti-Semites," published by the National Anti-Klan Network and the Klanwatch Project of the Southern Poverty Law Center, available through the Center for Democratic Renewal, Atlanta, Georgia.

    Weems' Klan background was never included in *Spotlight*'s coverage of the Populist Party but it was mentioned in an article about Weem's own 1981 Congressional campaign. "'White Elephant' Is People's Choice," *Spotlight*, June 22, 1981, p. 30.

25. "Party for Populists is Organized," *Spotlight*, March 12, 1984, p. 1.

26. "Populist Party Announces Platform," *Spotlight*, March 19, 1984, pp. 3, 29.

27. Leonard Zeskind report, "It's Not Populism," op cit.

28. "California Joins the Populist Party," *Spotlight*, June 4, 1984, p. 1. A supplement to the October 1, 1984 *Spotlight* included a listing of Populist Party chairpersons for forty-nine states; only in fourteen states did the party achieve ballot status.

29. "Populists Slate a National Meeting," *Spotlight*, June 4, 1984, p. 3; "Populists Tap Richards and Salaman," *Spotlight*, September 3, 1984, p. 1; and "Nominees Bring Experience to Race," *Spotlight*, September 3, 1984, p. 11.

30. Salaman, e.g., spoke at an October 1984 "prayer day" at the "Mo-Ark Christian Campgrounds" in Missouri. "National Prayer Day Planned," *Spotlight*, October 22, 1984, pp. 18–19. According to the Anti-Defamation League, the campground was part of a training facility for the anti-Semitic and paramilitary Christian Patriots Defense League. "The Populist Party: The Politics of Right-Wing Extremism," Anti-Defamation League of B'nai B'rith, Fall, 1985, p. 4.

31. "Populist Party Showing Fast Growth," *Spotlight*, January 7–14, 1985, p. 1, 46.

32. For the Liberty Lobby's perspective on the Populist Party split, see the following articles in the *Spotlight*: "Grass-Roots Populist Leaders Fighting National Level Coup," May 12, 1986, pp. 4–6; "Editorial," May 19, 1986, p. 26; "Party Saboteurs' Agenda Surfaces," June 30, 1986, p. 4.

33. "Populists run Duke for president," *The Monitor*, November 1988, pp. 4–5, published by The Center for Democratic Renewal, Atlanta, Georgia.

34. Among numerous sources on David Duke's background and ideology, the most useful are Douglas Rose, ed., *The Emergence of David Duke and the Politics of Race* (Chapel Hill: University of North Carolina Press, 1992); and "A Special Double Issue on David Duke," *The Texas Observer*, January 17–31, 1992 (available from Texas Observer Reprints, 307 West 7th St., Austin, TX 78701).

    The development and persistence of Duke's explicitly neo-Nazi ideology

396 • *Notes to Chapter 11* •

is traced in Lance Hill, "Nazi Race Doctrine in the Political Thought of David Duke," in Rose, op cit., pp. 94–111.

35. William V. Moore, "David Duke: The White Knight," in Rose, op cit., p. 48.
36. Ibid., pp. 49–51.
37. "Populists Select Duke and Gritz," and "'Rambo' gets Veep Nod in Cincinnati," *Spotlight*, March 28, 1988, pp. 4–5. Gritz and Duke were photographed clasping each other's hands.
38. "'Bo' Gritz Opts for House Race," *Spotlight*, April 18, 1988, p. 6.
39. Moore, in Rose, op cit., p. 51.
40. Ibid., p. 52. See also Lawrence N. Powell, "Slouching toward Baton Rouge: The 1989 Legislative Election of David Duke," in Rose, op cit., pp. 12–40.
41. Elizabeth A. Rickey, "The Nazi and the Republicans: An Insider View of the Response of the Louisiana Republican Party to David Duke," in Rose, op cit., pp. 65–66.
42. Douglas Rose with Gary Esolen, "DuKKKe for Governor," in Rose, op cit., p. 231.
43. The Populist Party did field numerous candidates; other racist Right activists ran for office as Republicans or Democrats. For a description of some of the candidacies, see "Populists seek Duke repeat," *The Monitor*, August 1990, p. 9, Center for Democratic Renewal, Atlanta, Georgia.
44. On the formation of the Populist Action Committee and, later, the Liberty Lobby's refusal to support Bo Gritz' campaign, see the following articles by Sara Diamond: "'Populists' Tap Resentment of the Elite," *Guardian*, July 3, 1991, p. 4; "The Right's Grass Roots," *Z Magazine*, March 1992, pp. 19–23; and "Patriots on Parade," *Z Magazine*, September 1992, pp. 20–22.
45. Duke's best-known associates during his 1988 presidential campaign were his campaign manager Ralph Forbes, a veteran of the Klan and American Nazi Party, and Don Black, who assumed national leadership of the Knights of the Ku Klux Klan when Duke himself abandoned the position in 1980.
46. See, generally, Michael Barkun, *Religion and the Racist Right: The Origins of the Christian Identity Movement* (Chapel Hill: University of North Carolina Press, 1994).
47. The above account is told in greater detail in Kevin Flynn and Gary Gerhardt, *The Silent Brotherhood: Inside America's Racist Underground* (New York: Free Press, 1989), pp. 46–68.
48. See Sara Diamond, *Spiritual Warfare*, pp. 134–141.
49. Flynn and Gerhardt, op cit.; Ridgeway, op cit.
50. Ibid.
51. The mainstream press covered the arrests, trial and sentencing in detail. See, e.g., *New York Times* dispatches for the following dates: April 4, 1985, 16, 22, 23, 24, and 28, 1985; September 9, 17, and 26, 1985; October 3, 1985; December 11 and 31, 1985; and February 7, 1986
52. The story is told in detail in Cheri Seymour, *Committee of the States: Inside the Radical Right* (Mariposa, CA: Camden Place Communications, 1991).
53. Ibid., p. 180.
54. Langer, op cit., p. 90.
55. Robert Miles, "From the Mountain," typed and mimeographed bimonthly

newsletter, author's collection. Miles made particular mention of the Liberty Lobby's failure to give the Fort Smith trial prominent coverage in *The Spotlight*. For the few sketchy reports, see *Spotlight* articles in the following issues: February 1, 1988; March 7, 1988; and April 25, 1988

56. On "Race and Reason," see Langer, op cit., pp. 85–87.

57. Ibid., pp. 98–99.

58. John Schrag, "Supremacy Verdict Hurts Civil Liberties," *In These Times*, October 31–November 6, 1990, p. 2.

59. Ibid., p. 104.

60. See the Center for Democratic Renewal's *When Hate Groups Come to Town*, op cit.; also CDR's *They Don't All Wear Sheets: A Chronology of Racist and Far Right Violence, 1980–86*, Atlanta, Georgia.

    One dimension of the rise of the "hate crime" phenomenon in the late 1980s was a dramatic increase in incidents of violence against homosexuals. See, e.g., "Record Level of Violence Against Gays Reported," *Los Angeles Times*, June 8, 1989; and "Forty-Two Percent Rise in Harassment of Gays Found," *Los Angeles Times*, June 7, 1988.

61. "Bush Signs Act Requiring Records on Hate Crimes," *Washington Post*, April 24, 1990.

62. Robert Miles' "From the Mountain" newletter, March–April 1988, p. 12, author's collection.

63. Douglas D. Rose with Gary Esolen, "DuKKKe for Governor," in Rose, op cit., pp. 218–22.

64. Ibid., pp. 210–211.

65. Ibid., pp. 212–213. One of Duke's campaign backers, Reverend Billy McCormack was also a leader of the Lousiana branch of Pat Robertson's Christian Coalition. On November 16, 1991, the day of Duke's run-off race for the governorship, McCormack was in Virginia at a Christian Coalition conference, where he told reporters of his support for Duke.

66. Douglas D. Rose, "Six Explanations in Search of Support," in Rose, op cit., pp. 156–196.

67. Ronald King, "On Particulars, Universals, and Neat Tricks," in Rose, op cit., pp. 245–246.

68. Samuel Francis, "The Education of David Duke," *Chronicles*, Feb. 1992, p. 8.

69. Ibid., p. 9.

70. Patrick Buchanan, "Duke's Challenge to the Right," *Washington Times*, Oct. 23, 1991, p. F1.

NOTES TO CHAPTER 12

1. "Conservatives Looking to Quayle As Their Top Ally in the White House," *New York Times*, November 17, 1988; and "Quayle Shuns Role as Right-Wing Link," *New York Times*, December 1, 1988.

2. "Bush Pleases Conservatives, Cuts into Democrats' Turf," *Washington Times*,

February 13, 1989, p. 3; and "Evangelicals Hear Bush Support for Tuition Tax Credits," *Washington Times*, April 19, 1989.

3. "Cheney Nomination Delights Conservatives," *Washington Times*, March 13, 1989.

4. Paul Craig Roberts, "Bringing Down the House That Reagan Built," *National Review*, July 23, 1990, p. 33.

5. "Bush's Surrender on Civil Rights," *Human Events*, November 9, 1991, pp. 1, 17.

6. "Where Do Conservatives Go From Here?" *Human Events*, November 10, 1990, pp. 1, 7.

7. Richard A. Viguerie and Steve Allen, "Bush Loses the Right Wing," *New York Times*, December 18, 1990. (This Steve Allen was not the famous comedian but rather the communications director for Viguerie's outfit, United Conservatives of America.)

8. "How Has the United States Met Its Major Challenges Since 1945?," *Commentary*, November 1985. The contributors were Lionel Abel, William Barrett, Peter L. Berger, Walter Berns, Midge Decter, Joseph Epstein, Suzanne Garment, Nathan Glazer, Owen Harries, Sidney Hook, Jeane Kirkpatrick, Joseph Kraft, Irving Kristol, Walter Laqueur, Michael Ledeen, Daniel P. Moynihan, Richard John Neuhaus, Robert Nisbet, Michael Novak, William Phillips, Richard Pipes, Eugene V. Rostow, Bayard Rustin, Edward Shils, John R. Silber, Robert W. Tucker, Ernest van den Haag, James Q. Wilson, and Albert Wohlstetter.

9. Elliot Cohen's introductory statement, excerpted in Ibid., p. 25.

10. Ibid., p. 36.

11. Ibid., p. 49.

12. Ibid., p. 57–58.

13. Ibid., p. 58.

14. Joseph Sobran, "Notes for the Reactionary of Tomorrow," *National Review*, December 31, 1985, p. 32.

15. Ibid., p. 33.

16. An important source on paleoconservatism is Paul Gottfried, *The Conservative Movement*, revised edition (New York: Twayne Publishers, 1993). The title is misleading as the bulk of the book is about paleoconservatives and their feud with neoconservatives. Gottfried, a humanities professor at Elizabethtown College, is himself one of paleoconservatism's leading advocates. Though ethnically Jewish himself, Gottfried routinely emphasizes the Jewish background of neoconservatives and others he disagrees with. In the book, p. 152, he erroneously categorizes me with two liberal writers, who also happen to be Jews, and claims we all favor "the cosmopolitan and pro-Israeli neoconservatives" over paleoconservatives. In my own case, such a claim is simply untrue and smacks of Jew-baiting.

17. John B. Judis, "The Conservative Wars," *New Republic*, August 11–18, 1986, pp. 15–16.

18. Clyde Wilson, "The Conservative Identity," *The Intercollegiate Review*, Spring 1986, pp. 6–7.

19. M. E. Bradford, "On Being Conservative in a Post-Liberal Era," *The Intercollegiate Review*, Spring 1986, pp. 15–16.
20. Jeffrey Hart, "Gang Warfare in Chicago," *National Review*, June 6, 1986, pp. 32–33.
21. Stephen J. Tonsor, "Why I Too am not a Neoconservative," *National Review*, June 20, 1986, pp. 54–56. See also Eugene B. Meyer, "The Case for Tolerance," *National Review*, July 18, 1986, p. 45.
22. Alexander Cockburn, "Beat the Devil" column, *The Nation*, July 5–12, 1986, p. 7.
23. Judis, op cit., p. 18.
24. Alexander Cockburn, "Beat the Devil," column for *The Nation*, June 7, 1986, p. 785.
25. Back issues of *Instauration*, author's collection.
26. William F. Buckley, Jr., "Notes and Asides," *National Review*, July 4, 1986, pp. 19–20.
27. Gottfried, op cit., p. 125.
28. Ibid., pp. 144–145.
29. "Rockford Rift Leads to a Showdown," *Washington Times*, May 18, 1989, pp. E1–2.
30. Ibid., and "Magazine Dispute Reflects Rift on U.S. Right," *New York Times*, May 16, 1989, p. 1, 12.
31. Ibid.
32. Kirk quoted in "Ugly accusations split conservatives," *Washington Times*, June 2, 1989, p. A1.
33. "Ugly accusations split conservatives," *Washington Times*, June 2, 1989, p. A6.
34. "As communism's ship takes on more water, conservatives tread it," *Washington Times*, December 27, 1989, pp. A1, 10.
35. "Conservatives war over dinner," *Washington Times*, February 5, 1990, pp. A1, 6.
36. "Conservatives seek 'new problems, threats,'" *Washington Times*, March 2, 1990, p. A5.
37. The Committee formally ceased existence at the end of 1990. Gary Dorrien, *The Neoconservative Mind: Politics, Culture, and the War of Ideology* (Philadelphia: Temple University Press, 1993), p. 350.
38. "Neoconservatives meet in search of common ground," *Washington Times*, April 24, 1990; and "Neoconservatives' 'peace dividend' is internal strife," *Washington Times*, April 30, 1990.
39. Patrick J. Buchanan, "America First—and Second, and Third," *The National Interest*, Spring 1990, p. 77, 81.
40. I detailed the neoconservative origins of NAS in "Readin,' Writin,' and Repressin," *Z Magazine*, February 1991. See also Jon Weiner, "Campus Voices Right and Left," *The Nation*, December 12, 1988, pp. 644–646; and Sara Diamond, "Notes on Political Correctness," *Z Magazine*, July–August, 1993.
41. On the anti-PC media campaign and its relation to multicultural education, see the Fall 1992 special issue of *Radical History Review*, esp., Michael Denning, "The Academic Left and the Rise of Cultural Studies," and Joan W. Scott, "The Campaign Against Political Correctness: What's Really at Stake."

42. See, e.g., "Cry of anti-Semitism seeps into Gulf debate," *Washington Times*, September 17, 1990, p. A1, 11; "Rosenthal vs. Buchanan—war of words keeps on getting hotter," *Washington Times*, September 20, 1990, p. 3; Patrick Buchanan, "Scarlet letter returned to sender," *Washington Times*, September 19, 1990, p. G1. A useful summary and analysis of the conflict is Eric Alterman, "The Pat and Abe Show," *The Nation*, November 5, 1990, pp. 517–520.

43. "U.S. Role in Gulf Splits Conservatives," *New York Times*, September 6, 1990, p. A11.

44. Ben Wattenberg, "Chicken hawks lay an egg?" *Washington Times*, September 12, 1990, p. G1, 4.

45. See, e.g., "Bush Backers Concerned About 'Land War' Talk," December 22, 1990; "Bush Should Rule Out Land War in Gulf Crisis," January 19, 1991. Later, *Human Events* published "Hail to the Chief!" as its March 9, 1991 cover editorial.

46. Joseph Sobran, "Why National Review is Wrong," *National Review*, October 15, 1990, p. 64, 92.

47. Norman Podhoretz, "Enter the Peace Party," *Commentary*, January 1991, p. 21.

48. Committee to Avert a Mideast Holocaust, Fall, 1990 through Spring, 1991 mailings, author's collection; "Conservative war opponents facing dilemma," *National Catholic Reporter*, January 25, 1991, p. 12.

49. Frederick Clarkson, "Money talks, but whose voice is it?" *In These Times*, January 30–February 5, 1991, p. 13.

50. Coalition for America at Risk, emergency action kit, postmarked November 27, 1990, author's collection. The Coalition's list of advisors included David Barron, Dr. Robert Billings, Lynn Bouchey, Colonel Samuel T. Dickens, Dr. Robert Grant, Benjamin Hart, Gary Jarmin, David Keene, Dr. Tim LaHaye, Ambassador Charles Lichenstein, Ralph Reed, John Rees, H. L. Bill Richardson, Duncan Sellars, Major General John K. Singlaub, Doug Wead, and Dr. Jack Wheeler.

51. "U.S. Charges Three As Kuwaiti Agents," *New York Times*, July 8, 1992; "Ex-Envoy Faces Charges Over Helping Kuwait," *San Francisco Chronicle*, July 8, 1992. Because Zakhem was a candidate for U.S. Senate from Colorado in June 1992, Denver's *Rocky Mountain News* published a series of reports on the revelations that Kuwait secretly financed advertisements through Zakhem, Kennedy, and Stanley. See dispatches for May 15, 17, 19, 22, 24, and 29 of 1992.

52. Pro-war rallies were described in "Backers of Policy Seize Initiative in the Streets," *New York Times*, February 6, 1991, p. 7.

53. Holly Sklar, "Brave New World Order," in Cynthia Peters, ed., *Collateral Damage: The 'New World Order' at Home and Abroad* (Boston: South End Press, 1992), p. 15. See also Ramsey Clark and others, *War Crimes: A Report on United States War Crimes Against Iraq* (Washington, DC: Maisonneuve Press, 1992).

54. Patrick J. Buchanan, *From the Right*, January 25, 1991, p. 7, author's collection.

55. In Sara Diamond, "After the Storm," *Z Magazine*, September 1991, pp. 31–35, I developed this distinction between the Quagmirists and the Opportunists.

56. Ibid. See also the Spring 1991 issue of the Heritage Foundation's *Policy Review*, including a number of opportunity-oriented analyses.

57. Burton Yale Pines, "A Primer for Conservatives," *The National Interest*, Spring 1991, p. 68.
58. "'Where Do Conservatives Go From Here?'" *Human Events*, February 23, 1991, p. 12.
59. Ibid., pp. 12–13.
60. "Building the New Establishment," Adam Meyerson's interview with Edwin J. Feulner, *Policy Review*, Fall 1991, pp. 6–9.
61. Ibid., p. 13.
62. "Bush link to right is fired," *Washington Times*, August 2, 1990, pp. 1, 8. The *Washington Times* daily political gossip column, "Inside the Beltway," focused on Wead's firing, August 3–9, 1990.
63. "Inside the Beltway," *Washington Times*, August 7, 1990, p. A6. Metzger was an evangelical herself. See the *National and International Religion Report*, December 17, 1990, p. 2, for the story of Metzger's defense of Bush following an October 30, 1990 report on Pat Robertson's Christian Broadcasting Network to the effect that the Bush administration discriminated against evangelical staffers. The *NIRR* listed numerous evangelicals appointed to administrative posts by Bush.
64. *National and International Religion Report*, November 5, 1990, p. 1.
65. Focus on the Family, *Citizen*, January 1990, pp. 1–8.
66. *National and International Religion Report*, July 2, 1990, p. 2. The first advertisement was featured in the *Washington Post* on June 20, 1990.
67. *National and International Religion Report* for these dates: July 29, 1991, p. 3; August 12, 1991, p. 7; August 26, 1991, p. 6; September 9, 1991, pp. 4–5.
68. *National and International Religion Report*, August 26, 1991, p. 2; and September 23, 1991, p. 7.
69. "Senate Approves Clarence Thomas," *Christian American*, November–December 1991, p. 3. *Christian American* is the bimonthly newspaper of the Christian Coalition.
70. "Robertson's phone corps boosted GOP," *The Virginia Pilot and Ledger-Star* (Norfolk), November 9, 1991, pp. 1–2.
71. Joe Conason, "The Religious Right's Quiet Revival," *The Nation*, April 27, 1992, p. 556.
72. Conason, p. 558. See also Frederick Clarkson, "The Christian Coalition: On the Road to Victory?" *Church and State*, January 1992, p. 4. Conason and Clarkson both stood with Duke supporters as they watched the television news returns.
73. *National and International Religion Report*, December 2, 1991, p. 7; March 9, 1992, p. 1.
74. Patrick J. Buchanan, speech before the 1992 Republican Party convention, excerpted in *Human Events*, August 29, 1992, p. 10.
75. "Goldwater Criticizes Anti-Abortion Plank," *New York Times*, August 7, 1992, p. 14.
76. "Bill Clinton: A Leader for America in the Post-Cold War Era," *New York Times*, August 17, 1992, p. 4. The list included the following: Paul Nitze, Samuel P. Huntington, Richard Schifter, John Bunzel, Henry Cisneros, Angier Biddle Duke, Rita Freedman, Edward Koch, Robert Leiken, Edward

Luttwak, Penn Kemble, R. James Woolsey, Martin Peretz, Joshua Muravchik, William Odom, Austin Ranney, Albert Shanker, Aaron Wildavsky, and Raymond Wolfinger.

77. Author's interview with Howard Phillips, September 1991. To my knowledge, I was the only one who reported Phillips' overtures to Buchanan. See Sara Diamond, "New Taxpayers Party to Push Bush from the Right," (New York) *The Guardian*, October 9, 1991, p. 4; Sara Diamond, "The Right's Grassroots," *Z Magazine*, March 1992, p. 22.

78. Patrick J. Buchanan, undated letter to supporters, including subscribers to his *From the Right* newsletter, author's collection.

79. "Buchanan Makes It Official," *Human Events*, December 21, 1991, p. 1.

80. "Buchanan Effort Grows," *Human Events*, November 30, 1991, p. 3; "Sununu's Departure Won't Help the White House," *Human Events*, December 14, 1991, p. 3. White House Chief of Staff John Sununu resigned abruptly at the end of 1991, in an apparent effort to distance unpopular policies from candidate George Bush's reelection efforts.

81. Patrick J. Buchanan, "Taking the High Ground on Tax Cuts," *Human Events*, November 30, 1991, p. 4.

82. "Buchanan's Splendid Showing in New Hampshire," *Human Events*, February 29, 1992, pp. 1, 7.

83. "Four More Years?" *National Review*, February 17, 1992, pp. 12–14; "Mr. Buchanan's Choice," *National Review*, March 2, 1992, pp. 12–15; William F. Buckley, "In Search of Anti-Semitism," *National Review*, December 30, 1991, excerpted from a book Buckley later published under the same title.

   In response to Buckley's article, Norman Podhoretz published "What is Anti-Semitism? An Open Letter to William F. Buckley, Jr.," *Commentary*, February 1992, pp. 15–20. Podhoretz thanked Buckley for the piece and for having led the push against anti-Semitism within the conservative movement during the 1950s.

84. Fred Barnes, "Heir Apparent," *New Republic*, March 30, 1992, pp. 20–21. Also from the ACU, Jeffrey Bell opposed Buchanan. See Jeffrey Bell, "The Wrong Man on the Right," *New York Times*, March 3, 1992, p. A15.

85. "The Disfiguring of Pat Buchanan," *Human Events*, March 14, 1992, p. 1.

86. Barnes, op cit., p. 22.

87. Norman Podhoretz, "Buchanan and the Conservative Crackup," *Commentary*, May 1992, pp. 30–34.

88. "Should Conservatives Shift to Ross Perot?" *Human Events*, June 13, 1992, pp. 1, 7.

89. "The Perot Phenomenon," *National Review*, June 22, 1992, pp. 16–17.

90. "Libertarian Marrou hits Perot," *Washington Times*, June 9, 1992, p. 4; "Inside the Beltway," *Washington Times*, June 8, 1992, p. 6.

91. "We Have Some Questions: Open Letter to Ross Perot From the Spotlight," *The Spotlight*, May 18, 1992, pp. 1, 3.

92. *National and International Religion Report*, June 15, 1992, p. 8.

93. "Perot assailied at right-to-life convention here," *Washington Times*, June 12, 1992, p. 8.

94. *National and International Religion Report*, June 15, 1992, p. 8.

95. See, e.g., Michael Lind, "The Exorcism," *New Republic*, December 14, 1992, pp. 20–21, (Lind was executive editor of *The National Interest*); and Joshua Muravchik, "Why the Democrats Finally Won," *Commentary*, January 1993, pp. 17–22.

96. See, e.g., Joseph Sobran, "Bracing for the morning after," *Washington Times*, October 3, 1992, p. B3; Phyllis Schlafly, "Mistakes of '92," *Washington Times*, November 21, 1992, p. C3.

97. September 1992 letter from the Institute for First Amendment Studies (publishers of *The Freedom Writer*, P.O. Box 589, Great Barrington, MA 01230), citing a report in *USA Today*, August 14, 1992.

98. "Platform Leans to Right of Bush," *San Francisco Chronicle*, August 18, 1992, p. 6.

99. People for the American Way, "Election Wrap-Up" report, available from PAW, 2000 M St. NW, Suite 400, Washington, D.C. 20036. The report was summarized in "Christian Conservatives Counting Hundreds of Gains in Local Votes," *New York Times*, November 21, 1992, p. 1. See also "Evangelicals Gain With Covert Candidates," *New York Times*, October 27, 1992, p. 1, 9.

100. "Christian Coalition to hand out 40 million voter guides Sunday," (Norfolk) *The Virginia Pilot and Ledger-Star*, October 31, 1992, p. D5.

101. Coalition for Human Dignity, *Rolling Back Civil Rights: A Study of the Oregon Citizen's Alliance* (P.O. Box 40344, Portland, OR 97240) provides overview and analysis of the anti-gay rights effort in Oregon.

102. Ibid. See also Jean Hardisty, "Constructing Homophobia," *The Public Eye*, March 1993 (Political Research Associates, 678 Massachusetts Ave., Suite 702, Cambridge, Massachusetts 02139).

103. *The Dignity Report*, June 15, 1993 and July 1, 1993, occasional newsletter produced by the Coalition for Human Dignity, P.O. Box 40344, Portland, OR 97240.

104. "Colorado Can't Ban Gay Rights Measures," *San Francisco Chronicle*, December 15, 1993, p. 1, 18.

105. "Gay-ban issue sends religious right to mailbox," *Washington Times*, March 1, 1993, p. 4; Frederick Clarkson, "The Anti-Gay Nineties," *The Freedom Writer*, March–April 1993.

106. Ralph Reed, Jr., "The Good News," *Christian American*, November–December 1992, p. 29.

107. "Religious Right Hopes Clinton Swells Ranks," *Washington Post*, November 8, 1992, p. A 34.

108. "Fordice won't retreat on 'Christian nation,'" *Washington Times*, November 20, 1992, p. 4.

109. "Political right warned to look to grass roots," *Washington Times*, November 25, 1992, p. A3.

110. Joe Barrett, "Perot and Conservatives," *Empowerment!* November 1992. *Empowerment!* was a monthly newsletter published by Weyrich's Free Congress Foundation.

111. "GOP Moderates State 'Inclusive' Movement," *San Francisco Chronicle*, December 16, 1992, p. 3; "Republicans Trying to Shake Religious Right Image," *San Francisco Examiner*, December 20, 1992, p. 4.

112. See the following *Washington Times* articles: "Buchanan launches foundation, sets culture debate," March 20, 1993, p. 4; "Cultural warriors fault movies, TV, schools, press," May 14, 1993, p. 4., and "Artists enlist in Buchanan's cultural war," May 15, 1993, p. 4.

113. *The American Cause* (American Cause Foundation), vol. 1, no. 1, June 1993, p. 1. Buchanan's speech was excerpted in "Line drawn at the culture frontier," *Washington Times*, May 19, 1993, p. G1.

114. "An index of culture in decline," *Washington Times* March 16, 1993, pp. 1, 8.

115. "Kirkpatrick assails Clintons for leading 'cultural revolution,'" *Washington Times*, May 28, 1993, pp. 1, 8.

116. Author's observation based on newspaper monitoring and literature received on both groups' mailing lists.

117. James L. Guth, John C. Green, Lyman A. Kellstedt, and Corwin E. Smidt, "God's Own Party: Evangelicals and Republicans in the '92 Election," *Christian Century*, February 17, 1993, p. 172.

118. Lyman A. Kellstedt, John C. Green, James L. Guth, and Corwin E. Schmidt, "Religious Voting Blocs in the 1992 Election: The Year of the Evangelical?" paper prepared for the Annual Meeting of the American Political Science Association meeting, September 1993. In the previously cited *Christian Century* article, the authors reported that Bush received 62 percent of the evangelical vote and 72 percent of the regular churchgoer vote. In the authors' later paper, they revised the figures to 63 percent and 70 percent, respectively.

 The authors noted that their research was backed financially by the Pew Charitable Trust. Professors John Green and James Guth also shared their research findings and analysis with Republican Party and right-wing movement strategists at a Pew-sponsored conference held at the neoconservative Ethics and Public Policy Center in Washington in December 1993. EPPC newsletter, Winter 1994.

119. "Religious Voting Blocs in the 1992 Election," op cit.

120. Tony Fabrizio and John McLaughlin, "Stop the Soul Searching," *National Review*, April 4, 1994, p. 50.

121. Ralph Reed Jr., "Casting a Wider Net," *Policy Review*, Summer 1993, pp. 31–35. A short version of Reed's article appeared in "The Religious Right Reaches Out," *New York Times*, August 22, 1993. See also "Christian right puts new focus on economy," *Washington Times*, July 15, 1993, p. 1.

122. Mark O'Keefe, "Christian Coalition Expands Agenda," *Charisma*, October 1993, pp. 64–66.

123. "Religious Group to Run Ads Against Health Plan," *San Francisco Chronicle*, February 16, 1994, p. 3.

124. "Christian Coalition to court minorities," *Washington Times*, September 10, 1993, p. 5.

125. "Minority Myths Exploded," *Christian American*, October 1993, pp. 1, 4.

126. On the evangelicals' moves toward "racial reconciliation," see Sara Diamond, "Change in Strategy," *The Humanist*, January–February 1994, pp. 34–36.

127. "Virginia's Religious Right Flexes Political Muscles," *Washington Post*, November 14, 1993.

128. "Farris Rebounds From Loss to Become a Powerhouse," *Washington Post*, July 26, 1994, pp. B1, 5.
129. "Religious Conservatives Claim a Place in Virginia's Mainstream," *Washington Post*, November 4, 1993.
130. *Washington Post*, November 14, 1993, op cit. Family Research Council's *Washington Watch* newsletter, January 18, 1994.
131. "'Religious Bigotry' Alleged," *Christianity Today*, December 13, 1993, pp. 66–67; "Religious right claims moral victory in Farris' defeat," *Washington Times*, November 4, 1993, p. 1, 10.
132. Elizabeth Shogren and Douglas Frantz, "School Boards Become the Religious Right's New Pulpit," *Los Angeles Times*, December 10, 1993, pp. 1, 38.
133. Ibid. See also, Donna Minkowitz, "Wrong Side of the Rainbow," *The Nation*, June 28, 1993, pp. 901–904. For the Christian Right's critique of *Children of the Rainbow*, see "Beating the Big City Bureaucrats" in Focus on the Family's *Citizen* magazine, April 19, 1993.
134. "Fundamentalist School Board Adopts Its Own Sex Education," *San Francisco Chronicle*, March 19, 1994, pp. 1, 15; "Three R's in California School District Include Religious Right," *Washington Post*, May 12, 1994, pp. 1, 10; Marc Cooper, "Chastity 101," *Village Voice*, June 7, 1994.
135. "Battle Over Patriotism Curriculum," *New York Times*, May 15, 1994, p. 12.
136. Ralph Reed quoted in "Floridians Seize Initiatives in the Culture War," *Human Events*, May 27, 1994, p. 6.
137. "Florida Voters Thrash Religious Right, 'America-First' Curriculum," *San Francisco Chronicle*, October 8, 1994, p. A6.
138. "Voters Reject School Vouchers, Homosexual Rights," *Christianity Today*, December 13, 1993, pp. 55–56.
139. "Austin voters repeal domestic partner benefits," Associated Press dispatch in the *Washington Times*, May 9, 1994, p. 10; "Austin Voters Repeal 'Live-In' Benefits," *Human Events*, May 20, 1994.
140. "In petition drives, anti-gay rights groups fall short," Associated Press dispatch in the *Washington Times*, July 12, 1994, p. 8; Mindy Ridgway, "Anti-Gay Initiatives Fail to Make the Ballot in Eight out of Ten States," *San Francisco Bay Times*, July 14, 1994, p. 4.
141. "The Right Response: A Survey of Voters' Attitudes on Gay-Related Questions," National Gay and Lesbian Task Force memorandum, March 17, 1994. (NGLTF, 1734 14th St. NW, Washington, D.C. 20009.) The lengthy NGLTF memo summarized poll data from major survey data firms: Gallup, Princeton Survey Research Assoicates, the Roper Center for Public Opinion Research, plus the survey units of CBS and NBC broadcast networks.
142. For a summary and analysis of a number of anti-gay materials, see Sara Diamond, "The Christian Right's Anti-Gay Agenda," *The Humanist*, July–August 1994, pp. 32–34.
143. Ibid. See also "Gay Agenda's New Look," *Christianity Today*, June 21, 1993, p. 46. A similar video *Gay Rights, Special Rights*, was used to mobilize support for the passage of anti-gay measures in Cincinnati and in Cobb County, Georgia. See "Minorities Speak Out Against Gay Rights," Focus on the Family's *Citizen* magazine, November 15, 1993, p. 13.

144. Donna Minkowitz, "Mississippi is Burning," *Village Voice*, February 8, 1994, pp. 23–28.
145. John W. Kennedy, "Pro-Life Movement Struggles for Viability," *Christianity Today*, November 8, 1993, pp. 40–44.
146. Laura L. Sydell, "The Right-to-Life Rampage," *The Progressive*, August 1993, pp. 24–27; Sara Diamond, "No Place to Hide," *The Humanist*, September–October 1993, pp. 39–41.
147. K. Kaufmann, "Attacks on clinics hit all-time high," *San Francisco Weekly*, December 16, 1992, p. 6.
148. "Abortions, Bibles and Bullets, and the Making of a Militant," *New York Times*, August 28, 1993, p. 1, 8.
149. *Life Advocate* magazine was published by Andrew Burnett and Advocates for Life Ministries in Portland, Oregon. The *Prayer and Action Weekly News* was published by Dave Leach in Des Moines, Iowa. Paul Hill circulated literature advocating violence against doctors under the name "Defensive Action" from a post office box in Pensacola, Florida.
150. "Avenging the Unborn," *Time*, August 8, 1994, pp. 24–27.
151. See, e.g., Ralph Reed, "Christianity vs. Fanaticism," *Wall Street Journal*, March 16, 1993; and Betsy Powell, "Media faulted in killings," *San Francisco Examiner*, August 7, 1994, p. A15. Powell represented the National Right to Life Committee, which took the position that the mass media, by frequently interviewing Paul Hill on his support for Michael Griffin, encouraged Hill to kill abortionists.
152. "Open Season on Pro-Lifers?" *Christianity Today*, March 7, 1994, p. 52.
153. "Operation Rescue Says it Won't Pay 'One Penny' to Abortion Clinics," Evangelical Press Service, May 13, 1994; "Abortion Foes' Court Losses Are Frustrating the Victors," *New York Times*, June 11, 1994, pp. 1, 8.
154. "Law Protecting Abortion Clinics From Protests Draws Lawsuit," Evangelical Press Service, June 3, 1994.
155. "Keep Your Distance," *Time*, July 11, 1994, p. 25.
156. "Religious Right's Turnout Rises," *Washington Times*, November 11, 1994, p. 13; "Quick Changes Artists," *Christianity Today*, December 12, 1994, p. 50; "Christian Coalition Threatens GOP," *Washington Post*, February 11, 1995, p. A9; "Religious Right Candidates Gain as GOOP Turnout Rises," *New York Times*, November 12, 1994.
157. "Clinton's Visceral Opposition," *Los Angeles Times*, July 5, 1994, pp. 1, 8.
158. "Key House Democrat lashes out at Christian conservatives," *Washington Times*, June 22, 1994, p. 1; "GOP senators urge Clinton to disown attack," *Washington Times*, June 24, 1994, p. 1.
159. "87 Lawmakers Seek Ouster of Joycelyn Elders," *San Francisco Chronicle,*, June 25, 1994.
160. "Clinton Calls Show to Assail Press, Falwell and Limbaugh," *New York Times*, June 25, 1994, p. 1, 10.
161. See, e.g., the following syndicated columns: Pat Buchanan, "Bellicose barrage of Christian-bashing," *Washington Times*, June 15, 1994, p. A17; Suzanne Fields, "Just how radical are the 'religious right' Republicans?" *Washington Times*, June 16, 1994, p. A19; William Rusher, "Political demon mongers,"

Washington Times, June 23, 1994, p. A17; and R. Emmett Tyrrel, Jr., "Railers against the 'radical right,'" *Washington Times*, July 15, 1994, p. A18.

162. See, e.g., Rich Lowry, "Crucifying the Christian Right," *National Review*, August 1, 1994.

163. "Democrats Unveil Frantic 1994 Strategy," *Human Events*, July 1, 1994, p. 5.

164. "Dissatisfied Americans May Spell Democrat Losses," *Los Angeles Times*, July 28, 1994, p. A19. Another poll, taken by Time and the Cable News Network in June 1994, asked: "Are the positions taken by Christian conservatives on social issues too extreme?" Forty percent said "yes" and 43 percent said "no." *Time*, June 27, 1994, p. 38.

165. On the ADL spy scandal see Robert I. Freidman, "The Enemy Within," *Village Voice*, May 11, 1993; Dennis King and Chip Berlet, "ADLgate," *Tikkun*, vol. 8, no. 4, pp. 31–101. In the spring of 1993, the *San Francisco Chronicle* devoted extensive coverage to the unfolding scandal.

166. See, e.g., *National Review*, August 1, 1994, p. 10; Don Feder, "Anti-Defamation League Slanders Christian Right," *Human Events*, July 1, 1994, p. 15.

167. "Should Jews Fear the 'Christian Right'?" *New York Times*, August 2, 1994. The group included Elliott Abrams, Mona Charen, Midge Decter, Suzanne Fields, Chester Finn, Bruce Herschensohn, Gertrude Himmelfarb, David Horowitz, Irving Kristol, Michael Ledeen, Michael Medved, Max Singer, and others. Many of these were participants in Toward Tradition, a Seattle-based group of conservative Jews devoted to, among other things, working in alliance with the Christian Right.

168. "A Campaign of Falsehoods: The Anti-Defamation League's Defamation of Religious Conservatives, A Special Report from the Christian Coalition," July 28, 1994 (Christian Coalition, 1801-L Sara Drive, Chesapeake, Virginia 23320).

169. Pat Robertson, "700 Club" program, Christian Broadcasting Network, July 14, 1994. On that broadcast, Robertson lamented the loss of "dear friends" within ADL. His remarks were summarized in CBN's "The 700 Club" *Fact Sheet* for July 14, 1994.

• • •

A Postscript on Data Sources

The Bibliography lists sources cited in this book's footnotes. I based this study almost exclusively on printed sources, both primary and secondary, for reasons of access and evenness of data.

My first book *Spiritual Warfare* relied heavily on media monitoring, event attendance, and interviews I conducted over a five-year period (1983–1988). During those years I also collected contemporaneous data on and from the secular New Right, the racist Right, and the neoconservatives.

To expand the historical scope of the study then presented some problems. I needed to collect data back in time. I wanted to use data sources that would be accessible to readers who would like to do their own further study. Some of the people and organizations treated in this book are amenable to interviewing; many are simply not. Additionally, some movements have left behind a greater volume of publicly available data than others.

I tried to solve these problems by combing as much of the public printed record as was feasible. The combined use of primary and secondary sources offered several advantages. I wanted to address right-wing movements multidimensionally, in terms of their beliefs, actions, and significance. The latter dimension implies looking for movements' contexts, and to do that I needed to rely on relevant secondary sources on U.S. political history. I also found it important to incorporate most of the secondary sources available on the Right, per se, in order to situate my own newly discovered material and analysis within the body of existing literature. To understand movements' *beliefs* and *actions* required scrutiny of movement participants' own writings.

Readers will notice my frequent citations of *New York Times* and other major press dispatches on incidents pertinent to right-wing activity. My motive, again, has been to provide readers with an easily accessible trail to pursue should they choose to check facts or do additional reading. Certainly, the *New York Times* and its counterparts are no objective sources of information. Mainstream press coverage of right-wing movements, no less than reportage on any subject, has been spotty, sometimes inaccurate, and selectively driven by the prerogatives of editors and corporate sponsors. Thus, for example, I found extensive *New York Times* coverage of the John Birch Society during the 1960s when the group met disapproval from political elites. During the same time period, the newspaper of record scarcely reported on elite-oriented anticommunist groups. The same was true throughout the 1970s and 1980s.

The unreliability of press accounts increased my confidence in the wisdom of relying, as much as possible, on primary source material. Movements' own publications and ephemera are essential for some research questions, less useful for others. Were I to have been concerned with activists' interpersonal relationships, participant-observation and interviewing would have been appropriate. Instead, I pursued questions of the movements' central organizing principles and objectives, plus their stances toward the state. These questions were best answered by reading about movements in their own words, but within the context of the rest of the public historical record. Given the inherent biases of movement participants, one does not necessarily rely on their accounts of external events but, rather, on how their interpretations of events derive from and, thereafter, determine movement strategy.

Reliance on movement publications is not a scientific method, and I make no claims about having drawn a scientific data sample. I can say, however, that the data used and cited is representative of what the movements studied have produced.

For each of the movements studied, my method was to go through, and closely read much of, the major publications for the entire duration of their existence. This means that I perused *Human Events* from the 1940s to the present, *National Review* from 1955 to the present, *Christianity Today* from 1955 to the present, *Spotlight* from 1975 to the present, and so forth. I did not read every article in each issue of all major and minor publications; I did review all issues for the most important publication(s) produced by each movement tendency.

The idea was not to quantify how many times each publication treated issues x, y, and z. Quantification would have produced a distorted rendition of the movements' priorities. Anyone who has ever worked for a movement journal of opinion knows that what appears in publication is at least somewhat arbitrary, reflective of editors' preferences toward certain issues and writers, and dependent on writers' variable willingness to contribute. However, over a large frame of time and over as much published material as is available, it is likely that all salient issues will be covered, as editors respond to reader concerns and solicit contributions consistent with the movement's agenda.

With this view of how to interpret primary source materials, I embarked on reading and locating consistent themes from the movement publications listed in the Bibliography. I supplemented thorough study of the major publications with an invaluable set of primary source material, the Right-Wing Collection of the University of Iowa, available through inter-library loan. This set of 154 reels of microfilm consists of periodicals and ephemera from about 1,000 organizations, large and small, spanning from the pre-World War II period through 1978. In the Bibliography, I have listed, by organization and reel number, only the parts of this collection cited in the footnotes. The bulk of the material comes from the anticommunist and racist Right movements (with some early evangelical publications), and mostly from the 1950s and 1960s. The quantity of material is random and varied. For example, the collection includes the entire run of Willis Carto's *Right* newsletter (1955 to 1960) but only a sampling of the American Security Council's 1960s newsletter "Council Notes." Still, the sheer volume of material included gave me a couple of advantages: it filled in my data collection for the early decades of this study, and, even where skimpy, the inclusion of sample issues from a given group enabled me to decide whether to seek a fuller collection of a given publication through inter-library loan.

Finally, the Bibliography lists the collections I consulted at the Hoover Institution Archives at Stanford University. These, too, are of variable quality and utility given how such collections come to be. A number of prominent movement figures, some living and some deceased, have donated their personal papers to the Hoover Institution. The donors have been mostly well known veterans of the anticommunist movement (Marvin Liebman, Walter Judd, Stanley Hornbeck, Henry Regnery, et al.) and a few neoconservatives (Ernest LeFever, Midge Decter). The collections vary from a few to many boxes. The most useful collections consist largely of the donors' files of correspondence with fellow movement participants. The content of these letters may elude those uninitiated in the history of right-wing movements. But when studied by a specialist such as myself, these documents answer critical questions about key events, and activists' relationships with each other and with state elites. Many of the files include some startling and previously unknown revelations about the donors and their colleagues. But unless these new facts pertained directly to my narrative, I chose not to incorporate these findings into this book. Instead, I selected for inclusion Hoover documents that substantiated or elucidated incidents or tendencies already under consideration, so as not to have the writing of this history driven by the highly personal nature of this data source.

In the end, the large quantity of available primary source data presented its own challenge, namely the problem of selectivity. Relative to others, this study is an exhaustive historical chronicle of the U.S. Right. Of necessity, though, much detail was omitted, for the sake of shedding light on the broadest and most consistent patterns of development.

Bibliography

This bibliography lists the primary and secondary source materials cited in chapter footnotes. Citations of specific articles from movement publications, as well as references to secondary source newspaper and magazine articles, all of which appear in footnotes, are left out of the bibliography.

MOVEMENT PUBLICATIONS

The American Mercury
American Opinion (John Birch Society)
Battle Line (American Conservative Union)
Christian American (Christian Coalition)
Christian Economics
Christianity Today
The Citizen (Citizens' Councils of America)
Citizen (Focus on the Family)
Commentary
Conservative Digest
Encounter (Congress for Cultural Freedom)
Human Events
Intercollegiate Review (Intercollegiate Studies Institute)
Libertarian Forum
Libertarian Review
Liberty Letter (Liberty Lobby)
Modern Age
Moral Majority Report
The National Interest
National and International Religion Report
National Review
New America (Social Democrats, U.S.A.)
New Guard (Young Americans for Freedom)
New Individualist Review

The New Leader
Partisan Review
The Public Interest
Reason
Religious Broadcasting
Right (Liberty Lobby)
Spotlight (Liberty Lobby)
United Evangelical Action (National Association of Evangelicals)
Washington Report (American Security Council)
The Washington Times

SOURCE MATERIALS
FROM THE MICROFILMED RIGHT-WING
COLLECTION OF THE UNIVERSITY OF IOWA

American Afro-Asian Educational Exchange, Inc., Reel 12
American Coalition of Patriotic Societies, Reel 5
American Conservative Union, "ACU Report," Reel 155
American Council of Christian Laymen, "Challenge," Reel 19
Americans for Constitutional Action, Reel 13
Assembly of Captive European Nations, "ACEN News," Reel 1
Association of Citizens' Councils, Reel 9
Christian Crusade, (Billy James Hargis), newsletter, Reel 22
Christian Vanguard (New Christian Crusade Church), Reel 23
Church League of America, "News and Views," Reel 86
Coast Federal Savings, Reel 36
Committee for Constitutional Government, Reel 29
Committee of One Million, Reel 29
Congress of Freedom, Reel 36
Constitution Party, Reel 36
"Council Notes," American Security Council, Reel 13
Friends of Rhodesian Independence newsletter, Reel 69
Foundation for Economic Education, Reel 88
"Identity" newsletter (William Potter Gale), Reel 61
Liberty Amendment Committee, Reel 7
Liberty Bell, Reel 69
"Liberty Letter" (Liberty Lobby), Reel 69
"Liberty Lowdown" (Liberty Lobby), Reel 69
Moral Rearmament, "MRA Information Service," Reels 75 and 78
National States' Rights Party, Reel 89
National Youth Alliance ephemera, Reel 89
Right, Reel 103
"The Phyllis Schlafly Report," Reel 92
South Louisiana Citizens' Council, Reel 127
Young Americans for Freedom (YAF), Reel 154

HOOVER INSTITUTION ARCHIVES
COLLECTIONS (BY NAME OF DONOR)

Colonel Charles Bohannan
L. Francis Bouchey (Council for Inter-American Security)
John Bunzel
Midge Decter (Committee for the Free World)
Christopher Emmet
Stanley Hornbeck
Walter H. Judd
Marx Lewis
Marvin Liebman
Mont Pelerin Society
Stefan Possony
Henry Regnery

BOOKS BY MOVEMENT PARTICIPANTS

Brady, Tom P. 1955. *Black Monday*. Winona, MI: Association of Citizens' Councils.

Carto, Willis A. 1982. *Profiles in Populism*. Greenwich, CT: Flag Press.

Coleman, Peter. 1989. *The Liberal Conspiracy: The Congress for Cultural Freedom and the Struggle for the Mind of Postwar Europe*. New York: Free Press.

Flynn, John T. 1949. *The Road Ahead: America's Creeping Revolution*. New York: Devin-Adair.

Gilder, George. 1981. *Wealth and Poverty*. New York: Basic Books.

Goldwater, Barry. [1960] 1990. *The Conscience of a Conservative*. Washington, DC: Regnery Gateway.

Gottfried, Paul. 1993. *The Conservative Movement*, revised edition. New York: Twayne.

Hahn, Walter F., and John C. Neff, eds. 1960. *American Strategy for the Nuclear Age*. New York: Anchor Books.

Hayek, Friedrich A. 1944. *The Road to Serfdom*. Chicago: University of Chicago Press.

Heatherly, Charles L. ed. 1981. *Mandate for Leadership*. Washington, DC: The Heritage Foundation.

Hunter, Edward. 1958. *The Black Book on Red China*. New York: The Book-mailer.

Kirk, Russell. [1953] 1987. *The Conservative Mind: From Burke to Eliot*. Chicago: Regnery Books.

Klasen, Thomas G. Klasen. 1988. *A Pro-Life Manifesto*. Westchester, IL: Crossway Books.

Kristol, Irving. 1978. *Two Cheers for Capitalism*. New York: Basic Books.

Kristol, Irving. 1983. *Reflections of a Neoconservative*. New York: Basic Books.

Liebman, Marvin. 1992. *Coming Out Conservative: An Autobiography.* San Francisco: Chronicle Books.
North, Gary. 1989. *Political Polytheism: The Myth of Pluralism.* Tyler, TX: Institute for Christian Economics.
North, Gary, and Gary DeMar. 1991. *Christian Reconstructionism: What It Is, What It Isn't.* Tyler TX: Institute for Christian Economics.
Novak, Robert D. 1965. *The Agony of the G.O.P. 1964.* New York: Macmillan.
Podhoretz, Norman. 1980. *The Present Danger.* New York: Simon and Schuster.
Putnam, Carleton. 1961. *Race and Reason: A Yankee View.* Washington, DC: Public Affairs Press.
Roberts, Paul Craig. 1984. *The Supply-Side Revolution: An Insider's Account of Policymaking in Washington.* Cambridge, MA: Harvard University Press.
Rothbard, Murray N. 1973. *For A New Liberty.* New York: Macmillan.
Rusher, William A. 1975. *The Making of the New Majority Party.* New York: Sheed and Ward.
Rusher, William A. 1984. *The Rise of the Right.* New York: William and Morrow.
Schaeffer, Francis A. 1981. *A Christian Manifesto.* Westchester, IL: Crossway Books.
Scheidler, Joseph M. 1985. *Closed: 99 Ways to Stop Abortion.* Westchester, IL: Crossway Books.
Simon, William E. 1978. *A Time For Truth.* New York: Reader's Digest Press.
Stockman, David A. 1986. *The Triumph of Politics: How the Reagan Revolution Failed.* New York: Harper & Row.
Tuccille, Jerome. 1970. *Radical Libertarianism: A Right Wing Alternative.* Indianapolis: Bobbs-Merrill.
Tyroler, Charles II, ed. 1984. *Alerting America: The Papers of the Committee on the Present Danger.* Washington, DC: Pergamon-Brassey's International Defense Publishers.
Viguerie, Richard. 1981. *The New Right: We're Ready to Lead.* Falls Church, VA: The Viguerie Co.
Viguerie, Richard. 1983. *The Establishment vs. the People.* Chicago: Regnery Gateway.
Welch, Robert. 1959. *The Blue Book of the John Birch Society.* Belmont, MA: Western Islands.
White, F. Clifton. 1967. *Suite 3505: The Story of the Draft Goldwater Movement.* New Rochelle, NY: Arlington House.
White, F. Clifton and William J. Gill. 1981. *Why Reagan Won: A Narrative History of the Conservative Movement 1964-1981.* Chicago: Regnery Gateway.

SECONDARY SOURCE BOOKS AND ARTICLES

Abbott, Pamela, and Claire Wallace. 1992. *The Family and the New Right.* London: Pluto Press.
Adams, Sherman. 1961. *Firsthand Report: The Story of the Eisenhower Administration.* New York: Harper & Bros.

Adler, Selig. 1957. *The Isolationist Impulse: Its Twentieth Century Reaction.* New York: Abelard-Schuman.

Aho, James A. 1990. *The Politics of Righteousness: Idaho Christian Patriotism.* Seattle: University of Washington Press.

Anderson, Scott, and Jon Lee Anderson. 1986. *Inside the League.* New York: Dodd, Mead.

Bachrack, Stanley D. 1976. *The Committee of One Million: "China Lobby" Politics, 1953–1971.* New York: Columbia University Press.

Bagdikian, Ben. 1987. *The Media Monopoly.* New York: Beacon Press.

Barkun, Michael. 1994. *Religion and the Racist Right: The Origins of the Christian Identity Movement.* Chapel Hill: University of North Carolina Press.

Barron, Bruce. 1992. *Heaven on Earth: The Social and Political Agendas of Dominion Theology.* Grand Rapids, MI: Zondervan.

Bartley, Numan. 1969. *The Rise of Massive Resistance: Race and Politics in the South During the 1950s.* Baton Rouge: Louisiana State University Press.

Beck, Paul Allen. 1977. "Partisan Dealignment in the Postwar South," *American Political Science Review,* vol. 71.

Belfrage, Cedric. 1989. *The American Inquisition, 1945–1960: A Profile of the "McCarthy Era."* New York: Thunder's Mouth Press.

Bell, Daniel, ed. 1964. *The Radical Right.* New York: Anchor Books.

Bellant, Russ. 1991. *Old Nazis, the New Right, and the Republican Party.* Boston: South End Press.

Bellant, Russ. 1991. *The Coors Connection.* Boston: South End Press.

Bennett, David H. 1988. *The Party of Fear: From Nativist Movements to the New Right in American History.* New York: Vintage Books.

Bennett, Stephen Earl. 1971. "Modes of Resolution of a 'Belief Dilemma' in the Ideology of the John Birch Society," *Journal of Politics,* vol. 33, no. 3, August 1971, pp. 734–772.

Bibbly, Reginald W., and Merlin B. Brinkerhoff. 1973. "The Circulation of the Saints: A Study of People Who Join Conservative Churches," *Journal for the Scientific Study of Religion.* September 1973, pp. 273–283.

Blanchard, Dallas A., and Terry J. Prewitt. 1993. *Religious Violence and Abortion: the Gideon Project.* Gainesville: University Press of Florida.

Bloom, Alexander. 1986. *Prodigal Sons: The New York Intellectuals and Their World.* New York: Oxford University Press.

Blum, William. 1986. *The CIA: A Forgotten History.* London: Zed Books.

Blumenthal, Sidney. 1986. *The Rise of the Counter-Establishment: From Conservative Ideology to Political Power.* New York: Harper and Row.

Bodenheimer, Thomas, and Robert Gould. 1989. *Rollback! Right-wing Power in U.S. Foreign Policy.* Boston: South End Press.

Bolton, Richard, ed. 1992. *Culture Wars: Documents from the Recent Controversies in the Arts.* New York: New Press.

Boyer, Paul. 1992. *When Time Shall Be No More: Prophecy Belief in Modern American Culture.* Cambridge, MA: The Belknap Press of Harvard University Press.

Brady, David W., and Kent L. Tedin. 1976. "Ladies in Pink: Religion and

416 • *Bibliography* •

Political Ideology in the Anti-ERA Movement," *Social Science Quarterly*, March, pp. 564–575.

Brinkley, Alan. 1982. *Voices of Protest: Huey Long, Father Coughlin, and the Great Depression*. New York: Alfred A. Knopf.

Broyles, J. Allen. 1964. *The John Birch Society: Anatomy of a Protest*. Boston: Beacon Press.

Buhle, Mari Jo, Paul Buhle, and Dan Georgakas, eds. 1992. *Encyclopedia of the American Left*. Urbana: University of Illinois Press.

Burk, Robert Fredrick. 1984. *The Eisenhower Administration and Black Civil Rights*. Knoxville: University of Tennessee Press.

Burke, Vincent J., and Vee Burke. 1974. *Nixon's Good Deed: Welfare Reform*. New York: Columbia University Press.

Burnham, Walter Dean. 1970. *Critical Elections and the Mainsprings of American Politics*. New York: Norton.

Burris, Val. 1987. "Business Support for the New Right: A Consumer's Guide to the Most Reactionary American Corporations," *Socialist Review*. January–February, pp. 33–63.

Caldwell, Dan. 1991. *The Dynamics of Domestic Politics and Arms Control: The SALT II Treaty Ratification Debate*. Columbia: University of South Carolina Press.

Canfield, James Lewis. 1984. *A Case of Third Party Activism: The George Wallace Campaign Worker and the American Independent Party*. Lanham, MD: University Press of America.

Carlson, Jody. 1981. *George C. Wallace and the Politics of Powerlessness: The Wallace Campaigns for the Presidency, 1964–1976*. New Brunswick, NJ: Transaction Books.

Carpenter, Joel A. 1980. "Institutions and the Rise of Evangelical Protestantism, 1929–1942," *Church History*. March. pp 62–75.

Carter, Hodding, III. 1959. *The South Strikes Back*. New York: Doubleday.

Caute, David. 1978. *The Great Fear: The Anti-Communist Purge Under Truman and Eisenhower*. New York: Simon and Schuster.

Center for Democratic Renewal. 1992. *When Hate Groups Come to Town: A Handbook of Effective Community Responses*. Atlanta, GA: Center for Democratic Renewal.

Chalmers, David M. 1965. *Hooded Americanism: The History of the Ku Klux Klan*. New York: New Viewpoints.

Chavkin, Samuel. 1982. *The Murder of Chile: Eyewitness Accounts of the Coup, the Terror, and the Resistance Today*. New York: Everest House.

Chomsky, Noam. 1993. *Year 501: The Conquest Continues*. Boston: South End Press.

Clark, Ramsey, et al. 1992. *War Crimes: A Report on United States War Crimes Against Iraq*. Washington, DC: Maisonneuve Press.

Coates, James. 1987. *Armed and Dangerous: The Rise of the Survivalist Right*. New York: Hill and Wang.

Cole, Wayne S. 1974. *Charles A. Lindbergh and the Battle Against American Intervention in World War II*. New York: Harcourt Brace Jovanovich.

Conover, Pamela Johnston, and Virginia Gray. 1983. *Feminism and the New Right*. New York: Praeger.

Cook, Blanche Wiessen. 1984. "First Comes the Lie: C.D. Jackson and Political Warfare," *Radical History Review, 31*.

Cook, James Graham. 1962. *The Segregationists*. New York: Appelton-Century-Crofts.

Cooney, Terry A. 1988. *The Rise of the New York Intellectuals: Partisan Review and Its Circle*. Madison: University of Wisconsin Press.

Corcoran, James. 1990. *Bitter Harvest: Gordon Kahl and the Posse Comitatus, Murder in the Heartland*. New York: Penguin.

Coser, Lewis A., and Irving Howe. 1973. *The New Conservatives: A Critique from the Left*. New York: Quadrangle.

Crass, Philip. 1976. *The Wallace Factor*. New York: Mason Charter.

Crawford, Alan. 1980. *Thunder on the Right: The "New Right" and the Politics of Resentment*. New York: Pantheon.

Cruikshank, Margaret. 1992. *The Gay and Lesbian Liberation Movement*. New York: Routledge.

Davis, Flora. 1991. *Moving the Mountain: The Women's Movement In America Since 1960*. New York: Simon & Schuster.

Devigne, Robert. 1994. *Recasting Conservatism: Oakeshott, Strauss, and the Response to Postmodernism*. New Haven: Yale University Press.

Diamond, Sara. 1987. "Shepherding," *Covert Action Information Bulletin*. Spring, pp. 18–31.

Diamond, Sara. 1989. *Spiritual Warfare: The Politics of the Christian Right*. Boston: South End Press.

Diamond, Sara. 1991a. "Readin', Writin', and Repressin'," *Z Magazine*. February.

Diamond, Sara. 1991b. "After the Storm," *Z Magazine*, September.

Diamond, Sara. 1991c. "Endowing the Right-Wing Academic Agenda," *Covert Action Information Bulletin*, Fall 1991.

Diamond, Sara. 1991d. "Free Market Environmentalism," *Z Magazine*, December.

Diggins, John. 1994. *Up From Communism: Conservative Odysseys in American Intellectual History*. New York: Columbia University Press.

Dittberner, Job L. 1979. *The End of Ideology and American Social Thought: 1930–1960*. UMI Research Press.

Doenecke, Justus D. 1979. *Not to the Swift: the Old Isolationists in the Cold War Era*. Lewisburg, PA: Bucknell University Press.

Doenecke, Justus D., ed. 1990. *In Danger Undaunted: The Anti-Interventionist Movement of 1940–1941 as Revealed in the Papers of the America First Committee*. Stanford, CA: Hoover Institution Press, Stanford University.

Donner, Frank. 1981. *The Age of Surveillance*. New York: Vintage Books.

Dorrien, Gary. 1993. *The Neoconservative Mind: Politics, Culture, and the War of Ideology*. Philadelphia: Temple University Press.

D'Souza, Dinesh. 1984. *Falwell, Before the Millenium*. Chicago: Regnery Gateway.

Dykeman, Wilma, and James Stokeley. 1960. "The Klan Tries a Comeback," *Commentary*. January.

Edsall, Thomas B. 1984. *The New Politics of Inequality*. New York: Norton.

Edsall, Thomas Byrne, and Mary Edsall. 1991. *Chain Reaction: the Impact of Race, Rights, and Taxes on American Politics*. New York: Norton.

Edwards, Lee. 1990. *Missionary for Freedom: The Life and Times of Walter Judd*. New York: Paragon House.

Ehrenreich, Barbara. 1983. *The Hearts of Men: American Dreams and the Flight From Commitment*. New York: Anchor Books.

Elliott, Jeffrey M. 1973. "Exclusive Interview with William K. Shearer, American Independent Party," *Community College Social Science Quarterly*, vol. IV, no. 1, Fall.

Epstein, Benjamin R., and Arnold Forster. 1966. *The Radical Right: Report on the John Birch Society and Its Allies*. New York: Random House.

Evans, Les, ed. 1974. *Disaster in Chile: Allende's Strategy and Why it Failed*. New York: Pathfinder Press.

Ferguson, Thomas, and Joel Rogers, eds. 1981. *The Hidden Election*. New York: Pantheon.

Ferguson, Thomas, and Joel Rogers. 1986a. *Right Turn: The Decline of the Democrats and the Future of American Politics*. New York: Hill and Wang.

Ferguson, Thomas, and Joel Rogers. 1986 b. "The Myth of America's Turn to the Right," *The Atlantic*, May 1986, pp. 43–53.

Flynn, Kevin, and Gary Gerhardt. 1989. *The Silent Brotherhood: Inside America's Racist Underground*. New York: Free Press.

Formisano, Ronald P. 1991. *Boston Against Busing: Race, Class and Ethnicity in the 1960s and 1970s*. Chapel Hill: University of North Carolina Press.

Forster, Arnold. 1950. *A Measure of Freedom*. New York: Doubleday.

Forster, Arnold, and Benjamin R. Epstein. 1956. *Cross-Currents*. New York: Doubleday.

Forster, Arnold, and Benjamin R. Epstein. 1964. *Danger on the Right*. New York: Random House.

Freed, Donald, and Fred Landis. 1980. *Death in Washington: The Murder of Orlando Letelier*. Westport, CT: Lawrence Hill.

Freedland, Richard M. 1985. *The Truman Doctrine and the Origins of McCarthyism: Foreign Policy, Domestic Politics, and Internal Security, 1946–1948*. New York: New York University Press.

Fried, Richard M. 1990. *Nightmare in Red: The McCarthy Era in Perspective*. New York: Oxford University Press.

Frohnmayer, John. 1993. *Leaving Town Alive: Confessions of an Arts Warrior*. New York: Houghton Mifflin.

Gasper, Louis. 1963. *The Fundamentalist Movement*. The Hague, The Netherlands: Mouton and Co.

Gelbspan, Ross. 1991. *Break-ins, Death Threats and the FBI: The Covert War Against the Central America Movement*. Boston: South End Press.

George, Carol V. R. 1993. *God's Salesman: Norman Vincent Peale and the Power of Positive Thinking*. New York: Oxford University Press.

Gifford, Paul. 1991. *The Religious Right in Southern Africa*. London: Pluto Press.

Ginger, Ann Fagan, and David Christiano, eds. 1987. *The Cold War Against Labor*. Berkeley, CA: Meiklejohn Civil Liberties Institute.

Graham, Hugh Davis. 1992. *Civil Rights and the Presidency: Race and Gender in American Politics, 1960-1972*. New York: Oxford University Press.

Greider, William. 1981. "The Education of David Stockman," *The Atlantic Monthly*. December.

Griffith, Robert. 1987. *The Politics of Fear: Joseph R. McCarthy and the Senate*. Amherst: University of Massachusetts Press.

Guinier, Lani. 1994. *The Tyranny of the Majority: Fundamental Fairness in Representative Democracy*. New York: Free Press.

Grupp, Fred W., Jr. 1969. "The Political Perspectives of Birch Society Members," in Robert A. Schoenberger, *The American Right Wing: Readings in Political Behavior*. Holt, Rinehart, and Winston.

Hadden, Jeffrey K., and Anson Shupe. 1988. *Televangelism: Power and Politics on God's Frontier*. New York: Henry Holt.

Hallin, Daniel C. 1989. *The "Uncensored War": The Media and Vietnam*. Berkeley: University of California Press.

Herman, Edward S., and Gerry O'Sullivan. 1989. *The Terrorism Industry: The Experts and Institutions That Shape Our View of Terror*. New York: Pantheon.

Hill, Dilys M., Raymond A. Moore, and Phil Williams, eds. 1990. *The Reagan Presidency: An Incomplete Revolution?* New York: St. Martin's Press.

Himmelstein, Jerome L. 1990. *To the Right: The Transformation of American Conservatism*. Berkeley and Los Angeles: University of California Press.

Hirschmann, Albert O. 1991. *The Rhetoric of Reaction: Perversity, Futility, Jeopardy*. Cambridge, MA: The Belknap Press of Harvard University Press.

Hixson, William B., Jr. 1992. *Search for the American Right Wing: An Analysis of the Social Science Record, 1955-1987*. Princeton, NJ: Princeton University Press.

Hofstadter, Richard. 1967. *The Paranoid Style in American Politics and Other Essays*. New York: Vintage Books.

Horsfield, Peter G. 1984. *Religious Television: The American Experience*. New York: Longman.

Hunter, James Davison. 1983. *American Evangelicalism: Conservative Religion and the Quandary of Modernity*. New Brunswick, NJ: Rutgers University Press.

Jeansonne, Glen. 1988. *Gerald L. K. Smith: Minister of Hate*. New Haven: Yale University Press.

Jenkins, J. Craig, and Teri Shumate, 1985. "Cowboy Capitalists and the Rise of the 'New Right': An analysis of Contributors to Conservative Policy Formation Organizations," *Social Problems*, vol. 33, no. 2. December, pp. 130-145.

Jonas, Manfred. 1990. *Isolationism in America, 1935-1941*. Chicago: Imprint.

Jonas, Susanne. 1991. *The Battle for Guatemala: Rebels, Death Squads, and U.S. Power*. Boulder, CO: Westview Press.

Jones, J. Harry, Jr. 1968. *The Minutemen*. New York: Doubleday.

Jones, Lawrence. 1985. "Reagan's Religion," *Journal of American Culture*, vol. 8, pp. 59–70.

Judis, John B. 1988. *William F. Buckley, Jr.: Patron Saint of the Conservatives*. New York: Simon and Schuster.

Kelley, Dean M. 1972. *Why Conservative Churches Are Growing*. New York: Harper & Row.

Kelley, Dean M. 1978. "Why Conservative Churches Are Still Growing," *Journal for the Scientific Study of Religion*. June 1978, pp. 165–172.

Kelley, Jonathan. 1974. "The Politics of School Busing," *Public Opinion Quarterly*. Spring 1974, pp. 23–39.

Key, V. O., Jr. [1949] 1986. *Southern Politics in State and Nation*. Knoxville: University of Tennessee Press.

Keynes, Edward, and Randall K. Miller. 1989. *The Court vs. Congress: Prayer, Busing, and Abortion*. Durham, NC: Duke University Press.

Klare, Michael T., and Peter Kornbluh. 1988. *Low Intensity Warfare: Counterinsurgency, Pro-Insurgency, and Antiterrorism in the Eighties*. New York: Pantheon.

Klehr, Harvey, and John Earl Haynes. 1992. *The American Communist Movement*. New York: Twayne.

Koen, Ross Y. 1974. *The China Lobby in American Politics*. New York: Harper & Row.

Kolko, Gabriel. 1985. *Anatomy of a War*. New York: Pantheon.

Kolko, Joyce. 1974. *America and the Crisis of World Capitalism*. Boston: Beacon Press.

Kovel, Joel. 1994. *Red Hunting in the Promised Land: Anticommunism and the Making of America*. New York: Basic Books.

Kuhl, Stefan. 1994. *The Nazi Connection: Eugenics, American Racism, and German National Socialism*. New York: Oxford University Press.

Kuttner, Robert. 1980. *Revolt of the Haves: Tax Rebellions and Hard Times*. New York: Simon and Schuster.

Kwitny, Jonathan. 1984. *Endless Enemies: The Making of an Unfriendly World*. New York: Penguin.

Ladd, Everett Carl, Jr., and Charles D. Hadley. 1978. *Transformations of the American Party System: Political Coalitions from the New Deal to the 1970s*. New York: Norton.

Lamis, Alexander P. 1990. *The Two-Party South*. New York: Oxford University Press.

Landau, Saul. 1988. *The Dangerous Doctrine: National Security and U.S. Foreign Policy*. Boulder, CO: Westview Press.

Landis, Fred S. 1975. *Psychological Warfare and Media Operations in Chile, 1970–73*, unpublished doctoral dissertation, University of Illinois, Urbana.

Langer, Elinor. 1990. "The American Neo-Nazi Movement Today," *The Nation*. July 16–23.

Lasch, Christopher. 1969. *The Agony of the American Left*. New York: Penguin.

Liebman, Robert C., and Robert Wuthnow, eds. 1983. *The New Christian Right: Mobilization and Legitimation*. New York: Aldine.

Lipset, Seymour Martin. 1963. *Political Man*. New York: Doubleday.

Lipset, Seymour Martin, and Earl Raab. 1969. "The Wallace Whitelash," *Trans-Action*. December 1969, pp. 24-25.

Lipset, Seymour Martin, and Earl Raab. 1970. *The Politics of Unreason: Right-Wing Extremism in America, 1790-1970*. New York: Harper and Row.

Lipstadt, Deborah. 1993. *Denying the Holocaust: The Growing Assault on Truth and Memory*. New York: The Free Press.

Lyons, Gene M., and Louis Morton. 1961. "Schools for Strategy," *Bulletin of Atomic Scientists*. March.

Manis, Andrew Michael. 1987. *Southern Civil Religions in Conflict: Black and White Baptists and Civil Rights, 1947-1957*. Athens: University of Georgia Press.

Mansbridge, Jane J. 1986. *Why We Lost the ERA*. Chicago: University of Chicago Press.

Marine, Gene. 1955. "The U.N. Haters," *The Nation*. May 14.

Marks, John. 1980. *The Search for the Manchurian Candidate: the CIA and Mind Control*. New York: McGraw Hill.

Marsden, George M. 1980. *Fundamentalism and American Culture: The Shaping of Twentieth Century Evangelicalism 1870-1925*. New York: Oxford University Press.

Martin, John Bartlow. 1957. *The Deep South Says "Never."* New York: Ballantine Books.

Mathews, Donald G., and Jane Sherron De Hart. 1990. *Sex, Gender, and the Politics of ERA*. New York: Oxford University Press, 1990.

Mauss, Armand L. 1994. *The Angel and the Beehive: The Mormon Struggle with Assimilation*. Urbana: University of Illinois Press.

McAdam, Doug. 1982. *Political Process and the Development of Black Insurgency, 1930-1970*. Chicago: University of Chicago Press.

McAuliffe, Mary Sperling. 1978. *Crisis on the Left: Cold War Politics and American Liberals, 1947-1954*. Amherst: University of Massachusetts Press.

McCarthy, John D., and Mayer N. Zald. 1977. "Resource mobilization and social movements: a partial theory," *American Journal of Sociology*, vol. 82. May 1977, pp. 1212-1239.

McClintock, Michael. 1992. *Instruments of Statecraft: U.S. Guerrilla Warfare, Counter-insurgency, and Counter-terrorism, 1940-1990*. New York: Pantheon Books.

McKeegan, Michele. 1992. *Abortion Politics: Mutiny in the Ranks of the Right*. New York: Free Press.

McMillen, Neil R. 1971. *The Citizens' Council: Organized Resistance to the Second Reconstruction, 1954-64*. Urbana: University of Illinois Press.

Merton, Andrew H. 1981. *Enemies of Choice: the Right-to-Life Movement and its Threat to Abortion*. Boston: Beacon Press.

Miles, Michael W. 1980. *The Odyssey of the American Right*. New York: Oxford University Press.

Mintz, Frank P. 1985. *The Liberty Lobby and the American Right: Race, Conspiracy, and Culture*. Westport, CT: Greenwood Press.

Mitau, G. Theodore. 1967. *Decade of Decision: The Supreme Court and the Constitutional Revolution 1954–1964*. New York: Charles Scribner's Sons.

Moen, Matthew C. 1989. *The Christian Right and Congress*. Tuscaloosa: University of Alabama Press.

Moen, Matthew C. 1992. *The Transformation of the Christian Right*. Tuscaloosa: University of Alabama Press.

Moffett, George D., III. 1985. *The Limits of Victory: The Ratification of the Panama Canal Treaties*. Ithaca, NY: Cornell University Press.

Morris, Aldon D., and Carol McClurg Mueller, eds. 1992. *Frontiers in Social Movement Theory*. New Haven, CT: Yale University Press.

Nairn, Allan. 1981. "Reagan's Administration Links With Guatemala's Terrorist Government," *Covert Action Information Bulletin*, April 1981, pp. 16–21.

Nash, George H. 1976. *The Conservative Intellectual Movement in America Since 1945*. New York: Basic Books.

Oakley, J. Ronald. 1986. *God's Country: America in the Fifties*. New York: Dembner Books.

O'Reilly, Kenneth. 1989. *"Racial Matters": The FBI's Secret File on Black America, 1960–1972*. New York: Free Press.

Page, Ann L., and Donald A. Clelland. 1978. "The Kanawha County Textbook Controversy: A Study of the Politics of Life Style Concern," *Social Forces*. September, pp. 265–281.

Paige, Connie. 1983. *The Right to Lifers*. New York: Summit Books.

Parry, Robert, and Peter Kornbluh. 1988. "Iran-Contra's Untold Story," *Foreign Policy*, Fall 1988, pp. 3–30.

Patterson, James T. 1967. *Congressional Conservatism and the New Deal: The Growth of the Conservative Coalition in Congress, 1933–1939*. Lexington: University of Kentucky Press.

Paull, Philip. 1982. *"International Terrorism": The Propaganda War*, unpublished MA thesis, San Francisco State University.

Peschek, Joseph G. 1987. *Policy-Planning Organizations: Elite Agendas and America's Rightward Turn*. Philadelphia: Temple University Press.

Petchesky, Rosalind Pollack. 1981. "Antiabortion, Antifeminism, and the Rise of the New Right," *Feminist Studies*. Summer 1981.

Petchesky, Rosalind Pollack. 1990. *Abortion and Woman's Choice: The State, Sexuality and Reproductive Freedom*. Boston: Northeastern University Press.

Peters, Cynthia, ed. 1992. *Collateral Damage: The "New World Order" at Home and Abroad*. Boston: South End Press.

Phillips, Kevin. 1969. *The Emerging Republican Majority*. New Rochelle, New York: Arlington House.

Phillips, Kevin. 1983. *Post-Conservative America: People, Politics, & Ideology in a Time of Crisis*. New York: Vintage Books.

Phillips, Kevin. 1990. *The Politics of Rich and Poor*. New York: Harper Perennial.

Phillips, Kevin. 1993. *Boiling Point: Republicans, Democrats, and the Decline of Middle-Class Prosperity*. New York: Random House.

Pieterse, Jan P. Nederveen, ed. 1992. *Christianity and Hegemony: Religion and Politics on the Frontiers of Social Change*. Oxford, England: Berg.

Piven, Frances Fox, and Richard A. Cloward. 1977. *Poor People's Movements*. New York: Vintage Books.

Piven, Frances Fox, and Richard A. Cloward. 1985. *The New Class War: Reagan's Attack on the Welfare State and Its Consequences*. New York: Pantheon.

Quebedeaux, Richard. 1978. *The Wordly Evangelicals*. San Francisco: Harper & Row.

Radosh, Ronald. 1975. *Prophets on the Right: Profiles of Conservative Critics of American Globalism*. New York: Simon and Schuster.

Rae, Nicole C. 1989. *The Decline and Fall of the Liberal Republicans: From 1952 to the Present*. New York: Oxford University Press.

Rae, Nicol C. 1994. *Southern Democrats*. New York: Oxford University Press.

Rainwater, Lee, and William L. Yancey. 1967. *The Moynihan Report and the Politics of Controversy*. Cambridge: M.I.T. Press.

Reinhard, David W. 1983. *The Republican Right Since 1945*. Lexington: University Press of Kentucky.

Relyea, Harold C. 1972. "The American Security Council," *The Nation*. January 24.

Ribuffo, Leo P. 1983. *The Old Christian Right: The Protestant Far Right from the Great Depression to the Cold War*. Philadelphia: Temple University Press.

Rice, Arnold S. 1962. *The Ku Klux Klan in American Politics*. Washington, DC: Public Affairs Press.

Ridgeway, James. 1990. *Blood in the Face*. New York: Thunder's Mouth Press.

Robinson, William I. 1992. *A Faustian Bargain: U.S. Intervention in the Nicaraguan Elections and American Foreign Policy in the Post-Cold War Era*. Boulder, CO: Westview Press.

Rogin, Michael Paul. 1967. *The Intellectuals and McCarthy: the Radical Specter*. Cambridge, MA: MIT Press.

Rogin, Michael Paul. 1969. "Politics, emotion, and the Wallace vote," *British Journal of Sociology*, 20 (March).

Rogin, Michael Paul. 1988. *Ronald Reagan, the Movie, and Other Episodes in Political Demonology*. Berkeley: University of California Press.

Rose, Douglas, ed. 1992. *The Emergence of David Duke and the Politics of Race*. Chapel Hill: University of North Carolina.

Rothmyer, Karen. 1981. "Citizen Scaife," *Columbia Journalism Review*. July–August, pp. 41–50.

Roy, Ralph Lord. 1953. *Apostles of Discord*. Boston: Beacon Press.

Rudolph, Frederick. 1950. "The American Liberty League, 1934–40," *American Historical Review*, vol. LVI, no. 1, October.

Saloma, John S., III. 1984. *Ominous Politics: The New Conservative Labyrinth*. New York: Hill and Wang.

Sandeen, Ernest R. 1970. *The Roots of Fundamentalism: British and American Millenarianism, 1800–1930* Chicago: University of Chicago Press.

Sanders, Jerry. 1983. *Peddlers of Crisis: the Committee on the Present Danger and the Politics of Containment*. Boston: South End Press.

Schaller, Michael. 1992. *Reckoning with Reagan: America and Its President in the 1980s*. New York: Oxford University Press.

Scheer, Robert, and Warren Hinckle. 1965. "The 'Vietnam Lobby,'" *Ramparts*. July, pp. 16–24.

Schonbach, Morris. 1985. *Native American Fascism During the 1930s and 1940s: A Study of Its Roots, Its Growth and Its Decline*. New York: Garland.

Schrecker, Ellen W. 1986. *No Ivory Tower: McCarthyism and the Universities*. New York: Oxford University Press.

Schurmann, Franz. 1987. *The Foreign Politics of Richard Nixon: The Grand Design*. Berkeley, CA: Institute of International Studies.

Seymour, Cheri. 1991. *Committee of the States: Inside the Radical Right*. Mariposa, CA: Camden Place Communications, Inc.

Shupe, Anson, and John Heinerman. 1985. "Mormonism and the New Christian Right: An Emerging Coalition?" *Review of Religious Research*, vol. 27, no. 2. December, pp. 146–157.

Simpson, Christopher. 1988. *Blowback: the First Full Account of America's Recruitment of Nazis, and Its Disastrous Effect on Our Domestic and Foreign Policy*. New York: Weidenfeld and Nicolson.

Simpson, Christopher. 1994. *Science of Coercion: Communication Research and Psychological Warfare, 1945–1960*. New York: Oxford University Press.

Sklar, Holly. 1988. *Washington's War on Nicaragua*. Boston: South End Press.

Smith, Geoffrey S. 1973. *To Save a Nation: American Countersubversives, the New Deal, and the Coming of World War II*. New York: Basic Books.

Smith, Rodney K. 1987. *Public Prayer and the Constitution: A Case Study in Constitutional Interpretation*. Wilmington, DE: Scholarly Resources.

Spanier, John W. 1959. *The Truman-MacArthur Controversy and the Korean War*. Cambridge, MA: The Belknap Press of Harvard University Press.

Steinfels, Peter. 1979. *The Neoconservatives*. New York: Simon and Schuster.

Sundquist, James L. 1968. *Politics and Policy: The Eisenhower, Kennedy, and Johnson Years*. Washington, DC: Brookings Institution.

Tarrow, Sidney. 1994. *Power in Movement: Social Movements, Collective Action and Politics*. New York: Cambridge University Press.

Tilly, Charles. 1978. *From Mobilization to Revolution*. Reading, MA: Addison Wesley Publishing Co.

Turner, William W. 1971. *Power on the Right*. Berkeley, CA: Ramparts Press.

Useem, Michael. 1984. *The Inner Circle: Large Corporations and the Rise of*

Business Political Activity in the U.S. and U.K. New York: Oxford University Press.

Vander Zanden, James W. 1959. "A Note on the Theory of Social Movements," *Sociology and Social Research*, XLIV. September–October, pp. 3–7.

Vander Zanden, James W. 1965. *Race Relations in Transition: The Segregation Crisis in the South.* New York: Random House.

Wade, Wyn Craig. 1987. *The Fiery Cross: The Ku Klux Klan in America.* New York: Simon and Schuster.

Wald, Alan M. 1987. *The New York Intellectuals: The Rise and Decline of the Anti-Stalinist Left from the 1930s to the 1980s.* Chapel Hill: University of North Carolina Press.

Weber, Timothy P. 1983. *Living in the Shadow of the Second Coming: American Premillennialism, 1875–1982.* Grand Rapids, MI: Zondervan.

Westin, Alan F. 1961. "The John Birch Society: Fundamentalism on the Right," *Commentary*. August.

Westin, Alan F. 1963. "Anti-Communism and the Corporations," *Commentary*. December.

White, O. Kendall, Jr. 1986. "A Review and Commentary on the Prospects of a Mormon New Christian Right Coalition," *Review of Religious Research*, vol. 28, no. 2. December 1986, pp. 180–188.

White, O. Kendall, Jr. 1989. "Mormonism and the Equal Rights Amendment," *Journal of Church and State*.

White, Theodore H. 1965. *The Making of the President 1964.* New York: Atheneum.

Wilkinson, J. Harvie, III. 1979. *From Brown to Bakke: The Supreme Court and School Integration: 1954–1978.* New York: Oxford University Press.

Wills, Garry. 1990. *Under God: Religion and American Politics.* New York: Simon and Schuster.

Wolfinger, Raymond E., et al. 1964. "America's Radical Right: Politics and Ideology," in David E. Apter, ed., *Ideology and Discontent.* New York: Free Press.

Wolfinger, Raymond, and Robert B. Arsenau. 1978. "Partisan Change in the South, 1952–1976," in Louis Maisel and Joseph Cooper, eds., *Political Parties: Development and Decay.* Beverly Hills, CA: Sage.

Wolfskill, George. 1962. *The Revolt of the Conservatives: A History of the American Liberty League, 1934–40.* Boston: Houghton Mifflin.

Wright, Gerald C., Jr. 1977. "Contextual Models of Electoral Behavior: The Southern Wallace Vote," *American Political Science Review*, vol. LXXI. pp. 497–508.

Young, Perry Deane. 1982. *God's Bullies: Native Reflections on Preachers and Politics.* New York: Holt, Rinehart, and Winston.

Index

American Council of Christian Churches
(ACCC), 95
American Enterprise Institute (AEI), 199
American Federation of Labor, 192
American Freedom Coalition (AFC), 244
American Friends of the Captive Nations
(AFCN), 45–47, 321n37, 321n46
American Friends of Vietnam, 344n40
American Independent Party (AIP), 90,
127, 131, 140, 143–145, 195, 261–
262, 324n86
and Viguerie, 130, 146
American Institute for Free Labor Develop-
ment (AIFLD), 218
American Mercury (magazine), 59, 102,
326n104
American Opinion (magazine), 54, 114, 145,
147
American Party, 140, 144–145
American Pistol and Rifle Association
(APRA), 355n1
American Security Council (ASC), 46–47,
121, 196, 214, 216
and the Cold War, 46–51
and Eisenhower, 49
and the military–industrial complex, 46–
51
and Trevor, 47
American Vigilance Intelligence Foundation, 47
American Woman's Party, 85
Americanist movement, 140–152
and the American Pistol and Rifle Association, 355n1
decline of, 159–160
definition, 355n1
ideology and activism of, 146–152
and the John Birch Society, 355n1
and John Katz, 355n1
opposition to Nelson Rockefeller, 159
organizational development, 152–155
Americans for Constitutional Action
(ACA), 61, 112
Americans for Democratic Action (ADA),
182–183, 192
Americans for Intellectual Freedom, 183
Anderson, Thomas J., 144–146, 324n86. *see
also* John Birch Society
Andrews, T. Coleman, 87, 145
Angola, 136, 221–223
Anti-abortion movement. *see* Abortion
rights
Anti-Ballistic Missile (ABM) treaty, 121
Anti-Bolshevik Bloc of Nations (ABN), 45,
156
Anticommunism, 8–9, 20, 137–138, 229. *see
also* World Anti-Communist League

and *American Mercury,* 59–60
Carto and, 86
China Lobby and, 41
and the Christian Right, 98–99
and Church League of America, 101–102
and the Cold War, 20, 37–41, 275–276
and *Commentary,* 184–185
Committee for One Million and, 42–43
and *Conservative Digest,* 130
Evangelical movement and, 101
grassroots organizations of, 51–59
and the Heritage Foundation, 216
and John Birch Society, 12–14, 51–59,
117, 140
and *National Review,* 31–35, 37, 44
and Reagan, 207, 214–224
Republican Party influenced by, 59–62,
308
and right-wing movements, 109–111,
117–123, 151–152, 307–309
and segregationism, 66–67
and Taft, 59
Weyrich and, 285
and YAF, 61
Anti-Defamation League (ADL), 218, 305–
306, 325n98
Anti-Semitism, 22–24, 47, 150. *see also* Israel
and the America First Committee,
315n25, 316n32
and the *American Mercury,* 59, 102,
326n104
and Aryan Nations, 158–160
and Buchanan, 293–294
and Carto, 85, 150
and *Christianity Today,* 100
and the Christian Right, 93
and farm crisis of 1980s, 259–265
H. Jung and, 47
Liberty Lobby and, 99, 154, 157
National Review's intolerance of, 284, 294
Posse Comitatus and, 156, 158–160, 259–
260
and *The Primrose and Cattleman's Gazette,*
260
and the racist Right, 259–265
W. Regnery and, 47, 315n25
Aquino, Corazon, 223–224, 240
Arab–Israeli war. *see* Israel
Armageddon. *see* Christian Right; Evangeli-
cal movement
Armey, Richard, 254
Arnett, Alvin, 344n35
Aron, Raymond, 183
Aryan Nations, 158–159, 258. *see also* White
Aryan Resistance
strategy of violence, 265–269
ASC. *see* American Security Council

17 Telegraph